Making Choices

Making Choices

READING ISSUES IN CONTEXT

MICHAEL COOLEY

KATHERINE POWELL

BERRY COLLEGE

HOUGHTON MIFFLIN COMPANY

BOSTON   NEW YORK

CONTENTS

v

U N I T   T W O

The Promise of Education

UNIT THREE

Earning Our Daily Bread

UNIT FOUR

Truth and Lying

U N I T   F I V E

Responsibility

UNIT SIX

The Pursuit of Happiness
What Is the Good Life?

TO THE INSTRUCTOR

This book is based on the simple principle that students write best when they are informed. Like other thematic readers on the market, *Making Choices* offers students an opportunity to read, discuss, and write about matters important to them and their world. Unlike most thematic readers, however, *Making Choices* also offers students a context for understanding and examining those issues.

Following a thorough discussion of critical reading and the reading-to-writing connection, the book is divided into five thematic units, each focusing on an area of choice in our individual and collective lives: education, work, honesty, responsibility, and the good life. As we explain further in "To the Student," each unit is divided into two sections, "Contexts" and "Controversies." The Context essays do just what their name suggests—they provide a context for understanding related issues. That context could be in the form of necessary background information or an introduction to the ideas that shape debate. In each Controversies section, the readings focus on three questions for examination. Some are of a social or political nature: "How Should We Educate a Diverse Population?" or "Is the Work Ethic Dead?" Others are questions of a personal nature: "When Should You Keep a Secret?" or "What Are My Responsibilities Within My Family?"

The seventy-nine selections in *Making Choices* represent a variety of perspectives, voices, genres, and writing styles. We begin each thematic unit with "A Way In," a short story, poem, or advertisement to start students thinking about and discussing their own ideas about the unit topic and the way popular culture informs and shapes those ideas. First-person narratives, arguments, interviews, and articles are among the other genres found throughout the units.

The "Rereading for Understanding" questions that follow each selection are designed to help students take a second look at the text and reach an understanding of the ideas and information presented. The "Responding" questions are designed to help them analyze and critique those ideas and consider them in light of their own beliefs and experiences and other readings in the text. Most selections are also followed by one or two "Responding in Writing" suggestions that give students an opportunity to enter the ongoing discussion presented in the readings.

We have organized the readings to facilitate making connections and understanding selections in context. You will discover, however, that there are numerous other possible arrangements for these pieces and that the selections speak to each other in ways we have not anticipated. We would be interested in hearing about your experiences using this reader and we welcome your suggestions and comments. You may write to us care of Houghton Mifflin or contact us via e-mail: kpowell@berry.edu

ACKNOWLEDGMENTS

We are indebted to a great many people for their help and support on this project.

We are grateful to our editors at Houghton Mifflin: George Kane, who recognized something interesting in our proposal and worked closely and patiently with us to turn that something into this book; Martha Bustin, whose careful reading and thoughtful comments on the early selections helped shape the book; Dean Johnson, who took over the project midway and guided it to completion with sound advice and good humor; and Janet Young, our production editor, who skillfully and efficiently transformed our rough manuscript into a real book. We also thank Mary Furlong Healey and Nandana Sen for their help throughout the project.

The following reviewers offered helpful commentary on various portions of this book:

Marshall W. Alcorn, Jr., *George Washington University, DC*

John Heyda, *Miami University, OH*

Sarah King, *George Mason University, VA*

Marlo Miller, *University of Massachusetts, Lowell*

Kathy Parrish, *Southwestern College, CA*

Jon Quitslund, *George Washington University, DC*

David Rivard, *Tufts University, MA*

Kristen L. Snoddy, *Indiana University at Kokomo*

Andrew Woolf, *Northern Essex Community College, MA*

Special thanks are owed to Kathy Parrish at Southwestern College for suggesting the piece by Rita Henley Jensen for the unit on work.

Our colleagues in the English Department at Berry College have encouraged this project and been understanding when we found it difficult to focus on anything else. We are grateful to all of them, especially Emily Wright, who suggested the short story "Economics" for the unit on truth and lying. We are thankful, too, to colleagues in other departments who shared their bookshelves and their expertise with us: Wade Carpenter, Greg Garrison, Bill Hoyt, and David McKenzie. The staff at Memorial Library, especially Lance Foldes, Jane Garrison, and Martha Reynolds, gave us invaluable research assistance.

Much of what we know about teaching reading and writing we have learned from our students at Berry College, and so we thank each of them. We are especially grateful to our student-workers, Denise Lenze, Jennifer Bryant, Rachel Blanton, and Holly Dean, who gave long hours to tracking down pieces and to the tedious work of typing and copying the manuscript.

Our greatest debt, of course, is to our families: to Daniel, for patience and understanding that far exceed your years and for your own love of reading and writing that is always an inspiration; to David, for keeping a fire in the hearth and in the heart and for being the chief advocate of my every effort for ten years and counting. To Susan, whose patience for another book when promises for other sorts of summers had been given must be acknowledged, your summer is now.

In *The Devil's Dictionary*, Ambrose Bierce defines *friendship* as "truce," and indeed there have been times as we worked on this project when our friendship of many years was reduced to little more than a tacit agreement not to declare open warfare. So finally, we are grateful for friendship that endures all trials, even collaboration.

M. C.
K. P.

TO THE STUDENT

Daily you are asked to make choices. Some are personal and relatively insignificant: "Where shall I have lunch today?" "What shall I wear?" "Am I going to make my bed this morning or just crawl back into these rumpled sheets tonight?" Others are personal but of greater importance: "What major should I declare?" "Should I write my own history paper or buy one from the term-paper service advertised on the bulletin board?" And some are choices that affect others as well as yourself: "Should I vote for Candidate X or Candidate Y?" "Should I volunteer to work at the soup kitchen?" "Should I serve my jury duty or try to get out of it?"

Of course, as you know, it's quite possible to make any of these choices with very little thought. You know, too, that it's often the trivial choices that get most of our attention. Many of us give more consideration to choosing just the right outfit to wear for an important event than to voting for the person to represent us in local or national government. Many of us would like to make more thoughtful choices but feel overwhelmed—there's so much to decide, so much to think about, so much to know. More often than not we make decisions or take positions based on a "gut" feeling we have about the issue.

Consider, for example, the following problem, described in Sissela Bok's book *Lying: Moral Choice in Public and Private Life:*

> A seventeen-year-old girl visited her pediatrician, who had been taking care of her since infancy. She went to his office without her parents, although her mother had made the appointment for her over the telephone. She told the pediatrician that she was very healthy, but that she thought she had some emotional problems. She stated that she was having trouble sleeping at night, that she was very nervous most of the day. She was a senior in high school and claimed she was doing quite poorly in most of her subjects. She was worried about what she was going to do next year. She was somewhat overweight. This, she felt, was part of her problem. She claimed she was not very attractive to the opposite sex and could not seem to "get boys interested in me." She had a few close friends of the same sex.
>
> Her life at home was quite chaotic and stressful. There were frequent battles with her younger brother, who was fourteen, and with

xv

her parents. She claimed her parents were always "on my back." She described her mother as extremely rigid and her father as a disciplinarian, who was quite old-fashioned in his values.

In all, she spent about twenty minutes talking with her pediatrician. She told him that what she thought she really needed was tranquilizers, and that that was the reason she came. She felt that this was an extremely difficult year for her, and if she could have something to calm her nerves until she got over her current crises, everything would go better.

The pediatrician told her that he did not really believe in giving tranquilizers to a girl of her age. He said he thought it would be a bad precedent for her to establish. She was very insistent, however, and claimed that if he did not give her tranquilizers, she would "get them somehow." Finally, he agreed to call her pharmacy and order medication for her nerves. She accepted graciously. He suggested that she call him in a few days to let him know how things were going. He also called her parents to say that he had a talk with her and he was giving her some medicine that might help her nerves.

Five days later, the girl called the pediatrician back to say that the pills were really working well. She claimed that she had calmed down a great deal, that she was working things out better with her parents, and had a new outlook on life. He suggested that she keep taking them twice a day for the rest of the school year. She agreed.

A month later, the girl ran out of pills and called her pediatrician for a refill. She found that he was away on vacation. She was quite distraught at not having any medication left, so she called her uncle who was a surgeon in the next town. He called the pharmacy to renew her pills and, in speaking to the druggist, found out that they were only vitamins. He told the girl that the pills were only vitamins and that she could get them over the counter and didn't really need him to refill them. The girl became very distraught, feeling that she had been deceived and betrayed by her pediatrician. Her parents, when they heard, commented that they thought the pediatrician was "very clever."

Do you think the physician acted correctly? Do you think the patient was right to be upset when she discovered the truth? Would you agree with her parents that the doctor was "very clever"?

You surely have an answer for all these questions, even though the story is relatively brief and lacking in detail. If your professor asked you to write a brief essay defending or attacking the doctor's actions, you could probably do a credible job.

RESPONDING FROM PERSONAL EXPERIENCE

Your response to this story is probably influenced largely by your personal experiences. Perhaps someone has lied to you "for your own good" in the past.

Perhaps you have practiced a similar form of benign deception on someone else. Your own experience with doctors probably influences your response, too. If you've had difficulty getting a straight answer from a doctor or getting a doctor to treat you as an adult, you'll probably feel differently about this story than you would if your relationship with your doctor were one of trust and mutual respect, or if you were a doctor yourself.

Responding on the basis of personal experience is clearly one way to come to a decision about an issue. Certainly it is the best beginning point, and it may be that even after further examination and analysis you discover that your initial, personal response still makes the most sense. But this book takes the position that most of the choices and decisions we need to make in order to live full, meaningful, and responsible lives demand that we draw upon more than our limited personal experience and beliefs.

This book aims to help you develop larger perspective for the choices that face you. We hope to help you develop a context for consideration of the myriad decisions that you are called upon to make each day.

THE LARGER PERSPECTIVE

In her essay "Saving the Life That Is Your Own," Alice Walker observes:

> What is always needed in the appreciation of art, or life, is the larger perspective. Connections made, or at least attempted, where none existed before, the straining to encompass in one's glance at the varied world the common thread, the unifying theme through immense diversity, a fearlessness of growth, of search, of looking, that enlarges the private and public world. And yet, in our particular society, it is the narrowed and narrowing view of life that often wins.

Walker made that statement in 1970, but her fear that the narrowed and narrowing view would prevail remains. Increasingly, it seems, we view the important issues of our lives from a narrow, individual point of view. News programs that pit a welfare mother against a conservative lawmaker in a discussion of reforms in the Aid to Families with Dependent Children program seem more intent on highlighting the differences that separate the parties than in either searching for the common thread that unites them or promoting the understanding that might lead to resolution. Talk shows that encourage audience members to scream at the guests and guests to pummel each other verbally or physically likewise only serve to entrench individuals more firmly in their own prejudices rather than to search for a broader perspective by considering another point of view.

Our intention in gathering and assembling the readings in this book has been to help you gain that broader perspective on the choices and decisions you will have to make now and in the future. Each thematic unit is divided into "Contexts" and "Controversies" sections. The "Contexts" essays introduce the broad theme of each unit. As the name suggests, they provide a context for thinking about the specific questions presented in the subsequent "Controversies" selections.

To see how the relationship between the Context and Controversies readings might work, let's consider the question already raised in this preface: "Should doctors prescribe placebos?" To answer this question, you might find it helpful to know some background information about the responsibilities and obligations of the medical profession. In this case, we might include (as a Context essay) the Hippocratic Oath, which most doctors take upon completion of medical school. More frequently, the Context essays will provide an examination of the *larger* ideas behind each controversial issue. The question of whether or not it is appropriate for doctors to prescribe placebos goes beyond the concerns of medicine; it raises larger questions about the value of honesty and the morality of deception, questions that philosophers have contemplated through the ages. So the Context section would include some of those philosophical discussions, recognizing that our perspective on any problem is broadened not only by taking in information but also by seeing how other minds in other times and cultures have grappled with the same problems.

PULLING IT ALL TOGETHER

Reading other people's ideas about an issue can help us gain perspective, but real understanding comes when we put those ideas together, when we evaluate them in light of each other and in light of our own personal responses and come to some kind of decision or judgment. That pulling together of ideas, making connections among the pieces, is what we do when we go back and reread a text, when we discuss what we've read with others, and when we write about the ideas raised by our reading. Each selection in this text is followed by questions. Those labeled "Rereading for Understanding" are designed to help you go back into the text and reexamine key ideas and evidence. Those under "Responding" invite you to engage in a dialogue with the text and/or other readers, to evaluate the ideas that have been presented, and to compare them with ideas you've gained from other reading or from experience and observation. "Responding in Writing" questions offer you opportunities to draw conclusions about the readings and the ideas they raise and to contemplate your own beliefs and experiences in relation to the ideas of others.

If you've ever climbed to the top of a mountain, you know the exhilarating rush that comes with gaining perspective. Points that once seemed separate and isolated now appear related as part of a larger landscape. But gaining perspective takes some work, a lot of steady walking, and sometimes arduous climbing before that moment of breaking through the treeline and getting a glimpse of what it was all for. Gaining perspective through reading can be difficult, and demanding, too. Many of the readings in this text are lengthy and complex. To read them with understanding, to see connections among them, to gain from them a new perspective will not be easy, but you will find the rewards well worth the effort.

Making Choices

UNIT ONE

Reading and Writing

CRITICAL READING

BEYOND DECODING

My five-year-old son studies the array of artificial fishing lures in the sporting goods department at Wal-Mart. "We better get these, Dad," he says, indicating a package of glittering pink rubber night crawlers. "See? It says, 'Best for Bass.'"

Later at the grocery store, he points out the kind of peanut butter he wants. "Let's get this, Dad. Look—'Kids Love It.'"

Having only recently mastered the ability to decode the written word, Daniel believes that reading involves nothing more than sounding out the letters and knowing what each word means, and in a way, of course, he's correct. Reading any text, be it an ad for peanut butter or a treatise on liberal education, begins with making sense—extracting the literal meaning from the printed words. But as any experienced reader knows, real reading involves much more. No experienced reader would assume that an advertising claim is true simply because it appears in print. Even when we read solely for information, we make judgments about the truth or falsehood of what we read. Critical reading, the kind of reading that leads to genuine understanding, demands much more.

WHAT IS CRITICAL READING?

Critical reading goes beyond merely decoding the text, or knowing what it says on a literal level. Critical reading is active reading. It involves paying attention as we go along, taking time to understand, questioning what we read, even questioning our own response. In short, critical reading demands that we *engage* the text, not merely absorb it.

Engaging the Text

Critical readers engage a text in three important ways: analysis, interpretation, and response.

1. When we *analyze* a text, we examine its various pieces to discover the structure and meaning of the whole they create. We try to determine the main idea and the key points that support it.

2. We also *interpret* the main idea and the key supporting points in light of what we already know, not just information, but also values and opinions we may have gained from other reading or from our own experiences and observations. To the extent that our economic class, our race, and our gender have shaped our experience, they also shape our reading of a text.

3. Finally, we *respond* to the text. In thinking, discussing, and writing, we try to answer questions raised by the text. We work to reconcile one text with another or with our own ideas and beliefs. We make judgments about the merit of the author's position. Clearly, the more we know, the broader our experiences and reading are, the more we bring to our reading of any text and the better able we are to evaluate it, to determine its worth.

To list the three ways by which we engage a text is not to suggest that these are necessarily isolated steps. As a reader, you have certainly found yourself interpreting and responding to a text even while you are reading it through for understanding. The important point to remember is that fully understanding a text must precede making a judgment or coming to a final conclusion about it. Generally speaking, especially with the kinds of complicated texts you can expect to encounter as you continue your education, at least two readings are required: one to gain a literal and analytical understanding of the piece and one to evaluate the position it sets forth. If you get in the habit of allotting yourself enough time to read each assigned text at least twice, you will find yourself far better prepared to discuss, question, and write about that text when the time comes.

Before You Read

When you read a piece through for the first time, your intention is to determine the main points of the selection. Such *analysis* of the text starts even before you actually begin reading it. The title, the author, and even the date and place of publication can give you some idea of the subject matter and the intention of the piece. An excerpt from *The Prince* entitled "How Princes Should Honor Their Word" may sound like an argument for honest leadership; if you know, however, that author Niccolo Machiavelli believed that deceit and manipulation of the masses was justified if the ultimate end was to their benefit, you can assume that the essay will instruct rulers as to when they should *not* honor their word as well as to when they should. Knowing that Machiavelli's treatise was written in 1517 in Italy gives you another advantage: you realize you are reading a work in translation, and a fairly old one at that; you can anticipate language and allusions that may not be readily understood by a contemporary audience. In this book, a brief note before each selection tells you something about the author and the issues the selection addresses. Don't underestimate the insights you can gain even before you begin reading.

ANALYZING: READING FOR UNDERSTANDING

Perhaps you've had the following experience. You're assigned to read a lengthy essay for class. You read it carefully, stopping to look up each word you don't recognize and to puzzle over each sentence that doesn't seem to make sense. Still, when you get to class, you find you have nothing to add to the discussion; in fact, you can't even articulate the key point of the essay. Or, you may have read an essay through once, focusing on the parts that were clear but skimming over the difficult sections and ignoring unfamiliar words. You know you haven't grasped every minute detail of the essay, but you're confident you understand its general idea. When your class discussion begins, however, you realize that in failing to grasp the details of the essay, you have misunderstood its main point.

As you engage in a first reading, then, you have to do two things simultaneously. You must read to gain a literal understanding of each word, sentence, and paragraph, and you must keep track of the way those words, sentences, and paragraphs add up to a whole piece. If that sounds like a demanding task, it is. It requires that you read carefully, with a dictionary nearby and a pen in hand. As you encounter new words, look them up. When you find yourself struggling to make sense of a sentence, go back over it again and again until its meaning is clear. Make note of ideas that strike you as significant. Observe the way one idea builds on another. Even in this first reading, you may find yourself asking questions, making connections with other ideas—jot down those questions and connections, too. Don't be too heavy-handed in highlighting passages or scribbling notes in the margin at this point, however. Remember that you will be doing at least one more reading. The notes you make now should guide you through that second reading, not obscure it.

Here, with a student's first-reading annotations, is the opening of Sissela Bok's essay on placebos, from which the story in "To the Student" was taken.

Placebos

Thesis?

The common practice of prescribing placebos to unwitting patients illustrates the two miscalculations so common to minor forms of deceit: ignoring possible harm and failing to see how gestures assumed to be trivial build up into collectively undesirable practices. Placebos have been used since the

*definition

beginning of medicine. They can be sugar pills, salt-water injections—in fact, any medical procedure which has no specific effect on a patient's condition, but which can have powerful psychological effects leading to relief from symptoms such as pain or depression.

Placebos are prescribed with great frequency. Exactly how often cannot be known, the less so as physicians do not ordinarily talk publicly about using them. At times, self-deception enters in on the part of physicians, so that they have unwar-

When did this change? examples? like bleeding w/leeches?

ranted faith in the powers of what can work only as a placebo. As with salesmanship, medication often involves unjustified belief in the excellence of what is suggested to others. In the past, most remedies were of a kind that, unknown to the medical profession and their patients, could have only placebic benefits, if any.

The derivation of "placebo," from the Latin for "I shall please," gives the word a benevolent ring, somehow placing placebos beyond moral criticism and conjuring up images of hypochondriacs whose vague ailments are dispelled through adroit prescriptions of beneficent sugar pills. Physicians often give a humorous tinge to instructions for prescribing these substances, which helps to remove them from serious ethical concern. One authority wrote in a pharmacological journal that the placebo should be given a name previously unknown to the patient and preferably Latin and polysyllabic, and added:

many syllables

> [I]t is wise if it be prescribed with some assurance and emphasis for psychotherapeutic effect. The older physicians each had his favorite placebic prescriptions—one chose tincture of Condurango, another Fluidextract of *Cimicifuga nigra*.

After all, health professionals argue, are not placebos far less dangerous than some genuine drugs? And more likely to produce a cure than if nothing at all is prescribed? Such a view is expressed in a letter to the *Lancet:*

What's this?

> Whenever pain can be relieved with a ml of saline, why should we inject an opiate? Do anxieties or discomforts that are allayed with starch capsules require administration of a barbiturate, diazepam, or propoxyphene?

Costs:

① Such a simplistic view conceals the real costs of placebos, both to individuals and to the practice of medicine. First, the resort to placebos may actually prevent the treatment of an underlying, undiagnosed problem. And even if the placebo "works," the effect is often short-lived; the symptoms may recur, or crop up in other forms. Very often, the symptoms of which the patient complains are bound to go away by themselves, sometimes even from the mere contact with a health professional. In those cases, the placebo itself is unnecessary;

② having recourse to it merely reinforces a tendency to depend upon pills or treatments where none is needed.

③ In the aggregate, the costs of placebos are immense. Many millions of dollars are expended on drugs, diagnostic tests, and psychotherapies of a placebic nature. Even operations can be of this nature—a hysterectomy may thus be performed, not because the condition of the patient requires such surgery, but because she goes from one doctor to another seeking to have the surgery performed, or because she is judged to have a great fear of cancer which might be alleviated by the very fact of the operation.

Even apart from financial and emotional costs and the squandering of resources, the practice of giving placebos is wasteful of a very precious good: the trust on which so much in the medical relationship depends. The trust of those patients who find out they have been duped is lost, sometimes irretrievably. They may then lose confidence in physicians and even in bona fide medication which they may need in the future. They may obtain for themselves more harmful drugs or attach their hopes to debilitating fad cures.

Notice that the student's notes show a first attempt to find the structure of the essay—"Thesis?" "Costs 1, 2, 3"—as well as to define key terms and make sense of passages or references that are not clear.

Summary: Checking Your Understanding

One way to check whether your first reading has given you an understanding of the essay is to try to summarize it. You should be able to state the overall main idea of the essay and to identify the points that the author uses to support it. To do so, you must not only recognize the important ideas of the essay, but also understand how they work together, what they all add up to. That's why it is important to pay attention to structure as well as content as you read.

Now look at the essay "Placebos" one more time, this time in its entirety. Read it carefully, taking time to make notes, look up unfamiliar words, and puzzle out difficult passages.

Placebos

The common practice of prescribing placebos to unwitting patients illustrates the two miscalculations so common to minor forms of deceit: ignoring possible harm and failing to see how gestures assumed to be trivial build up into collectively undesirable practices. Placebos have been used since the beginning of medicine. They can be sugar pills, salt-water injections—in fact, any medical procedure which has no specific effect on a patient's condition, but which can have powerful psychological effects leading to relief from symptoms such as pain or depression.

Placebos are prescribed with great frequency. Exactly how often cannot be known, the less so as physicians do not ordinarily talk publicly about using them. At times, self-deception enters in on the part of physicians, so that they have unwarranted faith in the powers of what can work only as a placebo. As with salesmanship, medication often involves unjustified belief in the excellence of what is suggested to others. In the past, most remedies were of a kind that, unknown to the medical profession and their patients, could have only placebic benefits, if any.

The derivation of "placebo," from the Latin for "I shall please," gives the word a benevolent ring, somehow placing placebos beyond moral criticism and conjuring up images of hypochondriacs whose vague ailments are dispelled through adroit prescriptions of beneficent sugar pills. Physicians often give a humorous tinge to instructions for prescribing these substances, which helps to remove them from serious ethical concern. One authority wrote in a pharmacological journal that the placebo should be given a name previously unknown to the patient and preferably Latin and polysyllabic, and added:

> [I]t is wise if it be prescribed with some assurance and emphasis for psychotherapeutic effect. The older physicians each had his favorite placebic prescriptions—one chose tincture of Condurango, another the Fluidextract of *Cimicifuga nigra.*

After all, health professionals argue, are not placebos far less dangerous than some genuine drugs? And more likely to produce a cure than if nothing at all is prescribed? Such a view is expressed in a letter to the *Lancet:*

> Whenever pain can be relieved with a ml of saline, why should we inject an opiate? Do anxieties or discomforts that are allayed with starch capsules require administration of a barbiturate, diazepam, or propoxyphene?

Such a simplistic view conceals the real costs of placebos, both to individuals and to the practice of medicine. First, the resort to placebos may actually prevent the treatment of an underlying, undiagnosed problem. And even if the placebo "works," the effect is often short-lived; the symptoms may recur, or crop up in other forms. Very often, the symptoms of which the patient complains are bound to go away by themselves, sometimes even from the mere contact with a health professional. In those cases, the placebo itself is unnecessary; having recourse to it merely reinforces a tendency to depend upon pills or treatments where none is needed.

In the aggregate, the costs of placebos are immense. Many millions of dollars are expended on drugs, diagnostic tests, and psychotherapies of a placebic nature. Even operations can be of this nature—a hysterectomy may thus be performed, not because the condition of the patient requires such surgery, but because she goes from one doctor to another seeking to have the surgery performed, or because she is judged to have a great fear of cancer which might be alleviated by the very fact of the operation.

Even apart from financial and emotional costs and the squandering of resources, the practice of giving placebos is wasteful of a very precious good: the trust on which so much in the medical relationship depends. The trust of those patients who find out they have been duped is lost, sometimes irretrievably. They may then lose confidence in physicians and even in bona fide medication which they may need in the future. They may obtain for themselves more harmful drugs or attach their hopes to debilitating fad cures.

The following description of a case where a placebo was prescribed reflects a common approach.

> A seventeen-year-old girl visited her pediatrician, who had been taking care of her since infancy. She went to his office without her parents, although her mother had made the appointment for her over the

telephone. She told the pediatrician that she was very healthy, but that she thought she had some emotional problems. She stated that she was having trouble sleeping at night, that she was very nervous most of the day. She was a senior in high school and claimed she was doing quite poorly in most of her subjects. She was worried about what she was going to do next year. She was somewhat overweight. This, she felt, was part of her problem. She claimed she was not very attractive to the opposite sex and could not seem to "get boys interested in me." She had a few close friends of the same sex.

Her life at home was quite chaotic and stressful. There were frequent battles with her younger brother, who was fourteen, and with her parents. She claimed her parents were always "on my back." She described her mother as extremely rigid and her father as a disciplinarian, who was quite old-fashioned in his values.

In all, she spent about twenty minutes talking with her pediatrician. She told him that what she thought she really needed was tranquilizers, and that that was the reason she came. She felt that this was an extremely difficult year for her, and if she could have something to calm her nerves until she got over her current crises, everything would go better.

The pediatrician told her that he did not really believe in giving tranquilizers to a girl of her age. He said he thought it would be a bad precedent for her to establish. She was very insistent, however, and claimed that if he did not give her tranquilizers, she would "get them somehow." Finally, he agreed to call her pharmacy and order medication for her nerves. She accepted graciously. He suggested that she call him in a few days to let him know how things were going. He also called her parents to say that he had a talk with her and he was giving her some medicine that might help her nerves.

Five days later, the girl called the pediatrician back to say that the pills were really working well. She claimed that she had calmed down a great deal, that she was working things out better with her parents, and had a new outlook on life. He suggested that she keep taking them twice a day for the rest of the school year. She agreed.

A month later, the girl ran out of pills and called her pediatrician for a refill. She found that he was away on vacation. She was quite distraught at not having any medication left, so she called her uncle who was a surgeon in the next town. He called the pharmacy to renew her pills and, in speaking to the druggist, found out that they were only vitamins. He told the girl that the pills were only vitamins and that she could get them over the counter and didn't really need him to refill them. The girl became very distraught, feeling that she had been deceived and betrayed by her pediatrician. Her parents, when they heard, commented that they thought the pediatrician was "very clever."

The patients who do *not* discover the deception and are left believing that a placebic remedy has worked may continue to rely on it under the wrong circumstances. This is especially true with drugs such as antibiotics, which are sometimes used as placebos and sometimes for their specific action. Many parents, for example, come to believe that they must ask for the prescription of antibiotics every time their child has a fever or a cold. The fact that so many doctors accede to such requests perpetuates the dependence of these families on medical care they do not need and weakens their ability to cope with health problems. Worst of all, those children who cannot tolerate antibiotics may have severe reactions, sometimes fatal, to such unnecessary medication.

Such deceptive practices, by their very nature, tend to escape the normal restraints of accountability and can therefore spread more easily than others. There are many instances in which an innocuous-seeming practice has grown to become a large-scale and more dangerous one. Although warnings against the "entering wedge" are often rhetorical devices, they can at times express justifiable caution; especially when there are great pressures to move along the undesirable path and when the safeguards are insufficient.

In this perspective, there is much reason for concern about placebos. The safeguards against this practice are few or nonexistent—both because it is secretive in nature and because it is condoned but rarely carefully discussed in the medical literature. And the pressures are very great, and growing stronger, from drug companies, patients eager for cures, and busy physicians, for more medication, whether it is needed or not. Given this lack of safeguards and these strong pressures, the use of placebos can spread in a number of ways.

The clearest danger lies in the gradual shift from pharmacologically inert placebos to more active ones. It is not always easy to distinguish completely inert substances from somewhat active ones and these in turn from more active ones. It may be hard to distinguish between a quantity of an active substance so low that it has little or no effect and quantities that have some effect. It is not always clear to doctors whether patients require an inert placebo or possibly a more active one, and there can be the temptation to resort to an active one just in case it might also have a specific effect. It is also much easier to deceive a patient with a medication that is known to be "real" and to have power. One recent textbook in medicine goes so far as to advocate the use of small doses of effective compounds as placebos rather than inert substances—because it is important for both the doctor and the patient to believe in the treatment! This shift is made easier because the dangers and side effects of active agents are not always known or considered important by the physician.

Meanwhile, the number of patients receiving placebos increases as more and more people seek and receive medical care and as their desire for instant, push-button alleviation of symptoms is stimulated by drug advertising and by rising expectations of what science can do. The use of placebos for children grows as well, and the temptations to manipulate the truth are less easily resisted once such great inroads have already been made.

Deception by placebo can also spread from therapy and diagnosis to experimentation. Much experimentation with placebos is honest and consented to by the experimental subjects, especially since the advent of strict rules governing such experimentation. But grievous abuses have taken place where placebos were given to unsuspecting subjects who believed they had received another substance. In 1971, for example, a number of Mexican-American women applied to a family-planning clinic for contraceptives. Some of them were given oral contraceptives and others were given placebos, or dummy pills that looked like the real thing. Without fully informed consent, the women were being used in an experiment to explore the side effects of various contraceptive pills. Some of those who were given placebos experienced a predictable side effect—they became pregnant. The investigators neither assumed financial responsibility for the babies nor indicated any concern about having bypassed the "informed consent" that is required in ethical experiments with human beings. One contented himself with the observation that if only the law had permitted it, he could have aborted the pregnant women!

The failure to think about the ethical problems in such a case stems at least in part from the innocent-seeming white lies so often told in giving placebos. The spread from therapy to experimentation and from harmlessness to its opposite often goes unnoticed in part *because* of the triviality believed to be connected with placebos as white lies. This lack of foresight and concern is most frequent when the subjects in the experiment are least likely to object or defend themselves; as with the poor, the institutionalized, and the very young.

In view of all these ways in which placebo usage can spread, it is not enough to look at each incident of manipulation in isolation, no matter how benevolent it may be. When the costs and benefits are weighed, not only the individual consequences must be considered, but also the cumulative ones. Reports of deceptive practices inevitably leak out, and the resulting suspicion is heightened by the anxiety which threats to health always create. And so even the health professionals who do not mislead their patients are injured by those who do; the entire institution of medicine is threatened by practices lacking in candor, however harmless the results may appear in some individual cases.

This is not to say that all placebos must be ruled out; merely that they cannot be excused as innocuous. They should be prescribed but rarely, and only after a careful diagnosis and consideration of non-deceptive alternatives; they should be used in experimentation only after subjects have consented to their use.

You may not be able to summarize the whole essay accurately and fully at this point, but if your reading has been thorough and your notes appropriate, you should be able to identify the author's main idea and chief supporting points. A brief summary of each point would look something like this:

1. The practice of prescribing placebos is a dangerous form of deception because placebos may be harmful and viewing such deceit as insignificant will lead to increasingly greater deceptions.

2. It is hard to know how frequently placebos are prescribed because doctors are usually secretive about it. In many cases, they may not even realize themselves that the treatment they prescribe is only placebic.

3. The practice of prescribing placebos is not considered a serious moral issue because the only effects are believed to be beneficial.

4. There are, however, real costs attached to the practice:

5. It may keep the doctor from diagnosing and treating a problem that really does exist.

6. It may encourage patients to believe that only medication can heal their ailments.

7. Millions of dollars are spent on pills and procedures that have no real therapeutic benefit.

8. It diminishes patients' trust in their doctors.

9. Patients may develop an unhealthy dependency on placebos.

10. Because the practice is not openly discussed, it is likely to spread in ways that may be dangerous.

11. One danger is that instead of prescribing placebos that have no effect at all (inert), some doctors prescribe medicine that does have a noticeable effect (active).

12. The more people receive placebos for their illnesses, the more they come to expect a quick cure for every ailment; in turn, more placebos are prescribed to meet the patient's expectation.

13. The use of placebos can spread from therapy to experimentation. Because prescribing placebos as treatment is not regarded as harmful deception, it may lead some doctors to regard using placebos in experiments without patients' consent as likewise trivial and harmless.

14. When making a decision about the use of placebos, you have to consider the cumulative effect of the practice, not just the pros and cons of a single situation. The whole medical profession suffers when doctors engage in this deceptive practice.

15. It may be necessary to prescribe placebos occasionally, but we should not regard such deception lightly and should try other methods of solving the problem first.

Glancing over these brief point summaries, you will notice that Bok's main point, her *thesis*, is presented in the first paragraph, as the student tentatively suggested in her notes. Every other point is presented as illustration or explanation of that thesis. It is also clear that some points are subpoints of another. You can see, for example, that points 5 through 10 all serve to explain point 4, itemizing the serious costs attached to the practice of prescribing placebos. You can also see that points 11 through 14 serve to clarify point 10, illustrating the dangerous results of regarding placebo therapy as trivial. Where do points 2 and 3 fit in? Presenting the "conventional wisdom" about placebos that Bok challenges in her essay, they provide some necessary context for the thesis. You probably recognize that point 15 functions as the conclusion.

Structure: A Key to Understanding

Summarizing the points of a text serves to check your understanding of the thesis and its support. In doing so, you also begin to see the structure of the piece. And recognizing structure is not simply an academic exercise; it is a valuable aid in understanding what you read. If Bok had intended for you to appreciate a number of isolated ideas about placebos, she would have presented you with a list. (Adrienne Rich uses that technique in "Women and Honor: Some Notes on Lying," page 264.) Bok organized the ideas as she did because she intended them to add up to something greater than the cumulative effect of their individual impact. If we understand how the ideas are related to one another and to the thesis, we will have comprehended the whole text in a way that allows us to interpret and respond to it.

INTERPRETING: FILTERING THE TEXT

You can think of reading as a conversation between writer and reader. In the first reading you listen to the writer speak and, as you do in most normal conversations, you try to understand what he or she is telling you. When you move from a literal understanding of the text to thinking about what that text means, you begin to question the writer, just as you might question someone's comments in conversation. You are not yet ready to respond to the writer; in interpretation, you seek clarification.

Coming to Terms

Interpretation begins with recognizing the writer's key terms and understanding how he or she is using them. Earlier we advised you to have a dictionary at hand during the first reading and to look up the meanings of unfamiliar words. As you interpret a text, you move beyond this literal, dictionary definition of each word, to an understanding of the *significance* of particular words and phrases and the way they are used in the piece you are reading. To illustrate the difference between these two ways of reading, let's examine a piece of writing whose words, on a literal level, are easy to understand.

The Hippocratic Oath

I do solemnly swear by whatever I hold most sacred that I will be loyal to the profession of medicine, and just and generous to its members.

That I will lead my life and practice my art in uprightness and honor.

That into whatsoever home I shall enter, it shall be for the good of the sick and the well to the utmost of my power, and that I will hold myself aloof from wrong and from corruption and from tempting of others to vice.

That I will exercise my art solely for the care of my patients and the prevention of disease, and will give no drugs and perform no operation for a criminal purpose and far less suggest such a thing.

That whatsoever I shall see or hear of the lives of men which is not fitting to be spoken, I will keep inviolably secret.

These things I do promise and, in proportion as I am faithful to this oath, may happiness and good repute be ever mine, the opposite if I shall be forsworn.

Filling the Gaps

The Hippocratic Oath probably contains no words that are unfamiliar to you. Its structure is obvious, and you probably find it unnecessary to check your comprehension by summarizing it; in fact, the short oath would be difficult to reduce much further. Consider what happens, however, when you try to answer the following questions: Would the Hippocratic Oath prohibit a doctor from prescribing placebos? from performing an abortion? from assisting in the suicide of a terminally ill patient?

A literal understanding of the text is not enough to answer these questions. Dictionary definitions of key terms like "good" or "vice" or "whatsoever is unfitting to be spoken" are of limited use. To answer these questions, you need to *interpret* the key points.

According to Robert Scholes, a teacher and thinker who has written much about the way texts work on readers and vice versa, "Interpretation can be the result of either some excess of meaning in a text or some deficiency of knowledge in the reader". In other words, interpretation is an attempt to fill the gaps in understanding between reader and writer. In this case, the problem seems to be an excess of meaning in the text; the terms offered are so broad that they cannot be applied to particular situations unless you, the reader, impose a narrower meaning on them. To do so, you must use knowledge or beliefs that you have acquired on your own to help you engage the text.

For example, if you believe that life in any form is "good," then you would probably say that the Hippocratic Oath forbids doctors from assisting in a suicide because it instructs physicians to act "only for the good" of their patients. If, on the other hand, you believe that life is "good" only to those able to enjoy it, then you might argue that a doctor who assists in the suicide of a person no longer able to enjoy life is acting "only for the good" of that patient. A word of caution: When we say that personal beliefs and knowledge influence the way you interpret a text, we are not suggesting that you can make the text say anything you wish it to. For example, to claim that the Hippocratic Oath permits a doctor to deny treatment to a patient he or she finds personally distasteful would not be an interpretation but a misreading of the text; nothing in the oath supports such a conclusion. You can see now why we insist that reading for understanding *precedes* interpretation. Unless you have a literal and accurate understanding of the author's ideas, you cannot begin to interpret them, much less respond to them.

RESPONDING: READING FOR EVALUATION

If we continue with our metaphor of reading as conversation, responding would be the point in the conversation when you talk back to the writer. Thinking about reading as a conversation helps you to keep in mind the purpose of responding to a text. When you engage in conversation, your purpose is to give your ideas and take in someone else's. You do so, we hope, with the intention of gaining enlightenment, coming to a clearer understanding of the issue you are discussing, finding a reasonable solution to the problem under consideration. Unfortunately, we've all had the experience of trying to converse with someone who doesn't listen to what we say, who simply waits for us to stop talking so that he or she can start. That kind of reply isn't a response because it isn't addressed to what we've said. It's simply an alternate statement. Unless we're inclined to give a much more generous ear to the speaker than he or she has given us, neither of us gains anything from the "conversation." We leave it with nothing more than we brought to it.

Reading respectfully, trying not only to gain a literal understanding of the writer's position but also to follow his or her reasoning, is thus more than a matter of etiquette. It is something you do for yourself, to be sure that you take from your reading all that you can, to make the difficult task of critical reading worth the time and effort.

Talking Back

Let's assume that you *have* listened carefully to what the writer said. You *have* interpreted the writer's statements thoughtfully in light of your own beliefs and knowledge. Now consider the various ways you might respond. One way to respond is simply to agree. You accept what the writer has written if it seems reasonable and in keeping with what you already know and believe. Or, you might reconsider your own knowledge and beliefs in light of the new ideas or knowledge you've accepted. Or, you might respond by disagreeing with a part or all of the writer's presentation. You might challenge the information on which the writer's thesis relies, or you might accept the information but reject as unreasonable the conclusion the author draws from it. Still another way to respond is to extend the author's statement, to observe connections with your own ideas and experiences or with other texts. You may notice possibilities within the text that the author may not have considered.

Drawing Conclusions

As we've stated previously, you are likely to find yourself responding in some or all of these ways as you read a text the first time through for understanding and as you work to interpret it. Remember, however, to reserve your complete response until you have a full understanding of the text. If you look back at the student's annotations on Bok's essay on pages 5–7, you will note that in addition to identifying the structure of the essay and marking unfamiliar words, she has also raised some questions and offered some examples. Get in the habit of jotting questions or connections that occur to you as you read. Keeping track of your responses to individual sections of the text will help you formulate a full response to the entire text. You will probably find it easiest simply to make these jottings in the margins of your text. Some readers prefer to keep a reading log, a separate notebook or computer file of their responses to a text. A reading log is especially useful if you find yourself responding at length and generating more notes than will fit in the margin.

Making Sense of Your Responses

Sometimes you will find that even after reading for understanding and after interpreting what you have read, you are unable to articulate a full response to the whole text, even though you may have strong responses to specific points. At such times, you may find it useful to make double-entry notes on your reading.

Double-Entry Notes.   Assuming that you have really read for understanding, you should be able to identify the writer's main idea. Write it, or a paraphrase of it, at the top of your notes, to refer to as you work. Then, proceed systematically through the key supporting points of the essay. Write each important point, or a summary of each point, on the left-hand side of your paper. On the corresponding right-hand side, record your thoughts in response to each point.

An Idea Skeleton.   When finish, you will have not just a skeleton of the essay, as you might get with summary notes, you will also have a skeleton of your own thoughts, which will reveal certain patterns of response. You may note, for example, that you have disagreed with the writer's information at several points. In this case, you might decide that although his thesis *seems* reasonable, the information in the text does not support it. Conversely, you may find that your comments challenge not so much the writer's information but the significance he attaches to them. Again, you would respond by disagreeing with the thesis, but for a different reason. If you find that most of your observations are statements that affirm the writer's points or extend them, then your full response to the essay may be acceptance, even if you disagree with a point here or there.

In the following double-entry notes on "Placebos" by Sissela Bok, reprinted earlier, such an idea skeleton and pattern of response emerge. We have already summarized the key points and identified the text's main idea, so the note-taking task has been made simpler.

Thesis: Prescribing placebos is a dangerous practice because the treatment may cause harm to the patient + the acceptance of this kind of deceit may lead us to accept other deceptions.

1. Hard to know how often placebos are prescribed because drs don't discuss practice openly. Also, sometimes drs are unaware that the treatment they've prescribed	*1. The very fact that drs don't even discuss this practice in medical literature suggests they themselves recognize it as an inappropriate use of their power.*

has only placebic benefits Esp. true in past.

I don't see why Bok mentions those occasions when dr is unaware that what he/she prescribed is placebic. That's a case of ignorance, not deception. Her point in this essay is to show why this kind of <u>deception</u> is wrong.

2. Prescribing placebos not seen as serious moral issue because deception is believed to have only beneficial effects.

2. Little white lie? Like telling someone they look good in an out-fit that looks terrible on them or tricking kids to believe in Santa Claus. I still think most "white lies" are wrong, even if they do have a beneficial effect because when you you get right down to it, they're about power. I control you by keep-ing the truth from you, i.e., I trick you into feeling better by giving you sugar pills. I get you to act the way I want you to by telling you that Santa is watching. I let you face the world thinking you look good even though I know you don't. All of these lies take away some-one's right to choose based on the facts.

3. The costs:
A. Prevents drs from diagnosing real illness, treating real problem.

A. This is a matter of bad diagnosis, not the practice of prescribing placebos. If the dr fails to locate the real problem, it doesn't matter if the treatment he prescribes is placebic or not—it won't work.

B. May encourage patients to believe medical treatment answer to all ailments.

B. I think we're all guilty of this. We pop a pill for <u>everything</u>. Could this be reason for # of people on mood altering drugs, e.g., Prozac? Also, think of effect of this on cost of health care, insurance for everyone.

C. Millions of $ are spent on pills + procedures that have no therapeutic benefit.

C. See ↑ This isn't a harmless practice if it's raising health care costs for everyone.

D. Diminishes trust patients have in drs.

D. Lack of trust in drs (and all authority) growing. Drs should realize patients will have greater trust if they feel dr is honest, treating them like adults capable of making their own choices.

E. Patients develop unhealthy dependence on placebos.

E. Even vitamin pills in Bok's example could be potentially dangerous. Also, if patient is taking 1 kind of drug, but doesn't realize it, he/she may not observe necessary precautions for taking that drug w/ other drugs, alcohol, etc.

4. Because practice is not discussed, may lead to other kinds of deception—i.e., using placebos as part of experiment w/out patients' permission.

4. Well, this seems kind of far-fetched. Does one thing always lead to another? Withholding treatment that the patient doesn't really need is a _lot_ different, morally speaking, than w/holding treatment patient _does_ need, i.e., Tuskegee syphilis experiments: people died because they weren't getting treatment. I think most drs would find that kind of deception unacceptable, even if they occasionally prescribe placebos.

5. Drs may prescribe active drugs so patient will feel small effect.

5. Again, taking any drug when you don't need to is putting your body at unnecessary risk. I'd be furious if this happened to me.

6. More people expect treatment, more placebos are prescribed, more people expect treatment.

6. Yes. This makes a lot of sense. And again, it seems a matter of power. Drs + drug companies want us to think we need them.

7. Must consider cumulative effect, not just isolated cases.

7. I agree + I agree w/ Bok that the cumulative effect of this kind of deceit is too dangerous + just wrong to justify an occasional beneficial outcome. Most of us, given the choice, would not want to be lied to, even for our own good.

As you look over these notes, you see that the reader finds some of the evidence Bok included irrelevant to the discussion. She also disagrees with one of Bok's key points, that the use of placebos could spread from therapy to experimentation without the patient's consent. On most points, however, she agrees with Bok's evidence and conclusions, and she has even drawn conclusions that Bok does not explicitly make. At several points, this reader notes that prescribing placebos constitutes an abuse of power. What seems to upset her most about the practice is that it denies patients the information they need to make their own choices.

Keeping double-entry notes is time-consuming, and of course is not necessary for everything you read. However, the system can be a useful tool for responding to a difficult piece.

READING IMAGINATIVE TEXTS

So far, our discussion of critical reading has focused on reading essays, appropriately so as most of the selections in this book are essays. However, you will also encounter some short stories and poems here, as well as pictures and advertisements. Therefore, we now turn to a discussion of reading other kinds of texts.

Obviously, reading a short story or a poem is an experience quite different from reading an analytical or expository essay. Like any other text, a short story or poem offers us information and ideas, but its purpose is not so much to communicate abstract knowledge or persuade us to accept certain views, as it is to share with us particular experiences, observations, or conditions.

Because imaginative writing, what we commonly call "literature," differs in its intentions from essay writing, it would be a mistake to approach both kinds of texts the same way. Clearly, you would ruin the experience of reading a story or poem if you were to work your way through it looking for the main idea and key supporting points. Nevertheless, some of the observations we have already made about critical reading are useful when engaging an imaginative text.

Like any other text, an imaginative text should be read thoughtfully, respectfully, and more than once. Perhaps even more so than an essay, an imaginative work invites us to interpret and respond even in the first reading. Nevertheless, we should be wary of drawing a final conclusion about the text until we are certain we have understood it.

Just as we read through an essay for understanding of the specific ideas that lead to the general point, the best way to approach a first reading of an imaginative text is simply to read for understanding, paying attention to the general impression we take from the work.

Read the following short story by William Carlos Williams once; then read the discussion that follows. Williams, best known as a poet, also practiced medicine in his native Rutherford, New Jersey. The disease he mentions in this story, diphtheria, virtually unheard of today thanks to widespread immunization, is a highly contagious, rapidly spreading disease that would often move into a community, killing or causing permanent heart damage and paralysis to scores of its most vulnerable members, generally children. Prior to immunization, diphtheria was treated with an antitoxin that, though it could not reverse damage already done, could prevent further harm. Hence, early diagnosis was crucial to recovery.

The Use of Force

They were new patients to me, all I had was the name, Olson. Please come down as soon as you can, my daughter is very sick.

When I arrived I was met by the mother, a big startled-looking woman, very clean and apologetic who merely said, Is this the doctor? and let me in. In the back, she added. You must excuse us, doctor, we have her in the kitchen where it is warm. It is very damp here sometimes.

The child was fully dressed and sitting on her father's lap near the kitchen table. He tried to get up, but I motioned for him not to bother, took off my overcoat and started to look things over. I could see that they were all very nervous, eyeing me up and down distrustfully. As often, in such cases, they weren't telling me more than they had to, it was up to me to tell them; that's why they were spending three dollars on me.

The child was fairly eating me up with her cold, steady eyes, and no expression to her face whatever. She did not move and seemed, inwardly, quiet; an unusually attractive little thing, and as strong as a heifer in appearance. But her face was flushed, she was breathing rapidly, and I realized that she had a high fever. She had magnificent blonde hair, in profusion. One of those picture children often reproduced in advertising leaflets and the photogravure sections of the Sunday papers.

She's had a fever for three days, began the father and we don't know what it comes from. My wife has given her things, you know, like people do, but it don't do no good. And there's been a lot of sickness around. So we tho't you'd better look her over and tell us what is the matter.

As doctors often do I took a trial shot at it as a point of departure. Has she had a sore throat?

Both parents answered me together, No . . . No, she says her throat don't hurt her.

Does your throat hurt you? added the mother to the child. But the little girl's expression didn't change nor did she move her eyes from my face.

Have you looked?

I tried to, said the mother, but I couldn't see.

As it happens we had been having a number of cases of diphtheria in the school to which this child went during that month and we were all, quite apparently, thinking of that, though no one had as yet spoken of the thing.

Well, I said, suppose we take a look at the throat first. I smiled in my best professional manner and asking for the child's first name I said, come on, Mathilda, open your mouth and let's take a look at your throat.

Nothing doing.

Aw, come on, I coaxed, just open your mouth wide and let me take a look. Look, I said opening both hands wide, I haven't anything in my hands. Just open up and let me see.

Such a nice man, put in the mother. Look how kind he is to you. Come on, do what he tells you to. He won't hurt you.

At that I ground my teeth in disgust. If only they wouldn't use the word "hurt" I might be able to get someplace. But I did not allow myself to be hurried or disturbed but speaking quietly and slowly I approached the child again.

As I moved my chair a little nearer suddenly with one cat-like movement both her hands clawed instinctively for my eyes and she almost reached them too. In fact she knocked my glasses flying and they fell, though unbroken, several feet away from me on the kitchen floor.

Both the mother and father almost turned themselves inside out in embarrassment and apology. You bad girl, said the mother, taking her and shaking her by one arm. Look what you've done. The nice man . . . .

For heaven's sake, I broke in. Don't call me a nice man to her. I'm here to look at her throat on the chance that she might have diphtheria and possibly die of it. But that's nothing to her. Look here, I said to the child, we're going to look at your throat. You're old enough to understand what I'm saying. Will you open it now by yourself or shall we have to open it for you?

Not a move. Even her expression hadn't changed. Her breaths however were coming faster and faster. Then the battle began. I had to do it. I had to have a throat culture for her own protection. But first I told the parents that it was entirely up to them. I explained the danger but said that I would not insist on a throat examination so long as they would take the responsibility.

If you don't do what the doctor says you'll have to go to the hospital, the mother admonished her severely.

Oh yeah? I had to smile to myself. After all, I had already fallen in love with the savage brat, the parents were contemptible to me. In the ensuing struggle they grew more and more abject, crushed, exhausted while she surely rose to magnificent heights of insane fury of effort bred of her terror of me.

The father tried his best, and he was a big man but the fact that she was his daughter, his shame at her behavior and his dread of hurting her made him release her just at the critical moment several times when I had almost achieved success, till I wanted to kill him. But his dread also that she might have diphtheria made him tell me to go on, go on though he himself was almost fainting, while the mother moved back and forth behind us raising and lowering her hands in an agony of apprehension.

Put her in front of you on your lap, I ordered, and hold both her wrists.

But as soon as he did the child let out a scream. Don't, you're hurting me. Let go of my hands. Let them go I tell you. Then she shrieked terrifyingly, hysterically. Stop it! Stop it! You're killing me!

Do you think she can stand it, doctor! said the mother.

You get out, said the husband to his wife. Do you want her to die of diphtheria?

Come on now, hold her, I said.

Then I grasped the child's head with my left hand and tried to get the wooden tongue depressor between her teeth. She fought, with clenched teeth, desperately! But now I also had grown furious—at a child. I tried to hold myself down but I couldn't. I know how to expose a throat for inspection. And I did my best. When finally I got the wooden spatula behind the last teeth and just the point of it into the mouth cavity, she opened up for an instant but before I could see anything she came down again and gripping the wooden blade between her molars she reduced it to splinters before I could get it out again.

Aren't you ashamed, the mother yelled at her. Aren't you ashamed to act like that in front of the doctor?

Get me a smooth-handled spoon of some sort, I told the mother. We're going through with this. The child's mouth was already bleeding. Her tongue was cut and she was screaming in wild hysterical shrieks. Perhaps I should have desisted and come back in an hour or more. No doubt it would have been better. But I have seen at least two children lying dead in bed of neglect in such cases, and feeling that I must get a diagnosis, now or never I went at it again. But the worst of it was that I too had got beyond reason. I could have torn the child apart in my own fury and enjoyed it. It was a pleasure to attack her. My face was burning with it.

The damned little brat must be protected against her own idiocy, one says to one's self at such times. Others must be protected against her. It is a social necessity. And all these things are true. But a blind fury, a feeling of adult shame, bred of a longing for muscular release are the operatives. One goes on to the end.

In a final unreasoning assault I overpowered the child's neck and jaws. I forced the heavy silver spoon back on her teeth and down her throat till she gagged. And there it was—both tonsils covered with membrane. She had fought valiantly to keep me from knowing her secret. She had been hiding that sore throat for three days at least and lying to her parents in order to escape just such an outcome as this.

Now truly she *was* furious. She had been on the defensive before but now she attacked. Tried to get off her father's lap and fly at me while tears of defeat blinded her eyes.

Making the Reading Your Own: Interpretation

It's impossible to read very far into this story without engaging in interpretation. Questions are raised, gaps are opened between the world you know and the world of the story, and you find you must answer those questions and fill those gaps before you can go on.

For example, the very first paragraph prompts you to wonder where and when this story takes place. Most of us today live in communities where doctors no longer make house calls. The fact that the doctor could so easily be summoned to the home of new patients may suggest that the story is set sometime in the past.

The next paragraph raises more questions: Why is the kitchen warmer than the rest of the house? Why is the home very damp sometimes? These living conditions may suggest that the family is poor, that their house or apartment is not well insulated, that it lacks a central heat source.

As you read the second paragraph, no doubt other questions occurred to you—not about the content of the paragraph, but about the form. Did you have trouble, at first, distinguishing the narrator's voice from the mother's? As you've noticed, Williams does not observe the convention of setting apart direct speech by enclosing it in quotation marks from the rest of the text.

You can see, then, that interpretation of an imaginative text involves several different information "filters." The first we might call the cultural filter. That is, our own cultural background gives us certain expectations of society, of reality. "Doctors don't make house calls" may be one. "Homes have central heating" may be another. When the story doesn't meet those cultural expectations, we engage in interpretation to make sense of the discrepancies. "The story is set in the past." "This family is poor."

A second filter through which we interpret an imaginative text might be called the literary filter, or in this case, the fictional filter. As experienced readers, we have certain expectations about the form of a text. We expect a short story to have a different form than a poem, a novel, or a play. We expect quotation marks around lines of dialogue. When our literary expectations are not met, we must adjust our reading accordingly. In this case, you probably found, once you got used to the lack of quotation marks, that you could tell which lines were speech. Nevertheless, you probably found that the narrator's thoughts, the statements of the parents and the child, and the narrator's statements to the parents and the child, followed quickly upon one another, even ran together at times in your mind.

There is yet another filter through which the events and observations of a story or poem come to us, and that is the filter of the author. As we read an imaginative text, we must keep in mind that we are listening to a particular voice, a voice controlled by a writer who chooses not just what we will hear and see but *how* we will hear and see and what we will *not* hear or see. In "The Use of Force," for example, we listen to the voice of the narrator, who, like the author, is a doctor. All we know of the other characters and the house call episode is presented to us by and through that narrator. As we interpret the events and characters of the story, then, we need to consider how much faith to put in the narrator's impressions.

Look, for example, at paragraph 23, in which the narrator describes the father's attempts to help the doctor examine the child's throat:

> The father tried his best, and he was a big man but the fact that she was his daughter, his shame at her behavior and his dread of hurting her made him release her just at the critical moment several times when I had almost achieved success, till I wanted to kill him. But his dread also that she might have diphtheria made him tell me to go on, go on, though he himself was almost fainting, while the mother moved back and forth behind us raising and lowering her hands in an agony of apprehension.

Do you find it strange that the narrator describes not only the father's actions, but his motivation as well? It seems that the narrator himself is engaging in interpretation here, filling in the gaps between what he knows—that the father is unable to hold his daughter still—and what he does not know—why this big man cannot restrain a child. In doing so, the narrator imposes his own cultural expectations on the event. The motivation he ascribes to the father may or may not accurately explain the man's actions. But it certainly reveals something about the narrator. We might interpret these lines to suggest that the narrator sympathizes with the father, that the lines show how the narrator would feel in the father's place. Or, in contrast, we might think that the narrator's presuming to explain the father's feelings reveals an attitude of superiority, that he believes he knows all there is to know about this family.

However we interpret this passage, it affects our interpretation of the story as a whole. If we conclude that the narrator considers the other characters inferior to himself, then we must filter all that he tells us about them and their surroundings and their actions through that interpretation. On the other hand, if we sense he is sympathetic to the family, we view the whole story quite differently.

Every reader brings his or her own expectations to a given text, and so every reader will interpret the text differently. This is what we mean by making the reading your own. The text itself is fixed. Williams's words cannot be changed to have the story turn out as we might wish, but the meaning of the text is mutable, varying sometimes slightly, sometimes significantly, as it is filtered through each reader's interpretations.

In this book, stories and poems will sometimes be followed by questions labeled Rereading for Understanding that we hope will help you interpret what you read. The questions below about "The Use of Force" are examples.

1. The narrator mentions the family's name and gives us some description of them, especially of the child. What significance do you find in these details? What do they tell us about the family?

2. How would you describe the parents' behavior toward the doctor? Which passages in the text support this description? What does their behavior toward the doctor suggest about them?

3. Trace the changes in the narrator's attitude toward the situation, the child, and her parents throughout the story. What do you think causes each change?

Don't depend too much on these Rereading questions; your own questions may be far more useful in arriving at a meaningful understanding of the text because they reflect your own cultural and literary expectations, not ours. As you read, note your questions in the margin of the text or in a reading journal. They will guide your interpretation.

Responding to Imaginative Texts: Criticism

As we noted in our previous discussion of critical reading, it is hard to separate the reading process neatly into discrete steps. We cannot read for understanding without engaging in interpretation. In order to interpret, we ask questions of the text, which is a kind of response to it. And the questions we raise in order to interpret lead us to other questions. We find ourselves asking not simply what does this mean? but *why* does it mean this? Our attempts to answer that question are called criticism.

Criticism is a word that tends to make students uncomfortable. It suggests passing judgment, evaluating a literary work, and many students (and other readers), because they lack formal training in literary analysis, feel inadequate even to try. But if we think of criticism as responding to the text, as that point in the reader/writer exchange when you have listened carefully to understand what the writer is "saying" and are now ready to reply, it becomes a little less intimidating. An extensive vocabulary of literary terms or thorough familiarity with the author's life and times, although certainly useful for producing certain kinds of criticism, are not the only kinds of knowledge that qualify you to respond critically to a literary work.

Criticism begins when we try to understand why the author has made choices he or she has. For example, we have noted that Williams has not observed the convention of enclosing direct speech in quotation marks. Why has Williams made this choice? What effect does it have on our experience reading this story? To one reader, the failure to observe literary conventions is a distraction; it prevents him from following the story and from fully engaging with it. Another reader may find that eliminating the visual cues that separate one character's words from another and from the narrator's thoughts, creates the atmosphere of urgency and disorder that the narrator himself feels; it allows her to share more fully in the experience he describes. Both of these readers are engaging in criticism. That is, they are not just interpreting the writer's choices, but critiquing them as well.

Criticism is more, however, than measuring a work against a set of literary standards. Criticism can also involve judging the implicit and explicit ideas the work presents, the position the work takes on issues beyond itself. It may involve pointing out the writer's biases, showing where and how and to what effect the writer imposes his own cultural and literary expectations on the experience he shares with us.

Let's consider again the passage in "The Use of Force" we examined earlier, in which the narrator attempts to explain the father's inability to hold the child still while her throat is examined. We have already noted the impossibility of the narrator's actually knowing what is going on in the father's mind, and we suggested two possible interpretations of this passage. For the sake of discussion, let's accept for now the second interpretation, that the passage suggests an assumption of superiority on the part of the narrator, that he feels himself capable of reading the minds of the family. We might now ask, why has the author included this passage? Why has he allowed the narrator to make this presumptuous judgment?

One answer to this question may be that Williams has not made a conscious choice, that he himself does not see the narrator's explanation as presumptuous. We might even go so far as to say that the narrator's presumed superiority is shared by Williams himself. If this is the case, we may conclude that Williams, in this story, uncritically excuses brutality in the name of doing good.

Another response may be that Williams has deliberately revealed the narrator's arrogance in this passage to expose his arrogance throughout the story. From the beginning, the narrator draws our attention to his own cool, professional behavior, versus the hysterical, helpless, and ignorant behavior of his patient's parents. We might conclude that Williams wants his readers to question the power that comes with authority, to see how the strong, in the name of helping the weak, serve instead their own needs and desires.

Yet another way we might understand Williams's inclusion of this revealing passage is that like the story itself, it complicates our notion of power as a positive or negative force. Williams doesn't want us to categorize the final act of the story either as an assault of the powerful upon the powerless, or as the beneficent intervention of the strong and skilled to save the life of the weak and ignorant, but perhaps as a little of both.

Each of these statements is criticism because each involves not merely interpreting the passage but explaining and evaluating the author's choice. Again, we should point out that reading, interpretation, and criticism, are not isolated acts. However, we can see that sound criticism depends on reasonable interpretation, which in turn must be based on accurate analytical reading of the text.

Each literary work in this book will be followed by questions labeled Responding, which are designed to help you formulate a critical position. Again, keep in mind that your own questions are equally useful for this purpose. Get in the habit of paying attention to your own responses as you read and reread. We have already examined some critical responses to "The Use of Force." Here are two Responding questions to help you think of others.

1. Why do you think Williams chose "The Use of Force" as the title for this story?

2. How might this story be different if it were told from the point of view of the child or one of the parents? How would it change if the narrator were outside the story looking in rather than a participant in the event?

READING IMAGES

Can you "read" a painting? Is a photograph a text you can analyze and interpret? We answer yes to both of these questions. An image, as defined by art critic John Berger, "is a sight, which has been recreated or reproduced." As such, Berger goes on to say, "every image embodies a way of seeing".

In other words, any image, from da Vinci's *Mona Lisa* to Aunt Melba's videotape of her trip to Graceland, is a product of selection and interpretation. We don't see the real, human woman who sat as da Vinci's model; what we see is the way da Vinci saw her, or perhaps the way he wanted us to see her. To follow Aunt Melba's camera as it pans from the front gate, up the drive, and to Elvis's front door is not the same as walking through that gate ourselves. For everything da Vinci and Aunt Melba have shown us, there is much more that they have not shown us, much that they cannot show us.

To a much greater extent than any of the other kinds of texts we have considered so far, images are a part of our daily life. Although we have to decide to read an essay, a short story, or a poem, we don't need to make a conscious decision to look at images. We are surrounded by them. We need only to hit the ON button on the television set, pick up a newspaper, or drive down the freeway to see innumerable images. On a trip to the market or a walk in the park we'll probably encounter a dozen images just on the T-shirts of passers-by. Most of the images we see each day are in the form of advertisement, but even images that aren't trying to sell us a product are nonetheless trying to persuade us, to shape the way we see a part of reality. Because images are so prevalent and because we can take them in with so little effort, they generally don't invite a critical response. It is for those very reasons, however, that we should give the same thoughtful, critical reading to images as to any other kind of text.

Look carefully at the following painting by Norman Rockwell, making note of your first impressions. Then use the questions that follow as guides for analyzing and interpreting the painting.

1. What is happening in this picture? What has taken place just prior to the moment shown here? What will happen next?

2. Describe the facial expression of the adult and the child. What do their faces convey about each of them, about the event that is taking place, and about their relationship with each other?

3. Look beyond the faces at the other physical attributes of the two people in the painting. What effect is gained, for example, by making the adult chubby and rosy-cheeked, rather than thin and pale? Why do you think Rockwell dressed the child in outerclothes (coat, hat, mittens, galoshes)? How would the picture be different if the child were somewhat older or younger? a boy instead of a girl? What other distinctive physical features do you notice? How do those features shape your impression of the event in the painting?

4. Look at the objects Rockwell has included in the painting. Why do you think he has placed the doctor's black bag on the floor? Why is one candle

partially burned? What other objects do you note? What impression does each item convey?

5. What is missing from the painting? Can you think of other people or objects that would probably have been present if this encounter were actually taking place? Why do you think Rockwell has chosen to show us just this much of the scene?

Analyzing and Interpreting Image Clues

In looking at the image and answering these questions, you probably found yourself doing many of the same things you do when you read any other text. On first looking at the image, you form a general impression of it, gathering information that leads to an understanding. You also find yourself interpreting, filling in the gaps between what you know and expect and what the image shows or doesn't show you. As you discuss your reading with your classmates, you'll notice that each reader filters the image through personal knowledge and particular beliefs and expectations.

The title of this painting is *The Doctor and the Doll.* We've withheld the title until now because we wanted you to see how easily you are able to read this image. Without any accompanying text, you know who the two people are and what the event is. You don't need the title to know that the man in this painting is a doctor. A few key objects—the stethoscope, the black bag, the framed document—reveal his profession immediately. It's almost as if Rockwell were speaking to us in a kind of code. He doesn't have to open the black bag and show us the medical instruments inside; the bag itself signifies "doctor" to us. He doesn't need to show us what is written on the framed document behind the books. The frame, the script, the single word "registration" are enough to cue us that this is a diploma or certificate of the doctor's medical training.

Learning the Codes

One reason why Rockwell enjoyed such popularity as an artist is that he knew his audience and could depend on their being able to read the cultural coding in his work. Not everyone would "read" this painting the same way because cultural codes are not universal. Consider this opening paragraph from "The Sick Child" by Angela DeCora, a Winnebago Indian:

It was about sunset when I, a little child, was sent with a handful of powdered tobacco leaves and red feathers to make an offering to the spirit who had caused the sickness of my little sister. It had been a long, hard winter, and the snow lay deep on the prairies as far as the eye could reach. The medicine woman's directions had been that the offering must be laid upon the naked earth, and that to find it, I must face toward the setting sun.(27)

The narrator of this story would probably have a difficult time understanding what is happening in Rockwell's painting because her cultural codes for healing and medicine are quite different from ours. Likewise, we would have a difficult time decoding an image of a woman handing powdered tobacco leaves and red feathers to a child and sending her off into the snow.

Now here's the curious part. Try to remember when, if ever, you have actually seen a doctor carrying a black bag like the one in this painting. We who are old enough to remember a doctor calling at our homes haven't seen a bag like this in thirty years or more. A survey in our freshman English classes revealed that although only three students could recall actually seeing a real doctor carrying such a bag, every student in the class recognized the bag in the painting as a "doctor's black bag."

The question is, if the doctor's bag is not something we know about from real experience, how are we able to recognize its significance in the painting? The answer of course is that although we may never have seen such a bag in the hands of a real doctor, we've seen plenty of pretend doctors carrying one: doctors on television and in books, in magazine advertisements, in paintings like this one.

So you see that even as images like Rockwell's painting depend on us to *recognize* cultural codes, they also serve to *teach* us those codes. As you consider the images and other texts in this book, pay attention to the cultural codes embedded in them and the sources of those codes. The Responding questions following images in this text are designed to help you think about both how the images draw on our cultural and social expectations and how they instill them. These two Responding questions reflect on *The Doctor and the Doll:*

1. How is the medical profession in general presented in this painting? What, does the painting suggest, characterizes a good doctor? a good doctor/patient relationship?

2. The doctor in this painting seems to be deceiving the child, playing along with the girl's obviously serious belief that her doll needs medical attention. How do you think Rockwell intends us to judge the doctor's act of deception? How does this image influence our thinking about the issue of trust in the doctor/patient relationship?

FROM READING TO WRITING

ecently, a student in my composition class stopped by to apologize for having missed many of our class meetings. After explaining that he wasn't a "morning person" (the class meets at 8:00 A.M.), he added casually that, since we had "just been discussing the reading" on the days he'd been absent, he really didn't feel he'd missed anything important. I didn't know whether to be impressed or offended by his candor—imagine telling one of your instructors that you considered a good half of the class sessions to be insignificant! But after he'd left, promising to change his truant ways, I realized that his intention had been neither to insult nor to shock. He simply assumed that I shared his understanding of the relationship between reading and writing: that reading and writing were wholly separate activities, and because this was a "writing" class, discussing essays the class had read was somehow peripheral, if not irrelevant, to the true aims of the course.

THE CONNECTION BETWEEN READING AND WRITING

The connection between reading and writing becomes clearer when we consider the title given to most college writing courses—"Composition"—and examine the different origins of that word and the word "write." The latter comes from an Old English word *writan*, meaning "to score or engrave," and in its earliest uses, it connoted simply the act of making letters or marks. "Compose" comes from a combination of two words from Middle French: *com*, meaning "together," and *poser*, meaning "to place or put," and early uses of the word meant just that: "to put together." If we think of writing as merely inscribing, no more than the mechanical act of recording in the current medium, be it stone or floppy disk, then reading and writing are connected to each other only in that when we read we are deciphering someone else's markings. If we think of writing as composing, however, as putting together parts to construct a whole, then we can see that we engage in the same critical thinking activities when we write as when we read.

When we read critically, we try to put the pieces of the text together by listening to and trying to understand what the writer is saying. We consider ideas and images in light of each other and in light of the thoughts we bring to the reading. We seek logical as well as structural connections among the pieces of the text. We raise questions and look for answers. We draw conclusions. In short, when we read, we are not passively searching for hidden meanings, we are actively making meaning as we go.

Likewise, when we compose, we examine concepts and seek connections among them. We ask ourselves questions and try to answer them. We draw conclusions. We sort and select ideas and images that show our conclusions to be sound and present them in a way that our audience can follow. Writing is not the simple act of finding words to express meaning; like reading, it is the active making of meaning.

READING AND WRITING IN COLLEGE

Much of the writing you will do in college will require you to draw upon and respond to something you have read. Sometimes you will be asked to write simply to demonstrate your recall of knowledge: "Briefly explain the process of photosynthesis." But more frequently, you will be expected to use your reading for a specific purpose. You may be asked to evaluate or critique a single text in light of other texts and/or your own knowledge; you may be asked to apply ideas from your reading to a particular problem or set of problems; or your assignment might be to synthesize ideas from several sources and draw a conclusion.

Earlier in this unit, we suggested that critical reading is similar to a conversation between reader and writer. Academic writing, too, can be seen as a kind of ongoing conversation in which ideas are offered, challenged, defended, questioned, and improved. As you proceed in college, you will find that you are expected in your writing not simply to listen politely to that discussion, nor just to repeat others' ideas, but to contribute actively to the conversation.

THE WRITING PROCESS

Writing is a process, but it is not a tidy, straightforward process like jump-starting a battery or loading a program on your computer. We cannot offer you a step-by-step, foolproof system for writing perfect papers. What we can and will offer is a method for approaching and accomplishing writing tasks that views composing as making meaning.

Understanding the Writing Task

In college, most of the writing you do will be in response to an assignment. Sometimes that assignment will be quite specific in its demands: "Write a 2-page essay critiquing the President's proposal to ban cigarette vending machines in light of our study of the Bill of Rights." Other assignments will be more general: "Write an 8 to 10 page critical paper on one of the literary works we've read in class." In either case, if you are writing in response to an assignment, now for a professor or later on for your employer, your first task is to understand the demands and expectations of that writing task. Don't be afraid to ask for additional information. You may need to ask the instructor to clarify certain terms. In the first assignment, for instance, you may want an explanation of what your instructor means by "critique." If you have been assigned the longer literary criticism paper, you probably want to know if secondary sources are permitted, or even required.

Taking the Audience into Consideration

Your understanding of the audience you are addressing can guide the composing process. For example, if you know how knowledgeable your audience is about your subject, you can decide how much background information you will need to provide. Knowing how interested in your subject your audience is likely to be will help you shape your introduction so as to capture their attention. And being aware of the opinions your audience may bring to their reading of your essay forces you to consider those opinions and find reasonable ways to address them.

Invention

Writing that is worth reading offers original insights or fresh ways of understanding that challenge our conventional thinking and allow us to grow intellectually. A good writer, then, must be able to complicate what seems obvious, to raise questions, to turn ideas on themselves, to look at old ideas in new ways. *Invention* is a term that refers to all the various activities we engage in to complicate our thinking about the writing task. It is what we do when we read critically, when we engage the text and actively make meaning as we read, when we put one text in dialogue with another. Invention also takes place when we discuss our reading in class or outside of class and when we do research.

Get in the habit of taking "invention notes." Keep a response journal or double-entry notes as you read. Always take notes in class discussion, paying attention not only to the ideas offered by your instructor and other students, but also to your own responses to those ideas. You will find that the very act of writing down thoughts as they come to you not only helps you recall them when it comes time to draft, but also clarifies them. In order to articulate an idea, you have to understand it. When you look over your notes, abstractions will indicate to you ideas which require further investigation.

There are other techniques for generating invention notes. Your instructor may ask you to *brainstorm*, or free write, about a topic for a designated period of time, say ten or fifteen minutes. The objective in brainstorming is to keep writing without pausing to edit or evaluate. Many writers find this sustained focus helps them to tap into ideas that they would not otherwise discover.

Some writers write *discovery drafts* as a means of inventing. They begin writing a draft in response to the writing task, recognizing that their purpose is to discover ideas, not to produce the content or set the format of the final essay.

If you have not already discovered effective strategies for invention, experiment with different approaches. The more you write, the more you will see how your mind generates and examines ideas. The important thing about invention is not *how* you do it, but *that* you do it—that you make a point of complicating your response to the writing topic before drawing a conclusion about it.

Thesis

Invention describes that part of the writing process that is writer-centered. Whatever form your invention notes take, they are intended for and useful to you alone. An audience would probably be unable to make sense of them. When you begin the next phase of the writing process, *drafting*, your focus is on the audience. When you draft, your purpose is to present the ideas and conclusion you reached in invention in a format that will be clear and convincing to your intended audience. Summing up your response to the writing task in a *thesis* marks the transition between these two phases.

A thesis is a premise, the statement your essay will serve to develop and support. In this sense, formulating a thesis marks the beginning of the drafting stage. The thesis reflects your thinking about the writing task. In this sense, it is a conclusion to invention.

Not every composition will contain an explicit *thesis statement*, but it is a helpful practice to try to write your thesis out in one or more clear sentences, even if you do not intend to include those sentences in your essay. Forcing yourself to articulate the premise or purpose of your essay will help you, first of all, to be sure that you *have* a clear premise. If you cannot state what it is that you are intending to support or develop in the essay, then you probably need to give more thought to the writing task. Writing the thesis out also helps you to know what ideas and information your essay must include.

Drafting

If the purpose of invention is to complicate your thinking, the purpose of drafting is to clarify it: to present those complex thoughts as clearly and directly as you can so that your audience will accept them. Because writing tasks and audiences vary, we cannot offer you a formula like "Every essay should have five paragraphs," "Every paragraph should have eight sentences," or "Points should be arranged in order of importance" that will satisfy the demands of every writing assignment.

Rather we suggest that you be guided by the expectations of your audience, by the inherent demands of the writing task, and by the purpose that you have set for yourself in your thesis. Although almost every composition you write will share certain characteristics of format, each composition will take a different shape to accommodate the particular demands of the assignment. For example, every composition should have a thesis, but sometimes you will choose to state that thesis at the beginning of the draft, sometimes at the end of the paper, and other times you will choose not to state the thesis at all. Likewise, you will organize the content of every composition to show clear connections among the ideas, but the particular rationale for organization will depend on what those ideas are and what thesis you intend them to support, as well as on the needs of your audience.

Revision

Consider the word *revision*. Re-vision suggests re-seeing. When you revise your composition, you begin by looking at it again and seeing whether it fulfills your original purpose, whether it meets the needs of its audience, and whether it satisfies the requirements of the writing task as thoroughly as it might.

Revision demands perspective. It demands that you see your draft as your audience will see it. This perspective is hard to achieve. If time permits, set your first draft aside and don't look at it for a day or two. You may be surprised by how clearly wrong or right some of your choices seem when you return to the draft and read it anew.

If at all possible, ask others to read your draft and give you feedback. You don't need to ask your readers to evaluate your work or even to suggest changes. The most useful kind of feedback is simply descriptive. See if your readers are able to tell you what the premise or main point of the composition is. Ask them to point out any passages that they did not understand or ideas that were not clearly explained or illustrated. Ask if they understand why you arranged material as you did. Find out if your ideas are clearly connected.

This kind of feedback will help you identify the changes you need to make to improve your composition. Revising may involve a significant reworking of parts or all of the draft. You may find yourself discarding whole sections of the draft and/or adding major pieces. You may find yourself rearranging the draft. However, revision is *not* correcting or polishing. That process is another distinct stage of the composition process, editing.

Editing

Editing is presented here as the final stage in the writing process, but that in no way suggests that editing is insignificant. *Editing* refers to correcting and polishing the draft. Editing involves finding errors and fixing them, replacing ambiguous words or phrases with precise ones, transforming wordy, clumsy passages into concise and articulate statements.

Your audience expects you to meet the conventions of Standard Written English. If you fail to do so, not only are you likely to lose credibility as an educated, intelligent writer, you may also fail to make the point you mean to make. Consider, for example, the following sentence:

Woman without her man is nothing.

Now watch what happens when a single mark of punctuation is added.

Woman—without her man is nothing.

If you don't see the difference in meaning between these two sentences, try reading each one out loud, pausing at the dash.

Remember, composing is the act of making meaning. Editing ensures that what you say is what you mean.

Editing your language for precision and grace is no less important than correcting errors. To illustrate the difference that word choice and sentence structure can make in how your audience receives and remembers your message, try to restate a famous sentence like John F. Kennedy's "Ask not what your country can do for you; ask what you can do for your country." You will find it difficult, if not impossible, to find a combination of words that conveys Kennedy's point as clearly and memorably.

A Final Note on the Writing Process

We have discussed the writing process here as a series of stages, and to a certain degree, composing does proceed in a linear fashion. Any experienced writer knows, however, that the process is never as neat, the stages never as distinct, as this discussion suggests.

You will find yourself generating invention notes even as you draft, revising and editing certain passages before completing a first draft, and sometimes writing clear, concise, and powerful passages that remain unchanged from invention notes to the final draft. As we suggested earlier, when you write, you are participating in an ongoing discussion, and as in any discussion, there is always room to reconsider, to restate, and to clarify your remarks.

WRITING TASKS IN THIS BOOK

Following most of the readings in this book, you will find a selection of writing tasks called Responding in Writing. Think of these tasks, and others your instructor may assign, as invitations to participate in the discussion of ideas presented in the chapter.

All of the writing tasks in this book ask you to draw upon the reading in various ways. We may ask you to consider one text as a means of analyzing or critiquing another or as a means of examining your own beliefs and knowledge. For some of the writing tasks, you must apply ideas from the readings to a new problem. Some require that you do research, and others call for you to collaborate with classmates. The writing tasks vary, but all are based on the premises we outlined in the preface to this book: (1) that reaching a reasonable conclusion about any issue demands context and perspective, and (2) that one of the important functions of reading is to provide the context for thinking and writing. Here are three sample tasks that ask you to respond in writing to the readings in Unit One.

1. As Sisela Bok notes in "Placebos," doctors prescribe placebos with some frequency, yet there is little discussion of the practice within the medical profession and no clearly established guidelines for a physician to follow. Write an essay addressed to members of the American Medical Association in which you explain when, if ever, it is appropriate for doctors to prescribe placebos. Assume that your essay will appear in the *Journal of American Medicine*.

2. Recent research has examined the extent to which the placebo effect is a factor in all medical treatment. That is, researchers have studied the effect

of a patient's belief in a given treatment on his or her response to it. Do some research on the placebo effect in medicine. What implications do your findings have on the medical practice as a whole and on the practice of prescribing placebos in particular?

3. "The Use of Force" raises questions about the rights and responsibilities of patients and their doctors. Working in a group of three or four, write a Statement of Doctors' and Patients' Rights in which you specify the kinds of information, respect, and/or treatment each party is entitled to in any doctor/patient encounter.

The Promise
of Education

INTRODUCTION

*I*n many ways, American education is the envy of the world. No other country promises its citizens so much. Universal free education through grade twelve is regarded not as the privilege of a few but as the right of everyone. Open admissions and guaranteed student loans make it possible for anyone who desires to pursue a higher education to do so, regardless of financial means or even academic record.

The Context essays in this chapter offer historical and ideological perspectives on the purpose of education. Education in America has long been recognized as the foundation on which fulfillment of our national ideals depends. As long ago as 1779, Thomas Jefferson proposed that his state, Virginia, establish free schools in every ward to teach basic reading, writing, and arithmetic. In a letter to John Adams, Jefferson explains that the goal of this plan was to discover and cultivate "worth and genius," whether they be found in the wealthiest or the poorest of citizens, thereby ensuring that future leaders would represent the best minds, rather than the most affluent families. Jefferson realized, too, that universal education was essential to the survival and efficient functioning of democracy. If the people are to be the guardians of their own liberty, he wrote, then "their minds must be improved to a certain degree."

Although Jefferson's plan died on the floor of the Virginia legislature, the demand for universal public education did not. The common school movement, which began in the nineteenth century, eventually led to the establishment of state-funded public schools throughout the United States. The movement was fueled in part by economic concerns, as industrialization created the need for a better-educated work force, but it was also a response to the increased diversity created by a rise in immigration during that century. Advocates of the common school movement recognized the school's role in forming citizens and creating social harmony. If members of different social classes and ethnic groups shared a classroom, it was theorized, strife between those groups would be eliminated. In addition, providing a common education to everyone would guarantee fair competition for social and professional positions. It was this belief, that education should provide equal opportunity, that led the Supreme Court, in the 1954 case of *Brown* v. *the Board of Education*, to recognize the inherent inequity of "separate but equal" schools.

Equal opportunity is a cherished right in our democratic system, but no less so than freedom. In his address to college freshmen, Wayne C. Booth argues that education, specifically a liberal arts education, should liberate students from prejudice and ignorance and give them the knowledge and critical tools to choose freely and wisely.

The promise of education in America is great, but how effectively have American schools fulfilled that promise? Although it's true that free universal education is available to every child in America, the quality of that schooling varies widely from school to school. The disparity between private and public education is great, but no greater than the disparity between wealthy public school districts and poor ones.

Likewise, while open admissions and student loans make entry into college a possibility for every American, they in no way open the doors of every college to every student. Students who have had the advantage of qualified instructors, up-to-date textbooks, and the latest technological equipment certainly have more choices when it comes to higher education than students who have struggled to learn in unsafe, ill-equipped, and understaffed schools.

How well have our schools met the other goals of education: to foster community and civic duty, to prepare students for the demands of the workplace, to give students the information and critical tools they need to lead productive, satisfying lives?

The numbers are impressive. In 1995, 75 percent of Americans were high school graduates; 45 percent of the population had received some postsecondary education as well; and 20 percent held a bachelor's degree or higher. But even as more people attain higher degrees, there are indications that those degrees mean less and less. Employers report that high school and college graduates lack the basic skills and knowledge to perform the jobs for which they're hired, and the appallingly low voter turn-out for virtually every election suggests that schools are failing to instill the fundamentals of civic responsibility necessary for democracy.

The essays in the Controversies section invite you to consider some of these conflicts and contradictions in American education, and to assess some of the proposals that have been offered to solve them.

Some have proposed that giving students and their parents choice among public schools or providing tax vouchers to apply toward private school tuition would not only give all students an opportunity for quality education, but also lead to the ultimate improvement of the whole education system by forcing schools to compete for students. The first set of Controversies essays examines the efficiency and fairness of such proposals.

The second set of essays also deals with the question of equal opportunity, specifically, the challenge of providing an equal education to a multicultural population. These essays ask how schools should adjust traditional methods and curriculum to meet the needs and interests of students of diverse backgrounds.

The final set of essays examines whether technology can help us fulfill the great promise of American education. Educational software can accommodate individual abilities and learning styles, but does the computer phenomenon undermine opportunities for sharing knowledge and building community? Electronic communication has given students almost unlimited access to information, but can it help students to understand and evaluate that information, to use it in meaningful ways?

The unit begins with a poem by Langston Hughes that invites us to think about the give-and-take process of education.

A WAY IN

*B*efore you read Langston Hughes's "Theme for English B," think for a minute about what you're doing here, in college, reading this poem as an assignment in this writing class. What choices led you here? What sacrifices did you make to be here? What sacrifices and choices do you think you will have to make to complete your education at this institution? What do you hope to gain from the education you receive here? a job? greater understanding of the world you live in? deeper knowledge of yourself?

Think also about your role in the intellectual and social community of your college. What adjustments have you made to fit among your fellow students? What changes in attitude or discipline have been required of you to understand and learn from your instructors? How have others given way to accommodate you?

LANGSTON HUGHES

Langston Hughes (1902–1967) was born in Joplin, Missouri, and raised in Lawrence, Kansas. He attended Columbia University for one year, then got a job on a ship and spent the next five years traveling the world, holding a series of odd jobs, and writing poetry. After gaining some literary recognition, Hughes completed his education at Lincoln College in Pennsylvania. A playwright and journalist as well as a poet, Hughes is remembered today as one of the leading figures of the Harlem Renaissance, a literary and intellectual movement of the 1920s that gave voice to the experience of African-Americans.

Theme for English B

The instructor said,

> *Go home and write*
> *a page tonight.*
> *And let that page come out of you—*
> *Then, it will be true.*   5

I wonder if it's that simple?
I am twenty-two, colored, born in Winston-Salem.
I went to school there, then Durham, then here
to this college on the hill above Harlem.
I am the only colored student in my class.   10
The steps from the hill lead down into Harlem,
through a park, then I cross St. Nicholas,
Eighth Avenue, Seventh, and I come to the Y,
the Harlem Branch Y, where I take the elevator
up to my room, sit down, and write this page: 15

It's not easy to know what is true for you or me
at twenty-two, my age. But I guess I'm what
I feel and see and hear, Harlem, I hear you:
hear you, hear me—we two—you, me, talk on this page.
(I hear New York, too.) Me—who?   20
Well, I like to eat, sleep, drink, and be in love.
I like to work, read, learn, and understand life.
I like a pipe for a Christmas present,
or records—Bessie, bop, or Bach.
I guess being colored doesn't make me *not* like   25
the same things other folks like who are other races.
So will my page be colored that I write?
Being me, it will not be white.
But it will be
a part of you, instructor.   30
You are white—
yet a part of me, as I am a part of you.
That's American.
Sometimes perhaps you don't want to be a part of me.
Nor do I often want to be a part of you.   35
But we are, that's true!
As I learn from you,
I guess you learn from me—
although you're older—and white—

and somewhat more free.   40

This is my page for English B.

◢ REREADING FOR UNDERSTANDING

I. The narrator's response to the assignment appears in two parts. Examine
    the first part, lines 7–15. What sort of information does he give about him-
    self in this section? How does it differ from the information he provides in
    the next section, lines 16–40?

2. Where is the narrator's home in relationship to the college? Why does he give us this information in such detail?

3. Why does the narrator have difficulty fulfilling the instructor's assignment? What does he mean when he says, "It's not easy knowing what is true for you or me / at twenty-two, my age"?

4. Reread lines 34 to the end. What is the narrator suggesting about the relationship he has or hopes to have with his instructor? What words would you use to describe the tone of these lines? Are they optimistic? hopeful? depressing? bitter?

◢ RESPONDING

1. What do you think of the instructor's assignment? Would you find this assignment easy or difficult to fulfill? What problems, if any, would it pose for you?

2. The narrator notes that he is shaped, in part, by what he hears. He says he hears Harlem and then adds, "I hear New York, too." Why do you think he separates Harlem from the rest of New York? What does he suggest by placing "I hear New York, too" in parentheses?

3. A writing assignment should give students a chance to do more than simply show off what they already know or think. A good writing task allow students to learn and discover something new in the course of fulfilling the assignment. What do you think the narrator learns or discovers while writing his page for English B?

◢ RESPONDING IN WRITING

1. Write about a time when you felt out of place in a classroom or another learning environment. What conditions made you feel that way? What effect did those feelings have on your ability to learn and perform in that class? Did you finally become comfortable in that classroom? If so, how? If not, why not?

2. Try to recall a class assignment that was particularly challenging or frustrating. Write to the teacher who gave you the assignment, telling him or her why the assignment was difficult for you and what made it ultimately rewarding or defeating.

THOMAS JEFFERSON

Of his many achievements in government, agriculture, science, architecture, and philosophy, the three for which Thomas Jefferson (1743–1826) wanted to be remembered were writing the Declaration of Independence, founding the University of Virginia, and drafting Virginia's statute on religious freedom. Each of these accomplishments reflects Jefferson's belief that, given access to information and freedom to inquire and question, individuals could make rational and moral choices. Education, Jefferson believed, should provide the knowledge and skills to enhance the exercise of common sense. This proposal—to establish public schools in Virginia—was not adopted by the state, but his ideas about the role of education in a democratic society remain part of the American consciousness.

A Plan for Public Education in Virginia

Q UERY XIV—*The administration of justice and the description of the laws?* . . . Another object of the revisal is to diffuse knowledge more generally through the mass of the people. This bill proposes to lay off every county into small districts of five or six miles square, called hundreds, and in each of them to establish a school for teaching reading, writing, and arithmetic. The tutor to be supported by the hundred, and every person in it entitled to send their children three years gratis, and as much longer as they please, paying for it. These schools to be under a visitor who is annually to choose the boy of best genius in the school, of those whose parents are too poor to give them further education, and to send him forward to one of the grammar schools, of which twenty are proposed to be erected in different parts of the country, for teaching Greek, Latin, geography, and the higher branches of numerical arithmetic. Of the boys thus sent in any one year, trial is to be made at the grammar schools one or two years, and the best genius of the whole selected, and continued six years, and the residue dismissed. By this means twenty of the best geniuses will be raked from the rubbish annually, and be instructed, at the public expense, so far as the grammar schools go. At the end of six years' instruction, one-half are to be discontinued (from among whom the grammar schools will probably be supplied with future masters); and the other half, who are to be chosen for the superiority of their parts and disposition, are to be sent and continued three years in the study of such sciences as they shall choose, at William and Mary College, the plan of which is proposed to be enlarged, as will be hereafter explained, and extended to all the useful sciences. The ultimate result of the whole scheme of education would be the teaching all the children of the State reading, writing, and common arithmetic; turning out ten annually, of superior genius, well taught in Greek, Latin, geography, and the higher branches of arithmetic; turning out ten others annually, of still superior parts, who, to those branches of learning, shall have added such of the sciences as their genius shall have led them to; the furnishing to the wealthier part of the people convenient schools at which their children may be educated at their own expense. The general objects of this law are to provide an education adapted to the years, to the capacity, and the condition of every one, and directed to their freedom and happiness. Specific details were not proper for the law. These must be the business of the visitors entrusted with its execution. The first stage of this education being the schools of the hundreds, wherein the great mass of the people will receive their instruction, the principal foundations of future order will be laid here. Instead, therefore, of putting the Bible and Testament into the hands of the children at an age when their judgments are not sufficiently matured for religious inquiries, their memories may here be stored with the most useful facts from Grecian, Roman, European and American history. The first elements of morality too may be instilled into their minds; such as, when further developed as their judgments advance in strength, may teach them how to work out their own greatest happiness, by showing that it does not depend on the condition of life in which chance has placed them, but is always the result of a good conscience, good health, occupation, and freedom in all just pursuits. Those whom either the wealth of their parents or the adoption of the State shall destine to higher degrees of learning, will go on to the grammar schools, which constitute the next stage, there to be instructed in the languages. The learning [of] Greek and Latin, I am told, is going into disuse in Europe. I know not what their manners and occupations may call for; but it would be very ill-judged in us to follow their example in this instance. There is a certain period of life, say from eight to fifteen or sixteen years of age, when the mind like the body is not yet firm enough for laborious and close operations. If applied to such, it falls an early victim to premature exertion; exhibiting, indeed, at first, in these young and tender subjects, the flattering appearance of their being men while they are yet children, but ending in reducing them to be children when they should be men. The memory is then most susceptible and tenacious of impressions; and the learning of languages being chiefly a work of memory, it seems precisely fitted to the powers of this period, which is long enough, too, for acquiring the most useful languages, ancient and modern. I do not pretend that language is science. It is only an instrument for the attainment of science. But that time is not lost which is employed in providing tools for future operation; more especially as in this case the books put into the hands of the youth for this purpose may be such as will at the same time impress their minds with useful facts and good principles. If this period be suffered to pass in idleness, the mind becomes lethargic and impotent, as would the body it inhabits if unexercised during the same time. The sympathy between body and mind during their rise, progress and decline, is too strict and obvious to endanger our being misled while we reason from the one to the other. As soon as they are of sufficient age, it is supposed they will be sent on from the grammar schools to the university, which constitutes our third and last stage, there to study those sciences which may be adapted to their views. By that part of our plan which prescribes the selection of the youths of genius from among the classes of the poor, we hope to avail the State of those talents which nature has sown as liberally among the poor as the rich, but which perish without use, if not sought for and cultivated. But of all the views of this law none is more important, none more legitimate, than that of rendering the people the safe, as they are the ultimate, guardians of their own liberty. For this purpose the reading in the first stage, where *they* will receive their whole education, is proposed, as has been said, to be chiefly historical. History, by apprising them of the past, will enable them to judge of the future; it will avail them of the experience of other times and other nations; it will qualify them as judges of the actions and designs of men; it will enable them to know ambition under every disguise it may assume; and knowing it, to defeat its views. In every government on earth is some trace of human weakness, some germ of corruption and degeneracy, which cunning will discover, and wickedness insensibly open, cultivate, and improve. Every government degenerates when trusted to the rulers of the people alone. The people themselves, therefore, are its only safe depositories. And to render even them safe, their minds must be improved to a certain degree. This indeed is not all that is necessary, though it be essentially necessary. An amendment of our constitution must here come in aid of the public education. The influence over government must be shared among all the people. If every individual which composes their mass participates of the ultimate authority, the government will be safe; because the corrupting the whole mass will exceed any private resources of wealth; and public ones cannot be provided but by levies on the people. In this case every man would have to pay his own price. The government of Great Britain has been corrupted, because but one man in ten has a right to vote for members of parliament. The sellers of the government, therefore, get nine-tenths of their price clear. It has been thought that corruption is restrained by confining the right of suffrage to a few of the wealthier of the people; but it would be more effectually restrained by an extension of that right to such members as would bid defiance to the means of corruption.

Lastly, it is proposed, by a bill in this revisal, to begin a public library and gallery, by laying out a certain sum annually in books, paintings, and statues. □   2

◤ REREADING FOR UNDERSTANDING

1. Jefferson says that the primary objective of his plan is "to provide an education adapted to the years, to the capacity, and the condition of every one." What does he mean by "years," by "capacity," and by "condition"? Explain how the plan Jefferson lays out attempts to achieve this ambitious objective.

2. Although Jefferson says, "Specific details were not proper for the law," he goes on to elaborate in fairly specific terms what the content of each level of instruction should be. Why does Jefferson argue for teaching history, rather than the Bible and religion, to the youngest pupils? Why does he think the study of language is appropriate for grammar school students?

3. Under Jefferson's plan, education serves the state in two different ways. What are they? Which does he believe to be more important?

◤ RESPONDING

1. Do you think Jefferson's plan would be effective in achieving its stated objectives? What difficulties do you see in implementing such a plan?

2. Jefferson's plan would provide most of the population with just three years of schooling, much of that devoted to the study of history and, perhaps, "the first elements of morality." Yet Jefferson claims that the most important purpose of education should be to prepare citizens for self-government. Do you think that three years of study would be sufficient for such a purpose? Why do you think Jefferson does?

3. What assumptions about human nature are revealed in Jefferson's plan?

CHIEF JUSTICE EARL WARREN

When Earl Warren was appointed Chief Justice of the Supreme Court in 1953, he inherited one of the most difficult and controversial cases in the history of the court. The 1954 case of *Brown v. The Board of Education* was not the first case the Supreme Court heard regarding segregated schools, nor was it the first time the Court ruled in favor of the plaintiffs, agreeing that the schools in question denied equal educational opportunity to black children. What made the Brown case unique was that the plaintiffs argued not that the black schools in question were substantially inferior to the white schools, but that the very practice of segregation sent a message of inferiority to black children that kept them from receiving the same education as their white counterparts. Thus, in ruling in favor of the plaintiff in *Brown*, the Court ruled against all school segregation.

The Brown decision is important for its impact on education and beyond. Frustration and anger at the refusal of many school systems to integrate following *Brown* fueled the civil rights movement and led to the Civil Rights Act of 1964. Although *Brown* only specifically addressed segregation in public schools, the ruling served as precedent for subsequent rulings against other forms of discrimination.

The case is also noteworthy for what it shows about prevailing attitudes toward education. As you read this opinion, pay attention to the assumptions it makes about the purpose of education and the function of public schools.

Brown v. The Board of Education of Topeka

M r. Chief Justice Warren delivered the opinion of the Court.   1
These cases come to us from the States of Kansas, South Carolina,   2
Virginia, and Delaware. They are premised on different facts and different local conditions, but a common legal question justifies their consideration together in this consolidated opinion.

In each of the cases, minors of the Negro race, through their legal rep-   3
resentatives, seek the aid of the courts in obtaining admission to the public schools of their community on a nonsegregated basis. In each instance, they had been denied admission to schools attended by white children under laws requiring or permitting segregation according to race. This segregation was alleged to deprive the plaintiffs of the equal protection of the laws under the Fourteenth Amendment.* In each of the cases other than the Delaware case, a three-judge federal district court denied relief to the plaintiffs on the so-called "separate but equal" doctrine announced by this Court in *Plessy* v. *Ferguson*,† 163 U. S. 537. Under that doctrine, equality of treatment is accorded when the races are provided substantially equal facilities, even though these facilities be separate. In the Delaware case, the Supreme Court of Delaware adhered to that doctrine, but ordered that the plaintiffs be admitted to the white schools because of their superiority to the Negro schools.

The plaintiffs contend that segregated public schools are not "equal" and   4
cannot be made "equal," and that hence they are deprived of the equal protection of the laws. Because of the obvious importance of the question presented, the Court took jurisdiction. Argument was heard in the 1952 Term, and reargument was heard this Term on certain questions propounded by the Court.

---

* The Fourteenth Amendment to the U.S. Constitution, added shortly after the Civil War, states in part: "No state shall make or enforce any law which shall abridge the privileges or immunities of citizens of the United States; nor shall any state deprive any person of life, liberty, or property, without due process of law; nor deny to any person within its jurisdiction the equal protection of the law." †Homer Plessy, who was one-eighth black and seven-eighths white, protested that his right under the Fourteenth Amendment to equal protection under the law had been violated when he was arrested for sitting in the white section of a train. The Supreme Court ruled against Plessy in 1895, arguing that segregation did not violate the Fourteenth Amendment, provided that the separate facilities were equal. This so-called "separate but equal" doctrine became the precedent for subsequent segregation rulings.

Reargument was largely devoted to the circumstances surrounding the   5
adoption of the Fourteenth Amendment in 1868. It covered exhaustively consideration of the Amendment in Congress, ratification by the states, then existing practices in racial segregation, and the views of proponents and opponents
of the Amendment. This discussion and our own investigation convince us
that, although these sources cast some light, it is not enough to resolve the
problem with which we are faced. At best, they are inconclusive. The most avid
proponents of the post-War Amendments undoubtedly intended them to
remove all legal distinctions among "all persons born or naturalized in the
United States." Their opponents, just as certainly, were antagonistic to both the
letter and the spirit of the Amendments and wished them to have the most limited effect. What others in Congress and the state legislatures had in mind cannot be determined with any degree of certainty.

An additional reason for the inconclusive nature of the Amendment's   6
history, with respect to segregated schools, is the status of public education at
that time. In the South, the movement toward free common schools, supported by general taxation, had not yet taken hold. Education of white children was largely in the hands of private groups. Education of Negroes was
almost nonexistent, and practically all of the race were illiterate. In fact, any
education of Negroes was forbidden by law in some states. Today, in contrast,
many Negroes have achieved outstanding success in the arts and sciences as
well as in the business and professional world. It is true that public school
education at the time of the Amendment had advanced further in the North,
but the effect of the Amendment on Northern States was generally ignored in
the congressional debates. Even in the North, the conditions of public education did not approximate those existing today. The curriculum was usually
rudimentary; ungraded schools were common in rural areas; the school term
was but three months a year in many states; and compulsory school attendance
was virtually unknown. As a consequence, it is not surprising that there should
be so little in the history of the Fourteenth Amendment relating to its intended
effect on public education.

In the first cases in this Court construing the Fourteenth Amendment,   7
decided shortly after its adoption, the Court interpreted it as proscribing all
state-imposed discriminations against the Negro race. The doctrine of "separate but equal" did not make its appearance in this Court until 1896 in the case
of *Plessy* v. *Ferguson, supra,* involving not education but transportation.
American courts have since labored with the doctrine for over half a century. In
this Court, there have been six cases involving the "separate but equal" doctrine
in the field of public education. In *Cumming* v. *County Board of Education,* 175
U. S. 528, and *Gong Lum* v. *Rice,* 275 U. S. 78, the validity of the doctrine itself
was not challenged.* In more recent cases, all on the graduate school level,

---

* In the *Cumming* case, Negro taxpayers sought an injunction requiring the defendant school board
to discontinue the operation of a high school for white children until the board resumed operation
of a high school for Negro children. Similarly, in the *Gong Lum* case, the plaintiff, a child of Chinese
descent, contended only that state authorities had misapplied the doctrine by classifying him with
Negro children and requiring him to attend a Negro school.

inequality was found in that specific benefits enjoyed by white students were denied to Negro students of the same educational qualifications. *Missouri ex rel. Gaines* v. *Canada,* 305 U. S. 337; *Sipuel* v. *Oklahoma,* 332 U. S. 631; *Sweatt* v. *Painter,* 339 U. S. 629; *McLaurin* v. *Oklahoma State Regents,* 339 U. S. 637. In none of these cases was it necessary to re-examine the doctrine to grant relief to the Negro plaintiff. And in *Sweatt* v. *Painter, supra,* the Court expressly reserved decision on the question whether *Plessy* v. *Ferguson* should be held inapplicable to public education.

In the instant cases, that question is directly presented. Here, unlike *Sweatt* v. *Painter,* there are findings below that the Negro and white schools involved have been equalized, or are being equalized, with respect to buildings, curricula, qualifications and salaries of teachers, and other "tangible" factors. Our decision, therefore, cannot turn on merely a comparison of these tangible factors in the Negro and white schools involved in each of the cases. We must look instead to the effect of segregation itself on public education.   8

In approaching this problem, we cannot turn the clock back to 1868 when the Amendment was adopted, or even to 1896 when *Plessy* v. *Ferguson* was written. We must consider public education in the light of its full development and its present place in American life throughout the Nation. Only in this way can it be determined if segregation in public schools deprives these plaintiffs of the equal protection of the laws.   9

Today, education is perhaps the most important function of state and local governments. Compulsory school attendance laws and the great expenditures for education both demonstrate our recognition of the importance of education to our democratic society. It is required in the performance of our most basic public responsibilities, even service in the armed forces. It is the very foundation of good citizenship. Today it is a principal instrument in awakening the child to cultural values, in preparing him for later professional training, and in helping him to adjust normally to his environment. In these days, it is doubtful that any child may reasonably be expected to succeed in life if he is denied the opportunity of an education. Such an opportunity, where the state has undertaken to provide it, is a right which must be made available to all on equal terms.   10

We come then to the question presented: Does segregation of children in public schools solely on the basis of race, even though the physical facilities and other "tangible" factors may be equal, deprive the children of the minority group of equal educational opportunities? We believe that it does.   11

In *Sweatt* v. *Painter, supra,* in finding that a segregated law school for Negroes could not provide them equal educational opportunities, this Court relied in large part on "those qualities which are incapable of objective measurement but which make for greatness in a law school." In *McLaurin* v. *Oklahoma State Regents, supra,* the Court, in requiring that a Negro admitted to a white graduate school be treated like all other students, again resorted to intangible considerations: ". . . his ability to study, to engage in discussions and exchange views with other students, and, in general, to learn his profession." Such considerations apply with added force to children in grade and high schools. To separate them from others of similar age and qualifications solely   12 because of their race generates a feeling of inferiority as to their status in the community that may affect their hearts and minds in a way unlikely ever to be undone. The effect of this separation on their educational opportunities was well stated by a finding in the Kansas case by a court which nevertheless felt compelled to rule against the Negro plaintiffs:

> Segregation of white and colored children in public schools has a detrimental effect upon the colored children. The impact is greater when it has the sanction of the law; for the policy of separating the races is usually interpreted as denoting the inferiority of the negro group. A sense of inferiority affects the motivation of a child to learn. Segregation with the sanction of law, therefore, has a tendency to [retard] the educational and mental development of negro children and to deprive them of some of the benefits they would receive in a racial[ly] integrated school system.

Whatever may have been the extent of psychological knowledge at the time of *Plessy* v. *Ferguson*, this finding is amply supported by modern authority. Any language in *Plessy* v. *Ferguson* contrary to this finding is rejected.

We conclude that in the field of public education the doctrine of "separate   13
but equal" has no place. Separate educational facilities are inherently unequal. Therefore, we hold that the plaintiffs and others similarly situated for whom the actions have been brought are, by reason of the segregation complained of, deprived of the equal protection of the laws guaranteed by the Fourteenth Amendment. This disposition makes unnecessary any discussion whether such segregation also violates the Due Process Clause of the Fourteenth Amendment.

Because these are class actions, because of the wide applicability of this   14
decision, and because of the great variety of local conditions, the formulation of decrees in these cases presents problems of considerable complexity. On reargument, the consideration of appropriate relief was necessarily subordinated to the primary question—the constitutionality of segregation in public education. We have announced that such segregation is a denial of the equal protection of the laws. In order that we may have the full assistance of the parties in formulating decrees, the cases will be restored to the docket, and parties are requested to present further argument on Questions 4 and 5 previously propounded by the Court for the reargument this Term. The Attorney General of the United States is again invited to participate. The Attorneys General of the states requiring or permitting segregation in public education will also be permitted to appear as *amici curiae* upon request to do so by September 15, 1954, and submission of briefs by October 1, 1954.

It is so ordered. ☐   15

◢ REREADING FOR UNDERSTANDING

1. Warren notes that much of the argument the Court heard in this case regarded the history surrounding the adoption of the Fourteenth Amendment and its application in *Plessy* v. *Ferguson*. Why was this discussion ultimately of little use in arriving at a decision?

2. Warren says that, in deciding this case, the Court "must consider public education in the light of its full development and its present place in American life" (par. 8). According to Warren, what is the purpose of public education? Why does Warren conclude that education must be "made available on equal terms"?

3. After concluding that the state is obligated to provide equal education for all citizens, Warren then considers whether or not segregation on the basis of race deprives children to equal educational opportunities. What does he conclude? Why?

◢ RESPONDING

1. The Chief Justice argues that education "is the very foundation of good citizenship" (par. 10). What does he mean by this statement? Compare his vision of the relationship between education and citizenship with Jefferson's position in "Notes on the State of Virginia."

2. The *Brown* ruling was one of the most controversial rulings in Supreme Court history and remains a debated judgment today. Opponents point to this statement (par. 12): "Whatever may have been the extent of psychological knowledge at the time of *Plessy* v. *Ferguson*, this finding is amply supported by modern authority," to argue that the Court went beyond its duty to interpret the Constitution by relying on psychological evidence rather than historical precedent. Do you think psychological evidence is relevant and trustworthy in this case, perhaps even more so than historical precedent, as Chief Justice Warren suggests? What problems do you see in permitting such evidence to be the basis of legal decisions?

◢ RESPONDING IN WRITING

Although *Brown* v. *The Board of Education* rendered segregation by law unconstitutional, many blacks and other minorities were still excluded from many institutions of higher education. In the 1960s, affirmative action programs that required colleges to recruit formerly excluded minorities and, in some cases, to apply a different admission standard for those minorities were deemed necessary to make the equal opportunity promised by the *Brown* decision a reality. Today, those policies are under attack. Indeed, many argue that applying separate standards on the basis of race is itself racist. Find out what practices, if any, your college engages in to attract and admit minority students. Is preferential treatment given to any group? What rationale is offered for your school's affirmative action policy or lack thereof? Once you have discovered your school's policy, write an essay explaining why you think the policy is fair and should continue, or unfair and should be changed or discarded.

WAYNE C. BOOTH

Wayne C. Booth (1921–   ) has had a long and distinguished career in academia. A professor of English and author of numerous books on literature and higher education, Booth spent much of his teaching career at the University of Chicago. It was there that he delivered the following talk as part of a series of lectures to the freshman class. Like the other pieces in this section, Booth's essay examines the purpose of education. Specifically, he is concerned with the value of a liberal arts education.

What's Supposed to Be Going on Here?

Liberal education was originally called "liberal" because it was supposed to liberate men to apply their minds, their critical thinking, to the most important decisions of their lives; how to act, who or what to love, what to call good or true or beautiful. We all know, of course, that much that traveled under the name of liberal education did not in fact liberate, because it was not in fact a removal of ignorance but an indoctrination with new forms of ignorance; or because the ignorance it removed was trivial, and the knowledge substituted was not of how to use critical intelligence but of how to use a collection of information, more or less inaccurate, for social climbing. But these perversions do not destroy the value of the genuine article: in the great educational philosophers, from Plato and Aristotle through Newman and John Dewey to whoever is your favorite of today, we discover a kind of perennial philosophy of liberating education. They all say that only in knowledge, only in the right kind of knowledge, can we liberate ourselves to make free choices. Without knowledge we may have the illusion of free choice; we may embrace political programs and schools of art and world views with as much passion *as if* we knew what we were doing, but our seeming choices are really what other people have imposed upon us.

Now if you're listening to me critically—and I hope you are—you will already be troubled with a lot of questions. Some of you will be wondering whether I'm against spontaneity. Some will be worried about the possible selfishness of cultivating free minds while the world burns (what *use* is freedom?). Some will want to ask whether I'm not just delivering a disguised bit of brainwashing, trying to *impose* an institutional doctrine to protect you from the educational efforts of SDS or the Black Panthers or whomever. I like to think that I have answers to such questions—every speaker would like to think he could answer *all* questions—and I hope some of your objections will be met as I go along. Keep them in mind, in any case, so that we can then discuss them later on, and let me try for the moment to explain this notion of mental freedom, a notion which is not original with me by any means but which is different from much of what gets said these days.

There are many ways of talking about the arts of liberal education, the arts that genuinely liberate. At the risk of being gimmicky, I'd like to suggest a way of reviving that tired old list, the "three R's." Reading, 'riting and 'rithmetic made up a highly simplified, minimal list of the arts of liberation: to be able to read is to be free to learn what other men know; to be able to write is to be free to teach or move or change other men with your words; and to be able to calculate is to be freed from enslavement to other men's calculations. Without scrapping arithmetic, which raises additional problems I can't go into, I'd like to expand the first two of these into four. The new list would have reading and writing mixed up in every one of the four, and it would run like this: first, the art of Recovery of meanings, the seemingly simple but never finally mastered ability to learn what other men have known or believed; second, the art of Rejection of whatever is false or enslaving in other men's meanings—what is often called critical thinking; third, the art of Renewing or (the thesaurus yields lots of "R's" here) Renovating or Recognizing or Re-presenting what is valid or worthwhile in other men's meanings; and finally the art of Revising or Revolutionizing thought by discovering genuinely new truth.*

Both critics and defenders of current education seem these days to be far more interested in the last of these four, revolutionary novelty, than any of the others. Under the names of "creativity," "originality," or novelty, educationists often talk as if a little institutional doctoring would make it possible for everyone to become intellectually revolutionary, thinking bold new thoughts that nobody else has ever dared to think. Well, maybe. Nobody knows precisely the limits of our creativity. All I can say is that genuinely new ideas seem to me terribly rare, and if it is the goal of education to produce them most of us seem to be doomed to perpetual second-class citizenship. Maybe I can dramatize what I mean by saying that so far as I know, there are no original ideas in this speech. It is true that the whole thing is brand spanking new in one sense: my various sub-points under the theme of education for freedom have never been put together in quite this shape before. But anyone who has the slightest acquaintance with the history of thought will find all of my ideas expressed by many before me, often expressed in better form than I can manage. So I'm going to leave genuine revision or revolutions of thought to one side for awhile, and concentrate briefly on the three R's that to me are more important to liberal education: more important, first, because they must be mastered before creativity has a chance, and more important, second, because they are available, in some degree, to every student who is willing to seek them out, regardless of his past educational experience. If I offered to teach you how to be a genuine intellectual revolutionary, I would be a fraud, because I don't know how it is done (believe me, if I *did* know, the world would be paying more attention to me than I seem to be able to get it to). But I *can* look you in the eye tonight and promise you that here at Chicago, in classes or on your own in the library or in conversation, you can learn how to free yourselves, maybe a little, maybe a lot, never totally, but enough to make a difference—to free yourself by working on the arts of recovery, rejection, and renovation. In the process you will not necessarily

4

---

* Yes, I really uttered all of these *mens*, to an audience about half of whom were women! And I heard no protesting groans, then or later. . . .

make yourselves happy; the liberal arts will not save you from disease and death, or from anxious pride and personal anxieties and the suffering that all human beings seem to inflict on each other. But they might save you—could save *all* of you, and almost certainly will save *some* of you—from the special forms of slavery that only these arts can remove. Nobody can force you to become educated, nobody can even convince you in advance that to become educated is worth doing. But the curious fact is that most of you do not need to be convinced; you already want this mysterious thing. The big problem is how to go about getting it.

The first step toward this elusive kind of freedom is learning how to recover   5
other people's meanings and thus make available to oneself what others have already learned. You and I were born as ignorant as the most ignorant newborn baby in the most primitive corner in the most backward moment in man's history. We were born ignorant provincials in time and space. But we were thrust immediately into a world buzzing with knowledge (and with misinformation disguised as knowledge). We must either learn to recover what is really known or be doomed to drift through seas of confusion.

There is no reason to think that a modern college is the only place, or even   6
the best place, in which to earn this freedom. For some people a job as a newspaper reporter would be better, and for some others prisons are better places. I know of no more moving account of how freedom comes to a man when he learns how to recover meanings for himself, how really to listen to what is there on the page, than Malcolm X's story of his prison reading.

If you haven't read his *Autobiography*, you ought to, and you ought to pay   7
special attention to Chapter 11, which he calls "Saved."

First, he says, talking of how learning saved him, he literally re-copied every   8
word and definition in the prison dictionary, determined to master the world of words. Think of that, ye innovators. *There's* innovation for you, and interdisciplinary at that!

And suddenly, he says,   9

> for the first time [I could] pick up a book and read and *now begin to understand what the book was saying.* Anyone who has read a great deal can imagine the new world that opened. Let me tell you something: from then until I left that prison, in every free moment I had, if I was not reading in the library, I was reading on my bunk. You couldn't have gotten me out of books with a wedge. . . . Months passed *without my even thinking about being imprisoned.* In fact, up to then, *I never had been so truly free in my life. . . .* No university would ask any student to devour literature as I did when this new world opened to me, of being able to read and *understand.* . . . I have often reflected upon the new vistas that reading opened to me. I knew right there in prison that reading had changed forever the course of my life. As I see it today, the ability to read awoke inside me *some long dormant craving to be mentally alive. . . .* My homemade education gave me, with every additional book that I read, a little bit more sensitivity to the deafness, dumbness, and

blindness that was afflicting the black race in America. Not long ago, an English writer telephoned me from London, asking questions. One was, "What's your alma mater?" I told him, "Books." You will never catch me with a free fifteen minutes in which I'm not studying something I feel might be able to help the black man. . . . Where else but in a prison could *I have attacked my ignorance* by being able to study intensely sometimes as much as fifteen hours a day. [Except for the word *understand*, italics are mine.]*

Even in this isolated quotation we can sense the miracle of freeing that has occurred. Every time I read that chapter I feel that there in that strange moment of human history, there in those seemingly binding circumstances, lies the full wonder of what education ought to be about: "I had never *been so truly free in my life.*" Malcolm Little, freed to become Malcolm X, still had a lot of mental chains upon him, as he himself says; we all do. But he had begun to learn the *ways* of freeing, and he went on to new and surprising freedoms throughout the rest of his short life.

It is important to look closely at what really happened in that first moment. The curious thing is that Malcolm X in fact already knew how to read, in the usual sense, long before he went to prison. In chapter 2 we learn that in seventh grade he was at the top of his class. As a thirteen-year-old boy he could, it is clear, read and write far beyond the average of his age group. But what happened later in prison, as his own emphasis shows, is that he suddenly became "able to read and *understand*." What the words before him were really saying became for the first time available to him, and he "*attacked his ignorance*" and became freer than ever before in his life.

Unfortunately, freedom to recover meanings, freedom to understand, is not as simple as my account so far would suggest. As Malcolm X would have been the first to admit, there is understanding and understanding, and there is a tremendous problem, even for highly literate folk, of deciding what meanings are worth understanding. Even that voracious and highly intelligent prisoner sneaking his gulps of learning behind the backs of the patrolling guards far into the night could not cover more than a fraction of the books that are worth reading. Our library here contains more than two million volumes, every one of them thought by somebody—if only its own author—to be worth reading. Even the speed readers among you, reading an average of a book a day for four years, will cover at best only around a thousand of those books, fewer than one two-thousandth of what is available: and meanwhile, during those four years, something like 150 thousand more books will have been published in America alone, scores of times more than you have read in the four years. Clearly nobody is free to recover knowledge in that quantity, and if anybody tried to he would soon crack up under the strain.

I am frequently told that your generation is "better educated" than any previous generation, partly because you have picked up so much knowledge from TV. It may be true that you have recovered, in this sense, more information than

---

* *The Autobiography of Malcolm X*, edited by Alex Haley (New York, 1966), 172–73; 179–80.

your predecessors, though from what little I see on TV I would say that more of it is misinformation than not. Even if our minds are filled with information, we could still be totally enslaved in the sense I'm talking about (and that Malcolm X was in part talking about), unless we had mastered that very different kind of knowledge—the knowledge of how to reconstruct what other people really mean by what they say or write. And *that* includes the knowledge of how to guard against one's temptations to misunderstand. It sounds simple, but it is one of the most difficult arts in the world—the art of recovering what other people mean and not what we'd like them to mean. It is an art that is not highly honored in the world around us: all the value is usually placed on reacting to meanings without discovering first what the meanings actually are. Our intellectual lives are for the most part lived about on the level of our TV watching: you can tell the good guys from the bad guys by simple symbols, and the heroes and villains shift from day to day without real thought. One day [Herbert] Marcuse is our hero (though don't ask how many have actually *read* him) and the next day he is attacked, still without really being read. It is all done with simple catchwords and slogans: Is he *for* the movement or *against* it? One day Paul Goodman is so besieged with invitations to campuses that he can't keep up; the next day (still without really being read or listened to) he is down and out, because he has accidentally pushed this or that button marked "Bad Guy."

And poor Goodman is left, in a recent poem called "The Young," lamenting   14

When young proclaim Make Love Not War
I back them up because it's better
and some are brave as they can be,
but they don't make love to me.

He brought petunias to the Be-In
and fed a lump of sugar to a policeman's horse,
but me, he said, he didn't like my vibrations.
For this I didn't need to trudge to Central Park.

Sure I am heartened by my crazy allies
and their long hair looks very nice on some,
but frankly, more of them were interesting
before they all began to do their thing.*

If I am right, then, the chief threat to our intellectual freedom is not illiter-   15
acy, or censorship committees, or boards of trustees firing radical professors, or the heckling and shouting down of speakers without caring about what they have to say. Though all of these are bad, they are openly bad, as it were, and few of us are fooled into thinking that they are good. More threatening to you and me is the subtler mental violence that occurs when people who think they are listening with an open mind actually wrench complicated or new or unacceptable messages into simpler, ready-made categories of old ideas. The person who reacts passionately for or against what was not actually said or written is a slave

---

* Paul Goodman, "The Young," *The Nation*, June 20, 1970, 794. (Reprinted by permission of The Nation Company, Inc., copyright 1970.)

to his own ignorance, no matter how gloriously free and spontaneous and righteous he feels as he reacts. Yet the shameful fact is that most of us most of the time reduce other folks' meanings to nonsense that we *can* reject. After all, if it's shit already, I don't have to try to digest it.

Jim Hoge, the editor of the *Sun Times,* told some of us freshmen last week   16
that he often cannot recognize quotations attributed to him by other journals, particularly the weeklies. The fault of mis-hearing and mis-reading is indeed so common, among the so-called educated professors, journalists, and politicians, that it is difficult to find counter-examples, examples of the painstaking recovery of what the other person knows or claims to know. *You* think you are an exception, I'll warrant. But bright as you are, full of information as you are, clever as you are at checking the box marked "None of the above," quick as you are at deciding whether this or that item from the past is relevant to your lives, I would be very much surprised if there are three of you here who could read a dialogue of Plato or an essay by Hume and reconstruct what is said in a form that Plato or Hume would recognize. I look you in the eye, you marvelous promisers of future freedom, and say something even more insulting: I doubt that many of you could write a summary of a speech by President Nixon or Senator Fulbright that *he* would accept as a genuine recovery of his meanings. I have no doubt whatever that you could write colorful *criticisms* of what you *thought* he said, criticisms that would pass for relevant because they wouldn't miss the target any further than most of what gets printed these days. But you're not free to learn from Plato or Hume or Fulbright, or even Nixon, and therefore you are not free to accept or refute them, until you are free to find out who they really are.

Just to show you how serious I am in this arrogant little part of this arro-   17
gant little speech, I am going to make an offer: to any one of you first-year students who can write a summary of *this* speech, in 100 to 250 words, a summary that really reconstructs what *I* think I mean, I hereby offer twenty-five dollars, tax free. In case there is more than one more-or-less successful entry in the Booth Recovery-of-Meanings Prize Contest, twenty-five dollars will go to the best entry, and five dollars to each of the others. Just remember: all I want is a summary or précis, the kind of thing that English teachers used to ask for before they got up-to-date and began to ask students to do what they call "research." And all I ask is that I will be able to say, "Yes, that's what I really said."

Some of you at this point will be wanting to ask, "Who are *you* to judge?"   18
"How can *you* be objective?" To which I reply, "Who else?" For the contest, it's *my* meanings we're after. Then we can move on to your refutations. If anyone insists, however, I'll be glad to appoint a review court, students of your choice. Anyway, don't be afraid that I'll be trying to protect my twenty-five bucks. I'm pathetically eager to be understood; I am praying for a winner this time, because I want to feel that I have not been talking into that great, garbling meaning-chopper that often seems to swallow all our meanings at one end and spew out nonsense at the other.*

---

* To my surprise, there were three winners. The first prize went to a young man who wrote his summary in an excellently formed sonnet sequence!

Everyone who has ever been reported in the press, and especially in the   19
weeklies, has felt the effects of the meaning-chopper. Norman Mailer, who
almost always seems to me to misunderstand everyone else, is very good on the
subject of how it feels himself to go through the meaning-chopper of the
media: "The papers distorted one's actions, and that was painful enough, but
they wrenched and garbled and twisted and broke one's words and sentences
until a good author always sounds like an overcharged idiot in newsprint."
Mailer sometimes makes the mistake of talking as if the meaning-chopper
worked only out of malice—if people would only be friendly all would be well.
But finally he recognizes the truth: "The average reporter [can]not get a sentence straight if it [is] phrased more subtly than his own mind. . . ."* In our
terms, the "average reporter," whether a professional reporting for other readers, or simply you and I trying to record for our own future needs, is not free to
recover meanings that are richer *than his own mind.* And the first goal of education is thus to prepare your minds for the free conversation with other minds
that can only take place if you really know what those other minds are offering.

Unfortunately, this first freedom, freedom to understand, is even more   20
complicated than my examples have suggested. Even experts, dealing calmly
with issues that are not tied to survival or burdened with emotions or cluttered
with business, often have trouble understanding each other. Philosophers
always claim to be misunderstood by other philosophers. Hegel is said to have
lamented on his deathbed: "There never was but one man who understood
me—and even he did not understand me." The reviewer of scholarly books who
can discover what the books attempt before damning or praising is a rare bird
indeed. And of course none of us ever becomes free, in this sense, in very many
subjects. I cannot, for example, recover the meanings of current papers in
mathematics or atomic physics; even the popularized is papers on these subjects
in *Scientific American* frequently throw me. To this extent, I am unliberated in
these subjects; the only freedom I can hope for is the freedom that comes from
knowing my own ignorance. But this in itself is no mean thing, as Socrates
taught the world. To know *when* you don't know and *what* you don't know is in
fact probably the most important step in earning the first freedom, because
unless you know that you are ignorant, you will not know that you are enslaved,
and you will have no motive to "attack your ignorance."

My second and third "R's" are Rejection, on the one hand, and Renewal or   21
Renovation, on the other. I won't discuss them at length tonight, but just describe them briefly. It is obviously not enough just to feed back accurately and
justly what the other speaker or writer meant. We must be able to sort out, distinguish the sound from the unsound, and then *re*-present old meanings in
forms intelligible and useful in new situations. The freedom to reject falsehood
and renew truth by transmitting it to others is in effect the freedom to exercise
power over the world and over other men's minds, and it thus clearly includes

---

* Norman Mailer, *Armies of the Night* (New York, 1968), 80–81

(though it goes far beyond) what we mean when we talk about "learning how to speak and write."

There's a lot of talk in America these days about how we professorial igno- 22
ramuses have failed to teach you student ignoramuses how to write. Supervisors of Ph.D. dissertations blame college teachers, college teachers blame high school teachers, and the public blames us all. But most of the complaints I see from the public are trivial, concerned only with spelling and grammar. The real failure we ought to be concerned about is that hardly anybody seems to be concerned with writing in the sense of composition—com-posing in the sense of testing, with hard mental labor, whether ideas really fit together. The writer who matters to us is the one who has faced honestly what happens when ideas are recovered and set free in a free mind. What happens is that some of the ideas fit together and some do not. The complacent, uneducated mind does not worry when ideas do not fit. Such a mind can believe, or believe that it believes, both that all men are brothers, or children of the same divine father, and that a particular man, whose skin color is wrong, can be used as a machine convenient for economic purposes, thus ignoring his humanity and brotherhood. The mind struggling to free itself can't do that. It looks at the two ideas and they start nagging at him: "One of us two has gotta go." The uneducated mind can accommodate the belief that "the students must be put down" because they are all immature, dirty, paranoid revolutionaries with the knowledge that particular students—Jones, Kozol, and Grziack—are mature, clean, reasonable people, deeply devoted to their studies in a university of which they are proud. The uneducated mind will accept slogans like "students are the most exploited class in America today," even though it also knows that migrant workers and black workers have been immeasurably more exploited and have a right to be insulted by the comparison with affluent middle-class students. The mind struggling to free itself will never rest easy with such plain and living disharmonies of words with words and of words with deeds. It cannot believe that to napalm a village is to liberate it, that to destroy a country is to bring it a better way of life, or—on the other side of the political fence—that the misery or even death of this particular human being now standing innocently in my path does not matter, so long as it is required in order to build a beautiful revolution. From this point of view, the ultimate expression of the enslaved mind would be something like that of the fathers of the Inquisition, who could kill a man to save his own soul, or the California cultists, who are said to have killed in the name of liberating the victims. But most of us can find examples in our own ideas and practices of equally crude disharmonies.

Note that I am not saying that an educated man has no ideas that clash with 23
other ideas. All of us struggle throughout our lives, until we die or die on our feet, with many incompatibles or seeming incompatibles. But it is the mark of an educated, free mind to struggle with its seeming incompatibles and to try to remove them without cheating. And it is one mark of anyone with this special kind of freedom that he has developed some skill in doing it: some capacity to take the various notions in his head, clarify them, sharpen them, reshuffle them in application to the manifold new situations that come thrusting at him from all directions. Such skills can of course be used in evil causes, and just as it is

possible for an uneducated man to be a good man, it is quite possible for an educated man in this sense to be a bad man. But he will never be satisfied with the slavery of deceiving himself.

I don't have to remind you that what I am saying about rejection and renovation, old and tested as it is, conflicts with a great deal that we are told. Everywhere you look, in the press, in art and movies and novels and books and essays about where we are in this decade, you can find claims that the effort to reason about things in this sense is old-fashioned, irrelevant, or even downright destructive. The medium is the message; linear thought is passé. We are in a time of "electronic simultaneity," of "iconic vision." Don't try to sort out the various messages and think things through for yourself: let yourself go, sink blissfully into cosmic pools of illumination, and you will find truths beneath truths, mystical roads on which nonsense is sense, contradictions are harmonies, everything anyone says is equally beautiful and equally true. And if you need intellectual support for repudiating the intellectual endeavor and believing anything you damn please, why there is the Freudian tradition, teaching that ideas are simply superstructures for our deeper, and hence realer, psychological and sexual motives; and there is the Marxian tradition, teaching that ideas are really only superstructures for historical and sociological motives that are deeper, and hence realer. Or there is the tradition of popular sayings, like "A foolish consistency is the bugbear of little minds." Or there are the Spirovian prophets [the reference is to Spiro Agnew, the already disgraceful Vice President, who was only later publicly disgraced] who address their stirring words to members of the silent and blissfully unthinking majority, telling them in effect not to worry about relating notions of right and wrong to U.S. actions abroad: that if there were "only" one-hundred Americans killed in Viet Nam this week—how I marvel at that "only"—things are getting better all the time; or that the evils of American life are caused by the "reds" and "radicals" who insist on pointing them out. Or there are the current anti-theorists of mindless activism: "Principles-Schminciples," a "Weatherman" wrote two years ago, when some of his SDS critics argued that deliberate and unprovoked violence contradicted certain clear principles of SDS. Or there is the philosophical tradition, promulgated by men who claim to be educated, telling you that the universe is itself proved to be absurd, and that true intellectual power comes from recognizing and surrendering to its absurdity, not from trying to penetrate the fog and find islands of clarity. Or there is the message found in so much of contemporary fiction: not only the universe, but every institution in it is absurd. After all, all values are only relative anyway; even *Time* magazine teaches that these days, so it can hardly make sense to try to wrestle with seeming inconsistencies between value X and value Y.

When I consider the floods of mis-education of this kind that have baptized you daily since your birth on that unlikely (but of course star-studded) day back in 1951 or '52 or '53, I am almost surprised that you haven't lynched me by now for casting doubt on the true church of freedom-as-caprice. But of course nobody can ever be fully baptized into hopeless absurdity. We all come strangely equipped with Malcolm X's "dormant craving to be mentally alive," a hunger for reasonableness that can seldom be totally repressed. We are, it is

24

25

true, equipped with many other hungers that often overwhelm this one, and this kind of psychological disharmony has sometimes been used as evidence that disharmony is at the heart of things. But the fact is that we all have a natural re-sistance to contradictions, we all feel violated by them *once we see them clearly.* And if I am right, it is the main task of education to help us see our contradic-tions clearly and, more importantly, to teach the methods of bringing contra-diction to the surface, of working out genuine harmonies, and of presenting the results persuasively to our fellow men.

There are many complications to be explored in all this, if only we had time. 26 There is, first, the plain fact that if I spend too much time trying to get all my ideas clear before I act, I may never act, and while I cultivate my precious mind, the needed actions may not be performed by anyone. I can't pretend to a satis-factory solution to this problem, since I am often torn between the need to act *now* and the desire to think some more. But what I do know is that the conflict is not between simple and easily realizable impulses to act for good in the world and simple and selfish impulses to cultivate mental freedom. On the contrary, more harm is done in the world by well-intentioned and mindless action than by a failure to act. Arthur Koestler has argued that in fact the chief cause of man's suffering in all ages has been group-oriented altruism—that the man selflessly committed to a noble cause, acting—or so he thinks—for the good of his group, usually does more harm than good. Just as it is true that only the man who is free to love is of much use to those who need love, so it is true that only the man whose mind is free is of much use to his fellow men—in any task, but especially in the task of freeing their minds. Was Malcolm X being selfish when he spent his time mastering those books? In this, as in so many things, it turns out that true self-fulfillment yields the greatest possibility for true service.

There is, secondly, the complication that just as everything under the sun, in- 27 cluding slavery, travels under the name of freedom, so does everything under the sun, including grossly inhumane and irrational behavior, travel under the name of reasonableness. And there is the third complication, that pleas like mine to ed-ucate free critical intelligence imply a radically misleading notion of independent, isolated thinking "atoms." Modern western civilization has contributed to per-versions of "reason" by isolating an imaginary construct, the critical intelligence somehow belonging to an isolated individual ego. One of the main contradic-tions we moderns must wrestle with is between this fictional critical calculator of independent thoughts and the world of passion and feeling and shared values and traditions and collective inquiry that in fact creates what we call the "self" and makes it able to function in the first place. Much of the present youthful revolt against abstract rational calculation divorce from value is thus justified, and it would be a mistake to defend education of the critical intelligence without taking into account what we now know, or should know, about our "selves." In-dividu-als simply cannot go it alone intellectually, as autonomous logical calculators, any more than they can go it alone morally and emotionally, ignoring the needs and promptings of their brothers and sisters.

And there is a fourth complication: How do we preserve ourselves, as we 28 seek an education, from the influence of indoctrinators disguised as educators?

(Am I an indoctrinator, for example, or have I been an educator tonight?) Everything I have said implies that there is a sharp difference between indoctrination and education: indoctrination enslaves us to the opinions of others, often by making us believe that we have thought for ourselves; education—if there really is such a thing—liberates us to recover and renovate ideas by making them our own. Even if this difference is, as I am claiming, real and fundamental, it will never be an easy one to recognize.

Each of these four complications deserves hours of discussion, but I think none of them invalidates my general claim: It is the main goal of education to liberate minds otherwise enslaved, by developing the skills, first, of recovering meanings, then, of rejecting the ones that do not hold up under a close look, and finally, of renovating, re-synthesizing those that do. About the fourth "R," the art of intellectual Revolution, I really have nothing to say; we must leave it to the geniuses.

Well, my time is up—and I've necessarily only scratched the surface. There are no doubt worst disasters than never learning to think. Never learning to love, never learning to enjoy laughter or music, never knowing friendship— these kinds of binding would seem to me even more tragic than never learning to think. But if anything is clear about recent experiments in anti-rational lifestyles, it is that even loving and laughing and friendship and making music can be poisoned by thoughtlessness. I suppose that "every man trusts his own consciousness-expanding devices," and I know that I am preaching to a generation that wants to believe that there is more education in a sunset than in Plato. But I hope I have shown that whatever crisis we face in education is made of our own fears, not of any real lack of value in our disciplines. To pretend that college education is an empty farce is to make it into an empty farce. But the age-old task of imparting the four arts of freedom is at least as important as it ever was, and it is as important as anything else in the world. Let's get on with it, all of us, celebrating the good fortune of living in a time when what we are doing here is not only allowed by our society but encouraged and rewarded by it. What could be a better gift than to be freed, for the next few years, to pursue the meaning of freedom together here? □

◢ REREADING FOR UNDERSTANDING

1. Booth says that the intention of a liberal education is to liberate. In what sense does he use the term "liberate?" What kind of learning must take place, according to Booth, to liberate the mind?

2. What are the four R's that Booth claims comprise the essential arts of liberal education? Which of those arts is considered most important by most education theorists, according to Booth? Why does he believe the other three R's are really more important?

3. How does Booth use the example of Malcolm X to illustrate that learning to recover other people's ideas is the first step toward intellectual freedom?

4. Booth defines the art of Recovery as "the seemingly simple but never finally mastered ability to learn what other men have known or believed" (par. 3). What does he mean in saying that Recovery is an ability we can never finally master? What difficulties hinder anyone who sets about trying to recover knowledge?

5. Booth anticipates his audience's response to several points in his speech. Identify at least three passages in which he acknowledges the likely questions or criticism of his listeners. How does he respond in each case?

◤ RESPONDING

1. Booth remarks that the students he is addressing have, through television, picked up more information than their predecessors, yet he questions whether this information has made them "better educated." What is the difference between being well educated and being filled with information? Booth delivered this speech in 1967. What do you think Booth would say about the current technology that gives students greater and easier access to incredibly more information?

2. Booth offers the following metaphor to illustrate our tendency to reject others' ideas without considering them: "If it's shit already, I don't have to digest it." Do you agree that we try to "reduce other folks' meanings to nonsense we can reject"? Try constructing your own metaphor to illustrate ways people respond to others' ideas.

3. Booth illustrates his claim (par. 22) "that the complacent, uneducated mind does not worry when ideas do not fit" with references to incidents familiar and relevant to college freshmen in 1967. Can you find examples in current events of actions that do not fit with the stated ideas of the actors? Can you think of times when you have said or done things that betray contradictory ideas?

◤ RESPONDING IN WRITING

1. Booth challenges the freshmen listening to write a summary of his speech and offers $25 to the student who is best able to reconstruct his meaning. Unfortunately, we cannot offer a cash reward, but we encourage you to take up the challenge anyway. Write a 100–250-word summary of Booth's speech. Compare your summary with your classmates' versions.

2. Booth says that college may not be the best place to learn how to recover and understand other people's meanings. Write about a personal, non-school experience or encounter that taught you something you could not have learned in school or that helped you to understand or make sense of something you had learned in school.

CONTROVERSIES

Should We Be Able to Choose Our Schools?

JOHN E. CHUBB
TERRY M. MOE

School choice is an issue that has been debated in education circles at least as far back as the 1960s, when economist Milton Friedman proposed giving parents tax vouchers to apply toward tuition at private schools of their choice. Friedman theorized that forcing schools to operate within a competitive market would allow good schools to flourish and force bad schools to either improve or close. As public concern about the state of American education increased through the 70s and 80s, choice became an increasingly popular idea.

In 1990, John Chubb and Terry Moe, fellows at the Brookings Institute, a conservative think tank, published *Politics, Markets, and America's Schools*, a comparative study of five hundred private and public high schools, in which they argued that school choice was the only way to effectively reform public education. Chubb and Moe's book became a clarion call for a new generation of school choice advocates, among them former President George Bush and his secretary of education, Lamar Alexander. This excerpt from the book appeared in *The Brookings Review* in 1990.

Choice *Is* a Panacea

For America's public schools, the last decade has been the worst of times and the best of times. Never before have the public schools been subjected to such savage criticism for failing to meet the nation's educational needs—yet never before have governments been so aggressively dedicated to studying the schools' problems and finding the resources for solving them.

The signs of poor performance were there for all to see during the 1970s. Test scores headed downward year after year. Large numbers of teenagers continued to drop out of school. Drugs and violence poisoned the learning environment. In math and science, two areas crucial to the nation's success in the world economy, American students fell far behind their counterparts in virtually every other industrialized country. Something was clearly wrong.

During the 1980s a growing sense of crisis fueled a powerful movement for educational change, and the nation's political institutions responded with aggressive reforms. State after state increased spending on schools, imposed tougher requirements, introduced more rigorous testing, and strengthened teacher certification and training. And, as the decade came to an end, creative experiments of various forms—from school-based management to magnet schools—were being launched around the nation.

We think these reforms are destined to fail. They simply do not get to the root of the problem. The fundamental causes of poor academic performance are not to be found in the schools, but rather in the institutions by which the schools have traditionally been governed. Reformers fail by automatically relying on these institutions to solve the problem—when the institutions are the problem.

The key to better schools, therefore, is institutional reform. What we propose is a new system of public education that eliminates most political and bureaucratic control over the schools and relies instead on indirect control through markets and parental choice. These new institutions naturally function to promote and nurture the kinds of effective schools that reformers have wanted all along.

SCHOOLS AND INSTITUTIONS

Three basic questions lie at the heart of our analysis. What is the relationship between school organization and student achievement? What are the conditions that promote or inhibit desirable forms of organization? And how are these conditions affected by their institutional settings?

Our perspective on school organization and student achievement is in agreement with the most basic claims and findings of the "effective schools" literature, which served as the analytical base of the education reform movement throughout the 1980s. We believe, as most others do, that how much students learn is not determined simply by their aptitude or family background—although, as we show, these are certainly influential—but also by how effectively schools are organized. By our estimates, the typical high school student tends to learn considerably more, comparable to at least an extra year's worth of study, when he or she attends a high school that is effectively organized rather than one that is not.

Generally speaking, effective schools—be they public or private—have the kinds of organizational characteristics that the mainstream literature would lead one to expect: strong leadership, clear and ambitious goals, strong academic programs, teacher professionalism, shared influence, and staff harmony, among other things. These are best understood as integral parts of a coherent syndrome of organization. When this syndrome is viewed as a functioning whole, moreover, it seems to capture the essential features of what people normally mean by a team—principals and teachers working together, cooperatively and informally, in pursuit of a common mission.

How do these kinds of schools develop and take root? Here again, our own   9 perspective dovetails with a central theme of educational analysis and criticism: the dysfunctions of bureaucracy, the value of autonomy, and the inherent tension between the two in American public education. Bureaucracy vitiates the most basic requirements of effective organization. It imposes goals, structures, and requirements that tell principals and teachers what to do and how to do it—denying them not only the discretion they need to exercise their expertise and professional judgment but also the flexibility they need to develop and operate as teams. The key to effective education rests with unleashing the productive potential already present in the schools and their personnel. It rests with granting them the autonomy to do what they do best. As our study of American high schools documents, the freer schools are from external control the more likely they are to have effective organizations.

Only at this late stage of the game do we begin to part company with the   10 mainstream. While most observers can agree that the public schools have become too bureaucratic and would benefit from substantial grants of autonomy, it is also the standard view that this transformation can be achieved within the prevailing framework of democratic control. The implicit assumption is that, although political institutions have acted in the past to bureaucratize, they can now be counted upon to reverse course, grant the schools autonomy, and support and nurture this new population of autonomous schools. Such an assumption, however, is not based on a systematic understanding of how these institutions operate and what their consequences are for schools.

POLITICAL INSTITUTIONS

Democratic governance of the schools is built around the imposition of higher-   11 order values through public authority. As long as that authority exists and is available for use, public officials will come under intense pressure from social groups of all political stripes to use it. And when they do use it, they cannot blithely assume that their favored policies will be faithfully implemented by the heterogeneous population of principals and teachers below—whose own values and professional views may be quite different from those being imposed. Public officials have little choice but to rely on formal rules and regulations that tell these people what to do and hold them accountable for doing it.

These pressures for bureaucracy are so substantial in themselves that real   12 school autonomy has little chance to take root throughout the system. But they are not the only pressures for bureaucracy. They are compounded by the political uncertainty inherent in all democratic politics: those who exercise public authority know that other actors with different interests may gain authority in the future and subvert the policies they worked so hard to put in place. This knowledge gives them additional incentive to embed their policies in protective bureaucratic arrangements—arrangements that reduce the discretion of schools and formally insulate them from the dangers of politics.

These pressures, arising from the basic properties of democratic control, are compounded yet again by another special feature of the public sector. Its institutions provide a regulated, politically sensitive setting conducive to the power of unions, and unions protect the interests of their members through formal constraints on the governance and operation of schools—constraints that strike directly at the schools' capacity to build well-functioning teams based on informal cooperation. 13

The major participants in democratic governance—including the unions—complain that the schools are too bureaucratic. And they mean what they say. But they are the ones who bureaucratized the schools in the past, and they will continue to do so, even as they tout the great advantages of autonomy and professionalism. The incentives to bureaucratize the schools are built into the system. 14

MARKET INSTITUTIONS

This kind of behavior is not something that Americans simply have to accept, like death and taxes. People who make decisions about education would behave differently if their institutions were different. The most relevant and telling comparison is to markets, since it is through democratic control and markets that American society makes most of its choices on matters of public importance, including education. Public schools are subject to direct control through politics. But not all schools are controlled in this way. Private schools—representing about a fourth of all schools—are subject to indirect control through markets. 15

What difference does it make? Our analysis suggests that the difference is considerable and that it arises from the most fundamental properties that distinguish the two systems. A market system is not built to enable the imposition of higher-order values on the schools, nor is it driven by a democratic struggle to exercise public authority. Instead, the authority to make educational choices is radically decentralized to those most immediately involved. Schools compete for the support of parents and students, and parents and students are free to choose among schools. The system is built on decentralization, competition, and choice. 16

Although schools operating under a market system are free to organize any way they want, bureaucratization tends to be an unattractive way to go. Part of the reason is that virtually everything about good education—from the knowledge and talents necessary to produce it, to what it looks like when it is produced—defies formal measurement through the standardized categories of bureaucracy. 17

The more basic point, however, is that bureaucratic control and its clumsy efforts to measure the unmeasurable are simply *unnecessary* for schools whose primary concern is to please their clients. To do this, they need to perform as effectively as possible, which leads them, given the bottom-heavy technology of 18 education, to favor decentralized forms of organization that take full advantage of strong leadership, teacher professionalism, discretionary judgment, informal cooperation, and teams. They also need to ensure that they provide the kinds of services parents and students want and that they have the capacity to cater and adjust to their clients' specialized needs and interests, which this same syndrome of effective organization allows them to do exceedingly well.

Schools that operate in an environment of competition and choice thus have strong incentives to move toward the kinds of "effective-school" organizations that academics and reformers would like to impose on the public schools. Of course, not all schools in the market will respond equally well to these incentives. But those that falter will find it more difficult to attract support, and they will tend to be weeded out in favor of schools that are better organized. This process of natural selection complements the incentives of the marketplace in propelling and supporting a population of autonomous, effectively organized schools.

INSTITUTIONAL CONSEQUENCES

No institutional system can be expected to work perfectly under real-world conditions. Just as democratic institutions cannot offer perfect representation or perfect implementation of public policy, so markets cannot offer perfect competition or perfect choice. But these imperfections, which are invariably the favorite targets of each system's critics, tend to divert attention from what is most crucial to an understanding of schools: as institutional systems, democratic control and market control are strikingly different in their fundamental properties. As a result, each system structures individual and social choices about education very differently, and each has very different consequences for the organization and performance of schools. Each system puts its own indelible stamp on the schools that emerge and operate within it.

What the analysis in our book suggests, in the most practical terms, is that American society offers two basic paths to the emergence of effective schools. The first is through markets, which scarcely operate in the public sector, but which act on private schools to discourage bureaucracy and promote desirable forms of organization through the natural dynamics of competition and choice.

The second path is through "special circumstances,"—homogeneous environments free of problems—which, in minimizing the three types of political pressures just discussed, prompt democratic governing institutions to impose less bureaucracy than they otherwise would. Private schools therefore tend to be effectively organized because of the way their system naturally works. When public schools happen to be effectively organized, it is in spite of their system—they are the lucky ones with peculiarly nice environments.

As we show in our book, the power of these institutional forces is graphically reflected in our sample of American high schools. Having cast our net widely to allow for a full range of noninstitutional factors that might reasonably be suspected of influencing school autonomy, we found that virtually all of them fall by the wayside. The extent to which a school is granted the autonomy it needs to develop a more effective organization is overwhelmingly determined by its sectoral location and the niceness of its institutional environment.

Viewed as a whole, then, our effort to take institutions into account builds   24
systematically on mainstream ideas and findings but, in the end, puts a very different slant on things. We agree that effective organization is a major determinant of student achievement. We also agree that schools perform better the more autonomous they are and the less encumbered they are by bureaucracy. But we do not agree that this knowledge about the proximate causes of effective performance can be used to engineer better schools through democratic control. Reformers are right about where they want to go, but their institutions cannot get them there.

The way to get schools with effective organizations is not to insist that   25
democratic institutions should do what they are incapable of doing. Nor is it to assume that the better public schools, the lucky ones with nice environments, can serve as organizational models for the rest. Their luck is not transferable. The way to get effective schools is to recognize that the problem of ineffective performance is really a deep-seated institutional problem that arises from the most fundamental properties of democratic control.

The most sensible approach to genuine education reform is therefore to   26
move toward a true institutional solution—a different set of institutional arrangements that actively promotes and nurtures the kinds of schools people want. The market alternative then becomes particularly attractive, for it provides a setting in which these organizations take root and flourish. That is where "choice" comes in.

EDUCATIONAL CHOICE

It is fashionable these days to say that choice is "not a panacea." Taken literally,   27
that is obviously true. There are no panaceas in social policy. But the message this aphorism really means to get across is that choice is just one of many reforms with something to contribute. School-based management is another. So are teacher empowerment and professionalism, better training programs, stricter accountability, and bigger budgets. These and other types of reforms all bolster school effectiveness in their own distinctive ways—so the reasoning goes—and the best, most aggressive, most comprehensive approach to transforming the public school system is therefore one that wisely combines them into a multifaceted reformist package.

Without being too literal about it, we think reformers would do well to   28
entertain the notion that choice is a panacea. Of all the sundry education reforms that attract attention, only choice has the capacity to address the basic institutional problem plaguing America's schools. The other reforms are all system-preserving. The schools remain subordinates in the structure of public authority—and they remain bureaucratic.

In principle, choice offers a clear, sharp break from the institutional past. In   29
practice, however, it has been forced into the same mold with all other reforms. It has been embraced half-heartedly and in bits and pieces—for example,

through magnet schools and limited open enrollment plans. It has served as a means of granting parents and students a few additional options or of giving schools modest incentives to compete. These are popular moves that can be accomplished without changing the existing system in any fundamental way. But by treating choice like other system-preserving reforms that presumably make democratic control work better, reformers completely miss what choice is all about.

Choice is not like the other reforms and should not be combined with   30
them. Choice is a self-contained reform with its own rationale and justification. It has the capacity *all by itself* to bring about the kind of transformation that reformers have been seeking to engineer for years in myriad other ways. Indeed, if choice is to work to greatest advantage, it must be adopted *without* these other reforms, since they are predicated on democratic control and are implemented by bureaucratic means. The whole point of a thoroughgoing system of choice is to free the schools from these disabling constraints by sweeping away the old institutions and replacing them with new ones. Taken seriously, choice is not a system-preserving reform. It is a revolutionary reform that introduces a new system of public education.

A PROPOSAL FOR REAL REFORM

The following outline describes a choice system that we think is equipped to   31
do the job. Offering our own proposal allows us to illustrate in some detail what a full-blown choice system might look like, as well as to note some of the policy decisions that must be made in building one. More important, it allows us to suggest what our institutional theory of schools actually entails for educational reform.

Our guiding principle in the design of a choice system is this: public au-   32
thority must be put to use in creating a system that is almost entirely beyond the reach of public authority. Because states have primary responsibility for American public education, we think the best way to achieve significant, enduring reform is for states to take the initiative in withdrawing authority from existing institutions and vesting it directly in the schools, parents, and students. This restructuring cannot be construed as an exercise in delegation. As long as authority remains "available" at higher levels within state government, it will eventually be used to control the schools. As far as possible, all higher-level authority must be eliminated.

What we propose, more specifically, is that state leaders create a new system   33
of public education with the following properties.

The Supply of Schools

The state will be responsible for setting criteria that define what constitutes a   34
"public school" under the new system. These criteria should be minimal, roughly corresponding to the criteria many states now use in accrediting private schools—graduation requirements, health and safety requirements, and teacher certification requirements. Any educational group or organization that

applies to the state and meets these minimal criteria must then be chartered as a public school and granted the right to accept students and receive public money.

Existing private schools will be among those eligible to participate. Their 35
participation should be encouraged, because they constitute a supply of already effective schools. Our own preference would be to include religious schools too, as long as their sectarian functions can be kept clearly separate from their educational functions. Private schools that do participate will thereby become public schools, as such schools are defined under the new choice system.

School districts can continue running their present schools, assuming 36
those schools meet state criteria. But districts will have authority over only their own schools and not over any of the others that may be chartered by the state.

Funding

The state will set up a Choice Office in each district, which, among other things, 37
will maintain a record of all school-age children and the level of funding—the "scholarship" amounts—associated with each child. This office will directly compensate schools based on the specific children they enroll. Public money will flow from funding sources (federal, state, and district governments) to the Choice Office and then to schools. At no point will it go to parents or students.

The state must pay to support its own Choice Office in each district. 38
Districts may retain as much of their current governing apparatus as they wish —superintendents, school boards, central offices, and all their staff. But they have to pay for them entirely out of the revenue they derive from the scholarships of those children who voluntarily choose to attend district-run schools. Aside from the governance of these schools, which no one need attend, districts will be little more than taxing jurisdictions that allow citizens to make a collective determination about how large their children's scholarships will be.

As it does now, the state will have the right to specify how much, or by what 39
formula, each district must contribute for each child. Our preference is for an equalization approach that requires wealthier districts to contribute more per child than poor districts do and that guarantees an adequate financial foundation to students in all districts. The state's contribution can then be calibrated to bring total spending per child up to whatever dollar amount seems desirable; under an equalization scheme, that would mean a larger state contribution in poor districts than in wealthy ones.

While parents and students should be given as much flexibility as possible, 40
we think it is unwise to allow them to supplement their scholarship amounts with personal funds. Such "add-ons" threaten to produce too many disparities and inequalities within the public system, and many citizens would regard them as unfair and burdensome.

Complete equalization, on the other hand, strikes us as too stifling and re- 41
strictive. A reasonable trade-off is to allow collective add-ons, much as the current system does. The citizens of each district can be given the freedom to decide whether they want to spend more per child than the state requires them to spend. They can then determine how important education is to them and

how much they are willing to tax themselves for it. As a result, children from different districts may have different-sized scholarships.

Scholarships may also vary within any given district, and we strongly think   42
that they should. Some students have very special educational needs—arising from economic deprivation, physical handicaps, language difficulties, emotional problems, and other disadvantages—that can be met effectively only through costly specialized programs. State and federal programs already appropriate public money to address these problems. Our suggestion is that these funds should take the form of add-ons to student scholarships. At-risk students would then be empowered with bigger scholarships than the others, making them attractive clients to all schools—and stimulating the emergence of new specialty schools.

Choice Among Schools

Each student will be free to attend any public school in the state, regardless of   43
district, with the student's scholarship—consisting of federal, state, and local contributions—flowing to the school of choice. In practice most students will probably choose schools in reasonable proximity to their homes. But districts will have no claim on their own residents.

To the extent that tax revenues allow, every effort will be made to provide   44
transportation for students who need it. This provision is important to help open up as many alternatives as possible to all students, especially the poor and those in rural areas.

To assist parents and students in choosing among schools, the state will   45
provide a Parent Information Center within its local Choice Office. This center will collect comprehensive information on each school in the district, and its parent liaisons will meet personally with parents in helping them judge which schools best meet their children's needs. The emphasis here will be on personal contact and involvement. Parents will be required to visit the center at least once, and encouraged to do so often. Meetings will be arranged at all schools so that parents can see firsthand what their choices are.

The Parent Information Center will handle the applications process in a   46
simple fashion. Once parents and students decide which schools they prefer, they will fill out applications to each, with parent liaisons available to give advice and assistance and to fill out the applications themselves (if necessary). All applications will be submitted to the Center, which in turn will send them out to the schools.

Schools will make their own admissions decisions, subject only to non-   47
discrimination requirements. This step is absolutely crucial. Schools must be able to define their own missions and build their own programs in their own ways, and they cannot do that if their student population is thrust on them by outsiders.

Schools must be free to admit as many or as few students as they want,   48
based on whatever criteria they think relevant—intelligence, interest, motivation, special needs—and they must be free to exercise their own, informal judgments about individual applicants.

Schools will set their own "tuitions." They may choose to do so explicitly, 49
say, by publicly announcing the minimum scholarship they are willing to accept.
They may also do it implicitly by allowing anyone to apply for admission and
simply making selections, knowing in advance what each applicant's scholarship
amount is. In either case, schools are free to admit students with different-sized
scholarships, and they are free to keep the entire scholarship that accompanies
each student they have admitted. That gives all schools incentives to attract students with special needs, since these children will have the largest scholarships.
It also gives schools incentives to attract students from districts with high base-
level scholarships. But no school need restrict itself to students with special
needs, nor to students from a single district.

The application process must take place within a framework that guaran- 50
tees each student a school, as well as a fair shot at getting into the school he or
she most wants. That framework, however, should impose only the most minimal restrictions on the schools.

We suggest something like the following. The Parent Information Center 51
will be responsible for seeing that parents and students are informed, that they
have visited the schools that interest them, and that all applications are submitted by a given date. Schools will then be required to make their admissions decisions within a set time, and students who are accepted into more than one
school will be required to select one as their final choice. Students who are not
accepted anywhere, as well as schools that have yet to attract as many students
as they want, will participate in a second round of applications, which will work
the same way.

After this second round, some students may remain without schools. At 52
this point, parent liaisons will take informal action to try to match up these students with appropriate schools. If any students still remain unassigned, a special safety-net procedure—a lottery, for example—will be invoked to ensure
that each is assigned to a specific school.

As long as they are not "arbitrary and capricious," schools must also be free 53
to expel students or deny them readmission when, based on their own experience and standards, they believe the situation warrants it. This authority is essential if schools are to define and control their own organizations, and it gives
students a strong incentive to live up to their side of the educational "contract."

Governance and Organization

Each school must be granted sole authority to determine its own governing 54
structure. A school may be run entirely by teachers or even a union. It may vest
all power in a principal. It may be built around committees that guarantee representation to the principal, teachers, parents, students, and members of the
community. Or it may do something completely different.

The state must refrain from imposing *any* structures or requirements that 55
specify how authority is to be exercised within individual schools. This includes
the district-run schools: the state must not impose any governing apparatus on
them either. These schools, however, are subordinate units within district government—they are already embedded in a larger organization—and it is the

district authorities, not the schools, that have the legal right to determine how they will be governed.

More generally, the state will do nothing to tell the schools how they must   56
be internally organized to do their work. The state will not set requirements for career ladders, advisory committees, textbook selection, in-service training, preparation time, homework, or anything else. Each school will be organized and operated as it sees fit.

Statewide tenure laws will be eliminated, allowing each school to decide   57
for itself whether or not to adopt a tenure policy and what the specifics of that policy will be. This change is essential if schools are to have the flexibility they need to build well-functioning teams. Some schools may not offer tenure at all, relying on pay and working conditions to attract the kinds of teachers they want, while others may offer tenure as a supplementary means of compensating and retaining their best teachers.

Teachers, meantime, may demand tenure in their negotiations (individual   58
or collective) with schools. And, as in private colleges and universities, the best teachers are well positioned to get it, since their services will be valued by any number of other schools. School districts may continue to offer districtwide tenure, along with transfer rights, seniority preference, and whatever other personnel policies they have offered in the past. But these policies apply only to district-run schools and the teachers who work in them.

Teachers will continue to have a right to join unions and engage in collec-   59
tive bargaining, but the legally prescribed bargaining unit will be the individual school or, as in the case of the district government, the larger organization that runs the school. If teachers in a given school want to join a union or, having done so, want to exact financial or structural concessions, that is up to them. But they cannot commit teachers in other schools, unless they are in other district-run schools, to the same things, and they must suffer the consequences if their victories put them at a competitive disadvantage in supplying quality education.

The state will continue to certify teachers, but requirements will be mini-   60
mal, corresponding to those that many states have historically applied to private schools. In our view, individuals should be certified to teach if they have a bachelor's degree and if their personal history reveals no obvious problems. Whether they are truly good teachers will be determined in practice, as schools decide whom to hire, observe their own teachers in action over an extended period of time, and make decisions regarding merit, promotion, and dismissal.

The schools may, as a matter of strategy, choose to pay attention to certain   61
formal indicators of past or future performance, among them: a master's degree, completion of a voluntary teacher certification program at an education school, or voluntary certification by a national board. Some schools may choose to require one or more of these, or perhaps to reward them in various ways. But that is up to the schools, which will be able to look anywhere for good teachers in a now much larger and more dynamic market.

The state will hold the schools accountable for meeting certain procedural   62
requirements. It will ensure that schools continue to meet the criteria set out in their charters, that they adhere to nondiscrimination laws in admissions and

other matters, and that they collect and make available to the public, through the Parent Information Center, information on their mission, their staff and course offerings, standardized test scores (which we would make optional), parent and student satisfaction, staff opinions, and anything else that would promote informed choice among parents and students.

The state will not hold the schools accountable for student achievement or other dimensions that call for assessments of the quality of school performance. When it comes to performance, schools will be held accountable from below, by parents and students who directly experience their services and are free to choose. The state will play a crucial supporting role here in monitoring the full and honest disclosure of information by the schools—but it will be only a supporting role.   63

CHOICE AS A PUBLIC SYSTEM

This proposal calls for fundamental changes in the structure of American public education. Stereotypes aside, however, these changes have nothing to do with "privatizing" the nation's schools. The choice system we outline would be a truly public system—and a democratic one.   64

We are proposing that the state put its democratic authority to use in creating a new institutional framework. The design and legitimation of this framework would be a democratic act of the most basic sort. It would be a social decision, made through the usual processes of democratic governance, by which the people and their representatives specify the structure of a new system of public education.   65

This framework, as we set it out, is quite flexible and admits of substantial variation on important issues, all of them matters of public policy to be decided by representative government. Public officials and their constituents would be free to take their own approaches to taxation, equalization, treatment of religious schools, additional funding for disadvantaged students, parent add-ons, and other controversial issues of public concern, thus designing choice systems to reflect the unique conditions, preferences, and political forces of their own states.   66

Once this structural framework is democratically determined, moreover, governments would continue to play important roles within it. State officials and agencies would remain pivotal to the success of public education and to its ongoing operation. They would provide funding, approve applications for new schools, orchestrate and oversee the choice process, elicit full information about schools, provide transportation to students, monitor schools for adherence to the law, and (if they want) design and administer tests of student performance. School districts, meantime, would continue as local taxing jurisdictions, and they would have the option of continuing to operate their own system of schools.   67

The crucial difference is that direct democratic control of the schools—the very *capacity* for control, not simply its exercise—would essentially be eliminated. Most of those who previously held authority over the schools would have   68 their authority permanently withdrawn, and that authority would be vested in schools, parents, and students. Schools would be legally autonomous: free to govern themselves as they want, specify their own goals and programs and methods, design their own organizations, select their own student bodies, and make their own personnel decisions. Parents and student would be legally empowered to choose among alternative schools, aided by institutions designed to promote active involvement, well-informed decisions, and fair treatment.

DEMOCRACY AND EDUCATIONAL PROGRESS

We do not expect everyone to accept the argument we have made here. In fact, we expect most of those who speak with authority on educational matters, leaders and academics within the educational community, to reject it. But we will regard our effort as a success if it directs attention to America's institutions of democratic control and provokes serious debate about their consequences for the nation's public schools. Whether or not our own conclusions are right, the fact is that these issues are truly basic to an understanding of schools, and they have so far played no part in the national debate. If educational reform is to have any chance at all of succeeding, that has to change.   69

In the meantime, we can only believe that the current "revolution" in public education will prove a disappointment. It might have succeeded had it actually been a revolution, but it was not and was never intended to be, despite the lofty rhetoric. Revolutions replace old institutions with new ones. The 1980s reform movement never seriously thought about the old institutions and certainly never considered them part of the problem. They were, as they had always been, part of the solution—and, for that matter, part of the definition of what democracy and public education are all about.   70

This identification has never been valid. Nothing in the concept of democracy requires that schools be subject to direct control by school boards, superintendents, central offices, departments of education, and other arms of government. Nor does anything in the concept of public education require that schools be governed in this way. There are many paths to democracy and public education. The path America has been trodding for the past half-century is exacting a heavy price—one the nation and its children can ill afford to bear, and need not. It is time, we think, to get to the root of the problem. □   71

◢ **REREADING FOR UNDERSTANDING**

1. Chubb and Moe note that the 1980s witnessed a flurry of school reform. What reforms do they mention? Why do the authors doubt these reforms will improve public education?

2. The title of this essay makes a grand claim about the effectiveness of choice in reforming education. How do Chubb and Moe defend their argument that school choice is not just one of many possibily effective reforms, but *the* only effective reform?

3. Much of the fault Chubb and Moe find with the current school system is
    that it is too bureaucratic. Examine Chubb and Moe's proposed choice plan
    in paragraphs 31–63. Do you think this plan would reduce the current
    bureaucracy of public schools? Is it possible that such a plan could actually
    create more bureaucracy? Explain your answer.

◢ RESPONDING

1. Chubb and Moe say that they are not trying to privatize American schools.
    They claim, in fact, that the system they propose would be a democratic
    one. However, they also charge that democratic control of public schools is
    the source of much of what's wrong with the current system. How can a
    system that is not subject to democratic control be democratic? In what
    sense would Chubb and Moe's system be democratic? In what ways is their
    definition of "democracy" consistent—or irreconcilable—with your un-
    derstanding of that word?

2. The essays in the Contexts section of this unit offer different understand-
    ings of the purpose of education. What do you think Chubb and Moe
    would say is the purpose of education, specifically public education? How
    does their view compare with Jefferson's or Booth's, or with the assumption
    about the purpose of education offered in *Brown* v. *The Board of Education?*

3. Jonathan Kozol points out in the following selection, page 81, that school
    choice was a plan embraced by segregationists as a way of getting around
    government-mandated integration. Do you think a plan like the one Chubb
    and Moe offer would lead to the kind of segregation outlawed by *Brown* v.
    The Board of Education? What safeguards would you recommend?

◢ RESPONDING IN WRITING

Imagine that a plan has been proposed to give parents in your state the option
of either sending their child to any public school in the state or receiving a
$3,000 tax voucher per child to apply toward tuition at the private school of
their choice. The proposal will be voted on in a referendum in the next election.
Write a letter to the editor of the major newspaper in your state, explaining to
voters why they should or should not support the plan.

JONATHAN KOZOL, interviewed by
VICKI KEMPER

Jonathan Kozol (1936–   ) became aware of the great inequality in American education in 1964 when he worked as a substitute teacher in the
Boston public school system. Having attended a private prep school before
enrolling at Harvard, Kozol was shocked by the learning conditions his pupils

at the Christopher Gibson School in the largely black Roxbury neighborhood faced. His experiences there, and subsequent firing for teaching a poem by black poet Langston Hughes, were chronicled in Kozol's first book, *Death at an Early Age: The Destruction of the Hearts and Minds of Negro Children in the Boston Public Schools*. Kozol has remained a tireless advocate for equal education for all children. His 1991 book, *Savage Inequalities*, is an extensive comparison of the best and the worst of American public schools. In this interview with Vicki Kemper for *Common Cause*, Kozol expresses his opposition to school choice.

Rebuilding the Schoolhouse

When Bill and Hillary Clinton announced in early January that their daughter, Chelsea, would be attending an exclusive private school in the nation's capital, they ignited a firestorm of criticism—and rekindled the debate over public vs. private schools and school "choice." There is in Washington a public school good enough for the nation's First Child, many argued.

But such reasoning begs an important question: Even if the Clintons had chosen to send their daughter to one of the District's top-notch public schools, what about all the not-so-good public schools in Washington, and the 80,000 children who have no choice but to attend them—given that the best schools can accept only so many pupils?

It is that question author Jonathan Kozol wants Bill Clinton the president to address, even as Bill Clinton the parent makes other choices for his own child. A former teacher, Kozol is angered and saddened by the increasingly separate and unequal schooling in America, and he calls for a new back-to-basics education movement: public school systems that provide all their students with comfortable classrooms, textbooks, libraries, teachers and—most important—an equal opportunity to learn and succeed.

Kozol's most recent book, *Savage Inequalities*, is a profoundly disturbing look at conditions in the nation's schools, as well as the personal attitudes and political policies that have created them. Kozol spent two years visiting public and private schools in Chicago, New York, East St. Louis, San Antonio, Washington and Camden, N.J. He saw school buildings that had been flooded with sewage, closets serving as classrooms, classes with no teachers and buildings where even the toilets didn't work. He learned of state school-financing formulas that fund affluent districts at a rate 14 times greater than neighboring, low-income districts. He talked with fourth-graders studying logic and high school students who could barely read. He was struck by "the remarkable degree of racial segregation that persisted almost everywhere."

Advocate as well as author, the 56-year-old Kozol insists he will "not accept a rationing of excellence" for the nation's schoolchildren. He encourages elected officials, educators and parents to "stop making new lists [of education goals] and immediately get to work on essentials" such as the expansion of Head Start and reforms in state school-financing systems. He spoke from his home in Massachusetts.

COMMON CAUSE: *What kind of impact does the Clintons' sending Chelsea to private school have on the education reform debate?*   6

KOZOL: I don't condemn President Clinton for that decision. The daughter of a   7
president is likely to be overwhelmed with press scrutiny, and anything that can afford her some privacy makes sense to me. That's a truly unique situation.

If you're going to condemn President Clinton for that decision, then you'd   8
have to condemn the entire U.S. Senate and House of Representatives, as well as virtually the entire press corps in New York and Washington. Because very few of the journalists I know, certainly very few of the editors and publishers, send their kids to public schools.

I do feel heartsick at the growing inclination of not only the very wealthy but   9
also the upper-middle class to flee. A friend of mine in New York, a woman in one of the publishing houses, when she read the first draft of *Savage Inequalities*, looked at me in tears. She said, "I feel awful, I'm sending my child to a private school. . . . Would it do any good if I were to sacrifice her to public school? What difference would that make?"

The answer I gave is "no." If one person makes that decision, it doesn't   10
really change anything. But if all the editors and publishers of the *Wall Street Journal* and *The New York Times*, CBS, and NBC, and Random House, and Simon and Schuster, if all of them put their kids in the New York City public schools, those schools would change overnight. Because they would not allow their children to be destroyed, and therefore they would work like hell to guarantee that the public schools of New York City were the equal of any top suburban district in the country.

What I'm really getting at here is the increasing tendency of the privileged   11
to secede not simply from public schools, but increasingly from almost all the areas of shared experience in our society. The United States is already a highly stratified society. But at least until recently, there were many areas of what I call "shared democracy," where we met on some kind of common ground and had to negotiate our differences with one another in specific situations.

Nowadays, we see the affluent increasingly refusing to pay the taxes it   12
would take to maintain the public parks, and instead, spending their money to join private health clubs where they get their exercise in company with one another. They're reluctant to pay the money that it takes to provide police protection for the entire city, but increasingly spending a vast amount for private security to guarantee that their condominiums, their office buildings, their apartment houses are well protected.

In the same sense, they're saying that they cannot afford to tax themselves   13
to provide first-rate schools for the children of New York, and then spending $10-, $15-, or $20,000 to send their children to private school. This, as a trend, is alarming. We have always had private schools in the United States. Some of

them are wonderful schools, like Exeter. But we are now seeing something new, which is the growing tendency of much larger numbers of people to flee not only to elite schools, but to virtually any school they can get into that will spare their children the obligation, I call it the opportunity, to learn about democracy firsthand, by meeting children of other races and other economic levels. That saddens me very much.

We are already two nations, as far as race is concerned. I worry that we might become 10 or 20 different nations if this continues. I'm concerned about the Balkanization of our society into unique and insulated sectors that will no longer speak even a common language of democracy.   14

CC: *President Clinton, the teachers' unions and many others oppose tuition vouchers that would allow the use of public education funds for private schooling, yet they support the concept of choice within public schools.*   15

KOZOL: I am relieved that President Clinton has taken a strong stand against vouchers that would permit public funds to be used for private education. No matter what the advocates of vouchers say it is, and no matter how many neo-liberals climb on the bandwagon, vouchers originate in an ideology which is distinctly right-wing. Another historic origin of the voucher concept are the so-called "freedom of choice" schools started in the South by white segregationists after the *Brown* [v. *Board of Education*] decision. That element, either covert or subtle racism, is deeply rooted in the voucher concept.   16

The advocates for vouchers nowadays pose the issue in a clever, but I think dishonest, manner. They say something like this: "The rich have always had the opportunity to send their kids to private school. Why shouldn't we give poor people the same opportunity?" But when you ask them what kind of vouchers they have in mind, the amount of money they propose varies from about $1,000 to at most the amount that is spent in an inner city public school, maybe $5,000. None of them are suggesting the $10- or $15,000 voucher that it would take to send these kids to the prep schools the rich children attend.   17

So in effect, under the pretense of compassion for the poor, they are simply proposing a privatized caste system in which the rich will continue to go to elite prep schools, and the poor, at very best, would be able to go to another category of private schools, either parochial schools or very poorly funded sort of second-rate private academies.   18

CC: *But should there be choice within the public school system?*   19

KOZOL: First of all, our capacity for historical amnesia sometimes dazzles me. The [desire for "choice" is] exactly what we heard from white people in Mississippi after the *Brown* decision in 1954. The fact is the government coerces us to do a great many things for the general good in this society. Our absolute right to the individual pursuit of our own ambitions is curtailed in many areas. And this is another one where it should be.   20

The myth here of course is that the choices will be equal and that everybody will be equally well-informed about the choices available. But these conditions are, in fact, never met and are virtually impossible to meet. First of all, people can choose only from things they've heard of. Many poor parents are only semi-literate. They have no opportunity to read the materials that school   21 systems distribute, even the announcements calling them to meetings at which these matters might be explained in greater detail.

But even those who can read do not always read aggressively. The poorest 22 people I know are inundated with written materials which they read so passively it is almost impossible for them to overcome the paralysis that overwhelms many aspects of their lives.

The typical conservative answer to this is, "Wait a minute, Mr. Kozol sounds 23 very patronizing. He's telling us that the poor are too stupid to make good choices for their children." The best answer I can give you is that of a black woman in Boston who saw [John] Chubb [a leading proponent of choice] debating with me once on television and said, "We don't need our enemies explaining to our friends that we're not stupid." She said, "Stupidity isn't the issue, access is."

An awful lot of the sophisticated decisions that are made in school choice 24 programs by the middle class tend to be decisions that are arrived at by word of mouth, because they hear very quickly from their brother-in-law, who is the school superintendent, or their sister, who is assistant to the mayor. They hear very quickly about the "boutique" school that's got the terrific principal and the six wonderful young teachers.

In Boston, whenever they discuss school choice—we have a so-called "con- 25 trolled choice" plan in Boston—the press always points to the same school. I was curious as to why. Then I found as I talked with the few affluent white people I know who still have their kids in public school in Boston, that they all went to the same school. A black woman who lives in Roxbury calls me up every couple of weeks, and she's never heard of school choice, she's never heard of this neat little boutique school.

The reason school choice within a given school district has become so pop- 26 ular, especially with the press, is that it provides the opportunity for people who feel vaguely guilty about fleeing the public system to keep their kids in the public system in what are virtually de facto prep schools.

Now a pragmatic person might reply to me that if we didn't give them 27 those boutique schools, they'd flee the system altogether. And then they wouldn't be there to support the system. But in a sense they've fled the system already, in that they are fighting now only for the school that their child attends, and not for the schools attended by all the other children in the system. They are in a position to raise extra money for that school, to form a real neat local PTA, to volunteer for the library or book fair, do all those things. They can make it into a terrific school, but they have very little incentive to fight for tax support for all the other schools in the system.

There are other problems with intradistrict choice, which has been intro- 28 duced in Minnesota and in Massachusetts and is being discussed elsewhere. The most obvious one is that virtually none of these plans ever provide transportation money. And that certainly couldn't be an oversight. In general [advocates of intradistrict choice] are people who historically opposed school busing for integration. So it's logical that they would sort of leave that out at this point.

So who is able to take advantage of this plan? The first full year of school   29
choice in Massachusetts roughly 93 percent of those who transferred were white
and/or middle class. Twenty-seven percent were poor children. The people who
took advantage of it were the people who had your typical two-parent suburban family, with two cars. The poorest parents aren't doing it because they don't
have cars.

A classic example, and this doesn't involve race, just economics. Two adja-   30
cent towns: Gloucester, Mass., a rather poor school district, a lot of very low-
income families, and Manchester-by-the-Sea, one of the wealthiest school
districts in Massachusetts, which spends about $2,000 more per pupil than
Gloucester does.

What happened when the choice plan was announced? The more affluent   31
people who lived in Gloucester shifted their kids into the Manchester district.
Gloucester lost the money that went with those kids. It also lost the advocacy of
their parents for the Gloucester public school system. And the kids left behind
in Gloucester no longer have the stimulation of some of their most fortunate
classmates.

In all respects, Gloucester is the loser. Gloucester has lost several hundred   32
thousand dollars to Manchester. Manchester has in fact been able to hire one of
the best Gloucester teachers. They cut a program in Gloucester and added it in
Manchester.

I notice that even in some areas, sort of small industrial towns in Massa-   33
chusetts, where there are a great many black or Hispanic families, virtually the
only families that are using the choice option to go to suburban districts are the
white middle-class families. It's interesting that here you have white parents,
who 20 years ago opposed school busing for desegregation because, as they
always told us, it wasn't fair to poor little black children to have to spend an
hour on the bus every day to come out to our spectacular school. Now the same
people are putting their kids on buses for two hours twice a day in order to flee
from black and Hispanic children.

In Massachusetts I don't think there's one family that's transferred from a   34
rich district to a poor district. In virtually every case they transfer from a poor
district to a rich one. If you question them further, you usually find they speak
of sports facilities. In Minnesota you hear that a lot, kids transferred because
it's a better football field or better gym. Convenience is another—because it's
easier for the parents, they can drop the kid off on the way to work. Or simply
that they are choosing from classmates. That again brings us back to profoundly unsettling racial and class issues.

CC: *Should we not have magnet schools?*   35

KOZOL: Magnet schools are different for a number of reasons, the most impor-   36
tant one being that they were conceived as levers of desegregation. And they are
almost always created with very specific guidelines to guarantee that they cannot become sort of an escape valve for the upper-middle class.

CC: *An undercurrent of the choice movement is the belief that many, if not most,*   37
of the public schools in our cities are bad and can't be saved.

KOZOL: That's a wild exaggeration, a very dangerous one. There are terrific   38
schools in almost every city, and they're not just a few elite schools. Even in
poor neighborhoods, you can always find some wonderful schools. And there
are remarkable teachers and good administrators in virtually every city.

The fact of the matter is that if these school systems had the same kinds of   39
resources that are available in the wealthiest suburbs, not simply equal funding,
but funding that is equal to the relative needs that they face—if New York City,
instead of having something like $7,500 [a] year per pupil, had something like
$18,000 per year per pupil as they have in Great Neck, N.Y., there wouldn't just
be a couple of dozen terrific schools, there would be several hundred great
schools in New York City. And the wealthy would have no reason to flee.

Some critics say, well it's not just money, it's also administration. Frankly,   40
my belief is that the major reason that the inner-city public schools are facing
the kind of problems I described in *Savage Inequalities* has very little to do with
so-called bureaucratic problems. It has everything to do with inequality and
with racial isolation. The fact is that once inner-city kids are racially isolated
they get a message. The message is extremely clear, especially when they are in
schools, as most of these inner-city schools are now, that are 90 to 99 percent
black and Hispanic. The message they get is that they are scorned, they are
shunned, that they are viewed as contaminated, that they are viewed as carriers
of plague, almost. That's the message they get.

Some people, I believe, misread *Savage Inequalities* to imply I was arguing   41
for separate but equal schools. I was not. The point I was making was that
unless there are white and middle-class people in the urban school districts,
influential people in the media, lawyers, doctors, all those people, the inner-city
schools will never get equality. And unless the schools are equal, they won't ever
attract white people.

CC: *Conservatives argue that money is not the answer.*   42

KOZOL: I've always been amused by those arguments. If money is not the issue,   43
then the people who live in Great Neck, N.Y., must be crazy. If money is not the
issue, why are they spending $18,000 a year for the kids in their schools?
Obviously, money is the issue. It's bizarre that in this society, where nobody
questions the significance of money in any other area of life, these people want
us to believe that the laws of economics stop at the schoolhouse door.

Typically they'll say, "Well what are you going to do with more money?"   44
Well, to start with you could cut the classes in many New York City schools
from 40 kids in a class down to 19 children in a class. It's still more than they
have at Exeter, where they have 13 in a class, but it would be a small blessing.

Then they say sarcastically, "Is a small class going to make a bad teacher into   45
a good teacher?" No, of course not, but a teacher good with 40 kids is dynamite
with 20, because she's got twice as much time to spend with every one of them.

CC: *People fear that when you say equity, you're talking leveling, that all schools*   46
are going to become mediocre. Given that there is a limited pot of money, how do
you avoid that?

KOZOL: First of all, that argument is profoundly cynical, because the same peo-   47
ple who make that argument are precisely the people who vote against higher

taxes. Obviously I don't want to bring the best schools down. But if the people living in the wealthy districts, who also are those who have the most influence on elections and public policy, if these people refuse to contemplate a significant change in the tax structure in this country, which adds new resources, then unfortunately they are right. The only alternative is to take it from their schools.

But it seems to me that that represents a very penurious vision of our society. Listening to those people, you get the feeling that if we give the kids in Camden the beautiful schools that they deserve, the grass is going to turn black in Princeton. I think that this nation is not only wise but wealthy enough to give superb schools to all our children. I'm simply not going to accept what they're proposing, which is virtually a rationing of excellence. 48

Of course, there is no way to do it without new resources. The most obvious way we're going to get those resources is through more progressive income taxes, which are, for the first time, being discussed in Connecticut. And by significant transfer of federal resources from defense into domestic needs. I don't see any other way this can be done. 49

CC: *What can and should President Clinton do to improve the nation's schools?* 50

KOZOL: First of all, hold fast against the voucher advocates. Second, lend moral and personal support to the parents in over half the states in the United States who are now suing their states for financial equity in their public schools. 51

Third, I would hope he would at least contemplate the possibility of redirecting large amounts of federal money into educational equity. 52

He has talked about redirecting some of the military funds into areas of domestic infrastructure. I would propose, instead of bridges and highways, or in addition, that we redirect some of those funds to literally rebuilding the schoolhouses of America. I'm not speaking here of curriculum or testing. I'm speaking of bricks and mortar and technology. 53

An inspired proposal would be a one-time $50-billion school reconstruction act. Returning soldiers and laid-off employees of military contractors could be put to work building for peace, as it were. That would be an important symbolic victory for equality, and also put to work a lot of unemployed people, many of them the products of segregated and inferior schools 20 years ago. 54

CC: *There are so many issues when we talk about improving our schools, everything from national education goals to school restructuring, to teacher testing. What are the greatest needs?* 55

KOZOL: I think setting goals again, and again, and again, is coming to have a neurotic quality. I've been at this now for 30 years and it seems every five or 10 years we get a new list of goals, but never any talk about the resources it would take to realize them. I would stop making a list and just get to work on a couple of the essentials: Immediately expand Head Start to all three- and four-year olds. I'd like to see it be a full-day Head Start with an additional component for parent education, literacy, and political skills for the parents of these children. So they can be good advocates for their kids. 56

Number two: A federal reconstruction bill to rebuild the crumbling infrastructure of our schools. 57

Number three: A state-by-state drive for school equality. 58

Number four: I would like to see us take a new look at teacher education in   59
this country. That's probably the one area where I agree with some of the conservatives. I think our teachers are frequently denied the kind of full liberal arts
education they require, and given a far too mechanistic preparation.

To me the most important priority would be for this nation to reopen the   60
issue of educational apartheid. For many years now I've found it almost impossible even to get people to speak of it. I would come into a school and see
not a single white child all day long, and finally I'd say to the black principal,
"Hey, would you call this a segregated school?" And he'd smile at me and put
his hand on my shoulder, almost sympathetically, and say, "Gee, Jonathan, I
haven't been asked that question for 10 years. Of course it is. This is American
apartheid."

Is this to continue for another century? Are we at the very most going to try   61
to have site-based ghetto schools? Ghetto schools with more input from ghetto
parents? Or are we at last going to question the persistence of the ghetto school—
this permanent disfigurement on the horizon of American democracy?

cc: *What would your model school in a model school system look like?*   62

KOZOL: A school in the middle of the South Bronx like Exeter. A school with   63
beautiful brick buildings and handsome landscaped lawns, and 13 kids in a
class; with teachers who feel so comfortable with that small class size that they
don't need to lecture and can enjoy the pleasures of a seminar situation; in
which the atmosphere is so comfortable physically and psychologically, for kids
and adults alike, that the teachers needn't live and work in a state of psychological siege. I'd like to see the same rich curriculum. I'd like to see a day when we
would never dream of asking a black teenage girl to concentrate in cosmetology
or food preparation services, a time when we look at those kids from the age of
four and five and say, this little girl has the same chance to go to Vassar as the
great-granddaughter of John Rockefeller.

The school would have no tracking. We would give the least skilled children   64
the opportunity to learn from the more skilled children, and we'd give the latter
a chance to learn something about generosity by helping kids who need the help.

I speak about the physical look of a school a lot because I believe that phys-   65
ical conditions are not just facts in themselves, but they're also metaphors. They
tell people how we value them.

cc: *In all your discussions with children, what did you find are their greatest*   66
needs, desires, and goal for their education?

KOZOL: Well, kids generally, sooner or later, point to most of the things we've just   67
discussed. They'd like to be in a class that's small enough so the teacher has time
to give them attention and love. They'd like to be in a building which doesn't
insult them by its smell and its crowded atmosphere. They'd like to know from
an early age that they can be anything they want, and not have that just be rhetoric, but have that proven by the nature of the curriculum that's offered.

But most of all, the poorest kids want to feel respected. How do you tell   68
kids that we respect them? You prove it to them by putting them in beautiful
schools, you prove it to them by giving them the same things they know the
richest kids in our country get, because they see it on TV all the time. Most of

all, you do it by putting them in the same schools that our children attend, so they know to start with that we do not view them as contaminated human beings. That is a terrible crime that we are still committing in this country. □

◢ REREADING FOR UNDERSTANDING

1. Kozol says he does not blame parents like the Clintons for putting their children in private schools, yet he argues that public education would be dramatically improved if the children of the wealthy and influential attended them. Why?

2. Kozol is concerned about what he calls "the Balkanization of our society." What does he mean by this? Do you think the analogy is an apt description of what is happening in the United States?

3. Kozol charges that the argument presented by advocates for vouchers is dishonest. What evidence does he offer to support this charge? What does he suggest would be the true effect of a voucher system?

4. Kozol argues that so-called school choice proposals, whether they involve tax vouchers or simply giving children the option of going to another public school in their district or another district, seldom offer real choice to all parents and children. What evidence does he offer to support his criticism of each plan?

◢ RESPONDING

Kozol's vision of equal opportunity is not one in which everyone has an equal shot at the few best schools, but one in which every school offers what only the best now do. He imagines a model school system with "a school in the middle of the South Bronx like Exeter" (par. 63). What prevents our country from having such a system? What obstacles does Kozol acknowledge? Can you think of other factors that would prevent Kozol's dream from becoming reality?

◢ RESPONDING IN WRITING

1. Kozol argues that the physical conditions of a school are not insignificant. He says physical conditions of a school "tell people how we value them." Based on your own experience, how much of an impact do the physical conditions of a school have on students' self-respect? on their ability to learn? Write a brief essay discussing the effect of certain physical conditions on learning and self-esteem. Draw upon your own experiences as a student to support your essay.

2. How would John Chubb and Terry Moe respond to the ideas Kozol presents here? How would Kozol respond to some of the claims they make and the proposal they present? Rewrite a section or sections of this interview to include what you think Chubb and Moe's response would be to Kemper's questions and/or Kozol's responses. Try to imagine how Kozol might either refute or affirm their remarks.

HERBERT KOHL

Herbert Kohl (1937–   ) began his career in education as a public school teacher in New York City in 1962 and has been an advocate of school reform ever since. Like Jonathan Kozol, Kohl is committed to a public education system that serves the needs of all children. In this essay he examines some of the institutional causes of the failure of public education in America and suggests steps we must take to truly reform public education.

In Defense of Public Education
Can It Be Saved?

Over the past twelve years public education has come under an attack that is unique in our national history. For two hundred years there have been many criticisms of public schools, ranging from fundamentalist "back-to-basics" movements to the calls for updating and remaking the curriculum after Sputnik so that we could "keep up with the Russians." Progressive movements, beginning as early as the 1830s and gaining great influence over the public schools in the first years of the twentieth century and during the Great Depression of the 1930s, called for schools to take leadership in remaking society in an egalitarian and sometimes a socialist mode. The progressives in turn, were criticized by many Marxist educators who felt that public schools necessarily reproduced class relations in capitalist society and were therefore dubious candidates for its transformation.

In the late forties and early fifties a wave of patriotism led to calls for introducing "Americanism" into the public-school curriculum. In the sixties public schools were to be the vehicles of racial integration, and during the seventies there was a movement to have them become models of gender equity as well.

All of these attempts to remake public education, whether from the left or right, from the unions or the corporate sector, with the major exception of many Marxist critics, had a common premise: that public education as an enterprise was one of the centerpieces of democracy and as such was indispensable. This implied that all children deserved excellent education and should have opportunities to become whatever they dreamed of being. But that is no longer the case. Since the Reagan era, public schools have been increasingly treated as both a public financial burden and a potentially large market for private profit. Chris Whittle's avowed intent to build a thousand private schools to compete with the public sector, the corporate leasing of several Baltimore public schools to a Minneapolis corporation, and such diverse programs as Bush's Education 2000 program and the corporate-funded New American Schools Development Corporation created to administer it, and the contractual arrangement between the Chelsea, Mass., public schools and Boston University—all threaten publicly controlled free education. Parallel to these efforts is a nationwide thrust for vouchers, which represent, finally, a redistribution of public education funding into the private sector. This voucher movement, well financed and supported by conservative think tanks and previously by the Bush administration, draws upon all segments of the population—from home schoolers, poor people whose children are being badly served by existing public schools, scared middle-class parents who feel their children are not being given competitive skills in the public schools, as well as private and parochial schools that advocate government funding of their work. The National Catholic Educational Association, for example, just commissioned a Gallup poll on school choice, and the results, released in September 1992, indicated 70 percent support for a publicly funded voucher system so that parents could send their children to public, private, or parochial schools of their choice.

All of this represents an abandonment of a common commitment to all the   4
children in our society. Vouchers would provide only a small part of private and parochial school tuition and would draw money away from underfunded public schools. Those who could afford private schools in the first place would be subsidized while the poor would find their children in what would become residue schools for disposable children. Corporate schools such as Whittle's and the Education 2000 schools, which would control admissions, standards, and hiring, would signify a direct assault on teachers unions and be free to neglect the children with the greatest educational needs. As Linda Draling-Hammond, professor of education at Teacher's College, Columbia University, has said,

> . . . those who are proposing private school choice are frequently the same people who have been opposing equal funding to schools for the past 20 years.
>
>   The real equity issue is that there are radically unequal allocations of funds to schools. The unequal allocations routinely disadvantage schools in central cities and in poor rural areas. Private school choice . . . is a smoke-screen to avoid tackling this real equity issue.

Corporate arrangements such as those in Chelsea and Baltimore are no less   5
cynical. They eliminate community participation, are union busting, and have no obligation to serve all of the children equally. Taken together, these assaults on public education stand to divide our children into those chosen for a superior education and those left to fend for themselves in schools that would make the ones described by Jonathan Kozol in *Savage Inequalities* seem like havens of decency and light.

Voices in support of free and excellent public education for all the children   6
in our society must be mobilized if we are to remain a democratic society.

However, it is very difficult to mobilize such support. Public education is defensible, but the current state of the public schools is not. Over the past thirty years I've been working in public education—sometimes within school systems, sometimes on the margins, and even at times in opposition to those systems. In every case I have been in what can only be described as the belly of the beast. There has been a massive failure of public schools to educate poor children and children of color. Most public schools are boring lifeless places that serve a few students well, push most through, and get rid of challenging students who become identified as "problems."

My involvement has been centered on the attempt to create contexts for   7
learning that provide the hope, skills, and knowledge necessary for all children to live decent and rewarding lives. I began teaching fifth grade in the New York City public schools in 1961. That same year I was involved in a teachers strike that closed the system down. The strike was as much for working conditions as for salary increases, and my local, at least, considered that negotiating over conditions of teaching, supplies, control over curriculum, and self-accountability was as important as salary increases. The strike was won, union dues checkoff was approved, and the membership of the United Federation of Teachers went from 5,000 to about 35,000 in a day. But along with the increase in membership went abandonment of teaching issues as union issues. Money and benefits were the obsession of the leadership, which had become, and remains, more politically conservative and concerned almost exclusively with its maintenance of power rather than the quality and nature of the work performed by teachers.

In 1966 I worked for the IS 210 planning board and crossed union picket   8
lines in support of community control of schools that I saw as racist and failing the children they were created to serve. In California, from 1968 to 1971 I was a teacher and principal of a public alternative school that functioned under a contract with the district. Our students received Berkeley High School diplomas. The arrangement was irregular, but was created with the cooperation of the school board because it was publicly acknowledged that the high school was not serving all of its students.

Many other public school educators have been involved in the development   9
of alternative schools, open schools, schools-within-schools, community-based learning, and the creation of new schools with distinct, democratically oriented structures and curricula. In addition, public school teachers have developed curricula on their own. Practicing teachers have led in the development of feminist, antiracist, and multi-cultural curricula, as well as in the development of creative approaches to reading, mathematics, and other subjects. From *No More Teachers' Dirty Looks, This Magazine Is About Schools, Teacher Paper,* and *Through the Net* in the late 1960s and early 1970s to *Rethinking Schools, Democracy and Education, Our Schools/Our Selves,* and *Changing Schools* today, teachers have created journals for each other and for the communities they serve. These publications speak about teachers' experiences in the classroom, but also about larger education issues, and explicitly advocate equity, cultural diversity, democracy, and creativity.

Through freedom schools, boycotts, and at times union activities, voices   10
advocating decency and equity in education have constantly insisted upon

public education as a necessary component of a hopeful and democratic society. It is probably true that all of these efforts have reached no more than 10 percent of the public schools, most of which have yielded to bureaucratic subversion, fatigue, conservative attack, and administrative and collegial hostility. The central point, however, is that there has been and is, within public education, a continuing force for improvement of free education, equity, and empowerment for all children. This tradition of struggle within public education represents a commitment to the widest possible access to learning. Good teaching and effective learning are based on the belief that every child, as a right, should be provided with the fullest opportunity to develop intellectually, socially, and emotionally. This implies that time must be taken to know each child, programs must be adapted to each child's style of learning. The teacher must believe that each child has an unknown but great potential, and that none of life's options is to be excluded through tracking or other forms of educational stigma. Teaching well involves patience, the refusal to accept failure, and the ability to maximize children's strengths. Its goal, perhaps unrealizable, is to overcome poverty, eradicate inequity, and at the same time hold everyone up to a high standard of intelligence, sensitivity, and excellence. Thinking as a teacher means refusing to accept a marginalized life for any child. And it means embracing all children, in their wonderful diversity, and teaching from their strengths nurtured by our knowledge and resources.

Yet to defend public education in a way that is convincing to the public is not easy, given the obvious failure of so many of the public schools. Words will simply not be enough. Teachers, principals, and administrators, as well as their unions, will have to take major risks and speak directly to the public and the media about the value and potential quality of public education. Public schools that work must become visible, and those that fail must be scrutinized and changed. Educators have to become self-critical and straighten out their own schools before any convincing defense of public schools can be made. No theoretical defense of public education in the name of democracy will be convincing unless a defense can also be made of public schools.

There are a number of specific things we can do in defense of public schools. Here are five of them:

1. *Public schools or programs that work must be identified and made visible.* Educators must articulate what they consider to be good practice and show how they can be effective with all children. This is really a problem when you are part of a system that has produced so much failure. Nevertheless there is much good public educational practice, and books such as *Embracing Diversity,* edited by Laurie Olsen (California Tomorrow), *The Good Common School: Making the Vision Work for All Children* (National Coalition of Advocates for Students, Boston, Mass.), and George Wood's *Schools that Work: America's Most Innovative Public Education Programs* (Dutton, 1992) show how public education can succeed.

The resources of teachers' unions and other organizations should be used to reach out to a wider public with visions of public schools that work. Right now, these organizations are too insular and do not relate to the communities they are supposed to serve or speak in ordinary language to parents and concerned citizens about quality public schooling. The reason may be that quality schools may embarrass schools that are failing; but it is time to admit failure in public education and do something about it. If educators can't hold each other accountable for the quality of their work, there will be no work for them to do.

2. *All categories of educational stigma must be re-examined and eliminated.*   15
Stigmatizing students because of teachers' inability to educate is a common strategy in the public schools and is perhaps one of the central causes of community resentment. This is also reinforced by the media. For example, Chris Sajac, the teacher in Tracy Kidder's book *Among Schoolchildren,* is given pats on the back for feeling bad about referring one of her students to special education since she knows that it is equivalent to an educational death sentence.

Funding programs based on the continued existence of students who fail is   16
another. In the early 1970s I was asked to help a group of Chicano college students in southern California set up a reading and writing program in a local public school. The school district had agreed to enter into a partnership with the college, and several third- and fourth-grade classes were chosen for the experiment. Almost all of the children in the classes were designated Title IV children—that is, they were poor, predominantly minority students who were functioning below grade level and therefore qualified for extra federal funding under Title IV of the Elementary and Secondary Education Act of 1964.

After a year of hard work the program began to bear fruit. One by one, and   17
then in small groups, the students began to perform on grade level until a critical mass of about two-thirds of the students involved were on or above grade level. At that point some of the college students called and asked me to return to southern California to help plan the next step, which was to expand their program up to the fifth and sixth, and down to the first and second grades.

A few days before my visit I received another call telling me that the pro-   18
gram had been destroyed. It turned out that because the program had succeeded in getting a number of third and fourth graders up to grade level, those students no longer qualified for Title IV money. The district's Title IV budget was cut, and there was no more financial support for the program. And the school district administration was angry at the students and the college for messing up its supplemental funding. One of the district administrators even told a public meeting that the district had to increase the number of its Title IV qualified students in order to maintain its programs. Less than one academic year later the school had reconstituted enough failure to get its full Title IV funding again.

Title IV programs, and other programs that tie money to student failure,   19
have no mechanism for dealing with success. Programs that depend upon financial support predicated on the existence of failure or pathology have to maintain the condition they are designed to eliminate in order to survive. Consider the case of the so-called "educationally handicapped" (EH). EH children are identified by teachers as needing special treatment. Most of them have problems reading, writing, or doing math, but there are a substantial number

of children designated EH simply because they do not like to sit still or stay quiet when they work or because their teachers feel uncomfortable with them.

Stigmatizing children as a cover for educational incompetence is not lim- 20 ited to the children of the poor. Recently a new category of stigma has been constructed: Attention Deficit Disorder. Students designated as ADD often refuse to listen quietly and without response when a teacher or another person in authority is talking, resist following instructions blindly, and refuse to do boring worksheets and other assignments if they already know the material. Interestingly enough, these conditions are positive qualifications for future participatory citizenship. An argument can be that ADD is one way that public school authorities are suppressing the spirit of democracy.

Some of the symptoms of ADD are fidgeting, getting out of one's seat 21 without permission, and doodling instead of doing boring assignments. The primary victims of this syndrome are middle-class children who can perform academically but refuse to when they are not challenged. The category was invented as an extension of the idea that educators do not need to examine their practice and change it when it fails. Instead, the strategy is to spread stigma throughout the student population and blame the victims of pedagogical incompetence.

Gerald Coles, a neurologist, establishes in his well-documented book on the EH 22 phenomena, *The Learning Mystique,* that there is no physiological or medical condition that EH children share. His remarks hold true for ADD as well. According to Coles, EH is not a condition of brain pathology. There is no proof that there is anything wrong with the mental functioning of EH children. There is no common underlying pathology. Instead of adjusting the classroom to fit these children's styles of learning or changing the curriculum, schools invest the children with pathology and treat them as deficient.

Once designated EH, children are removed from the classroom for the 23 whole or part of the day; some of them are drugged with Ritalin; most of them are subjected to simplified versions of the learning material that they had already failed to master in their original classrooms. The classes they are sent to are smaller than regular classes and funded through laws and regulations providing for special education. The teachers are EH specialists, which means that they have taken special classes in the education of the EH child and have certificates or even master's degrees in the field. However, the substance of what is taught in classes on the education of the EH child is not much different from what is taught in ordinary teacher education classes.

Thus the EH child is surrounded by an entire social system entailing laws, 24 regulations, funding, college classes, degrees, and certification. The inability of regular classrooms to educate all children (and in particular minority, working-class and poor children) has led to the construction of a profession that depends upon the existence of children who are pushed out of "normal" classrooms and made pathological. Once an EH program is rooted in a school, staffed by certified EH teachers, funded by EH laws, using ordinary educational materials specially labeled as appropriate for EH children, the children have to be found. There is no mechanism for the elimination of EH programs if they happen to be successful. Nor is there a mechanism for the elimination of dysfunctional professions. Yet degrees in the education of the handicapped are no more than artifices dependent upon suspect stigmatization of children.

Not surprisingly, the existence of the EH subsystem has not led to a wide-   25 scale increase in the levels of performance of EH children. In fact, once the idea is established that school failure is always the fault of the child and that one can get away with blaming the victims of failed practice, the way is open for the constant creation of new categories of pathological behavior as well as for a proliferation of new professions. And when school failure reaches massive proportions, the climate is created for going beyond individual systems of pathology to the development of categories of social stigmatization that turn societal prejudices into pseudoscientific systems of behavior control. We are, unfortunately, now at that point. The category of "at risk," though applied to individual children, is actually a form of social stigmatization that is at times difficult to distinguish from racism.

I have not been able to find a clear and unambiguous definition of what   26 is meant by "at-risk behavior." The closest I've come appears in a book published in the National Education Association's Professional Library Series, *At-Risk, Low-Achieving Students in the Classroom,* by Judy Brown Lehr and Hazel Wiggins Harris. The authors admit at the very beginning that a "review of the literature does not indicate a published definition of the at-risk, low-achieving student." Then they go on to give a list of possible labels without bothering to question whether accepting the concept without a definition is intellectually responsible. In fact, the whole book proceeds on the assumption that, definition or not, the category is useful. Here are some of the labels they come up with:

> disadvantaged, culturally deprived, underachiever, non achiever, low ability, slow learner, less able, low socioeconomic status, language-impaired, drop-out-prone, alienated, marginal, disenfranchised, impoverished, underprivileged, low-performing and remedial.

The authors then go on to list characteristics that can be used to identify   27 students as at risk (not all of which need be present, they tell us, in order to identify a student as at risk):

> academic difficulties, lack of structure (disorganized), inattentiveness, distractibility, short attention span, low self-esteem, health problems, excessive absenteeism, dependence, discipline problem, narrow range of interest, lack of social skills, inability to face pressure, fear of failure (feels threatened by learning), and lack of motivation.

To identify children as "at risk" is to pick them out for special treatment   28 *not for what they have done but for what they might do.* A child who is merely doing poorly in school is not necessarily "at risk." Nor is a child who has any of the above characteristics. So what makes a child at risk, what is the hidden agenda of the people who have manufactured the at risk category? What are such children at risk of doing?

In plain language, at-risk children are at risk of turning the poverty and   29
racism they experience against the society rather than learning how to conform
and take their proper place. One strong way for educators to defend public education is to repudiate all categories like this and assume responsibility for changing their practice until it works for children they have previously been unable to
serve. If not, the voucher option, the private or parochial school, or corporate
learning center is bound to be more attractive than public schools of stigma.

3. *Advocate genuine educational choice within the public schools.* Allow   30
teachers, parents, and other groups of educators to create small schools within
the context of large public school systems and give them freedom and resources. Evaluate them, for sure, but on criteria that parents and teachers agree
upon, not those mandated by a central authority that might be irrelevant to
their practice and goals.

It is easy to create bogus choice systems in public schools. The first experi-   31
ment with choice and vouchers within a public school system that I heard
about took place in the Alum Rock School District in San Jose, California in the
early 1970s. The district, which served many children of color and was experiencing major failure, was to be a model of school choice. Parents would be
given vouchers covering the cost of their children's education that could be re-
deemed at any school in the district that they chose. The experiment fell apart
in less than three years for the following reasons:

- the few decent schools were immediately oversubscribed and the communities they served didn't want to give up any places to outsiders.

- the worst schools stayed just as they were and became residue schools, where
students who couldn't get into the schools of their choice were assigned.

- no training materials were provided, nor were physically depressing sites
rebuilt.

- the teachers, community groups, and parents who wanted to create innovative schools were denied access to funds or facilities, and

- a combination of teacher organizations and administrators made sure that
no person or school, no matter how dismal, was evaluated or forced to
change or declare itself out of business.

Public school choice in Alum Rock, and in many other districts I have ob-   32
served over the years, became, for the majority of underserved people, no
choice at all. Business as usual was restored to the district—meaning failure
without accountability.

Public schools must open themselves up to the uncomfortable fact that   33
many children have been failed by their efforts, and new blood and new life must
enter the process if public education in not to be undone by private choice.

4. *Go on the offensive and let parents know that the corporate agenda for their*   34
children is cynical and undemocratic. The current rhetoric pushing schools to
prepare students for the work world is a sham. Corporations cannot possibly
employ hundreds of thousands of well-qualified technical and professional
workers who command high salaries and still squeeze out the profits their

stockholders demand. The corporations want to train a small elite of middle-level workers; they take no responsibility for the rest of the people. This was dramatically illustrated to me last year when I was asked to make a presentation at a meeting of business people and educators who were restructuring schools in a large southern city. The theme of the meeting was "Education and Vocation for the 21st Century." My presentation was preceded by a luncheon, and I was seated with the CEO of a sponsoring corporation. We hit it off immediately and shared personal experiences, stories about our children's struggles in their schooling, and ideas for new schools that would provide young people with creative and critical skills. I was amazed at the convergence of our views and asked him what would happen if, through restructuring, most of the students developed technological and critical thinking skills. I wondered aloud if these young people would become fully employed and have decent salaries and challenging work.

I sensed some distress as he composed an answer. Yes, some of the youngsters would get good jobs, but even his corporation, which was committed to the development of the community, had a limited number of new jobs and was reducing staff. In addition, there was no guarantee that the company, which was part of a multinational corporation, would remain in the state. Education and economics were not in sync, and the ability of students to benefit from educational reform was dependent upon conditions that had nothing to do with what happened in schools. Painfully, he admitted that finding jobs for all well-qualified people was simply not his or his corporation's responsibility.

Corporate education partnerships also pretend to encourage critical thinking. But in the current anti-union and anti-worker climate, putting education in the hands of the corporations is a form of workercide.

5. *Parents should become more knowledgeable about public education.* Work to make what happens in your children's school transparent so that stigma is exposed, incompetence revealed, and excellence discovered. Create progressive, multiracial, and cross-class coalitions with other parent groups, caring teachers, and principals to change schools. Run people for the school board, and make it known to school bureaucrats, from the superintendent down, that they are accountable for their performance and that blaming your children for their failure is simply not acceptable if they are to receive public funds. Fight the stigmatization of children—refuse it as a substitute for adequate funding, caring teachers, and good pedagogy. Scrutinize school budgets—and rewrite them from the bottom up—from the perspective of services provided directly to students and the community, not from the perspective of supporting a central Board of Education and the services it mandates.

There are two national groups that provide support and information for coalitions committed to progressive school change. One is the National Coalition of Education Activists (P.O. Box 405, Rosedale, N.Y. 12472). The other is the National Coalition of Advocates for Students (100 Boylston St., Suite 737, Boston, MA 02116-4610), which has twenty-two member organizations. Each will send free information.

Finally, in defense of public education, we need to reaffirm that we care   39
about other people's children, about *all* of the children born in our society. I
hope that people will begin to speak more intelligently and courageously
about ideas like freedom and democracy, reaffirming the essential role of public education. □

◢ REREADING FOR UNDERSTANDING

1. Kohl, while admitting that public schools have always been targets of criti-
    cism, notes that there is an essential difference between the kind of criti-
    cism public education has generally received and criticism that has been
    launched against it in the last decade. What is that difference?

2. Explain the distinction Kohl makes when he says, "No theoretical defense
    of public education in the name of democracy will be convincing unless a
    defense can also be made of public schools" (par. 11).

3. Kohl notes the ironic effect of the successful Title IV program he helped
    implement in southern California. What point does he make about educa-
    tional bureaucracy with this anecdote? How does this story lead into his
    discussion of children labeled EH (emotionally handicapped) or ADD (at-
    tention deficit disorder)?

4. Kohl claims that the category "at risk" is a form of social stigmatization and
    racism. What evidence does he offer to support this claim? Why does he call
    on educators to reject this category and others in order to defend public
    education?

◢ RESPONDING

1. Kohl says that "Good teaching and effective learning are based on the belief
    that every child, as a right, should be provided with the fullest opportunity
    to develop intellectually, socially, and emotionally" (par. 10). Consider the
    implications of this statement. Do you agree that all children are entitled to
    such opportunities? Should schools provide opportunity for social and
    emotional development, or is their primary obligation to promote intellec-
    tual development in their pupils?

2. Kohl says that teaching well involves the refusal to accept failure: "Thinking
    as a teacher means refusing to accept a marginalized life for any child" (par.
    10). How do you understand this statement, based on your own experi-
    ences and observations in school? Is Kohl placing too much responsibility
    on teachers for students' failure or success? What does his observation sug-
    gest about the teaching occupation? Does this statement describe any of the
    teachers you have had? Tell about them.

3. Kohl contends that corporate partnerships in education are cynical. Why? Do you think it is appropriate for businesses to be involved in the funding of public education? Defend your answer.

◢ RESPONDING IN WRITING

1. Kohl charges that designating students as ADD (attention deficit disorder) has become a way for educators to avoid blame for failing to motivate or interest students. Rather than examining their own practices to understand students' shortcomings, Kohl says, teachers use the ADD label to "spread stigma throughout the student population and blame the victims of peda-gogical incompetence" (par. 21). Indeed, ADD is a controversial issue in ed-ucation and in psychology today. Many argue, as Kohl does, that it is a convenient label for any child who presents a challenge. Others claim that it is a clearly diagnosable and treatable disorder that should be taken seri-ously. Do some research on ADD in your library and, if possible, by inter-viewing an elementary or secondary school teacher and/or a psychologist or counselor at your college. Write an essay in reply to Kohl's charge.

2. Kohl is concerned with the responsibility of teachers and administrators for making public education work. He argues that too often students are blamed for the failures of the system. What responsibility *do* students have for the success or failure of public education? Write an essay addressed to students at your former high school. Point out to them what you believe are the major obstacles your school faces in trying to provide an education for every student, and suggest specific steps that they as students could take to remedy the situation.

CONTROVERSIES

How Should We Educate
a Diverse Population?

MIKE ROSE

The only child of Italian immigrants, Mike Rose (1944–   ) was his parents' hope of achieving the American dream. They wanted him to receive the education they never had and leave behind the poverty of South Los Angeles where he grew up. But Rose did poorly in school and was quickly placed in that large category of children of whom little is expected. In high school he was put in the vocational track, where the work was unchallenging and the teachers' attitudes demeaning. One exception was his biology teacher, who recognized that Rose belonged in the college prep track. There, he met an English teacher who encouraged him to aim for college despite his poor academic background and helped him get accepted on a probationary status at Loyola. Although he struggled at Loyola to make up for the education he had missed in high school, Rose did earn his degree and received a graduate fellowship in English at UCLA. Rose didn't complete his graduate work, however; instead, he joined the Teacher Corps and returned to South L.A. to help children from backgrounds much like his own. He went on to teach returning Vietnam veterans and other adults in evening classes. Later he became director of the Tutorial Center at UCLA, working with college students who, like his younger self, wanted to learn but lacked the academic background and confidence to succeed in college classes. In his 1989 book *Lives on the Boundary,* Rose shares some of the lessons he learned helping underprepared students such as the ones to whom he refers in the excerpt that follows.

The Politics of Remediation

During the time I was working with . . . Lucia and the others, all hell was breaking loose in American education. The literacy crisis that has become part of our current cultural vocabulary was taking shape with a vengeance. It was in December 1975 that *Newsweek* informed America that Johnny couldn't write, and in the fall of 1976 the *Los Angeles Times* declared a "Drop in Student Skills Unequalled in History." California, the *Times* article went on to reveal, had "one of the most pronounced drops in achievement of all." Reports on the enrollment and retention of students are a long-standing tradition in the way education conducts its business, but it seemed that every month now a new document was appearing on my desk: reports from a vice-chancellor or the university president's office or from some analyst in the state legislature. What percentage of people from families below a certain income level were entering college? What were their SAT scores? What were the SAT scores of blacks? Chicanos? Asians? More locally, how many UCLA students were being held for remedial English? Remedial math? Were there differences by race or income?

This was a new way for me to look at education. My focus had been on particular students and their communities, and it tended to be a teacher's focus, rich in anecdote and observation. Increasingly, my work in the Tutorial Center required that I take a different perspective: I had to think like a policy-maker, considering the balance sheet of economics and accountability. Chip would sit with me in the late afternoon, going over the charts and tables, showing me how to use them to argue for our programs, for in an academic bureaucracy admissions statistics and test scores and retention rates are valued terms of debate. All teaching is embedded in a political context, of course, but the kind of work I had done before coming to the Tutorial Center tended to isolate me from the immediate presence of institutions: working with a group of kids in the corner of a cafeteria, teaching veterans in a dingy satellite building. I was learning from Chip and from a shrewd vice-chancellor named Chuck Ries how to work within the policy-maker's arena. And though it was, at times, uncomfortable for me and though I would soon come to question the legitimacy of the vision it fostered, it provided an important set of lessons. Probably the central value of being at the Tutorial Center was that it forced me to examine the broad institutional context of writing instruction and underpreparation.

The work in the center led to other projects, and during my four years in Campbell Hall, I would be invited to participate in them. One was the Writing Research Project, initiated by Vice-Chancellor Ries, and its purpose was to study the uses of writing and the way it was taught at UCLA. Another was the Freshman Summer Program, six intensive weeks before the freshman year during which students took a writing course linked to an introductory course in political science or psychology or history. There is a lot to tell about these ventures—the politics of evaluating a curriculum at a university, the strains of initiating a curriculum that requires people to cross departmental lines—but the most important thing about both projects was that they led me to do something rarely achieved at a research university. I had to stand on the borders of a number of disciplines and study the way knowledge is structured in the academy and, as well, detail what it means to be unprepared to participate in that disciplinary structure.

Students were coming to college with limited exposure to certain kinds of writing and reading and with conceptions and beliefs that were dissonant with those in the lower-division curriculum they encountered. And that curriculum wasn't doing a lot to address their weaknesses or nurture their strengths. They needed practice writing academic essays; they needed opportunities to talk about their writing—and their reading; they needed people who could quickly determine what necessary background knowledge they lacked and supply it in comprehensible ways. What began troubling me about the policy documents and the crisis reports was that they focused too narrowly on test scores and tallies of error and other such measures. They lacked careful analysis of the students' histories and lacked, as well, analysis of the cognitive and social demands of the academic culture the students now faced The work I was doing in the Tutorial Center, in the Writing Research Project, and in the Summer Program was guiding me toward a richer understanding of what it meant to be underprepared in the American research university. It seemed to me there were five overlapping problem areas—both cognitive and social—that could be used to explain the difficulties experienced by students like . . . Lucia. These by no means applied equally to all the students whom I came to know, but taken together they represent, better than pie charts and histograms, what it means to be underprepared at a place like UCLA. Many young people come to the university able to summarize the events in a news story or write a personal response to a play or a movie or give back what a teacher said in a straightforward lecture. But they have considerable trouble with what has come to be called critical literacy: framing an argument or taking someone else's argument apart, systematically inspecting a document, an issue, or an event, synthesizing different points of view, applying a theory to disparate phenomena, and so on. The authors of the crisis reports got tremendously distressed about students' difficulty with such tasks, but it's important to remember that, traditionally, such abilities have only been developed in an elite: in priests, scholars, or a leisure class. Ours is the first society in history to expect so many of its people to be able to perform these very sophisticated literacy activities. And we fail to keep in mind how extraordinary it is to ask *all* our schools to conduct this kind of education—not just those schools with lots of money and exceptional teachers and small classes—but massive, sprawling schools, beleaguered schools, inner-city schools, overcrowded schools. It is a charge most of them simply are not equipped to fulfill, for our educational ideals far outstrip our economic and political priorities.

We forget, then, that by most historical—and current—standards, the vast majority of a research university's underprepared students would be considered competently literate. Though they fail to meet demands made of them in their classes, they fail from a literate base. They are literate people straining at the boundaries of their ability, trying to move into the unfamiliar, to approximate a kind of writing they can't yet command. And as they try, they'll make all the blunders in word choice and sentence structure and discourse strategy that regularly get held up for ridicule, that I made when I was trying to write for my teachers at Loyola. There's a related phenomenon, and we have research evidence of this: As writers move further away from familiar ways of expressing themselves, the strains on their cognitive and linguistic resources increase, and the number of mechanical and grammatical errors they make shoots up. Before we shake our heads at these errors, we should also consider the possibility that many such linguistic bungles are signs of growth, a stretching beyond what college freshmen can comfortably do with written language. In fact, we should *welcome* certain kinds of errors, make allowance for them in the curricula we develop, analyze rather than simply criticize them. Error marks the place where education begins.

Asked to produce something that is beyond them, writers might also fall   6
back on strategies they already know. Asked to take a passage critically apart, they'll summarize it. We saw this with James, the young man distressed with his C–, but as with so much else in this book, the principle applies to more than just those labeled underprepared. I was personally reminded of it when I was writing my dissertation. My chairman was an educational research methodologist and statistician; my background straddled humanities and social science, but what I knew about writing tended to be shaped by literary models. When it came time to report on the procedures I was using in my study—the methods section of the dissertation—I wrote a detailed chronology of what I did and how I did it. I wanted to relay all the twists and turns of my investigation. About a week later I got it back covered with criticism. My chairman didn't want the vagaries of my investigative life; he wanted a compressed and systematic account. "What do you think this is," he wrote alongside one long, dancing stretch of narrative, "*Travels with Charley?*"

Associated with these difficulties with critical literacy are students' diverse orientations toward inquiry. It is a source of exasperation to many freshmen that   7
the university is so predisposed to question past solutions, to seek counterexplanations—to continually turn something nice and clean and clear into a problem. English professor David Bartholomae recalls a teacher of his suggesting that, when stuck, student writers should try the following "machine": "While most readers of _____ have said _____, a close and careful reading shows that _____." The teacher's machine perfectly expresses the ethos of the university, a fundamental orientation toward inquiry. University professors have for so long been socialized into this critical stance, that they don't realize how unsettling it can be to students who don't share their unusual background.

There is Scott sitting in an Astronomy tutorial, his jaw set, responding to   8
another student's question about a finite versus an infinite universe: "This is the kind of question," he says, "that you'll argue and argue about. It's stupid. No one wins. So why do it?" And there is Rene who can't get beyond the first few sentences of her essay for Speech. She has to write a critical response to an address of Ronald Reagan's. "You can't criticize the president," she explains. "You've

gotta support your president even if you don't agree with him." When students come from other cultures, this discordance can be even more pronounced. Our tutors continually encouraged their students to read actively, to ask why authors say what they say, what their claims are, what assumptions they make, where you, the reader, agree or disagree. Hun's tutor is explaining this to him, then has him try it, has him read aloud so she can guide him. He reads a few lines and stops short. After two more abortive trials, she pulls out of Hun the explanation that what gets written in books is set in tradition, and he is not learned enough to question the authority of the book.

Remember Andrea? She was the distressed young woman who was failing   9
chemistry. Andrea could memorize facts and formulas but not use them to solve problems—and her inability was representative of a whole class of difficulties experienced by freshmen. What young people come to define as intellectual competence—what it means to know things and use them—is shaped by their schooling. And what many students experience year after year is the exchange of one body of facts for another—an inert transmission, the delivery and redelivery of segmented and self-contained dates and formulas—and thus it is no surprise that they develop a restricted sense of how intellectual work is conducted. They are given Ancient History one year and American History the next, and once they've displayed knowledge of the Fertile Crescent and cuneiform and Assyrian military campaigns, there is little need for them to remember the material, little further opportunity to incorporate it, little reason to use these textbook facts to engage historical problems. Next year it will be American History: a new textbook, new dates and documents and campaigns, new tests—but the same rewards, and the same reasons to forget. John Dewey saw the difficulty long ago: "Only in education, never in the life of the farmer, sailor, merchant, physician, or laboratory experimenter, does knowledge mean primarily a store of information aloof from doing."

Students like Andrea are caught in a terrible bind. They come to the university with limited experience in applying knowledge, puzzling over solutions,   10
solving problems. Many of the lower-division courses they encounter—their "general education" or "breadth" requirements—will involve little writing or speaking or application, will rely on so-called objective tests that, with limited exception, stress the recall of material rather than the reasoned elaboration of it. But the gatekeeper courses—the courses that determine entrance to a major—they up the intellectual ante. Courses like Andrea's bête noire, Chemistry 11-A, are placed like land mines in the uneven terrain of the freshman year. The special nature of their demands is not made the focus of attention that it should be; that is, the courses are not taught explicitly and self-consciously as courses on how to think as a chemist or a psychologist or a literary critic. And there are few opportunities for students to develop such ability before they enroll in those courses. The faculty, for the most part, do not provide freshmen with instruction on how to use knowledge creatively—and then penalize them when they cannot do so.

It is not unusual for students to come to the university with conceptualiza-   11
tions of disciplines that are out of sync with academic reality. . . . A lot of
entering freshmen assume that sociology is something akin to social work, an
applied study of social problems rather than an attempt to abstract a theory
about social interaction and organization. Likewise, some think psychology
will be a discussion of human motivation and counseling, what it is that
makes people do what they do—and some coverage of ways to change what
they do. It comes as a surprise that their textbook has only one chapter on personality and psychotherapy—and a half dozen pages on Freud. The rest is
animal studies, computer models of thought, lots of neurophysiology. If they
like to read novels, and they elect a literature course, they'll expect to talk
about characters and motive and plot, but instead they're asked to situate the
novel amid the historical forces that shaped it, to examine rhetorical and styl-
istic devices and search the prose for things that mean more than they seem to
mean. Political science should be politics and government and current events—
nuclear treaties, trade sanctions, the Iran-Contra scandal—but instead it's Marx
and Weber and political economy and organizational and decision-making
models. And so goes the litany of misdirection. This dissonance between the
academy's and the students' definitions of disciplines makes it hard for students to get their bearings with material: to know what's important, to see how
the pieces fit together, to follow an argument, to have a sense of what can be
passed over lightly. Thus I would see notebooks that were filled—in frantic
script—with everything the professor said or that were scant and fragmented,
records of information without coherence.

The discourse of academics is marked by terms and expressions that represent   12
an elaborate set of shared concepts and orientations: alienation, authoritarian
personality, the social construction of the self, determinism, hegemony, equi-
librium, intentionality, recursion, reinforcement, and so on. This language
weaves through so many lectures and textbooks, is integral to so many learned
discussions, that it's easy to forget what a foreign language it can be. Freshmen
are often puzzled by the talk they hear in their classrooms, but what's important to note here is that their problem is not simply one of limited vocabulary.
If we see the problem as knowing or not knowing a list of words, as some quick-
fix remedies suggest, then we'll force glossaries on students and miss the complexity of the issue. Take, for example, *authoritarian personality.* The average
university freshman will know what *personality* means and can figure out
autoritarian; the difficulty will come from a lack of familiarity with the conceptual resonances that *authoritarian personality* has acquired in the discussions of
sociologists and psychologists and political scientists. Discussion . . . you could
almost define a university education as an initiation into a variety of powerful
ongoing discussions, an initiation that can occur only through the repeated use
of a new language in the company of others. More than anything, this was the
opportunity people like Father Albertson, my Shakespeare teacher at Loyola,
provided to me. The more comfortable and skillful students become with this

kind of influential talk, the more they will be included in further conversations and given access to further conceptual tools and resources—the acquisition of which virtually defines them as members of an intellectual community.

All students require such an opportunity. But those coming to the univer-   13
sity with less-than-privileged educations, especially those from the lower classes, are particularly in need. They are less likely to have participated, in any extended way, in such discussions in the past. They won't have the confidence or the moves to enter it, and can begin to feel excluded, out of place, put off by a language they can't command. Their social marginality, then, is reinforced by discourse and, as happened to me during my first year at Loyola, they might well withdraw, retreat to silence.

This sense of linguistic exclusion can be complicated by various cultural   14
differences. When I was growing up, I absorbed an entire belief system—with its own characteristic terms and expressions—from the worried conversations of my parents, from the things I heard and saw on South Vermont, from the priest's fiery tales. I thought that what happened to people was preordained, that ability was a fixed thing, that there was one true religion. I had rigid notions about social roles, about the structure of society, about gender, about politics. There used to be a rickety vending machine at Manchester and Vermont that held a Socialist Workers newspaper. I'd walk by it and feel something alive and injurious: The paper was malevolent and should be destroyed. Imagine, then, the difficulty I had when, at the beginning of my senior year at Mercy High, Jack MacFarland tried to explain Marxism to us. How could I absorb the language of atheistic materialism and class struggle when it seemed so strange and pernicious? It wasn't just that Marxist terms-of-art were unfamiliar; they felt assaultive. What I did was revert to definitions of the social order more familiar to me, and Mr. McFarland had to draw them out of me and have me talk about them and consider them alongside Marx's vision and terminology, examining points of conflict and points of possible convergence. It was only then that I could appropriate Marx's strange idiom.

Once you start to think about underprepared students in terms of these over-   15
lapping problem areas, all sorts of solutions present themselves. Students need more opportunities to write about what they're learning and guidance in the techniques and conventions of that writing—what I got from my mentors at Loyola. They need more opportunities to develop the writing strategies that are an intimate part of academic inquiry and what has come to be called critical literacy—comparing, synthesizing, analyzing—the sort of thing I gave the veterans. They need opportunities to talk about what they're learning: to test their ideas, reveal their assumptions, talk through the places where new knowledge clashes with ingrained belief. They need a chance, too, to talk about the ways they may have felt excluded from all this in the past and may feel threatened by it in the present. They need the occasion to rise above the fragmented learning the lower-division curriculum encourages, a place within a course or outside it to hear about and reflect on the way a particular discipline conducts its inquiry:

Why, for example, *do* so many psychologists who study thinking rely on computer modeling? Why is mathematics so much a part of economics? And they need to be let in on the secret talk, on the shared concepts and catchphrases of Western liberal learning.

There is nothing magical about this list of solutions. In fact, in many ways, 16 it reflects the kind of education a privileged small number of American students have received for some time. The basic question our society must ask, then, is: How many or how few do we want to have this education? If students didn't get it before coming to college—and most have not—then what are we willing to do to give it to them now? Chip and I used to talk about our special programs as attempts to create an Honors College for the underprepared. People would smile as we spoke, but, as our students would have said, we were serious as a heart attack. The remedial programs we knew about did a disservice to their students by thinking of them as *remedial*. We wanted to try out another perspective and see what kind of program it would yield. What would happen if we thought of our students' needs and goals in light of the comprehensive and ambitious program structures more often reserved for the elite? ☐

◪ REREADING FOR UNDERSTANDING

1. Rose says his job as an administrator at the Tutorial Center made him look at education in a whole new way. What does he mean?

2. What does Rose find troubling about national reports and measurements of students' abilities and knowledge?

3. Rose discovered five overlapping problems that contributed to students' difficulties in the college classroom. What are those five problems?

4. How does Rose explain students' lack of what he calls "critical literacy"— the ability to engage with, talk back to, synthesize, and question ideas presented in reading or lectures? How does this lack of critical literacy explain some of the errors students make, according to Rose? How should instructors respond to such errors?

◪ RESPONDING

1. Rose says, "It is a source of exasperation to many freshmen that the university is so predisposed to question past solutions, to seek counterexplanations—to continually turn something nice and clean and clear into a problem" (par. 7). Have you found that your college courses tend to raise questions and consider multiple perspectives more than your high school courses did? If so, are you exasperated by this tendency, as Rose suggests many students are?

2. According to Rose, students often see little connection between what they learn in one course and what they learn in another. Consider your own

schedule this semester. Do you find any ways in which the course material you are studying connects or overlaps? Can you think of ways in which material you learned in previous semesters or in high school applies to what you are learning this semester? Do you agree with Rose that students tend to forget what they've learned in a course once the course is over?

3. Rose says that students often have inaccurate notions of what an academic discipline involves. They may, for example, believe that Sociology is the study of social problems or that Political Science will be a discussion of current political issues. Did you find any of your introductory college courses were out of sync with your expectation or understanding of that discipline?

4. One of the primary obstacles to success in college, according to Rose, is that students are unfamiliar with the language of academic discourse, even if they are intellectually capable of understanding and responding to the ideas. As a result, those students often withdraw from discussion and do poorly in their written assignments. Have you found the language of your college courses to be an obstacle to learning and to demonstrating what you know? What have your instructors done to familiarize students with the conventions of academic discourse and the specialized language of their fields?

▨ RESPONDING IN WRITING

1. Rose says, "Error marks the place where learning begins." Do you recall a time when an error led to new understanding or discovery? Write an essay in which you tell about a specific mistake you made and show what you learned as a result.

2. How well did your prior education prepare you for college? In an essay addressed to the principal or headmaster of your high school, evaluate the education you received in light of your college experience so far. In what ways did your high school education prepare you for the demands of college? In what ways do you believe it failed to prepare you? Recommend a specific change in the curriculum and/or practices of the school based on your observations.

BELL HOOKS

bell hooks (1952–) is a prolific and controversial writer of numerous books and essays examining racism and sexism in American life as a whole and in education in particular. Born Gloria Jean Watkins, hooks went to segregated schools until she reached high school age, at which time she was bussed to an integrated high school, an experience she mentions in this essay. While an undergraduate at Stanford University, hooks began work on her first book, *Ain't I a Woman? Black Women and Feminism,* which was published in 1981. She chose the pen name "bell hooks" in honor of her great-grandmother and opted for lower case spelling of that name in order to call attention to the work, not its author. Hooks has taught at Yale University and Oberlin College and is currently a distinguished professor of English at City College of New York.

In this piece, taken from her 1994 book *Teaching to Transgress,* hooks examines the challenge of transforming institutions of higher education to reflect our nation's diversity of cultures.

A Revolution of Values
The Promise of Multicultural Change

Two summers ago I attended my twentieth high school reunion. It was a last-minute decision. I had just finished a new book. Whenever I finish a work, I always feel lost, as though a steady anchor has been taken away and there is no sure ground under my feet. During the time between ending one project and beginning another, I always have a crisis of meaning. I begin to wonder what my life is all about and what I have been put on this earth to do. It is as though immersed in a project I lose all sense of myself and must then, when the work is done, rediscover who I am and where I am going. When I heard that the reunion was happening, it seemed just the experience to bring me back to myself, to help in the process of rediscovery. Never having attended any of the past reunions, I did not know what to expect. I did know that this one would be different. For the first time we were about to have a racially integrated reunion. In past years, reunions had always been segregated. White folks had their reunion on their side of town and black folks had a separate reunion.

None of us was sure what an integrated reunion would be like. Those periods in our adolescent lives of racial desegregation had been full of hostility, rage, conflict, and loss. We black kids had been angry that we had to leave our beloved all-black high school, Crispus Attucks, and be bussed halfway cross town to integrate white schools. We had to make the journey and thus bear the responsibility of making desegregation a reality. We had to give up the familiar and enter a world that seemed cold and strange, not our world, not our school. We were certainly on the margin, no longer at the center, and it hurt. It was such an unhappy time. I still remember my rage that we had to awaken an hour early so that we could be bussed to school before the white students arrived. We were made to sit in the gymnasium and wait. It was believed that this practice would prevent outbreaks of conflict and hostility since it removed the possibility of social contact before classes began. Yet, once again, the burden of this transition was placed on us. The white school was desegregated, but in the classroom, in the cafeteria, and in most social spaces racial apartheid prevailed. Black and white students who considered ourselves progressive rebelled against the unspoken racial taboos meant to sustain white supremacy and racial apartheid even in the face of desegregation. The white folks never seemed to understand that our parents were no more eager for us to socialize with them than they were to socialize with us. Those of us who wanted to make racial equality a reality in every area of our life were threats to the social order. We were proud of ourselves, proud of our willingness to transgress the rules, proud to be courageous.

Part of a small integrated clique of smart kids who considered ourselves 3 "artists," we believed we were destined to create outlaw culture where we would live as Bohemians forever free; we were certain of our radicalness. Days before the reunion, I was overwhelmed by memories and shocked to discover that our gestures of defiance had been nowhere near as daring as they had seemed at the time. Mostly, they were acts of resistance that did not truly challenge the status quo. One of my best buddies during that time was white and male. He had an old gray Volvo that I loved to ride in. Every now and then he would give me a ride home from school if I missed the bus—an action which angered and disturbed those who saw us. Friendship across racial lines was bad enough, but across gender it was unheard of and dangerous. (One day, we found out just how dangerous when grown white men in a car tried to run us off the road.) Ken's parents were religious. Their faith compelled them to live out a belief in racial justice. They were among the first white folks in our community to invite black folks to come to their house, to eat at their table, to worship together with them. As one of Ken's best buddies, I was welcome in their house. After hours of discussion and debate about possible dangers, my parents agreed that I could go there for a meal. It was my first time eating together with white people. I was 16 years old. I felt then as though we were making history, that we were living the dream of democracy, creating a culture where equality, love, justice, and peace would shape America's destiny.

After graduation, I lost touch with Ken even though he always had a warm 4 place in my memory. I thought of him when meeting and interacting with liberal white folks who believed that having a black friend meant that they were not racist, who sincerely believed that they were doing us a favor by extending offers of friendly contact for which they felt they should be rewarded. I thought of him during years of watching white folks play at unlearning racism but walking away when they encountered obstacles, rejection, conflict, pain. Our high school friendship had been forged not because we were black and white but because we shared a similar take on reality. Racial difference meant that we had to struggle to claim the integrity of that bonding. We had no illusions. We knew there would be obstacles, conflict, and pain. In white supremacist capitalist patriarchy—words we never used then—we knew we would have to pay a price for this friendship, that we would need to possess the courage to stand up for our belief in democracy, in racial justice, in the transformative power of love. We valued the bond between us enough to meet the challenge.

Days before the reunion, remembering the sweetness of that friendship, I 5 felt humbled by the knowledge of what we give up when we are young, believing that we will find something just as good or better someday, only to discover that not to be so. I wondered just how it could be that Ken and I had ever lost contact with one another. Along the way I had not found white folks who understood the depth and complexity of racial injustice, and who were as willing to practice the art of living a nonracist life, as folks were then. In my adult life I have seen few white folks who are really willing to go the distance to create a world of racial equality—white folks willing to take risks, to be courageous, to live against the grain. I went to the reunion hoping that I would have a chance to see Ken face-to-face, to tell him how much I cherished all that we had shared, to tell him—in words which I never dared to say to any white person back then—simply that I loved him.

Remembering this past, I am most struck by our passionate commitment to a vision of social transformation rooted in the fundamental belief in a radically democratic idea of freedom and justice for all. Our notions of social change were not fancy. There was no elaborate postmodern political theory shaping our actions. We were simply trying to change the way we went about our everyday lives so that our values and habits of being would reflect our commitment to freedom. Our major concern then was ending racism. Today, as I witness the rise in white supremacy, the growing social and economic apartheid that separates white and black, the haves and the have-nots, men and women, I have placed alongside the struggle to end racism a commitment to ending sexism and sexist oppression, to eradicating systems of class exploitation. Aware that we are living in a culture of domination, I ask myself now, as I did more than twenty years ago, what values and habits of being reflect my/our commitment to freedom.

In retrospect, I see that in the last twenty years I have encountered many folks who say they are committed to freedom and justice for all even though the way they live, the values and habits of being they institutionalize daily, in public and private rituals, help maintain the culture of domination, help create an unfree world. In the book *Where Do We Go From Here? Chaos or Community,* Martin Luther King, Jr. told the citizens of this nation, with prophetic insight, that we would be unable to go forward if we did not experience a "true revolution of values." He assured us that

> the stability of the large world house which is ours will involve a revolution of values to accompany the scientific and freedom revolutions engulfing the earth. We must rapidly begin the shift from a "thing"-oriented society to a "person"-oriented society. When machines and computers, profit motives and property rights are considered more important than people, the giant triplets of racism, materialism and militarism are incapable of being conquered. A civilization can flounder as readily in the face of moral and spiritual bankruptcy as it can through financial bankruptcy.

Today, we live in the midst of that floundering. We live in chaos, uncertain about the possibility of building and sustaining community. The public figures who speak the most to us about a return to old-fashioned values embody the evils King describes. They are most committed to maintaining systems of domination—racism, sexism, class exploitation, and imperialism. They promote a perverse vision of freedom that makes it synonymous with materialism. They teach us to believe that domination is "natural," that it is right for the strong to rule over the weak, the powerful over the powerless. What amazes me is that so many people claim not to embrace these values and yet our collective rejection of them cannot be complete since they prevail in our daily lives.

These days, I am compelled to consider what forces keep us from moving   8
forward, from having that revolution of values that would enable us to live differently. King taught us to understand that if "we are to have peace on earth"
that "our loyalties must transcend our race, our tribe, our class, and our nation."
Long before the word "multiculturalism" became fashionable, he encouraged us
to "develop a world perspective." Yet, what we are witnessing today in our everyday life is not an eagerness on the part of neighbors and strangers to develop a
world perspective but a return to narrow nationalism, isolationisms, and xeno-
phobia. These shifts are usually explained in New Right and neoconservative
terms as attempts to bring order to the chaos, to return to an (idealized) past.
The notion of family evoked in these discussions is one in which sexist roles are
upheld as stabilizing traditions. Nor surprisingly, this vision of family life is
coupled with a notion of security that suggests we are always most safe with
people of our same group, race, class, religion, and so on. No matter how many
statistics on domestic violence, homicide, rape, and child abuse indicate that, in
fact, the idealized patriarchal family is not a "safe" space, that those of us who
experience any form of assault are more likely to be victimized by those who are
like us rather than by some mysterious strange outsiders, these conservative
myths persist. It is apparent that one of the primary reasons we have not experienced a revolution of values is that a culture of domination necessarily promotes addiction to lying and denial.

That lying takes the presumably innocent form of many white people (and   9
even some black folks) suggesting that racism does not exist anymore, and that
conditions of social equality are solidly in place that would enable any black
person who works hard to achieve economic self-sufficiency. Forget about the
fact that capitalism requires the existence of a mass underclass of surplus labor.
Lying takes the form of mass media creating the myth that feminist movement
has completely transformed society, so much so that the politics of patriarchal
power have been inverted and that men, particularly white men, just like emas-
culated black men, have become the victims of dominating women. So, it goes,
all men (especially black men) must pull together (as in the Clarence Thomas
hearings) to support and reaffirm patriarchal domination. Add to this the
widely held assumptions that blacks, other minorities, and white women are
taking jobs from white men, and that people are poor and unemployed because
they want to be, and it becomes most evident that part of our contemporary
crisis is created by a lack of meaningful access to truth. That is to say, individuals are not just presented untruths, but are told them in a manner that enables
most effective communication. When this collective cultural consumption of
and attachment to misinformation is coupled with the layers of lying individuals do in their personal lives, our capacity to face reality is severely diminished as is our will to intervene and change unjust circumstances.

If we examine critically the traditional role of the university in the pursuit   10
of truth and the sharing of knowledge and information, it is painfully clear that
biases that uphold and maintain white supremacy, imperialism, sexism, and
racism have distorted education so that it is no longer about the practice of
freedom. The call for a recognition of cultural diversity, a rethinking of ways of

knowing, a deconstruction of old epistemologies, and the concomitant demand that there be a transformation in our classrooms, in how we teach and what we teach, has been a necessary revolution—one that seeks to restore life to a corrupt and dying academy.

When everyone first began to speak about cultural diversity, it was exciting.   11
For those of us on the margins (people of color, folks from working class backgrounds, gays, and lesbians, and so on) who had always felt ambivalent about our presence in institutions where knowledge was shared in ways that reinscribed colonialism and domination, it was thrilling to think that the vision of justice and democracy that was at the very heart of civil rights movement would be realized in the academy. At last, there was the possibility of a learning community, a place where difference could be acknowledged, where we would finally all understand, accept, and affirm that our ways of knowing are forged in history and relations of power. Finally, we were all going to break through collective academic denial and acknowledge that the education most of us had received and were giving was not and is never politically neutral. Though it was evident that change would not be immediate, there was tremendous hope that this process we had set in motion would lead to a fulfillment of the dream of education as the practice of freedom.

Many of our colleagues were initially reluctant participants in this change.   12
Many folks found that as they tried to respect "cultural diversity" they had to confront the limitations of their training and knowledge, as well as a possible loss of "authority." Indeed, exposing certain truths and biases in the classroom often created chaos and confusion. The idea that the classroom should always be a "safe," harmonious place was challenged. It was hard for individuals to fully grasp the idea that recognition of difference might also require of us a willingness to see the classroom change, to allow for shifts in relations between students. A lot of people panicked. What they saw happening was not the comforting "melting pot" idea of cultural diversity, the rainbow coalition where we would all be grouped together in our difference, but everyone wearing the same have-a-nice-day smile. This was the stuff of colonizing fantasy, a perversion of the progressive vision of cultural diversity. Critiquing this longing in a recent interview, "Critical Multiculturalism and Democratic Schooling" (in the *International Journal of Educational Reform*), Peter McLaren asserted:

> Diversity that somehow constitutes itself as a harmonious ensemble of benign cultural spheres is a conservative and liberal model of multiculturalism that, in my mind, deserves to be jettisoned because, when we try to make culture an undisturbed space of harmony and agreement where social relations exist within cultural forms of uninterrupted accords we subscribe to a form of social amnesia in which we forget that all knowledge is forged in histories that are played out in the field of social antagonisms.

Many professors lacked strategies to deal with antagonisms in the class-   13
room. When this fear joined with the refusal to change that characterized the stance of an old (predominantly white male) guard it created a space for disempowered collective backlash.

All of a sudden, professors who had taken issues of multiculturalism and [14] cultural diversity seriously were backtracking, expressing doubts, casting votes in directions that would restore biased traditions or prohibit changes in faculty and curricula that were to bring diversity of representation and perspective. Joining forces with the old guard, previously open professors condoned tactics (ostracization, belittlement, and so on) used by senior colleagues to dissuade junior faculty members from making paradigm shifts that would lead to change. In one of my Toni Morrison seminars, as we went around our circle voicing critical reflections on Morrison's language, a sort of classically white, blondish, J. Crew coed shared that one of her other English professors, an older white man (whose name none of us wanted her to mention), confided that he was so pleased to find a student still interested in reading literature—words— the language of texts and "not that race and gender stuff." Somewhat amused by the assumption he had made about her, she was disturbed by his conviction that conventional ways of critically approaching a novel could not coexist in classrooms that also offered new perspectives.

I then shared with the class my experience of being at a Halloween party. A [15] new white male colleague, with whom I was chatting for the first time, went on a tirade at the mere mention of my Toni Morrison seminar, emphasizing that *Song of Solomon* was a weak rewrite of Hemingway's *For Whom the Bell Tolls*. Passionately full of disgust for Morrison he, being a Hemingway scholar, seemed to be sharing the often-heard concern that black women writers/thinkers are just poor imitations of "great" white men. Not wanting at that moment to launch into Unlearning Colonialism, Divesting of Racism and Sexism 101, I opted for the strategy taught to me by that in-denial-of-institutionalized-patriarchy, self- help book *Women Who Love Too Much*. I just said, "Oh!" Later, I assured him that I would read *For Whom the Bell Tolls* again to see if I would make the same con- nection. Both these seemingly trivial incidents reveal how deep-seated is the fear that any de-centering of Western civilizations, of the white male canon, is really an act of cultural genocide.

Some folks think that everyone who supports cultural diversity wants to re- [16] place one dictatorship of knowing with another, changing one set way of think- ing for another. This is perhaps the gravest misperception of cultural diversity. Even though there are those overly zealous among us who hope to replace one set of absolutes with another, simply changing content, this perspective does not accurately represent progressive visions of the way commitment to cultural diversity can constructively transform the academy. In all cultural revolutions there are periods of chaos and confusion, times when grave mistakes are made. If we fear mistakes, doing things wrongly, constantly evaluating ourselves, we will never make the academy a culturally diverse place where scholars and the curricula address every dimension of that difference.

As backlash swells, as budgets are cut, as jobs become even more scarce, [17] many of the few progressive interventions that were made to change the acad- emy, to create an open climate for cultural diversity are in danger of being undermined or eliminated. These threats should not be ignored. Nor should our collective commitment to cultural diversity change because we have not yet devised and implemented perfect strategies for them. To create a culturally diverse academy we must commit ourselves fully. Learning from other movements for social change, from civil rights and feminist liberation efforts, we must accept the protracted nature of our struggle and be willing to remain both patient and vigilant. To commit ourselves to the work of transforming the academy so that it will be a place where cultural diversity informs every aspect of our learning, we must embrace struggle and sacrifice. We cannot be easily discouraged. We cannot despair when there is conflict. Our solidarity must be affirmed by shared belief in a spirit of intellectual openness that celebrates diversity, welcomes dissent, and rejoices in collective dedication to truth.

Drawing strength from the life and work of Martin Luther King, Jr., I am   18
often reminded of his profound inner struggle when he felt called by his religious beliefs to oppose the war in Vietnam. Fearful of alienating conservative bourgeois supporters, and of alienating the black church, King meditated on a passage from Romans, chapter 12, verse 2, which reminded him of the necessity of dissent, challenge and change: "Be not conformed to this world but be ye transformed by the renewal of your minds." All of us in the academy and in the culture as a whole are called to renew our minds if we are to transform educational institutions—and society—so that the way we live, teach, and work can reflect our joy in cultural diversity, our passion for justice, and our love of freedom. □

◢ REREADING FOR UNDERSTANDING

1. Hooks begins this essay with a personal narrative about attending her twentieth high school reunion. Why did hooks decide to attend the reunion? Why was she apprehensive about what she would find there?

2. Hooks says that we remain a culture of domination because we are addicted to lying and denial. In other words, we haven't changed because we believe there is no need to change. What specific lies does hooks claim we have accepted? Do you agree with hooks that these ideas are, in fact, lies?

3. What does hooks mean when she calls the demand for recognition of cultural diversity in the classroom and re-thinking of traditional methods of teaching and learning "a necessary revolution"? In what sense was this call for educational reform necessary? In what ways was it revolutionary?

4. How does hooks explain the reluctance of many within the academic community to embrace the concept of cultural diversity in their classrooms?

◢ RESPONDING

1. Why do you think hooks opens this piece with a personal narrative? How does that introduction serve the ideas she sets forward later in the essay?

2. Hooks recalls the early days of integration as "an unhappy time." What made them unhappy? Does hooks's memory of the early years of integration

surprise you? Do you think her perception of that time was shared by other black students?

3. Hooks argues that education is "never politically neutral." What does she mean? From your own educational experience, can you think of subjects or courses that were free from political interpretation? Can you think of others that clearly reflected a certain political bias?

4. Hooks acknowledges a common fear that proponents of cultural diversity "hope to replace one set of absolutes with another" (par. 16). Do you think this fear is justified, or do you agree with hooks that our fear of a few extremists should not prevent us from trying to "make the academy a culturally diverse place"?

◢ RESPONDING IN WRITING

1. The passage that hooks cites from *Where Do We Go from Here?* by Martin Luther King, Jr., sounds very much like the calls for traditional family values that we hear from politicians and religious leaders today. Yet hooks says that the "public figures who speak the most to us about a return to old-fashioned values embody the evils King describes" (par. 7). Using your library, find an example of a speech on values by a prominent political or religious figure such as Louis Farrakhan, Hillary Rodham Clinton, or Pat Buchanan. Write an essay analyzing the speech in light of hooks's charge. Is the speaker calling for a return to practices that encourage racism, sexism, and class exploitation disguised as values, as hooks claims? Or is the speaker calling for us to "transcend our race, our tribe, our class, and our nation" to become the "person-oriented society" King called for?

2. Hooks says, "I have encountered many folks who say they are committed to freedom and justice for all even though the way they live, the values and habits of being they institutionalize daily, in public and private rituals, help maintain the culture of domination" (par. 7). Write an essay examining your own "habits of being" or those of someone you know well. Is the way you live consistent with the beliefs you hold? Look for specific, day-to-day habits or behaviors that either confirm or contradict the values that matter to you.

LINDA CHAVEZ

Former director of the U.S. Commission of Civil Rights under President Reagan, Linda Chavez (1947–   ) is a senior fellow at the Manhattan Institute for Policy Research. She is the author of *Out of the Barrio: Toward a New Politics of Hispanic Assimilation.* Linda Chavez's outspoken opposition to affirmative action and bilingual education have made her the target of criticism to some and a hero to others.

The Real Aim of Cultural Diversity Is Exclusion

Cultural Diversity" has become the shibboleth of the 90's on college cam-   1
puses. Few critics are willing to challenge the values of diversity and pluralism lest they be branded reactionary or, worse, racist. The promoters
of cultural diversity tell us that theirs is an ideology of inclusion. But the politics of cultural diversity as they are practiced on campus today have very little
to do with inclusion or diversity.

My own experience with the promoters of this new ideology suggests that   2
their real aim is to keep out certain ideas and certain people, to foreclose debate, to substitute their own catechism for the free inquiry usually associated
with a university.

In May of this year, I was scheduled to be the commencement speaker at   3
the University of Northern Colorado. The topic of my address to graduating
seniors was to have been the movement toward democracy occurring in Eastern
Europe and elsewhere and what special challenges this posed to those of us living in the United States, the world's oldest democracy. However, when word
spread of my invitation to speak, a group of Hispanic students and community
activists launched a protest. They objected to my views on affirmative action
and bilingual education—I am critical of both. They also objected to my past
association with the Reagan Administration (I was director of the U.S. Commission on Civil Rights under President Reagan and later joined the senior staff
of the White House). And they objected to my past affiliation with U.S. English,
a public-policy group that promotes laws to make English the official language
of the United States.

At first, the university president, Robert Dickeson, held firm, stating the   4
university's commitment to honor its invitation. I offered to come to campus a
day early and meet with the protesters—under any conditions they might
choose—to discuss my views on affirmative action, bilingual education, or any
other topic, even though these subjects had nothing to do with the speech I intended to give. Mr. Dickeson declined my offer but reiterated his commitment
to have me speak.

Less than 10 days later, Mr. Dickeson rescinded the university's invitation.   5
He apparently changed his mind after a marathon listening session in the
student lounge, where he heard from 95 of the university's 9,500 students. In
revoking the invitation, he issued an extraordinary statement, which said in
part: "The intent of the university in inviting Linda Chavez to be the commencement speaker was to be sensitive to cultural diversity, and the committee
making the decision intended to communicate the importance of cultural pluralism. It is clear that the decision was both uninformed and gave the appearance of being grossly insensitive."

In trying to explain how my selection as a commencement speaker was incon-   6
sistent with the university's commitment to cultural diversity and pluralism,

Mr. Dickeson later wrote in an opinion piece for *The Rocky Mountain News:* "[T]he people who had selected Chavez honestly thought they were picking a positive role model for Hispanic women leaders, and that she would be received as such. They were obviously wrong."

Cultural pluralists claim to want diversity, but the diversity they seek is certainly not in opinions different from their own. In the ideology of cultural pluralism, one's world view is determined by race, ethnicity, gender, and class. To be black or Hispanic or female or working class is to think a certain way. In the cultural pluralists' model, no one is really capable of escaping his or her cultural determinants. In this view, getting beyond one's own cultural reference point requires exposure to people who exemplify the thinking of other groups. Since blacks, Hispanics, and women differ so profoundly from white men, the ideology assumes, the products of black, Hispanic, and female thought must be added to the curriculum; universities must comprise sufficient numbers of such persons as students and faculty members; and such people must be presented as "role models" on ceremonial occasions.

The problem with the cultural pluralists' model, of course, is that not all blacks, Hispanics, or women think alike. Neither do white males, for that matter. How could they? None of these groups is homogenous. Among Hispanics, for example, are people who were born in the United States and speak barely a word of Spanish, as well as others born thousands of miles away who speak not a word of English. What does a Peruvian immigrant from Cuzco have in common with a third-generation Mexican-American born in Chicago? Do we really expect these two to share a common world view because we define both as Hispanic?

Much as the cultural pluralists might regret it, right-mindedness is not passed along in the DNA. Not every black person embraces affirmative action, nor every Hispanic bilingual education. So the cultural pluralists think they must define which blacks, Hispanics, and women are acceptable role models—who among them may be heard, and under what circumstances. Thus the decision to bar me as a commencement speaker.

Censorship is beginning to masquerade as diversity.

The trend is not only to limit which outsiders such as myself may speak in the university but, more important, to limit what those within academe may say and do. Several universities recently have adopted policies restricting what they see as racially or sexually offensive speech—Emory University, the University of Pennsylvania, the University of Michigan, the University of Wisconsin, and Stanford University, to name a few.

At Stanford, a student apologist for the new "anti-harassment" restrictions on that campus said: "What we are proposing is not completely in line with the First Amendment. But I'm not sure it should be. We at Stanford are trying to set a different standard from what society at large is trying to accomplish."

Roger Kimball, in describing such restrictions in his book *Tenured Radicals* (Harper and Row, 1990), asks: "But what does it mean that the university, traditionally a bastion of free speech and a place where controversial ideas may freely circulate, has begun to encroach even on these ideals in the name of a certain vision of political rectitude?"

What it means, unfortunately, is that universities will become more homo-   14
geneous institutions—not more diverse—when it comes to certain ideas, particularly those ideas that impinge on race, ethnicity, or gender. Everyone—students and professors—will learn to tiptoe around certain subjects deemed too sensitive to explore.

Cultural pluralists may favor an environment where professors feel constrained   15
from introducing "any sort of thing that might hurt a group," as one of them admonished his colleagues at a Harvard seminar on racial insensitivity last year. But what kind of teaching can take place in such an environment?

At a speech I gave recently at Grinnell College, a young black woman in-   16
formed me that she was tired of reading about slavery in American history courses because it gave her white classmates the "wrong impression" about blacks and their contribution to this nation. In the name of cultural diversity, should we revise our history books to remove painful lessons? And how will these new culturally sensitive institutions deal with the growing numbers of blacks, Hispanics, and women who break ranks with the orthodoxies of their groups?

Recently, Shelby Steele, associate professor of English at San Jose State Uni-   17
versity, wrote in *The New York Times Magazine* of his disillusionment with preferential employment and admissions policies, which he feels stigmatize blacks.

Other black intellectuals have criticized at least some forms of racial pref-   18
erence: among them are Thomas Sowell, Glenn Loury, Walter Williams, Julius Lester, Randall Kennedy, and Stephen Carter. Will these men be driven from the academy for their heretical views? Or ostracized within it?

The cultural pluralists have embarked on a dangerous course. Inevitably,   19
however, the tide will begin to turn as more and more people resist their bullying tactics. In the meantime, those claiming to want diversity and pluralism will have done great damage to the liberal traditions of the university. Let's hope that academic freedom can survive the assault. □

◢ REREADING FOR UNDERSTANDING

1. What does Chavez mean when she says, "'Cultural diversity' has become the shibboleth of the '90s on college campuses" (par. 1)? Look up "shibboleth" if you do not know what the word means.

2. What do proponents of cultural diversity claim is their goal? What is their true goal, according to Chavez? What is it? How does Chavez define "diversity"?

3. Chavez suggests that proponents of cultural diversity have a narrow definition of "diversity." What is it? How does Chavez define "diversity"?

4. What logical flaw does Chavez claim underlies the current model of cultural diversity on most campuses?

RESPONDING

1. According to bell hooks in the previous selection (par. 16), "In all cultural revolutions there are periods of chaos and confusion, times when grave mistakes are made. If we fear mistakes, doing things wrongly, constantly evaluating ourselves, we will never make the academy a culturally diverse place where scholars and the curricula address every dimension of that difference." How do you think hooks would view Chavez's experience with the University of Northern Colorado? Was the university's withdrawal of its invitation to speak a "grave mistake" in the name of an ultimately worthwhile goal? Or was it further evidence of the "great damage to the liberal traditions of the university," as Chavez claims? Defend your answer.

2. How does your own college recognize and encourage cultural diversity inside and outside the classroom? Working in small groups, try to list the different kinds of people represented on your campus. Then discuss whether these groups are equally and adequately represented in the curriculum and in campus activities. What constitutes equal and adequate representation?

RESPONDING IN WRITING

Imagine that Chavez has been invited to speak at your college campus and that her appearance is being protested for the same reasons the Colorado students offered. Write a letter to your college president explaining why you think the college should or should not withdraw its invitation.

NICHOLASA MOHR

Nicholasa Mohr (1935–   ) is an artist and writer whose novels and stories depict the lives of working-class people in the neighborhoods of New York, where she grew up and where she lives today.

The English Lesson

Remember our assignment for today everybody! I'm so confident that you will all do exceptionally well!" Mrs. Susan Hamma smiled enthusiastically at her students. "Everyone is to get up and make a brief statement as to why he or she is taking this course in Basic English. You must state your name, where you originally came from, how long you have been here, and . . . uh . . . a little something about yourself, if you wish. Keep it brief, not too long; remember, there are twenty-eight of us. We have a full class, and everyone must have a chance." Mrs. Hamma waved a forefinger at her students. "This is, after all, a democracy, and we have a democratic class; fairness for all!"

Lali grinned and looked at William, who sat directly next to her. He winked and rolled his eyes toward Mrs. Hamma. This was the third class they had attended together. It had not been easy to persuade Rudi that Lali should learn better English.

2

"Why is it necessary, eh?" Rudi had protested. "She works here in the store with me. She don't have to talk to nobody. Besides, everybody that comes in speaks Spanish—practically everybody, anyway."

3

But once William had put the idea to Lali and explained how much easier things would be for her, she kept insisting until Rudi finally agreed. "Go on, you're both driving me nuts. But it can't interfere with business or work—I'm warning you!"

4

Adult Education offered Basic English, Tuesday evenings from 6:30 to 8:00, at a local public school. Night customers did not usually come into Rudi's Luncheonette until after eight. William and Lali promised that they would leave everything prepared and make up for any inconvenience by working harder and longer than usual, if necessary.

5

The class admitted twenty-eight students, and because there were only twenty-seven registered, Lali was allowed to take the course even after missing the first two classes. William had assured Mrs. Hamma that he would help Lali catch up; she was glad to have another student to make up the full registration.

6

Most of the students were Spanish-speaking. The majority were American citizens—Puerto Ricans who had migrated to New York and spoke very little English. The rest were immigrants admitted to the United States as legal aliens. There were several Chinese, two Dominicans, one Sicilian, and one Pole.

7

Every Tuesday Mrs. Hamma traveled to the Lower East Side from Bayside Queens, where she lived and was employed as a history teacher in the local junior high school. She was convinced that this small group of people desperately needed her services. Mrs. Hamma reiterated her feelings frequently to just about anyone who would listen. "Why, if these people can make it to class after working all day at those miserable, dreary, uninteresting, and often revolting jobs, why, the least I can do is be there to serve them, making every lesson count toward improving their conditions! My grandparents came here from Germany as poor immigrants, working their way up. I'm not one to forget a thing like that!"

8

By the time class started most of the students were quite tired. And after the lesson was over, many had to go on to part-time jobs, some even without time for supper. As a result there was always sluggishness and yawning among the students. This never discouraged Mrs. Hamma, whose drive and enthusiasm not only amused the class but often kept everyone awake.

9

"Now this is the moment we have all been preparing for." Mrs. Hamma stood up, nodded, and blinked knowingly at her students. "Five lessons, I think, are enough to prepare us for our oral statements. You may read from prepared

10

notes, as I said before, but please try not to read every word. We want to hear you speak; conversation is what we're after. When someone asks you about yourself, you cannot take a piece of paper and start reading the answers, now can you? That would be foolish. So . . . "

Standing in front of her desk, she put her hands on her hips and spread her   11
feet, giving the impression that she was going to demonstrate calisthenics.

"Shall we begin?"   12

Mrs. Hamma was a very tall, angular woman with large extremities. She   13
was the tallest person in the room. Her eyes roamed from student to student until they met William's.

"Mr. Colón, will you please begin?   14

Nervously William looked around him, hesitating.   15

"Come on now, we must get the ball rolling. All right now . . . did you hear   16
what I said? Listen, 'getting the ball rolling' means getting started. Getting things going, such as—" Mrs. Hamma swiftly lifted her right hand over her head, made a fist, then swung her arm around like a pitcher and, with an underhand curve forcefully threw an imaginary ball out at her students. Trying to maintain her balance, Mrs. Hamma hopped from one leg to the other. Startled, the students looked at one another. In spite of their efforts to restrain themselves, several people in back began to giggle. Lali and William looked away, avoiding each other's eyes and trying not to laugh out loud. With assured countenance, Mrs. Hamma continued.

"An idiom!" she exclaimed, pleased. "You have just seen me demonstrate   17
the meaning of an idiom. Now I want everyone to jot down this information in his notebook." Going to the blackboard, Mrs. Hamma explained, "It's something which literally says one thing, but actually means another. Idiom . . . idiomatic." Quickly and obediently, everyone began to copy what she wrote. "Has everyone got it? OK, let's GET THE BALL ROLLING, Mr. Colón!"

Uneasily William stood up; he was almost the same height standing as sit-   18
ting. When speaking to others, especially in a new situation, he always preferred to sit alongside those listening; it gave him a sense of equality with other people. He looked around and cleared his throat; at least everyone else was sitting. Taking a deep breath, William felt better.

"My name is William Horacio Colón," he read from a prepared statement.   19
"I have been here in New York City for five months. I coming from Puerto Rico. My town is located in the mountains in the central part of the island. The name of my town is Aibonito, which means in Spanish 'oh how pretty.' It is name like this because when the Spaniards first seen that place they was very impressed with the beauty of the section and—"

"Make it brief, Mr. Colón," Mrs. Hamma interrupted, "there are others, you   20
know."

William looked at her, unable to continue.   21

"Go on, go on, Mr. Colón, please!"   22

"I am working here now, living with my mother and family in Lower East   23
Side of New York City." William spoke rapidly. "I study Basic English por que . . . because my ambition is to learn to speak and read English very good. To get

a better job. Y—y también, to help my mother y familia." He shrugged. "Y do better, that's all."

"That's all? Why, that's wonderful! Wonderful! Didn't he do well, class?" Mrs. Hamma bowed slightly toward William and applauded him. The students watched her and slowly each one began to imitate her. Pleased, Mrs. Hamma looked around her; all together they gave William a healthy round of applause.   24

Next, Mrs. Hamma turned to a Chinese man seated at the other side of the room.   25

"Mr. Fong, you may go next."   26

Mr. Fong stood up; he was a man in his late thirties, of medium height and slight build. Cautiously he looked at Mrs. Hamma, and waited.   27

"Go on, Mr. Fong. Get the ball rolling, remember?"   28

"All right. Get a ball rolling . . . is idiot!" Mr. Fong smiled.   29

"No, Mr. Fong, idio*mmmmmm!*" Mrs. Hamma hummed her *m*'s, shaking her head. "Not an—It's idiomatic!"   30

"What I said!" Mr. Fong responded with self-assurance, looking directly at Mrs. Hamma. "Get a ball rolling, idiomit."   31

"Never mind." She cleared her throat. "Just go on."   32

"I said OK?" Mr. Fong waited for an answer.   33

"Go on, please."   34

Mr. Fong sighed, "My name is Joseph Fong. I been here in this country United States New York City for most one year." He too read from a prepared statement. "I come from Hong Kong but original born in city of Canton, China. I working delivery food business and live with my brother and his family in Chinatown taking the course in Basic English to speak good and improve my position better in this country. Also to be eligible to become American Citizen."   35

Mrs. Hamma selected each student who was to speak from a different part of the room, rather than in the more conventional orderly fashion of row by row, or front to back, or even alphabetical order. This way, she reasoned, no one will know who's next; it will be more spontaneous. Mrs. Hamma enjoyed catching the uncertain looks on the faces of her students. A feeling of control over the situation gave her a pleasing thrill, and she made the most of these moments by looking at several people more than once before making her final choice.   36

There were more men than women, and Mrs. Hamma called two or three men for each woman. It was her way of maintaining a balance. To her distress, most read from prepared notes, despite her efforts to discourage this. She would interrupt them when she felt they went on too long, then praise them when they finished. Each statement was followed by applause from everyone.   37

All had similar statements. They had migrated here in search of a better future, were living with relatives, and worked as unskilled laborers. With the exception of Lali, who was childless, every woman gave the ages and sex of her children; most men referred only to their "family." And, among the legal aliens, there was only one who did not want to become an American citizen, Diego Torres, a young man from the Dominican Republic, and he gave his reasons.   38

" . . . and to improve my economic situation." Diego Torres hesitated, look-   39
ing around the room. "But is one thing I no want and is to become American
citizen"—he pointed to an older man with a dark complexion, seated a few
seats away—"like my fellow countryman over there!" The man shook his head
disapprovingly at Diego Torres, trying to hide his annoyance. "I no give up my
country, Santo Domingo, for nothing," he went on, "nothing in the whole
world. OK, man? I come here, pero I cannot help. I got no work at home. There,
is political. The United States control most the industry which is sugar and
tourismo. Y—you have to know somebody. I tell you, is political to get a job,
man! You don't know nobody and you no work, eh? So I come here from necessity, pero this no my country—"

"Mr. Torres," Mrs. Hamma interrupted, "we must be brief, please, there   40
are—"

"I no finish lady!" he snapped. "You wait a minute when I finish!"   41

There was complete silence as Diego Torres glared at Susan Hamma. No   42
one had ever spoken to her like that, and her confusion was greater than her
embarrassment. Without speaking , she lowered her eyes and nodded.

"OK, I prefer live feeling happy in my county, man. Even I don't got too   43
much I live simple but in my own country I be contento. Pero this is no possible in the situation of Santo Domingo now. Someday we gonna run our own
country and be jobs for everybody. My reasons to be here is to make money,
man, and go back home buy my house and property. I no be American citizen,
no way. I'm Dominican and proud! That's it. That's all I got to say." Abruptly,
Diego Torres sat down.

"All right." Mrs. Hamma had composed herself. "Very good; you can come   44
here and state your views. That is what America is all about! We may not agree
with you, but we defend your right to an opinion. And as long as you are in this
classroom, Mr. Torres, you are in America. Now, everyone, let us give Mr. Torres
the same courtesy as everyone else in this class." Mrs. Hamma applauded with
a polite light clap, then turned to find the next speaker.

"Bullshit," whispered Diego Torres.   45

Practically everyone had spoken. Lali and the two European immigrants   46
were the only ones left. Mrs. Hamma called upon Lali.

"My name is Rogelia Dolores Padillo. I come from Canovanas in Puerto   47
Rico. Is a small village in the mountains near El Yunque Rain Forest. My family
is still living there. I marry and live here with my husband working in his business of restaurant. Call Rudi's Luncheonette. I been here New York City Lower
East Side since I marry, which is now about one year. I study Basic English to
improve my vocabulario and learn more about here. This way I help my husband in his business and I do more also for myself, including to be able to read
better in English. Thank you."

Aldo Fabrizi, the Sicilian, spoke next. He was a very short man, barely five   48
feet tall. Usually he was self-conscious about his height, but William's presence
relieved him of these feelings. Looking at William, he thought being short was
no big thing; he was, after all, normal. He told the class that he was originally

from Palermo, the capital of Sicily, and had gone to Milano, in the north of Italy, looking for work. After three years in Milano, he immigrated here six months ago and now lived with his sister. He had a good steady job, he said, working in a copper wire factory with his brother-in-law in Brooklyn. Aldo Fabrizi wanted to become an American citizen and spoke passionately about it, without reading from his notes.

"I be proud to be American citizen. I no come here find work live good and   49 no have responsibility or no be grateful." He turned and looked threateningly at Diego Torres. "Hey? I tell you all one thing, I got my nephew right now fighting in Vietnam for this country!" Diego Torres stretched his hands over his head, yawning, folded his hands, and lowered his eyelids. "I wish I could be citizen to fight for this country. My whole family is citizens—we all Americans and we love America!" His voice was quite loud. "That's how I feel."

"Very good," Mrs. Hamma called, distracting Aldo Fabrizi. "That was well   50 stated. I'm sure you will not only become a citizen, but you will also be a credit to this country."

The last person to be called on was the Pole. He was always neatly dressed   51 in a business suit, with a shirt and tie, and carried a briefcase. His manner was reserved but friendly.

"Good evening fellow students and Madame Teacher." He nodded politely   52 to Mrs. Hamma. "My name is Stephan Paczkowski. I am originally from Poland about four months ago. My background is I was born in capital city of Poland, Warsaw. Being educated in capital and also graduating from the University with degree of professor of music with specialty in the history of music."

Stephan Paczkowski read from his notes carefully, articulating every word.   53 "I was given appointment of professor of history of music at University of Krakow. I work there for ten years until about year and half ago. At this time the political situation in Poland was so that all Jewish people were requested by the government to leave Poland. My wife who also is being a professor of economics at University of Krakow is of Jewish parents. My wife was told she could not remain in position at University or remain over there. We made arrangements for my wife and daughter who is seven years of age and myself to come here with my wife's cousin who is to be helping us.

"Since four months I am working in large hospital as position of porter in   54 maintenance department. The thing of it is, I wish to take Basic English to improve my knowledge of English language, and be able to return to my position of professor of history of music. Finally, I wish to become a citizen of United States. That is my reasons. I thank you all."

After Stephan Paczkowski sat down, there was a long awkward silence as   55 everyone turned to look at Mrs. Hamma. Even after the confrontation with Diego Torres, she had applauded without hesitation. Now she seemed unable to move.

"Well," she said, almost breathless, "that's admirable! I'm sure, sir, that you   56 will do very well . . . a person of your . . . like yourself, I mean . . . a professor . . . after all, it's really just admirable." Everyone was listening intently to what she said. "That was well done, class. Now, we have to get to next week's assignment." Mrs. Hamma realized that no one had applauded Stephan Paczkowski. With a slightly pained expression, she began to applaud. "Mustn't forget Mr. Paczkowski; everybody here must be treated equally. This is America!" The class joined her in a round of applause.

As Mrs. Hamma began to write the next week's assignment on the board, 57 some students looked anxiously at their watches and others asked about the time. Then they all quickly copied the information into their notebooks. It was almost eight o'clock. Those who had to get to second jobs did not want to be late; some even hoped to have time for a bite to eat first. Others were just tired and wanted to go home.

Lali looked at William, sighing impatiently. They both hoped Mrs. Hamma 58 would finish quickly. There would be hell to pay with Rudi if the night customers were already at the luncheonette.

"There, that's next week's work, which is very important, by the way. We 59 will be looking at the history of New York City and the different ethnic groups that lived here as far back as the Dutch. I can't tell you how proud I am of the way you all spoke. All of you—I have no favorites, you know."

Mrs. Hamma was interrupted by the long, loud buzzing sound, bringing 60 the lesson to an end. Quickly everyone began to exit.

"Good night, see you all next Tuesday!" Mrs. Hamma called out. "By the 61 way, if any of you here wants extra help, I have a few minutes this evening." Several people bolted past her, excusing themselves. In less than thirty seconds, Mrs. Hamma was standing in an empty classroom.

William and Lali hurried along, struggling against the cold, sharp March 62 wind that whipped across Houston Street, stinging their faces and making their eyes tear.

In a few minutes they would be at Rudi's. So far, they had not been late 63 once.

"You read very well—better than anybody in class. I told you there was 64 nothing to worry about. You caught up in no time."

"Go on. I was so nervous, honestly! But, I'm glad she left me for one of the 65 last. If I had to go first, like you, I don't think I could open my mouth. You were so calm. You started the thing off very well."

"You go on now. I was nervous myself!" He laughed, pleased. 66

"Mira, Chiquitin," Lali giggled, "I didn't know your name was Horacio. 67 William Horacio. Ave Maria, so imposing!"

"That's right, because you see, my mother was expecting a valiant warrior! 68 Instead, well"—he threw up his hands—"no one warned me either. And what a name for a Chiquitin like me."

Lali smiled, saying nothing. At first she had been very aware of William's 69 dwarfishness. Now it no longer mattered. It was only when she saw others reacting to him for the first time that she was once more momentarily struck with William's physical difference.

"We should really try to speak in English, Lali. It would be good practice 70 for us."

"Dios mio . . . I feel so foolish, and my accent is terrible!" 71

"But look, we all have to start some place. Besides, what about the Americanos? When they speak Spanish, they sound pretty awful, but we accept it. You know I'm right. And that's how people get ahead, by not being afraid to try."   72

They walked in silence for a few moments. Since William had begun to work at Rudi's, Lali's life had become less lonely. Lali was shy by nature; making friends was difficult for her. She had grown up in the sheltered environment of a large family living in a tiny mountain village. She was considered quite plain. Until Rudi had asked her parents for permission to court her, she had only gone out with two local boys. She had accepted his marriage proposal expecting great changes in her life. But the age difference between her and Rudi, being in a strange country without friends or relatives, and the long hours of work at the luncheonette confined Lali to a way of life she could not have imagined. Every evening she found herself waiting for William to come in to work, looking forward to his presence.   73

Lali glanced over at him as they started across the wide busy street. His grip on her elbow was firm but gentle as he led her to the sidewalk.   74

"There you are, Miss Lali, please to watch your step!" he spoke in English.   75

His thick golden blond hair was slightly mussed and fell softly, partially covering his forehead. His wide smile, white teeth, and large shoulders made him appear quite handsome. Lali found herself staring at William. At that moment she wished he could be just like everybody else.   76

"Lali?" William asked, confused by her silent stare. "Is something wrong?"   77

"No." Quickly Lali turned her face. She felt herself blushing. "I . . . I was just thinking how to answer in English, that's all."   78

"But that's it . . . don't think! What I mean is, don't go worrying about what to say. Just talk natural. Get used to simple phrases and the rest will come, you'll see."   79

"All right," Lali said, glad the strange feeling of involvement had passed, and William had taken no notice of it. "It's an interesting class, don't you think so? I mean—like that man, the professor. Bendito! Imagine, they had to leave because they were Jewish. What a terrible thing!"   80

"I don't believe he's Jewish; it's his wife who is Jewish. She was a professor, too. But I guess they don't want to be separated . . . and they have a child."   81

"Tsk, tsk, los pobres! But, can you imagine, then? A professor from a university doing the job of a porter? My goodness!" Lali sighed. "I never heard of such a thing!"   82

"But you gotta remember, it's like Mrs. Hamma said, this is America, right? So . . . everybody got a chance to clean toilets! Equality, didn't she say that?"   83

They both laughed loudly, stepping up their pace until they reached Rudi's Luncheonette.   84

The small luncheonette was almost empty. One customer sat at the counter.   85

"Just in time," Rudi called out. "Let's get going. People gonna be coming in hungry any minute. I was beginning to worry about you two!"   86

William ran in the back to change into his workshirt.   87

Lali slipped into her uniform and soon was busy at the grill.   88

"Well, did you learn anything tonight?" Rudi asked her.   89

"Yes."   90

"What?"   91

"I don't know," she answered, without interrupting her work. "We just   92
talked a little bit in English."

"A little bit in English—about what?"   93

Lali busied herself, ignoring him. Rudi waited, then tried once more.   94

"You remember what you talked about?" He watched her as she moved,   95
working quickly, not looking in his direction.

"No." Her response was barely audible.   96

Lately Rudi had begun to reflect on his decision to marry such a young   97
woman. Especially a country girl like Lali, who was shy and timid. He had never
had children with his first wife and wondered if he lacked the patience needed
for the young. They had little in common and certainly seldom spoke about
anything but the business. Certainly he could not fault her for being lazy; she
was always working without being asked. People would accuse him in jest of
overworking his young wife. He assured them there was no need, because she
had the endurance of a country mule. After almost one year of marriage, he felt
he hardly knew Lali or what he might do to please her.

William began to stack clean glasses behind the counter.   98

"Chiquitin! How about you and Lali having something to eat? We gotta few   99
minutes yet. There's some fresh rice pudding."

"Later . . . I'll have mine a little later, thanks."   100

"Ask her if she wants some," Rudi whispered, gesturing toward Lali.   101

William moved close to Lali and spoke softly to her.   102

"She said no." William continued his work.   103

"Listen, Chiquitin, I already spoke to Raquel Martinez who lives next door.   104
You know, she's got all them kids? In case you people are late, she can cover for
you and Lali. She said it was OK."

"Thanks, Rudi, I appreciate it. But we'll get back on time."   105

"She's good, you know. She helps me out during the day whenever I need   106
extra help. Off the books. I give her a few bucks. But, mira, I cannot pay you and
Raquel both. So if she comes in, you don't get paid. You know that then, OK?"

"Of course. Thanks, Rudi."   107

"Sure, well, it's a good thing after all. You and Lali improving yourselves.   108
Not that she really needs it, you know. I provide for her. As I said, she's my wife,
so she don't gotta worry. If she wants something, I'll buy it for her. I made it
clear she didn't have to bother with none of that, but"—Rudi shrugged—"if
that's what she wants, I'm not one to interfere."

The door opened. Several men walked in.   109

"Here they come, kids!"   110

Orders were taken and quickly filled. Customers came and went steadily   111
until about eleven o'clock, when Rudi announced that it was closing time.

The weeks passed, then the months, and this evening, William and Lali sat with   112
the other students listening to Mrs. Hamma as she taught the last lesson of the
Basic English course.

"It's been fifteen long hard weeks for all of you. And I want you to know how proud I am of each and every one here." 113

William glanced at Lali; he knew she was upset. He felt it too, wishing that this was not the end of the course. It was the only time he and Lali had free to themselves together. Tuesday had become their evening. 114

Lali had been especially irritable that week, dreading this last session. For her, Tuesday meant leaving the world of Rudi, the luncheonette, that street, everything that she felt imprisoned her. She was accomplishing something all by herself, and without the help of the man she was dependent upon. 115

Mrs. Hamma finally felt that she had spent enough time assuring her students of her sincere appreciation. 116

"I hope some of you will stay and have a cup of coffee or tea, and cookies. There's plenty over there." She pointed to a side table where a large electric coffeepot filled with hot water was steaming. The table was set for instant coffee and tea, complete with several boxes of assorted cookies. "I do this every semester for my classes. I think it's nice to have a little informal chat with one another; perhaps discuss our plans for the future and so on. But it must be in English! Especially those of you who are Spanish-speaking. Just because you outnumber the rest of us, don't you think you can get away with it!" Mrs. Hamma lifted her forefinger threateningly but smiled. "Now, it's still early, so there's plenty of time left. Please turn in your books." 117

Some of the people said good-bye quickly and left, but the majority waited, helping themselves to coffee or tea and cookies. Small clusters formed as people began to chat with one another. 118

Diego Torres and Aldo Fabrizi were engaged in a friendly but heated debate on the merits of citizenship. 119

"Hey, you come here a minute, please," Aldo Fabrizi called out to William, who was standing with a few people by the table, helping himself to coffee. William walked over to the two men. 120

"What's the matter?" 121

"What do you think of your paisano. He don't wanna be citizen. I say—my opinion—he don't appreciate what he got in this country. This a great country. You the same like him, what do you think?" 122

"Mira, please tell him we no the same," Diego Torres said with exasperation. "You a citizen, pero not me. Este tipo no comprende, man!" 123

"Listen, you comprendo . . . yo capito! I know what you say. He be born in Puerto Rico. But you see, we got the same thing. I be born in Sicily—that's another part of the country, separate. But I still Italiano, capito?" 124

"Dios mio!" Diego Torres smacked his forehead with an open palm. "Mira"—he turned to William—"explain to him, por favor." 125

William swallowed a mouthful of cookies. "He's right. Puerto Rico is part of the United States. And Sicily is part of Italy. But not the Dominican Republic, where he been born. There it is not the United States. I was born a citizen, you see?" 126

"Sure!" Aldo Fabrizi nodded. "Capito. Hey, but you still no can vote, right?" 127

"Sure I can vote; I got all the rights. I am a citizen, just like anybody else." William assured him. 128

"You some lucky guy then. You got it made! You don't gotta worry like the   129
rest of—"

"Bullshit," Diego Torres interrupted. "Why he got it made, man? He forced   130
to leave his country. Pendejo, you no capito nothing, man . . . "

As the two men continued to argue, William waited for the right moment   131
to slip away and join Lali.

She was with some of the women, who were discussing how sincere and   132
devoted Mrs. Hamma was.

"She's hardworking . . . "   133

"And she's good people . . . " an older woman agreed.   134

Mr. Fong joined them, and they spoke about the weather and how nice and   135
warm the days were.

Slowly people began to leave, shaking hands with their fellow students and   136
Mrs. Hamma, wishing each other luck.

Mrs. Hamma had been hoping to speak to Stephan Paczkowski privately   137
that evening, but he was always with a group. Now he offered his hand.

"I thank you very much for your good teaching. It was a fine semester."   138

"Oh, do you think so? Oh, I'm so glad to hear you say that. You don't know   139
how much it means. Especially coming from a person of your caliber. I am confident, yes, indeed, that you will soon be back to your profession, which after all,
is your true calling. If there is anything I can do, please . . . "

"Thank you miss. This time I am registering in Hunter College, which is in   140
Manhattan on Sixty-eighth Street in Lexington Avenue, with a course of English
Literature for beginners." After a slight bow, he left.

"Good bye," Mrs. Hamma sighed after him.   141

Lali, William, and several of the women picked up the paper cups and nap-   142
kins and tossed them into the trash basket.

"Thank you so much, that's just fine. Luis the porter will do the rest. He   143
takes care of these things. He's a lovely person and very helpful. Thank you."

William shook hands with Mrs. Hamma, then waited for Lali to say good-   144
bye. They were the last ones to leave.

"Both of you have been such good students. What are your plans? I hope   145
you will continue with your English."

"Next term we're taking another course," Lali said, looking at William.   146

"Yes," William responded, "it's more advance. Over at the Washington   147
Irving High School around Fourteenth Street."

"Wonderful." Mrs. Hamma hesitated. "May I ask you a question before you   148
leave? It's only that I'm a little curious about something."

"Sure, of course." They both nodded.   149

"Are you two related? I mean, you are always together and yet have differ-   150
ent last names, so I was just . . . wondering."

"Oh, we are just friends," Lali answered, blushing.   151

"I work over in the luncheonette at night, part-time."   152

"Of course." Mrs. Hamma looked at Lali. "Mrs. Padillo, your husband's place   153
of business. My, that's wonderful, just wonderful! You are all just so ambitious.
Very good . . ."

They exchanged farewells.   154

Outside, the warm June night was sprinkled with the sweetness of the new   155
buds sprouting on the scrawny trees and hedges planted along the sidewalks
and in the housing project grounds. A brisk breeze swept over the East River on
to Houston Street, providing a freshness in the air.

This time they were early, and Lali and William strolled at a relaxed pace.   156

"Well," Lali shrugged, "that's that. It's over!"   157

"Only for a couple of months. In September we'll be taking a more ad-   158
vanced course at the high school."

"I'll probably forget everything I learned by then."   159

"Come on, Lali, the summer will be over before you know it. Just you wait   160
and see. Besides, we can practice so we don't forget what Mrs. Hamma taught
us."

"Sure, what do you like to speak about?" Lali said in English.   161

William smiled, and clasping his hands, said, "I would like to say to you   162
how wonderful you are, and how you gonna have the most fabulous future . . .
after all, you so ambitious!"

When she realized he sounded just like Mrs. Hamma, Lali began to laugh.   163

"Are you"—Lali tried to keep from giggling, tried to pretend to speak in   164
earnest—"sure there is some hope for me?"

"Oh, heavens, yes! You have shown such ability this"—William was begin-   165
ning to lose control, laughing loudly—"semester!"

"But I want"—Lali was holding her sides with laughter—"some guarantee   166
of this. I got to know."

"Please, Miss Lali," William was laughing so hard tears were coming to his   167
eyes. "After . . . after all, you now a member in good standing . . . of the proper
future!"

William and Lali broke into uncontrollable laughter, swaying and limpings   168
oblivious to the scene they created for the people who stared and pointed at
them as they continued on their way to Rudi's. □

◢ RESPONDING

1. Mrs. Hamma asks her class to tell why they are taking the course in Basic
   English. With the exception of Mr. Torres, most of the students make somewhat perfunctory statements. What motives, in addition to the ones offered
   in their statements, do you think Lali and William have for enrolling in the
   class? What do you think motivates Mrs. Hamma to teach the course?

2. How would you describe Rudi and Lali's relationship? Why do you think he
   is at first reluctant to let her take the Basic English course? Why do you
   think he relents?

3. Why do you think Mohr made William a dwarf? What does this detail add
   to our understanding of him and of his relationship with Lali? Of what
   significance is this physical detail to the ideas presented by the story?

4. In "A Revolution of Values" (p. 109), bell hooks argues that education is never politically neutral. Do you think Mrs. Hamma would agree with this statement? Would she see her classroom as a place for political indoctrination or an open forum for political ideas?

5. Education always involves more than simply learning the content material of a course. What do the participants in Mrs. Hamma's English class gain from their experience, beyond familiarity with the English language? In what ways is their experience representative of all education?

Can Computers Help
American Education Fulfill
Its Promise?

NEIL POSTMAN

Although he is best known today for his writing on media and technology, Neil Postman is no stranger to educational reform movements. In 1969, he and his colleague Charles Wiengartner published *Teaching as a Subversive Activity,* in which they argued for a student-centered curriculum that emphasized flexibility, creativity, innovation and tolerance—as opposed to memorization of facts and figures. A decade later, Postman published *Teaching as a Conserving Activity,* which reflected a reversal of many of his previous positions on education, arguing now for more rigorous intellectual content in school curriculum. Postman is currently chairperson of the Department of Culture and Communication at New York University and the author of several books and numerous articles examining the role of technology and television in contemporary life. This selection from *TECHNOS* illustrates Postman's continuing concern that technology is making us lose sight of the real goals of education.

Of Luddites, Learning, and Life

LUDDITES

I think it is a fair guess to say that my role in the pages of TECHNOS is to serve as the resident Luddite. If this is so, then there are two things you need to know. The first is that I do not regard my association with Luddism as, in any way, a disgrace. As perhaps readers will know, the Luddite movement flourished in England between 1811 and 1818 as a response to the furious growth of machines and factories. Notwithstanding the excesses of their zeal, the Luddites seemed to be the only group in England that could foresee the catastrophic effects of the factory system, especially on children. They did not want their children to be deprived of an education—indeed, of childhood itself—for the purpose of their being used to fuel the machines of industry. As William Blake put it, they did not want their children to labor in the "dark Satanic Mills."

It is true that the Luddites busted up some textile machinery from which their unsavory reputation originates, but when did we decide to mock or despise people who try to protect their children and preserve their way of life?

The second thing you need to know is that despite the respect I have for them, I am not at all a Luddite. I have, for example, no hostility toward new technologies and certainly no wish to destroy them, especially those technologies, like computers, that have captured the imagination of educators. Of course, I am not enthusiastic about them, either. I am indifferent to them. And the reason I am indifferent to them is that, in my view, they have nothing whatever to do with the fundamental problems we have to solve in schooling our young. If I do harbor any hostility toward these machines, it is only because they are distractions. They divert the intelligence and energy of talented people from addressing the issues we need most to confront.

Let me begin, then, to make my case by telling you about a conversation I had with an automobile salesman who was trying to get me to buy a new Honda Accord. He pointed out that the car was equipped with cruise control, for which there was an additional charge. As is my custom in thinking about the value of technology, I asked him, "What is the problem to which cruise control is the answer?" The question startled him, but he recovered enough to say, "It is the problem of keeping your foot on the gas." I told him I had been driving for 35 years and had never found that to be a problem. He then told me about the electric windows. "What is the problem," I asked, "to which electric windows are the answer?" He was ready for me this time. With a confident smile, he said, "You don't have to wind the windows up and down with your arm." I told him that this, too, had never been a problem, and that, in fact, I rather valued the exercise it gave me.

I bought the car anyway, because, as it turns out, you cannot get a Honda Accord without cruise control and electric windows—which brings up the first point I should like to mention. It is that, contrary to conventional wisdom, new technologies do not, by and large, *increase* people's options but do just the opposite. For all practical purposes, you cannot go to Europe anymore by boat, which I can report is a thrilling and civilized way to go. Now you have to take an airplane. You cannot work for a newspaper unless you use a word processor, which eliminates me, since I do all of my composing with a pen and yellow pad and do not wish to change. You cannot buy records anymore; you must use CDs. I can go on with a thousand examples which demonstrate the point that new technologies drive old technologies out of business; which is to say that there is an imperialistic thrust to technology, a strong tendency to get everyone to conform to the requirements of what is new. Now, this is not always a bad thing, although sometimes it is very bad. I bring it up to call attention to the fact that what we too easily call "progress" is always problematic. The word comes trippingly to the tongue, but when you examine what it means, you discover that technology is always a Faustian bargain. It giveth and it taketh away. And we would all be clearer about what we are getting into if there were less cheerleading about, let us say, the use of computers in the classroom and more sober analysis of what may be its costs intellectually and socially.

A second point my Honda story illuminates is that new technologies may   6
not always solve significant problems or any problem at all. But because the technologies are *there,* we often invent problems to justify our using them. Or sometimes we even pretend we are solving one problem when, in fact, the reason for building and employing a new technology is altogether different. There are two expensive examples I can think of on this point. The first concerns the construction of the superconducting supercollider in Texas. It was justified by no less a person than Stephen Hawking, who told us that the research the supercollider would permit would give us entry to the mind of God. Since Hawking is an avowed atheist, he cannot possibly believe this; but even if he were not, it is equally sure he does not believe it. Nonetheless, it was good public relations. A Christian nation would be likely to go for it (though its Congress, after a $2 billion investment, did not), since the mysterious ways of the Lord have always been a serious problem for most of us. This is not to say that there aren't some interesting problems in cosmology that the supercollider might have solved. But since the people who would have been required to pay for this machine did not have any background or interest in these problems, it was best to talk about the mind of God.

The second example is the information superhighway that President Clin-   7
ton and especially Vice President Gore are so ardently promoting. I have not yet heard a satisfactory answer to the question "What is the problem to which this $50 billion investment is the solution?" I suspect that an honest answer would be something like this: "There *is* no social or intellectual problem, but we can stimulate the economy by investing in new technologies." That is not at all a bad answer, but it is not the answer the vice president has given. He is trying to sell the idea by claiming that it solves the problem of giving more people greater access to more information faster, including providing them with 500 TV channels (or even a thousand.)

LEARNING

This leads me directly to the question of schools and technology. In reading   8
Lewis Perelman's book, *School's Out,* and the work of those who are passionate about the educational value of new technologies, I find that their enthusiasm is almost wholly centered on the fact that these technologies will give our students greater access to more information faster, more conveniently, and in more various forms than has ever been possible. That is their answer to the question "What is the problem to which the new technologies are the solution?" I would suggest a modification of the question by putting it this way: "What *was* the 19th-century problem to which these technologies are an irrelevant solution?"

By putting it this way, I mean to say that the problem of getting information to people fast and in various forms was the main technological thrust of the 19th century, beginning with the invention of telegraphy and photography in the 1840s. It would be hard not to notice that the problem was solved and is therefore no longer something that any of us needs to work at, least of all, become worked up about. If anyone argues that technology can give people access to more information outside of the classroom than could possibly be given inside the classroom, then I would say that has been the case for almost 100 years. What else is new?

In other words, the information-giving function of the schools was rendered obsolete a long time ago. For some reason, more than a few technophiles (like Perelman) have just noticed this and are, in some cases, driven to favor eliminating our schools altogether. They err in this, I think, for a couple of reasons. One is that their notion of what schools are for is rather limited. Schools are not now and in fact have never been *largely* about getting information to children. That has been on the schools' agenda, of course, but has always been way down on the list.

One of the principal functions of school is to teach children how to behave in groups. The reason for this is that you cannot have a democratic, indeed, civilized, community life unless people have learned how to participate in a disciplined way as part of a group. School has never been about individualized learning. It has always been about how to learn and how to behave as part of a community. And, of course, one of the ways this is done is through the communication of what is known as social values. If you will read the first chapter of Robert Fulghum's *All I Ever Really Needed to Know I Learned in Kindergarten*, you will find an elegant summary of the important business of schools. The summary includes the following: Share everything, play fair, don't hit people, put things back where you found them, clean up your own mess, wash your hands before you eat, and, of course, flush. The only thing wrong with Fulghum's book is that no one has learned all these things, along with an affection for one's country, at kindergarten's end. We have ample evidence that it takes many years of teaching these values in school before they have been accepted and internalized. Some would say that this function of schooling is the most difficult task educators must achieve. If it is not, then the function of providing the young with narratives that help them to find purpose and meaning in learning and life surely is.

By a narrative I mean a story of human history that gives meaning to the past, explains the present, and provides guidance for the future. If there is a single problem that plagues American education at the moment, it is that our children no longer believe, as they once did, in some of the powerful and exhilarating narratives that were the underpinning of the school enterprise. I refer to such narratives as the story of our origins in which America is brought forth out of revolution, not merely as an experiment in governance but as part of God's own plan—the story of America as a moral light unto the world. Another great narrative tells of America as a melting pot where the teeming masses, from anywhere, yearning to be free, can find peace and sustenance.

Still another narrative—sometimes referred to as the Protestant Ethic—tells of how hard work is one of the pathways to a fulfilled life. There are many other such narratives on which the whole enterprise of education in this country has rested. If teachers, children, and their parents no longer believe in these narratives, then schools become houses of detention rather than attention.

LIFE

What I am driving at is that the great problems of education are of a social and   12
moral nature and have nothing to do with dazzling new technologies. In fact, the new technologies so loudly trumpeted in TECHNOS and in other venues are themselves not a solution to anything, but a problem to be solved. The fact is that our children, like the rest of us, are now suffering from information glut, not information scarcity. In America there are 260,000 billboards, 17,000 newspapers, 12,000 periodicals, 27,000 video outlets for renting tapes, 400 million television sets, and well over 400 million radios, not including those in automobiles. There are 40,000 new book titles published every year, and every day in America 41 million photographs are taken. And, just for the record (thanks to the computer), over 60 billion pieces of advertising junk mail come into our mailboxes every year. Everything from telegraphy and photography in the 19th century to the silicon chip in the 20th has amplified the din of information. From millions of sources all over the globe, through every possible channel and medium—light waves, air waves, ticker tapes, computer banks, telephone wires, television cables, satellites, and printing presses—information pours in. Behind it in every imaginable form of storage—on paper, on video and audio tape, on disks, film, and silicon chips—is an even greater volume of information waiting to be retrieved. Information has become a form of garbage. It comes indiscriminately, directed at no one in particular, disconnected from usefulness. We are swamped by information, have no control over it, and don't know what to do with it.

And in the face of all of this, there are some who believe it is time to aban-   13
don schools.

Well, if anyone is wondering whether or not the schools of the future have   14
any use, here is something for them to contemplate. The role of the school is to help students learn how to ignore and discard information so that they can achieve a sense of coherence in their lives; to help students cultivate a sense of social responsibility; to help students think critically, historically, and humanely; to help students understand the ways in which technology shapes their consciousness; to help students learn that their own needs sometimes are subordinate to the needs of the group. I could go on for another three pages in this vein without any reference to how machinery can give students access to information. Instead, let me summarize in two ways what I mean. First, I'll cite a remark made repeatedly by my friend Alan Kay, who is sometimes called "the father of the personal computer." Alan likes to remind us that any problems the schools cannot solve without machines, they cannot solve with them. Second, and with this I shall come to a close: If a nuclear holocaust should occur some place in the world, it will not happen because of insufficient information; if children are

starving in Somalia, it's not because of insufficient information; if crime terror-
izes our cities, marriages are breaking up, mental disorders are increasing, and
children are being abused, none of this happens because of a lack of information. These things happen because we lack something else. It is the "something
else" that is now the business of schools. ☐

◢ REREADING FOR UNDERSTANDING

1. What is a Luddite? Why is Postman frequently called a Luddite? Why doesn't
    he object to the label? Why does he think the label is inaccurate?

2. What does Postman mean when he says that technology is always a "Faus-
    tian bargain" (par. 5)? In what sense is computer technology in schools
    such a bargain, according to Postman?

3. What is the main benefit cited by those who advocate the use of comput-
    ers in education? Why does Postman claim that computer technology is
    addressing a problem that does not exist?

4. Why do some individuals argue that computers have made schools obso-
    lete? Why does their argument fail, according to Postman?

◢ RESPONDING

1. Do you agree with Postman's claim that the real problems we face, prob-
    lems like crime, war, starvation, and social decay, are not the result of a
    lack of information, and therefore computers cannot help us learn to solve
    them? Does he accurately present the nature of the major problems we
    face? Does his analysis reflect an understanding of the many uses of com-
    puter technology?

2. Postman insists he is not hostile to computer technology in the school, but
    indifferent to it: he believes it distracts from the real goals of education,
    that is, to teach students to think critically about the information that sur-
    rounds them and to help them make judgments and decisions in a his-
    torical and moral context. Think about your own education. Do you think
    the goals that Postman cites were the goals of most of your high school
    courses? If computer technology was used in any of your courses, what role
    did it serve? Based on your own experience, discuss whether computers
    "divert the intelligence and energy of talented people from addressing the
    issues we need most to confront" (par. 3).

3. In his plan for establishing public schools in Virginia (p. 46), Thomas
    Jefferson notes that young children lack the maturity for religious or philo-
    sophical inquiry. Instead, he suggests, "their memories may here be stored
    with the most useful facts from Grecian, Roman, European and American
    history. The first elements of morality too may be instilled into their minds;

such as, when further developed as their judgments advance in strength, may teach them to work out their own happiness . . . ." Given Jefferson's notions of the purposes of early education, how would he regard computer technology and its function in schooling?

◢ RESPONDING IN WRITING

Postman's question, "What is the problem to which this is the answer?" is a good beginning point for analyzing any new idea or technological innovation. Choose one such innovation that you've encountered recently, and use Postman's question to judge its value. Does the new thing really offer a solution to an existing problem, or does it, in fact, create problems?

NICHOLAS NEGROPONTE

Nicholas Negroponte (1943–   ) is a senior columnist for *WIRED* and the founder and director of the Media Lab at MIT, a research center devoted to studying and experimenting with future forms of human communication. Negroponte lectures widely in the United States and abroad on the role of computers in communication and other areas of daily life. In his 1995 book *Being Digital*, from which this selection is taken, Negroponte observes: "Computing is not about computers anymore. It's about living." In this essay, Negroponte discusses the ways computers have already transformed education and speculates about their future impact on teaching and learning.

Hard Fun

TEACHING DISABLED

When the Media Lab premiered its LEGO/Logo work in 1989, kids, kinder-   1
garten through sixth grade from the Hennigan School, demonstrated their projects before a full force of LEGO executives, academics, and the press. A zealous anchorwoman from one of the national TV networks, camera lights ablazing, cornered one child and asked him if this was not just all fun and games. She pressed this eight-year-old for a typical, "cute," sound-bite reply.

The child was obviously shaken. Finally, after her third repetition of the   2
question and after considerable heat from the lights, this sweaty-faced, exasperated child plaintively looked into the camera and said, "Yes, this is fun, but it's hard fun."

Seymour Papert is an expert on "hard fun." Early on he noted that being   3
"good at" languages is an odd concept when you consider that any run-of-the-mill five-year-old will learn German in Germany, Italian in Italy, Japanese in Japan. As we get older, we seem to lose this ability, but we cannot deny we had it in our youth.

Papert proposed that we think about computers in education, literally and   4
metaphorically, as if creating a country called, say, Mathland, where a child
will learn math the same way she learns languages. While Mathland is an odd
geopolitical concept, it makes perfect computational sense. In fact, modern
computer simulation techniques allow the creation of microworlds in which
children can playfully explore very sophisticated principles.

At Hennigan, one six-year-old boy in the so-called LEGO/Logo class built   5
a clump of blocks and placed a motor on top. He connected the two wires of
the motor to his computer and wrote a one-line program that turned it on and
off. When on, the blocks vibrated. He then attached a propeller to the motor,
but for some reason mounted it eccentrically (i.e., not centered, maybe by mistake). Now, when he turned on the motor, the blocks vibrated so much, they
not only jumped around the table but almost shook themselves apart (solved
by "cheating"—not always bad—with a few rubber bands).

He then noticed that if he turned the motor so that the propeller rotated   6
clockwise, the pile of LEGOs would first jerk to the right and then go into random motion. If he turned it on counterclockwise, the pile would first jerk to
the left and then go into random motion. Finally, he decided to put photocells
underneath his structure and then set the blocks on top of a black squiggly line
he had drawn on a large white sheet of paper.

He wrote a more sophisticated program that first turned on the motor   7
(either way). Then, depending on which photocell saw black, it would stop the
motor and start it up clockwise, to jerk right, or counterclockwise, to jerk left,
thereby getting back onto the line. The result was a moving pile of blocks that
followed the black squiggly line.

The child became a hero. Teachers and students alike asked how his inven-   8
tion worked and looked at his project from many different perspectives, asking
different questions. This small moment of glory gave him something very important: the joy of learning.

We may be a society with far fewer learning-disabled children and far   9
more teaching-disabled environments than currently perceived. The computer
changes this by making us more able to reach children with different learning
and cognitive styles.

DON'T DISSECT A FROG, BUILD ONE

Most American children do not know the difference between the Baltics and the   10
Balkans, or who the Visigoths were, or when Louis XIV lived. So what? Why are
those so important? Did you know that Reno is west of Los Angeles?

The heavy price paid in countries like France, South Korea, and Japan for   11
shoving many facts into young minds is often to have students more or less dead
on arrival when they enter the university system. Over the next four years they
feel like marathon runners being asked to go rock climbing at the finish line.

In the 1960s, most pioneers in computers and education advocated a   12
crummy drill-and-practice approach, using computers on a one-on-one basis,
in a self-paced fashion, to teach those same God-awful facts more effectively.
Now, with the rage of multimedia, we have closet drill-and-practice believers

who think they can colonize the pizzazz of a Sega game to squirt a bit more information into the heads of children, with more so-called productivity.

On April 11, 1970, Papert held a symposium at MIT called "Teaching Children Thinking," in which he proposed using computers as engines that children would teach and thus learn by teaching. This astonishingly simple idea simmered for almost fifteen years before it came to life through personal computers. Today, when more than a third of all American homes contain a personal computer, the idea's time has really come.   13

While a significant part of learning certainly comes from teaching—but good teaching and by good teachers—a major measure comes from exploration, from reinventing the wheel and finding out for oneself. Until the computer, the technology for teaching was limited to audiovisual devices and distance learning by television, which simply amplified the activity of teachers and the passivity of children.   14

The computer changed this balance radically. All of a sudden, learning by doing became the rule rather than the exception. Since computer simulation of just about anything is now possible, one need not learn about a frog by dissecting it. Instead, children can be asked to design frogs, to build an animal with frog-like behavior, to modify that behavior, to simulate the muscles, to play with the frog.   15

By playing with information, especially abstract subjects, the material assumes more meaning. I remember when my son's third-grade teacher reported to me sadly that he could not add or subtract a pair of two- or three-digit numbers. How odd, I thought, as he was always the banker when we played Monopoly, and he seemed to do a dandy job at managing those numbers. So I suggested to the teacher that she try posing the same addition as dollars, not just numbers. And, behold, he was suddenly able to add for her three digits and more in his head. The reason is because they were not abstract and meaningless numbers; they were dollars, which related to buying Boardwalk, building hotels, and passing Go.   16

The computer-controllable LEGO goes one step further. It allows children to endow their physical constructs with behavior. Current work with LEGOs at the Media Lab includes a computer-in-a-brick prototype, which demonstrates a further degree of flexibility and opportunity for Papert's constructivism, and includes interbrick communications and opportunities to explore parallel processing in new ways.   17

Kids using LEGO/Logo today will learn physical and logical principles you and I learned in college. Anecdotal evidence and careful testing results reveal that this constructivist approach is an extraordinarily rich means of learning, across a wide range of cognitive and behavioral styles. In fact, many children said to have been learning disabled flourish in the constructionist environment.   18

STREET SMARTS ON THE SUPERHIGHWAY

During the fall break, when I was in boarding school in Switzerland, a number of children including myself could not go home because home was too far away. But we could participate instead in a *concours,* a truly wild goose chase.   19

The headmaster of the school was a Swiss general (in the reserves, as are   20
most of the Swiss armed forces) and had both cunning and clout. He arranged
a five-day chase around the country, where each team of four kids (twelve to
sixteen years old) was equipped with 100 Swiss francs ($23.50 at the time) and
a five-day railroad pass.

Each team was given different clues and roamed the country, gaining   21
points for achieving goals along the way. These were no mean feats. At one
point we had to show up at a certain latitude and longitude in the middle of the
night, whereupon a helicopter dropped the next message in the form of a quar-
ter-inch tangled audiotape in Urdu, telling us to find a live pig and bring it to a
location that would be given at a certain phone number (which we had to
determine by a complex number puzzle about the dates when seven obscure
events took place, whose last seven digits made up the number to call).

This kind of challenge has always had an enormous appeal to me, and,   22
sorry to brag, my team did win—as I was convinced it would. I was so taken by
this experience, I did the same for my son's fourteenth birthday. However, without the American army at my beck and call, I made it a one-day experience in
Boston for his class, broken up into teams, with a fixed budget and an unlimited subway pass. I spent weeks planting clues with receptionists, under park
benches, and at locations to be determined through telephone number puzzles.
As you might probably guess, those who excelled in classwork were not necessarily the winners—in fact, usually the opposite. There has always been a real
difference between street smarts and smart smarts.

For example, to get one of the clues in my wild goose chase, you had to   23
solve a crossword puzzle. The smart-smart kids zoomed to the library or called
their smart friends. The street-smart kids went up and down the subway asking
people for help. Not only did they get the answers more quickly, but they did so
while moving from A to B and gaining distance and points in the game.

Today kids are getting the opportunity to be street smart on the Internet,   24
where *children are heard and not seen*. Ironically, reading and writing will benefit. Children will read and write on the Internet to communicate, not just to
complete some abstract and artificial exercise. What I am advocating should
not be construed as anti-intellectual or as a disdain for abstract reasoning—it
is quite the opposite. The Internet provides a new medium for reaching out to
find knowledge and meaning.

A mild insomniac, I often wake up around 3:00 a.m., log in for an hour, and   25
then go back to sleep. At one of these drowsy sessions I received a piece of e-mail
from a certain Michael Schrag, who introduced himself very politely as a high
school sophomore. He asked if he might be able to visit the Media Lab when he
was visiting MIT later in the week. I suggested that he sit in the back of the
room of my Friday "Bits Are Bits" class, and that we match him with a student
guide. I also forwarded a copy of his and my e-mail to two other faculty members who agreed to see him (ironically so: they thought he was the famous
columnist Michael Schrage, whose name has an *e* at the end).

When I finally met Michael, his dad was with him. He explained to me   26
that Michael was meeting all sorts of people on the Net and really treated it the
way I treated my *concours*. What startled Michael's father was that all sorts of

people, Nobel Prize winners and senior executives, seemed to have time for Michael's questions. The reason is that it is so easy to reply, and (at least for the time being) most people are not drowning in gratuitous e-mail.

Over time, there will be more and more people on the Internet with the   27
time and wisdom for it to become a web of human knowledge and assistance. The 30 million members of the American Association of Retired Persons, for example, constitute a collective experience that is currently untapped. Making just that enormous body of knowledge and wisdom accessible to young minds could close the generation gap with a few keystrokes.

PLAYING TO LEARN

In October 1981 Seymour Papert and I attended an OPEC meeting in Vienna.   28
It was the one at which Sheik Yamani delivered his famous speech about giving a poor man a fishing rod, not fish—teach him how to make a living, not take a handout. In a private meeting with Yamani, he asked us if we knew the difference between a primitive and an uneducated person. We were smart enough to hesitate, giving him the occasion to answer his own question, which he did very eloquently.

The answer was simply that primitive people were not uneducated at all,   29
they simply used different means to convey their knowledge from generation to generation, within a supportive and tightly knit social fabric. By contrast, he explained, an uneducated person is the product of a modern society whose fabric has unraveled and whose system is not supportive.

The great sheik's monologue was itself a primitive version of Papert's con-   30
structivist ideas. One thing led to another and both of us ended up spending the next year of our lives working on the use of computers in education in developing countries.

The most complete experiment in this period was in Dakar, Senegal, where   31
two dozen Apple computers with the programming language Logo were introduced into an elementary school. The children from this rural, poor, and underdeveloped west African nation dove into these computers with the same ease and abandon as any child from middle-class, suburban America. The Senegalese children showed no difference in adoption and enthusiasm due to the absence of a mechanistic, electronic, gadget-oriented environment in their normal life. Being white or black, rich or poor, did not have any bearing. All that counted, like learning French in France, was being a child.

Within our own society we are finding evidence of the same phenomenon.   32
Whether it is the demographics of the Internet, the use of Nintendo and Sega, or even the penetration of home computers, the dominant forces are not social or racial or economic but generational. The haves and the have-nots are now the young and the old. Many intellectual movements are distinctly driven by national and ethnic forces, but the digital revolution is not. Its ethos and appeal are as universal as rock music.

Most adults fail to see how children learn with electronic games. The com-   33
mon assumption is that these mesmerizing toys turn kids into twitchy addicts

and have even fewer redeeming features than the boob tube. But there is no question that many electronic games teach kids strategies and demand planning skills that they will use later in life. When you were a child, how often did you discuss strategy or rush off to learn something faster than anybody else?

Today a game like Tetris is fully understandable too quickly. All that changes is the speed. We are likely to see members of a Tetris generation who are much better at rapidly packing the trunk of a station wagon, but not much more. As games move to more powerful personal computers, we will see an increase in simulation tools (like the very popular SimCity) and more information-rich games.

Hard fun. ☐

34

35

◢ **REREADING FOR UNDERSTANDING**

1. What is Negroponte's thesis? Where does he state it?

2. Negroponte notes that the only use to which many educators have put multimedia technologies is to glamorize the old "drill-and-practice" programs of the 1960s. He shows, however, that there are many more innovative uses to which computers can be put in the classroom. What are some of these uses? How do they enhance learning, according to Negroponte?

3. What does Negroponte mean by his comment, "There has always been a real difference between street smarts and smart smarts" (par. 22)? How might the Internet help children acquire *both* street smarts and smart smarts?

◢ **RESPONDING**

1. In "Of Luddites, Learning, and Life" (p. 134), Neil Postman claims that computers' primary contribution to education is to provide faster access to more information, but that such access solves no educational problem. How would Negroponte respond to Postman's argument? What does Negroponte see as the chief contributions of computers to education?

2. In "The Politics of Remediation" (p. 101), Mike Rose notes that many students are unprepared to participate in the intellectual exchange of higher education. He says the students he observed "needed practice writing academic essays; they needed opportunities to talk about their writing—and their reading; they needed people who could quickly determine what necessary background knowledge they lacked and supply it in comprehensible ways" (par. 4). Do you think the kind of constructivist, interactive learning Negroponte describes here would be useful in addressing the problems Rose describes? Can you think of other ways in which computer technology might tackle some of the problems of students who are unprepared for college work? How might computer technology, rather than resolving college students' problems, make matters worse for them?

3. Negroponte's essay is rich in anecdotal evidence. How effective is that evidence in leading you to accept his thesis? Do you think other kinds of evidence, statistics say, would be more or less useful in supporting his claims?

◢ RESPONDING IN WRITING

1. Negroponte says that although some learning can occur within the traditional active teacher/passive student classroom, "a major measure comes from exploration, from reinventing the wheel and finding out for oneself" (par. 14). What do you think are the essential factors that encourage learning? Imagine you are writing an essay to teachers who want to create classroom environments conducive to learning. Based on your experiences as a student and a learner, write an essay in which you describe the conditions in which learning best takes place.

2. Write an essay about a learning experience you had that was "hard fun." What was hard about the experience? What was fun? What did you learn?

SVEN BIRKERTS

Sven Birkerts (1951–   ) is a literary critic and essayist. In his 1995 book *The Gutenberg Elegies*, Birkerts considers the impact of the on-line revolution and asks us to consider what may be lost in the shift from printed text to hypertext. In changing the way we see and receive information, Birkerts asks, aren't we also changing our experience and definition of learning and reading?

Perseus Unbound

Like it or not, interactive video technologies have muscled their way into the formerly textbound precincts of education. The videodisc has mated with the microcomputer to produce a juggernaut: a flexible and encompassing teaching tool that threatens to overwhelm the linearity of print with an array of option-rich multimedia packages. And although we are only in the early stages of implementation—institutions are by nature conservative—an educational revolution seems inevitable.

Several years ago in *Harvard Magazine*, writer Craig Lambert sampled some of the innovative ways in which these technologies have already been applied at Harvard. Interactive video programs at the Law School allow students to view simulated police busts or actual courtroom procedures. With a tap of a digit they can freeze images, call up case citations, and quickly zero-in on the relevant fine points of precedent. Medical simulations, offering the immediacy of video images and instant access to the mountains of data necessary for diagnostic assessment, can have the student all but performing surgery. And language classes now allow the learner to make an end run around tedious drill repetitions and engage in protoconversations with video partners.

The hot news in the classics world, meanwhile, is Perseus 1.0, an interactive 3 database developed and edited by Harvard associate professor Gregory Crane. Published on CD-ROM and videodisc, the program holds, according to its publicists, "the equivalent of 25 volumes of ancient Greek literature by ten authors (1 million Greek words), roughly 4,000 glosses in the on-line classical encyclopedia, and a 35,000-word on-line Greek lexicon." Also included are an enormous photographic database (six thousand images), a short video with narration and "hundreds of descriptions and drawings of art and archeological objects." The package is affordable, too: Perseus software can be purchased for about $350. Plugged in, the student can call up a text, read it side by side with its translation, and analyze any word using the Liddell-Scott lexicon; he can read a thumbnail sketch on any mythic figure cited in the text, or call up images from an atlas, or zoom in on color Landsat photos; he can even study a particular vase through innumerable angles of vantage. The dusty library stacks have never looked dustier.

Although skepticism abounds, most of it is institutional, bound up with 4 established procedures and the proprietorship of scholarly bailiwicks. But there are grounds for other, more philosophic sorts of debate, and we can expect to see flare-ups of controversy for some time to come. For more than any other development in recent memory, these interactive technologies throw into relief the fundamental questions about knowledge and learning. Not only what are its ends, but what are its means? And how might the means be changing the ends?

From the threshold, I think, we need to distinguish between kinds of 5 knowledge and kinds of study. Pertinent here is German philosopher Wilhelm Dilthey's distinction between the natural sciences (*Naturwissenschaften*), which seek to explain physical events by subsuming them under causal laws, and the so-called sciences of culture (*Geisteswissenschaften*), which can only understand events in terms of the intentions and meanings that individuals attach to them.

To the former, it would seem, belong the areas of study more hospitable to 6 the new video and computer procedures. Expanded databases and interactive programs can be viewed as tools, pure and simple. They give access to more information, foster cross-referentiality, and by reducing time and labor allow for greater focus on the essentials of a problem. Indeed, any discipline where knowledge is sought for its application rather than for itself could only profit from the implementation of these technologies. To the natural sciences one might add the fields of language study and law.

But there is a danger with these sexy new options—and the rapture with 7 which believers speak warrants the adjective—that we will simply assume that their uses and potentials extend across the educational spectrum into realms where different kinds of knowledge, and hence learning, are at issue. The realms, that is, of *Geisteswissenschaften*, which have at their center the humanities.

In the humanities, knowledge is a means, yes, but it is a means less to in- 8
strumental application than to something more nebulous: understanding. We study history or literature or classics in order to compose and refine a narrative, or a set of narratives about what the human world used to be like, about how the world came to be as it is, and about what we have been—and are—like as psychological or spiritual creatures. The data—the facts, connections, the texts themselves—matter insofar as they help us to deepen and extend that narrative. In these disciplines the process of study may be as vital to the understanding as are the materials studied.

Given the great excitement generated by Perseus, it is easy to imagine that 9
in the near future a whole range of innovative electronic-based learning pack-ages will be available and, in many places, in use. These will surely include the manifold variations on the electronic book. Special new software texts are al-ready being developed to bring us into the world of, say, Shakespeare, not only glossing the literature, but bathing the user in multimedia supplements. The would-be historian will step into an environment rich in choices, be they visual detailing, explanatory graphs, or suggested connections and sideroads. And so on. Moreover, once the price is right, who will be the curmudgeons who would deny their students access to the state-of-the-art?

Being a curmudgeon is a dirty job, but somebody has to do it. Someone has 10
to hoist the warning flags and raise some issues that the fast-track proselytizers might overlook. Here are a few reservations worth pondering.

1. Knowledge, certainly in the humanities, is not a straightforward matter 11
of access, of conquest via the ingestion of data. Part of any essential under-standing of the world is that it is opaque, obdurate. To me, Wittgenstein's famous axiom, "The world is everything that is the case," translates into a recog-nition of otherness. The past is as much about the disappearance of things through time as it is about the recovery of traces and the reconstruction of vistas. Say what you will about books, they not only mark the backward trail, but they also encode this sense of obstacle, of otherness. The look of the printed page changes as we regress in time; under the orthographic changes are the changes in the language itself. Old-style textual research may feel like an un-necessarily slow burrowing, but it is itself an instruction: It confirms that time is a force as implacable as gravity.

Yet the multimedia packages would master this gravity. For opacity they 12
substitute transparency, promoting the illusion of access. All that has been said, known, and done will yield to the dance of the fingertips on the terminal keys. Space becomes hyperspace, and time, hypertime ("hyper-" being the fashionable new prefix that invokes the nonlinear and nonsequential "space" made possible by computer technologies). One gathers the data of otherness, but through a medium which seems to level the feel—the truth—of that oth-erness. The field of knowledge is rendered as a lateral and synchronic enter-prise susceptible to collage, not as a depth phenomenon. And if our media restructure our perceptions, as McLuhan and others have argued, then we may

start producing generations who know a great deal of "information" about the past but who have no purchase on pastness itself. . . .

2. Humanistic knowledge, as I suggested earlier, differs from the more instrumental kinds of knowledge in that it ultimately seeks to fashion a comprehensible narrative. It is, in other words, about the creation and expansion of meaningful contexts. Interactive media technologies are, at least in one sense, anticontextual. They open the field to new widths, constantly expanding relevance and reference, and they equip their user with a powerful grazing tool. One moves at great rates across subject terrains, crossing borders that were once closely guarded. The multimedia approach tends ineluctably to multidisciplinarianism. The positive effect, of course, is the creation of new levels of connection and integration; more and more variables are brought into the equation.

But the danger should be obvious: The horizon, the limit that gave definition to the parts of the narrative, will disappear. The equation itself will become nonsensical through the accumulation of variables. The context will widen until it becomes, in effect, everything. On the model of Chaos science, wherein the butterfly flapping its wings in China is seen to affect the weather system over Oklahoma, all data will impinge upon all other data. The technology may be able to handle it, but will the user? Will our narratives—historical, literary, classical—be able to withstand the data explosion? Or will the knowledge of the world become, perforce, a map as large and intricate as the world itself?

3. We might question, too, whether there is not in learning as in physical science a principle of energy conservation. Does a gain in one area depend upon a loss in another? My guess would be that every lateral attainment is purchased with a sacrifice of depth. The student may, through a program on Shakespeare, learn an immense amount about Elizabethan politics, the construction of the Globe theater, the origins of certain plays in the writings of Plutarch, the etymology of key terms, and so on, but will this dazzled student find the concentration, the will, to live with the often burred and prickly language of the plays themselves? The play's the thing—but will it be? Wouldn't the sustained exposure to a souped-up cognitive collage not begin to affect the attention span, the ability if not willingness to sit with one text for extended periods, butting up against its cruxes, trying to excavate meaning from the original rhythms and syntax? The gurus of interaction love to say that the student learns best by doing, but let's not forget that *reading* a work is also a kind of doing.

4. As a final reservation, what about the long-term cognitive effects of these new processes of data absorption? Isn't it possible that more may be less, and that the neural networks have one speed for taking in—a speed that can be increased—and quite another rate for retention? Again, it may be that our technologies will exceed us. They will make it not only possible but irresistible to consume data at what must strike people of the book as very high rates. But what then? What will happen as our neural systems, evolved through millennia to certain capacities, modify themselves to hold ever-expanding loads? Will we simply become smarter, able to hold and process more? Or do we have to reckon with some other gain/loss formula? One possible cognitive response—

call it the "S.A.T. cram-course model"—might be an expansion of the short-term memory banks and a correlative atrophying of long-term memory.

But here our technology may well assume a new role. Once it dawns on us, [17] as it must, that our software will hold all the information we need at ready access, we may very well let it. That is, we may choose to become the technicians of our auxiliary brains, mastering not the information but the retrieval and referencing functions. At a certain point, then, we could become the evolutionary opposites of our forebears, who, lacking external technology, committed everything to memory. If this were to happen, what would be the status of knowing, of being educated? The leader of the electronic tribe would not be the person who knew most, but the one who could execute the broadest range of technical functions. What, I hesitate to ask, would become of the already antiquated notion of wisdom?

I recently watched a public television special on the history of the computer. [18] One of the many experts and enthusiasts interviewed took up the knowledge question. He explained how the formerly two-dimensional process of book-based learning is rapidly becoming three-dimensional. The day will come, he opined, when interactive and virtual technologies will allow us to more or less dispense with our reliance on the sequence-based print paradigm. Whatever the object of our study, our equipment will be able to get us there directly: inside the volcano or the violin-maker's studio, right up on the stage. I was enthralled, but I shuddered, too, for it struck me that when our technologies are all in place—when all databases have been refined and integrated—that will be the day when we stop living in the old hard world and take up residence in some bright new hyperworld, a kind of Disneyland of information. I have to wonder if this is what Perseus and its kindred programs might not be edging us toward. That program got its name, we learn from the brochure, from the Greek mythological hero Perseus, who was the explorer of the limits of the known world. I confess that I can't think of Perseus without also thinking of Icarus, heedless son of Daedalus, who allowed his wings to carry him over the invisible line that was inscribed across the skyway. ☐

◢ REREADING FOR UNDERSTANDING

1. Birkerts says that the introduction of interactive video technologies to education demands that we confront fundamental questions about education. What are those questions?

2. Explain the distinction Birkerts notes between natural sciences and sciences of culture. Why does he think new video and computer technology is more suitable for the natural sciences than for the sciences of culture?

3. What four concerns raised by electronic learning does Birkerts enumerate?

◢ RESPONDING

1. Examine Birkerts's first reservation about electronic learning. Is his concern that electronic images will restructure our perception of the past a serious concern? What weaknesses, if any, do you see in his claim that as a result of computer technology in schools, "we may start producing generations who know a great deal of 'information' about the past but who have no purchase on pastness itself" (par. 12)?

2. One of the difficulties that many underprepared college students have, according to Mike Rose (p. 104), is that "they come to the university with limited experience in applying knowledge, puzzling over solutions, solving problems." In high school and in introductory college courses, students are not encouraged to see connections between subjects or to apply learning from one area to another. Birkerts acknowledges that interactive media technologies tend to encourage connections across fields of study. He says, "The positive effect, of course, is the creation of new levels of connection and integration; more and more variables are brought into the equation" (par. 13). Yet he also warns that there are obvious dangers with the connections and multidisciplinary approach that such technology makes possible. What are those dangers? Do you think they are serious concerns? How do you think Rose would respond?

3. Respond to Birkerts's fear that, as it becomes easier for us to store and retrieve information from machines, we will lose our desire and perhaps our ability to remember anything other than how to operate those machines.

4. In a completely electronic world in which all information was easily accessed, Birkerts wonders, "What would happen to the already antiquated idea of wisdom?" What is the difference between information, knowledge, and wisdom? Is Birkerts correct to worry that wisdom will be sacrificed on the altar of easy access to information? Explain.

5. What is the point of Birkerts's reference to Icarus at the end of his essay?

UNIT THREE

Earning Our Daily Bread

INTRODUCTION

"What do you want to be when you grow up?" It's a question most of us recall being asked when we were children and there are certainly many ways to answer: "I want to be smart . . . rich . . . happy . . . loved." But somehow, even as children, we knew how to respond: "I want to be a taxi-driver . . . a teacher . . . a nurse . . . a paleontologist."

The familiarity of the question and the automatic response it elicits, from even the youngest children, reveal a great deal about our attitudes toward work.

Consider first of all the way the question is phrased: "What do you want to BE?" rather than "What do you want to DO?" suggests that who we are *is* what we do; that is, our occupations, not our characters, define us.

Implicit in the question, too, is the assumption that of course we *will* do *something*. We may be encouraged to do whatever kind of work we choose, to believe that any chosen profession is attainable, but choosing not to work is never an option.

And what do we mean by work? In its most common usage, the word has come to mean wage labor done outside the home. Although we recognize that there are other kinds of productive activities, we distinguish these from "real" work by the titles we give them: *housework, yardwork, volunteer work, homework*.

Our lives revolve around the work we do, or will do, or have done. We are encouraged to do well in school so that we can go to a college or vocational school that will prepare us for future work. We choose a college and course of study based on the profession we hope to enter upon graduation. And frequently even our choice of nonwork activities, such as playing a sport or doing community service, is guided by what will look good on a job résumé. We expect to be employed most of our adult lives, and when we finally leave our professional duties behind, we refer to ourselves as *retired*, as if the main activity of our lives were clearly over.

To a great degree, we identify ourselves and others by our professions. "What do you do?" is one of the first questions we ask of someone we are getting to know, and we are quick to make assumptions about education, economic status, social class, and even intelligence based on the answer. Because our work is so much a part of our sense of who we are, losing a job can be personally devastating.

So ingrained are these attitudes about work that we tend to think they are universal. We don't question where they came from or whether there are other ways to understand the phenomenon that we call work. The Contexts essays in this unit examine our beliefs about work and the historical and cultural bases for them. The Controversies section poses current questions about work in light of the ideas and images presented in the Contexts essays. The first group of essays, "Is the Work Ethic Dead or Is It Killing Us?" examines the claim that the work ethic is declining in America versus the conflicting evidence that, in fact, Americans are working longer and harder and with less reward than they did a generation ago. The second section, "Can the Work Ethic Survive in a Welfare State?" focuses on the continuing debate about welfare reform in the United States, particularly the ongoing efforts to return welfare recipients to the work force. The final essays examine the changing job market of today and tomorrow and ask, "Will There Be a Job for Me?"

The "A Way In" piece for this unit is an advertisement that invites you to consider the way cultural images shape our vision of and attitudes about work.

A   W A Y   I N

hat does the word "work" mean to you? Is it synonymous with "job"? How does a job differ from a career? What role does your work, job, or career play in your life at this point? What proportion of your time and energy is devoted to work as opposed to other things like family, friends, recreation? Do you expect work to take a larger or smaller percentage of your time and energy in the future?

When you consider the questions above, think also about the sources of your ideas about work. To what extent have your family, your community, your education shaped your ideas about work? What other factors have influenced your vision of work? To what extent have your notions of work been influenced by the way work is depicted in popular culture?

    SOUTHERN COMFORT

Do What You Love

◢ RESPONDING

1. What attitude about work does the ad on the next page suggest? In what way is it a realistic or unrealistic view of work?

2. Every image in this ad, from the model to the instrument he is playing to the way he is dressed, has been chosen to imply a particular lifestyle with

which the advertisers want Southern Comfort to be associated. Describe that lifestyle and explain how the images and text of the ad suggest it.

3. Images of work surround us in popular culture. Can you think of another advertisement, a television show, a movie, or a song that, in addition to selling a product or telling a story, also presents an image of work, either what it is or what it ought to be? What attitude toward work is conveyed? How?

PERRY PASCARELLA

"Work ethic" is a term used loosely today. Indeed, we most frequently hear it used to describe a particularly hard-playing athlete. While Michael Jordan or Cal Ripkin may be displaying some kind of work ethic driving down the court or taking the field, it would certainly not be recognized as such by the Puritans who settled in New England in the seventeenth century, bringing with them the belief that there was a moral purpose and justification for their labors. In this excerpt from *The New Achievers: Creating a Modern Work Ethic,* Perry Pascarella examines the religious roots of that belief and its secularization and eventual decline in America. Pascarella is a business journalist who is concerned with the role business plays in shaping and responding to the changing demands of society.

What Happened to the Old Protestant Ethic?

An individual comes to work to meet economic needs, belonging needs, the need to feel a sense of self-worth, the need to serve others, or the need for self-development and self-expression—any or all in their many shades. He or she may respond to different needs at different times. In earlier times, the reason for working was more clear-cut: economic necessity reinforced by a moral imperative.

The need to earn a living still drives people to seek a job, but work no longer seems to have that same transcendental connection for many Americans. It is impossible to measure the religious commitment of a society at any point in time and make a sound comparison with some time in the past; however, there is little doubt that religion is playing a lesser role in our public lives today than in early America and during the early years of industrialization. In the past two or three decades, the nation has become highly sensitized to any laws, regulations, or national policies—extant or proposed—that would bring church and state closer together. Religious beliefs, or the absence of them, are protected by barring discussion of religious or moral considerations in the official public arena.

Americans still consider themselves religious, however. Regardless of their church affiliation or nonaffiliation, regardless of the degree to which their daily lives are governed by transcendent considerations, they believe in a god, they say. In a study of American values done for the Connecticut Mutual Life Insurance Co., 94 percent of adults said they occasionally feel God loves them; 73 percent feel that frequently. Although only 44 percent of these people attend church regularly, 73 percent consider themselves "religious."   3

Other studies have shown, year after year, that over 90 percent of Americans believe in God but that fewer than 50 percent regularly attend worship services. There is little evidence, then, that most Americans are deeply and continuously influenced by the religious word. In fact, the analysts working on the Connecticut Mutual study call only one-fourth of the respondents "highly religious."   4

Religious commitment may no longer be the all-embracing force it once was, but the Connecticut Mutual report's authors conclude that it is still the "strongest predictor" of a person's satisfaction and involvement with his or her work. Of the most religious respondents to the survey, nearly all feel dedicated to their work while only two-thirds of the "least religious" feel that way.   5

Although religion may influence some people's attitudes toward work today, we are far from reaching a consensus on any of the troublesome questions that would be provided answers by a common ideology of work. There is little agreement about the relationship of work to life's purpose, of individual interests versus those of the community, or of working to perfect life here on earth versus relying on God's salvation. There is disagreement not only between "religious" and not-so-religious persons but even within the ranks of those with strong religious beliefs.   6

The effect of differing spiritual views on people's attitudes toward work was revealed in a survey done for the Continental Group. A high correlation appeared among those who engage in traditional religious activities, those who believe in giving a high priority to economic growth, and those who place a high priority on work that makes a contribution to society. We might call this the more traditional view of economic growth and the meaning of work. On the other hand, there is a growing number of people who favor more cautious economic growth and who give a high priority to preserving the earth's resources. People in this group are likely to regard themselves as "driven" individuals. They tend to be less content with their work situations and more aggressive in demanding that their expectations be met. We have, then, at least two work ethics shaping people's behavior. One leads its adherents to accept traditional work structures and rewards while the other leads to resistance.   7

MONEY AND MORALS

In early America there was an obvious need to work for one's economic survival and a dominant moral obligation to work as well. This obligation was the basis   8 for what is referred to as the "Protestant ethic" or "Puritan ethic." The blend of economic necessity—for the individual and the community—and the moral force weaved its way through much of American history. In time, however, this fabric became unraveled. Why?

Two powerful and competing movements laid the ideological foundation 9 for American life: the Reformation and the Enlightenment. Both were reactions against the traditional church. Both carried strong messages regarding the individual in relation to the universe, his work, and his wealth.

The Reformation began with Martin Luther (1483–1546) challenging the 10 notion that individual salvation could be earned through good works as prescribed by the church. Salvation could come only through God's grace, said Luther. While the Roman Church had an "elect"—the priests—Luther and other Protestant leaders taught that the "elect" could be anyone. Anyone, but not all. John Calvin (1509–1564) said that those who would be granted salvation had already been predetermined. Material success, he allowed, is a sign that one has been designated by God for salvation.

Luther saw no particular virtue or evil in poverty. "God does not condemn 11 the possession of wealth, but the evil use of it, that is, its use merely to satisfy one's selfish desire. . . ." Man is in the world to be of service to his fellow man and to God, said Luther. A person who conducts himself accordingly will not lose his heart to wealth and will use his riches for the good of all, he believed. He advanced the revolutionary concept of a worldly "calling"—the keystone of what was to become the Protestant work ethic. Prior to that, in the teachings of the Roman Church, the highest calling had been the monastic life of contemplation. But Luther's "calling" was to action in the secular world as an expression of brotherly love. ". . . this moral justification of worldly activity was one of the most important results of the Reformation," wrote Max Weber, the German sociologist, in his classic book *The Protestant Ethic and the Spirit of Capitalism.*

For many centuries, man had regarded work as a curse. For early Hebrews, 12 it was atonement for original sin. For early Christians, "labor" or "toil" was not something to be pursued with all one's energies. But Luther and Calvin brought significance to work. They presented it as the bridge between heaven and earth.

Calvin went one step further in drawing man into worldly activity for spir- 13 itual purpose. He preached "maximum effort"; when a person produces more than he needs, said Calvin, this surplus should not be wasted on personal appetites. It should serve the glory of God by being reinvested to improve one's work and provide even greater surpluses for the glory of God. For centuries, Christianity had condemned profit-making; but early Protestantism supported a profound social and economic shift. Wealth had long been associated with oppressors; now it was taken as a sign that one was among God's elect.

Early Lutheranism and Calvinism coincided with secular, economic changes 14 that were occurring in Europe. People were rising above the subsistence level. A middle class was developing. The "calling" to work justified a working class. The division of people into classes and occupations was, for Luther, the result of Divine Will. It is man's duty to persevere in his assigned place, he taught. Protestantism supported another aspect of the new economic system by discouraging wasteful consumption and the enjoyment of possessions. Calvin's concept of "maximum effort" laid a spiritual foundation for amassing capital. This powerful religious movement thus generated a high-production, high-investment mentality. It made self-denial in production and consumption both ethically right and economically effective.

SELF-DESTRUCTING ETHIC

Two centuries after the thinking of Luther and Calvin had begun working their effect on society, John Wesley (1703–1791) foresaw the likely negative outcome of such expressions of faith. Religion, he said, will produce industry and frugality which will lead to riches; as riches increase, so will pride, anger, and desire. Religion thus brings on its own decay. It would be futile to try to prevent people from working and accumulating wealth, Wesley realized. His practical solution was to encourage them to do so and then to share their wealth so they would grow in grace.   15

Later, in young America, riches did indeed increase. Work and wealth became signs of respectability—a principal motivating force in people's lives. Religious forces drew people's attention to the secular life, but, in time, many lost sight of the treasures in heaven. Attempts to make the church of the saved visible in this world shifted people's concern from the hereafter to the here and now. Material success became an end in itself.   16

While Protestantism served early America well and laid the foundation for industrialization with its justification of work and investment, the industrial system eventually abused and then lost touch with that ethic. The notion of work as a spiritual calling fell out of sync with the mechanized work of mass production. The objective of work centered on economic gain, and even that was beyond the reach of many people. Industrialization eventually eroded the certainty that work would bring success to the individual. Semiskilled workers, trapped in the mills of the nineteenth century, realized that no amount of hard work would lift them to wealth or self-improvement. Thus came the mounting negative feelings toward work and demands for more and more economic compensation in exchange for surrendering to such meaningless activity.   17

Work was no longer done for God's glorification; it took on a more utilitarian meaning. Ironically, what had been the foundation for industrialization was eventually eroded by it. American industry progressed, from that point, not on the work ethic but despite it. The Protestant ethic had taught people to work hard, save their money, and get their rewards in the future or the hereafter. But that message became perverted to a consumption ethic: "Work as little as possible, spend your money because it's shrinking in value, and demand your rewards now." By the 1960s, this trend culminated in the "me generation"—people devoted to self-gratification. The me-generation mentality affected more than just the youth of this country. Their parents had led the way in the scramble for houses, cars, appliances, and leisure-time goods; the youth merely expected more and then turned to new experiences when goods no longer satisfied their hunger.   18

MIXED MESSAGES

The American brand of capitalism succeeded in creating such widespread pros-   19
perity relative to anything the world had ever seen that the imperative came to
be one of consumption, not production. Demand for goods and services became the flywheel that kept the economic engine running fast and smooth. The
spiritual dimension, meanwhile, faded as a justification for the accumulation of
wealth. Whereas the Protestant view of work and wealth was once clear and present, it is now mixed at best. The individual seeking guidance in the Bible regarding those messages encounters some popular passages that admonish him
to work and others that suggest that work is unimportant. For example, most
Americans with any exposure to the New Testament will have heard Matt.
6:26—"Look at the birds of the air; they neither sow nor reap nor gather into
barns, and yet your heavenly Father feeds them." The message seems to be: don't
worry about working or storing up wealth. On the other hand, they may hear 2
Thess. 3:11–12—" . . . we hear that some of you are living in idleness, mere
busybodies, not doing any work. Now such persons we command and exhort in
the Lord Jesus Christ to do their work in quietness and to earn their own living." And there is 1 Tim. 1:4—"If any would not work, neither should he eat."

Few verses are more widely known that those regarding the curse of wealth   20
such as Matt. 19:23–24—" . . . it will be very hard for rich people to enter the
kingdom of heaven. Again I tell you, it is easier for a camel to go through the eye
of a needle than for a rich man to enter the kingdom of God." Yet people may be
led in the other direction by Matt. 25:29—"For to every person who has something, even more will be given, and he will have more than enough; but the person who has nothing, even the little that he has will be taken away from him."

Literal interpretations of selected passages from the New Testament do not   21
necessarily convey the central message of Christianity. When people attempt to
set guidelines for living and working in such a manner, they do not all arrive at
the same conclusions. As a result, even those who are listening to "The Word"
do not necessarily share a common ethic. In addition, biblical stories regarding
wealth and poverty or servant and master seem hardly relevant to a society in
which wealth is widespread and servant-master relationships have long since
disappeared.

As John Wesley had feared, the Protestant ethic came to support an eco-   22
nomic system that led to its own undoing. Today, our economic system is in
danger of failing because it has no spiritual foundation despite the fact that
many Americans assume a spiritual ethic is built into their political-economic
system. After all, they believe, the United States is essentially a Christian nation.

A CHRISTIAN NATION?

The nation's founders provided a philosophical base but not a religious one—   23
especially not a specifically Christian one. Our founding fathers were influenced
by Enlightenment thinking which matured in the eighteenth and nineteenth
centuries. They believed that all men were created equal and that, given the

proper material and social conditions, fully realized human beings would evolve. If our institutions would conform to "natural law," man would develop his natural perfection, according to this utopian line of thought.

Enlightenment thinking also meshed well with the rise of science. By the eighteenth century, man's view of nature was changing in the Western world. Nature was no longer mysterious and divine. It had been reduced to a scientific machine, and man's place was to master this machine to produce wealth. America's seemingly unbounded resources and new frontiers promised material gain and freedom for man to fully realize his potential far beyond what some of the earlier Enlightenment thinkers may ever have dreamed. Economic expansion became part of America's destiny. 24

The Declaration of Independence, signed a century and a half after the white man began to settle the land, is a most humanitarian document, but it is not a Christian document. Thomas Jefferson, Benjamin Franklin, and George Washington rank among the greatest statesmen of all time, but they were deists out of the Enlightenment fashion, allowing that supreme power had created the world but was no longer acting in its unfolding. The great document that launched America toward nationhood contains only three references to a divine being: 25

1. "equal station to which the Laws of Nature and of Nature's God entitle them"

2. "that they are endowed by their Creator"

3. "with a firm reliance on the protection of Divine Providence"

In its single reference to spiritual matters, our other great document, The Constitution, reads: "Congress shall make no law respecting an establishment of religion, or prohibiting the free exercise thereof." The reference was not made in the original articles, but added in the First Amendment! This nation, which so may citizens regarded as having built-in Christian values, was launched officially according to deist concepts but made no official recognition of a particular religion. We were given the foundation for a liberal society. 26

In time, the Protestant's concern for salvation gave way to the liberal's notion that society is perfectible. As man learned to read some of nature's laws, there seemed to be less need for divine intervention. Even Christians suspected that the Kingdom was coming on earth, that it was happening right here, and that one could be concerned with self-pursuits because "the system" would take care of thy neighbor. Moralists like Ben Franklin spoke of work and wealth in terms of usefulness rather than the Glory of God. Protestantism had begun to elevate the concept of wealth, and the pragmatism that developed in America raised it still higher. The old Protestant ethic was being secularized. 27

RIGID RULES

Eighteenth- and nineteenth-century America did have a strong Christian thrust despite the lack of official direction. The churches that took root in this land of 28 freedom did not allow man to follow nature's laws, despite the intentions of the founding fathers. Quite the contrary! The early Protestants were no longer subject to the rule of the priests, but they lived under strict rules for daily conduct. Protestantism allowed everyone to be part of the "elect," but it enforced rigid rules for involvement in the secular world.

Early American churches left little room for the individual to fall victim to   29
his wicked natural inclinations. "The core of Puritanism . . . was an intense moral zeal for the regulation of everyday conduct," says Daniel Bell. "Given the external dangers and psychological strains of living in a closed world, the individual had to be concerned not only with his own behavior but with the community." Spiritual values were central to people's lives and tied all the elements of life into a meaningful whole.

Despite the tight religious rules for social conduct, preoccupation with in-   30
dividual salvation sometimes justified a person's acquisitiveness at the expense of others rather than as a blessing to be shared with others. Thus there was a religious "justification" for the inhumanities of the early days of the Industrial Revolution. Max Weber discussed the development of a bourgeois ethic which permitted the businessman to pursue his financial interests, enjoy a supply of industrious workers, and assure himself that unequal economic distribution was the result of Divine Providence. By the twentieth century, increased prosperity and the attainment of greater economic and social equality had undermined the notion of high calling for both businessman and laborer. Even at the beginning of this century, Weber was able to note that the idea of duty in one's calling "prowls about in our lives like the ghost of dead religious beliefs."

Protestantism has carried within itself a fundamental conflict between in-   31
dividualism and community. When economic interests conflict with the central Christian message of love and sharing, some Protestants divorce their private life and their religion from their public activities. They focus on individual religious experiences. For some, this leads to concern for grace and being one of the "elect" and generates hostility rather than compassion for sinners. Martin Marty, in *Righteous Empire,* describes the division between personal and community concern. "Private" Protestantism, beginning especially in the early nineteenth century, stressed individual salvation and the moral life of the "saved." Its followers were concerned with conversion and reaffirmation of faith. They were out to save souls. "Public" Protestantism, on the other hand, was more concerned with social order and man's social role. Adherents worked for transformation of the world; they were out to save society.

In recent years, religion has become an internalized, private affair for   32
many Americans. Following the peak of public party Protestantism in the 1960s, with its highly visible mobilization for civil rights and against war, the private side has returned to the fore. Perhaps, with the rise of big systems— government, business, and labor unions—the individual has seen little choice but to retreat inward.

The interplay of religion, social development, and economic growth over   33
American history is much too complex to treat fully here. Cause and effect are not easily distinguished and invite oversimplification. We can safely conclude,

however, that the underlying spiritual dimension to work and the predominant view of man have changed significantly over the past two centuries. As people turn inward, many find their work has no meaning. Although some embrace the more traditional, self-denial values that provide meaning for their work, far more find the contrast between what they believe they are and what the workplace expects of them too great to bear. They may rebel at the pressures that threaten to compress or extinguish their spirituality. The workplace is one of the principal places where they strike out against their loss of power and the fragmentation of their lives. The old Protestant ethic taught people to deny their selfish desires and work for greater social and spiritual glory, but denying oneself does not seem to make sense in an era of rational and scientific thinking. Many, including a significant portion of those in the ranks of traditional religions, embrace the humanist notion that man's highest goal is progress here on earth. Their concerns, whether personal or societal, are essentially secular.

Many of us stand naked with neither spiritual connection nor social agreement to give purpose to our work. In the late nineteenth century, we had regarded ourselves as the chosen nation. Less than a century later, the country which had fought World War II convinced that God was on its side waged a nonwar in Vietnam that it hoped God wouldn't hear about. Blood-letting in the ghettos and on the campuses revealed our inner conflicts and suggested that we were hypocrites who could no longer hide our selfish, inhumane, un-Christian tendencies. Scarcities and uncertainties have risen up to dampen our traditional eagerness to meet the future. Rather than striking at the heart of the problem, we expect to do little more than cope with an undesirable situation. We have given up the notion of the perfectibility of man. We try instead to fine-tune our institutions to compensate for our individual shortcomings. Our institutions are of less and less help in the struggle, however, because they were designed to serve an ethic of consumption rather than the earlier calling to work that opposed immediate gratification of desires. The early success of capitalism had been built, not on the "impulse to acquisition," but on the restraint of that impulse. But that discipline of worker and businessman has been lost.

While the old Protestant ethic or some vestige of it is still at work in some people's lives, it is not the predominant influence on attitudes toward work today. After centuries of its undoing there is little reason to expect a return to widespread acceptance of the old ethic. We should, instead, look to see if there is a new work ethic that can be articulated for our time. We should look, too, at why our organizations are failing to bring together the work that needs to be done and the needs that people could satisfy through work. □

▲ REREADING FOR UNDERSTANDING

1. According to Pascarella, early Americans had two powerful motives to work. What were they? How do they compare with our reasons for working today?

2. Explain how the Protestant Reformation led to a change in attitude toward work.

3. Pascarella says that differing spiritual views have led to the emergence of two separate work ethics. Explain in your own words what those two ethics are and describe the spiritual views that spawned them.

4. Pascarella suggests that the Protestant work ethic contained the seeds of its own destruction. Explain.

◢ RESPONDING

1. Pascarella cites a Connecticut Mutual Life Insurance report that found religious commitment to be the strongest predictor of a person's satisfaction or involvement with his or her work. On what evidence is this conclusion based? Can you think of other reasons that might explain this relationship between commitment to religion and commitment to work?

2. Today, we hear a great deal of discussion from politicians and others about the need to return to the traditional values on which our country was founded. Indeed, some argue that we need to return to the Christian values which they purport were the spiritual foundation for our nation. Based on the brief history of thought in early America that Pascarella provides, do you think this country can claim a specifically Christian heritage? If a return to traditional values is needed, which particular values need to be re-embraced? Why?

◢ RESPONDING IN WRITING

What rewards do you think work should provide? What sorts of benefits have you received from jobs you have held? What kinds of rewards do you hope to gain from future work? Write an essay addressed to employers who want to encourage productivity and commitment from their workers. Explain to your readers what factors make work rewarding.

JULIET B. SCHOR

Juliet Schor is a senior lecturer on economics and director of studies in the Women's Studies Program at Harvard University. In the preface to her 1991 book *The Overworked American*, from which this excerpt is taken, she confesses that for much of her professional life she was caught up in the "time squeeze" that has become an accepted part of the American worker's daily life. Her marriage to an Indian immigrant who did not share the American attitude toward work and leisure, and her own studies of the labor market, led her to undertake a serious inquiry into the established belief that capitalism has resulted in greater leisure for more people. Her findings, recorded in *The Overworked American*, suggest that far from increasing leisure, capitalism has demanded greater and greater human effort. In fact, she reports, since 1960, the average working American has added 160 hours—or one month of work—to his year. In this chapter, Schor explores a belief that many of us hold: that our ancestors were harder and more willing workers than we are.

"A Life at Hard Labor"
Capitalism and Working Hours

> *The labouring man will take his rest long in the morning; a good piece of the day is spent afore he come at his work; then he must have his breakfast, though he have not earned it, at his accustomed hour, or else there is grudging and murmuring: when the clock smiteth, he will cast down his burden in the midway, and whatsoever he is in hand with, he will leave it as it is, though many times it is marred afore he come again; he may not lose his meat, what danger soever the work is in. At noon he must have his sleeping time, then his bever in the afternoon, which spendeth a great part of the day; and when his hour cometh at night, at the first stroke of the clock he casteth down his tools, leaveth his work, in what need or case soever the work standeth.*

—THE BISHOP PILKINGTON

One of capitalism's most durable myths is that it has reduced human toil. This myth is typically defended by a comparison of the modern forty-hour week with its seventy- or eighty-hour counterpart in the nineteenth century. The implicit—but rarely articulated—assumption is that the eighty-hour standard has prevailed for centuries. The comparison conjures up the dreary life of medieval peasants, toiling steadily from dawn to dusk. We are asked to imagine the journeyman artisan in a cold, damp garret, rising even before the sun, laboring by candlelight late into the night.

These images are backward projections of modern work patterns. And they are false. Before capitalism, most people did not work very long hours at all. The tempo of life was slow, even leisurely; the pace of work relaxed. Our ancestors may not have been rich, but they had an abundance of leisure. When capitalism raised their incomes, it also took away their time. Indeed, there is good reason to believe that working hours in the mid-nineteenth century constitute the most prodigious work effort in the entire history of humankind.

Therefore, we must take a longer view and look back not just one hundred years, but three or four, even six or seven hundred. . . .

Consider a typical working day in the medieval period. It stretched from dawn to dusk (sixteen hours in summer and eight in winter), but, as the Bishop Pilkington has noted, work was intermittent—called to a halt for breakfast, lunch, the customary afternoon nap, and dinner. Depending on time and place, there were also midmorning and midafternoon refreshment breaks. These rest periods were the traditional rights of laborers, which they enjoyed even during

Eight Centuries of Annual Hours

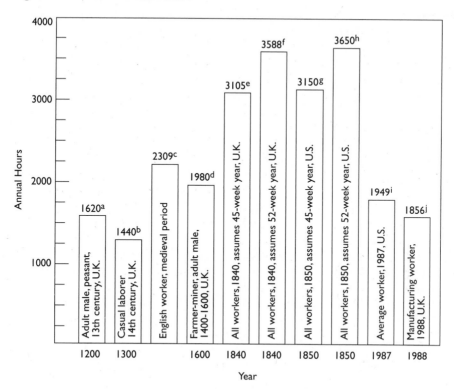

[a]Calculated from Gregory Clark's estimate of 150 days per family, assumes 12 hours per day, 135 days per year for adult male ("Impatience, Poverty, and Open Field Agriculture," mimeo, 1986).

[b]Calculated from Nora Ritchie's estimate of 120 days per year. Assumes 12-hour day. ("Labour Conditions in Essex in the Reign of Richard II," in E. G. Carus-Wilson, ed., *Essays in Economic History*, vol. II [London: Edward Arnold], 1962.)

[c]Calculated from Ian Blanchard's estimate of 180 days per year. Assumes 11-hour day. ("Labour Productivity and Work Psychology in the Engish Mining Industry, 1400–1600," *Economic History Review*, 31 [1, (1978)]: 23.)

[d]Author's estimate of average medieval laborer working two-thirds of the year at 9.5 hours per day.

[e]Average worker in the United Kingdom, assumes 45-week year, 69 hours per week (weekly hours from W. S. Woytinsky, "Hours of Labor," in *Encyclopedia of the Social Sciences*, vol. III [New York: Macmillan], 1935).

[f]Average worker in the United Kingdom, assumes 52-week year, 69 hours per week (weekly hours from ibid.).

[g]Average worker in the United States, assumes 45-week year, 70 hours per week (weekly hours from Joseph Zeisel, "The Workweek in American Industry, 1850–1956," *Monthly Labor Review*, 81 [January 1958]: 23–29).

[h]Average worker in the United States, assumes 52-week year, 70 hours per week (weekly hours from ibid.).

[i]From table 2.4.

[j]Manufacturing worker in the United Kingdom, calculated from Bureau of Labor Statistics data, Office of Productivity and Technology.

peak harvest times. During slack periods, which accounted for a large part of the year, adherence to regular working hours was not usual. According to Oxford Professor James E. Thorold Rogers, the medieval workday was not more than eight hours. The worker participating in the eight-hour movements of the late nineteenth century was "simply striving to recover what his ancestor worked by four or five centuries ago."

The pace of work was also far below modern standards—in part, because   5
the general pace of life in medieval society was leisurely. The French historian Jacques LeGoff has described precapitalist labor time "as still the time of an economy dominated by agrarian rhythms, free of haste, careless of exactitude, unconcerned by productivity—and of a society created in the image of that economy, *sober and modest*, without enormous appetites, undemanding, and incapable of quantitative efforts." Consciousness of time was radically different. Temporal units we take for granted today—such as the hour, or the minute— did not exist. There was little idea of time saving, punctuality, or even a clear perception of past and future. Consciousness of time was much looser—and time had much less economic value.

But the pace of work was slow not only for cultural reasons. On the basis   6
of our knowledge of caloric intake, we can infer that work had to have been a low-energy affair. The food consumption of all but the rich was inadequate to sustain either a rapid pace or continuous toil. (This may be why lords provided substantial meals to laborers during harvests.) A long, hard day of agricultural labor requires well over three thousand calories per day, an amount out of the range of common people. As more food became available over the nineteenth and twentieth centuries, a significant fraction of those additional calories have been burned up by an accelerated pace of work.

The contrast between capitalist and precapitalist work patterns is most   7
striking in respect to the working year. The medieval calendar was filled with holidays. Official—that is, church—holidays included not only long "vaca-tions" at Christmas, Easter, and midsummer but also numerous saints' and rest days. These were spent both in sober churchgoing and in feasting, drinking, and merrymaking. In addition to official celebrations, there were often weeks' worth of ales—to mark important life events (bride ales or wake ales) as well as less momentous occasions (scot ale, lamb ale, and hock ale). All told, holiday leisure time in medieval England took up probably about one-third of the year. And the English were apparently working harder than their neighbors. The *ancien régime* in France is reported to have guaranteed fifty-two Sundays, ninety rest days, and thirty-eight holidays. In Spain, travelers noted that holi-days totaled five months per year.

The peasant's free time extended beyond officially sanctioned holidays.   8
There is considerable evidence of what economists call the backward-bending supply curve of labor—the idea that when wages rise, workers supply less labor. During one period of unusually high wages (the late fourteenth century), many laborers refused to work "'by the year or the half year or by any of the usual terms but only by the day.'" And they worked only as many days as were neces-sary to earn their customary income—which in this case amounted to about

120 a year, for a probable total of only 1,440 hours annually (this estimate assumes a 12-hour day because the days worked were probably during spring, summer, and fall). A thirteenth-century estimate finds that whole peasant families did not put in more than 150 days per year on their land. Manorial records from fourteenth-century England indicate an extremely short working year—175 days—for servile laborers. Later evidence for farmer-miners, a group with control over their worktime, indicates they worked only 180 days a year.

The short workyear reveals an important feature of precapitalist society: the absence of a culture of consumption and accumulation. There was far less interest in and opportunity for earning or saving money. Material success was not yet invested with the overriding significance it would assume. And consumerism was limited—both by the unavailability of goods and by the absence of a middle class with discretionary income. Under these circumstances, the lack of compulsion to work is understandable. Of course, those who object to this characterization argue that free time in the middle ages was not really leisure but underemployment. If work effort was low, they claim it is because the economy provided few opportunities for earning money.

What are we to make of these claims? It is certainly true that holidays were interspersed throughout the agrarian calendar, falling after the peak periods of planting, sowing, and harvesting. And in both agriculture and industry, the possibilities for earning additional income were limited. Yet cause and effect are hard to untangle. If more work had been available, it is not obvious that many people would have taken it. The English case provides considerable evidence that higher incomes led to less not more labor—for example, the casual laborers of the thirteenth century, the farmer-miners of the sixteenth, and even the early industrial workers who resisted work whenever their incomes allowed it. Just after wages were paid, as employers learned, absenteeism, failure to work, and much-decried "laziness" resulted. But wherever one stands on the causes of medieval leisure, one fact remains: steady employment, for fifty-two weeks a year is a modern invention. Before the nineteenth—and, in many cases, the twentieth—century—labor patterns were seasonal, intermittent, and irregular.

The argument I will be making is that capitalism created strong incentives for employers to keep hours long. In the early stages, these incentives took the form of a fixed wage that did not vary with hours. In the twentieth century, this incentive would reappear in the guise of the fixed annual salary, which proved to be a major reason for the white-collar worker's long hours. Other incentives also came into play by the end of the nineteenth century, such as employers' desires to keep machinery operating continuously, and the beneficial effects of long hours on workplace discipline. Later, peculiarities in the payment of fringe benefits would have an impact. Each of these factors has been important in keeping hours long. Of course, there have been countervailing pressures, the most important of which was the trade union movement, which waged a successful hundred-year struggle for shorter hours. But once this quest ended after the Second World War, reductions in hours virtually ceased. Not long after unions gave up the fight, the American worker's hours began to rise.

CAPITALISM AND THE EROSION OF LEISURE

Moments are the elements of profit.
—LEONARD HORNER,
ENGLISH FACTORY INSPECTOR

Capitalism steadily eroded the leisure that pervaded medieval society. Telltale   12
signs—in the form of modern conflicts over time—appeared in at least one
"capitalist" enclave as early as the fourteenth century, when the textile industry
was faced with an economic crisis. The first response of the cloth makers to this
crisis was predictable: they announced reductions in wages. But they also tried
something new: the imposition of a longer, "harsher" working day. To enforce
this new regime, employers introduced what historians believe are the first
public clocks, which appeared in textile centers across Europe. These work
clocks—or *Werkglocken*, as they came to be called—signaled to workers when
they should arrive at work, the timing of meals, and the close of the day. The
idea was that the clock would replace the sun as the regulator of working hours.
But unlike the sun, the clocks would be under the control of the employer.

As soon as the *Werkglocken* were introduced, they became objects of bitter   13
antagonism. As they were actually not mechanical clocks but bells which were
rung manually, workers, employers, and city officials vied for control of them.
Workers staged uprisings to silence the clocks, fighting what the historian
Jacques LeGoff has termed "the time of the cloth makers." City officials responded by protecting employers' interests. Fines were levied against workers
who disobeyed the injunctions of the bells, by coming late to work or leaving
early. Harsher penalties—including death—awaited those who used the bell to
signal a revolt. Faced with the alliance of employers and state, the workers' resistance failed; and they resigned themselves to the longer hours, the higher
pace of work, and the regimentation of the clocks.

The crisis of labor time in the textile industry illustrates two important   14
points about capitalism and work. First, employers used *time* itself to regulate
labor. In medieval Europe, consciousness of time was vague. The unit of labor
time was the "day." It was tied to the sun and, as I have noted, tended to be
approximate. Modern time consciousness, which includes habituation to clocks,
economy of time, and the ownership of time, became an important weapon
which employers used against their employees. In the words of the English historian E. P. Thompson, time became "currency: it is not passed but spent." As
employers consolidated control over their workforces, the day was increasingly
split into two kinds of time: "owners' time, the time of *work*"; and "their own
time, a time (in theory) for *leisure.*" Eventually, workers came to perceive time,
not as the milieu in which they lived their life, but "as an objective force within
which [they] were imprisoned."

The second point is that working time became a crucial economic variable,   15
profoundly affecting the ability of businesses to survive and prosper. In the textile case, the impetus of the employers to raise hours emanated from an immediate crisis in their geographically widening and fiercely competitive market. In
order to earn sufficient profits to survive, employers took advantage of an in-
tensification of labor. They learned that the market system has a structural

imperative to exploit labor: those who do not succeed in raising hours of work or accelerating the pace of production may very well be driven out of business by their competitors. The rigors of the market are particularly demanding during the inevitable depressions in trade which lower prices and choke off demand for products.

As capitalism grew, it steadily lengthened worktime. The change was felt in   16
earnest by the eighteenth century. The workday rose in the cottage industries which sprang up throughout the English countryside. Rural people, especially women, took on spinning, weaving, lacemaking, and other handicrafts, in their own cottages, in order to earn a little cash to survive. The time commitment ranged from a few hours a day for the better-off, to eight, ten, or twelve hours a day for those who were poor. And this was in addition to regular domestic responsibilities. Outside the cottage, workdays rose as employers encroached on customary periods for eating and resting. Farm laborers, hired by the day, week, or season, were subjected to tighter discipline and stricter schedules. The invention of factories, in the late eighteenth century, allowed employers to squeeze out the vestiges of precapitalist work habits. Eventually, when artificial lighting came into use, the working "day" stretched far into the night, and scheduled hours climbed.

Some workers—such as the most highly skilled, well-organized male craft   17
workers in England—were able to withstand increases beyond the ten-hour mark. But even in some skilled trades, such as baking and potteries, the men could not hold out. In any case, skilled male workers were a minority of the workforce. The majority of laboring people, in both England and America, would eventually work longer days. Men, women, and children in home-based and factory labor, farm laborers, slaves, domestic servants, and even a large fraction of male craftsmen experienced a progressive lengthening of work hours. Twelve-, fourteen-, even sixteen-hour days were not uncommon.

A second change was the loss of nearly all the regular holidays medieval   18
people had enjoyed. The Puritans launched a holy crusade against holidays, demanding that only one day a week be set aside for rest. Their cause was aided by the changing economic incentives of the market economy, particularly the growing commercialization of agriculture which resulted in more year-round activity. In the sixteenth century, the long rise in holidays was arrested; and during the seventeenth, reversed. The eighteenth saw the demise of the laborer's long-honored Saturday half-holiday. By the nineteenth century, the English agricultural laborer was working six days per week, with only Good Friday and Christmas as official time off. A similar process occurred in the United States, during the nineteenth century, as steady employment grew more common.

Taken together, the longer workday and the expanding workyear increased   19
hours dramatically. Whereas I estimate a range of 1,440 to 2,300 hours per year for English peasants before the seventeenth century, a mid-nineteenth-century worker in either England or the United States might put in an annual level of between 3,150 and 3,650 hours.

Workers' progressive loss of leisure stemmed from structural imperatives   20
within capitalism which had no counterpart in the medieval economy. The European manor survived on its own efforts, mainly consuming what it produced

itself. Neither peasants nor their lords were dependent on markets for basic subsistence. They were not exposed to economic competition, nor driven by a profit motive. Their time was their own. Medieval industry was also protected from market pressures. Guilds had strictly defined hours of work, and apparently "few conflicts arose over the time of work." Custom, rather than competition, dictated economic activity. And custom dictated strictly limited work effort.

The growth of markets, both national and international, thrust workers out   21
of their world of custom and into a competitive dynamic. Capitalist businesses, in contrast to medieval manors, strove for maximum profits. They lived or died by the bottom line. Time off was costly, hence bitterly resisted. Whenever one employer managed to squeeze a bit more work out of his workers, others were compelled to follow. As long as a critical mass of employers was able to demand longer hours, they could set the standard. Workers became victims in a larger-than-life struggle for financial dominance. When textile workers in Manchester lost an hour a day, the repercussions would be felt in Lancashire or maybe far across the seas in Lowell. As local outposts were knitted together into a world market, an economic relay system was created—and it operates to this day. American textile workers, who enjoy paid vacations and official five-day weeks, are rapidly losing out to their counterparts in China, where daily, weekly, and hourly schedules are far more arduous.

Given the high value medieval people placed on a leisurely way of life, why   22
did they accede to grueling hours and the loss of their free time? The answer is straightforward. Capitalists were successful because workers lacked alternatives. In the medieval economy, peasants—whether serfs or freepersons—had secure, time-honored access to land. And land was what nearly everyone depended on for survival. Crop failures might lead to hunger or starvation, but most ordinary people retained *social* rights to some part of their manor's holdings, and hence to food. They were not dependent on the market for their "subsistence." Indeed, a "market" in land did not even exist. Custom dictated its use and disposition.

The growth of a world market led to the uprooting of the peasantry from   23
the land that had sustained them for centuries. Lords enclosed open fields, in order to claim ownership to carry out commercial schemes. Peasants lost control over what had once been a "common treasury" from which they had derived a measure of independence. Now their survival depended on participation in the market in labor. They had become proletarians, reduced to selling time and toil. An analogous fate befell artisans, with the elimination of the more or less assured upward mobility of journeymen into masters promised by the guild system. Increasingly, masters turned themselves into small capitalists and permanently hired apprentices and journeymen. The labor practices enforced by guild traditions were jettisoned in favor of reliance on "what the market would bear."

These changes degraded the status of many common people: "To lose con-   24
trol over one's own (and one's family's) labour was to surrender one's independence, security, liberty, one's birthright." In England, this "commodification" of labor had occurred by the seventeenth century. In the United States, the process took place much later and followed a different path; but by the mid-nineteenth century, similar pressures were operating. In the words of E. P. Thompson,

"enclosure and the growing labour-surplus at the end of the eighteenth century tightened the screw for those who were in regular employment; they were faced with the alternatives of partial employment and the Poor Law, or submission to a more exacting labour discipline." As a result, living standards were depressed, and widespread poverty developed. Observers in seventeenth-century England suggest that between a quarter and a half of the rural population lived in poverty. Many commentators maintained that poverty was necessary: "It is only hunger which can spur and goad [the poor] on to labour." The struggle for subsistence had become the paramount fact of life for many people—and in the process, leisure time became an unaffordable luxury.

The Daily Wage and the Expansion of Worktime

The growth of a world market and the creation of a proletariat were major   25
social developments which formed the backdrop for the rise of working hours. Specific features of the emerging labor markets also exacerbated pressures toward long hours. For example, capitalists followed the centuries-old custom of fixing wages by the day, the week, or even the month—in contrast to the modern practice of payment by the hour, which had not been introduced. The daily wage was largely invariant to hours or intensity of labor, a worker earning neither more nor less as the working day expanded or contracted. This flexibility of working hours was a departure from past practice. On medieval manors, serfs' labor obligations to their lords were spelled out in detail, and a certain amount of effort was expected. But with the decline of serfdom, these labor obligations faded away.

The fact that daily wages were fixed gave employers a simple incentive to   26
raise worktime: *each additional hour worked was free.* And because workers were unable to resist the upward pressure on hours, worktime rose dramatically—especially in factories in England and the United States. Marx's famous description of early factories was a harsh reality to the laborers in them: "The 'House of Terror' for paupers, only dreamed of by the capitalist mind in 1770, was brought into being a few years later in the shape of a gigantic 'workhouse' for the industrial worker himself. It was called the factory. And this time the ideal was a pale shadow compared with the reality."

In these "Satanic mills," the custom of a fixed daily wage led the owners to   27
extend hours of toil by whatever means they could manage. They tried "petty pilferings of minutes." They "nibbl[ed] and cribbl[ed] at mealtimes." These methods produced pure profit. One factory operative explained:

In reality there were no regular hours: masters and managers did with us as they liked. The clocks at the factories were often put forward in the morning and back at night, and instead of being instruments for the measurement of time, they were used as cloaks for cheatery and oppression. Though this was known amongst the hands, all were afraid to speak, and a workman then was afraid to carry a watch, as it was no uncommon event to dismiss any one who presumed to know too much about the science of horology.

Testimony of this sort was not uncommon:

> We worked as long as we could see in summer time, and I could not say at what hour it was that we stopped. There was nobody but the master and the master's son who had a watch, and we did not know the time. There was one man who had a watch. . . . It was taken from him and given into the master's custody because he had told the men the time of day.

Similar strategies were in use in the United States, where factory hours might range from seventy-five to ninety hours a week by the second quarter of the nineteenth century.

Of course, workers did not passively accept the theft of their time. Resistance was widespread and took a variety of forms as workers acquired their own timepieces, failed to show up at work on time, or went on strike to recoup lost leisure. In a New Jersey factory, the young hands went on strike to protest the shifting of the dinner hour. One observer noted: "the children would not stand for it, for fear if they assented to this, the next thing would be to deprive them of eating at all." However, until the second half of the nineteenth century, factory hours in both Britain and the United States rose rather than fell. Workers' position in the market where they sold their labor was not favorable enough to win back their leisure time.   28

Although the state stepped in, in both countries, government legislation to limit hours was often ineffective. Factory inspectors found themselves unable to enforce the laws: "'The profit to be gained by it' (over-working in violation of the [Factory] Act) 'appears to be, to many, a greater temptation than they can resist . . . In cases where the additional time is gained by a multiplication of small thefts in the course of the day, there are insuperable difficulties to the inspectors making out a case.'"   29

The incentives to increase hours operated in other parts of the economy as well. Servants were also paid fixed wages. Taken together, farm servants and domestics in middle-class homes made up a significant proportion of workers in both England and the United States in the second half of the nineteenth century. Servants were given room and board, plus some payment, either weekly or perhaps by the season. If their hours of work went up, they received no extra pay. It should come as no surprise, then, that their hours of work were particularly arduous. They would rise in the early hours of the morning and work until evening. The hours of domestic servants frequently expanded to fourteen or fifteen hours a day and were typically above those of factory workers. "I used to get up at four o'clock every morning, and work until ten P.M. every day of the week," recounted one Minneapolis housemaid. "Mondays and Tuesdays, when the washing and ironing was to be done," she began at 2 A.M. Time off was often minimal, as families were reluctant to do without their "help." In the United States, free time was one evening or half-day every week or every other week until the 1880s, after which Sundays were added. But even on a "day off," servants were required to do an average of seven and a half hours.   30

Similar dynamics operated where labor was formally enslaved. Slaves in the American South received a subsistence living—meager food, clothing, and shelter, which did not vary with their hours of work. Field hands worked "every   31 day from 'fore daylight to almost plumb dark"; and during picking season, lighting kept them going at night, often sixteen hours a day. One slave noted: "Work, work, work. . . . I been so exhausted working, I was like an inchworm crawling along a roof. I worked till I thought another lick would kill me." If the owners were able to squeeze out an extra hour here or there, it was purely to their benefit. Slaves' "wages" did not rise.

Employers (and slaveowners) managed to push working hours to the brink   32
of human endurance because they were far more powerful than the common people they hired (or owned). They had the law on their side, to punish those who went on strike or fled the plantation. They had superior resources, to outlast a work stoppage or buy off opposition. They could also invoke the discipline of the market. When businesses are squeezed from above, workers below may find it impossible to resist. In the end, labor lost the battle over working time because it was just too dependent on capital for its very survival.

Piece Rates: "Under-Pay Makes Over-Work"

Not all workers were paid by daily rates. Where it is possible to measure an indi-   33
vidual's output, as in the sewing of garments or the cutting of machine tools, there can be payment by the "piece"—that is, on the basis of actual work accomplished. This form of labor contract would seem to vitiate the pressure toward long hours. In theory, the worker can choose a level of effort, and the employer can pay for only what is done. There is no obvious incentive to long hours.

Piece rates were common in the first phase of industrialization in both Eng-   34
land and the United States. As I have noted, this phase did not take place in factories but was a small scale, low-tech affair, operating out of cottages in the countryside. Similar arrangements also developed in cities. Because the work took place in a worker's own dwelling, this arrangement has come to be called the "putting out," "domestic," or "outwork" system. Workers received raw materials from a capitalist entrepreneur and returned finished goods. In both countries, the bulk of putting out was in textiles, but it was also used for other handicrafts.

Unlike the factory, where the boss or his representatives kept watch over the   35
worker, in the putting-out system the laborer would appear to retain control over the pace and conditions of work. This is certainly the classic interpretation: after turning in finished goods and receiving their pay on Friday or Saturday, workers might spend the next few days drinking, relaxing, and working at a leisurely pace, if at all. Only on Wednesday or Thursday, as the deadline for handing unfinished goods approached, did the pace of work pick up. "Whatever else the domestic system was, however intermittent and sweated its labour, it did allow a man a degree of personal liberty to indulge himself, a command over his time, which he was not to enjoy again." In fact, this "degree of personal liberty" was enjoyed mainly by adult men and mainly in the early days of the system. The system's freedom was illusory. Eventually piece rates would spawn a rise in work effort even more prodigious than that engendered by the factory.

Piece rates led to long hours partly because the rates were set so low. These   36
low rates had a variety of causes. For one thing, the system was dominated by women, whose pay has always been low. A second factor was that there were

virtually no barriers to participating in putting out: there was little capital, and materials were advanced by the capitalist "putters-out." With so many people involved, the putters-out could easily reduce rates. Finally, the structure of these industries has typically been highly competitive, often leaving the capitalist with a small profit margin. Margins were frequently squeezed during downturns in trade, and rates cut to compensate.

For the many piece-rate workers who were perched perilously close to the line between survival and starvation, work was a veritable imperative. The historian J. D. Chambers has provided an apt description of an English village swept up in the system: "They knitted as they walked the village streets, they knitted in the dark because they were too poor to have a light; they knitted for dear life, because life was so cheap." In New York City tenements, women all but sewed themselves to death. They often toiled fifteen or sixteen hours a day in cold, badly ventilated tenements. The introduction of the sewing machine further drove down rates, by increasing productivity and consequently the supply of garments. The system also extended working lives. Both the very old and the very young were led to participate, to raise family income. Three- and four-year-olds were put to work, helping their parents in the cottages or slum dwellings. In England, "schools" were started, where, by age five or six, girls would be taught the discipline of twelve- to fifteen-hour days of lacemaking, knitting, or sewing. [37]

The piece-rate workers were caught in a vicious downward spiral of poverty and overwork, a veritable catch-22. When rates were low, they found themselves compelled to make up in extra output what they were losing on each piece. But the extra output produced glutted the market and drove rates down farther. The system kept them poor. A pair of aphorisms summarized their dilemma: "Over-work makes under-pay" and "Under-pay makes over-work." [38]

Eventually the putting-out system declined in importance in both England and the United States. Piece rates did not disappear but were introduced in factories, spurred on in the early twentieth century by reformer Frederick Winslow Taylor's philosophy of "scientific management." Taylor aimed to eliminate the conflict between capital and labor, by paying strictly on the basis of actual work done—that is, by the piece. In order to make the setting of rates "scientific," and thereby insulate them from conflict, scientific management pioneered the use of time-and-motion studies to determine the pacing of individual tasks within factories, or what were termed "standard times." Piece rates were then calculated on the basis of these standards. [39]

But scientific management was unable to eliminate workplace conflict. The process of discovering standard times became a game of cunning between the operative and the man with the stopwatch. An operative in a machine tool shop explains: "If you expect to get any kind of a price, you got to outwit that son-of-a-bitch! . . . You got to add in movements you ain't going to make when you're running the job! . . . They figure you're going to try to fool them, so they make allowances for that. . . . It's up to you to figure out how to fool them more than they allow for." Once a rate is set, the conflict does not end. Management can always change it. When workers show that they can do more than they have been allocated for, the company frequently reduces its rate: thus, "a couple of [40] operators (first and second shift on the same drill) got to competing with each other to see how much they could turn in. They got up to $1.65 an hour, and the price [rate] was cut in half." With lower rates, they had to work more. The tendency for underpay to create overwork thus reappeared in another guise.

WAGE WORKERS' RISING HOURS

The resistance of workers to long hours did not lead back to the earlier, more relaxed patterns of work but to cementing the link between hours of work and pay. As employers demanded more work, workers demanded more money. Eventually, the principle of paying by the hour (or even smaller units) became the dominant form of labor contracting. Although tying wages to workhours would seem to eliminate the employer's preference for long hours, with extra hours no longer being free, other factors perpetuated the employer's interest in long hours. These were increased mechanization in the second half of the nineteenth century, the use of long hours and the concept of employment rent, to promote workplace discipline, by the twentieth century, and the bias created by the structure of fringe benefits since the Second World War. □

41

◢ REREADING FOR UNDERSTANDING

1. What is Schor's thesis? Where do you find it?

2. If, as Schor claims, it is a myth that our forebears worked longer and harder than we do, why have we believed it?

3. How did the medieval concept of time differ from our present-day view? What accounts for that difference?

4. In addition to greater leisure, another important feature of the precapitalist society, Schor claims, was the lack of consumerism and materialism. To what does she attribute this absence? What effect did it have on people's attitudes toward work?

5. Trace the various factors that combined with the growth of capitalism to make the workday longer and longer.

◢ RESPONDING

1. Discuss the picture of medieval life that Schor paints. Do you believe her portrayal of the average worker's existence to be complete and honest? Has she overlooked or ignored anything in suggesting that medieval workers were free from materialistic concerns and enjoyed greater leisure than their modern-day counterparts?

2. If you have read Perry Pascarella's piece, "What Happened to the Old Protestant Ethic?", evaluate Schor's thesis that capitalism is responsible for long working hours and the loss of leisure time. Does a study of the

Protestant work ethic suggest that there may have been other forces behind this phenomenon?

3. Schor notes that the commodification of labor resulted in increasing numbers of people living in poverty. She notes that "many commentators maintained that poverty was necessary: 'It is only hunger which can spur and goad [the poor] to labour'" (par. 24). To what extent do we accept that statement as true today? You may want to read some of the essays on welfare and workfare in the Controversies section of this chapter.

ARUNODAY SAHA

In 1992, Japanese Prime Minister Kiichi Miyazawa caused a minor international furor when, in response to a comment by Japanese House Speaker Yushio Sakurauchi that American workers were "lazy" compared to their Japanese counterparts, he suggested that Americans "may lack a work ethic." American labor unions and both political parties jumped to refute the prime minister's claim, but Miyazawa had simply given voice to what many Americans and others had secretly assumed to be true: Japanese business is more productive than American business because the Japanese work harder than Americans. The Japanese work ethic is legendary and many American corporations have tried to emulate Japanese managerial practices to get the same loyalty and industry from their workers. In this essay, Arunoday Saha, a professor at the National Institute for Training in Industrial Engineering in Bombay, India, suggests that the hard work and dedication of the Japanese worker have their source not in any particular management strategy, but in the values associated with Zen Buddhism that inform all aspects of Japanese culture.

Zen and the Japanese Work Ethic

The essence of Japanese culture is said to lie in the group rather than in the individual. According to the viewpoint favoured in most writings on Japanese society and culture, the Japanese are a group-oriented people; they like to work in groups and have always worked in association with one another, and social pressures on the individual to conform happen to be irresistible. The nail that sticks out, as the popular saying goes, gets hammered down.

However, like any generalisation about large complex societies, excessive emphasis on the primacy of collective behaviour in Japan is prone to oversimplification, overshadowing the fact that the country's ethos also stresses the importance of the individual, and has a place for strong persons. The individualism inherent in Japanese culture, of course, differs from the Western; it is less assertive, seeking not separateness but harmony with society. Japanese individualism has roots in indigenous tradition, more specifically that component of indigenous tradition known as Zen Buddhism.

As is well-known, art forms such as tea-ceremony, *haiku* poetry, *sumiye*   3
painting, miniature gardening, and judo are peculiar to Japan. Experts agree
that Zen provides the source of inspiration in these fields of endeavour.

In the case of work behaviour and certain other aspects of industrial func-   4
tioning—also unique to Japan—similar claims are not made. Yet, values associated with Zen may be shown to operate in the sphere of industry and business,
shaping, among other things, the famous Japanese work ethic.

HISTORICAL BACKGROUND

Though popularly believed to have originated in India modern scholarship   5
holds the view that the Zen sect of Buddhism developed wholly in China
through the fusion of classical Mahayana and Taoist ideas. The central feature
of Zen (derived from the Chinese word, *Chan* which in turn is a corruption of
the Sanskrit, *dhyana*, meaning meditation) consists in its exclusive reliance on
meditation for achieving "enlightenment," conceived of as "the realisation of the
Buddha nature inherent in each individual."

The historical founder of the important southern school of Zen or Rinzai   6
was the reputedly illiterate, practical-minded farmer, Hui-neng (637–713 A.D.).
His stress on the dynamic nature of the meditation process against the older
emphasis on quietism (the Indian *samadhi*) set the revolutionary iconoclastic
tone of Zen. Quietism, according to Hui, is synonymous with death. Hui also
preached forthrightness, self-reliance, the doctrine of "no-mind" and avoidance
of book learning.

Around 750 A.D. Pai-cheng, in another major ideological shift from the   7
main current of Buddhism introduced manual work in his monastery. He
required monks to devote part of the day to hard physical labour. This feature,
entirely alien to Indian Buddhism, later found expression in the maxim, "No
work, no food," becoming a cardinal tenet of the faith.

Introduced into Japan during the thirteenth century, Zen quickly found   8
favour with the samurai warriors of the time as suiting their needs best. Soldiers
flocked to Zen monasteries eager to be taught by the priests; they wanted a philosophy that would inculcate in them the quality of bravery and help them
overcome fear of death. The instructions, moreover, had to be direct and practical. And Zen masters met these requirements effectively.

Non-military, commercial activities also engaged the attention of the Zen   9
clergy. During the Ashikaga period (1338–1573) they actively participated in
trading ventures with China. It was in the Zen monastery called Myoshinji that
a new method of accountancy was perfected. Thus, almost from the beginning
the religion had been associated with economic activities.

The long peace imposed by the Tokugawa shoguns (1600–1867) greatly de-   10
creased opportunities for actual combat, encouraging Zen priests to increase
their preoccupation with mundane matters. Worldly pursuits became imbued
with a kind of religious spirit as masters like Takuan (1573–1645) and Shozan
Suzuki (1579–1655) consistently preached that if a man puts his heart and soul
into his secular profession, he was in fact serving Buddha as well. "Farming is
nothing but the doings of a Buddha," Shozan taught farmers. To merchants he

told, "Renounce desires and pursue profits wholeheartedly, but you should never enjoy the fruits of your own labour." Each individual could gain salvation by doing his own task well—as long as he kept away from "the three poisons of greed, anger and idle complaint."

Zen became increasingly popular after 1868, the year of restoration of the   11
Meiji emperor, which marked the entry of Japan into the modern era. Though the proportion of population declaring themselves as Zen Buddhists remained a minority, the religion came to be identified with Japanese culture as such. In more recent times, Zen has achieved popularity in the West as an exotic product of the Eastern mind.

THE PHILOSOPHY AND THE TECHNIQUE

As mentioned, the central feature of Zen is meditation (*zazen*). Though derived   12
from Indian sources the objective of meditation in Zen Buddhism is not, as in Indian *yoga*, the suspension of mental faculties in a trance. On the contrary, Zen seeks to augment the powers of the mind "by focusing them through the most intensive exercise into a state of one-pointedness."

In a typical *zazen* session the meditator sits cross-legged in an erect posture   13
keeping his spine straight and controlling his breath. Consciousness is first sought to be swept clean of all previous perceptions and ideas, bringing about the so-called "no-mind" state. This implies "liberation from preoccupation with the self" as well as exclusion of the intellect. According to Zen Buddhism, knowledge is derived, not from reasoning or exercise of the intellectual faculties, but from intuition and experience. By excluding outward sensations Zen seeks to lead the empirical consciousness to its deeper unconscious sources. And in *satori*—the end-objective of meditation efforts—the meditator achieves "enlightenment," the ultimate indescribable experience of fulfilment. The effect of these practices on the individual has been summed up by Buddhist scholar, C. Humphreys: "With clarity of mind whence emotion and passion have ebbed away comes an inward certainty of purpose and the right way to achieve it, and the certainty is quite impersonal."

The technique and the philosophy described above may be applied to any   14
task. This is facilitated by the fact that Zen has no special doctrines; it is, for instance, without such common religious conceptions as sin, God, grace, salvation, a future life. "Clear-sighted" Zen masters have been known to avoid fixed doctrines. They teach—and their teachings are often borrowed from non-Zen sources—whatever the situation demands. But the individual situation in each case is emphasised, along with the fact that the activity one happens to be engaged in should be performed with resolution, dedication and with single-minded sense of purpose.

Modern Zen protagonists recommend the practice of *zazen* to practical   15
persons devoid of religious intent as a means of controlling the mind and locating hidden sources of energy. Writes Albert Low: "Through the practice of ordinary (non-religious) Zen, a manager could learn to control his mind and mobilise his energy in a way that he could never imagine to be possible. This

mobilisation of energy would make way for a more persistent yet dynamic approach to work, for greater flexibility and for a deep awareness of our place in the scheme of things which come from liberation."

Many Japanese managers practice *zazen*. One famous practitioner of the [16] technique has been Konosuke Matsushita. Following his example, executives of the Matsushita Company are known to meditate regularly. Early in his career, during a visit to a Zen temple, Matsushita had realised "the power drawn forth by religion at work among men." Everything worked in the place with such smoothness and clockwork precision that he called it the "epitome of skilful management." The industrialist then began to emphasise "spiritual values" in running his enterprises.

Some Japanese firms send their fresh recruits to Zen temples where, apart [17] from the skills of meditation, they acquire physical discipline. Apparently, like the samurai of old, modern company soldiers still learn how to fight battles— this time of economic competition—from Zen masters.

That living in a Zen monastery for some time can be very helpful in instill- [18] ing the values of Japanese culture is borne out by the following description by an American initiate who spent a few days there: "It was grim. We had to get up at four every morning and meditate for a whole hour. That means kneeling bolt upright and not moving a muscle. If you do, the *roshi*—that's the Zen master— comes and beats you with a stick. We had three meals a day: unsalted rice gruel and sour pickled plum for breakfast. . . . When we weren't meditating we had to chop wood and dig for vegetables. We were also sent out each weekend to go around the district with a begging bowl asking for alms. The *roshi* explained this was to teach us humility".

TRAINING AND WORKMANSHIP

Since historical times meditation techniques developed in Zen monasteries [19] have been applied to training for practical pursuits. Samurai warriors wishing to perfect their skills in the art of fencing, first used this method which was later extended to other crafts, such as sword-forging. Takuan, one of the greatest fig- ures in the Zen world of the Tokugawa period, gave lessons in fencing. "What is most important in the art of fencing is to acquire a certain mental attitude. . . . This [attitude] is intuitively acquired after a great deal of training," he taught.

Zen stresses training of both mind and body, the former being more im- [20] portant. Meditation aims at training the mind, and the body is conditioned through long, exhaustive exercise. Upon attaining mastery of craft the learner achieves *satori*.

The emphasis is not upon striving for physical dexterity but on obtaining [21] identity of the mind, body and the task being performed. Zen believes that as long as effort exists, duality of the physical abilities and skill hinders mastery; in a state of perfection, the performance of a task is rendered effortless.

Doing a job should not only be effortless but unconscious as well. [22] Conforming to the notion of "no-mind," consciousness is first purged of all dis- tracting ideas; and the mental powers, the physical faculties and the task at hand are brought into unity. This type of mastery (wherein the three are undifferentiated) is know as *muga*, literally non-ego. "*Muga*," to quote D. T. Suzuki, Zen's most famous modern exponent, "is something identified with a state of ecstasy in which there is no sense of 'I am doing it.' The feeling of self is a great hindrance to the execution of a work."

These ideas ingrained in the cultural tradition, it is postulated, have influenced modern-day Japanese attitudes toward training and work. In no country is learning emphasised as in Japan. "An obsessive concern for training is a distinctly Japanese ethos," observe Pascale and Athos. Japanese managers tend to think that the key to improved performance and virtually all industrial problems lies in training. This conviction has sometimes been carried to seemingly unrealistic limits—as when one company which felt dissatisfied with its performance decided to subject its entire staff to an intensive development programme lasting from 6.30 A.M. to 11.00 P.M., every day, six days a week, for a period of three years.   23

In Japanese organisations training constitutes an inextricable part of work, continuing throughout the employee's career. A wage or salary-earner in a manufacturing enterprise in Japan, it has been estimated, spends about eight hours per week in activities related to self-improvement, half of which is on his personal time. Almost everybody, from the lowest category of workman to the company president, participates in some form of learning or other. Operatives train not only in their own job skills but in allied tasks as well, thereby becoming multifunctional, and managerial staff may be shifted to many different departments within the organisation.   24

As in training, the influence of Zen is felt in the performance of work. The fifteenth century tale of the sword-maker, Yoshihiro illustrates the traditional ideal of a manual worker. Yoshihiro is angered when another sword-maker, Masamune bags the prize in a sword-making competition. Suspecting an unfair decision and wishing to find out the truth himself, he travels a long distance to Masamune's place. There he finds Masamune's workshop, "like a sacred shrine every nook and cranny having been purified." The master swordsmith and his two assistants dressed in ceremonial robes "put their heart and soul into each stroke of the hammer." Says Yoshihiro, kneeling before his rival, "I am ashamed at my self-conceit. I had no idea of the spiritual factor in the art of sword forging. Mere skill cannot produce a masterpiece."   25

An identical spirit may be observed in modern factories. Reports Leddihn: "My visit to the new plant at Noritaka, the china and ceramics manufacturer at Nagoya was equally impressive. The atmosphere in the still highly individualised workshops, where skilled personnel paint and design on each object, resembles that of a hospital. Everything is white and spotless; there is no noise, no loud noise, utmost concentration."   26

Another observer states: "The factories I visited were exceptionally quiet and orderly, regardless of the type of industry, the age of the company, its location or whether it was a US subsidiary. Clearly, this orderliness was not accidental. . . ."   27

A factor that contributes to the cleanliness of the factory floor is the virtual absence of inventories. This achievement has partly been the result of just-in-   28 time, a method of manufacturing devised by Toyota Motors, following the 1973 oil crisis, which since then has spread to other companies. Just-in-time means receiving and producing the right units in the right quantities at the right time. As delays are unacceptable, JIT requires, above all, strict control and iron discipline at all stages of the production process. Care must, at the same time, be taken to make fault-free items since, in the absence of inventories, defectives would upset the entire system. Though, following Japan's example, variations of JIT have been introduced in other countries, only Japanese society seems capable of generating the degree of precision and co-ordination required for the success of just-in-time in its real sense.

Both in manual skills as well as in the care and dedication operatives bestow on every aspect of production, ordinary workers in Japanese industry appear to excel over their competitors in other countries. The post-war reputation of Japanese products for quality and reliability arises mostly out of superiority of human factors rather than from advanced technology. 29

Underlying much of Japanese successes in economic endeavours has been the quest for becoming better and better. *Kaizen*, a word frequently heard in Japanese organisations, best expresses this notion of continuous striving for excellence. *Kaizen* implies endless effort at improvement as an end in itself. Perfection is to be achieved through group co-ordination and through intensive, continuous training. 30

The psychological mechanism behind the Japanese pursuit of excellence may be understood with the help of the concept of "imperfectionism," proposed by Hiroshi Minami. The word "imperfectionism" describes a typical Japanese conviction that unhappiness and misfortune are not to be negatively endured or diverted but are rather to be positively accepted as desirable for self-cultivation. Consequently, a person experiences a perceptual sense of dissatisfaction with his performance and strives for betterment but is never satisfied with the results obtained. In fact, he dislikes the possibility of becoming satisfied, a sentiment that essentially reflects the pessimistic world-view of Buddhism whose main teaching, "Life is suffering" has conditioned Japanese thinking for centuries. The theme that life consists overwhelmingly of pain and endurance occurs frequently in Buddhist literature. A hymn composed by the Zen monk, Hakuin reads, "This world of ours is but a world of endurance, and nothing turns out as we wish." 31

Opinion surveys amply support the viewpoint that the majority of Japanese remain dissatisfied with their performance at work. Lincoln, who conducted a study of work attitudes of manufacturing employees in Japan and the USA, found large differences in job satisfaction scores. American employees seem more satisfied with their jobs than do the Japanese. This, as the author suggests, may mean "restless striving for perfection and ongoing quest for fulfilment of lofty work values" on the part of the Japanese. In the case of Americans, greater satisfaction scores possibly reflect low job expectations and pre-occupation with leisure-time pursuits. Besides, the American impulse is to put the best face on things, to be upbeat and cheerful even in situations of high uncertainty and when the future looks bleak. The Japanese, it appears, bias their assessments in the opposite direction, colouring their evaluation of almost 32 everything with a large dose of pessimism, humility and understatement. The word "happiness", for instance, rarely occurs in their conversation. If a person were to declare that he is happy, to his listeners the statement would sound quaint and affected.

ETHIC OF HARD WORK AND SIMPLE LIVING

That the Japanese are a very diligent and hard-working people is possibly the strongest and most persistent stereotype about them in other countries. And this view coincides with the opinion most Japanese hold about themselves; responses to questionnaires reveal that the majority prefer to characterise themselves as *kin ben* (diligent, hard-working). The Japanese also surpass the Americans, the Germans and the British in considering work as the central interest of their lives. The "workaholism" of the Japanese people, one often hears the complaint, encourages unfair competition as it increases production for export while maintaining domestic demand at a low level.   33

Despite their country's status as the world's biggest creditor nation, employees in Japan continue to put in the greatest amount of work time than any industrialised country; on the average, they spend 200 hours per year more than their counterparts in the United States. Only 1 out of 3 workers enjoys a 5-day week and employees, by and large, spend just half their vacation time, generally 15 days a year.   34

Statistics alone does not convey the full picture. In offices, staying at one's desk long after quitting time is common. Unlike other parts of the world, the typical Japanese office does not wear a deserted look following scheduled working hours. And many executives lodge near their workplaces, visiting their families only on weekends.   35

The roots of this intense predilection for keeping busy may be traced to Zen Buddhism which not only esteems work but emphasises its indispensability for survival. Zen literature abounds in such phrases as "in the marketplace," "in the middle of the crossroads," meaning busily engaged in all kinds of activities, "the face smeared with dirt and the head covered with ashes," describing a man who toils. "An idle man in the daylight" represents an expression of contempt.   36

In Judeo-Christian tradition, on the other hand, the attitude toward work is basically negative. God in wrath punished Adam and all his progeny to earn their daily bread through strenuous labour. The later Protestant ethic inverted the approach. "Idleness is bad," "Being busy is good" or so, taught the Protestants.   37

Not surprisingly, the Japanese language does not contain a word for leisure. The word *yoka* used to convey the idea of leisure literally means "leftover time," and has negative connotations. A person with *yoka* in his hands would thus be understood to be not doing too well. This contrasts with the normal pattern one finds in Europe and the United States of dividing time into two distinct sectors, leisure and work—a division also prevalent in ancient Rome where *otium* (idleness) represented the time segment allotted to non-productive matters whereas *negotium* was the segment dedicated to business.   38

In Japan, work and leisure are not sharply differentiated; a grey area usu-   39
ally lies between business and pleasure. Playing golf with business associates on
company time, treating clients to a sumptuous meal on expense account or
spending an evening at the bar with colleagues may not be directly productive
or be regarded as work in the conventional sense but can hardly be counted as
free leisure. Such activities, however, alleviate the strain of continuous exertion,
reducing the necessity for off-duty time.

In recent years, the Japanese government and large corporations have been   40
encouraging employees to consume their days of paid leave. This has led to the
growth of leisure-time businesses such as tourism. The new-found desire to
enjoy oneself is partly a natural outcome of affluence, and partly the result of
sensitivity to foreign criticism. Yet, the idea of devoting long hours to work remains so firmly embedded in Japanese life that in a survey conducted in 1987
by the Prime Minister's Office, 53 percent of the respondents said they felt
"guilty" about taking time off. Moreover, by characterising themselves as industrious and the rest of the world as prone to laziness the Japanese render it
difficult for themselves to make the transition to a life of greater leisure, since
by doing so they run the risk of losing a large part of their distinctiveness.

In addition to hard work, simple living is emphasised in Zen Buddhism,   41
which has an important place for monastic life. "The monastery is not meant
to be a hiding place from the worries of the world; on the contrary, it is a training station where a man equips himself for life's battlefield," writes D. T. Suzuki.

The attitude of "this-worldly" asceticism, advocated by Zen, has filtered into   42
modern economic activity. Since the Meiji Restoration, till the economic boom
of the 1960s, the average Japanese consumer did not display what economists
call the "demonstration effect", or the desire to imitate more lavish consumption
patterns prevalent in affluent countries (a phenomenon that plagues development efforts in most Third World nations). In fact, so deep-seated and widespread has been the ideal of asceticism that the immensely wealthy *zaibatsu*
families, who dominated the Japanese economy in pre-war times, severely limited their personal expenditure. Elaborate house rules prohibited conspicuous
consumption. In the Yasuda *zaibatsu*, for example, a fixed stipend was allotted
annually to each of the thirteen families and every individual was required to
enter all his personal expenses in a register which was audited every six months
by the head office.

Even in present-day Japan, the average individual is said to be "not a good   43
consumer" (by Western standards). His savings ratio remains one of the highest in the world. In other countries mostly the well-to-do save, but not in Japan
where ordinary wage and salary earners willingly forego consumption. The savings of ordinary men and women in banks served as the major source of in-
vestible funds required for the nation's post-war economic growth. . . .

INDEPENDENCE AND SELF-RELIANCE

In a typical Zen meditation session the personal efforts of the initiate assume   44
utmost importance; the master merely points in the right direction. (This

incidentally contrasts with the master-disciple relationship prevalent in India where dependence on the guru is indispensible for the disciple's spiritual welfare). Zen also considers scriptures, relics and other familiar religious paraphernalia as "useless encumbrances". Neither is there any dependence on God or other supernatural agencies. The spirit of independence and self-reliance fostered by these beliefs and practices finds expression in economic endeavours. . . .

The careers of numerous Meiji industrialists bear ample evidence to the fact   45 that those who transformed Japan from a technologically backward country into a modern state were independent-minded persons possessed of extraordinary initiative and drive. Emerging often from obscure and non-commercial backgrounds, men such as Asano Soichiro, Yasuda Zenjiro and Iwasaki Yataro ventured into hitherto unexplored fields of economic activity and struggling frequently against prodigious odds succeeded in establishing industrial and commercial empires.

The pattern of post Second World War reconstruction resembled the earlier   46 industrialisation effort. Though numerous old business houses staged a comeback, there were many new entrepreneurs—Ibuka Masaru, Soichiro Honda, Konosuke Matsushita and others. These men displayed a self-determination and drive no less remarkable than that of the Meiji pioneers, enabling Japan to rise from defeat and destruction to become a dominant industrial power.

The tendency toward independence and self-reliance is further manifested   47 in Japan's assimilation of Western science and technology. Oya Shin'ichi mentions an interesting case of the difference between Chinese and Japanese methods of translating Western scientific books into their respective languages, during the initial period of contact with the West. In China the job was usually done by a team of two persons. A foreigner fluent in spoken Chinese would read aloud the contents of a book which a Chinese colleague recorded in written Chinese. Using this method the translations were rendered accurate right from the beginning but the Chinese failed to develop independent translation skills.

The Japanese, on the other hand, did not adopt this system of collaboration   48 with foreigners. They welcomed opportunities for instruction in European languages but for translations into the Japanese language one person by himself or in co-operation with his other countrymen would do the work. Consequently, the initial results were quite clumsy with many distortions, but there was cumulative improvement in skills, and translations gradually became more fluent and accurate.

Ever since the Japanese became aware of the superiority of Western tech-   49 nology and were convinced about the necessity of learning it, they have opted for a more difficult approach aimed at attaining self-reliance instead of settling down into a relationship of permanent dependence (as is preferred by most presently developing countries). The objective has always been to master foreign technology quickly and then dispense with the tutelage. Wrote Valentine Chirol at the turn of the century: "At first they no doubt applied themselves merely to copy the products of European industry, and as with all beginners, their first attempts were often clumsy and imperfect but with unswerving tenacity of purpose they kept on plodding away until they had in most cases remedied their defects and in some improved even upon their models."

For example, when the Japanese government bought its first Jacquard loom, it engaged craftsmen to dismantle and assemble the machine time after time until the technology had been fully learnt. They could then think of safely substituting some of the metal parts with wood.   50

The flow of scientific and technological know-how from the West came to a halt following Japanese political adventures in Asia during the mid-thirties. This forced the country to become self-reliant. Massive investment in research and development followed, and soon factories were turning out guns, tanks, ships and airplanes of a standard capable of challenging the military might of the most industrially advanced nations on earth.   51

After war-time devastation the Japanese once again felt the need to extensively borrow technology from the West. During the last two decades after 1945, they bought the bulk of new knowledge produced abroad, paying for it in royalties, outright purchases and equity participation. But the contracts came to an end soon after local technicians had mastered all the patented processes. Japanese companies then began investing in research and development to improve production methods and product designs; innovations were mostly dictated by the need to reduce costs, improve quality and marketability. And successes in these fields gave them an edge in international competition. Since the mid-eighties, having learnt all that the West could offer, R&D investment has been directed toward invention or discovery of new processes and products. The century-old Japanese quest for technological self-reliance may thus be said to have reached a successful conclusion.   52

CONCLUSION

Underpinning many of the factors that have contributed to Japanese economic success of modern times—the unique work ethic, pragmatic orientation, emphasis on training, entrepreneurial boldness, quest for technological self-sufficiency—has been the ideology of Zen Buddhism, transferred to the sphere of industry and commerce. This may not be obvious to the superficial observer. Culture is essentially a background phenomenon, shaping human values and institutions and thereby influencing behaviour. To understand Japanese economic practices—particularly those that are not borrowed from the West—one must therefore analyse the cultural environment to which the roots of most of these methods can be traced.   53

Such an exercise, however, does not mean that other countries cannot learn from the Japanese experience; it only implies that the underlying values must be understood and transported, as far as practicable, so that variance between functional methods and the value system is minimised. This is likely to improve the effectiveness of Japanese originated industrial and management practices in other countries. □   54

◢ REREADING FOR UNDERSTANDING

1. Most of us think of Japan as having a group-oriented culture; however, Saha suggests that Japanese culture also places considerable importance on the individual. Japanese individualism and Western individualism are different, however, he points out. Explain that difference. How did Zen Buddhism help to shape the Japanese concept of individualism?

2. The central feature of Zen is *zazen*, or meditation from which one receives enlightenment (par. 12). How could this practice of quiet contemplation be the driving force behind the legendary hard work and diligence of the Japanese worker?

3. What does *yoka* mean (par. 38)? How does it differ from the word "leisure"? What dᵒ ʾe terms tell us about the attitudes of their respective cultures toward work and spare time?

4. Saha compares the way the Japanese and the Chinese have translated Western scientific books. What do the different methods illustrate about each culture? What national Japanese character trait does he suggest is illustrated by this example?

◢ RESPONDING

1. What similarities, if any, do you find between the work ethic inspired by Zen and the Protestant work ethic described by Perry Pascarella in "What Happened to the Old Protestant Ethic?"

2. Saha notes that the Japanese place great importance on training as a necessary component of successful business. To your knowledge, does American business place a similar emphasis on training? Does American education place a strong emphasis on job training?

3. Saha says that Japanese workers are encouraged never to feel satisfied with their efforts, but constantly to seek improvement. He claims this discontent leads to increased productivity and better quality of work. On the contrary, he notes, a far greater percentage of Americans report feeling satisfied with their jobs, resulting in lower expectations of themselves and lower quality of work. Do you agree with the cause/effect equation Saha sets forth here? Are there other positive or negative effects of either way of thinking that he fails to examine?

CONTROVERSIES

Is the Work Ethic Dead
or Is It Killing Us?

BARBARA BRANDT

At the beginning of this century, labor unions pushed for increasingly shorter working hours for Americans. By the end of World War II, the workweek was down to forty hours, and most economists predicted the thirty-five-hour workweek would soon follow. It didn't. Economists like Benjamin Hunnicutt (see next selection) and Juliet Schor (see p. 167) have noted that Americans are spending more time than ever on the job. Barbara Brandt is a writer and member of the Shorter Work-Time Group of Boston, a political action group dedicated to achieving a shorter workweek for American workers. In this essay she examines some of the forces that have served to establish and keep in place a long workweek, and she urges workers to take action on their own behalf to attain more reasonable working hours.

Less Is More
A Call for Shorter Work Hours

America is suffering from overwork. Too many of us are too busy, trying to squeeze more into each day while having less to show for it. Although our growing time crunch is often portrayed as a personal dilemma, it is in fact a major social problem that has reached crisis proportions over the past 20 years.

The simple fact is that Americans today—both women and men—are spending too much time at work, to the detriment of their homes, their families, their personal lives, and their communities. The American Dream promised that our individual hard work paired with the advances of modern technology would bring about the good life for all. Glorious visions of the leisure society were touted throughout the '50s and '60s. But now most people are working more than ever before, while still struggling to meet their economic commitments. Ironically, the many advances in technology, such as computers and fax machines, rather than reducing our workload, seem to have speeded up our lives at work. At the same time, technology has equipped us with "conveniences" like microwave ovens and frozen dinners that merely enable us to adopt a similar frantic pace in our home lives so we can cope with more hours at paid work.

A recent spate of articles in the mainstream media has focused on the new   3
problems of overwork and lack of time. Unfortunately, overwork is often portrayed as a special problem of yuppies and professionals on the fast track. In reality, the unequal distribution of work and time in America today reflects the decline in both standard of living and quality of life for most Americans. Families whose members never see each other, women who work a double shift (first on the job, then at home), workers who need more flexible work schedules, and unemployed and underemployed people who need more work are all casualties of the crisis of overwork.

Americans often assume that overwork is an inevitable fact of life—like   4
death and taxes. Yet a closer look at other times and other nations offers some startling surprises.

Anthropologists have observed that in pre-industrial (particularly hunting   5
and gathering) societies, people generally spend 3 to 4 hours a day, 15 to 20 hours a week, doing the work necessary to maintain life. The rest of the time is spent in socializing, partying, playing, storytelling, and artistic or religious activities. The ancient Romans celebrated 175 public festivals a year in which everyone participated, and people in the Middle Ages had at least 115.

In our era, almost every other industrialized nation (except Japan) has   6
fewer annual working hours and longer vacations than the United States. This includes all of Western Europe, where many nations enjoy thriving economies and standards of living equal to or higher than ours. Jeremy Brecher and Tim Costello, writing in *Z Magazine* (Oct. 1990), wrote that "European unions during the 1980s made a powerful and largely successful push to cut working hours. In 1987 German metalworkers struck and won a 37.5-hour week; many are now winning a 35-hour week. In 1990, hundreds of thousands of British workers have won a 37-hour week."

In an article about work-time in the Boston Globe, Suzanne Gordon notes   7
that workers in other industrialized countries "enjoy—as a statutory right— longer vacations [than in the U.S.] from the moment they enter the work force. In Canada, workers are legally entitled to two weeks off their first year on the job. . . . After two or three years of employment most get three weeks of vacation. After 10 years, it's up to four, and by 20 years, Canadian workers are off for five weeks. In Germany, statutes guarantee 18 days minimum for everyone, but most workers get five or six weeks. The same is true in Scandinavian countries, and in France."

In contrast to the extreme American emphasis on productivity and com-   8
mitment, which results in many workers, especially in professional-level jobs,
not taking the vacations coming to them, Gordon notes that "In countries that
are America's most successful competitors in the global marketplace, all working people, whether lawyers or teacher, CEOs or janitors, take the vacations to
which they are entitled by law. 'No one in West Germany,' a West German em-
bassy's officer explains, 'no matter how high up they are, would ever say they
couldn't afford to take a vacation. Everyone takes their vacation.'"

And in Japan, where dedication to the job is legendary, Gordon notes that   9
the Japanese themselves are beginning to consider their national workaholism
a serious social problem leading to stress-related illnesses and even death. As a
result, the Japanese government recently established a commission whose goal
is to promote shorter working hours and more leisure time.

Most other industrialized nations also have better family-leave policies   10
than the United States, and in a number of other countries workers benefit
from innovative time-scheduling opportunities such as sabbaticals.

While the idea of a shorter workweek and longer vacations sounds appeal-   11
ing to most people, any movement to enact shorter work-time as a public policy will encounter surprising pockets of resistance, not just from business
leaders but even from some workers. Perhaps the most formidable barrier to
more free time for Americans is the widespread mind-set that the 40-hour
workweek, 8 hours a day, 5 days a week, 50 weeks a year, is a natural rhythm of
the universe. This view is reinforced by the media's complete silence regarding
the shorter work-time and more favorable vacation and family-leave policies of
other countries. This lack of information, and our leaders' reluctance to suggest
that the United States can learn from any other nation (except workaholic
Japan) is one reason why more Americans don't identify overwork as a major
problem or clamor for fewer hours and more vacation. Monika Bauerlein, a
journalist originally from Germany now living in Minneapolis, exclaims, "I
can't believe that people here aren't rioting in the streets over having only two
weeks of vacation a year."

A second obstacle to launching a powerful shorter work-time movement is   12
America's deeply ingrained work ethic, or its modern incarnation, the workaholic syndrome. The work ethic fosters the widely held belief that people's work
is their most important activity and that people who do not work long and hard
are lazy, unproductive, and worthless.

For many Americans today, paid work is not just a way to make money but   13
is a crucial source of their self-worth. Many of us identify ourselves almost entirely by the kind of work we do. Work still has a powerful psychological and
spiritual hold over our lives—and talk of shorter work-time may seem somehow morally suspicious.

Because we are so deeply a work-oriented society, leisure-time activities—   14
such as play, relaxation, engaging in cultural and artistic pursuits, or just quiet
contemplation and "doing nothing"—are not looked on as essential and worth-

while components of life. Of course, for the majority of working women who must work a second shift at home, much of the time spent outside of paid work is not leisure anyway. . . . Also much of our non-work time is spent not just in personal renewal, but in building and maintaining essential social ties—with family, friends, and the larger community.

Today, as mothers and fathers spend more and more time on the job, we are   15
beginning to recognize the deleterious effects—especially on our young people—of the breakdown of social ties and community in American life. But unfortunately, our nation reacts to these problems by calling for more paid professionals—more police, more psychiatrists, more experts—without recognizing the possibility that shorter work hours and more free time could enable us to do much of the necessary rebuilding and healing, with much more gratifying and longer-lasting results.

Of course, the stiffest opposition to cutting work hours comes not from cit-   16
izens but from business. Employers are reluctant to alter the 8-hour day, 40-hour workweek, 50 weeks a year because it seems easier and more profitable for employers to hire fewer employees for longer hours rather than more employees—each of whom would also require health insurance and other benefits—with flexible schedules and work arrangements.

Harvard University economist Juliet B. Schor, who has been studying issues   17
of work and leisure in America, reminds us that we cannot ignore the larger relationship between unemployment and overwork: While many of us work too much, others are unable to find paid work at all. Schor points out that "workers who work longer hours lose more income when they lose their jobs. The threat of job loss is an important determinant of management's power on the shop floor." A system that offers only two options—long work hours or unemployment—serves as both a carrot and a stick. Those lucky enough to get full-time jobs are bribed into docile compliance with the boss, while the spectre of unemployment always looms as the ultimate punishment for the unruly.

Some observers suggest that keeping people divided into "the employed"   18
and "the unemployed" creates feelings of resentment and inferiority/superiority between the two groups, thus focusing their discontent and blame on each other rather than on the corporations and political figures who actually dictate our nation's economic policies.

Our role as consumers contributes to keeping the average work week from   19
falling. In an economic system in which addictive buying is the basis of corporate profits, working a full 40 hours or more each week for 50 weeks a year gives us just enough time to stumble home and dazedly—almost automatically—shop; but not enough time to think about deeper issues or to work effectively for social change. From the point of view of corporations and policymakers, shorter work-time may be bad for the economy, because people with enhanced free time may begin to find other things to do with it besides mindlessly buying products. It takes more free time to grow vegetables, cook meals from scratch, sew clothes, or repair broken items than it does to just buy these things at the mall.

Any serious proposal to give employed Americans a break by cutting into   20
the eight-hour work day is certain to be met with anguished cries about international competitiveness. The United States seems gripped by fear that our nation has lost its economic dominance, and pundits, policymakers, and business
leaders tell us that no sacrifice is too great if it puts America on top again.

As arguments like this are put forward (and we can expect them to increase   21
in the years to come), we need to remember two things. First, even if America
maintained its dominance (whatever that means) and the economy were
booming again, this would be no guarantee that the gains—be they in wages, in
employment opportunities, or in leisure—would be distributed equitably between upper management and everyone else. Second, the entire issue of competitiveness is suspect when it pits poorly treated workers in one country
against poorly treated workers in another; and when the vast majority of economic power, anyway, is in the control of enormous multinational corporations
that have no loyalty to the people of any land.

Many people are experimenting with all sorts of ways to cope with gruel-   22
ing work schedules. Those with enough money use it to "buy time." They find
child care, order take-out meals, and hire people to pick their children up from
school and do the family shopping. Other options being pursued by both men
and women include actively looking for good part-time jobs; sharing jobs; ar-
ranging more flexible work schedules; going into business for themselves;
working at home; and scaling back on consumption in order to work fewer
hours for lower pay. While these ideas work in some cases, they are often
stymied by a lack of support from employers, and they aren't available to many
people, especially those with lower incomes.

But perhaps the major shortcoming of all these individual responses is pre-   23
cisely that: They are individual. The problem of overwork is a broad problem
of our economic system. It cannot be solved by just one individual, family, or
business. Individual approaches ignore the many larger causes of the problem.

A number of solutions now discussed for the overwork crisis are actually   24
steps in the wrong direction.

The conservative climate of the '80s and '90s has spawned a neotraditional   25
cultural movement that holds up the 1950s as a golden age from which we have
unwisely strayed. Their simplistic solution to the complex set of social issues involved with overwork is to force women back into the home. While we all
should support the right of any woman to freely choose home and family as her
primary responsibility and source of fulfillment, we need to oppose social and
economic policies that either seek to keep women at home or offer them only
limited opportunity—low-paying, low-status, part-time jobs—outside the
home. Such policies are not only unfair to women themselves, they are economically harmful to the many families supported by working women.

The idea of a four-day, 10-hour-a-day workweek has frequently been sug-   26
gested as a superior alternative to the current five-day workweek. But this is no
shortening of work hours, and it ignores the fact that many people who do paid

work also need to care for home and family when they get home. Lengthening the workday would add considerably to the burden these people already carry.

Finally, we should be wary of programs supposedly aimed at helping working parents and their families when the ultimate outcome is to keep parents at work longer—day care for sick children and corporate day care centers open on weekends to accommodate parents who want to work extended hours, for example.   27

Now that public attention is beginning to take note of the mounting personal, economic, and social toll of overwork, it is time to treat overwork as a major political and social issue. To accomplish this, the Shorter Work-Time Group of Boston—a multicultural group of women's and labor activists—proposes a national campaign for shorter work hours that could foster a formidable alliance of unions, community groups, women's groups, and workers in all fields. To begin this campaign, we propose a 10-point plan that could help heal the problems of overwork in its many forms and enhance the quality of all our lives—at home, on the job, and in the community.   28

1. **Establish a 6-hour day/30-hour week.** We propose that a 6-hour day/30-hour week be made the new standard for "full-time work." This new policy would not only give America's workers more time to devote to our families, friends, and personal and community lives, but would also provide benefits to employers in increased efficiency and productivity, reduced accidents and absenteeism, improved morale, lower turnover, and retention of valuable employees.   29

Annual Vacation Time (in weeks)

	By law	By bargaining agreement
Austria	4	4–5
Denmark	—	5
Finland	5	5–6
France	5	5–6
Germany	3	4–6
Greece	4	
Ireland	3	4
Italy	—	4–6
Netherlands	3	4–5
Portugal	4	
Spain	5	5
Sweden	5	5–8
Switzerland	4	4–5
United States	—	2–4
United Kingdom	—	4–6

Source: "Reduction of Working Time in Europe," *European Industrial Relations Review,* No. 127, August 1984: 9–13.

So that workers do not suffer financially from reduction of their work-time, we also propose that any reduction in hours be accompanied by a corresponding increase in hourly income—that the six-hour day be compensated by what was formerly eight-hour pay. Since numerous studies have shown shortened workdays improve productivity, this would not be economically unrealistic.

2. **Extend paid vacations for all American workers.** American workers should enjoy what their counterparts around the world take for granted—four to six weeks of paid vacation each year. Vacation should be based on overall years in the work force rather than tied to the number of years a person has been employed in a particular firm.

3. **Improve family-leave policies.** The Family and Medical Leave Act, vetoed last year by President Bush, needs broad national support so that politicians would fear reprisals from an angry public if they did not support it. This bill would provide job security for people who have to leave work for extended periods in order to care for newborn children or seriously ill family members. Although it does not provide for pay during such leaves, paid leave should be an eventual goal.

4. **Establish benefits for all workers.** At present, employers of part-time and temporary workers are not legally required to provide health insurance, vacations, pensions, or any other benefits. This is especially insidious because women and many low-income workers are most likely to hold part-time and temporary jobs. Congresswoman Pat Schroeder has introduced HR 2575, the Part-Time and Temporary Workers Protection Act, to rectify this situation at the national level.

5. **Discourage overtime work.** Since overtime is detrimental to workers, their families, and the other workers it replaces, we would like to see it eliminated as much as possible. This can be done by mandating the elimination of compulsory overtime and raising the pay rate to double time for voluntary overtime.

6. **Support alternative working arrangements.** We encourage business to increase flex-time and other innovative work-time arrangements that enable employees to better meet their personal and family needs.

7. **Acknowledge workaholism as a social disorder.** In Japan, they even coined a word—*karoshi* (death from overwork) to show this is a serious disease.

8. **Promote awareness that our citizens and our nation as a whole will benefit from shorter work-time.** We need a public education campaign to raise public consciousness about the devastating effects that overwork is having on our health, our families, our communities, and especially on our young people. American workers must have more time to care for their families and restore their communities. This does not mean sending women back home. It means giving all people the time and resources to create their own solutions. If we had more time for ourselves, for example, we would probably see a wide variety of child-care options. In some families women would do this exclusively: in others, women and men would share child-care responsibilities; some people would hire paid help; and others would develop cooperative or community-based programs for their children; many people would take advantage of a mix

of options. The same would probably occur with regard to a wide range of family and community issues.

9. **Look at how the issue of overwork influences the problems of under-** 38 **employment and unemployment.** Because of increasing economic pressures, many corporations are developing a two-tier work force: a core of workers who enjoy good salaries, job security, and full benefits, and another group of lower paid part-time and temporary workers who have no benefits or job security.

10. **Challenge the assertion that we have to enslave ourselves to our jobs in** 39 **order to keep America competitive.** Germany, for example, has mandated shortened work hours, and clearly has not lost its competitive edge in the world economy. ☐

◢ REREADING FOR UNDERSTANDING

1. What is Brandt's thesis? Where do you find it?

2. Brandt notes that the media, though it has paid some attention to the crisis of overwork, has not accurately presented the problem. Explain.

3. If Americans are as overworked as Brandt claims, why aren't more people upset about their long working hours? Why are Americans not demanding workweeks comparable to those of their European counterparts?

4. According to Brandt, what forces serve to keep the long workweek a fact of life in America?

◢ RESPONDING

1. Brandt claims that long working hours not only cause problems for those who are employed, but also contribute to unemployment. Explain this cause/effect relationship. Do you think her logic is sound? Are there other explanations for unemployment that Brandt's equation overlooks?

2. How does Brandt address the fear that America has lost its economic dominance in the world and that only through demanding more of our workers will we regain our place on top?

◢ RESPONDING IN WRITING

Review the ten-part plan that the Shorter Work-Time Group of Boston has proffered to address the problems of overwork. Write an essay critiquing the plan. Which, if any, of these proposals would you support? Why? If there are proposals you could not support, tell why not.

WENDELL BERRY

Poet, novelist, essayist, Wendell Berry (1934–   ) lives and farms in eastern Kentucky a few miles from where his parents and grandparents lived. In his writing, Berry is concerned with our increasing distance from the earth and the kind of work that sustains us physically and spiritually. He has called for a return to traditional methods of agriculture, and to the traditional, mutually supportive agricultural community in which he was raised. In this excerpt from his 1981 book *The Gift of Good Land: Further Essays Cultural and Agricultural*, he argues that a world without real work would be a world without real satisfaction.

Looking Ahead

The university intellectuals are increasingly preoccupied with the future. They are not especially interested in *preparing* for the future—which is something that people do by behaving considerately, moderately, conservatively, and decently in the present—but in *predicting* the future, saying now what will happen then. But one of the fundamental truths of human experience is that we can never be sure what will happen in the next minute, much less in the next century. So what are the reasons for all these botherings of the future by the so-called "futurologists"? I will suggest several.

First, "futurology" is a new academic profession; as such, it provides a lot of new "job openings." The universities, in order to give their graduate faculties work appropriate to their dignity, have turned out too many doctors of philosophy. One way to deal with such a surplus is to featherbed: if the market for these people's brains is oversupplied in the present, then put them to work in the future. Thus is born, or contrived, the "futurologist." He escapes present un- or underemployment by going to work in the future *now*.

Second, "futurology" has suddenly become a very lucrative and glamorous specialty. "Futurologists" are much in demand as conferees and consultants. What they say or write is almost certain to attract public attention. And they give academic prestige to the purposes and ambitions of the corporations. Their "projections" and "worlds of the future" almost invariably rest on the assumption that society cannot help but become more centralized and mechanized, and that people will become more dependent on products that they cannot produce for themselves.

Third, the future is the best of all possible settings for the airy work of academic theorists—simply because neither nature nor human nature has yet taken place there. If you build a castle in the air *now*, people will notice that it does not exist, and you will be accused of pipedreaming; people will think you are crazy. But if you build it in the future, which does not exist, you can call it a "logical projection," your colleagues will talk learnedly about it, you can hope to get a promotion, a salary increase, and to earn large fees as a lecturer and consultant.

These "logical projections" remind me of what farmers sometimes call   5
"winter crops." A winter crop is the crop that a farmer grows in his mind while he sits by the stove in the winter. They are always perfect crops. They are perfect because no sweat has been shed in them, and they are safe from pests, human frailty, and bad weather. Summer crops are another matter. "Futurology" is a way to secure a professional salary for a grower of winter crops; a "futurologist" is a person who *never* needs to worry about growing a crop in the summertime. "That ain't what I call a job," says a neighbor of mine. "That's what I call a position."

The most recent "logical projection" that I have seen is the work of eleven   6
engineering professors at Purdue University. This one proposes to tell us what American life will be like at the beginning of the twenty-first century, and I venture to say that nobody has ever pipedreamed a more dismal "logical projection." The account I read offers a glimpse of the daily life in 2001 of "the fictitious Niray family, living in the imaginary Midland City, U.S.A." A few samples of the text will be enough to show what a perfect "world of the future" this is—for machines.

The hero of this fiction, Dave Niray, breakfasted on a "cylinder of Nutri-   7
Juice"; in 2001 nobody cooked at home but a few eccentrics: gourmets and old-fashioned people. (For some unexplained reason, the future is here described in the past tense.)

After drinking his breakfast, Dave began work. "Dave was an editor and fea-   8
ture writer of Trans Com News Service, one of the world's largest electronic news organizations. Although he routinely worked on stories of national and international events, he seldom left the apartment. His video screen gave him access to all of Trans Com's files. He could interview almost anyone in the world—from prime minister to Eskimo trader—via Vision-Phone."

By Vision-Phone, Dave interviewed "the minister of agriculture in Buenos   9
Aires," composed his article, and then "activated the house monitor computer system," which reminded him "that Rent-A-Robot would be coming in to clean."

Ava, Dave's wife, worked in a factory. She did her work in a "control room"   10
before "an enormous array of keyboards, video screens, and ranks and files of tiny lights." Her work was "kept track of" by a "central computer" known as "the front office." The members of "Ava's crew . . . were, of course, machines." "Although she was called a supervisor, she really did no supervision."

In the evening, the Nirays and their son, Billy, played electronic games on   11
their video-screens.

This is a remarkable world in several respects. These people are apparently   12
able to live an entire day without fulfilling directly any necessity of their lives. They do not take pleasure in any physical contact with anything or anybody. It is not recorded that they ever touch or speak to each other. Nor, apparently, do they ever think a thought. Their entire mental life is devoted to acquiring things, getting promoted, and being electronically amused.

Although this world is enormously sophisticated technologically, it is bio-   13
logically cruder and more irresponsible than our own. The Nirays drank "water
recycled directly from sewage" because "there was really little choice. The wells
had gone dry . . . years ago, and only an idiot would try to purify the stuff that
came out of lakes and streams in the year 2001."

The engineers at Purdue assume that technology can be substituted for   14
biology (as for everything else) with perfect adequacy and safety. There is not
an ecological, economic, political, esthetic, or social consideration anywhere in
the account. In this world, as we see from the Niray's job descriptions, words do
not mean what they say: Ava is a supervisor, not because she supervises, but because she is *called* a supervisor. And knowledge has become simply news. No
one needs to write or speak with authority. It is normal procedure for a reporter
to write an article about a country he has never seen. Technology has thus replaced truth; it has perfected the public lie. (I am writing this, come to think of
it, on Washington's *official* birthday. His *real* birthday is day after tomorrow.)

This "future" society is built exclusively on the twin principles of "con-   15
venience" and "control"—built, that is, on the dread of any kind of physical
activity remotely classifiable as work. "Convenience," raised to this power,
means the exchange of dependence (on oneself, on other people, on other creatures) for "control." It means not needing anything or anybody in particular.
"Control" means, ultimately, *being* controlled, for in this world every room is a
"control room," and no one is ever beyond control.

This "future" is so dismal, I think, because it is so nearly lifeless. The only liv-   16
ing creatures, or the only ones on view, are humans, and humans are rigidly isolated from one another. They make no direct connections. They deal with each
other, as they deal with the material world, only through technology. They live by
"remote control." In nothing else I have read has the meaning of that phrase come
so clear. Remote control is *pure* control—control without contact, without feeling, without fellow-feeling, therefore without satisfaction. Or is it without satisfaction to any but the totalitarian personality that enjoys control for its own sake.

And so the first question raised by the work of these fanciful engineers is: 17
Where does satisfaction come from? They apparently think it comes from living in a state of absolute control and perfect convenience, in which one would
never touch anything except push buttons.

The fact is, however, that a great many people have gladly turned off the   18
road that leads to "Midland City, U.S.A." They are the home gardeners, the
homesteaders, the city people who have returned to farming, the people of all
kinds who have learned to do pleasing and necessary work with their hands, the
people who have undertaken to raise their own children. They have willingly
given up considerable amounts of convenience, and considerable amounts of
control, too, and have made their lives more risky and difficult than before.

Why? For satisfaction, I think. And where does satisfaction come from? I   19
think it comes from contact with the materials and lives of this world, from the
mutual dependence of creatures upon one another, from fellow feeling. But you

cannot talk about satisfaction in abstract terms. There is no abstract satisfaction. Let me give an example.

Last summer we put up our second cutting of alfalfa on an extremely hot, 20
humid afternoon. Our neighbors came in to help, and together we settled into what could pretty fairly be described as suffering. The hay field lies in a narrow river bottom, a hill on one side and tall trees along the river on the other. There was no breeze at all. The hot, bright, moist air seemed to wrap around us and stick to us while we loaded the wagons.

It was worse in the barn, where the tin roof raised the temperature and held 21
the air even closer and stiller. We worked more quietly than we usually do, not having breath for talk. It was miserable, no doubt about it. And there was not a push button anywhere in reach.

But we stayed there and did the work, were even glad to do it, and experi- 22
enced no futurological fits. When we were done, we told stories and laughed and talked a long time, sitting on a post pile in the shade of a big elm. It was a pleasing day.

Why was it pleasing? Nobody will ever figure that out by "logical projec- 23
tion." The matter is too complex and too profound for logic. It was pleasing, for one thing, because we got done. That does not make logic, but it makes sense. For another thing, it was good hay, and we got it up in good shape. For another, we like each other and we work together because we want to.

And yet you cannot fully explain satisfaction in terms of just one day. 24
Satisfaction rises out of the flow of time. When I was a boy I used to dread the hay harvest. It seemed an awful drudgery: the lifting was heavy and continuous; the weather was hot; the work was dusty; the chaff stuck to your skin and itched. And then one winter I stayed home and I fed out the hay we had put up the summer before. I learned the other half of the story then, and after that I never minded. The hay that goes up in the heat comes down into the mangers in the cold. That is when its meaning is clearest, and when the satisfaction is completed.

And so, six months after we shed all that sweat, there comes a bitter cold 25
January evening when I go up to the horse barn to feed. It is nearly nightfall, and snowing hard. The north wind is driving the snow through the cracks in the barn wall. I bed the stalls, put corn in the troughs, climb into the loft and drop the rations of fragrant hay into the mangers. I go to the back door and open it; the horses come in and file along the driveway to their stalls, the snow piled white on their backs. The barn fills with the sounds of their eating. It is time to go home. I have my comfort ahead of me: talk, supper, fire in the stove, something to read. But I know too that all my animals are well fed and comfortable, and my comfort is enlarged in theirs. On such a night you do not feed out of necessity or duty. You never think of the money value of the animals. You feed and care for them out of fellow feeling, because you want to. And when I go out and shut the door, I am satisfied.

That leaves a lot unexplained. A lot is unexplainable. But the satisfaction is 26
real. We can only have it from each other and from other creatures. It is not available from any machine. The "futurologists" do not see it in the future because they do not understand it now. ☐

◢ REREADING FOR UNDERSTANDING

1. According to the Purdue researchers, what will work be like in the twenty-first century? Why does Berry find this future world "remarkable"?

2. Why does Berry call the future described by the Purdue professors "dismal"?

3. Berry says the Purdue model of the future raises this question: "Where does satisfaction come from?" (par. 17). How would the makers of the model answer this question? How does Berry answer it?

4. The meaning of Berry's summer work harvesting hay did not become clear until he raked the hay down from the loft to feed the horses the following winter. Explain.

◢ RESPONDING

1. Reread Berry's description of the hypothetical Niray family. He says that "nobody has ever pipedreamed a more dismal 'logical projection'" (par. 6). Do you agree? Is there anything about the Nirays' existence that seems attractive to you?

2. Berry wrote this essay in 1981; today, we are much closer to the beginning of the twenty-first century. How close have we come to fulfilling the predictions of the Purdue researchers?

3. In "Less Is More: A Call for Shorter Work Hours" (p. 191), Barbara Brandt sees a relationship between our consumer culture and our long workweek. She warns, "In an economic system in which addictive buying is the basis of corporate profits, working a full 40 hours or more for 50 weeks a year gives us just enough time to stumble home and dazedly—almost automatically—shop; but not enough time to think about deeper issues or to work effectively for social change" (par. 19). What similarities do you see between Brandt's theory and the concerns raised by Wendell Berry in "Looking Ahead"? Do you think Berry would agree with Brandt's central claim that Americans spend too much time on the job?

◢ RESPONDING IN WRITING

Berry describes the difficult task of haying as an example of the satisfaction that only hard physical labor in the service of necessity can bring. Can you think of work you've performed that has brought you similar satisfaction? Write an essay about the most rewarding work you have done. Describe the task or job and explain what made it satisfying. What general conclusions about work can you draw from that experience?

BENJAMIN K. HUNNICUTT
GARY BURTLESS

These two essays are presented together, as they originally appeared in *The Wall Street Journal*. Benjamin Hunnicutt, a professor of leisure studies at the University of Iowa, has been researching the loss of leisure and increase of worktime in America for over ten years. His 1988 book *Work Without End: Abandoning Shorter Hours for the Right to Work* was published by Temple University Press. Gary Burtless is an economist at the Brookings Institute in Washington, D.C.

Are We All Working Too Hard?

NO TIME FOR GOD OR FAMILY (Benjamin K. Hunnicutt)

Recently there have been some indications that work-time is increasing. According to Louis Harris and Associates, the average American works 20% more today than in 1973 (up from 40.6 hours to 48.8 hours) and has 32% less free time per week (down from 17.7 hours per week to 8.5). Harris discovered, for example, that small-business people now work over 57 hours a week on average, professional people and those with incomes over $50,000 over 52 and the people whom Harris terms "baby boomers" nearly 52.

The average is up partly because there are more women entering the work force (56% of adult women are now employed). Women, including those who work in the home, put in an average of nearly 49 hours a week. Also, many retired people are returning to the workforce.

News like this is usually welcome, and is sometimes seen as a vindication of President Reagan's tax policies. But the idea that "the more work, the better," is hardly a product of Reaganomics. Not so long ago, however, the Harris report would have been seen by most of us as an indication of retrogression—a time in living memory when most Americans saw human advance in continual work reduction, not continual work creation.

The work-reduction movement began in the early 19th century. Workers adopted the American Revolution's vision of liberty and applied it to their own lives. Shorter hours came to represent a distinctive working-class brand of Jeffersonian liberalism, in which leisure was liberation from bosses, capitalists and toil and was freedom for religion, culture, family life and a host of other nonpecuniary activities.

From sunup to sundown, six days a week and sometimes even seven, the work-week gradually shrank to 60 hours a week by the turn of the century. Over the next two decades, hours fell sharply to 50 hours a week at the end of the First World War. Progress slowed during the 1920s, but accelerated during the Great Depression, when the five-day week became widely accepted. As the average workweek reached 35 hours in the 1930s, unions began to press, unsuccessfully, for a six-hour day. The Second World War inflated hours to an average of 44 a week, and after the war the Fair Labor Standards Act, which had been enacted in 1938 but had been suspended for the duration of the war, set 40 hours as the national norm. And there the workweek has stood.

Intellectuals, politicians and social critics in the century before the Great   6
Depression welcomed work reduction because they believed it would free men and women from the machine and material concerns. Economists such as John Stuart Mill and Simon Patten believed that human needs for material things were limited, and thus could be met in real human history. Freed from economic necessity by industrial progress, ordinary people, Mill hoped, might begin to enjoy "mental culture, moral and social progress . . . and the Arts of Living."

Almost a century later, John Maynard Keynes concluded that working   7
hours would continue to shrink. Keynes wrote that when "the economic problem is solved [to him an immediate possibility in 1933] . . . for the first time since his creation man will be faced with his real, his permanent problem—how to use his freedom from . . . economic cares, how to occupy leisure . . . to live wisely and agreeably and well."

But the work reduction movement ended just after the Depression. Organ-   8
ized labor abandoned the cause. Politicians forgot it. State and federal lawmakers stopped passing laws to reduce hours. Today, shorter work hours are considered by the economists at the Commerce Department to be a negative "leading economic indicator." Intellectuals and writers have ceased dreaming of further work reductions and "necessity's obsolescence," pining instead for a world full of enough work for everyone or brooding about the "work famine" to come. Instead of viewing progress as a means of transcending work, Americans now view work as an end in itself—the more of it the better. No longer is it thought that needs are finite—progress is ever higher levels of consumption, not higher levels of freedom from "necessity."

If anything, most Americans find free time too free. The possibility of the   9
gradual reduction of human labor to its lowest terms forces an increasingly secular people to confront traditional religious questions such as "what is worth doing for its own sake? How is purpose, seriousness, or meaning found in life when it is not given by earthly necessity or external authority?" Americans thus run headlong from free time back to the relative security of finding new problems to solve, new and "serious" tasks to perform, new frontiers to open and more work to do.

Something like a Theology of Work has ensued; Americans now tend to an-   10
swer traditional religious questions (Who am I? Where am I going? What do I need to do to get out of the mess I am in?) in terms of work instead of traditional religions. The new work ethic is not Protestant; there is little or no God-talk associated with it. It is a distinctively modern and secular work ethic/religion.

Over a century ago John Stuart Mill predicted that if the Western world took the road we have in fact taken, the environment must eventually be destroyed: "the earth must lose that great portion of its pleasantness which it owes to things that the unlimited increase in wealth . . . would extirpate from it. . . . I sincerely hope, for the sake of posterity, that [future generations] will be content to be stationary, long before necessity compels them to it."

Mill made the inescapable point: unlimited increases in work and wealth in   11
a limited world is simply impossible. Sooner or later humans will have to deal with freedom from working—either accepting inevitable limits and voluntarily taking time off or, kicking against the traces of limits, plunge themselves into a wasteland of exhausted nature where an epidemic of forced unemployment rages. Freedom from work will come—as William Green the former head of the AFL said, the only choice is "leisure or unemployment."

Whether or not the Harris poll is accurate in its specific findings, there is   12
no doubt that our economy and culture are based on expanding need, consumption and work. Reversing these large-scale historical trends would involve what the British historian E. P. Thompson has called "a novel dialectic," in which we might relearn what workers in the 19th century knew: Work and economic growth are not ends in themselves but are means to healthy living and superior earthly and heavenly values.

IT'S BETTER THAN WATCHING OPRAH (Gary Burtless)

Americans have too little time for leisure. That at least is what they tell poll tak-   13
ers sent around by the Harris organization. According to a recent Harris report, the typical workweek, including the commute to and from work, has risen by six hours—about 15%—since 1975. The amount of time left for leisure has shrunk nearly 10 hours a week, or more than a third.

With a growing scarcity of leisure, Americans are thought to feel more har-   14
ried than ever. They are too driven by the demands of work to enjoy the wholesome pleasures of healthful recreation and quiet family life. Although I have not yet seen the word "crisis," a spate of newspaper and magazine articles informs me that present trends are a matter for grave concern. Yale psychologist Edward Zigler told *Time* magazine last spring that the shortage of leisure means "we're at the breaking point as far as family is concerned."

It is not altogether clear why leisure has suddenly become so scarce. *Time*   15
magazine blames technology, which has sped up the tempo of life, both on and off the job. In "Work Without End," Benjamin Hunnicutt argues that intellectuals, labor leaders and liberal-minded politicians have abandoned the struggle to improve work life through reductions in work hours. In the modern religion of paid work, honest toil is virtuous and leisure disreputable.

But the best available evidence flies in the face of the assertion that leisure   16
is diminishing, Harris polls and anecdotal data notwithstanding. While we lack reliable information about how much time our forebears devoted to leisure, we have a fair idea of how long they worked.

In the middle of the last century the typical workweek was 70 hours—a   17
bit more on the farm and a bit less in urban areas. From 1850 until 1900 the

workweek declined gradually to about 60 hours. The trend toward shorter weekly hours accelerated in the first four decades of this century, with the typical paid workweek falling to just 40 hours in the 1940s, where it has remained ever since.

While the typical paid workweek has remained stuck around 40 hours, it is not strictly accurate to say that average weekly hours at work have stayed constant over the past five decades. There are many fewer workers, like farmers, who work extremely long hours each week. There are many more workers, like women and students, who work fewer hours. Even among full-time workers, hours spent on the job have fallen as sick leave, paid holidays and vacation benefits have become more generous. Taking all of these factors into account, average time spent on the job has *fallen* more than five hours a week—roughly 13%—since 1950. 18

To be sure, work for pay involves far more people in 1989 than it did in 1950. Women typically work fewer than 40 hours a week, bringing down the length of the average workweek. But women are far more likely to work for pay in the 1980s than they were in the 1950s. Over the course of a lifetime, Americans today can probably expect to devote slightly more time to paid work than they did in 1950 because women now spend substantially more hours in paid work even though men spend less. 19

Do these trends mean that Americans have less time for leisure? Surprisingly, the amount of time devoted to leisure has risen rather than shrunk in recent decades. The best evidence for this comes from careful studies in which respondents fill out time diaries showing exactly how they spend each minute of the day. This painstaking procedure is expensive and unquestionably burdensome to respondents. But there is little doubt that it provides more accurate information than a phone call from Louis Harris asking people how many hours they think were spent on leisure during the preceding week. 20

Sociologists in the Survey Research Centers at the University of Michigan and the University of Maryland have administered time diary studies using reasonably consistent methods since 1965. These surveys suggest that among working age adults free time is up, while time devoted to work (including commuting and housework) is down.

Among men, a rise in time devoted to housework and family tasks has been more than offset by a dip in time devoted to paid work, including the commute to a job. Among women, the gain in paid employment has been outweighed by a drop in housework and family responsibilities. Between 1965 and 1985 free time among women rose four hours a week, or about 11%, while time devoted to paid and unpaid work fell about six hours, or 10%. Gains in free time and reductions in time devoted to work were also enjoyed by working-age men, primarily because of a trend toward early retirement. 21

For those who believe leisure is ennobling, I should mention one other finding from these studies. In the past 20 years, the amount of time devoted to watching television has climbed faster than the average amount of free time. To judge by their actual behavior, most Americans who complain they enjoy too 22 little leisure are struggling to find a few extra minutes to watch Oprah Winfrey and "L.A. Law,"

Mr. Hunnicutt argues that labor leaders and politicians have failed in their 23 responsibility to fight for a shorter workweek. This view might be persuasive if we could discover evidence that Americans would prefer to work shorter hours but are prevented from doing so by legal, institutional or technical constraints at the work place. When asked whether they are satisfied with their hours, however, most workers report either that they are satisfied or that they would prefer to work even longer if additional hours were available at the same wage rate. Only a handful of workers report dissatisfaction because hours are too long. In fact, workers who would prefer longer hours outnumber those who would prefer shorter by more than 4 to 1.

Those distressed by the shortage of leisure might consider a heretical 24 thought. Perhaps most people in this country actually like what they do in their jobs. Annual hours of work in the U.S. are higher than in most other countries that have a similar standard of living, but workers here seem to prefer it that way.

Whatever our attitudes toward work, most of us would probably choose to 25 enjoy more leisure if extra leisure had no cost. For nearly all of us, though, additional leisure does have a cost. Those who work for a living would have to give up some time on our jobs and forfeit some wages. Those who cook or work around the house might have to tolerate less palatable meals, less attractive lawns, and less sanitary kitchens. Given these tradeoffs, most of us strike the best bargain we can, compromising our desire for more leisure with our wish to put food on the table (and our need to clean up the mess afterward).

The suggestion that a mandated drop in the workweek eliminates the unpleasant tradeoff between more leisure and less money is fatuous. Shorter hours would leave us with more time but less money to enjoy our leisure. Those who prefer this combination are welcome to choose it. I see no compelling reason to urge political leaders to force it on the rest of us. □

◢ REREADING FOR UNDERSTANDING

1. Hunnicutt says in the first essay that the figures indicating that worktime is increasing would not have been welcome news a century or even a half-century ago. Why not?

2. Hunnicutt claims (par. 10) that a "Theology of Work" has evolved. What does he mean by this?

3. What are some of the costs attached to the increase in worktime, according to Hunnicutt?

4. Burtless, in the second essay, does not dispute that the average workweek has lengthened in the last half of this century; however, he claims that average time on the job has nonetheless fallen since 1950. Explain his reasoning.

5. What research method does Burtless rely on to determine how much leisure time people actually have? Why does he find this method more reliable than the Harris poll Hunnicutt cites?

6. Burtless makes special note of the fact that the amount of time people spend watching television has increased in the past twenty years. Why is this information significant for his argument?

◢ RESPONDING

1. Burtless and Hunnicutt not only present different interpretations of the same information, but also each presents information that seems directly to contradict the other's findings. Can both be right? If so, how? If not, whom are you inclined to believe, and why?

2. Hunnicutt, like Juliet Schor (p. 167) and Barbara Brandt (p. 191), believes that Americans would choose to work fewer hours if they were given that option. Burtless argues that Americans work as much as they do because they enjoy their work. Based on your own experiences with work and your own career expectations, whose argument is more persuasive?

◢ RESPONDING IN WRITING

How do you spend your time? Do you have an accurate perception of the way your time is divided between work and leisure activities? To find out, first try to estimate how you use your time on an average school day. How much time do you spend studying outside class? sleeping? eating? meeting daily needs like shopping, cleaning, cooking, or doing laundry? Do you spend time caring for a family? Do you have a job? How much time do you spend watching television? Then, keep a time diary of the kind Burtless describes for one day. Rather than recording every minute of your time, divide your day into fifteen-minute blocks. As you complete an activity, mark off how many blocks that activity consumed. Compare your estimated time use to your actual time diary. Are you satisfied with the way you spend your time?

CONTROVERSIES

Should People Be Made to Work?

MICKEY KAUS

The demand for welfare reform is almost as old as the program itself. Although there are many forms of welfare subsidies, the program that is most often the target of such demands is Aid to Families with Dependent Children (AFDC). Politicians have, for decades, played to many working Americans' perception that their taxes were being used to support able-bodied people who were simply unwilling to work. In 1992, Bill Clinton campaigned on a promise to "end welfare as we know it" and as president introduced legislation that would have required welfare recipients to leave the welfare rolls within two years. In 1995, the newly elected Republican majority in Congress proposed a similar reform, but unlike Clinton's proposal, Congress's plan provided no job training for welfare recipients and no child-care for those receiving such training. As this book goes to press, the President has agreed to sign a welfare reform bill that, among other things, requires healthy adults to find jobs within two years of entering welfare programs and limits lifetime benefits to five years.

The notion of putting welfare recipients to work is hardly a new one. In 1986, Mickey Kaus, a senior editor at *The New Republic*, published a lengthy and controversial article called "The Work Ethic State" in which he claimed that although the existing welfare system may not have actually caused an antiwork attitude among welfare recipients, it had certainly helped to sustain that mentality. Previous attempts to overhaul welfare programs to include a work component had failed, he said, because they had not addressed that fundamental attitude. Kaus argued that the entire welfare system—including AFDC, food stamps, and housing subsidies—should be dismantled and replaced by a mandatory work-for-aid program modeled on Franklin Roosevelt's Work Projects Administration (WPA), created to provide government jobs for unemployed workers during the Depression. In this excerpt from "The Work Ethic State," Kaus explains how such a program would work.

Only Work Works

What would a program that had a real chance of undermining the underclass look like? The deficiencies in the efforts currently underway give us some idea. First, it would be a program that expects women to work even if they have young children. Second, it would offer work to ghetto men and single women as well as to the welfare mothers. Third, it will have to deal with the related Take Away and Low Wage dilemmas: how can you require welfare recipients to accept private jobs if they pay less than welfare? How can you avoid making workfare or training more lucrative than private sector work?

Solving these problems will take something more radical than any existing workfare plan. It must be far bigger, in order to offer jobs to men, and far tougher in its dealings with young mothers. Above all, the program must unambiguously announce the cultural norm it seeks to promote in place of the culture of welfare.

What is required, I think, is something like this: replacing all cash-like welfare programs that assist the able-bodied poor (AFDC, general relief, Food Stamps, and housing subsidies, but not Medicaid) with a single, simple offer from the government—an offer of employment for every American citizen over 18 who wants it, in a useful public job at a wage slightly below the minimum wage. If you could work, and needed money, you would not be given a check (welfare). You would not be given a check and then cajoled, instructed, and threatened into working it off or "training it off" (workfare). You would be given the location of several government job sites. If you showed up, and worked, you would be paid for your work. If you don't show up, you don't get paid. Simple.

Unlike "workfare" jobs, these jobs would be available to everybody, men as well as women, single or married, mothers and fathers alike. No perverse "anti-family" incentives. No "means test" either. If David Rockefeller showed up, he could work too. But he wouldn't. Most Americans wouldn't. The low wage itself would "ration" the jobs to those who needed them most, and preserve the incentive to look for better work in the private sector. Instead of paying what in effect are high workfare "wages" and then relying on the stigma of welfare to encourage people to leave, this program would pay low wages but remove the stigma. Those who worked in the jobs would be earning their money. They could hold their heads up. They would also have something most unemployed underclass members desperately need: a supervisor they could give as a job reference to other employers. Although the best workers could be promoted to higher paying public service positions, for most workers movement into the private sector would take care of itself. If you have to work anyway, why do it for $3 an hour?

Those who didn't take advantage of these jobs, however, would be on their own. No cash doles. Mothers included. (Remember, we're only talking here about those able to work.) People who show up drunk for their jobs, who show up high, or who pick a fight with their supervisor could be fired (though they could show up again after a decent interval). There would be no need to "require" work. Work would be all that was offered. The problem of having to take away high benefits to force low-wage work would be solved by simply not providing those benefits in the first place.

This is not a new idea. Similar proposals have been advanced in the past by Russell Long and (of all people) Arthur Burns. Basically, it makes the same decision Franklin Roosevelt made in 1934, when he decided to replace a system of cash relief for the able-bodied with the Work Projects Administration, the WPA. Liberals who invoke Roosevelt's "compassionate" legacy tend to forget this anti-dole decision. Meanwhile, Reagan gleefully quotes Roosevelt's description of the dole as "a narcotic," somehow failing to mention that FDR said it in the speech where he proposed the largest government jobs program in the nation's history. In fact, FDR's anti-dole and pro-WPA opinions were of a piece, a decision in favor of work-welfare and against cash-welfare.

Of course, Roosevelt's WPA was designed to combat general unemployment at a time when most of those needing "relief" were veteran workers and nobody imagined that the tiny AFDC program, nestled unnoticed in the New Deal structure, would one day sustain millions of husbandless mothers. Our goal, in contrast, is to break the culture of poverty by providing jobs for ghetto men and women who may have no prior work habits, at the same time as we end the option of a life on welfare for single mothers. It is the transformation of the welfare state into the Work Ethic State, in which status, dignity, and government benefits flow only to those who work, but in which the government steps in to make sure work is available to all. There are a number of obvious objections to so simple a solution:

Will the wage be enough to support a family? No. This is the Low Wage dilemma. The poverty line for a family of three is $8,570. A full-time, minimum-wage job brings in only $7,000, and the government jobs proposed here would pay less than that. But there are ways to supplement the incomes of low-wage workers outside the welfare system (while preserving an incentive to seek better pay). The current Earned Income Tax Credit is one, the innovative Wage Rate Subsidy system of Brandeis professor Robert Lerman (which would pay half the difference between the family breadwinner's wage and $6 an hour) is another. Even Ronald Reagan once proposed this approach while testifying against the guaranteed income in 1972.

A subsidized wage would, in effect, be a guaranteed income *for those who work* (a far more affordable proposition than an income guarantee that doesn't have a base of wages to start from). There is no objection, in the Work Ethic State, to the government sending out checks as long as able-bodied people only get them if they work. Supplementing wages is a much better solution to the

Low Wage problem than pretending the underclass can get "good jobs" that pay enough in themselves to support a family.

Will people be allowed to starve? The state's basic obligation, in this scheme, 10 is to provide dignified work for all who can work, and a decent income for the disabled. There will be those who refuse work. Many ghetto men, at least initially, will prefer the world of crime, hustle, and odd jobs to working for "chump change." One advantage of the Work Ethic State is that criminals can be treated as criminals, without residual guilt about the availability of jobs. Others—the addled and addicted—will simply fail at working, or not even try. Even a fraction of welfare mothers, the most employable underclass group, will have trouble. "The workplace is so foreign to so many people who are second- and third-generation dependents," says Tom Nees, a Washington, D.C., minister whose Community of Hope works with welfare families poor enough to be homeless.

The first underclass generation *off* welfare will be the roughest. Those peo- 11 ple who fail at work will be thrown into the world of austere public in-kind guarantees—homeless shelters, soup kitchens, and the like—and the world of private charitable organizations like Nees's. This aid would be stigmatizing (as it must be if work is to be honored), but it could be compassionate. Nobody would starve. Counseling, therapy, training, could be offered, even subsidized by the government, in order to help these people back on their feet. The one thing the government would not offer them is cash.

What about mothers with young children? The government would announce 12 that, after a certain date, single mothers would no longer qualify for cash welfare payments. The central ambiguity of our welfare system—whether single mothers should work—would be resolved cleanly and clearly in favor of work. This hard choice is a key way the Work Ethic State would hope to break the self-perpetuating culture of poor, single-parent families. Teenage mothers who had babies could no longer count on welfare to sustain them. They would have to work like everyone else, and the prospect of juggling motherhood and a not-very-lucrative job would make them think twice, although it would also offer a way out of poverty that Charles Murray's starvation solution would deny.

What would the children do when their mothers were working? If the gov- 13 ernment is going to expect poor mothers to work, then it will have to provide day care for all those who need it. This will be expensive (Massachusetts pays $2,800 a year for each day-care slot). But it won't be as prohibitively expensive as many who raise the day-care issue seem to believe. In every state in which free day care has been offered to AFDC mothers, demand has fallen below predictions. "It is never utilized to the extent people thought it would be," says Barbara Goldman of MDRC. Most mothers, it seems, prefer to make their own arrangements. Whether those arrangements are any good is another question. The government might actually have to take steps to encourage day care, as part of the general trend toward getting kids out of underclass families and into school at an early age.

What about mothers with very young children, two years and under? A desti- 14 tute mother with a newborn infant presents the basic AFDC dilemma in its starkest form. It *is* a dilemma, meaning there are arguments on both sides. One alternative is to allow temporary cash welfare for the first two years of a child's life, with a three-year limit to avoid the have-another-kid loophole. A two-year free ride is better than a six-year free ride. Teenagers are likely to be friends with someone in their community who has a two-year-old kid and is "up against it," as Murray puts it. On the other hand, no free ride at all (except for in-kind nutritional assistance during pregnancy and infancy to avoid disastrous health problems) would clearly have stronger impact. It would also put mothers into the world of work without letting them grow accustomed to dependency. Oklahoma applies its soft workfare requirement to mothers as soon as their kids are born, with no apparent ill effects.

And if a mother refuses? The short, nasty answer is that if a mother turns down   15
the state's offer of a job with which she might support her children, and as a re-
sult her children live in squalor and filth, then she has neglected a basic task of parenthood. She is subject to the laws that already provide for removal of a child from an unfit home.

What about teenagers who haven't even finished high school? They could re-   16
ceive free day care while finishing, and in-kind nutritional assistance, but no cash. To obtain any extra cash necessary to support a baby, they would have to work, in one of the guaranteed government jobs if necessary. Again, the government could offer as many free training programs as it wanted, but without cash entitlement. Since training would no longer be an alternative to working, trainees would have every incentive to make the most of it.

Will there be enough jobs these people can do? As noted above, the objection   17
can't be that there aren't enough worthwhile jobs to be done. The crumbling "in-
frastructure" that preoccupied Washington three years ago hasn't been patched up overnight. All around the country governments have stopped doing, for financial reasons, things they once thought worthwhile, like opening libraries on Saturday and picking up trash twice a week. Why not do them again?

But there are plausible doubts whether the welfare recipients who would need   18
public service employment are suited to doing all these worthwhile jobs. One objection has to do with women and physical labor. Are we really going to have teenage girls repairing potholes and painting bridges? One response is, why not? Women can fill potholes and paint bridges (and water lawns and pick up garbage), just as women can be telephone repairmen and sailors. Feminism has rightly destroyed the sex stereotypes that used to surround much physical work. Anyway, there are many non-arduous "women's" jobs that need doing—nurses' aides, Xerox operators, receptionists, clerks, coat checkers, cooks, and cleaners. Private schools often require parents to keep order on playgrounds twice a month. Public schools might employ one or two parents to do the same full-
time. Day-care centers could too. Is there any point in offering women free day care and then putting some of them to work in day-care centers? Yes. First, that would still free up a lot of women for employment. Second, and more important, the day-care jobs would exist within the culture of work—with alarm clocks to set, appointments to keep, and bosses to please—rather than the cul-
ture of welfare.

A second objection has to do with competence. Can an illiterate, immature   19
high school dropout be trusted to work in a hospital as a nurses' aide, or in a
public office as a clerk? Maybe not. But who can't sweep a floor? The liberals
who make this objection often seem to have an opinion of underclass capabil-
ity that makes William Shockley look generous. In fact, supervisors of soft-
workfare workers polled by MDRC rated welfare recipients as productive as
regular entry-level workers. For those with severe limitations—well, even a leaf-
raking job rakes leaves. It that's all someone's capable of doing, does that mean
she shouldn't be paid for doing it? The alternative, remember, is to pay her to
stay home and raise children. . . .

Won't it cost a fortune? The WPA, at its peak, employed 3.3 million people   20
full time. CETA, at its peak, 750,000. At the pit of the past recession, there were
11.4 million unemployed (4.6 million for more than 15 weeks). What fraction
of them would want subminimum-wage jobs—and how many of those not in
the labor force would come out of the woodwork to claim those jobs—is anybody's guess. It's usually more expensive, at least initially, to give people jobs
than it is to give people cash welfare. Jobs require materials and expensive supervisors. A reasonable estimate, based on previous programs, is about $10,000
per job. That's $10 billion for every million jobs. Pretty soon you're talking real
money. The long-run savings, of course, would be huge if the welfare culture
was absorbed into the working, taxpaying culture. In the short run, however,
welfare savings would be less, and the benefit of the work done would show up
as savings only if it was work the government would be doing anyway. Would
these short-term savings balance out the extra short-term costs? Probably not.
Who cares? The point isn't to save money.

The point is to enforce the work ethic. This is a long-term cultural offensive, not   21
a budget-control program or an expression of compassion. The sharpness and
simplicity of its choices—no cash welfare for the able-bodied, no exceptions for
parenthood—are its main virtue, because they embody with unmistakable clarity the social norms that are in danger of disappearing in the underclass culture.

Liberals, in particular, should leap at the chance to reassert those values.   22
The Work Ethic State proclaims the equal dignity of all who work, an idea that
seems more Democratic than Republican. In any case, it's very American. If it
helps, ambitious liberals might note that every poll ever taken shows that cash
for the disabled and jobs for the able-bodied is what the public supports. Now
is a propitious moment to appeal to these sentiments, because the current
workfare boom gives liberals a chance to achieve, through the back door, the
ancient Democratic dream of a guaranteed job. Indeed, workfare, expanded to
include everyone and not just single mothers, *is* a guaranteed job. But I won't
tell if you won't. □

◢ REREADING FOR UNDERSTANDING

I. Briefly explain the major difference between Kaus's proposed program and
other systems of providing aid to the poor. How does the "workfare"

described in this essay differ from previous attempts to encourage welfare recipients to seek training and employment?

2. Kaus proposes that a public job be given to every American citizen over eighteen who wants one. Wouldn't such a system go bankrupt on its first day? How does Kaus defend such a seemingly expensive government program? Kaus claims that whether such a program costs more or less money than the existing program is unimportant. Why?

3. The jobs Kaus proposes would not allow a family of three to live above the poverty level. If a worker is unable even to support his or her family, what is the incentive to take such a job?

◤ RESPONDING

1. Does Kaus's proposal seem reasonable? What problems does he anticipate in implementing such a program? Has he adequately addressed these problems? Can you think of other concerns he has not considered?

2. Kaus's argument rests on the implicit assumption that the accessibility of government aid is the main reason that welfare recipients don't work. Might there be other factors for high welfare dependency among single mothers (the recipients of AFDC payments and the primary target of welfare reform)? Does Kaus's proposal address any of these other factors?

◤ RESPONDING IN WRITING

Kaus advocates returning to a relief system similar to the Work Projects Administration implemented by Franklin Roosevelt in 1934. As he notes, many politicians, both liberal and conservative, point to the WPA as a model government-assistance program. But how successful was the WPA in providing relief and in instilling the work ethic in participants? Use your library to find articles and commentary from 1934 to 1939 about the WPA, as well as contemporary analysis of the program. Write an essay in response to the following question: Is the WPA a worthy model for welfare reform?

NEIL GILBERT

Neil Gilbert is Chernin Professor of Social Welfare at the University of California, Berkeley, and author of numerous works on social policy. In this article from *Commentary*, he offers an unfavorable critique of the welfare reform proposal President Clinton set forth in his 1994 State of the Union address.

Why the New Workfare
Won't Work

Almost everyone agrees that work must replace welfare. Following President Clinton's lead, both Democrats and Republicans have embraced the idea of a two-year limit on welfare, during which recipients of Aid to Families with Dependent Children (AFDC) would be given education, training, child care, and job-placement services. Afterward, when entering the labor force, they would continue to qualify for transitional services like Medicaid and child care during the first year of employment, as is currently the case under the Family Support Act.

This approach is a variation on workfare experiments that have disappointed policy-makers since the 1967 work-incentive program. Although the reforms now in fashion are more stringent in their demands, and more generous in their incentives, they are no more likely to succeed than earlier schemes.

The ultimate question is: what happens to welfare recipients who follow the program, but are unable to secure employment after the two years? According to current thinking, they should be required to participate in some form of public-works program established by the state. This is a tough-sounding quick fix that will surely create more problems than it solves. For those who have not found a job after two years are likely to include many AFDC mothers who are among the least skilled and least motivated in the welfare population. The social and economic costs of employing them in public works will be staggering.

Thus, estimates by the Congressional Budget Office indicate that expenditures for on-the-job supervision of these workers and day care for their children would amount to $6,300 per participant. With the average AFDC grant already about $5,000, participation in mandatory work programs would hence more than double the costs for each welfare recipient. Smoke-and-mirrors proposals to finance this plan through taxing food stamps and cutting other welfare benefits suggest just how desperate the administration is becoming as it starts to calculate the costs of public works. And beyond fiscal concerns, the cynicism and demoralization bred by make-work would surely undermine the already shaky standards of public bureaucracies.

Other aspects of the current thinking on welfare reform are also hardly likely to go according to plan. In particular, proposals for reform organized around incentives to work and a two-year limit on public support are plagued by three problems: they ignore success; they create perverse effects; and they require a level of callousness that social-agency personnel are unlikely to countenance.

For many families, AFDC serves not as a poverty trap, but as a temporary support in hard times; in fact, about 48 percent of all AFDC spells last less than two years. True, this success rate can be somewhat misleading, since one-third of short-term cases will enroll in AFDC again some time in the future and, in any event, most AFDC costs are attributable to long-term recipients. Nevertheless, reform measures that ignore the substantial number of successful cases are only likely to increase program expenses still further. By providing various transitional services and other incentives to work, they will raise the costs of public support for families who previously, in the absence of these benefits, would have left the rolls.

At the same time, if incentives are high enough, they may perversely encourage those who are already in low-paying occupations to leave work for AFDC, and then recycle back into the labor force in order to qualify for the transitional benefits.   7

Finally, for those welfare recipients who refuse to participate in either training or public works, how are public agencies to enforce mandatory work requirements? Answers to this question are harsh and unsatisfactory. The Republican Task Force on Welfare Reform, for example, would impose sanctions on those who fail to participate by initially reducing the family's AFDC grant and food stamp benefits by 25 percent, and after six months dropping them from AFDC altogether. But proposals of this sort disregard the question of what will happen to the children on welfare, for whom the AFDC program was originally devised.   8

Whatever hard lines policy-makers may draw, moreover, workers in welfare agencies are unlikely to impose sanctions that would virtually drive families with children onto the street. And if these sanctions *were* enacted, one may confidently predict that the two-year limit would become to welfare in the 1990's what deinstitutionalization was to mental illness in the 1960's, the deferred costs of which now plague our cities.   9

The essential problem with the transitional-incentives and time-limits approach to welfare reform is that it deals too generously with those recipients who are most competent and motivated, and too harshly with those who are least competent and motivated. I would suggest an alternative—one that begins with the need to distinguish among AFDC families, and seeks to ensure the well-being of children.   10

Families enter the AFDC program for different reasons and remain on the rolls for varying periods of time. About 60 percent of AFDC spells begin because of either a decline in family earnings or a divorce (or separation) of married couples with children. I would argue that these cases should be treated differently from the 30 percent of AFDC spells that begin when an unmarried woman has a child.   11

The reason is simple. Welfare applicants who were married or employed for some period of time prior to enrollment in AFDC are generally independent citizens who had been abiding by social conventions and trying to follow the rules. It is reasonable to presume that they are competent and motivated to become self-sufficient. Thus, they should be considered a separate group, awarded AFDC benefits, and left alone for two years to reorganize their lives. A high proportion of them will be among the 48 percent of recipients who leave the welfare rolls of their own volition in less than two years. Those remaining on AFDC after two years could then be enrolled in the first phase of intervention, leading to what might be termed "managed dependency."   12

As for women who enter the AFDC program because of out-of-wedlock   13
births, they are another matter. For one thing, they are younger and more likely
to become long-term recipients than those in the other group. For another
thing, their children are at great risk of harm. Children in single-parent families are twice as likely to be abused as those in households where both parents
are present; when the single parent is a teenager, the risk is even higher. This
group should be targeted for special intervention, if for no other reason than to
protect the children.

Instead of forced labor and make-work schemes, however, the intervention   14
would be divided into two phases. In the first, practical assistance would be
offered to mothers and protection would be provided for their children by
means of regular home-health visits, assistance in home management, encouragement of school drop-outs to complete their high-school requirements, and
development of systematic plans for reintegration into the labor force.

After three years, those still on AFDC would enter the second phase. Here,   15
greater social controls would be employed, reflecting the recipients' emerging
status as "wards of the state." Home visiting to supervise child-care practices
would continue, and the level of public-assistance grants would remain the
same. But during this phase, a case manager would be assigned to exercise increased regulation over each family's financial affairs, which would entail payment of rent and utilities and weekly allocations of food stamps. There would
also be increased monitoring of outside resources available to recipients, which
would reduce their AFDC grants.

Tightening social control through case managers and home-health visitors   16
would certainly raise the costs of AFDC. But this would still be a relatively inexpensive way for society to protect vulnerable children, while giving notice
that long-term public dependence would be accompanied by greater public
surveillance. Increasing the role of public authority in recipients' lives would
make welfare less attractive to some who might otherwise be employed.

This is a modest goal, but those who demand more would do well to recognize   17
that tinkering with AFDC is not the answer. Although AFDC may help to sustain the never-married, single-parent culture of poverty, it did not create this
unhealthy pattern of behavior, and forces larger than those generated by welfare
reform will be required to eliminate it.

Indeed, a serious effort to reduce welfare must go well beyond adjustments   18
in the AFDC program. The best and fairest incentive would be to increase the
work-related benefits of low-paying jobs of the kind that many welfare recipients might perform. Progress along these lines is already under way with the
expansion of tax-based social transfers, such as the earned income-tax credit.
Working families also need the security of medical protection, which those on
welfare receive through Medicaid. Finally, there is widespread agreement that
absent fathers should be held responsible for the financial support of their
children (though resources for such support are often quite limited among
fathers of children in the AFDC population).

Even with all this, dependency will not disappear. Whether due to personal   19
deficiencies or forces beyond their control, people in need of care will always be
with us. At the very least, however, social policies aimed at alleviating dependency should not condemn children for the hard luck or personal frailties of
their parents. ☐

◢ REREADING FOR UNDERSTANDING

1. Gilbert and many other critics of Clinton's welfare reform proposal believe
   that the program would be far costlier than the current system. Why?

2. Although Gilbert points out that the high cost of Clinton's proposal is
   problematic, the cost is not his primary concern. He also contends that the
   proposal ignores success (par. 6). What does he mean by this? In what way
   does this shortcoming add to the costs of the program?

3. Gilbert says that, in order to work, Clinton's proposal will "require a level
   of callousness" on the part of social policymakers and enforcers. Describe
   the kind of difficult decisions that would have to be made and executed.

4. One problem of the Clinton proposal, according to Gilbert, is that it assumes a common reason for families entering the AFDC program. Gilbert
   suggests that there are two categories of AFDC recipients. Who comprises
   each group, and why should they be treated differently?

◢ RESPONDING

1. It is hard to disagree with Gilbert's claim that the administration's program
   would be more expensive than the current system, but does that fact alone
   condemn the effort? Are there benefits that might justify the cost? Consider
   Mickey Kaus's argument in the previous selection for the long-term benefits of creating a new American work ethic.

◢ RESPONDING IN WRITING

Write an essay critiquing Gilbert's alternative proposal for welfare reform. Do
you think it is more or less reasonable, humane, and/or feasible than Clinton's
plan? Why?

RITA HENLEY JENSEN

A former welfare mother, Rita Henley Jensen is now a respected investigative journalist whose work has appeared in *The New York Times, The
Washington Times,* and the American Bar Association's *ABA Journal.* In this

essay, which appeared in *Ms.*, she tells of her struggle to earn a degree and work her way out of welfare, and she analyzes the social, political, economic, and psychological forces that continue to make the transition from welfare to work so difficult.

Welfare

I am a woman. A white woman, once poor but no longer. I am not lazy, never 1
was. I am a middle-aged woman, with two grown daughters. I was a welfare mother, one of those women society considers less than nothing.

I should have applied for Aid to Families with Dependent Children when I 2
was 18 years old, pregnant with my first child, and living with a boyfriend who slapped me around. But I didn't.

I remember talking it over at the time with a friend. I lived in the neigh- 3
borhood that surrounds the vast Columbus campus of Ohio State University. Students, faculty, hangers-on, hippies, runaways, and recent émigrés from Kentucky lived side by side in the area's relatively inexpensive housing. I was a runaway.

On a particularly warm midsummer's day, I stood on High Street, directly 4
across from the campus' main entrance, with an older, more sophisticated friend, wondering what to do with my life. With my swollen belly, all hope of my being able to cross the street and enroll in the university had evaporated. Now, I was seeking advice about how merely to survive, to escape the assaults and still be able to care for my child.

My friend knew of no place I could go, nowhere I could turn, no one else I 5
could ask. I remember saying in a tone of resignation, "I can't apply for welfare." Instead of disagreeing with me, she nodded, acknowledging our mutual belief that taking beatings was better than taking handouts. Being "on the dole" meant you deserved only contempt.

In August 1965, I married my attacker. 6

Six years later, I left him and applied for assistance. My children were 18 7
months and five and a half years old. I had waited much too long. Within a year, I crossed High Street to go to Ohio State. I graduated in four years and moved to New York City to attend Columbia University's Graduate School of Journalism. I have worked as a journalist for 18 years now. My life on welfare was very hard—there were times when I didn't have enough food for the three of us. But I was able to get an education while on welfare. It is hardly likely that a woman on AFDC today would be allowed to do what I did, to go to school and develop the kind of skills that enabled me to make a better life for myself and my children.

This past summer, I attended a conference in Chicago on feminist legal 8
theory. During the presentation of a paper related to gender and property rights, the speaker mentioned as an aside that when one says "welfare mother" the listener hears "black welfare mother." A discussion ensued about the underlying racism until someone declared that the solution was easy: all that had to

be done was have the women in the room bring to the attention of the media the fact that white women make up the largest percentage of welfare recipients. At this point, I stood, took a deep breath, stepped out of my professional guise, and informed the crowd that I was a former welfare mother. Looking at my white hair, blue eyes, and freckled Irish skin, some laughed; others gasped—despite having just acknowledged that someone like me was, in fact, a "typical" welfare mother.

Occasionally I do this. Speak up. Identify myself as one of "them." I do so   9
reluctantly because welfare mothers are a lightning rod for race hatred, class prejudice, and misogyny. Yet I am aware that as long as welfare is viewed as an *African American* woman's issue, instead of a *woman's* issue—whether that woman be white, African American, Asian, Latina, or Native American—those in power can continue to exploit our country's racism to weaken and even elim-inate public support for the programs that help low-income mothers and their children.

I didn't have the guts to stand up during a 1974 reception for Ohio state   10
legislators. The party's hostess was a leader of the Columbus chapter of the National Organization for Women and she had opened up her suburban home so that representatives of many of the state's progressive organizations could lobby in an informal setting for an increase in the state's welfare allotment for families. I was invited as a representative of the campus area's single mothers' support group. In the living room, I came across a state senator in a just-slightly-too-warm-and-friendly state induced by the potent combination of free booze and a crowd of women. He quickly decided I looked like a good per-son to amuse with one of his favorite jokes. "You want to know how a welfare mother can prevent getting pregnant?" he asked, giggling. "She can just take two aspirin—and put them between her knees," he roared, as he bent down to place his Scotch glass between his own, by way of demonstration. I drifted away.

I finally did gather up my courage to speak out. It was in a classroom dur-   11
ing my junior year. I was enrolled in a course on the economics of public pol-icy because I wanted to understand why the state of Ohio thought it desirable to provide me and my two kids with only $204 per month—59 percent of what even the state itself said a family of three needed to live.

For my required oral presentation, I chose "Aid to Families with Dependent   12
Children." I cited the fact that approximately two thirds of all the poor families in the country were white; I noted that most welfare families consisted of one parent and two children. As an audiovisual aid, I brought my own two kids along. My voice quavered a bit as I delivered my intro: I stood with my arms around my children and said, "We are a typical AFDC family."

My classmates had not one question when I finished. I don't believe anyone   13
even bothered to ask the kids' names or ages.

If I were giving this talk today, I would hold up a picture of us back then   14
and say we still represent typical welfare recipients. The statistics I would cite to back up that statement have been refined since the 1970s and now include "Hispanic" as a category. In 1992, 38.9 percent of all welfare mothers were white, 37.2 percent were black, 17.8 percent were "Hispanic," 2.8 percent were Asian, and 1.4 percent were Native American.

My report, however, would focus on the dramatic and unrelenting reduc-   15
tion in resources available to low-income mothers in the last two decades.

Fact: In 1970, the average monthly benefit for a family of three was $178.   16
Not much, but consider that as a result of inflation, that $178 would be ap-
proximately $680 today. And then consider that the average monthly payment
today is only about $414. That's the way it's been for more than two decades:
the cost of living goes up (by the states' own accounting, the cost of rent, food,
and utilities for a family of three has doubled), but the real value of welfare payments keeps going down.

Fact: The 1968 Work Incentive Program (the government called it WIN;   17
we called it WIP) required that all unemployed adult recipients sign up for job
training or employment once their children turned six. The age has now been
lowered to three, and states may go as low as age one. What that means is you
won't be able to attend and finish college while on welfare. (In most states a college education isn't considered job training, even though experts claim most
of us will need college degrees to compete in the workplace of the twenty-first
century.)

Fact: Forty-two percent of welfare recipients will be on welfare less than   18
two years during their entire lifetime, and an additional 33 percent will spend
between two and eight years on welfare. The statistics haven't changed much
over the years: women still use welfare to support their families when their children are small.

In 1974, I ended my talk with this joke: A welfare mother went into the   19
drugstore and bought a can of deodorant. I explained that it was funny because
everyone knew that welfare mothers could not afford "extras" like personal
hygiene products. My joke today would be: A welfare mother believed that if
elected public officials understood these facts, they would not campaign to cut
her family's benefits.

The idea that government representatives care about welfare mothers is as   20
ridiculous to me now as the idea back then that I would waste my limited funds
on deodorant. It is much clearer to me today what the basic functions of welfare public policy are at this moment in U.S. history.

By making war on welfare recipients, political leaders can turn the public's   21
attention away from the government's redistribution of wealth to the wealthy.
Recent studies show that the United States has become the most economically
stratified of industrial nations. In fact, Federal Reserve figures reveal that the
richest 1 percent of American households—each with a minimum net worth of
$2.3 million—control nearly 40 percent of the wealth, while in Britain, the rich-
est 1 percent of the population controls about 18 percent of the wealth. In the
mid-1970s, both countries were on a par: the richest 1 percent controlled 20
percent of the wealth. President Reagan was the master of this verbal shell
game. He told stories of welfare queens and then presided over the looting of
the nation's savings and loans by wealthy white men.

Without a doubt, the current urgency for tax cuts and spending reductions   22
can be explained by the fact that President Clinton tried to shift the balance
slightly in 1992 and the wealthy ended up paying 16 percent more in taxes the
following year, by one estimate.

The purpose of this antiwelfare oratory and the campaigns against sex edu- 23
cation, abortion rights, and aid to teenage mothers is to ensure a constant supply of young women as desperate and ashamed as I was. Young women willing
to take a job at any wage rate, willing to tolerate the most abusive relationships
with men, and unable to enter the gates leading to higher education.

To accomplish their goals, political leaders continually call for reforms 24
that include demands that welfare recipients work, that teenagers don't have
sex, and that welfare mothers stop giving birth (but don't have abortions).
Each "reform" addresses the nation's racial and sexual stereotypes: taking care
of one's own children is not work; welfare mothers are unemployed, promis-
cuous, and poorly motivated; and unless the government holds their feet to the
fire, these women will live on welfare for years, as will their children and their
children's children.

This type of demagoguery has been common throughout our history. 25
What sets the present era apart is the nearly across-the-board cooperation of
the media. The national news magazines, the most prestigious daily newspapers, the highly regarded broadcast news outlets, as well as the supermarket
tabloids and talk-radio hosts, have generally abandoned the notion that one of
their missions is to sometimes comfort the afflicted and afflict the comfortable. Instead, they too often reprint politicians' statements unchallenged,
provide charts comparing one party's recommendations to another's without
really questioning those recommendations, and illustrate story after story,
newscast after newscast, with a visual of an African American woman (because
we all know they're the only ones on welfare) living in an urban housing project (because that's where all welfare recipients live) who has been on welfare
for years.

When *U.S. News & World Report* did a major story on welfare reform this 26
year, it featured large photographs of eight welfare recipients, seven of whom
were women of color: six African Americans and one Latina or Native American (the text does not state her ethnicity). Describing the inability of welfare
mothers to hold jobs (they are "hobbled not only by their lack of experience but
also by their casual attitudes toward punctuality, dress, and coworkers"), the
article offers the "excuse" given by one mother for not taking a 3 P.M. to 11 P.M.
shift: "'I wouldn't get to see my kids,'" she told the reporter. You can't win for
losing—should she take that 3-to-11 job and her unsupervised kids get in trouble, you can be sure some conservative would happily leap on her as an example of one of those poor women who are bad mothers and whose kids should
be in orphanages.

Why don't the media ever find a white woman from Ohio or Iowa or 27
Wisconsin, a victim of domestic violence, leaving the father of her two children
to make a new start? Or a Latina mother like the one living in my current neighborhood, who has one child and does not make enough as a home health care
attendant to pay for her family's health insurance? Or a Native American
woman living on a reservation, creating crafts for pennies that will be sold by
others for dollars?

Besides reinforcing stereotypes about the personal failings of welfare re- 28
cipients, when my colleagues write in-depth pieces about life on welfare they

invariably concentrate on describing welfare mothers' difficulties with the world at large: addictions, lack of transportation, dangerous neighbors, and, most recently, shiftless boyfriends who begin beating them when they do get jobs—as if this phenomenon were limited to relationships between couples with low incomes.

I wonder why no journalist I have stumbled across, no matter how well   29
meaning, has communicated what I believe is the central reality of most women's lives on welfare: they believe all the stereotypes too and they are ashamed of being on welfare. They eat, breathe, sleep, and clothe themselves with shame.

Most reporting on welfare never penetrates the surface, and the nature of   30
the relationship between the welfare system and the woman receiving help is never explored. Like me, many women fleeing physical abuse must make the welfare department their first stop after seeking an order of protection. Studies are scarce, but some recent ones of women in welfare-to-work programs across the U.S. estimate that anywhere from half to three fourths of participants are, or have been, in abusive relationships. And surveys of some homeless shelters indicate that half of the women living in them are on the run from a violent mate.

But if welfare is the means of escape, it is also the institutionalization of the   31
dynamic of battering. My husband was the source of my and my children's daily bread and of daily physical and psychological attacks. On welfare, I was free of the beatings, but the assaults on my self-esteem were still frequent and powerful, mimicking the behavior of a typical batterer.

As he pounds away, threatening to kill the woman and children he claims to   32
love, the abuser often accuses his victims of lying, laziness, and infidelity. Many times, he threatens to snatch the children away from their mother in order to protect them from her supposed incompetence, her laziness, dishonesty, and sexual escapades.

On welfare, just as with my husband, I had to prove every statement was   33
not a lie. Everything had to be documented: how many children I had, how much I paid for rent, fuel, transportation, electricity, child care, and so forth. It went so far as to require that at every "redetermination of need" interview (every six months), I had to produce the originals of my children's birth certificates, which were duly photocopied over and over again. Since birth certificates do not change, the procedure was a subtle and constant reminder that nothing I said was accepted as truth. Ever.

But this is a petty example. The more significant one was the suspicion that   34
my attendance at Ohio State University was probably a crime. Throughout my college years, I regularly reported that I was attending OSU. Since the WIN limit at that time was age six and my youngest daughter was two when I started, I was allowed to finish my undergraduate years without having to report to some job-training program that would have prepared me for a minimum-wage job. However, my caseworker and I shared an intuitive belief that something just had to be wrong about this. How could I be living on welfare and going to college? Outrageous! Each day I awoke feeling as if I were in a race, that I had to complete my degree before I was charged with a felony.

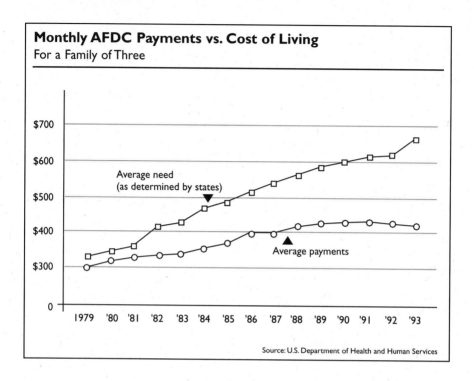

Monthly AFDC Payments vs. Cost of Living
For a Family of Three

Average need
(as determined by states)

Average payments

$700
$600
$500
$400
$300
0

1979 '80 '81 '82 '83 '84 '85 '86 '87 '88 '89 '90 '91 '92 '93

Source: U.S. Department of Health and Human Services

As a matter of fact, I remember hearing, a short time after I graduated, that a group of welfare mothers attending college in Ohio were charged with food stamp fraud, apparently for not reporting their scholarships as additional income.   35

Batterers frequently lie to their victims—it's a power thing. Caseworkers do too. For example, when I moved to New York to attend graduate school and applied for assistance, I asked my intake worker whether I could apply for emergency food stamps. She told me there was no emergency food program. The kids and I scraped by, but that statement was false. I was unaware of it until welfare rights advocates successfully sued the agency for denying applicants emergency food assistance. In another case, when someone gave me a ten-year-old Opel so I could keep my first (very low paying) reporting job, my caseworker informed me in writing that mere possession of a car made me ineligible for welfare. (I appealed and won. The caseworker was apparently confused by the fact that although I was not allowed to have any assets, I did need the car to get to work. She also assumed a used car had to have some value. Not this one.)   36

Then there's the issue of sexual possessiveness: states rarely grant assistance to families with fathers still in the home. And as for feeling threatened about losing custody, throughout the time I was on welfare, I knew that if I stumbled at all, my children could be taken away from me. It is widely understood that any neighbor can call the authorities about a welfare mother, making a charge of neglect, and that mother, since she is less than nothing, might not be able to prove her competency. I had a close call once. I had been hospitalized for ten   37 days and a friend took care of my children. After my return home, however, I was still weak. I would doze off on the sofa while the kids were awake—one time it happened when they were outside playing on the sidewalk. A neighbor, seeing them there unattended, immediately called the child welfare agency, which sent someone out to question me and to look inside my refrigerator to see if I had any food. Luckily, that day I did.

Ultimately, leaving an abusive relationship and applying for welfare is a little like leaving solitary confinement to become part of a prison's general population. It's better, but you are still incarcerated.   38

None of this is ever discussed in the context of welfare reform. The idiot state legislator, the prosecutor in Ohio who brought the charges against welfare mothers years ago, Bill Clinton, and Newt Gingrich all continue to play the race and sex card by hollering for welfare reform. They continue to exploit and feed the public's ignorance about and antipathy toward welfare mothers to propel their own careers. Sadly, journalists permit them to do so, perhaps for the same reason.   39

Lost in all this are the lives of thousands of women impoverished by virtue of their willingness to assume the responsibility of raising their children. An ex-boyfriend used to say that observing my struggle was a little like watching someone standing in a room, with arms upraised to prevent the ceiling from pressing in on her. He wondered just how long I could prevent the collapse.   40

Today, welfare mothers have even less opportunity than I did. Their talent, brains, luck, and resourcefulness are ignored. Each new rule, regulation, and reform makes it even more unlikely that they can use the time they are on welfare to do as I did: cross the High Streets in their cities and towns, and realize their ambitions. Each new rule makes it more likely that they will only be able to train for a minimum-wage job that will never allow them to support their families.   41

So no, I don't think all we have to do is get the facts to the media. I think we have to raise hell any way we can.   42

Our goal is simple: never again should there be a young woman, standing in front of the gates that lead to a better future, afraid to enter because she believes she must instead choose poverty and battery. ☐   43

◢ REREADING FOR UNDERSTANDING

1. Jensen says that it is unlikely that a woman would be able to get a college education while on welfare today. Why?

2. According to Jensen, why is it so important that the media do all it can to discredit the myth that most welfare recipients are African Americans?

3. In what way has the welfare program changed since the 1970s? In what ways has it stayed the same, according to Jensen?

4. Jensen charges that calls for welfare reform appeal to America's racial and sexual stereotypes. How? In what way is the media responsible for promoting these stereotypes?

◢ RESPONDING

1. Why didn't Jensen apply for welfare when she was pregnant with her first child, as she now admits she should have? What point does she make about the system by opening her essay with this personal dilemma?

2. Why is welfare reform a perennial political issue according to Jensen? What do politicians gain from attacking the welfare system? How does she explain current antiwelfare rhetoric? Do you think the explanation she offers is reasonable? Why or why not?

3. Jensen says that journalists should keep in mind "that one of their missions is to sometimes comfort the afflicted and afflict the comfortable" (par. 25). What does she mean by this statement? Is this an appropriate mission for journalism?

4. Jensen observes that being on welfare is not very different from being in an abusive marriage. What similarities does she note between the two situations?

◢ RESPONDING IN WRITING

1. Working in groups of three or four, collect a sampling of news coverage on welfare from recent periodicals and television programs. Analyze the data you've collected in light of Jensen's charge the media is responsible for promoting stereotypes of welfare recipients rather than realistic portrayals. Write a letter to the editor or station manager of one of the news sources you've used, presenting an analysis of your findings.

2. In August 1996, President Clinton signed into law a welfare reform bill that changed welfare from a Federal entitlement program for the poor to a temporary assistance program controlled primarily by the states. Do some research to discover how this change has affected welfare recipients in your state. Based on your reading of Kaus, Gilbert, and Jensen, write an essay analyzing and critiquing this change in the welfare program.

CONTROVERSIES

Will There Be a Job for Me?

ROBERT E. SULLIVAN, JR.

Twenty-five years ago, a diploma and a decent transcript were virtual guarantees of employment following graduation. As corporate America continues to downsize and as technological advances have reduced the number of
workers needed for industrial production, the prospects for employment
have grown dim and the competition for good jobs has become cutthroat.
Many college graduates are finding that not only do they have to settle for
jobs for which they are overqualified, but they often have to fight fiercely for
even these positions. In this article from *Rolling Stone,* Robert Sullivan looks
at some of the causes of the current job dearth and some of its effects on
the unemployed and underemployed.

Greatly Reduced Expectations

After Jim McKay graduated from the University of Washington, in 1992, he
couldn't land any of the kinds of jobs that he always figured a college
graduate with an English major should be able to land, at one of the area's
daily or weekly newspapers, perhaps, or in the sports-information department
of his university or even, as time went on, as a sales representative for Rainier
beer. But with his school loans looming, he managed to find a position with
Coca-Cola. Now he earns $10.68 an hour stacking product on Seattle grocery-
store shelves.

At first he thought that his predicament was his own doing, that he hadn't
tried hard enough. Then he thought it was his choice of major. But after a while,
sharing an apartment with a similarly underemployed accounting major and
meeting more and more recent grads in the same boat, he realized something
bigger was going on. Now, working among men who for the most part didn't
go to college and wondering if his future will include the back surgery that so

many of them have had, McKay has all but given up on finding any job that uses what he learned in college. "I feel angry about the whole thing," he says. "I guess when you're told your whole life that something's gonna happen and then the opposite happens, you feel cheated."

In the career-counseling center of McKay's alma mater, the same fear is striking the science majors, the very students who five years ago were expected to be in insatiable demand in the high-tech Nineties. "Right now, I'm taking every interview I can get," says Brian McCoy, a chemical-engineering major graduating this spring, as he emerges from an interview with a paper company. "I'm just trying to eat up everything I can and hope I land something. I'm thinking I may have to demote myself to a sales position, though. They say they have enough engineers, and I guess they figure that it's easier to teach a technical person how to sell than to teach a salesperson to be technical. And I may have to move." 3

Even people with more than four years of schooling are having trouble. With a six-year architecture degree from the University of Cincinnati, Jamie Hurd, 31, has so far found only part-time work in her field. When she looks elsewhere for office work, she sometimes feels the need to play down her schooling. "Here you've got this professional degree, and it's almost a hindrance," she says. "I have a friend who's an architect, and he couldn't get a job in a deli because he had never worked a cash register. I mean, he could size beams, but he couldn't work a register. Sometimes you feel overqualified." 4

"Things have changed drastically in the economy over the past two or three years," says Robert Thirsk, director of career counseling at the University of Washington. A few years ago, Thirsk and his colleagues were dreaming about the rise in the salary curve expected to continue into the Nineties; about the anticipated shortage of college graduates (especially those with specialized technical degrees); about a booming service economy chock-full of the kind of lower- and midlevel management jobs perfect for all those liberal-arts and business graduates; even about the coming of the thirty-hour workweek. Now, they talk about corporate America's continued downsizing and lower wages. 5

To a certain extent, this is a problem in the short term, the result of a deep recession. There are plenty of economists who argue that college graduates are doing relatively well and that when the economy gets up and running again, when companies begin rehiring, they will again be leading the statistical pack. "This is temporary," says John Bishop, an economist at Cornell. "I'd bet a lot on that." 6

But to a larger extent, it appears that the value of the diploma—once a general-admission ticket to the economy—is dropping with each quarter and each crop of grads, leaving a lot of people standing at the door, unable to get in. More studies are reporting permanent rather than temporary job losses, and economists are theorizing that no matter how fast the economy recovers, it may never resume spitting out the kinds of jobs that the college educated want or are best suited for. 7

Magazines and newspapers spend their time addressing this problem by raving about generational battles and trying to decide if young people are lackadaisical, angry or just stupid. Politicians and corporate executives handle it by 8 banging their fists for more worker training. But the economic fact of the matter remains that the best and brightest of the labor force can't get the right kinds of jobs.

"It turns out that there aren't going to be all the vacancies that require a   9 college degree that they said there would be," Thirsk says. "That's going to force people with college degrees to lower occupations. And then there's going to be a lot more competition for all those jobs." In many cases, this all means that people who just graduated are going to have to return immediately to school— and pay more—for job-specific skills, a wholly demoralizing thought for a well-grade-pointed twenty-two-year-old trying to begin a career. "They get discouraged," Thirsk says. "They say, 'Gosh, you're telling me that I've spent four years getting a degree and a year from now I may be taking courses and doing something I never thought I'd do.'"

It's at this point that a lot of Thirsk's students walk out of the University of   10 Washington's Center for Career Services, think about their last four years and all the money college cost them and ask themselves if they've just wasted a whole lot of time.

"I see a lot of anger," says Jim McKay a few hours before he heads off to his   11 Coca-Cola job. "I see it in some people who give up after a while. I see it in people who work as coffee clerks in a law firm. I mean, basically I see a lot of people with college degrees doing the same thing as a person with just a high-school degree. I know there's more to a college education than getting a job, and you don't see yourself as being above these people or anything, and yet they didn't do anything to get where they are." In hopes of bettering his position in the labor force, McKay, like many of the people his age who feel underemployed, plans to do what makes sense in an economy that has traditionally emphasized skills: go to graduate school for yet more training.

When scores of economic bigwigs assembled in December for Bill Clinton's   12 economic teach-in in Little Rock, Arkansas, they all sat around discussing, among other things, the need for a better-educated work force. Robert Solow, a professor of economics at MIT, called education and training the two keys to raising the nation's productivity rates. Robert Reich, soon to become labor secretary, lamented that only nine percent of the federal budget went to, among other things, education. "We need an education system that will educate all of our students," said John Sculley, chairman and CEO of Apple Computer, sounding a populist Clintonian note, "not just the top fifteen or twenty percent." By the end of all the charts and note taking, it seemed as if the United States could simply educate its way out of its economic mess.

Yet statistics are piling up that show those in that top fifteen or twenty per-   13 cent, those who worked to get degrees, are, in a reversal of a decades-long trend, finding it increasingly difficult to get jobs. Young men who wanted to get into bank-training programs are now working cash registers; young women who looked forward to careers in marketing are now working in supermarkets. According to the most recent estimates, one out of every five college graduates in the Eighties took a job that requires no college degree. In the Sixties, only one out of every ten graduates did. By 1990, according to the Labor Department, 5.8 million people were "educationally underutilized." In 1991, according to a study by the National Center for Education Statistics, forty percent of all college-educated workers felt the jobs they were in did not require a college degree.

All this underemployment takes place against a backdrop of falling wages   14 Economic Policy Institute said that white-collar college graduates' salaries fell 3.1 percent between 1987 and 1991. This was the first postwar recession where unemployment rose more among white-collar workers than among blue-collar workers, a fact that many economists believe indicates a high incidence of permanent job loss. In fact, compared with the 1979–83 recession, the 1987–91 recession (assuming it is over) saw fifty percent more permanent job loss, a figure that translates to significantly more permanent trouble for the economy's hopeful entrants. In "The End of the White-Collar Job Boom," from a recent issue of *International Economic Insights*, economist Lawrence Mishel notes that the faltering demand for college-educated workers actually preceded the recession by several years. That white-collar wages initially appeared to continue rising turns out to say more about the tremendous wage losses endured by the seventy-five percent of the work force that didn't have four years of college education.

Since at least the time of the GI Bill, which made it possible for returning   15 World War II veterans to further their education, the American Dream has been predicated on a trip to college. For forty years, a college degree was essential for most white-collar jobs. But current trends fly in the face of old practices. "For college graduates entering the job market, the last couple of years have been the bleakest years we've ever seen," says Larry Katz, a Harvard economist. Now graduating from college is a little like graduating from high school was in the Thirties as far as white-collar employers are concerned, and the more than 1 million people who graduated from four-year colleges last spring—the largest crop in U.S. history—are guaranteed little more than an acute awareness of the hole they may end up climbing into.

All during her four years at Lewis and Clark College in Portland, Oregon,   16 Meggan Baron figured that she had a fairly pragmatic attitude about her studies. She liked to paint and draw, but rather than starve as an artist, she designed a major that was half art, half business. Commerce and art, she called it. After graduation she hoped for a job in a department store—maybe buying, maybe using her artistic skills, but at least working her way up the management ladder. And during her senior year she even managed to wrangle a three-month internship at Nordstrom, the department store of her career dreams. But it didn't lead where she thought.

"To be honest, when I graduated, at first I couldn't even get a job," Baron   17 says, "and then I finally got something at Nordstrom, but it was only part time, selling women's clothing. I mean, I think they're one of the best department stores in the country and all, and I know that they like to start everybody out on the bottom, you know, and then work them up, but I wasn't even permanent. And then it was hard working with customers. Customers don't always treat you so nicely, and that's harder when you're feeling like you're not going anywhere. It took me five months to realize that I wasn't going to get a permanent job, that I wasn't going to get promoted. And the reason was, there were all these people on the bottom who were willing to keep their jobs; they didn't want to give them up. We're talking people who had made selling on the floor their career, which is something I never really wanted to do. Here I was, twenty-three-years old, and they were probably all in their late thirties at least, several of them without any education, really. I mean, you have people saying, 'You should be lucky with the job you have.' But, well, I want more."

Baron's career counselor at Lewis and Clark, Sara Hamilton, sees Baron's   18 situation as representative of the deeper structural problems in the economy. "Historically," Hamilton says, "business organization was highly linear, and people, after they entered the company, were groomed and usually moved up. Now things are much more horizontal, which is good for productivity and good for participatory management but not good for the rookies, the people who don't have experience and want to get in."

Whereas once the first-time job seeker looked to climb up the corporate   19 ladder behind advancing older employees, now many of the thirty- and forty-year-olds are struggling simply to hang onto their rungs. They've watched their middle-aged colleagues get downsized into early retirement or onto the unemployment line. The young job seekers, meanwhile, are inexperienced next to those older employees. Ten years ago, scores of large companies like IBM toured college campuses snapping up business majors; today IBM is laying thousands of people off. Last spring, the *New York Times* reported that a third of all entry-level jobs for new graduates had "evaporated."

Gary Neilson, a vice-president at Booz, Allen and Hamilton, a manage-   20 ment-consulting firm, sees these losses, in part, as the result of firms reacting to the need for quicker decision-making processes and lower operating costs in the global economic markets. "What's going on in a lot of companies is that there is a recognition of a need for fewer levels in management," he says.

Most of the economy's growth, moreover, is coming from companies often   21 too small to recruit, to pay high wages or even to offer health insurance—companies whose investments in new technologies sometimes seem more cost-effective than hiring new, young workers. As C. Emily Feistritzer of the National Center for Education Information wrote recently, "What is really needed in this country is a focus on creating jobs that utilize the brainpower the nation is producing in ever-increasing numbers."

For graduates facing this new landscape, career counselors are preaching   22 flexibility and liberal-arts degrees. "If someone is interested in economic research, they can work at a coffee shop and use that experience somehow," Hamilton says. "I mean, your long-term goal should inform the kind of work you choose even in a setting that may not be ideal. If you want to, you can find what you need in any kind of setting." In other words, if you approach it correctly, that first job selling blazers at the Gap can be your eventual ticket to success. The other option is to scale down your concept of success. Of course, neither of these approaches is a hallmark of the postwar American imagination.

"The attitude has always been 'Well, I should have had it yesterday,'" Hamilton says. "And right now the sky, from a historical point of view, anyway, is falling for these kids."   23

Seattle is a city full of people who feel like Jim McKay. The coffee shops are manned by thousands of B.A.s and B.S.s from the big state schools and the small liberal-arts colleges, and college diplomas are to waiters and caterers there what acting lessons are to the same professions in New York. But the phenomenon of underemployment is not quarantined to a particular region or grade point or status.   24

Graduates of the country's most competitive schools are succumbing to these fears, too. At Duke University, Larry Goodwyn, a history professor, sees more and more of his top students beginning to worry. "We're talking about a very large shift in outlook for the future," Goodwyn says, "There is a growing sense among them that they can be the first generation in America who can look forward to a decline in their living standards from their parents."   25

Colleges are starting to respond: President Clinton's alma mater, Georgetown University, for example, has begun to hold retreats and seminars at which its students are urged to think about their career choices earlier, and its president, Leo J. O'Donovan, S.J., emphasizes the idea that not everyone has to be a high-salaried investment banker, that teaching second grade is just as worthwhile. And even at Yale, another of the new president's alma maters, career counselors are telling their students that a Yale diploma is not necessarily a guarantee of anything.   26

Some educators and a few economists say the fix is in the lower schools, with more emphasis on basic education and the introduction of mentoring programs sponsored by businesses so that college can be a more career-oriented time. "It seems to me that maybe what's wrong is that people are not getting a good basic education at lower levels," says Nabeel Alsalam of the National Center for Education Statistics. "For quite a few people, college seems to be a place to learn what they should have learned in high school." The flip side of that argument, of course, is that despite what has been guidance-counselored into most students since the sixth grade, not everyone may need to go to college.   27

Or they need to think about different purposes for their college learning. Phyllis Eisen, a senior policy director at the National Association of Manufacturers, is waging a one-woman campaign to eradicate the term *blue collar*. She's trying to persuade counselors from high school on to put a good spin on factory jobs—mostly because factory jobs, characterized as they are by new technological and decision-making powers, are less and less what they used to be. "The twenty percent of people who go to college rarely want to work on a factory floor, no matter how good the job is," Eisen says. "They've been told it's no good for them. It's counterculture. And then you have people going into   28 factories, and it turns out that now you need to know geometry, algebra and trig to read a blueprint to run a robot."

There is also the theory that seems in sync with President Clinton's call for investment in people, especially workers—though it reeks of either socialism or surrender, depending on your preference. It says that if there are going to be more seemingly less-fulfilling jobs, then make them more fulfilling.   29

Starbucks Coffee, Seattle's flagship espresso server, knew that all those frus-trated college grads in Seattle and the West Coast cities it brews in, if properly enticed, would be the perfect people to sell things billed as gourmet. As a result, Starbucks became one of the first companies to offer medical benefits to part-time employees (the major of its employees, in fact) and plenty of opportunity for upward movement. Also, it was the first company in the country to offer part-timers membership in a stock-option plan. In the food-retail business, where employee-attrition rates vary between 200 and 400 percent, Starbucks manages a turnover rate of only 60 percent. And the company's productivity—the magic word in economic circles these days—is booming, a possible lesson for employers of the young and old.   30

Says Howard Schultz, Starbucks's president: "If I were labor secretary, I would lobby heavily for companies to realize that by providing comprehensive benefits for employees, their performance levels will exceed the level of expecta-tion of management, and all three constituencies will win: employees, manage-ment and, if it's a public company, the stockholders. I believe the prototypical American company has to be reinvented, and the employee has to be given the same level of commitment as the customers. When it comes to productivity, mediocrity just won't do."   31

Imagine a world thirty years from now in which both of those theories have become, somehow, fact. Imagine an America where everyone goes to college and biotechnical engineers working in soda factories meet for coffee served by sixty-year-old espresso hands ready to cash in their stock options and retire. The Democratic presidential candidate campaigns on a platform of master's degrees for everyone, and America is winning despite cheap-labor world markets by virtue of high productivity rates and products of exceptional quality. In a way, it would be like America in the Fifties, where a good factory job was all anyone could hope for, except that the factories, technologized to their roofs, would be more like office jobs and everyone would have taken freshman English. If you wanted to pull ahead, you'd probably have to spend decades in graduate school, and there would be a whole new and unimaginable American Dream. □   32

◤ REREADING FOR UNDERSTANDING

1. According to Sullivan, what factors have contributed to the declining job prospects for college graduates? What effect has this downturn had on those without college degrees?

2. How is the recession of the late eighties and early nineties different from previous postwar recessions? Why is the difference significant?

3. This article suggests that the pattern of advancement on the job has changed in recent years. Explain the new trend. Why has the change been good for management but bad for employees?

◢ RESPONDING

1. Many politicians and business executives argue that better education for all United States citizens would make the country economically stronger. In light of Sullivan's article, do you agree with this argument?

2. Sullivan points to changes in the corporate world and the national economy as the chief cause of underemployment, but his article suggests that other factors may be at work as well. For example, more people than ever before are going to college. In other words, many of today's underemployed college graduates would not even have attended college a generation ago. Should fewer people be encouraged to go to college? Consider the future Sullivan projects at the end of the article. Would the life he describes be desirable? Would pursuing a college education be worthwhile under these conditions?

3. What is your response to the testimonies of the underemployed college graduates in this article? Do you sympathize with these people, or do they strike you as complainers?

◢ RESPONDING IN WRITING

Given the job prospects described in Sullivan's article, do you think a college degree is a good investment of time and money? Write an essay addressed to high school students either (1) explaining why you think a college education remains a good investment despite diminished employment opportunities, or (2) proposing alternatives to going to college that are more sensible in light of the current and future job market.

ROBERT REICH

Before becoming secretary of labor under President Clinton, Robert Reich was a lecturer in political economy at the John F. Kennedy School of Government at Harvard University. Both as a scholar and in his cabinet position, Reich has called for government investment in education and job training. Although he acknowledges the same declining job market that Robert E. Sullivan describes in "Greatly Reduced Expectations" (p. 228), Reich argues that the same factors that are causing some jobs to disappear forever will produce an abundance of brand new jobs. These new jobs, however, will require considerably more skill than the ones they replace.

Jobs
Skills Before Credentials

Nearly 50 years ago, the specter of long-term mass joblessness unnerved America. World War II had ended in triumph, but the outbreak of peace held its own perils. The Great Depression had been submerged by war rather than resolved, and there seemed little reason to believe that 1948 would look much different from 1938. The returning GIs, it was thought, must either displace the new workers who had run the wartime economy or else face unemployment themselves as the Depression set in again. It seemed perfectly plain, to experts and ordinary citizens alike, that prospects were grim for a huge number of American workers.

Yet this period of apparently well-founded pessimism gave way to an era of rapid growth and rising living standards. The transition was by no means painless. But the main story, still, is the enormous discrepancy between the fearful expectations of the postwar years and the positive turn that history actually took.

The explanation seems simple: Americans at the time had a vivid picture of imperiled old jobs and only dim inklings of better jobs to come. The economy's capacity to create new jobs simply exceeded the mind's capacity to imagine them.

UNNECESSARY PESSIMISM

We may be at such a juncture once again. Global competition, defense downsizing, corporate restructuring and technological change have put many established jobs at risk. Even informed Americans despair that there will ever be enough good jobs for new entrants to the labor force or for displaced workers. Anxious voices—"Where are the jobs?" "Training for what?"—greet proposals to reform education and deliver competitive job skills.

The future, to be sure, is ultimately as unknowable in 1994 as it was in 1949. But we may be able to use the lessons of the past—as well as some modest advances in economic forecasting—to gain a degree of insight into the jobs of the future. A clearer view of employment prospects may prevent pessimism from undermining concrete measures that would make the good jobs of the future come faster and more surely for American workers.

All the evidence points to strong, long-term growth in demand for workers with problem-solving skills. In the Clinton administration's first 11 months, the economy created more than 1.6 million private-sector jobs. Over the past year, nearly half of the employment growth has been in managerial and professional jobs. The Bureau of Labor Statistics predicts that the number of jobs for technicians will grow 37% between 1990 and 2005.

Yet these familiar categories are only approximate labels for the skill-centered work that is emerging. Distinctions are eroding. The old hierarchy of mid-level managers, lower-level supervisors and low-skilled drones is blurring into a broad class of workplace problem-solvers. Expertise and authority seep away from the front office and are dispersed throughout the productive team. "Goods" and "services" are becoming less distinct, as more and more of the value of a product is embedded in related services delivered both before it is manufactured (design, programming, process engineering) and after it is sold (targeted distribution, customized installation, training in applications).

Credentialism is breaking down. Many of the fastest-growing good jobs—   8
factory technician, data-processor—don't require a college degree. But as formal credentials become less essential, up-to-date skills become ever more crucial—even in jobs where the unskilled could formerly thrive.

Workers without skills, meanwhile, find their options shrinking. More than   9
ever before, what you earn depends on what you learn. Americans without training beyond high school have suffered a continuing decline in earnings over the past 15 years. High-school dropouts have been hit even harder, with collapsing wage rates and rising unemployment.

Like comparable periods before, our current era of rapid economic change   10
opens new opportunities. Every American can develop the skills to make it in the new economy. The winners won't be limited to college graduates. A recent study by economists Tom Kane and Cecilia Rouse found that every year of post-secondary training in universities or community colleges, and whether leading to a degree or not, boosts annual earning power by 5% to 10%. The good jobs of the future won't fit neatly into our current categories of "manager/managed" or "high-tech/low-tech."

Examples abound. There's a new kind of delivery truck driver equipped   11
with a computer and modem in her cab, so she can time deliveries to exactly when customers need them, and then custom-assemble the complex machinery she's delivering. She shares little more than a job title with the trucker of 10 years ago. She's a high-skilled service technician, and she's making good money.

Throughout the economy, familiar-sounding jobs are becoming more   12
demanding, and more rewarding, as job descriptions metamorphose. In 1990, just 18% of the functions in a typical Ford automobile were computer-controlled. In 1994, the proportion is 82%. This technological shift has profound consequences for the number and nature of good jobs. Auto mechanics skilled in computer diagnostics can command annual salaries ranging from $30,000 to $75,000. In the same way, assembly work is transformed, as a new kind of factory worker sits behind a computer, programming and reprogramming a robot that does the pulling and twisting that human beings used to do.

The bad news about our current juncture in economic history is real   13
enough: More and more old jobs are imperiled by global economic integration and technological change. Fewer and fewer Americans can count on holding a single job throughout their careers, and the unskilled face worsening odds for sustainable prosperity.

SKILLS PAY OFF

But the good news is equally real, if less obvious: The payoff to skills is surging.   14
Technological evolution is spawning a profusion of good new jobs. Integrated,

expanding global markets create many more opportunities than they close off. And the skills needed for many of these high-skill, high-wage jobs can be learned, often through two-year associate's degrees, apprenticeship programs and on-the-job training.

Hard questions remain. How do we ensure that the right kinds of training   15 are available, at the right time, as Americans struggle with work-force transitions? How do we buffer the shock of change for workers who now depend on vulnerable jobs and industries? The Clinton administration is working hard to answer these questions.

But one question—"training for what?"—is easier to answer than it seems.   16 The evidence shows that skills pay off. The evidence shows that American workers can learn. "Training for what?" For the high-skill work taking shape all around us today. America's economy is racing into the future. There is no excuse for leaving a single citizen behind. □

◢ REREADING FOR UNDERSTANDING

1. According to Reich, in what way are the mid-1990s similar to the late 1940s? What lesson from the post–World War II economy should we consider when contemplating today's gloomy job market?

2. Reich says that the traditional categories of jobs and distinctions of hierarchy are changing. How?

3. What is "credentialism"(par. 8)? Why does Reich believe it is less important now than it used to be?

◢ RESPONDING

Reich sees the current job market in a much more optimistic light than Robert L. Sullivan ("Greatly Reduced Expectations," p. 228) does. What reasons does each writer offer to support his outlook? Who do you think presents the more credible argument?

ERIC ZICKLIN

Although the jobless rate has dropped somewhat as the economy has improved in the mid-1990s, the corporate restructuring and downsizing in the 1980s and early 1990s resulted in permanent changes in the job market. No longer does a college degree guarantee an interview, much less a job. Nevertheless, as the college graduates featured in this article from *Rolling Stone* testify, there are still opportunities for rewarding work.

Mod Jobs

Y ou've been hearing it since high school: Work is scarce these days; you'll   1
be lucky to get a job answering someone's phones. Take whatever you
can get.

Well, it's all true. The number of jobs offered to the college class of '94 was   2
down more than 30 percent from pre-recession levels. In fact, every year of the
'90s so far has seen a drop in the percentage of graduating seniors hired. What's
worse is that according to the most recent U.S. Bureau of Labor Statistics survey,
20 percent of college grads were either unemployed or working jobs that don't require college diplomas. In 1970 only 11 percent of graduates fell into that category.

Pretty bleak. But there *is* hope. Even as the social contract of education for   3
prosperity continues to disintegrate, people recently sprung from college are
improvising strange and twisted paths to contentment and security. They're
doing it without mentors in fields they didn't always intend to join. They are
trusting their instincts to guide them along the unmarked trail that some still
call a job market.

Here are four examples of such people. They are strangers to one another,   4
but they share a spirit of persistence and innovation that is critical to finding
(or in some cases creating) good work. They also enjoy the odd privilege of
holding jobs that their parents could never have filled, because these occupations didn't even exist a generation ago.

CHRISTOPHER KEISER

Christopher Keiser is about the happiest person he knows. "I've met so many   5
lawyers and accountants who say, 'Man, you've got the greatest job.' And I say
'Yeah, I do.'"

Keiser's job is to teach those lawyers and accountants how to avoid physi-   6
cal disaster when they step into their in-line roller skates and attempt the
street's most dangerous sport. As an instructor at the Rollerblade Inc.-spon-
sored Blade School, in Los Angeles, Keiser, 25, has found a way to make money
doing exactly what he loves to do—skating.

There are about 1,500 in-line instructors nationwide, but that number is   7
ultimately expected to hit 20,000. The fastest-growing sport of the '90s, in-line
skating has created an industry that has quadrupled during the past five years
and is now worth an estimated $400 million a year. The sport has more partic-
ipants than alpine skiing; blading also has a startling injury rate, so people like
Keiser are in demand, fetching $12–$35 per hour for lessons.

Like most people in their 20s, Keiser has struggled through brain-numbing   8
jobs behind store counters. Unlike most he has also worked on the crews of
touring yachts, and he even juggled on the streets to pay for his two years at
Northern Colorado University. "I wasn't too happy," he says of those times.

Now, though, Keiser acknowledges that he sometimes laughs at his good   9
fortune. "I live 10 blocks from the beach," he says. "I just bought a new road

bike, and my patio is bigger than my entire first apartment. Something's definitely going right."

With his teaching experience and encyclopedic knowledge of in-line prod-   10
ucts, Keiser is qualified to take a step up the corporate ladder. "I just declined
an extremely lucrative offer from another company to be a sales rep," he says,
"which made me realize that I'm pretty marketable in this business. That was
an eye-opener. I mean, I could really have a future here."

So could many other people. According to the Bureau of Labor Statistics'   11
Occupational Outlook Quarterly, recreation-related jobs are expected to grow
"faster than average in response to population growth, increased interest in
health and fitness and rising demand for organized recreational activities." Dr.
Victor R. Lindquist, former dean of placement at Northwestern University and
the executive director of Career Management Research Institute, in Oak Brook,
Ill., agrees. "There is a tremendous market of people who are looking for new
ways to take care of their bodies."

Although Keiser races professionally, consistently placing in the top 5 per-   12
cent, his athleticism did not win him his position at Blade School. Teaching
skills—rather than blinding speed or airborne stunts—separate competent
skaters from employable instructors. "You have to love to skate, and you have to
want to teach," Keiser says of his job's most important requirements. "A couple
of our instructors actually learned how to skate right here at Blade School. So
you don't have to be a superstar."

The school's instructors learn how to teach through training programs   13
sponsored by the International In-line Skating Association, in Atlanta. A weekend of intensive clinics (and a $275 fee) can turn anyone with skating profi-
ciency into a certified instructor.

On the subject of instructing, Keiser is downright evangelical. "It's the most   14
incredible feeling to watch the beginners learn," he says. "They're always so
shocked that they're actually skating. Then they're hooked on the sport, and
that's such a rush. I mean, I'm turning people on to good stuff here. It's like taking someone to your favorite restaurant and watching them discover how great
it is. I do that with 20 people every day."

Keiser's excitement hasn't been lost on the people around him. His father   15
recently told him how impressed he was with his son's enthusiasm for work.
"He told me for the first time that he was proud of me," the younger Keiser says.
"He's pretty miserable with his job, and he said he was proud that I'm taking
care of myself and enjoying it at the same time. He was amazed by that, and I
said, 'I am, too.'"

JILL BAUER

As the 500-channel future quickly becomes a cluttered reality, entirely new   16
genres of television programming are being unveiled each year, creating thousands of jobs out of thin air, or cable, anyway. Jill Bauer is already exploiting this
programming revolution to find more fun and fatter paychecks for herself.

You've seen Bauer before—probably more than once. She's an on-air host   17
at QVC, the largest home-shopping channel in the world. Bauer is one of those
smiling people who can effortlessly explain the merits of exfoliating cream,
nylon sweat suits or autographed portraits of Pete Maravich without the slightest hesitation, all while callers are patched in to offer their own breathless testi-
monials, and the sales total climbs to levels that nearly match the 800 number.
"I've always had the gift of gab, and I love to shop," she says, "so I guess this is
the perfect job for me."

As one of the untiring personalities whom viewers trust and respond to,   18
Bauer, 26, is part of the reason her employer was able to coax $1.2 billion out
of America's credit cards last year. In 1993 viewers coughed up $8 billion for
products that were offered on television and mailed to their homes.

After graduating from the University of Missouri, Bauer worked for four   19
years as a television news reporter and weekend anchor in Lafayette, Ind. "The
reality of the TV news industry," she says, "is that you've got to be ready to start
at $200 a week. And you've got to be ready to do it in places like Yakima [Wash.]
or Dubuque [Iowa]."

That all changed for Bauer when stations like QVC started filling out the   20
cable dial. Now working in West Chester, Pa., she earns nearly three times what
she used to make in Lafayette. And she's happier in the new job. "In that anchor
chair, I could never be Jill," she says. "But I can be myself on QVC. I can be silly,
laugh out loud and just let go. I can let Jill be Jill."

And she says the perks are better these days, too. "I get to go to New York   21
City fashion shows in a limo," Bauer says. "I mean, do I love this job or what?"

Though Bauer is the youngest on-air host at QVC, she is hardly the token   22
twentysomething among the staff and crew. In fact, 30 percent of the company's
employees are between 20 and 30, including producers, buyers, graphic designers, photographers, publicists, copywriters and one senior vice president of programming, who is only 29. In an industry as young as electronic retailing,
young people define the spirit of the workplace. "This company is only 8 years
old," Bauer says. "It's just a baby. I know the business is huge, but there's still a
lot more to come."

Most of that growth, say experts like Lindquist, will be in *behind*-the-camera   23
personnel. "People who have the technical background to handle the multimedia," he says, "are never out of work for long."

Bauer's work so far has generally been scheduled for the graveyard shift,   24
sometimes for nine consecutive nights. "At 3 a.m. I start to drag," she says, "especially when I'm selling the Vornado air circulator for the 28th time."

So don't anyone say that Bauer's job is cushy. "This is the hardest job I've   25
ever had," she says. "It's a zillion times harder than TV news, because I do so
much prep work to learn about all the products I'm going to be selling that
night. Plus I go to the factories to see how everything is made, so I can explain
why this doll costs $300, even though the other one was $75."

Such discipline pays off when Bauer smoothly chats her way through an-   26
other three- to four-hour shift of live television without a script, a TelePromp-
Ter or cue cards. "I forget that I'm selling," she says. "I just go out there, shop and
talk about the items. That's when Jill is Jill."

ERIK LEVY

Erik Levy couldn't wait for his diploma before getting down to work. "I always   27
knew I wanted to start a business of some kind," he says, "and I had taken all the
economics classes I could stand. So I left college without a degree and moved
on. I *had* to move on."

And Levy hasn't looked back since. As the founder and president of Save   28
That Stuff, Levy, 26, manages a cardboard-recycling business in Boston that
grosses $15,000–$20,000 a month. "In 1990," he says, "I grossed $15,000 for the
whole year. So right now I'm completely psyched about the business."

At Denison University, in Granville, Ohio, Levy worked on the school's   29
recycling truck, which collected corrugated cardboard from around campus
then delivered it to a nearby mill that would transform it onto chipboard.
Spaghetti boxes, pizza boxes, note-pad covers and game boards all are made
of chipboard.

When he first moved to Boston, Levy sought work with a cardboard-   30
recycling company, but he couldn't find a single one. So he started his own. "I
knew Save That Stuff would work even when I had only one customer," he says.
"I remember they paid me $120 a month to pick up their cardboard, and as a
result, they lowered their trash bill $500 a month."

Local garbage services charge about $6–$15 per cubic yard to cart away any   31
kind of refuse, according to Levy. Save That Stuff charges $3 per cubic yard
strictly for cardboard. So by hiring Levy, business owners are able to save money
while simultaneously helping the environment. "I always say to new customers,
'Why do you want to pay top dollar for the trash company to dump your cardboard in a landfill, when you can pay me half as much and know that it's being
recycled?"

It's tough logic to argue with. Yet even now, with more than 200 accounts,   32
including four Kmarts and three Tower Records outlets, Levy meets plenty of
resistance. "It's hard to convince the older people," he says. "Mention the word
recycle to them, and they think, 'That doesn't work, and it's gonna cost me
extra.'

"I have to educate people that recycling cardboard isn't just the charitable   33
thing," Levy says. "It's good business."

It's certainly been good for Levy's business. Save That Stuff collects 250 tons   34
of cardboard a month, each ton of which he sells for $50. "That's why we call it
brown gold," he says.

Whatever its color, the gold doesn't come easy. Levy works six-day, 80-hour   35
weeks, wooing new customers and managing the paperwork in addition to collecting cardboard. The business has grown enough to allow him to purchase a
10-wheel packer garbage truck, the appearance of which caused one competitor
to anonymously phone Levy. "He told me, 'You've got some balls buying a
packer. After you go bankrupt, I'm going to buy that truck off the repo company,'" Levy recalls, laughing.

Lindquist, the career expert, shares Levy's cheerful outlook. "As people   36
make the personal commitment to choose recycled products," he says, "the economics of recycling companies will become better and better."

Levy guesses that Lindquist's outlook will mean selling Save That Stuff to   37
one of the bigger trash companies, perhaps even to his mysterious caller. But he
isn't looking forward to that day. Instead, he wants to continue collecting more
cardboard and converting more business owners to a recycling way of life.

Levy knows that this kind of work matters. He's got evidence: "I've recycled   38
more than 3,500 tons of cardboard with this business," he says. "So I've saved
about 60,000 trees. That's a small forest, I guess. And that's the most rewarding
thing in the world. To help. To know that you've helped."

REGINA JOSEPH

"Older people like to say that if you've got the skills and the energy, you'll always   39
find work. Well, that's bullshit. Total bullshit," says Regina Joseph.

"I know plenty of people with master's degrees in journalism who are in-   40
telligent and vigorous," she says, "and they're working as bartenders. There's no
room for them in the conventional publishing world.'"

Joseph, a 29-year-old New Yorker who graduated from Hamilton College,   41
in Clinton, N.Y., is one of the leaders of the *un*conventional publishing world
as the co-founder and editor in chief of *Blender,* a CD-ROM magazine about
pop culture due out in late October. She believes she's found a work source for
young writers, designers, photographers and filmmakers who may be frustrated
with mixing margaritas for a living. "Digital technology has revealed a brand-
new world," she says. "If you're smart, and you've got a good idea, there's a ton
of opportunity at this end of the media."

Comparable measures of weight can be found on the crowded shelves of   42
computer stores, where more than 8,000 titles, including *The Lifestyles of the
Rich and Famous Cookbook* and the collection of London's National Gallery, are
now available on CD-ROM. There is also the startling success of *Myst,* a CD-
ROM adventure game that has unexpectedly sold approximately 500,000 units
so far on little more than work-of-mouth publicity.

Even implacable job experts are giddy about the future of CD-ROM. Lind-   43
quist predicts that the machines will soon be as common as the three and half
inch computer drive. "In the next five years, it's going to blow us away," says
Charlie Drozdyk, author of *Hot Jobs* (HarperCollins). Already CD-ROM titles
are selling at a rate four times faster than in 1993.

"It's not linear the way that print is," Joseph says of the CD-ROMs, each of   44
which holds as much information as 300 floppies. "And it's not passive the way
that TV and film are, where your only two choices are to watch or not watch."

The first issue of *Blender* (price: $19.95) proves Joseph's point, as every   45
article is chockablock with options. In the cover story you are presented with a
floor plan to Henry Rollins' house, where his publishing company is based. Pick
any room and you are greeted with video images of the artist himself, guiding
you through his living and working space. He even lets you look into his fridge.

Each album review in the issue is accompanied by audiovisual samples of   46
the artists so that the bands' sounds can be experienced instead of merely
described, as they are in print publications. And to enhance the unpredictability

of "reading" *Blender*, there are trapdoors scattered throughout the magazine that lead to live-performance footage and other treats. "This isn't like a regular magazine," Joseph says, "where all of the content is readily apparent. You're going to have to use your brain to find the hidden parts, the secret areas."

Joseph estimates that it will take three to four hours to see and hear every-   46
thing in an issue of *Blender*. Finding an investor for the magazine, however, took Joseph quite a bit longer. "It's been two full years from making a prototype to launching the first issue," she says. "And there were months—not moments, *months*—when I thought it would never work. There were so many rejections, so many presentations that led nowhere. It was almost too frustrating to bear."

But Dennis Publishing, which is one of the largest publishers of computer   47
magazines in England, ultimately signed on, and Joseph was rescued from her life in print publications, where, she says, there was so much fear of unemployment among the young staffers that they forgot to have fun. "Two years ago I was working at *Spin*," she recalls, "and I knew that I was lucky to be there. But when I looked around the industry, I saw people my age settling, working for people they despised and doing jobs that they didn't even enjoy.

"The thought of spending my life like that scared me," Joseph says. "Better   48
to take a chance, and try to do your own ideas."

If the country's 6 million CD-ROM owners embrace Joseph's current idea,   49
she may change the way we read magazines. The stress of self-employment, however, has already changed parts of Joseph. "This job has given me a nice John Davidson streak in my hair," she says. "It's going to have me gray by the time I'm 30." ☐

◢ RESPONDING

1. Compare the individuals profiled in this piece with those interviewed in "Greatly Reduced Expectations" (p. 228). What similarities and differences do you find in their situations, attitudes, and approaches to work?

2. Do the "mod jobs" in this article give credibility to Robert Reich's claim that the new economy is creating new jobs for people with the right skills? Are these four individuals just lucky, or are they pioneers in the new job market?

◢ RESPONDING IN WRITING

1. Do you have a special interest or talent that you wish you could turn into an occupation? Write an essay describing your ideal job, one that would allow you to do the things that you do best and enjoy most.

2. Like the people profiled in Zicklin's article, many of us have talents and skills that may not come to light on a job application or in an interview, but that could be applied in useful ways in a variety of jobs. Make a list of your hobbies, talents, and special interests. For each item on your list, try to think of at least one kind of work for which it could be usefully applied.

3. Have you considered the kind of work you hope to do when you graduate from college? Given the competitive job market described in the readings in this section, you'll need to be able to demonstrate abilities, training, or traits that will set you apart from the competition. Choose an employer for whom you would like to work in the future, and write a letter of recommendation on your own behalf to that individual or corporation. Tell what qualifications make you the best candidate in contention.

McDONALD'S

Check Out the Flip Side of Flippin' Burgers

At McDonald's, we're flippin' the script on what you think about flippin' burgers. McDonald's crew members have lots of opportunities for career advancement and growth. More than 60% of McDonald's restaurant managers and more than a third of McDonald's restaurant owners began as crew members. And McDonald's devotes millions of dollars to ongoing employee training. But the most important thing is, this training equips crew members with a variety of job skills that can be used at McDonald's, or anywhere else.

Have you had your break today?

RESPONDING

1. Who is the target audience for this ad? How can you tell?

2. What preconceived ideas or stereotypes about jobs does this ad assume? How does the ad attempt to counter those ideas?

Truth and Lying

INTRODUCTION

t's 10 P.M. the night before the toughest exam of the semester. You're studying in your dorm room with a couple of friends, looking over class notes, texts, and old exams from previous semesters. Another friend comes in with a copy of an exam that you haven't seen before. You add it to the stack of study materials, answer the questions, share your answers. The next morning, when you open your exam, you discover that it is the test you studied from the night before.

You're living in a foreign city as a student in a study-abroad program. In your hotel lives a retired American, a prominent and highly respected figure. During your stay, this individual repeatedly attempts to initiate a sexual relationship with you. You refuse his advances as politely as you can, but you are relieved when your studies are over and you leave him behind. Months later you hear that another student has charged this person with sexual harassment. You are disturbed to learn that her accusations of unwanted sexual advances are regarded by most people as lies or fantasy.

You're the news editor at your local television station. The lead story one night is flooding in a nearby community. Only a few minutes remain before air time, and your camera crew has not returned with footage of the flood. Then you remember that the same area flooded two years ago and that you still have footage of that flood.

What would you do in any of these situations? Would you explain to your professor that you had unwittingly studied an advance copy of the exam? Would you speak up in defense of your fellow student and victim and tell of your own experience? Would you broadcast a major story without accompanying visuals?

The answer *should* be simple. Just tell the truth. Haven't we all been told from a very early age that honesty is the best policy? And yet we also learn quite early in life that telling the truth—or even knowing what the truth is—is often not as easy as it seems.

We all know, because we've all lied at one time or another, that there are times when concealing the truth or even lying seems more practical, safer, perhaps ultimately better for the cause of truth than disclosing all we know or think. Consider the three situations that open this unit. In each case, telling the truth would have serious consequences. In the first, to admit to having seen an advance copy of the exam would be, at the very least, to implicate others in a serious academic offense. In the second, to speak up about the sexual advances you had to fend off would mean having to talk publicly about something that was personally embarrassing and distasteful, and to risk having your own honesty questioned. The third may seem the most clear-cut; obviously, it would be wrong to mislead an audience by showing film of something that happened two years ago and suggesting it was a current event. On the other hand, the third situation may be the least clear-cut: as long as you do not *say* the pictures are of this year's flood, are you really lying? If the pictures are simply shown concurrently with the story, are you responsible for the conclusions the audience draws?

Recognizing that there are often strong motives for concealing or distorting the truth leads us to recognize the difficulty of knowing the truth. Much of the information we receive comes to us from other sources, and even if those sources are not deliberately misleading, they are at least subjective. Can we ever know the truth about an event that happened in the past, for example, or an experience that happened to someone else? Any information that comes to us second-hand, whether it be about the Battle of Gettysburg or a friend's fight with her boyfriend, has already been interpreted by at least one other person by the time we receive it. Even when we witness or experience an event first-hand, we cannot be certain that our understanding of that event is complete or even accurate.

The Contexts essays in this unit present three different perspectives on the acceptability and advisability of deception as a general practice. The Controversies essays then provide opportunities to consider specific problems we face both in trying to discover the truth and in deciding whether to reveal, conceal, or distort what we know.

Because much of the information we take in comes to us through broadcast or print media, the first group of Controversies essays asks whether it's possible to learn the truth from these sources. Can a television news story fairly and fully represent the event it reports? Can we expect advertisements to tell us any true or useful information about the products we must choose among?

The second group of essays focuses on the question of cheating. Most of us face enormous pressure to succeed and compete, and dishonesty in and out of the academic world is therefore a powerful temptation. In a 1992 survey of 6,000 students, 76 percent reported cheating in high school or college. Of course, the academy isn't the only setting for cheating, as numerous scandals in business and government confirm.

The last set of Controversies essays considers the problem of keeping secrets. Is failure to disclose all you know equivalent to lying? What should you do when lying is necessary to protect yourself or someone else?

A WAY IN

*H*onesty is regarded as a virtue almost universally. Most of us would say that we try to be honest in dealing with others as well as in judging ourselves. But have you ever stopped to notice the number of small deceptions you engage in on any given day? How many times today have

you given a compliment you didn't really mean, kept silent in the face of opposition, equivocated to avoid taking responsibility? In "The Uses of Fiction," poet
Naomi Shihab Nye presents one of those moments when honesty may *not* be the
best policy.

NAOMI SHIHAB NYE

The daughter of a Palestinian father and a German-American mother,
Naomi Shihab Nye spent most of her childhood in St. Louis, Missouri. When
she was in high school, Nye's family moved to Jerusalem for a year, then to
San Antonio, Texas, where she lives today. Nye says she draws inspiration for
her poetry from "local life, random characters met on the streets, our own
ancestry sifting down to us through small essential daily tasks."

The Use of Fiction

A boy claims he saw you on a bicycle last week,
touring his neighborhood. "West Cypress Street!" he shouts,
as if your being there and his seeing you
were some sort of benediction.

To be alive, to be standing outside   5
on a tender February evening . . .
"It was a blue bicycle, ma'am, your braid was flying,
I said hello and you laughed, remember?"

You almost tell him your bicycle seat is thick with dust,
the tires have been flat for months.   10
But his face, that radiant flower, says you are his friend,
he has told his mother your name!
Maybe this is a clear marble
he will hide in his sock drawer for months.
So who now, in a world of figures,   15
would deny West Cypress Street,
throwing up clouds into this literal sky?
"Yes, Amigo"—hand on shoulder—
"It was I."

◢ REREADING FOR UNDERSTANDING

I. Explain the metaphor in lines 13 and 14: "Maybe this is a clear marble/he
    will hide in his sock drawer for months." What is "this"? What does the
    comparison suggest about the narrator? about the boy?

2. What is the significance of the title? In what sense is "fiction" synonymous with "lying"? In what way are the terms different?

◢ RESPONDING

1. What do you think is the relationship between the narrator and the boy? Have they met before?

2. Why does the narrator decide not to tell the boy the truth? Would you have done the same in her place? Why or why not?

◢ RESPONDING THROUGH WRITING

Try to recall a time when you agonized over whether or not to tell the truth. Describe the situation, explaining why it was such a dilemma, what you finally decided, and why.

NICCOLO MACHIAVELLI

Niccolo Machiavelli (1469–1527) dedicated *The Prince* to Lorenzo de Medici in 1513, explaining that of the many possessions he might offer to win the favor of the new duke of Florence, none was more valuable than "the knowledge of the actions of men, learned by me from long experience with modern things and a continuous reading of ancient ones." The short treatise suggests the qualities a prince must exhibit in order to acquire and maintain power. Machiavelli recognized that the prince's power depends on both the love and the fear of his subjects. Thus, Machiavelli advised, the prince must *appear* to be morally virtuous in the eyes of his subjects, even as he must resort to vice as needed to subdue and control them. In this chapter, he discusses the importance of the prince's word.

In What Mode Faith Should Be Kept by Princes

How laudable it is for a prince to keep his faith, and to live with honesty and not by astuteness, everyone understands. Nonetheless one sees by experience in our times that the princes who have done great things are those who have taken little account of faith and have known how to get around men's brains with their astuteness; and in the end they have overcome those who have founded themselves on loyalty.

Thus, you must know that there are two kinds of combat: one with laws, the other with force. The first is proper to man, the second to beasts; but because the first is often not enough, one must have recourse to the second. Therefore it is necessary for a prince to know well how to use the beast and the man. This role was taught covertly to princes by ancient writers, who wrote that Achilles, and many other ancient princes, were given to Chiron the centaur to be raised, so that he would look after them with his discipline. To have as teacher a half-beast, half-man means nothing other than that a prince needs to know how to use both natures; and the one without the other is not lasting.

Thus, since a prince is compelled of necessity to know well how to use the beast, he should pick the fox and the lion, because the lion does not defend itself from snares and the fox does not defend itself from wolves. So one needs to be a fox to recognize snares and a lion to frighten the wolves. Those who stay simply with the lion do not understand this. A prudent lord, therefore, cannot observe faith, nor should he, when such observance turns against him, and the causes that made him promise have been eliminated. And if all men were good, this teaching would not be good; but because they are wicked and do not observe faith with you, you also do not have to observe it with them. Nor does a prince ever lack legitimate causes to color his failure to observe faith. One could give infinite modern examples of this, and show how many peace treaties and promises have been rendered invalid and vain through the infidelity of princes; and the one who has known best how to use the fox has come out best. But it is necessary to know well how to color this nature, and to be a great pretender and dissembler; and men are so simple and so obedient to present necessities that he who deceives will always find someone who will let himself be deceived. 3

I do not want to be silent about one of the recent examples. Alexander VI never did anything, nor ever thought of anything, but how to deceive men, and he always found a subject to whom he could do it. And there never was a man with greater efficacy in asserting a thing, and in affirming it with greater oaths, who observed it less; nonetheless, his deceits succeeded at his will, because he well knew this aspect of the world. 4

Thus, it is not necessary for a prince to have all the above-mentioned qualities in fact, but it is indeed necessary to appear to have them. Nay, I dare say this, that by having them and always observing them, they are harmful; and by appearing to have them, they are useful, as it is to appear merciful, faithful, humane, honest, and religious, and to be so; but to remain with a spirit built so that, if you need not to be those things, you are able and know how to change to the contrary. This has to be understood: that a prince, and especially a new prince, cannot observe all those things for which men are held good, since he is often under a necessity, to maintain his state, of acting against faith, against charity, against humanity, against religion. And so he needs to have a spirit disposed to change as the winds of fortune and variations of things command him, and as I said above, not depart from good, when possible, but know how to enter into evil, when forced by necessity. 5

A prince should thus take great care that nothing escape his mouth that is not full of the above-mentioned five qualities and that, to see him and hear him, he should appear all mercy, all faith, all honesty, all humanity, all religion. And nothing is more necessary to appear to have than this last quality. Men in general judge more by their eyes than by their hands, because seeing is given to everyone, touching to few. Everyone sees how you appear, few touch what you are; and these few dare not oppose the opinion of many, who have the majesty of the state to defend them; and in the actions of all men, and especially of princes, where there is no court to appeal to, one looks to the end. So let a prince win and maintain his state: the means will always be judged honorable, 6 and will be praised by everyone. For the vulgar are taken in by the appearance and the outcome of a thing, and in the world there is no one but the vulgar; the few have a place there when the many have somewhere to lean on. A certain prince of present times, whom it is not well to name, never preaches anything but peace and faith, and is very hostile to both. If he had observed both, he would have had either his reputation or his state taken from him many times. □

◪ REREADING FOR UNDERSTANDING

1. In paragraph 1, Machiavelli sets forth the paradox that the rest of the essay addresses. What is that paradox? Do you think it applies to political leadership today?

2. What does Machiavelli mean when he says that a prince "must know well how to use the beast and the man" (par. 2)? Why does he recommend the fox and lion (par. 3) as the beasts a prince should use? Why is it necessary to be able to use both, not merely one or the other?

3. Machiavelli says that it is impossible for a prince, especially a new prince, actually to embody the virtues he should *appear* to possess. Why? Why is it more important, according to Machiavelli, to *appear* "merciful, faithful, humane, honest, and religious" (par 5.) than to *be* so?

◪ RESPONDING

1. In paragraph 3, Machiavelli presents an argument that says, essentially, it's OK to lie to people who lie to you. Do you agree with this justification? Would it apply to other vices as well? For example, is it OK to steal from people who steal from you?

2. Machiavelli argues (par. 6): "Let a prince win and maintain his state: the means will always be judged honorable, and will be praised by everyone." Do you think this is an accurate observation of human nature? Do people tend to forgive wrongdoing if they benefit from its consequences? Do you agree with this advice for rulers? If you can, give an example of circumstances in which it might be acceptable for a ruler to lie to the people "for their own good."

HARRIET GOLDHOR LERNER

In her book *The Dance of Deception*, psychotherapist Harriet Goldhor Lerner looks at the strategies we use to keep from facing the truth. Acknowledging that total honesty with others may not be possible in every situation, Lerner nevertheless suggests that continually pretending that problems don't exist or denying the complexity of our feelings only leads to more problems. In this chapter, she discusses the problem of benevolent lies, those lies we tell to protect others.

To Do the Right Thing

In 1970, Dr. Robert Wolk and Arthur Henley published a book called *The Right to Lie,* the first "how-to" guide on using deceit in everyday life. The authors provide numerous examples of "constructive" and "worthwhile" lies that purportedly strengthen intimate relationships.

There is the case of Evelyn G., for example, who with her husband consults a doctor after trying unsuccessfully for a year to become pregnant. Following fertility tests, the doctor telephones Evelyn and asks her to visit him privately. He then informs her that her husband is sterile, but asks her to consider whether her husband should be told. The authors continue:

> Evelyn is deeply disappointed. She has an impulse to tell her husband, "See, I'm not to blame! It's all your fault!" But she knows that this will strike at the heart of his self-esteem. The doctor agrees, adding that such an accusation might possibly even make Paul G. impotent.
>
> To preserve her sex life and her husband's sensibilities, Evelyn decides to tell a lie. She takes full blame for her inability to conceive. It is a "loving" lie, that protects the marriage. As Evelyn had expected, her husband is sympathetic and tells her not to feel badly, that he will be just as happy to adopt a baby. That is **his** loving lie and concludes an even exchange of deceits that strengthens the relationship.

According to the authors, the "constructive lies" that Evelyn and Paul exchange are born of necessity and kindness, and serve to reinforce the loving bond between them. Happily, the specifics of their story is dated[.] . . . If nothing else, a physician who joins with one spouse to falsify medical facts to the other might fear a malpractice suit. People still justify lying, however, if they believe it serves a protective end or a greater good. What has changed are cultural norms, and we have changed with them. As creatures of culture and context, our beliefs about "constructive lies" shift with the political climate of the day.

I have thought hard about the impact of culture and context, particularly as I watched the televised congressional hearings in 1991 that turned into a painful and outrageous attack on Anita Hill, as she tried to tell the truth about Supreme Court Justice nominee Clarence Thomas. In the midst of the moral outrage I felt on her behalf, I recalled an experience I had in 1962, more than a quarter of a century ago.

I was spending my junior year of college in Delhi, India, in a program sponsored by the University of Wisconsin, where I was an undergraduate. Midway through the year, I moved from Miranda House, a college dorm in Old Delhi, to a room in a nearby hotel. At this same hotel lived a distinguished

American, perhaps forty years my senior, who had retired from a high government position. He was, in his own words, "a very important man." Indeed, he was the most important man I had ever encountered close up.

For months he pursued me aggressively and inappropriately for sex. Later that year, when I came down with malaria, he made advances toward a close woman friend who was caring for me at the time, and was also an American student in the program. After my recovery, I was relieved to find that he continued to pursue her rather than me. 6

I always found this man's advances unwelcome and discomfiting. Yet never for a moment did I question the "right" of so prominent a man—a veritable force in history, as I saw it—to persist in his efforts to get what he wanted. I was always more attuned and vigilantly protective of his feelings than of my own. My friend and I discussed his advances only with each other. We said nothing to the leader of our program in Delhi. 7

The following year, back in Madison, Wisconsin, my friend and I sat with this same program leader in the cafeteria of the Student Union. He was visiting briefly from Delhi and was about to return there. Suddenly departing from small talk, he told us that a student was currently reporting sexual advances from this same man. He quickly added that this honorable gentleman would never do such a thing. The student could only be mistaken. 8

"Right?" he said in our direction. It may well have been meant as a question, but I heard it as a declaration or challenge. My friend and I nodded affirmatively and nothing more was said on the subject. It wasn't until 1991, as I watched, in astonishment, the enemies of Anita Hill, that I thought with sorrow and disbelief about my nod and subsequent silence. Why did I leave that brave student, halfway across the world, in a position of isolation and vulnerability? What was her name? What price did she pay for speaking the truth? Why had I not spoken out? I felt ashamed of myself—particularly because I had felt not the slightest hint of shame at the time. 9

I'm sure that I lied for many of the usual reasons people lie: to make myself most comfortable at the moment, to escape disapproval and censure, to avoid complexity and complication, to keep at bay my own emotions, which were linked to my earlier experience. My friend and I feared, perhaps rightfully so, that our disclosure might also be discounted or held against us. Our program head was a compassionate and intelligent man, but the cultural climate of the day enforced denial. 10

More to the point, I thought at the time that I was doing *the right thing*. I believed that it was my responsibility to protect the reputation of this very important man. I figured that the woman, whoever she was, could handle the situation. But the public image (and personal feelings) of an older man of high status was another matter. Like Evelyn G., who lied to protect her husband from injury and impotence, I believed that my lie was "constructive," even honorable. 11

How could I have thought this way? Or, given that I did think this way, why is my current perspective so radically different? A generous friend explains, "Well, you're obviously much braver now." I share her view that courage, like good taste, is acquired with age. But I was courageous during my college years, and was not one to submit to injunctions that violated my conscience. No, my 12 individual bravery was not the issue here. Rather, the bravery of other women transformed cultural norms.

The first to speak out about abuses of power must be particularly brave or   13
thick-skinned. When I was in college, terms such as "sexual harassment," "date rape," "sexual abuse," and even "sexism" had not yet been invented. The word "patriarchy" wasn't in my vocabulary. We called these things "life," and I never considered the necessity, or even the possibility, of women creating and codifying language. Without the vocabulary, however, I was unable to name, much less protest, what was happening inside and around me. Also, as more women told the truth, my beliefs about what constitutes "honorable lying" changed, and I began to reexamine the question of who needs protection from whom. Watching Anita Hill reminded me of how much—and how little—has changed in the world since my undergraduate days.

If even one heroic male senator had stood up in eloquent outrage at the   14
abusive treatment of Anita Hill, the "ordinary folks" watching television might have been better able to open their eyes to the abuses of our patriarchal fathers. Yet when it comes to interpreting the motivations of others, we can never know the whole story. In protecting the president's nominee, these politicians might also have convinced themselves that they were engaging in an honorable lie or a noble silence. They might have believed that protecting "a very important man"—and the collective rule of men—served a greater good. Perhaps they believed that they were acting on behalf of higher principles, such as "loyalty" or "solidarity."

Does the epidemic of lying, duplicity, and concealment on the part of "hon-   15
orable men"—the leaders of our country—make it easier for us to rationalize our own private departures from the truth? Most of us do see our lies in a benevolent light. So how can we decide in our daily lives whether deception in its countless manifestations is right, or harmless, or justified, or necessary, or good for somebody? How accurately do we observe ourselves and take note of the times we are less than honest or forthright, even over the course of a single day?

WHAT'S YOUR HQ?

I recently came across a quiz in a women's magazine that invited readers to   16
assess their "HQ" (Honesty Quotient) by ranking themselves on a scale of 1 to 10 for truthfulness. Obviously, this rating scale—like others of its kind—could not begin to do justice to human experience or the complexity of even a day in the life of a real human being. Real life is complicated, messy, contextual, unquantifiable, full of paradoxes and contradictions. In a single conversation, I may be truthful, untruthful, and sort of truthful, without even noticing the discrepancies.

Consider the scene that followed a talk I had with my younger son, Ben,   17
about the importance of being honest. As we leave the shopping mall, we pass a video arcade and he demands to play a game. I tell Ben that I have no change, and I pull him along with me toward the exit. I probably do have the change, but we're both in a terrible mood and it seems easier to put it this way than risk

a fight. When we get home, the phone rings and I overhear Ben's impatient response: "Why do you keep bothering me? I don't want you to come over!" I'm mad at Ben for this display of tactlessness, and I whisper to him: "Why don't you just tell him you're busy and can't have friends over today?"

On my better days, I behave more solidly. I tell Ben why I'm not giving him   18
money for a video game and I deal directly with his reaction. I approach the subject of his telephone etiquette without coaching him to fib to a friend. This may seem like a small distinction, but perhaps not. True enough, no single trivial lie undermines my integrity or my relationship with my son. But fibbing, including "polite" or social lies, can become part of the daily fabric of living—a way of avoiding conflict and complication that becomes so habitual we fail to notice even the fact of it and its imperceptible erosion of our integrity and our relationships.

In the abstract, people almost unanimously applaud honesty, which, as popu-   19
lar wisdom has it, is "the best policy." If we actually could measure a person's "HQ," we would each aspire to a high score and would strive to surround ourselves with others who rate high on our ten-point scale. Honesty, like authenticity, is one of our culture's most deeply held values. It is always a slur to say, "She is a dishonest woman," or, "This man does not tell the truth." It is always a compliment to speak of someone's honesty and commitment to the truth.

But what happens when we move away from abstract values and focus in-   20
stead on specific incidents in the lives of real human beings? Then we have Evelyn and Paul exchanging their "loving lies" on the infertility problem; we have me back in my college days nodding my head in the wrong direction to protect "a very important man." Or, more recently, fourteen white, male senators protecting the president's Supreme Court nominee.

Within my own profession, psychologists hold widely divergent views on   21
whether lies harm or benefit their recipients. Some years ago, this news item appeared in the *San Francisco Chronicle*:

> A pale, slight 11-year-old boy, injured but alive, was pulled yesterday from the wreckage of a small plane that crashed Sunday in the mountains of Yosemite National Park. The boy had survived days of raging blizzards and nights of sub-zero temperatures at the 11,000-foot-high crash site, swaddled in a down sleeping bag in the rear seat of the snow-buried wreckage.... "How is my mom and dad?" asked the dazed fifth-grader. "Are they all right?" Rescuers did not tell the boy that his stepfather and his mother were dead, still strapped into their seats in the airplane's shattered cockpit, only inches from where he lay.

Dr. Paul Ekman, a professor of psychology and noted expert on lying,   22
selected this news item to illustrate "an altruistic lie, benefiting the target, not providing any gains to the rescuers." He stated that few would deny this fact. But when my husband (also a psychologist and family therapist) and I discuss the same news clipping, we imagine that this lie made the rescuers feel more comfortable and perhaps occurred at the expense of the child. Had we been at the

scene, we would not have volunteered the facts. But we try to imagine what the rescuers did tell the boy, who undoubtedly feared (or knew) the worst and asked directly for information about his family.

For days after reading that news item, I found myself thinking about the as- 23 sault on this boy's reality and on his future capacity to trust that adults would tell him the truth. While knowing more details might shift my perspective, I question the same lie that my fellow psychologist applauds.

It has been fascinating for me to listen to women voice their moral judg- 24 ment on a range of examples of deception and truth-telling. Sometimes there is a predictably shared response, as when a colleague tells how her parents invented a web of lies and trickery to hide a Jewish family in their home from the Nazis. Her story is unarguably one of courageous and honorable deception in the service of a higher ideal.

But more commonly, and more interestingly, we differ in our responses to 25 the myriad ways that people deliberately distort or conceal the truth—and to how they reveal it, for that matter. What one woman considers a necessary revelation, another considers an inappropriate disclosure. While one person claims, "He deserves to have the facts," another insists that "he should be protected from the truth." What one woman calls a "healthy venting of true feelings," another labels a "hostile, inappropriate outburst."

In regard to tolerating or even inviting deceit, we also differ. In her book, *Lying,* 26 the philosopher Sissela Bok claims that everyone, even deceivers, wants to avoid being deceived. Yet some of us consistently demand the truth, while others ask to be "spared." Consider some examples of the second option.

The wife of a university professor says to me, "If my husband is sleeping 27 with other women, I don't ever want to know it."

A mother in a family therapy session looks her daughter directly in the eye 28 and says, "If you're on drugs, don't tell me about it. I can't handle it."

A woman who has been sexually abused by two maternal uncles attends a 29 movie with her mother that includes the theme of incest. As they leave the theater, her mother says, "If anything like that ever happened in our family, I wouldn't want to know about it."

A therapy client tells me she is worried that her brother might be suicidal 30 but then adds, "I really don't want to know. There's nothing I can do anyway."

No one *wants* to be tricked, manipulated, or duped. But we may feel, at a 31 particular moment, that we can't handle a more direct confrontation with what we already suspect or know. We are unlikely to seek "more truth" if we feel unable to manage it, or if we are not confident that potentially painful information is ultimately empowering and could lead to productive problem solving, more informed decision making, and a more solid self in relationships. We vary widely in the degree to which we are in touch with our competence to manage painful facts, and our readiness and willingness to move toward them.

We differ, too, in our capacity to detect deception and, more generally, in 32 our ability to observe and name reality. We all repress, deny, project, distort, tune out, and get sleepy. Our knowledge and interpretation of "the truth" is, at best, partial, subjective, and incomplete. But we do have varying capacities for empathy, intuition, reflection, autonomy, objectivity, integrity, maturity, clarity, and courage—all of which enhance our ability to detect deception and incongruity in ourselves and in others.

We also differ from each other in our subjective experience of lying. One   33
friend tells me, "When I don't tell the truth, I feel it in my body. So I don't get off the phone, for example, by making excuses, like someone's at the door or I'm late for an appointment. Telling a big lie, like faking sexual pleasure, would make me physically sick." She adds, "My body keeps me honest, even if my head wants to get away with things."

This friend describes herself as being committed to the principle of veracity at "a cellular level." She seeks an honest way to express herself, no matter how   34
inconsequential the issue or insignificant the interaction. In contrast, another woman tells me that she comfortably engages in every variety of "social" and "face-saving" lie. She reports feeling fine about this behavior "as long as no one is hurt." . . .

How often do we articulate our differing philosophy on the many rich and   35
complex dimensions of deception and truth-telling, of speaking and holding back? Since the beginning of recorded time, philosophers and scholars from varied disciplines have debated the nature of truth, as well as the moral, ethical, legal, psychological, and evolutionary aspects of deception and the forces that drive it. But despite the profundity, centrality, and immediacy of this subject in everyday private and public life, we may avoid discussing with others our own personal beliefs about it. Perhaps we should initiate and sustain more such conversations. Clarifying our commonalities and differences helps us examine how we are choosing to live in the world and how we are making decisions about doing "the right thing."

HIDING A LIFE

An attorney named Lena who was flying from Miami to Boston was engaged in   36
friendly conversation with an older woman next to her. They talked about their respective jobs, then the woman showed Lena a photo of her family, which included a new grandson she was visiting for the first time. Midway into their flight, she asked Lena, "Are you married?" "No," Lena responded matter-of-factly, "but I've been living with a woman for five years and we think of ourselves as married." The woman stared at her blankly, so Lena explained further, "I'm a lesbian. My partner, Maria, is a woman." Her flight companion fell silent and kept her eyes riveted to a magazine for the remainder of the flight.

Lena had left a distant, unsatisfactory marriage that had lasted for nine   37
years. When she came out as a lesbian three years later, she decided that she would never again "live a lie." From that time forward, she has been open about her lesbianism, resisting all temptations to pass as a heterosexual. Some of Lena's friends believe she makes herself unnecessarily vulnerable, but this is what Lena chooses, explaining: "If I'm quiet about Maria in any situation where I would have mentioned my husband or son, I'm acting as if my life and loving

is shameful and wrong." Lena will have no part in this, no part in hiding or in pretending through silence to be what she is not.

Lena's family "love her anyway," as they collectively put it, which is among   38
the milder of the homophobic responses she has encountered over the years. There have been more dramatic consequences of her dedication to being truthful: Lena's car has been vandalized by high school students, she has been sexually harassed in her neighborhood, and she almost lost custody of her son, who is now eleven. But the ignorance and hatred she has faced have only strengthened her resolve to be more open. Even to avoid the pain of prejudice, Lena says she would no sooner hide her life than would a black civil rights leader pretend to be white. This deeply held value of living without deception or concealment does not allow Lena to hide the honest affections of her good heart.

Lena believes that silence about her sexual orientation constitutes a lie. "It   39
is lying," Lena argues, "because heterosexuals deny not just our right to love openly but the very fact of our existence." Sure, Lena could have said to her flight companion, "No, I'm not married." But that factually correct statement would have been, from Lena's perspective, intended to mislead. "Silence is a lie," Lena insists, "if you are deliberately going along with another person's false belief. In this case, the false belief happens to erase and degrade the lives of ten percent of the population."

Moreover, Lena reminds me, passing for what one is not never involves a   40
solitary lie. As many have observed, it is easy to tell a lie, but it is almost impossible to tell only one. The first lie may need to be protected by others as well. Concealing something important takes attention and emotional energy that could otherwise serve more creative ends. When we must "watch ourselves," even when we do so automatically and seemingly effortlessly, the process dissipates our energy and erodes our integrity. "It also creates a disturbance in the air," Lena tells me. "Before I was out, I'd bring Maria to office parties and I knew everyone was saying behind my back, 'Are they? Aren't they?' Now they know. And they know that I know they know. It's less crazy-making."

As we discuss the airplane conversation, Lena talks about how trivialities   41
add up. One doesn't say, "Oh, my partner is in the same field as your husband!" One doesn't pull out a photo of one's own to show. One doesn't mention, even if asked, that the purpose of one's flight is to attend a concert to benefit gay and lesbian rights. One doesn't step off the plane and freely embrace one's lover. One doesn't hold hands by the baggage claim. Any of these ways of holding back, of not speaking, of not acting, may seem trivial. But the life this adds up to, Lena says, is a life half-lived. . . .

Fortunately, we don't have to be rated (or to rate others) on a scale that measures   42
our "HQ" because even close friends or colleagues won't necessarily view a specific incident of revelation or concealment in the same light. We might not even agree on the meaning of such terms as "truth" or "authenticity." At times I have felt like throwing up my hands in the face of seemingly endless unravelings.

Yet I don't really believe, or, more to the point, I don't live as if decisions   43
about truth-telling and deception are hopelessly subjective, infinitely complex,

and ultimately unquantifiable. Instead, I decide with confidence that some people and some sources of information are more trustworthy than others. I choose with conviction friends whom I think are open, authentic, and real. I make assessments about which contexts—public or private—provide individuals with more (or less) opportunity to discover, invent, and share their own truths. I observe the power of context to shape and limit the stories we tell. But I also observe the power of individuals to transcend and shape context, to create new stories, and to find new meanings in even the most oppressive circumstances. My work as a clinical psychologist and psychotherapist is guided by these convictions.

And sometimes—such as when watching Anita Hill and Clarence Thomas   44
on television—the question of what is right, what is true, and what is real, appears simple and obvious after all. □

◤ REREADING FOR UNDERSTANDING

1. Consider the case study at the opening of this essay. How do you feel about Evelyn G.'s lie? What point is Lerner trying to illustrate with this example?

2. Lerner offers an example of a "noble lie" from her own experience. What was that lie? What made her reconsider it?

3. Lerner suggests that seeing our lies in a benevolent light makes us unable to "observe ourselves and take note of the times we are less than honest or forthright, even over the course of a single day" (par. 15). Why should we keep track of our lies? How might failing to acknowledge our little lies make us less wary of the big lies we tell?

4. Lerner discusses several types of deception in this essay—deliberately making an untruthful statement, not inquiring after the truth ("I don't want to know"), and choosing not to reveal all unless asked directly. Do you agree that all of these choices constitute lying? Are they all equally acceptable or unacceptable? Why?

◤ RESPONDING

1. Consider the story Lerner tells about the boy whose parents were killed in a plane crash. Lerner faults the rescuers for not telling the 11-year-old his parents were dead. Do you agree? When, if ever, might it be acceptable to lie to someone for his or her own benefit?

2. Lerner tells about Lena, who openly acknowledges her lesbian lover in any situation in which she would have mentioned a husband. She believes that to keep quiet about her relationship would be the same as lying about it. Is Lena's honesty necessary? Is it commendable? What effects has it had and might it have on those around her? Think of a time when you withheld the truth about yourself or someone else. Why did you do it? Would you do it again?

RESPONDING IN WRITING

Lerner suggests that the little fibs we tell to protect others or ourselves, or simply out of convenience, can lead to a habit of lying that may eventually hurt our relationships. Try to keep a one-day "journal of fibs and white lies." At the end of the day, count how many times you lied or withheld the truth. Is the number consistent with what you expected, or did you surprise yourself? Why did you lie in each circumstance? As you look over your list, are there any lies that you would like to correct? any that you would tell again? any that commit you to further deceit? Write a brief analysis of your lies. What did you learn by studying them?

ADRIENNE RICH

As one of America's most distinguished poets, Adrienne Rich (1929–   ) has, through her poetry and prose, questioned and attempted to redefine the role of women in our traditionally patriarchal culture. In these notes from her book *On Lies, Secrets, and Silences,* she examines the duplicity that has often marked women's relationships with one another and with the culture at large, and calls for a new level of honesty among women.

Women and Honor
Some Notes on Lying

(These notes are concerned with relationships between and among women. When "personal relationship" is referred to, I mean a relationship between two women. It will be clear in what follows when I am talking about women's relationships with men.)

The old, male idea of honor. A man's "word" sufficed—to other men—   1
without guarantee.

"Our Land Free, Our Men Honest, Our Women Fruitful"—a popular colo-   2
nial toast in America.

Male honor also having something to do with killing: *I could not love thee,*   3
Dear, so much/Lov'd I not Honour more, ("To Lucasta, On Going to the Wars").
Male honor as something needing to be avenged: hence, the duel.

Women's honor, something altogether else: virginity, chastity, fidelity to a   4
husband. Honesty in women has not been considered important. We have been
depicted as generically whimsical, deceitful, subtle, vacillating. And we have
been rewarded for lying.

Men have been expected to tell the truth about facts, not about feelings.   5
They have not been expected to talk about feelings at all.

Yet even about facts they have continually lied.   6

We assume that politicians are without honor. We read their statements try-   7
ing to crack the code. The scandals of their politics: not that men in high places
lie, only that they do so with such indifference, so endlessly, still expecting to be
believed. We are accustomed to the contempt inherent in the political lie.

* * *

To discover that one has been lied to in a personal relationship, however,   8
leads one to feel a little crazy.

* * *

Lying is done with words, and also with silence.   9

The woman who tells lies in her personal relationships may or may not   10
plan or invent her lying. She may not even think of what she is doing in a calculated way.

A subject is raised which the liar wishes buried. She has to go downstairs,   11
her parking meter will have run out. Or, there is a telephone call she ought to
have made an hour ago.

She is asked, point-blank, a question which may lead into painful talk: "How   12
do you feel about what is happening between us?" Instead of trying to describe
her feelings in their ambiguity and confusion, she asks, "How do *you* feel?" The
other, because she is trying to establish a ground of openness and trust, begins
describing her own feelings. Thus the liar learns more than she tells.

And she may also tell herself a lie: that she is concerned with the other's   13
feelings, not with her own.

But the liar is concerned with her own feelings.   14

The liar lives in fear of losing control. She cannot even desire a relationship   15
without manipulation, since to be vulnerable to another person means for her
the loss of control.

The liar has many friends, and leads an existence of great loneliness.   16

* * *

The liar often suffers from amnesia. Amnesia is the silence of the un-   17
conscious.

To lie habitually, as a way of life, is to lose contact with the unconscious. It   18
is like taking sleeping pills, which confer sleep but blot out dreaming. The unconscious wants truth. It ceases to speak to those who want something else
more than truth.

In speaking of lies, we come inevitably to the subject of truth. There is   19
nothing simple or easy about this idea. There is no "the truth," "a truth"—truth
is not one thing, or even a system. It is an increasing complexity. The pattern of
the carpet is a surface. When we look closely, or when we become weavers, we
learn of the tiny multiple threads unseen in the overall pattern, the knots on the
underside of the carpet.

This is why the effort to speak honestly is so important. Lies are usually   20
attempts to make everything simpler—for the liar—than it really is, or ought
to be.

In lying to others we end up lying to ourselves. We deny the importance of   21
an event, or a person, and thus deprive ourselves of a part of our lives. Or we

use one piece of the past or present to screen out another. Thus we lose faith even with our own lives.

The unconscious wants truth, as the body does. The complexity and fecundity of dreams come from the complexity and fecundity of the unconscious struggling to fulfill that desire. The complexity and fecundity of poetry come from the same struggle.   22

* * *

An honorable human relationship—that is, one in which two people have the right to use the word "love"—is a process, delicate, violent, often terrifying to both persons involved, a process of refining the truths they can tell each other.   23

It is important to do this because it breaks down human self-delusion and isolation.   24

It is important to do this because in so doing we do justice to our own complexity.   25

It is important to do this because we can count on so few people to go that hard way with us.   26

* * *

I come back to the questions of women's honor. Truthfulness has not been considered important for women, as long as we have remained physically faithful to a man, or chaste.   27

We have been expected to lie with our bodies: to bleach, redden, unkink or curl our hair, pluck eyebrows, shave armpits, wear padding in various places or lace ourselves, take little steps, glaze finger and toe nails, wear clothes that emphasized our helplessness.   28

We have been required to tell different lies at different times, depending on what the men of the time needed to hear. The Victorian wife or the white southern lady, who were expected to have no sensuality, to "lie still"; the twentieth-century "free" woman who is expected to fake orgasms.   29

We have had the truth of our bodies withheld from us or distorted; we have been kept in ignorance of our most intimate places. Our instincts have been punished: clitoridectomies for "lustful" nuns or for "difficult" wives. It has been difficult, too, to know the lies of our complicity from the lies we believed.   30

The lie of the "happy marriage," of domesticity—we have been complicit, have acted out the fiction of a well-lived life, until the day we testify in court of rapes, beatings, psychic cruelties, public and private humiliations.   31

Patriarchal lying has manipulated women both through falsehood and through silence. Facts we needed have been withheld from us. False witness has been borne against us.   32

And so we must take seriously the question of truthfulness between women, truthfulness among women. As we cease to lie with our bodies, as we cease to take on faith what men have said about us, is a truly womanly idea of honor in the making?   33

* * *

Women have been forced to lie, for survival, to men. How to unlearn this among other women?   34

"Women have always lied to each other."   35

"Women have always whispered the truth to each other."   36
Both of these axioms are true.   37
"Women have always been divided against each other."   38
"Women have always been in secret collusion."   39
Both of these axioms are true.   40

In the struggle for survival we tell lies. To bosses, to prison guards, the   41
police, men who have power over us, who legally own us and our children,
lovers who need us as proof of their manhood.

There is a danger run by all powerless people: that we forget we are lying,   42
or that lying becomes a weapon we carry over into relationships with people
who do not have power over us.

* * *

I want to reiterate that when we talk about women and honor, or women   43
and lying, we speak within the context of male lying, the lies of the powerful,
the lie as false source of power.

Women have to think whether we want, in our relationships with each   44
other, the kind of power that can be obtained through lying.

Women have been driven mad, "gaslighted," for centuries by the refuta-   45
tion of our experience and our instincts in a culture which validates only
male experience. The truth of our bodies and our minds has been mystified
to us. We therefore have a primary obligation to each other: not to undermine
each others' sense of reality for the sake of expediency; not to gaslight each
other.

Women have often felt insane when cleaving to the truth of our experience.   46
Our future depends on the sanity of each of us, and we have a profound stake,
beyond the personal, in the project of describing our reality as candidly and
fully as we can to each other.

* * *

There are phrases which help us not to admit we are lying: "my privacy,"   47
"nobody's business but my own." The choices that underlie these phrases may
indeed be justified; but we ought to think about the full meaning and consequences of such language.

Women's love for women has been represented almost entirely through   48
silence and lies. The institution of heterosexuality has forced the lesbian to dis-
semble, or be labeled a pervert, a criminal, a sick or dangerous woman, etc., etc.
The lesbian, then, has often been forced to lie, like the prostitute or the married
women.

Does a life "in the closet"—lying, perhaps of necessity, about ourselves to   49
bosses, landlords, clients, colleagues, family, because the law and public opinion are founded on a lie—does this, can it, spread into private life, so that lying
(described as *discretion*) becomes an easy way to avoid conflict or complication? can it become a strategy so ingrained that it is used even with close
friends and lovers?

Heterosexuality as an institution has also drowned in silence the erotic feel-   50
ing between women. I myself lived half a lifetime in the lie of that denial. That
silence makes us all, to some degree, into liars.

When a woman tells the truth she is creating the possibility for more truth 51
around her.

* * *

The liar leads an existence of unutterable loneliness. 52
The liar is afraid.
But we are all afraid: without fear we become manic, hubristic, self- 53
destructive. What is this particular fear that possesses the liar? 54
She is afraid that her own truths are not good enough. 55
She is afraid, not so much of prison guards or bosses, but of something un- 56
named within her.
The liar fears the void. 57
The void is not something created by patriarchy, or racism, or capitalism. 58
It will not fade away with any of them. It is part of every woman.
"The dark core," Virginia Woolf named it, writing of her mother. The dark 59
core. It is beyond personality; beyond who loves us or hates us.
We begin out of the void, out of darkness and emptiness. It is part of the 60
cycle understood by the old pagan religions, that materialism denies. Out of
death, rebirth; out of nothing, something.
The void is the creatrix, the matrix. It is not mere hollowness and anarchy. 61
But in women it has been identified with lovelessness, barrenness, sterility. We
have been urged to fill our "emptiness" with children. We are not supposed to
go down into the darkness of the core.
Yet, if we can risk it, the something born of that nothing is the beginning 62
of our truth.
The liar in her terror wants to fill up the void, with anything. Her lies are a 63
denial of her fear; a way of maintaining control.

* * *

Why do we feel slightly crazy when we realize we have been lied to in a 64
relationship?
We take so much of the universe on trust. You tell me: "In 1950 I lived on 65
the north side of Beacon Street in Somerville." You tell me: "She and I were
lovers, but for months now we have only been good friends." You tell me: "It is
seventy degrees outside and the sun is shining." Because I love you, because there
is not even a question of lying between us, I take these accounts of the universe
on trust: your address twenty-five years ago, your relationship with someone I
know only by sight, this morning's weather. I fling unconscious tendrils of belief,
like slender green threads, across statements such as these, statements made so
unequivocally, which have no tone or shadow of tentativeness. I build them into
the mosaic of my world. I allow my universe to change in minute, significant
ways, on the basis of things you have said to me, of my trust in you.
I also have faith that you are telling me things it is important I should 66
know; that you do not conceal facts from me in a effort to spare me, or yourself, pain.
Or, at the very least, that you will say, "There are things I am not telling you." 67
When we discover that someone we trusted can be trusted no longer, it 68
forces us to reexamine the universe, to question the whole instinct and concept

of trust. For awhile, we are thrust back onto some bleak, jutting ledge, in a dark 68
pierced by sheets of fire, swept by sheets of rain, in a world before kinship, or
naming, or tenderness exist; we are brought close to formlessness.

* * *

The liar may resist confrontation, denying that she lied. Or she may use 69
other language: forgetfulness, privacy, the protection of someone else. Or, she
may bravely declare herself a coward. This allows her to go on lying, since that
is what cowards do. She does not say, *I was afraid,* since this would open the
question of other ways of handling her fear. It would open the question of what
is actually feared.

She may say, *I didn't want to cause pain.* What she really did not want is to 70
have to deal with the other's pain. The lie is a short-cut through another's
personality.

* * *

Truthfulness, honor, is not something which springs ablaze of itself; it has 71
to be created between people.

This is true in political situations. The quality and depth of the politics 72
evolving from a group depends in very large part on their understanding of
honor.

Much of what is narrowly termed "politics" seems to rest on a longing for 73
certainty even at the cost of honesty, for an analysis which, once given, need not
be reexamined. Such is the deadendedness—for women—of Marxism in our
time.

Truthfulness anywhere means a heightened complexity. But it is a move- 74
ment into evolution. Women are only beginning to uncover our own truths;
many of us would be grateful for some rest in that struggle, would be glad just
to lie down with the sherds we have painfully unearthed, and be satisfied with
those. Often I feel this like an exhaustion in my own body.

The politics worth having, the relationships worth having, demand that we 75
delve still deeper.

* * *

The possibilities that exist between two people, or among a group of peo- 76
ple, are a kind of alchemy. They are the most interesting thing in life. The liar is
someone who keeps losing sight of these possibilities.

When relationships are determined by manipulation, by the need for con- 77
trol, they may possess a dreary, bickering kind of drama, but they cease to be interesting. They are repetitious; the shock of human possibilities has ceased to
reverberate through them.

When someone tells me a piece of the truth which has been withheld from 78
me, and which I needed in order to see my life more clearly, it may bring acute
pain, but it can also flood me with a cold, sea-sharp wash of relief. Often such
truths come by accident, or from strangers.

It isn't that to have an honorable relationship with you, I have to under- 79
stand everything, or tell you everything at once, or that I can know, beforehand,
everything I need to tell you.

It means that most of the time I am eager, longing for the possibility of tell- 80
ing you. That these possibilities may seem frightening, but not destructive, to me.
That I feel strong enough to hear your tentative and groping words. That we both
know we are trying, all the time to extend the possibilities of truth between us.

The possibility of life between us. ☐   81

◢ REREADING FOR UNDERSTANDING

1. Rich describes truth as "an increasing complexity" and lying as an attempt
   to make things simpler than they really are. Do you agree with this definition of truth? Can you think of evidence from your own experience or
   from your observation of public life that illustrates the accuracy or inaccu-
   racy of Rich's definition?

2. What does Rich mean when she says, "The liar often suffers from amnesia"
   (par. 17)?

3. Rich contends that women have been expected to lie with their bodies in
   various ways. Reread this section, paragraphs 27–33. Do you agree that the
   things Rich describes are lies? If not, why not? If so, why do you think
   women have participated in such lies for so long?

4. Rich claims that the liar acts out of fear. What is it, according to Rich, that
   the liar really fears?

◢ RESPONDING

1. Rich calls this piece "notes" rather than an essay. Why do you think she has
   chosen this format? What effect does the format have on the way you understand and interpret the ideas in this piece? Can you articulate the thesis? Is
   there one? If you believe there is, is it stated or implied?

2. Rich introduces this selection with a disclaimer: "These notes are concerned with relationships among and between women. When 'personal
   relationship' is referred to, I mean a relationship between two women."
   Reread the third section (pars. 9–16) and the closing lines (pars. 76–79). Do
   you think Rich's comments here and elsewhere might apply to *any* personal
   relationships? Explain your answer.

3. Rich suggests in this essay that women need to create a new system of
   honor for themselves in their relationships with each other. What kind of
   honor does she mean? How does it differ from the traditional idea of honor
   among women? How does it differ from honor among men?

◢ RESPONDING IN WRITING

Choose one observation from these notes—such as "The liar has many friends,
and leads an existence of great loneliness"—as the starting point of a journal

entry or free-writing exercise. Think of examples from your own experiences and observations that illustrate the statement. Think about what it suggests, what it makes you think of. You may wish to turn your notes into an essay about lying.

ELIZABETH SEYDEL MORGAN

Elizabeth Seydel Morgan is a poet and fiction writer who lives in Richmond, Virginia. This story first appeared in *The Virginia Quarterly* in 1991.

Economics

Our mother taught us to substitute the word "tiger" for the word "nigger" when the neighborhood gang chose up teams. Sitting here on my brother's porch, watching my nieces play in the yard with their friends, I think how much has changed since he and I grew up in Atlanta—for one thing, two of their playmates are black. Yet children, their summer games, even this ancient choosing rhyme—catch a tiger by the toe—haven't changed at all.

Back then my brother and I said tiger, but we didn't have much influence on our next door neighbor, Carson Foster. He poked his finger in our chests as he chanted "eenie, meenie, miney, moe" and emphasized the forbidden word even more. "If he hollers, let him go." He also added codas if "moe" brought his finger to one of us girls. "Eu-gene Talmadge told me so," or "My father said. To pick the. Very. Best. Man."

But then my mother said a variation of the word herself. "Can you imagine a nigra named Queen Esther Parris?" I overheard her say to Daddy, who answered, "Is that her name or her title?"

"Name," said Mama. "Wants her checks written out to Queen Esther Parris."

"Checks?" I heard his low voice repeat.

"Queen Esther wants to be paid by check."

"Strange," said my Dad.

This fact, which I now understand to have been phenomenal in the forties, was strange to me, too, because I thought I knew what checks were—money that was not real, the pale blue of Great Aunt Tisha's Christmas check for a million dollars that Daddy stuck in his mirror frame, the many-colored money that stuck out from under the Monopoly board at the Foster's next door. When we weren't playing softball or strip poker, we'd gather around the board on the Foster's screen porch and play Monopoly. Though sometimes he let a boy get to the hotel stage, Carson Foster usually won all the money, his pile of gold thousands as big as our worthless pink fives and white singles.

Queen Esther, paid by check (how much? I wonder) on Fridays, worked for us when I was around ten. I remember my age because I can picture and hear the moment in my back yard when Carson laughed at my mother working in her garden and said behind her back, "Your mother's a hoer. Get it?"

I didn't get it, but I was certain he had insulted my mother, and I was sick 10 of him and sick of his games. That day in the garden as my mother hoed the border, I stood, I imagine, with my hands on my hips and told Carson, "Look. I'm almost ten years old and I'm not doin' that strip poker and movie-love stuff with you anymore." I have no memory of exactly what he looked like—except that he was big, and he had long square fingers that he liked to put on me—but today I can hear my own words perfectly: "I'm almost ten years old." And I know I didn't say them until after Queen Esther had been with us awhile.

"Hey Mary Meade . . . your maid's sure some Ubangi," Carson had jeered 11 over the hedge when she first came. Later I saw a movie, *King Solomon's Mines*, I think it was, and there were those six or seven foot Negroes—blacks I mean— and true, I guess Queen Esther might have come from such a tall African tribe. She was at least six feet. She towered over me (though now I'm very tall myself); I remember most her pink palmed hand turned slightly outward at her side, and what would I have been then—maybe four feet tall? We'd walk to Connell's with me skipping at her side to match her long strides, my younger brother and sometimes other children trailing behind, Queen Esther tickling her nose all the while with her triffle.

Queen Esther's triffle was a piece of cotton, frayed into a fringe at the end, 12 that she wound around her forefinger and used to tickle her lips or nose or cheeks. Now I know that it was the same kind of habit as smoking, or fingering a blanket's satin edge, as I do every night to get to sleep; then it was mysterious, like her height and her name.

"Queen Esther, why you have that whatcha-callit?" one of us would ask. 13

"That's my triffle," she'd reply. 14

"What's a triffle?" 15

"Your business is to direct us all to this drug store. My triffle is to help me 16 following you, so we get there."

But she never followed us, and after the first time we walked to Buckhead, 17 she never needed help to get there. I suppose she meant the triffle habit was to help her be where she was.

Queen Esther ironed. She did everything else, too: the vacuuming, the 18 laundry, the beds, the scraping scrambled eggs out of the iron skillet left in the mornings before she came, the picking up of toys and children's clothes and grown-up underwear in the sheets when she changed the beds, the tossing of empty bottles, scraps of hardened cheese on Chinese plates left from Sunday on the screen porch, the emptying trash cans of Modess and deposit slips and green Coca-Cola bottles.

When Queen Esther ironed, she put books under the legs of the ironing 19 board. After she'd tried the Atlanta phone books once, she never used them again. She'd go to the bookshelf in the den or the living room and try a differ-ent selection every Tuesday. I was pretty much loving books myself then, so I'd notice, sitting on the floor by the ironing board, just what was raising it up to her arms. I think back now to the selection of books available to her for lifting the ironing board:

Readers Digest novels, *Up Front, Gone With the Wind,* volumes of Colliers' 20 Encyclopedia, *Clothes Make the Man, Leave Her to Heaven, The Decameron, Southern Textiles,* and *Warp Sizing,* the last two either written or given to us by our uncle.

She came to use only the brown encyclopedias, eight to an ironing, and I 21 think she and I were probably the first in our house to crack every one open and look at it. We'd find a picture or more often a map she'd be interested in, and while she was sprinkling down the sheets, I'd read about it out loud. After a time, we started reading a little together—I'd read some words, then she'd read some words—"while the iron heats up," she said.

One day before she placed "E" on the floor, we discovered Esther, the Biblical 22 queen of Xerxes who saved her people from destruction. After we read the short column aloud, her namesake read it over to herself.

"Left out the best part, Mary Meade," she said. 23

"Tell," I said. 24

"Esther, she knows her husband kicked out his first wife on account of she 25 didn't come when he called her."

"They got a divorce?" 26

"No. He the king, she out on the street." 27

"Oh." 28

"But even so, when time comes to save her people, Esther said, 'Then I will 29 go to the king though it be against the law and if I perish, I perish.'"

She pronounced the quotation slowly, like a teacher. 30

"That straight out of the Bible . . . from Esther's own book." 31
Then she said quickly in her getting-down-to-work voice, "Now you read your own story for a while."

I remember the brown books under the wooden legs, the scratch of the rug 32 through my cotton underpants, the book in my lap—probably one of the Black Stallion novels—as I sat by the ironing board, reading while Queen Esther intoned the throaty songs that repeated every line with just a little change. *When you get up tomorrow I'll be gone, babe, when you wake up tomorrow, I'll be gone.*

After Queen Esther found out I could charge money at Connell's Drug Store, 33 we walked to Buckhead every Friday, just the two of us. Doc Connell, or Miss Presson, would write my father's name on the pad with carbon paper, write "money" on the first line and "$1.00" beside "total." Then he'd hand me the dollar bill. For several weeks, I'm not sure how long, Queen Esther would stand tall and silent behind me as I made my transaction. After the first surprised look from Doc Connell and Miss Presson, they didn't look at her at all. It was clear she was my maid. "Thanks a lot," I'd say politely. "You're welcome, Mary Meade," he or both of them would answer. If it was Doc Connell, he usually added something about how come I never spent my money in his store, and I always said the same thing, that it was for the Saturday double feature and serial.

I'd pocket the dollar and walk past cosmetics with Queen Esther, out the   34
screen door to Peachtree, down to the corner at Paces Ferry Road where we
waited for her bus. "Well, bye," I'd say when the Five Points bus to downtown
Atlanta came, "see you Monday." She'd nod her head to the side with this way
she had, and I'd start back to our neighborhood to hand over the money to
Carson.

One Friday afternoon, standing at Connell's counter, I was surprised by the   35
long black arm extending from behind me, Queen Esther's bony fingers holding out three beige checks to Miss Presson. Miss Presson looked from my face
way up over my head and then down at the checks in the black hand. "We don't
cash checks," she said to me.

"Those are Mama-an-Daddy's," I said.   36

"No, Sweetie, those are your maid's. And Doc don't allow cashing except for   37
charge customers."

"Mary Meade a charge customer," said Queen Esther.   38

"What's cashing?" I suppose I asked, because it was then I got a lesson in fi-   39
nance from Miss Presson, learned the difference between my parents' checks
and Aunt Tisha's, and watched Queen Esther's arm retreat. As we walked to the
bus stop, I asked her how she was going to get real money in place of those beige
checks. She stopped still and swivelled her head around on her long neck, looking up and down Peachtree Street. "Some how," she answered.

Who knows who called my parents, Doc or Miss Presson. "We have to have a   40
talk," said Daddy in his lowest voice, guiding me with a pinch of the back of my
neck into the den. "It looks like, Mary Meade, that we need to talk some economics tonight."

"Yes, sir," I said.   41

"Do you know what I mean?"   42

"No, sir."   43

"Economics is a big word for, uh, hmmm. Uh, money. Things about   44
money."

I remember his hemming and hawing more than his exact words. But   45
Daddy always kept you standing for a long time, getting to the point, and I remember the word "economics" so well from that evening that even today it
gives me a catch in the stomach.

"I've been letting you charge a dollar here and there at Connell's—figured   46
it would teach you something—but it looks like you been at it every week. And
I would like to ask just why you need so many dollars. I know about the shows
at the Buckhead and all, but you also have your allowance, and your money for
sitting with Robert."

"Yes."   47

"Yes, what."   48

"Yes, sir."   49

"I mean yes, what are you doing with the money, Mary Meade?"   50

I looked at Daddy and opened my mouth. Probably the only two times I've   51
ever been as terrified as that was the time with Carson and the day before my

wedding when I told Clifford Sealew that I could not go through with it. Without planning to, I had lied to Clifford, told him there was someone else.

"Well?" said my father.   52

From my opened mouth the words slipped easy as a prayer. "I gave the   53
money to Queen Esther."

Unlike Cliff, Daddy didn't explode or break down. He said something along   54
the lines of "I thought so" and went on to question me about Queen Esther going in Connell's with me and trying to cash checks. Then he came back around to my lie. He asked me if she'd forced me to give her money.

"Oh, no, no, no!" I saw immediately what I'd gotten into. I saw his angry   55
look gathering, and I knew it was directed at her. "No, Daddy. I wanted to give it to her. She can't get real money for your checks. She tried, and she can't."

He said something like "so I heard" and changed into being real sweet to me.   56
He praised me that night, which I'll always remember, and my fears subsided. We hugged and kissed and I was sent on somewhere, having learned that lying pays, while Daddy stayed in the den in his leather armchair, smoking a cigarette.

That Friday afternoon I ran to catch up with Queen Esther, who'd already   57
started for Buckhead without me. Even after I caught up with her, breathless, she walked faster than I could keep up beside her.

"What you running for?" she called loud enough to keep from turning her   58
head. "You don't need to go to Connell's anymore. Your charging days are over."

I remember the back of her, its motion—slim thighs, boxy rear end, long,   59
long spine showing through something like jersey, wide shoulders. I think of her in something grey or tan, with a shiney red belt—probably patent leather. I think of her moving, her hips moving smoothly, and me running behind her, eye level to her red belt.

"How do you know?" I yelled at her shoulders, the long loops of earrings   60
touching them.

"Your Daddy."   61

"He wouldn't tell *you*."   62

"Oh yes he would. He did." She wore a sort of glittery turban that day, and   63
she turned her head in a flash of shine and swinging earrings. Running, looking up, I saw the profile of her moving lips.

"You are a liar." she said.   64

"You are a hoer," Carson had rasped slowly at the opening we'd made in the la-   65
gustrum hedge.

"Un uh," I said, shaking my head and toeing the soft dirt with my bare foot.   66

"Yes you are."   67

"Un UH." I was getting scared. Fear was suffusing my body the way plea-   68
sure had when Carson and I had been in the bushes.

"A hoer is a girl who does stuff like you did with me. A bad girl."   69

"I'm not a bad girl."   70

"You let me tickle you . . . down there."   71

"No."   72

"Come on, you already forgetting movie-love?" He pointed at a bunch of   73
tall azaleas in his back yard. "Under there? Those times you let me tickle you
with my finger? A long time. And you said it felt good."

"No."   74

"Well you can say no all you want to, girl. But I'm telling."   75

The fear was pushing out at my surfaces. I know my pale white skin was   76
red.

"You liked it," Carson said real low, looking up and down my red skin.   77

"I said I wasn't . . . . I said stop it, you know I did."   78

"Yeah—later you say *'I'm ten.'* Big deal. You're still a hoer. You still *liked* it.   79
And I'm telling."

"Ah, Carson. Please don't," I whined. I wonder now why I didn't say "tell   80
who?", "tell what?" but to a child "I'm telling" needs no who.

He reached through the opening in the hedge and yanked down the elastic   81
top of my sundress, pulling my bare chest into the pruned branches.

"What'll you pay me?"   82

"Huh?"   83

"What'll you pay me to never tell?"   84

I had no idea what he meant.   85

"You get an allowance, dontcha?"   86

I just stood there burning with this new, unbearable feeling.   87

"Listen!" he spat. "Do you?"   88

"What?" The backs of my legs prickled like poison ivy.   89

"Do you get an allowance? Do you get lunch money? Movie money?"   90

"Movie . . . allowance."   91

"I want one dollar a week."   92

"Why?" I'm pretty sure I said. I remember being completely confused.   93

"Why! To keep me from telling you're a hoer. That's why."   94

"Okay."   95

He seemed surprised. "Okay?"   96

"Okay." It seemed easy that afternoon to stop the burning. Just pay my next   97
door neighbor one dollar and he would never tell that I let him put his finger
between my legs and move it around and make me feel good, and bad.

"Wait a minute, Queen Esther," I yelled, catching up. "Please wait!"   98

She didn't exactly wait, but she must have slowed her long-legged stride a   99
little because I came up alongside her, puffing.

"Queen Esther, I really wish I could give my dollars to *you*."   100

Far above me I saw the whites of her eyes as she rolled them. She just kept   101
walking, getting ahead of me again.

"If you can't get cashed."   102

She looked over her shoulder. "If you knew somethin beside nothin, you'd   103
be trouble." And then she raised her arm as if to swat me backward, but she only
stroked her upraised chin with her triffle.

That slowed her a little and I caught up. My heart was thudding with run-   104
ning and what I was about to do.

"Queen Esther—I have to give all my dollars to Carson!"   105

"Say?"   106

"Carson. The charge money. I give it to him."   107

She stopped. "Wuf fo?" she said in the language I knew as well as I know   108
French now.

What I told Queen Esther as we stopped on the road to Buckhead was   109
surely not the whole story. I never told anyone about feeling the sweet sensation
that had spread over my body and made me bad.

I told her we'd played strip poker and "doctor" and I had to pay to keep it   110
a secret.

"Blackmail!" sang Queen Esther. "Bluemail, man-mail, exto. Strongarm,   111
Strong, strong."

It sounded like a chant. Whatever she was saying or chanting, her stride had   112
slowed to let me stay beside her.

We walked together, past my school, past the bungalows smaller than my   113
house, to Paces Ferry Road. Her bus stop was ahead, down at Peachtree.

"Don' pay'm mo," she said, and I heard this clearly as *Don't pay Carson any*   114
more dollars.

"But how?" I looked up and she heard that clearly as *Without his telling*   115
Mama and Daddy I'm a hoer.

"Say: I'm good. And I know it. And I ain't givin' you a cent. Say: You boy, I   116
am a good girl."

I thought about it. "He'll still tell."   117

"No. He won't." Said Queen Esther.   118

We'd come to Connell's Drug Store and both tried to look the other way.   119

"I won't be coming back, Mary Meade. I been let go."   120

"Where you going?"   121

"Some other house."   122

"Where you cashing?"   123

"I knows a man." She looked down at me. "If I perish, I perish. . . ."   124

"Oh. Can I wait with you for Five Points Bus?"   125

We waited with the group of maids and yardmen at the corner. Queen   126
Esther was taller than all of them, and the men looked embarrassed to have her
standing like a giraffe in their midst. The women seemed ashamed to be dressed
so ugly. Every one of them looked drab and dusty. Queen Esther, in her shining
turban and earrings and glowing skin, was beautiful. I remember understanding that for the first time.

We watched the bus make a circle around the Buckhead traffic island to head   127
back downtown. Queen Esther looked down and said, with no smile or sadness,
no emotion at all, "Tell the boy no mo dollars, and tell your daddy they never
were for me."

Then she took the steps up the bus with one step, ducked her head and was   128
gone.

All the black people around me moved toward the bus, and I turned toward   129
Paces Ferry Road.

I went home and lied to Carson that my Daddy had found out anyway so I   130
couldn't pay him anymore, and I lied to Daddy by never saying another word
about it. I never told anyone, then or now, that I am good. □

◢ REREADING FOR UNDERSTANDING

1. Why is Queen Esther's request to be paid by check considered so strange?
Why do you think she wants to be paid this way?

2. There are a number of deceptions in this story. Skim the story again, and
list every instance of lying or dishonesty you find.

◢ RESPONDING

1. In the previous selection, Adrienne Rich cautions, "There is a danger run by
all powerless people: that we forget we are lying, or that lying becomes a
weapon we carry over into relationships with people who do not have power
over us" (par. 42). Consider this statement in the context of "Economics."
Who are the powerless people in this story? How do they use deceit to deal
with both those who have power over them and those who do not?

2. Mary Meade says she learned from her exchange with her father "that lying
pays." Do you think she still believes that? What evidence in the story indicates whether she still practices deception?

3. Consider the significance of the title. What does "economics" literally
mean? What are some of the connotations of this word? How are the various denotations and connotations relevant to the story?

To Tell the Truth: Can We Find the Truth in the Media?

LESLIE SAVAN

Leslie Savan is a critic for the *Village Voice*. This piece is an excerpt from the introduction to her 1995 book *The Sponsored Life*, a collection of her weekly columns on advertising and popular culture. Unlike the media critics whose warnings to watch out for hidden lies and empty claims in advertising assume a certain naiveté in their audience, Savan assumes the audience she is addressing is sophisticated and savvy about advertising. She points out that advertisers have twisted even our ironic detachment and resistance to advertising into a sales pitch.

The Bribed Soul

Television-watching Americans—that is, just about *all* Americans—see approximately 100 TV commercials a day. In that same 24 hours they also see a host of print ads, billboard signs, and other corporate messages slapped onto every available surface, from the fuselages of NASA rockets right down to the bottom of golf holes and the inside doors of restroom stalls. Studies estimate that, counting all the logos, labels, and announcements, some 16,000 ads flicker across an individual's consciousness daily.

Advertising now infects just about every organ of society, and wherever advertising gains a foothold it tends to slowly take over, like a vampire or a virus. When television broadcasting began about 50 years ago, the idea of a network that would air nothing but commercials was never seriously considered, not even when single-sponsor shows were produced straight out of the sponsor's ad agency. But today, by the grace of cable, we have several such channels, including MTV, stylistically the most advanced programming on the air, and FYI, a proposed new channel that would run only ads—infomercials, home-shopping shows, regular-length commercials, and, for a real treat, programs of "classic" ads. Similarly, product placement in the movies started small, with the occasional Tab showing up in a star's hand, but now it's grown big enough to eat the whole thing. In its 1993 futuristic thriller *Demolition Man,* Warner Bros. not only scattered the usual corporate logos throughout the sets but it also rewrote the script so that the only fast-food chain to survive the "franchise wars" of the 20th century was Taco Bell—which, in return, promoted the movie in all its outlets.

Even older, far statelier cultural institutions have had their original values hollowed out and replaced by ad values, leaving behind the merest fossil of their founders' purpose. Modernist masters enjoy art museum blockbusters only when they can be prominently underwritten by an oil company or a telecommunications giant; new magazines are conceived not on the basis of their editorial content but on their ability to identify potential advertisers and groom their copy to fit marketing needs. In the process, the function of sponsored institutions is almost comically betrayed. The exotic bug exhibit at the Smithsonian Museum's new O. Orkin Insect Zoo, for example, opens with the red diamond logo of Orkin Pest Control and displays various little beasties, ever so subtly planting the suggestion that if they were to escape their glass cages you'd know who to call. Though the Smithsonian would never be so crass as to actually recommend Orkin's services, it is crass enough to never once mention in its exhibits the dangers of pesticides.

As for all those television-watching Americans, hit on by those 16,000 paid (and tax-deductible) messages a day, they're even more vulnerable than their institutions. Most admakers understand that in order sell to you they have to know your desires and dreams better than you may know them yourself, and they've tried to reduce that understanding to science. Market research, in which psychologists, polling organizations, trends analysts, focus group leaders, "mall-intercept" interviewers, and the whole panoply of mass communications try to figure out what will make you buy, has become a $2.5 billion annual business growing at a healthy clip of about 4.2 percent a year (after adjustment for inflation). Yet even this sophisticated program for the study of the individual consumer is only a starter kit for the technological advances that will sweep through the advertising-industrial complex in the 1990s. Today, the most we can do when another TV commercial comes on—and we are repeatedly told that this is our great freedom—is to switch channels. But soon technology will take even that tiny tantrum of resistance and make it "interactive," providing advertisers with information on the exact moment we became bored—vital data that can be crunched, analyzed, and processed into the next set of ads, the better to zap-proof *them.*

Impressive as such research may be, the real masterwork of advertising is the way it uses the techniques of art to seduce the human soul. Virtually all of modern experience now has a sponsor, or at least a sponsored accessory, and there is no human emotion or concern—love, lust, war, childhood innocence, social rebellion, spiritual enlightenment, even disgust with advertising—that cannot be reworked into a sales pitch. The transcendent look in a bride's eyes the moment before she kisses her groom turns into a promo for Du Pont. The teeth-gnashing humiliation of an office rival becomes an inducement to switch to AT&T.

In short, we're living the sponsored life. From Huggies to Maalox, the necessities and little luxuries of an American's passage through this world are provided and promoted by one advertiser or another. The sponsored life is born when commercial culture sells our own experiences back to us. It grows as those experiences are then reconstituted inside us, mixing the most intimate processes of individual thought with commercial values, rhythms, and expectations. It has often been said by television's critics that TV doesn't deliver products to viewers but that viewers themselves are the *real* product, one that TV delivers to its advertisers. True, but the symbiotic relationship between advertising and audience goes deeper than that. The viewer who lives the sponsored life—and that is most of us to one degree or the other—is slowly recreated in the ad's image.

Inside each "consumer," advertising's all-you-can-eat, all-the-time, all-dessert buffet produces a build-up of mass-produced stimuli, all hissing and sputtering to get out. Sometimes they burst out as sponsored speech, as when we talk in the cadences of sitcom one-liners, imitate Letterman, laugh uproariously at lines like "I've fallen and I can't get up," or mouth the words of familiar commercials, like the entranced high school student I meet in a communications class who moved his lips with the voiceover of a Toyota spot. Sometimes they slip out as sponsored dress, as when white suburban kids don the baggy pants and backward baseball caps they see on MTV rappers. Sometimes they simply come out as sponsored equations, as when we attribute "purity" and "honesty" to clear products like Crystal Pepsi or Ban's clear deodorant.

To lead the sponsored life you don't really have to do anything. You don't need to have a corporate sponsor as the museums or the movies do. You don't even have to buy anything—though it helps, and you will. You just have to live in America and share with the nation, or at least with your mall-intercept cohorts, certain paid-for expectations and values, rhythms and reflexes. . . .

The chief expectation of the sponsored life is that there will and always should be regular blips of excitement and resolution, the frequency of which is determined by money. We begin to pulse to the beat, the one-two beat, that moves most ads: problem/solution, old/new, Brand X/hero brand, desire/gratification. In order to dance to the rhythm, we adjust other expectations a little here, a little there: Our notions of what's desirable behavior, our lust for novelty, even our visions of the perfect love affair or thrilling adventure adapt to the mass consensus coaxed out by marketing. Cultural forms that don't fit these patterns tend to fade away, and eventually *everything* in commercial culture—not just the 30-second spot but the drama, news segment, stage performance, novel, magazine layout—comes to share the same insipid insistence on canned excitement and neat resolution.

What's all the excitement about? Anything and nothing. You know you've entered the commercial zone when the excitement building in you is oddly incommensurate with the content dangled before you: Does a sip of Diet Coke really warrant an expensive production number celebrating the rebel prowess of "ministers who surf," "insurance agents who speed," and "people who live their life as an exclamation not an explanation"?!? Of course not. Yet through the sympathetic magic of materialism we learn how to respond to excitement: It's less important that we purchase any particular product than that we come to expect resolution *in the form of* something buyable.

The way ads have of jacking up false excitement in the name of ultimately   11
unsatisfying purchases has given Western societies a bad case of commercial blue balls. You're hit on, say, by yet another guy on TV hawking fabric whitener, but—wait a minute—he "can't be a man" because he packs a different brand of smokes. And maybe you moan, "I can't get no, no no no . . . "

Anyway, that's how the Rolling Stones put it in that seminal semiotic text   12
"(I Can't Get No) Satisfaction" back in 1965. Commercials are tinny jingles in our heads that remind us of all we've abandoned in exchange for our materially comfortable lives—real extended families, real human empathy, real rebel prowess. The result of stale promises endlessly repeated is massive frustration.

But Mick Jaggar is younger than that now: Long after "Satisfaction" had   13
dropped off the charts, the Rolling Stones became the first major band to tour for a corporate sponsor, Jovan perfumes, in 1981. By then Jagger had become a symbol of the most popular postmodern response to advertising's dominant role in our culture: the ironic reflex.

Irony has become a hallmark of the sponsored life because it provides a cer-   14
tain distance from the frustration inherent in commercial correctness. For some time now the people raised on television, the baby boomers and the "Generation Xers" that followed, have mentally adjusted the set, as it were, in order to convince themselves that watching is cool. They may be doing exactly what their parents do—but they do it *differently*. They take in TV with a Lettermanesque wink, and they like it when it winks back. In many cases (as Mark Crispin Miller has described so well in *Boxed In*), the winkers have enthusiastically embraced the artifice, even the manipulativeness, of advertising as an essential paradox of modern life, a paradox that is at the crux of their own identity.

The winkers believe that by rolling their collective eyes when they watch   15
TV they can control *it*, rather than letting it control them. But unfortunately, as a defense against the power of advertising, irony is a leaky condom—in fact, it's the same old condom that advertising brings over every night. A lot of ads have learned that to break through to the all-important boomer and Xer markets they have to be as cool, hip, and ironic as the target audience likes to think of itself as being. That requires at least the pose of opposition to commercial values. The cool commercials—I'm thinking of Nike spots, some Reeboks, most 501s, certainly all MTV promos—flatter us by saying we're too cool to fall for commercial values, and therefore cool enough to want their product.

If irony is weak armor, how do we ward off the effect of billions of words   16
and images from our sponsors? No perfect wolfsbane exists, but I can suggest some tactics to keep in mind:

When watching, watch out. Literally. Watch as an outsider, from as far a   17
distance as you can muster (farther even than irony)—*especially* when watching ads that flatter you for being an outsider, as more and more are doing.

Big lie, little lie. All advertising tells lies, but there are little lies and there are 18 big lies. Little lie: This beer tastes great. Big lie: This beer makes *you* great. Not all ads tell little lies—they're more likely to be legally actionable (while big lies by definition aren't). And many products do live up to their modest material claims: This car runs. But all ads *must* tell big lies: This car will attract babes and make others slobber in envy. Don't be shocked that ads lie—that's their job. But do try to distinguish between the two kinds of lies.

Read the box. Look not just at whether an ad's claims are false or exag- 19 gerated, but try to figure out what portion of an ad is about the culture as opposed to the product. Read the contents as you would a cereal box's: Instead of how much sugar to wheat, consider how much style to information. Not that a high ratio of sugar to wheat is necessarily more malevolent than the other way around. But it's a sure sign that they're fattening you up for the shill.

Assume no relationship between a brand and its image. Marlboro was 20 originally sold as a woman's cigarette, and its image was elegant, if not downright prissy. It wasn't until 1955 that the Marlboro Man was invented to ride herd on all that. The arbitrary relationship between a product and its ads becomes even clearer when you realize how much advertising is created to overcome "brand parity"—a plague more troubling to marketers than bodily odors. Brand parity means that there's little or no difference between competing brands and that the best a brand can do is hire a more appealing image. When advertising works at all, it's because the public more or less believes that something serious is going on between a product and its image, as if the latter reveals intrinsic qualities of the former. Peel image off item, and you too can have more of the freedom that ads are always promising. Likewise . . .

We don't buy products, we buy the world that presents them. Over the 21 long run, whether you actually buy a particular product is less important than that you buy the world that makes the product seem desirable. Not so long ago a BMW or Mercedes was required if you seriously bought the worldview that their ads conveyed. Still, buying an attitude doesn't automatically translate into product purchase. If your income precluded a BMW, you might have bought instead a Ralph Lauren polo shirt or even a Dove bar (which is how yuppie snack foods positioned themselves—as achievable class). Sure, GE wants you to buy its bulbs, but even more it wants you to buy the paternalistic, everything's-under-control world that GE seems to rule. Buying *that* will result, GE is betting, not only in more appliance sales but also in more credibility when spokesmen insist that defrauding the Pentagon is not *really* what GE's all about. That is to say . . .

The promotional is the political. Each world that commercials use to sell 22 things comes packed with biases: Entire classes, races, and genders may be excluded for the coddling of the sponsored one. Lee Jeans's world (circa 1989) is a place where young people are hip, sexual, and wear jeans, while old people are square, nonsexual, and wear uniforms. The class and age politics here is more powerful than the Young Republicans'. There is politics in all advertising (and, more obviously, advertising in all politics). It makes sense that these two professions call what they do "campaigns."

Advertising shepherds herds of individuals. When Monty Python's mistaken messiah in *The Life of Brian* exhorts the crowd of devotees to "Don't follow me! Don't follow anyone! Think for yourselves! . . . You are all individuals!" they reply in unison, "We are all individuals!" That is advertising in a nutshell.   23

Advertising's most basic paradox is to say: Join us and become unique.   24
Advertisers learned long ago that individuality sells, like sex or patriotism. The urge toward individualism is a constant in America, with icons ranging from Thomas Jefferson's yeoman farmer to the kooky girl bouncing to the jingle "I like the Sprite in you!" Commercial nonconformity always operates in the service of . . . conformity. Our system of laws and our one-man-one-vote politics may be based on individualism, but successful marketing depends on the exact opposite: By identifying (through research) the ways we are alike, it hopes to convince the largest number of people that they need the exact same product. Furthermore, in modern pop culture, we construct our individuality by the unique combination of mass-produced goods and services we buy. I sip Evian, you slug Bud Light; I drive a Geo, you gun a Ford pickup; I kick sidewalk in cowboy boots, you bop in Reeboks. Individuality is a good angle for all advertising, but it's crucial for TV commercials. There you are sitting at home, not doing anything for hours on end, but then the very box you're staring at tells you that you are different, that you are vibrantly alive, that your quest for freedom—freedom of speech, freedom of movement, freedom to do whatever you damn well choose—will not be impeded! And you can do all that, says the box, without leaving your couch.

It's the real ad. The one question I'm most often asked is, Does advertising   25
shape who we are and what we want, or does it merely reflect back to us our own emotions and desires? As with most nature-or-nurture questions, the answer is both. The real ad in any campaign is controlled neither by admakers nor adwatchers; it exists somewhere between the TV set and the viewer, like a huge hairball, collecting bits of material and meaning from both. The real ad isn't even activated until viewers hand it their frustrations from work, the mood of their love life, their idiosyncratic misinterpretations, and most of all, I think, their everyday politics. On which class rung do they see themselves teetering? Do they ever so subtly flinch when a different race comes on TV? In this way, we all coproduce the ads we see. Agency people are often aghast that anyone would find offensive meanings in their ads because "that's not what we intended." Intention has little to do with it. Whatever they meant, once an ad hits the air it becomes public property. That, I think, is where criticism should aim—at the fluctuating, multimeaning thing that floats over the country, reflecting us as we reflect it.

Follow the flattery. I use the word *flattery* a lot. When trying to understand   26
what an ad's really up to, following the flattery is as useful as following the money. You'll find the ad's target market by asking who in any 30-second drama is being praised for qualities they probably don't possess. When a black teenager plays basketball with a white baby boomer for Canada Dry, it's not black youth that's being pandered to. It's white boomers—the flattery being that they're cool enough to be accepted by blacks. Ads don't even have to put people on stage to

toady up to them. Ads can flatter by style alone, as do all the spots that turn on hyperquick cuts or obscure meanings, telling us—uh, *some* of us—that we're special enough to get it.

We participate in our own seduction. Once properly flattered, all that's left 27 is to close the sale—and only we can do that. Not only do we coproduce ads, but we're our own best voiceover—that little inner voice that ultimately decides to buy or not. The best ads tell us we're cool *coolly*—in the other meaning of the word. McLuhan used to say that a cool medium, like television, involves us more by not giving us everything; the very spaces between TV's flickering dots are filled in by our central nervous system. He refers to "the involvement of the viewer with the completion or 'closing' of the TV image." This is seduction: We're stirred to a state so that not only do we close the image but, given the right image at the right time, we open our wallet. All television is erotically engaged in this way, but commercials are TV's G-spot. The smart ads always hold back a little to get us to lean forward a little. Some ads have become caricatures of this tease, withholding the product's name until the last second to keep you wondering who could possibly be sponsoring such intrigue. The seduction may continue right to the cash register, where one last image is completed: you and product together at last. It'd be nice to say that now that you've consumed, you've climaxed, and everyone can relax. But sponsorship is a lifetime proposition that must be renewed every day.

The themes singled out in this introduction run throughout the book, each 28 chapter illustrating them with a different category of ad. If category's the right word. The chapters are loosely organized around various topics, and I chose columns that seemed to best illustrate the topic at hand—though commercials often invoke many issues and therefore occasionally overlap several chapters. But to a certain extent that's inevitable. Advertising daily, hourly, overlaps with everything else on TV, in the home, at the store, on the street.

The first chapter, "Too Cool for Words," deals the most directly with style, 29 aesthetics, and technique in advertising. The last 10 years or so have seen a frantic scramble of all the visual, audial, and temporal elements in ads. Footage shakes, is chopped up, reverts to black and white, and—as if the image itself were in retreat—explodes into words. This chapter also includes the unbearably trendy ads: Maybe they ride a trendy slogan ("It's the right thing to do") or an emotional trend (nostalgia for "place" or hype over "lifestyle"). Because the ads in this section strain so hard to be "cutting edge," you'll find among them the arty (some sneaker spots, ads that use opera), the artsy-fartsy (Obsession, Infiniti), and the 100 percent ironic (Joe Isuzu, subliminal spoofs). The chapter starts with a piece not about advertising per se but about a typeface, Helvetica, that at the time permeated ad attitude.

Chapter 2, "Corporate Image Adjustment," is about the true star of the '80s 30 (and the poster boy of the '90s): Big Business. Often there's a bad rep (Dow, Drexel Burnham, E. F. Hutton) or, almost worse, a stale rep (John Hancock, Miller beer, Coca-Cola) that a corporation must advertise its way out of. The past decade was full of businesses heavy into S&M: hostile takeovers, arbitrage, greenmail, corporate fraud. Growing out of the go-for-it, that's-*his*-problem, Reagan-endorsed ethos came the ulcer-producing anxiety sell (as in AT&T, Merrill Lynch, and Apple computer ads). But this is also the land of the corporate crocodile tear and the Vaseline-smeared lens, and all that fear and greed was more commonly transmogrified into visions of goodness and warmth—like the agency melodramas for Perrier, Chevrolet, and Hands Across America, to name a few. Sappy, however, is not always safe—it can tempt the muckraker in each of us—and so other companies simply produced the most unassailable version of themselves possible: funny animals or cartoony humans. That is, they let their mascots handle their PR, Joe Camel doing the most phallic, uh, facile job.

"Real Problems, Surreal Ads" looks at the spin fib-friendly corporations put   31
out when they butt up against the real world. These columns recount how advertising tries to confront, evade, or capitalize on controversial national and international issues, among them: the fall of communism, the gulf war, defense contracts, environmentalism, business ethics, boycotts, and the geopolitical news closest to ad people's hearts, the recession.

"Our Bodies, Our Sells" focuses on advertising's portrayal of women.   32
Women and advertising are ensnarled (though I hate the trendy word, it fits) co-dependently. After all, modern advertising and the modern woman's sense of identity grew hand in hand: Mass market consumerism was largely invented for lady customers by the great 19th-century department stores. Because women still do most of the nation's shopping, advertising still aims primarily at them. And since so many ads are built on a problem/solution structure, a structure that leads from the unenviable to the ideal, advertising is powerfully and frighteningly integrated into the formation of female identities. (And by advertising, I also mean women's magazines, where editorial unabashedly plugs advertisers. It's a phenomenon that promotes not only Calvin and Revlon, but dumbness and dependency—relying as it does on the assumption that we won't make the connection, and if we do, we won't care.) These columns aren't so much about the notorious stereotypes—the yellow, waxy build-up housewife or the babe draped over the car (an endangered species since women now make almost half of all new car purchases)—as about the newer stereotypes that evolved as a reaction to all that: the career dominatrix, the gals who find "empowerment" by stomping asphalt in Reeboks.

Chapter 5, "Shock of the Hue," is about how advertising presents "the   33
Other"—and how some ads use the momentary shock of seeing someone who's "different" appear on the same tube that's usually so busy defining "normal." The Other is usually racially or ethnically different, but the Other may also be someone who has AIDS, is homeless, does drugs, or is simply square. Except when they're target-marketed for their "purchasing power," Others often function in advertising to make the mainstream look good: The square tells everyone else they're hip, African-Americans certify white soul, the Japanese are machine to American mensch. But the notion that difference is suspect doesn't jibe with what advertising *also* tells us: You are all individuals! Dare to be different! Some campaigns try to clip the contradiction by presenting models of

generic individualism, like the cartoon character Fido Dido. But whenever advertising volunteers to fix problems like drugs or racism, the contradiction only winds tighter. Commercial infrastructure militates against it really fixing anything that has to do with addiction or prejudice, since commercialism must addict and prejudice us to products, to ways of reacting, and to itself. Advertising must create and maintain needs, as drugs do. It must also posit "others"— whether "Brand X" or other values countering the hero brand's—as basically inferior or even threatening, as racism does. So much of advertising is set up on those Manichean good/bad, problem/solution, threat/security structures that even when an Other person isn't on the scene, an otherness is.

The last chapter, "The Sponsored Life," harkens back to the beginning of   34
this introduction. Advertising is always hitching rides onto other vehicles— tying its products in with movie and charity promotions or, as has been proposed, sticking its messages onto a mile-long satellite that from Earth would look like a moon-sized logo. Forward-thinking agencies have also extended the definition of an ad vehicle to include Hurricane Hugo, the San Francisco earthquake, and the coming millennium. Advertising's even buying its way into people's urge for a more spiritual life—until recently one of the few ways out of the sponsored life.

But the sponsored life is more than finding corporate sponsorship under   35
every rock (musician). It's also revising our concept of what an ad is—and what an ad's consciousness of *itself* is. And so this chapter considers something like office design as an ad for a corporate approach to life, warns about PSAs that warn you not to watch so much TV, treats popular catchphrases as slogan spores, and takes on phenomena that mess with the relationship between consumer and commercial—such as the commercial-parodying Energizer Bunny, the ad-loving Jordache girl, and all the TV commercials that show people watching TV commercials. . . .

I hope this book does two things: provides a sense of how specific ads, campaigns, and marketing trends got to be the way they are, and lends some cumulative insight into the symbiotic relationship between modern consciousness and advertising. Ads have been playing with our sensibilities for quite a while now. As long ago as 1902, William James, in *The Varieties of Religious Experience*, wrote that, with the universal acceptance of material comfort as the ultimate good, "We have lost the power even of imagining what the ancient idealization of poverty could have meant: the liberation from material attachments, the unbribed soul." How advertising spreads and deepens this uniquely American form of spiritual graft is the real subject of this book. □

◢ REREADING FOR UNDERSTANDING

I. Savan's essay is notable for its use of figurative language. For example, in paragraph 2 she suggests that advertising is like "a vampire or a virus."

What does she mean by this simile? Cite other examples of figurative language throughout the essay and explain their meaning. How effective are these passages in establishing Savan's points?

2. Savan says "the chief expectation of the sponsored life is that there will and always should be regular blips of excitement and resolution" (par. 9). How does advertising create and fulfill such an expectation? How does that expectation affect other areas of our life, according to Savan?

3. Throughout the essay, Savan insists that getting the audience to purchase the particular product being advertised is not the most important objective of advertising. What *is* the most important objective? Why?

◤ RESPONDING

1. Savan claims that "virtually all of modern experience now has a sponsor" (par. 5). Do you agree? Can you think of significant aspects of your personal experience that are untouched by advertising? Can you cite evidence from your own experience of the way advertising pervades popular culture?

2. Do you agree with Savan that "commercial nonconformity always operates in the service of . . . conformity" (par. 15)? Can you think of ads that either exemplify or challenge her claim?

3. Savan claims that "there is no human emotion or concern—love, lust, war, childhood innocence, social rebellion, spiritual enlightenment, even disgust with advertising—that cannot be reworked into a sales pitch" (par. 5). Working in groups of three or four, see if you can think of an advertisement that exploits each of the concerns Savan lists. Then generate your own list of emotions and concerns. Exchange lists among groups and try to think of advertisements that turn one another's listed items into sales pitches.

◤ RESPONDING IN WRITING

1. Savan maintains that all advertising assumes certain cultural biases in its intended audience and exploits those biases. Choose a magazine or newspaper ad or a television commercial in which a particular bias about a certain group (for example, teenagers, the elderly, women, men, children) is either reinforced or debunked. Write an essay describing and analyzing the commercial text and images to show how the ad perpetuates or undermines that bias.

2. Try your hand at ad criticism. Analyze one of the ads on the following pages or in one of the other units in this book. Assume you are writing for an audience of your peers who have grown up surrounded by advertisements but who may not be in the habit of thinking critically about them.

PIG'S EYE PILSNER

A Brutally Honest Beer

Elvis really is dead.

A BRUTALLY HONEST BEER.

"Kemo Sabe" means "soggy shrub" in Navajo.

A BRUTALLY HONEST BEER.

RESPONDING

1. As Leslie Savan points out in "The Bribed Soul" (p. 297), those of us who grew up with television in our homes and advertising in almost every facet of our lives are neither shocked nor surprised to be told that ads are intentionally misleading; we have never assumed otherwise. To reach this savvy audience, Savan suggests, advertisers have had to change their tactics, to take a more tongue-in-cheek approach. Study these two ads for Pig's Eye Pilsner. Who is their intended audience? What assumptions do they make about the audience's sophistication? about their self-image? about their expectations of advertising?

2. What do the ads actually tell us about the product? Do you think these ads would be effective in promoting the product? Why or why not?

3. Leslie Savan claims that all ads lie. Do these ads lie? What lie is explicitly or implicitly communicated?

NEIL POSTMAN
STEVE POWERS

In their 1992 book *How To Watch TV News*, Neil Postman and Steve Powers combine an academic perspective (Postman is the chair of New York University's Department of Communication Arts) with professional expertise (Powers has over thirty years of experience in radio and television news). In this chapter from their book, Postman and Powers examine the phenomenon of recreating actual events to accompany or, in some cases, replace news reports.

Reenactment and Docudramas, or No News Is Still News

On several occasions, former President Ronald Reagan enjoyed telling how he re-created Chicago Cubs' games in his years as a baseball announcer. In the early days of radio, details of baseball games were telegraphed down the line to radio stations where announcers would re-create the game without seeing it. When the information was slow in coming, the announcers were forced to use their imaginations to fill in the details. They would, for example, describe how the pitcher was taking his time, was picking up the resin bag and checking the new ball thrown to him by the umpire. In other words, the announcer would kill time until the telegraph details started flowing again. What the announcer said might not have been truth but it was good theater. To make even better theater, the announcer would hit a stick against a piece of wood to simulate the sound of a bat hitting a ball. It sounded real but it wasn't. It was a baseball game as imagined by the announcer, a re-creation—we might even say, a docudrama.

Re-creations were used from time to time on radio programs other than baseball games. For example, the program "The March of Time" was a form of docudrama employing actors who impersonated historic figures such as Hitler, Churchill, and Roosevelt. The tradition carried over to television. "You Are There" aired from 1953 to 1957 and again in 1971 for one season. Its host was Walter Cronkite. The program re-created various historical events complete with conversations no one had ever heard. To his credit, Cronkite is on record as believing that historical re-creations have "no place in a news division," that, in effect, they are devices to be used to entertain, and not for anything else.

But that was long ago, before the line separating news and entertainment became blurred, before news programming became a "cash cow." Television's need to fill the blank screen brought re-creations back in ways that might even surprise Ronald Reagan. Instead of an anchor simply talking about an event on camera, reenactments allow actors and other masters of stagecraft to formulate a scene that approximated events from the past. Instead of a blank screen we have a simulation of reality, a reenactment.

Generally speaking, television executives don't see reenactments as a prob-   4
lem, primarily because reenactments make engrossing television. But some
critics claim that re-creations mislead the viewer into thinking he or she is
watching a recording of the real thing. Perhaps the most famous example of a
re-creation gone astray took place in July 1989. ABC's "World News Tonight"
showed footage of U.S. diplomat Felix Bloch handing a briefcase to a Soviet
agent. The scene was not labeled as a re-creation. The word "simulation" or
some other warning, such as "what you are seeing, we made up," was accidentally left off the screen, leaving viewers with the impression they were watching the actual taped event. The entire scene was broadcast for only ten seconds
but its impact was great. It focused attention on the problem inherent in "recreating" reality.

These problems do not disappear even when a re-creation is properly   5
labeled. For example, the CBS news series "Saturday Night with Connie Chung"
presented the story of Abbie Hoffman's last days. Hoffman, after a colorful career as an activist for various causes, committed suicide. The program pur-
ported to reveal the last moments of Hoffman's life. His last words, reenacted,
were as follows:

> ABBIE: I'm okay, Jack. I'm okay. Yeah, I'm out of bed. I got my feet on the
> floor. Yeah. Two feet. I'll see you Wednesday? Thursday. I'll always be with
> you, Jack. Don't worry.

Viewers knew, of course, that Hoffman was already dead so that they could   6
not be hearing his last words as he spoke them. But many believed, and had a
right to believe, that someone had recorded the event and that these were
Hoffman's actual words. They weren't. They were words pieced together by interviews and then scripted by a writer. Does it matter that the words attributed
to Abbie Hoffman in his last moments were never uttered?

Some say it doesn't. In fact, besides using re-creations for short segments   7
on news shows, TV producers have created whole programs of simulated reality. They are called docudramas. These usually use real news stories for the
starting point of a story line, then weave in events created by a writer. These
events may or may not be true, but producers defend docudramas by arguing
that the audience understands that it is not watching the actual event. The fact
that studies show that audiences tend to absorb information from television
even though they forget where that information originated does not trouble
producers of docudramas.

Producers like docudramas for a variety of reasons. For one thing, they take   8
the form of a theatrical event with a beginning, middle, and end, with "time
outs" for commercials. Actual news events, of course, are not always so tidy. In
real-life dramas, heroes get killed, hostages are sometimes not released, and the
villain is not always brought to justice. Most newsworthy events are not concluded in neat thirty- or sixty-minute segments. A docudrama can remedy unhappy or unjust conclusions by packaging them in palatable forms.

Another reason some producers like docudramas is their low cost. A re-   9
created one-hour docudrama might cost $400,000–$500,000, or roughly half of

what a similar theatrical drama would cost using popular actors, good writers, scenic designers, and directors.

The lines between re-creations and reality are so muddled that some news   10 programs have even used Hollywood films to illustrate news stories. There is nothing producers or news directors fear more than a void, a black hole in a newscast, as for example, when the anchor is talking about a subject and there is no newsreel footage to go with the comments. What to do? One answer is simply to use excerpts from Hollywood films. On one CBS network newscast, while Dan Rather reported on a new exploration of the *Titanic* wreckage, the picture on the screen was of a movie depicting the sinking of the *Titanic*, complete with wet actors manning the lifeboats. It was enough to give serious journalists a sinking feeling. On "NBC News with Tom Brokaw," a reporter used footage from the movie *The Spy Who Came in from the Cold* to illustrate the changing roles of the CIA now that the Soviet Union's menace seems to be fading. The next logical step would be to run a clip of a John Wayne movie showing battle footage when discussing the fighting during World War II, or any war that happened to be around. To our knowledge, that hasn't happened . . . yet.

So where should the lines be drawn? Is it acceptable for applause to be   11 dubbed in on footage of a concert, or sirens in a police-car chase scene, or gunfire in battle footage? Is it ethical for a television journalist to use a "reverse question," that is, the technique of taking pictures of a reporter asking the questions he used during an earlier interview, then splicing the questions into a finished tape? We know what answers Edward R. Murrow would give to most of these questions. He once addressed them, and made the following unambiguous remark: "There will always be some errors in news gathering, but the tricks that microphones, cameras, and film make possible must never be contrived to pass off as news events that were fabricated to document an event that we missed or which may never have happened."

Murrow is generally regarded as the man who established the standards of   12 TV news, and we can assume his microphone would short out were he to know about the uses made of re-creations today. Indeed, we can imagine he would have some harsh words for "pseudo-news" shows such as Phil Donahue's and Geraldo Rivera's. These programs are not under the control of news departments but draw part of their appeal from the fact that they involve real people and real events. They are television's version of "yellow journalism," typically dealing with sensational, weird, or perverse stories.

During one ratings period in 1989, the "Geraldo" show featured the fol-   13 lowing subjects: "Prison Motherhood," "Lady Lifers: Bad Girls Behind Bars," "Teen Prostitutes," "Women Who Date Married Men," "Girls Who Can't Say 'No!,'" "Murderers Who Should Never Get Out of Prison," "Campus Rape," "Illicit, Illegal, Immoral: Selling of Forbidden Desires," "Parents of Slain Prostitutes," "Cocaine Cowgirls," "Chippendales," "Battered Lesbians," "Contract to Kill: Running from the Mafia," "Men Who Marry Prostitutes," "Transsexual Transformations," "Angels of Death," and "Secret Lives of Stars"—all this within one three-week period.

The defense for this kind of programming proceeds along the following   14 lines. First, such programming draws huge audiences, which suggests that people are interested in both the subject matter and the subjects. Second, the high profitability of the shows allows the hosts to include programs devoted to more acceptable news content—for example, an interview with the Secretary of Defense or a discussion of industrial pollution. The audience is attracted by the promise of the bizarre, then is exposed to serious issues. Third, programs about battered lesbians, girls who can't say "no," and parents of slain prostitutes *are* news, and serious news, at that. They tell as much or more about the state of our society than do 90 percent of the stories on any daily network news show. They are a form of documentary journalism; they reveal to us the pain, humiliation, and confusion of real people trying to cope with an intractable reality.

The answer to these arguments is that such programming is nothing more than a highly profitable freak show, exploiting the insatiable curiosity of audiences for what is strange and forbidden. The audience members are voyeurs, peeking, as it were, into the bedrooms or living rooms of people who are desperately seeking a momentary sense of celebrity. Besides, all of this serves as a diversion from the urgent issues of the day. What people don't know can kill them (to borrow from Fred Friendly, formerly of CBS News). To this might be added that what people do know can keep them from knowing what they must know. In other words, the "psuedo-news" show fixes people's attention on what is peripheral to an understanding of their lives, and may even disable them from distinguishing what is relevant from what is not.   15

In fact, a somewhat similar set of arguments is made against the docudramas and re-creations (especially those done within the context of news shows). It proceeds as follows: A re-creation can be as engrossing as a program about men who marry prostitutes. But as the latter diverts attention from what is necessary to know, the former severs the trust that citizens must have in their sources of information. For example, consider the following lead sentence from a story in *The New York Times*, August 5, 1991: "More than 500 passengers and crew members were saved yesterday in a tense rescue operation when the Greek cruise liner *Oceanos* . . . foundered and sank in high winds and heavy seas two miles off the South African coast."   16

Now, let's pretend that you learned that the *Times* story was in error;—that only 324 passengers were saved (500 makes the rescue operation appear more effective); that there were no high winds and heavy seas (that was included to make the event more dramatic); and that the boat did not sink after the passengers were removed but made it safely back to port (a sinking boat makes a better story than a merely damaged boat). You would, we imagine, abandon whatever trust you have in *The New York Times* as a reliable source of news. We imagine further that you would not be impressed with an explanation claiming that the alterations were made to give the story more drama. Moreover, if you think our example exaggerates the extent to which a TV docudrama may depart from reality, we should observe that in the mini-series depicting the life of Peter the Great, there was a scene in which Peter meets with Isaac Newton, a meeting which never took place except in the imaginations of the writer, director, and producer of the program. The two of them did live, roughly, at the same time; Peter died in 1725, Newton in 1727. Is this a justification for a scene in which   17 they have a conversation? Perhaps—if you take the view that *all* television is only a form of entertainment. Not at all—if you take a more rigorous position, that when entertainment conflicts with truth, truth must prevail. ☐

◢ REREADING FOR UNDERSTANDING

1. The authors begin by offering examples of reenactments from the early days of broadcasting. How are these examples different from the reenactments and docudramas of today?

2. Powers and Postman claim that the objective of broadcast news has changed since the early days of television. What is that change? How does the current approach to television news explain the popularity of reenactments and docudramas?

3. What potential problem do Postman and Powers see in reenactments?

4. Why do the authors include a discussion of television talk shows like *Geraldo* and *Donahue*, which do not claim to be news programs? What parallels do the authors draw between talk show and news reenactments?

◢ RESPONDING

One of the dangers of re-creations of actual events, the authors suggest, is that these re-creations "sever the trust that citizens must have in their sources of information" (par. 16). That is, when we know that some of what is presented as news is not true, we may come to doubt the veracity of all news reports. Do you think this concern is as significant as Postman and Powers believe, or do they overestimate the credulity of the viewing public? Can you find evidence in your own experience as a viewer of television news to support or challenge their belief?

◢ RESPONDING IN WRITING

Working in a group, spend one week gathering data on television news. Assign each member a different program to watch each day. Try to choose a range of programs, from tabloid TV like *A Current Affair* to network and local news shows. Decide as a group what data to look for, such as the number of "serious" stories versus distractions, or the number of reenactments included per broadcast. You might also want to note the length of time given to each story covered. Have each member keep a viewing log to record his or her observations. At the end of the week, combine your data and write a group report analyzing and comparing the programs. Which is the most informative? the most believable? the most entertaining? Which would you recommend and why?

HENRY LOUIS GATES, JR.

Henry Louis Gates is a professor of English and chairman of Afro-American studies at Harvard University and the author of several books of literary and cultural criticism. Gates was born and raised in Piedmont, West Virginia, a small mill town with a population of 2,500. In the days before integration, the 1950s and 1960s when Gates was growing up, the town's 380 black citizens inhabited their own community, separate in many ways from the rest of the town. In his 1994 memoir *Colored People*, from which this piece is taken, Gates tells what it was like to live in a segregated world. In this chapter, Gates examines the role that television played in shaping his vision of life beyond Piedmont.

Prime Time

Actually, I first got to know white people as "people" through their flick- 1
ering images on television shows. It was the television set that brought
us together at night, and the television set that brought in the world outside the Valley. We were close enough to Washington to receive its twelve channels on cable. Piedmont was transformed from a radio culture to one with the
fullest range of television, literally overnight. During my first-grade year, we'd
watch *Superman, Lassie,* Jack Benny, Danny Thomas, *Robin Hood, I Love Lucy,
December Bride,* Nat King Cole (of course), *Wyatt Earp, Broken Arrow,* Phil
Silvers, Red Skelton, *The $64,000 Question, Ozzie and Harriet, The Millionaire,
Father Knows Best, The Lone Ranger,* Bob Cummings, *Dragnet, The People's
Choice, Rin Tin Tin, Jim Bowie, Gunsmoke, My Friend Flicka, The Life of Riley,
Topper, Dick Powell's Zane Grey Theater, Circus Boy,* and Loretta Young—all in
prime time. My favorites were *The Life of Riley,* in part because he worked in a
factory like Daddy did, and *Ozzie and Harriet,* in part because Ozzie never
seemed to work at all. A year later, however, *Leave It to Beaver* swept most of the
others away.

With a show like *Topper,* I felt as if I was getting a glimpse, at last, of the life 2
that Mrs. Hudson, and Mrs. Thomas, and Mrs. Campbell, must be leading in
their big mansions on East Hampshire Street. Smoking jackets and cravats,
spats and canes, elegant garden parties and martinis. People who wore suits to
eat dinner! This was a world so elegantly distant from ours, it was like a voyage
to another galaxy, light-years away.

Leave It to Beaver, on the other hand, was a world much closer, but just out 3
of reach nonetheless. Beaver's street was where we wanted to live, Beaver's
house where we wanted to eat and sleep, Beaver's father's firm where we'd have
liked Daddy to work. These shows for us were about property, the property that
white people could own and that we couldn't. About a level of comfort and ease
at which we could only wonder. It was the world that the integrated school was
going to prepare us to enter and that, for Mama, would be the prize.

If prime time consisted of images of middle-class white people who looked   4
nothing at all like us, late night was about the radio, listening to *Randy's Record
Shop* from Gallatin, Tennessee. My brother, Rocky, kept a transistor radio by his
bed, and he'd listen to it all night, for all I knew, long after I'd fallen asleep. In
1956, black music hadn't yet broken down into its many subgenres, except for
large divisions such as jazz, blues, gospel, rhythm and blues. On *Randy's,* you
were as likely to hear The Platters doing "The Great Pretender" and Clyde
McPhatter doing "Treasure of Love" as you were to hear Howlin' Wolf do
"Smokestack Lightning" or Joe Turner do "Corrine, Corrine." My own favorite
that year was the slow, deliberate sound of Jesse Belvin's "Goodnight, My Love."
I used to fall asleep singing it in my mind to my Uncle Earkie's girlfriend, Ula,
who was a sweet caffè latté brown, with the blackest, shiniest straight hair and
the fullest, most rounded red lips. Not even in your dreams, he had said to me
one day, as I watched her red dress slink down our front stairs. It was my first
brush with the sublime.

We used to laugh at the way the disc jockey sang "Black Strap Lax-a-teeves"   5
during the commercials. I sometimes would wonder if the kids we'd seen on TV
in Little Rock or Birmingham earlier in the evening were singing themselves to
sleep with *their* Ulas.

Lord knows, we weren't going to learn how to be colored by watching tele-   6
vision. Seeing somebody colored on TV was an event.

"Colored, colored, on Channel Two," you'd hear someone shout. Somebody   7
else would run to the phone, while yet another hit the front porch, telling all the
neighbors where to see it. And *everybody* loved *Amos 'n' Andy*—I don't care
what people say today. For the colored people, the day they took *Amos 'n' Andy*
off the air was one of the saddest days in Piedmont, about as sad as the day of
the last mill pic-a-nic.

What was special to us about *Amos 'n' Andy* was that their world was *all* col-   8
ored, just like ours. Of course, *they* had their colored judges and lawyers and
doctors and nurses, which we could only dream about having, or becoming—
and we *did* dream about those things. Kingfish ate his soft-boiled eggs delicately, out of an egg cup. He even owned an acre of land in Westchester County,
which he sold to Andy, using the facade of a movie set to fake a mansion. As far
as we were concerned, the foibles of Kingfish or Calhoun the lawyer were the
foibles of individuals who happened to be funny. Nobody was likely to confuse
them with the colored people we knew, no more than we'd confuse ourselves
with the entertainers and athletes we saw on TV or in *Ebony* or *Jet,* the magazines we devoured to keep up with what was happening with the race. And people took special relish in Kingfish's malapropisms. "I denies the allegation, Your
Honor, and I resents the alligator."

In one of my favorite episodes of *Amos 'n' Andy,* "The Punjab of Java-   9
Pour," Andy Brown is hired to advertise a brand of coffee and is required to
dress up as a turbaned Oriental potentate. Kingfish gets the bright idea that if
he dresses up as a potentate's servant, the two of them can enjoy a vacation at
a luxury hotel for free. So attired, the two promenade around the lobby, running up an enormous tab and generously dispensing "rubies" and "diamonds"
as tips. The plan goes awry when people try to redeem the gems and discover

them to be colored glass. It was widely suspected that this episode was what prompted two Negroes in Baltimore to dress like African princes and demand service in a segregated four-star restaurant. Once it was clear to the management that these were not American Negroes, the two were treated royally. When the two left the restaurant, they took off their African headdresses and robes and enjoyed a hearty laugh at the restaurant's expense. "They weren't like our Negroes," the maître d' told the press in explaining why he had agreed to seat the two "African princes."

Whenever the movies *Imitation of Life* and *The Green Pastures* would be 10 shown on TV, we watched with similar hunger—especially *Imitation of Life*. It was never on early; only the late *late* show, like the performances of Cab Calloway and Duke Ellington at the Crystal Palace. And we'd stay up. Everybody colored. The men coming home on second shift from the paper mill would stay up. Those who had to go out on the day shift and who normally would have been in bed hours earlier (because they had to be at work at 6:30) would stay up. As would we, the kids, wired for the ritual at hand. And we'd all sit in silence, fighting back the tears, watching as Delilah invents the world's greatest pancakes and a down-and-out Ned Sparks takes one taste and says, flatly, "We'll box it." Cut to a big white house, plenty of money, and Delilah saying that she doesn't want her share of the money (which should have been *all* the money); she just wants to continue to cook, clean, wash, iron, and serve her good white lady and her daughter. (Nobody in our living room was going for *that*.) And then Delilah shows up at her light-complected daughter's school one day, unexpectedly, to pick her up, and there's the daughter, Peola, ducking down behind her books, and the white teacher saying, I'm sorry, ma'am, there must be some mistake. We have no little colored children here. And then Delilah, spying her baby, says, Oh, yes you do. Peola! Peola! Come here to your mammy, honey chile. And then Peola runs out of the room, breaking her poor, sweet mother's heart. And Peola continues to break her mother's heart, by passing, leaving the race, and marrying white. Yet her mama understands, always understands, and, dying, makes detailed plans for her own big, beautiful funeral, complete with six white horses and a carriage and a jazz band, New Orleans style. And she dies and is about to be buried, when, out of nowhere, comes grown-up Peola, saying, "Don't die, Mama, don't die, Mama, I'm sorry, Mama, I'm sorry," and throws her light-and-bright-and-damn-near-white self onto her mama's casket. By this time, we have stopped trying to fight back the tears and are boo-hooing all over the place. Then we turn to our *own* mama and tell her how much we love her and swear that we will *never, ever* pass for white. I promise, Mama. I promise.

Peola had sold her soul to the Devil. This was the first popular Faust in the 11 black tradition, the bargain with the Devil over the cultural soul. Talk about a cautionary tale.

The Green Pastures was an altogether more uplifting view of things, our 12 Afro Paradiso. Make way for the Lawd! Make way for the Lawd! And Rex Ingram, dressed in a long black frock coat and a long white beard, comes walking down the Streets Paved with Gold, past the Pearly Gates, while Negroes with the whitest wings of fluffy cotton fly around Heaven, playing harps, singing spirituals, having fish fries, and eating watermelon. Hard as I try, I can't stop seeing God as that black man who played Him in *The Green Pastures* and see-ing Noah as Rochester from the Jack Benny show, trying to bargain with God to let him take along an extra keg of wine or two.

Civil rights took us all by surprise. Every night we'd wait until the news to see what "Dr. King and dem" were doing. It was like watching the Olympics or the World Series when somebody colored was on. The murder of Emmett Till was one of my first memories. He whistled at some white girl, they said; that's all he did. He was beat so bad they didn't even want to open the casket, but his mama made them. She wanted the world to see what they had done to her baby.   13

In 1957, when I was in second grade, black children integrated Central High School in Little Rock, Arkansas. We watched it on TV. All of us watched it. I don't mean Mama and Daddy and Rocky. I mean *all* the colored people in America watched it, together, with one set of eyes. We'd watch it in the morn-ing, on the *Today* show on NBC, before we'd go to school; we'd watch it in the evening, on the news, with Edward R. Murrow on CBS. We'd watch the Special Bulletins at night, interrupting our TV shows.   14

The children were all well scrubbed and greased down, as we'd say. Hair short and closely cropped, parted, and oiled (the boys); "done" in a "perma-nent" and straightened, with turned-up bangs and curls (the girls). Starched shirts, white, and creased pants, shoes shining like a buck private's spit shine. Those Negroes were *clean*. The fact was, those children trying to get the right to enter that school in Little Rock looked like black versions of models out of *Jack & Jill* magazine, to which my mama had subscribed for me so that I could see what children outside the Valley were up to. "They hand-picked those children," Daddy would say. "No dummies, no nappy hair, heads not too kinky, lips not too thick, no disses and no dats." At seven, I was dismayed by his cynicism. It bothered me somehow that those children would have been chosen, rather than just having shown up or volunteered or been nearby in the neighborhood.   15

Daddy was jaundiced about the civil rights movement, and especially about the Reverend Dr. Martin Luther King, Jr. He'd say all of his names, to drag out his scorn. By the mid-sixties, we'd argue about King from sunup to sundown. Sometimes he'd just mention King to get a rise from me, to make a sagging evening more interesting, to see if I had *learned* anything real yet, to see how long I could think up counter arguments before getting so mad that my face would turn purple. I think he just liked the color purple on my face, liked producing it there. But he was not of two minds about those children in Little Rock.   16

The children would get off their school bus surrounded by soldiers from the National Guard and by a field of state police. They would stop at the steps of the bus and seem to take a very deep breath. Then the phalanx would start to move slowly along this gulley of sidewalk and rednecks that connected the steps of the school bus with the white wooden double doors of the school. All kinds of crackers would be lining that gulley, separated from the phalanx of children by rows of state police, who formed a barrier arm in arm. Cheerleaders from the all-white high school that was desperately trying to stay that way were dressed in those funny little pleated skirts, with a big red *C* for "Central" on their chests, and they'd wave their pom-poms and start to cheer: "Two, four, six, eight—We   17 don't want to integrate!" And all those crackers and all those rednecks would join in that chant as if their lives depended on it. Deafening, it was: even on our twelve-inch TV, a three-inch speaker buried along the back of its left side.

The TV was the ritual arena for the drama of race. In our family, it was located in the living room, where it functioned like a fireplace in the proverbial New England winter. I'd sit in the water in the galvanized tub in the middle of our kitchen, watching the TV in the next room while Mama did the laundry or some other chore as she waited for Daddy to come home from his second job. We watched people getting hosed and cracked over their heads, people being spat upon and arrested, rednecks siccing fierce dogs on women and children, our people responding by singing and marching and staying strong. Eyes on the prize. Eyes on the prize. George Wallace at the gate of the University of Alabama, blocking Autherine Lucy's way. Charlayne Hunter at the University of Georgia. President Kennedy interrupting our scheduled program with a special address, saying that James Meredith will *definitely* enter the University of Mississippi, and saying it like he believed it (unlike Ike), saying it like the big kids said "It's our turn to play" on the basketball court and walking all through us as if we weren't there.

Whatever tumult our small screen revealed, though, the dawn of the civil rights era could be no more than a spectator sport in Piedmont. It was almost like a war being fought overseas. And all things considered, white and colored Piedmont got along pretty well in those years, the fifties and early sixties. At least as long as colored people didn't try to sit down in the Cut-Rate or at the Rendezvous Bar, or eat pizza at Eddie's, or buy property, or move into the white neighborhoods, or dance with, date, or dilate upon white people. Not to mention try to get a job in the craft unions at the paper mill. Or have a drink at the white VFW, or join the white American Legion, or get loans at the bank, or just generally get out of line. Other than that, colored and white got on pretty well. □

REREADING FOR UNDERSTANDING

1. In the opening paragraph, Gates says he first got to know white people as people by watching them on TV. What does he mean by "as people"? How was his knowledge of white people on TV different from his knowledge of the white people in his hometown?

2. Gates makes a distinction between the vision of white people presented in *Topper* and that presented in *Leave It to Beaver*. Which show seems to have had more of an impact on him? Why?

RESPONDING

1. Gates states "Civil rights took us all by surprise" (par. 13). Why do you think this small community of blacks in West Virginia was surprised that

other blacks were challenging segregation laws elsewhere in the South? What does their surprise suggest about the black citizens of Piedmont? What does it suggest about the effects of segregation?

2. Gates says that his father was "jaundiced about the civil rights movement, and especially about the Reverend Dr. Martin Luther King, Jr." (par. 16). What do you think Gates means by "jaundiced"? What does the word suggest about the source of the senior Gates's cynicism?

3. This excerpt from Gates's memoir can be divided into two sections: the first focuses on entertainment media, the second on information media. Reread each section. Aside from the change in topic, can you find other differences in each section? How would you characterize the tone of each? Consider especially the last paragraph, and the last sentence in particular: "Other than that, colored and white got on pretty well." How do you think Gates intends that sentence to be read? Why?

4. What does this essay say about the possibility of discovering truth on television? What perceptions does the young Gates draw about his own life and the lives of others, both white and black, from the various images he sees on television? How accurate are those perceptions? Would you say that television plays a positive or negative role in this essay?

◢ RESPONDING IN WRITING

Try writing a brief memoir, similar to Gates's, in which you examine a period of your life by recalling the television programs (or particular program) you watched regularly during that time. Consider what influence, if any, the programs had in shaping your ideas about yourself, your family, the world you lived in. In retrospect, how truthful were the impressions you gleaned from TV? An alternative to this assignment might be to examine how a significant book or movie influenced you at one stage in your life.

CONTROVERSIES

Does Everybody Cheat?

CHARLES VAN DOREN

When he appeared on the cover of *Time* in 1957, Charles Van Doren seemed to have it all. Barely thirty, he was a well-liked instructor at Columbia University where he shared an office with his famous father, scholar Mark Van Doren. Charles Van Doren seemed guaranteed a successful future in academia, but more important to most Americans, he was the reigning champion on the television quiz show *Twenty-one*. *Twenty-one* was one of several quiz programs that fascinated American viewers in the late 1950s, and Van Doren was easily the most popular and widely recognized contestant. Good-looking, charming, and seemingly endlessly knowledgeable, Van Doren was undefeated for fifteen weeks, collecting $129,000 in winnings. Even after losing, Van Doren remained a television personality on NBC's *Today* show. All that changed in 1959 when Van Doren, testifying before a House of Representatives subcommittee investigating the quiz shows, admitted that *Twenty-one*'s producers had supplied him with answers to the questions before each show. Van Doren read the statement that follows before being questioned by the subcommittee.

I Have Deceived My Friends

I would give almost anything I have to reverse the course of my life in the last three years. I cannot take back one word or action; the past does not change for anyone. But at least I can learn from the past.

I have learned a lot in those three years, especially in the last three weeks. I've learned a lot about life. I've learned a lot about myself, and about the responsibilities any man has to his fellow men. I've learned a lot about good and evil. They are not always what they appear to be. I was involved, deeply involved, in a deception. The fact that I, too, was very much deceived cannot keep me from being the principal victim of that deception, because I was its principal symbol.

There may be a kind of justice in that. I don't know. I do know, and I can say it proudly to this committee, that since Friday, Oct. 16, when I finally came to a full understanding of what I had done and of what I must do, I have taken a number of steps toward trying to make up for it.   3

I have a long way to go. I have deceived my friends, and I had millions of them. Whatever their feelings for me now, my affection for them is stronger today than ever before. I am making this statement because of them. I hope my being here will serve them well and lastingly.   4

TELLS OF RECANTING

Since Oct. 16 I have informed my immediate family of the facts I will disclose today. I have appeared before District Attorney [Frank S.] Hogan [of New York] and Assistant District Attorney [Joseph] Stone and told them that my testimony before the grand jury last January was not in accord with the facts. And I appear before you today prepared to tell the whole truth about my association with the quiz program "Twenty-one."   5

Let me start at the very beginning. A friend first suggested that I might apply to be a contestant on "Tic Tac Dough," and told me the address of the producers, Barry & Enright, Inc. I have always had a good memory, and I had a reputation among my friends for a wide range of knowledge and for being good at quizzes of all sorts. I hesitated for several weeks and finally went to the office and applied.   6

I was given an examination which I passed easily. I was then given a much longer and harder one, the purpose of which I did not know, but which I also completed. I left the office and was told that I would be called if wanted. In the hall outside I met Albert Freedman, whom I had met socially two or three times. He told me that he was the producer of "Tic Tac Dough" and I said that I had applied to be a contestant.   7

I was called the next week and told that I had been chosen to be a contestant on "Twenty-one," a program of which I had never heard. I learned that "Twenty-one" was Barry & Enright's new nighttime quiz show, and that it was supposedly an honor to be so chosen. I returned to the office and was instructed in the rules of "Twenty-one" by, I think, Daniel Enright.   8

Following orders, I came to the studio several hours before air time. I worked hard at memorizing lists of facts and figures, and carried with me a book of facts. I was frightened and excited. I did not appear on the program that night, which was, I believe, Nov. 7, 1956. I continued to be a stand-by contestant for two more weeks.   9

Before my first actual appearance on "Twenty-one" I was asked by Freedman to come to his apartment. He took me into his bedroom where we could talk alone. He told me that Herbert Stempel, the current champion, was an "unbeatable" contestant because he knew too much. He said that Stempel was   10 unpopular, and was defeating opponents right and left to the detriment of the program. He asked me if, as a favor to him, I would agree to make an arrangement whereby I would tie Stempel and thus increase the entertainment value of the program.

HONESTY "IMPOSSIBLE"

I asked him to let me go on the program honestly, without receiving help. He   11
said that was impossible. He told me that I would not have a chance to defeat Stempel because he was too knowledgeable. He also told me that the show was merely entertainment and that giving help to quiz contestants was a common practice and merely a part of show business. This of course was not true, but perhaps I wanted to believe him. He also stressed the fact that by appearing on a nationally televised program I would be doing a great service to the intellectual life, to teachers and to education in general, by increasing public respect for the work of the mind through my performances.

In fact, I think I have done a disservice to all of them. I deeply regret this,   12
since I believe nothing is of more vital importance to our civilization than education. Whenever I hesitated or expressed uneasiness at the course events were taking during my time on the program the same sort of discussion ensued, and, foolishly and wrongly, I persuaded myself that it was all true. Freedman guaranteed me $1,000 if I would appear for one night. I will not bore this committee by describing the intense moral struggle that went on inside me. I was sick at heart. Yet the fact is that I unfortunately agreed, after some time, to his proposal.

GOT QUESTIONS IN ADVANCE

I met him next at his office, where he explained how the program would be   13
controlled. He told me the questions I was to be asked, and then asked if I could answer them. Many of them I could. But he was dissatisfied with my answers. They were not "entertaining" enough.

He instructed me how to answer the questions: to pause before certain of   14
the answers, to skip certain parts and return to them, to hesitate and build up suspense, and so forth. On this first occasion and on several subsequent ones he gave me a script to memorize, and before the program he took back the script and rehearsed me in my part.

This was the general method which he used throughout my fourteen   15
weeks on "Twenty-one." He would ask me the questions beforehand. If I could not answer them he would either tell me the answers or, if there was sufficient time before the program, which was usual, he would allow me to look them up myself. A foolish sort of pride made me want to look up the answers when I could, and to learn as much about the subject as possible. When I could answer the questions right off he would tell me that my answers were not given

in an entertaining and interesting way, and he would then rehearse me in the manner in which I was to act and speak.

GUARANTEED CASH

After the first program, on which I tied Stempel three times, Freedman told me   16
that I would win the next evening and be the new champion. My guarantee was increased to $8,000. I again agreed to play, and I did defeat Stempel. At this point my winnings totaled $20,000. For the next twelve programs I continued to play in this manner, Freedman guaranteeing that I would end up winning no less than a certain amount.

I was deeply troubled by the arrangement. As time went on the show bal-   17
looned beyond my wildest expectations. I had supposed I would win a few thousand dollars and be known to a small television audience. But from an un-known college instructor, I became a celebrity.

I received thousands of letters and dozens of requests to make speeches, ap-   18
pear in movies, and so forth—in short, all the trappings of modern publicity. To a certain extent this went to my head.

I was almost able to convince myself that it did not matter what I was doing   19
because it was having such a good effect on the national attitude to teachers, education, and the intellectual life. At the same time, I was winning more money than I had ever had or ever dreamed of having: I was able to convince myself that I could make up for it after it was over.

Again, I do not wish to emphasize my mental and moral struggles. Yet the   20
public renown also made me terribly uncomfortable. I hoped people would not think I could do nothing besides stand in an isolation booth and answer questions.

I realized that I was really giving a wrong impression of education. True   21
education does not mean the knowledge of facts exclusively. I wrote articles try-ing to express this feeling, but few were interested. Instead I was referred to as a "quiz-whiz," a "human book of knowledge," a "walking encyclopedia."

I wanted to be a writer and a teacher of literature. I seemed to be moving   22
farther and farther away from that aim.

I didn't know what to do nor where to turn and, frankly, I was very much   23
afraid. I told Freedman of my fears and misgivings, and I asked him several times to release me from the program. At the end of January, 1957, when I had appeared eight or ten times, I asked him once more to release me, and this time more strongly.

He agreed to allow me to stop, but it was some time before it could be   24
arranged. He told me that I had to be defeated in a dramatic manner. A series of ties had to be planned which would give the program the required excite-ment and suspense.

On February 18, I played a tie with Mrs. Vivienne Nearing, and the fol-   25
lowing week played two more ties with her. Freedman then told me that she

was to be my last opponent, and that I would be defeated by her. I thanked him. . . .

26 The next program was on March 11. . . . Mrs. Nearing defeated me in the first game played that night. My total winnings after fourteen appearances were $129,000. . . .

27 One result of my appearance on "Twenty-one" was a contract with N. B. C. I hoped this would give me the chance to do something else besides answer questions in an isolation booth. I never wanted to see another quiz show. The opportunity came in October, 1958, when I was assigned to the Dave Garroway program. I am grateful to Mr. Garroway and to N. B. C. for letting me appear on this program for a year and talk for five minutes every morning about some subject which I considered interesting and important.

28 I spoke about science, poetry, history and famous people, as well as many other things. At least once a week during my five minutes I read poetry and talked about it as I would do to a Columbia class. I think I may be the only person who ever read seventeenth-century poetry on a network television program—a far cry from the usual diet of mayhem, murder and rape. I hoped that television viewers would judge me on what I did on the Garroway show and forget my role on "Twenty-one."

29 All the time I was appearing on television I continued to teach at Columbia. People told me I was impractical to do so, but teaching seemed to me much more important. I have always wanted to be a teacher, and I hoped to be one when my quiz show experience was forgotten.

30 I completed the requirement for a Ph. D. last spring, and on July 1 I was made an Assistant Professor of English. This was the fulfillment of a lifelong desire. I hoped that it would be possible to slide slowly from my public life back to the life of teaching and writing that I had always wanted. But things didn't work out that way.

"HORROR-STRUCK"

31 In August, 1959, Stempel and others charged that some quiz shows, including "Twenty-one," had been rigged. I was at that time appearing on the Garroway program as a replacement for Mr. Garroway, who was on vacation.

32 The news of Stempel's charges was like a blow. I was horror-struck. I have said I received many letters. Thousands more were from school children and students. All expressed their faith in me, their hope for the future, their dedication to knowledge and education.

33 These letters and all they stood for were like a vast weight. I could not bear to betray that faith and hope. I felt that anything that might happen to me was preferable to betraying them. I felt that I carried the whole burden of the honor of my profession.

34 And so I made a statement on the Garroway program the next morning to the effect that I knew of no improper activities on "Twenty-one" and that I had

received no assistance. I knew that most people would believe me. Most people did. I honestly thought I was doing the right thing.

I was, of course, very foolish. I was incredibly naïve. I couldn't understand 35
why Stempel should want to proclaim his own involvement. I could hardly believe what he said, though I knew it must be true, from my own experience.

"LIKE A CHILD"

In a sense, I was like a child who refuses to admit a fact in the hope that it will 36
go away. Of course, it did not go away, and an investigation was begun by the office of the District Attorney of New York.

I was called by Mr. Joseph Stone of that office and was interrogated. I 37
denied any knowledge of improper activities. After my interview with Mr. Stone, I engaged a lawyer, Carl Rubino. In my folly, I did not even tell him the truth. I supposed that an attorney could defend me if he did not know what I had done. I appeared before the grand jury in January, 1959, and still denied any involvement. I guess I did not fully understand the seriousness of this action, but even if I had, I am not sure I would have been physically able to admit what I had done. . . .

TRIED TO SAVE JOB

My life and career, it appeared, were being swept away in a flood. I tried to save 38
whatever part seemed in the most immediate danger. First, I hoped to save the [NBC] contract. I was just unable to walk out and slam the door on a $50,000-a-year job, a job which I enjoyed and thought extremely important. But, I was to lose things of greater value as time went on. . . .

"CONFUSED AND DISMAYED"

Thus, I could not face the situation on Thursday night. I was completely con- 39
fused and dismayed. I did not know what to do. Since I had been relieved from my assignment on the Garroway show the same day, I asked Columbia if I might miss the following day's class.

The university offered me a week's leave of absence, and I simply ran away. 40
There were a dozen newsmen outside my door, and I was running from them, too. I couldn't think when everywhere I went there were people trying to interview me and flashing bulbs in my face.

Most of all, I was running from myself. I realized that I had been doing it 41
for a long time. I had to find a place where I could think, in peace and quiet. I knew now that I could not lie any more, nor did I want to.

But, I was not yet at the point where I could tell the whole story. My wife and 42
I drove up into New England. I drove aimlessly from one town to another, trying to come to some conclusion. But I still could not face up to what I had done.

I returned to New York on Tuesday, Oct. 13, and the next day, the 14th, by   43
arrangement between Mr. Lishman and Mr. Rubino, I was served with a sub-
peona by a representative of the committee. I spent the rest of the week trying
hopelessly to seek a way out. There was no way, but even though my mind knew
there was none, I could not face the prospect emotionally.

ONLY ONE WAY OUT

There was one way out which I had, of course, often considered, and that was   44
simply to tell the truth. But, as long as I was trying to protect only myself and
my own reputation, and, as I thought, the faith people had in me, I could not
believe that was possible. But I was coming closer and closer to a true understanding of my position.

I was beginning to realize what I should have known before, that the truth   45
is always the best way, indeed it is the only way, to promote and protect faith.
And the truth is the only thing with which a man can live.

My father had told me this, even though he did not know the truth in my   46
case. I think he didn't care what it was so long as I told it. Other people said the
same thing, even thought they, too, did not know what the truth was.

In the end, it was a small thing that tipped the scales. A letter came to me   47
which I read. It was from a woman, a complete stranger, who had seen me on
the Garroway show and who said she admired my work there. She told me that
the only way I could ever live with myself, and make up for what I had done—
of course, she, too, did not know exactly what that was—was to admit it, clearly,
openly, truly.

Suddenly, I knew she was right, and this way, which had seemed for so   48
long the worst of all possible alternatives, suddenly became the only one.
Whatever the personal consequences, and I knew they would be severe, this
was the only way.

In the morning I telephoned my attorney and told him my decision. He   49
had been very worried about my health and, perhaps, my sanity, and he was
happy that I had found courage at last. He said, "God bless you." □

◢ REREADING FOR UNDERSTANDING

1. Van Doren says that he was both the principal victim of the quiz show deception, and its principal symbol. In what way did he fit both of these roles?

2. Van Doren says that at first he was able to rationalize his participation in
the deception because he felt he was serving the greater cause of education.
What positive effect do you think he may have had on education in general? Even before the quiz show scandal broke, he admits he realized that he
was giving people the wrong impression of education. How?

3. In the course of this statement, Van Doren confesses to not one but several
deceptions. What are they? How does he rationalize each?

◢ RESPONDING

1. Van Doren's confession seems deeply personal. He not only describes the events that took place, but also his emotional state beginning with his first appearance on *Twenty-one* through to his final decision to tell the truth. What effect do you think that disclosure of his own feelings had on his audience in the House of Representatives? on the American public? How does the personal nature of this statement affect your understanding and acceptance of it?

2. For his participation in the quiz show scandal, Charles Van Doren lost both his position as a commentator on the *Today* show and his teaching position at Columbia. Do you think this punishment was appropriate, too lenient, or too harsh? Defend your answer.

3. The revelation that quiz shows routinely fed answers to contestants came as a shock to television viewers in 1959. Do you think the same revelation would shock viewers today? Why or why not?

4. In "Women and Honor" (p. 264), Adrienne Rich observes that "the liar often suffers from amnesia. Amnesia is the silence of the unconscious." To what extent does this statement apply to Charles Van Doren?

◢ RESPONDING IN WRITING

1. Imagine that you are a student at Columbia University in 1959 and that Charles Van Doren is your instructor. Van Doren has appeared before Congress and confessed to participating in the quiz show deception. Write a letter to Columbia's board of trustees, explaining why you think Van Doren should or should not lose his position on the Columbia faculty.

2. Look for articles and commentary about this quiz show fiasco in newspapers and periodicals of the time. Then view Robert Redford's 1994 movie *Quiz Show*, which purports to tell the story of the scandal. Write a review of Redford's movie, critiquing how effectively and accurately it depicts this moment in history.

HANS J. MORGENTHAU

Charles Van Doren's dismissal from Columbia University for participating in the quiz show scandal was met with considerable protest by students who pleaded that their professor be given a second chance. Hans J. Morgenthau, then a professor at the University of Chicago, published an article in *The New York Times Magazine* in support of the university's decision. After receiving many anonymous letters from Columbia students in response to his article, Morgenthau addressed them all in a statement that appeared in *The*

New Republic. The piece that follows is a condensed version of that statement, reprinted in *The New Republic* in 1994, when the movie *Quiz Show* renewed interest in the Van Doren case.

Quisling Show

You are stung by my assertion that you are unaware of the moral problem posed by the Van Doren case, and you assure me that you disapprove of his conduct. But my point is proved by the very arguments with which you try to reconcile your disapproval of Van Doren's conduct with your petition to rehire him. Your concern is primarily with the misfortune of an attractive teacher, your regret in losing him and the rigor of the university's decision. You support your position by five main arguments: the confession has swept the slate clean, Van Doren will not do it again, his teaching was above reproach, academic teaching is not concerned with substantive truth and the university acted with undue haste. These arguments, taken at face value and erected into general principles of conduct, lead of necessity to the complete destruction of morality.

If confession can undo the deed, no evil could ever be condemned and no evil-doer ever brought to justice. If wrong could be so simply righted and guilt so painlessly atoned, the very distinction between right and wrong, innocence and guilt, would disappear; for no sooner would a wrong be committed than it would be blotted out by a confession. Confession, even if it is freely rendered as an act of contrition and moral conversion, can mitigate the guilt but cannot wipe it out.

The argument that the morally objectionable act is not likely to be repeated assumes that the purpose of moral condemnation is entirely pragmatic, seeking to prevent a repetition of the deed. Yet while it is true that according to the common law a dog is entitled to his first bite, it is nowhere written that a man is entitled to his first murder . . . or his first lie. The moral law is not a utilitarian instrument aiming at the protection of society, even though its observance has this effect. . . . Oedipus did not think that it was all right to marry his mother once since he did not do it again. Or would you suggest that evil-doers like Leopold and Loeb should have gone free because it was most unlikely that they would repeat what they had done?

The arguments of the good teacher and of teaching not being concerned with substantive truth go together. You assume . . . that the teacher is a kind of intellectual mechanic who fills your head with conventionally approved and required knowledge, as a filling station attendant fills a tank with gas. You don't care what the teacher does from 10 a.m. to 9 a.m. so long as he gives you from 9 to 10 a.m. the knowledge which he has been paid to transmit. You recognize no relation between a teacher's general attitude toward the truth and his way of transmitting knowledge, because you do not recognize an organic relation between transmitted knowledge and an objective, immutable truth. Yet the view that knowledge is but conventional—one conception of truth to be superseded by another—while seemingly supported by the radical transformations of physics, finds no support in the fields of knowledge dealing with man. If it were otherwise, Plato and Aristotle, Sophocles and Shakespeare . . . could mean nothing to us, except as objects for antiquarian exploration.

[The argument] that the trustees of Columbia University acted with undue   5
haste is the most curious of all, and it gives the show away. . . . You look for reasons which justify your unwillingness to transcend that three-cornered relationship among yourself, your teacher and your university and to judge the obvious facts by the standards of morality rather than adjust them for your and your teacher's convenience. You are sorry about losing an attractive teacher and you hate to see that teacher suffer; nothing else counts. But there is something else that counts and that is the sanctity of the moral law.

All men—civilized and barbarian—in contrast to the animals, are born   6
with a moral sense; that is to say, as man is by nature capable of making logical judgments, so is he capable by nature of making moral judgments. . . . Civilized man shares with the barbarian the faculty of making moral judgments, but excels over him in that he is capable of making the right moral judgments, knowing why he makes them. He knows—as Socrates, the Greek tragedians . . . the Biblical prophets and the great moralists and tragedians of all the ages know—what is meant by the sanctity of the moral law.

The moral law is not made for the convenience of man, rather it is an in-   7
dispensable precondition for his civilized existence. It is one of the great paradoxes of civilized existence that . . . it is not self-contained but requires for its fulfillment transcendent orientations. The moral law provides one of them.

You will become aware of the truth of that observation. For when you look   8
back on your life in judgement, you will remember it, and you will want it to be remembered, for its connection with the things that transcend it. And if you ask yourself why you remember and study the lives and deeds of great men, why you call them great in the first place, you will find that they were oriented in extraordinary ways and to an unusual degree toward the things that transcend their own existence. That is the meaning of the passage from the Scriptures, "He that findeth his life shall lose it; and he that loseth his life for my sake shall find it."

This connection between our civilized existence and the moral law explains   9
the latter's sanctity. By tinkering with it, by sacrificing it for individual convenience, we are tinkering with ourselves as civilized beings, we are sacrificing our own civilized existence.

The issue before you, when you were asked to sign that petition on Van   10
Doren's behalf then, was not the happiness of a particular man nor, for that matter, your own, but whether you and your university could afford to let a violation of the moral law pass as though it were nothing more than a traffic violation. Socrates had to come to terms with that issue, and he knew how to deal with it. You did not know how to deal with it. And this is why you hide your faces and muffle your voices. For since your lives have lost the vital contact with the transcendence of moral law, you find no reliable standard within yourself by which to judge and act. . . . But once you have restored that vital connection with the moral law from which life receives its meaning, you will no longer be

afraid of your shadow and the sound of your voices. You will no longer be afraid of yourself. For you will carry within yourself the measure of yourself and of your fellows and the vital link with things past, future and above. ☐

◪ REREADING FOR UNDERSTANDING

1. Morgenthau begins by listing the five arguments the Columbia students offer against firing Van Doren. What are those arguments?

2. What is Morgenthau's *thesis*, the main claim of his essay? Where is it found?

3. Why does Morgenthau disagree with the student's asserting that Van Doren's confession has "wiped the slate clean"?

4. Reread paragraphs 6 and 7. What connection between moral law and civilization does Morgenthau make?

◪ RESPONDING

1. Morgenthau takes issue with the argument that Van Doren should be reinstated because he has learned from his mistake and is certain never to repeat his action. This line of reasoning, he says, changes our understanding of moral law and its purpose. What does he mean by this? What examples and comparisons does he offer to support this point? How persuasive is this evidence?

2. Morgenthau suggests that it is because Van Doren is a teacher that he must be dismissed from his job. He says that a teacher is accountable not only for his performance in the classroom, but for his conduct outside the classroom as well. Why? Do you agree that honesty is more important in teaching than in other occupations? Can you think of other occupations that hold their members to a higher moral standard? Are such practices fair?

3. Morgenthau calls for an absolute adherence to moral principles. He warns that if we try to adapt moral law to suit our own convenience, "we are sacrificing our own civilized existence" (par. 9). Do you believe he is correct? Can you think of examples from your own experience or from history that support or contradict Morgenthau's claim?

4. In the selection from *The Prince* (p. 253), Machiavelli notes that "the princes who have done great things are those who have taken little account of faith and have known how to get around men's brains with their astuteness; and in the end they have overcome those who have founded themselves on loyalty" (par. 1). How do you think Machiavelli would see Morgenthau's view of moral law? How do you think he would have regarded the whole quiz show scandal?

POPE BROCK

A friend of ours was recently accepted at a prestigious university. During his interview with the admissions officer, he was asked where he ranked in his high school class of approximately 300. He replied with some pride that he was second in his class. The interviewer's response? "Why aren't you first?"

The pressure to succeed in school is enormous, and although teachers and alumni may claim that what matters is how much you learn, not what grades you receive, in reality grades mean a great deal, as our friend's experience indicates. Increasingly, grades are viewed as a measure of ability and potential for success and a few points more or less on your GPA can determine whether or not you are accepted into a graduate program or get a job after graduation.

Given this pressure, it's hardly surprising that academic dishonesty seems to be rising. In this article, which first appeared in *Esquire*, Pope Brock explores how the pressure to succeed academically, intensified by the pressure of military life and a rigorous honor code, erupted in scandal at the U.S. Naval Academy in 1994.

The Extremes of Honor

As is true every spring, the sun-drenched campus of the United States Naval Academy in Annapolis, Maryland, was in bloom. The cherry trees were laden with pink popcorn, and the tulips were out. Along the winding brick walkways—past the cannons, the gazebo, the venerable buildings, the domed chapel—scores of midshipmen crossed the yard, impressive in their dark-blue uniforms. Everybody was striding tall. There was no hint on this sparkling morning that the academy was locked in a torturous cheating scandal and that in just days, the secretary of the Navy, John Dalton, would announce which of the midshipmen would be expelled. In many ways, the placid face of the campus was a credit to how well the academy conducted its business. The students had been taught to stand tall. They had been taught to handle pressure.

Handling pressure is what the academy is all about. That's why plebes— first-year students—shout out reams of memorized trivia on command and do push-ups until their biceps cramp. "One guy in my year went completely bald from the stress," said Christopher Rounds, class of '94. "He had brown hair, and it all fell out for four or five months, and then it grew back white and fuzzy, like fur." The purpose of all the pounding is to impart a bedrock lesson of military life: how to perform correctly under intense strain.

Still, it's safe to say no one at the academy ever anticipated the kind of pressure that the class of 1994 would have to withstand. For sixteen months, scores of its students had been engulfed in the worst cheating scandal in the academy's 149-year history. The basic accusation—stealing and studying a copy of an exam for a notoriously difficult course—eventually enmeshed 133 midshipmen, including the class president, the captains of half a dozen varsity teams, and members of the '94 Honor Staff.

But if the scandal embarrassed the academy, the investigation shamed it. At first, the case was grossly underexplored by a school administration that seemed afraid of what it might find. Later, it overreacted as agents from the Pentagon showed up. Hundreds of students were interrogated by thugs in little rooms. This seemed to work: The investigation uncovered the guilty hardcore, but it also sucked in many others who were far less involved or completely innocent, as well as all their anguished families. Victims became as random as the casualties of war. 4

THE RUTHLESSNESS OF INTEGRITY

The young people who come here arrive by and large with a fierce faith in honor and country. After all, these are kids who want to fly jets and command ships. "I like being out front—leadership stuff," said Brian Pirko, twenty-two, from Dryden, New York, one of those mixed up in the scandal. Most have dreamed for years of attending the academy, which has produced an armada of astronauts and admirals, seventy-three Medal of Honor winners, and such ostentatious achievers as Jimmy Carter and Ross Perot. They arrive ready for a place where simply going to lunch is executed like a halftime formation. They are also ready to embrace the school's pristine Honor Concept: "Midshipmen are persons of integrity: They do not lie, cheat, or steal." 5

But for many, something goes wrong. As Richard L. Armitage, chairman of a board that recently studied the Honor Concept, put it, midshipmen "are much more idealistic when they arrive at the Naval Academy than when they leave." A major reason is the ruthless way that integrity has often been taught there. 6

Nobody quarrels with teaching would-be warriors honor ("Your word is my life," as they say), but many mids soon discover that the Honor Concept can eat them alive. The slightest infraction may have drastic consequences. A mid used a fake ID in a bar and was expelled. A tubby female midshipman who underreported her weight by six pounds was expelled. A midshipman spotted a pretty girl on campus one day, told her the guy she was looking for wasn't free, and took her out for a milk shake; he was expelled. 7

Administration officials insist that all cases aren't judged so harshly, but the mids say that's not true. "The problem is fear," said Justin Jones-Lantzy, now twenty-three, another member of the class of '94 implicated in the cheating scandal. "People don't adhere to the honor code because of honor. They're just afraid. Break it and you're out. There are no gray areas." 8

Oddly, there's the parallel Administrative Conduct System, which judges violations of conduct as opposed to honor. Here, entirely different rules seem to apply. A few years back, a midshipman, driving drunk, crashed his car and killed a passenger. All he received were demerits. Midshipmen have "gotten away with some pretty heinous things," says one alumnus, "as long as they were conduct and not honor offenses." 9

Many midshipmen do enjoy the challenge of discipline and carry the ideal-   10
ism they brought with them through graduation. But many develop a fear of
the "honor Nazis" and a corrosive, us-versus-them attitude. That contributed
substantially to the cheating scandal—a tale that began on December 11, 1992,
when a copy of the final exam for Electrical Engineering 311 fell into the hands
of an enterprising midshipman.

"IT SEEMED FISHY, BUT I DIDN'T ASK"

Double-E, wires, whatever they called it, the mids loathed that course. A re-   11
quirement widely viewed as irrelevant to most Navy careers, it was a crusher
that had damaged many a mid's class rank, crucial in determining who gets the
plum assignments after graduation.

On or about December 11, 1992, a civilian who worked in the campus   12
copying center secretly sold the exam to a midshipman; according to a source
close to the case, the price was $5,000. This midshipman—the Navy has not
released his name—gave two or three others a peek for a price; then he squir-
reled away the exam and waited. At about 9:00 P.M. on December 13, the night
before the exam, he and his friends released the test like a virus into the academy dormitory, Bancroft Hall.

A gargantuan building made of granite, Bancroft is the largest college dor-   13
mitory in America, with nearly five miles of corridors. Everyone in the academy's 4,100-student brigade lives there; on that particular evening, almost all of
the 663 juniors slated to take the exam were under one roof. Some worked
alone, others in groups. Along with their textbooks, students were pawing
through "gouge"—academy lingo for study aids, such as old exams kept on file
at the library. As one mid told *The Washington Post*: "It's the way we study. . . .
We're used to using old exams, we're used to working in groups, because that's
the way we're going to work in the fleet."

By now, Midshipman X had slipped copies to a knot of friends, some of   14
whom began selling the test for fifty bucks a pop. Then a few distributors began
working the halls. Investigators later identified two of them as Christopher
Rounds and Rodney Walker. (Rounds acknowledged that he was among the
first to get the exam but declined to say whether he had cheated. Walker refused
to be interviewed for this article unless he was paid.) But any hope of additional
sales vaporized in the next few minutes. The exam hit a pocket of football players and then blew like a back draft down several corridors. In moments, the
price dropped like a stone—twenty-five dollars, ten dollars—and then the exam
was everywhere. People started copying questions in longhand, passing them
around, E-mailing bits and pieces. The longer this blast echoed and re-echoed
throughout Bancroft, the vaguer the source of the questions became. Some
knew what they had. Some suspected. Some just thought it was more gouge—
maybe "football gouge," the very best, given to players by friendly professors.
Who knew? But the word was that it was hot stuff. Beyond the core conspira-
tors, there were a lot of midshipmen in the shadowlands. Pirko was one.

"There were seven of us in my room studying," said Pirko, then a top student on track to become a jet pilot. "A guy comes in with a copy of something. He says, 'This is good stuff. Study it.' It seemed fishy, but I didn't ask." What Pirko did know was that "you'd feel stupid if you didn't use it." Since the problems came without answers, he and his friends worked on them until nearly dawn.

By morning, shards of the exam—from half a dozen or so hard copies— had penetrated twenty-nine of the thirty-six companies living in Bancroft. During breakfast, there were mids who, not knowing what they were getting, were handed questions while they ate.

The Double-E students opened their tests together at 7:45 A.M. "That's when I saw I'd had the actual test the night before," Pirko said. "I froze up. I didn't know what to think or do." What he did was take the test and turn it in. Elsewhere in the room was Justin Jones-Lantzy, from North East, Pennsylvania. He had studied the night before with a group outside Bancroft into which, he said later, "my roommate, a major star on the football team, had brought portions of the test unbeknownst to us." Now, as he toiled over the exam, Jones-Lantzy noticed that three or four of the questions were "similar" to what he'd seen the night before. He didn't think anything of it. After completing the test (which, as it turned out, he failed), he climbed into his car and started home for Christmas break.

At 5:02 P.M., as Jones-Lantzy was cruising along a Pennsylvania highway, an E-mail message appeared in the office of an electrical-engineering professor at the academy: "Urgent!!!! . . . re: possible honor violation."

"IT WAS INCOMPREHENSIBLE TO ME"

When he took over as superintendent of the Naval Academy, Rear Admiral Thomas C. Lynch was, after service in the Mediterranean, the Middle East, and Washington, one of the Navy's rising stars. He was a political animal—"more show horse than workhorse," one academy grad said—but well liked, and he had a strong talent for leadership.

Much was expected of Lynch. He had been posted in June 1991 with a mission to reinvigorate the academy after an ugly sexual-harassment episode in which a female midshipman was chained to a urinal and taunted by a gang of eight male classmates. He also had another mission, one dearer to his heart: bringing back Navy football. He had been center and cocaptain of the academy's 1963 team—the year when Roger Staubach passed his way to a Heisman Trophy, when Navy was ranked second in the country and went to the Cotton Bowl. But Navy football had fallen on hard times since then—lousy, losing seasons for more than a decade. Lynch, along with others, was bent on seeing the blue and gold come roaring back.

News of possible cheating on the Double-E exam landed on his desk on December 15, the day after the test. "It was incomprehensible to me," Lynch said long afterward. "It's still incomprehensible to me. But I tried to handle it as forthrightly as possible." The next day, he called in the Naval Criminal

Investigative Service (NCIS)—because crimes such as theft and sale of government documents had possibly occurred. This news sent a jolt through the class of '94.

What to do? Given the brutal way in which the Honor Concept had often   22
been applied—sentence first, trial afterward—not just the ringleaders but anyone tainted by the events of the night or anyone who thought that he might even *look* tainted was afraid of being expelled if he talked. As one midshipman put it: "To come forward was a career-ending decision."

There was another powerful reason to keep quiet: the stricture against   23
"bilging a classmate," the academy expression for making a buddy look bad, something midshipmen are drilled to avoid. There's even a Bilger's Gate on campus through which, by tradition, no midshipman ever goes.

Add this: "There was an underlying physical threat," Jones-Lantzy said,   24
"especially involving the football team. There was a fear that if you ratted out a football player, you would be . . . very unliked."

As the midshipmen went into damage control, the NCIS agents went to   25
work. Tough and professional, they took care to inform the more than two hundred people they interviewed of their constitutional rights. In time, a couple of mids gave the first glimpses into the conspiracy—a name or two, an exchange of cash. Then, on January 8, the NCIS interviewed Rodney Walker, one of the top lieutenants in the scheme. He couldn't stop talking.

Walker was, as a classmate said, "smooth and very smart." Exactly why he   26
decided to talk remains muddy, but Walker, according to this mid, "was prior-enlisted, so he'd been in the fleet. He just saw the academy as a nice break from real life. And his persona was, I'm gonna do whatever it takes to get out of trouble." Whatever the impulse, Walker appeared to be the kind of garrulous case buster investigators love. In a four-page sworn statement, Walker named twenty-three midshipmen who had had the exam and said he sold it to four of them himself. He also said, "I know a majority of the varsity junior-class football players had the exam." He said he was ready to testify against everybody.

The NCIS completed its report on February 4, and twenty-four cases of   27
possible honor violations were referred to the student Honor Staff of the class of '93—the senior class. Once the hearings started, several began to suspect that the administration wasn't really interested in learning the truth—not the whole truth, anyway. As Brigade Honor Secretary Brendon Dibella later told Navy investigators, "There were conspiracies of lying, bribes, and threats" among mids and "obvious collusion on the part of the accused," but the committee couldn't tear into most of it because faculty advisers drastically curtailed testimony and refused to pursue leads. "Censorship of the evidence," Dibella said, "plagued the board."

To top it off, on March 17, Rodney Walker repudiated his own statement,   28
claiming it had been coerced (his signed acknowledgement that he had been read his rights notwithstanding). Whether he had been threatened or bribed—once he said he'd been offered $15,000 by some mids to take the fall—or whether, as one Navy official suggested, "he just liked to jerk people around," Walker disavowed his evidence at sixteen separate board hearings. "He wanted to tell the

truth, not rat, and save his hide, all at the same time," said a board member who saw him perform. "It was like watching a guy with multiple personalities."

Ultimately, Dibella reported, "the Honor Staff unanimously agreed the entire process had been an abortion." Though convinced the "cheating tree" spread far wider, the board could find only eleven of the twenty-four accused midshipmen in violation. "The worst part of it all," according to Dibella, "was the administration appeared satisfied that a thorough job had been done. . . ." [29]

The eleven cases went to Commandant John Padgett, Lynch's deputy, who cleared four more—including, to the shock of the Honor Staff, one of the best-known figures on campus: Duncan "Duke" Ingraham Jr., a fullback on the football team and the son of one of Admiral Lynch's 1963 teammates. In addition, Duke Ingraham and Lynch's son, Thomas, were good friends. (According to Dibella's report, when asked by an honor-board member whether he feared expulsion, Ingraham, known to some classmates as Teflon, replied, "I was never worried. They weren't going to get rid of me." Ingraham declined to be interviewed for this article.) [30]

The last seven cases—none football players—went to Admiral Lynch in mid-April. By then, he must have been aware of a huge uneasiness roiling the school. A Catholic chaplain at the academy, J. William Hines, had just written him about the torment many midshipmen were going through over the cheating and about "the extensive lying by many members of the brigade." On April 21, Lynch received a letter from Annapolis attorney William Ferris, who represented five of the accused. "I am sure you are aware," Ferris wrote, "that there were almost surely over a hundred midshipmen involved." [31]

Starting early the next morning, on April 22, Lynch interviewed the seven accused midshipmen and their distraught parents, in half-hour shifts. He expelled six. That evening, he strode across the campus toward Alumni Hall for a Superintendent's Call, at which he would address the full forty-one-hundred-member brigade. He was going to tell them that the incident was over. [32]

THE LID BLEW OFF ANYWAY

What's so remarkable now is that Lynch seems to have thought he could make it stick. But why try in the first place? Some believe Lynch succumbed to what one lieutenant commander called "the wimp syndrome." After the *Iowa* and Tailhook episodes, this officer says, "The Navy will do anything to avoid exposure and embarrassment." Certainly by tossing these six midshipmen into the volcano, Lynch hoped to appease the gods of justice. [33]

Standing in the well of the hall, looking up at forty-one hundred solemn faces, Lynch summarized the episode. Then he announced the expulsion, adding that he was "glad" to report that no football players were involved. [34]

A low but dangerous surge of noise passed through the student body. Then Rodney Walker, a man with nothing to lose, sprang to his feet, shouting. He attacked the admiral, demanding to know why Midshipman Ingraham had visited Lynch's house the very night before his case was to be heard by Commandant Padgett. [35]

Lynch denied having seen Ingraham that night. There was snickering and   36
hooting from the audience. But Ingraham had been talking about the visit himself, Walker retorted.

The superintendent, angered, replied that he had only said hello to Ingra-   37
ham and had discussed nothing of substance with him. A sarcastic chant broke
out in the brigade: "Duke, Duke, Duke . . ." Other mids sat shocked, white-faced,
and confused. But there was more.

Walker wasn't through. Now he asserted that he had been approached   38
about wearing a wire to record other midshipmen and that Lynch knew all
about it. Furious, Lynch cut him short. The room broke into an uproar. A senior
midshipman took the mike and reminded the brigade that they were in the
presence of an admiral.

Lynch tried to respond to other questions, but it was heavy weather. The   39
football-player issue wouldn't go away: The team had long been resented for its
special privileges—basically, more food and less abuse—but now Lynch seemed
to be shielding the whole team. The mood in the hall stayed ugly. Finally, Lynch
ended the meeting by declaring that the case would remain open. If any leads
emerged, he said, they would be pursued. The midshipmen spilled out of
Alumni Hall, many more cynical than ever.

Within a week, the lid blew off anyway. "Far and away, the heroes of this   40
story are the midshipmen themselves," said an academy graduate close to the
case. "They're the people who consistently wanted justice. They faxed and
leaked and kept this story alive."

A mid from the class of '94 buttonholed Cory Culver, the '93 honor-board   41
chairman who had overseen the original hearings, and laid out in detail the
copying and collusion he knew about. Culver—ramrod straight in ethical matters—immediately took this news to academy officials. He got nowhere, but
during the next two weeks, he kept pushing. ("Padgett must have wet his pants
every time Culver knocked on the door," one alumnus remarked.)

Too late. On May 26, *The Baltimore Sun* reported that new information on   42
the scandal had turned up that officials seemed to be ignoring. That brought
action. Two days later, Senator Richard Shelby of Alabama, chairman of an
Armed Services subcommittee, called for an investigation by the inspector general of the Pentagon. On June 4, the chief of naval operations, Frank Kelso II,
ordered IG investigators to the campus.

"I read in the paper that the IG was coming in," Jones-Lantzy said. "I was   43
very uneasy. I was under a contract of loyalty to my roommate and half a dozen
others"—to keep silent about what he knew—"and things were getting thicker
and thicker." Just how thick they would get, he and the rest of the academy
could not have imagined. Unlike their relatively polite predecessors, IG agents
treated interrogations as a blood sport, a game with no rules. This time, the
midshipmen would have no right to remain silent, no right to a lawyer, and no
right to leave the room.

The IG agents set up shop on the third floor of Nimitz Library and set   44
about scaring the hell out of everybody. Usually, two or three interrogators
worked on each "midshipman suspect." Jones-Lantzy recalled his first interview

this way: "We were in a very small room at the library. There were no windows. I remember the buzzing of the fluorescent light in the ceiling. One guy was like my best friend for the first five minutes. Then suddenly he was banging on the table and calling me scum. It was like a POW session. He said, 'We can keep you here forever.' Finally, I said to them, 'Why don't you hook me up to electric shock? It would be quicker.'"

Soon, horror stories were pouring out of those little rooms in the library; some of the tales can now be found in sworn affidavits filed in the U.S. district court in Washington. "I was told I had no rights except to tell the truth," said one of these college students. "I was told that if I lied I would be 'thrown out of the academy and sent to Leavenworth.'" The investigators "screamed and cursed at me. They told me they 'knew I had the fucking exam,' that I was 'a lying sack of shit.' They told me that the only thing I would be doing in the future was 'scrubbing floors at McDonald's.'" 45

"At one point," said a female midshipman, one of the few women caught up in the scandal, "I got up and tried to leave, stating that I was most certainly being accused and that I would come back with a lawyer. The investigators yelled at me and told me that I could not leave. I felt intimidated. 46

"The investigators asked questions regarding my personal life that were un-related to the 311 EE exam. They put up a picture of my boyfriend in the inter-view room" and "asked me personal questions about my boyfriend and laughed at our [E-mail] messages. . . . The investigators repeatedly told me that 'people like you make us sick.'" 47

For the midshipmen, the pressure had moved into the red zone. A few crumbled, but most still stonewalled. "Lie till you die" was a popular refrain at Bancroft. Still, anxiety about who could be trusted was becoming intense, along with a vivid fear among parents that one or more mids would commit suicide. "My son called me once, crying like a baby," one mother said, "He told me, 'I feel like getting into a car and driving into a tree.'" One midshipman accused of cheating checked into Bethesda Naval Hospital. He had no feeling in half his body. "The doctors thought it was multiple sclerosis," his mother said. "It was stress." Another became so withdrawn he took to sleeping under his bed. Sup-port groups sprang up, complete with rosary beads, inspirational poetry, and midshipmen clasping one another's hands. 48

On top of everything else, it became known that a few midshipmen were acting as informants. "Some mids were adopted by the IG"—i.e., recruited as spies—said one high-ranking Navy lawyer, enabling the interrogators to make "lucky guesses" during questioning. This ratcheted up the level of paranoia. "Everybody thought the rooms were bugged," Jones-Lantzy said. Under this barrage, long-standing friendships cracked. "It became friends versus friends, roommates versus roommates," said Christopher Rounds. "Backstabbing be-came rampant. It was me, me, me. If I turn in enough people, maybe they'll keep me. You're up against the wall. It's your senior year. You'll do anything. You minimize personal involvement and try to put it on someone else. And then guys would say, like, 'I stabbed you in the back, but you have to understand, it was my best move.'" 49

"There was such turmoil," Jones-Lantzy recalls. "I had headaches every   50
day." In October 1993, he finally had enough. Guilty of stonewalling the investigation but not of cheating (he had never known about the illegal gouge, he
said, until many days after he took the test), he decided to abandon his contract
of loyalty and just tell the truth.

Thus Jones-Lantzy became a pariah. "Guys I'd been friend with for four or   51
five years wouldn't look me in the eye. My roommate and I said ten words over
the whole next semester, then I got a new roommate. College friends are supposed to be the ones you keep, and now I have none."

On January 24, 1994, the IG released a thirty-page report implicating 133   52
midshipmen in wholesale cheating and lying that "exposed their shallow commitment to the Honor Concept." But the report also roasted Admiral Lynch and
his staff for the way they handled the issue, saying it "constituted mismanage-
ment" and created a climate in which midshipmen "did not feel the truth was
found or even seriously sought." Lynch was further embarrassed by the report's
comments on him and the football team, how on August 3, 1993, he told agents
that if their probe couldn't be completed by the end of the summer, "then the
investigators should take their time and do a thorough job because the Army-
Navy game was December 5, 1993." As for the Duke Ingraham case, the IG
found "no actual conflict of interest. . . . However, there was a definite perception of a conflict or lack of impartiality among the midshipmen, and the academy officials were not sensitive to this perception. . . ."

"WHAT IS THE MESSAGE?"

Of course, the question still hanging was what to do with the 133 midshipmen   53
implicated in the cheating. After more than a year of suffering, everybody
wanted a quick resolution. So for the first time in its history, the academy lost
its authority over its own honor cases. Admiral Kelso appointed a five-member
panel, headed by Rear Admiral Richard C. Allen, to rule on them.

Simultaneously, the judge advocate general (JAG) assigned fourteen defense   54
attorneys, headed by Lieutenant Commander Jo King, to help the mids. "I had
expected to find a bunch of spoiled cheaters," King said, "but there were some
very special kids here caught up in something with very few clear lines and all
these shadings of gray." She was also appalled by the IG's interrogation techniques. "I was flabbergasted by the contempt and abuse," she said, "especially in
something of this magnitude, with the potential damage to lives, loss of careers.
It still baffles me. These were college kids, not cracked-out criminals."

With hearings set for mid-February, time was scarce. The JAG lawyers had   55
to prepare dozens of defenses in a matter of days, and it didn't help that most
of their young clients were now deeply suspicious of anyone in uniform. "We
did a lot of hand-holding," said Lieutenant Commander Julie Tinker, a JAG attorney who represented nine mids. Meanwhile, Allen and his board were working through the landfill of evidence already collected and sorting through
hundreds of testimonial letters and appeals. "I understand that Admiral Lynch
was quoted in an Annapolis newspaper as saying, 'We want to save the mids

worth saving,'" ended one mother's letter. "I'd like to think all mids are worth saving; I know my mid is worth saving. . . ."

The hearings opened at Alumni Hall on February 24. In the lobby, parents, friends, and midshipmen milled in a pall of agitation and dread. Inside sat Admiral Allen and his four colleagues. Over the next month, they would work twelve hours a day, six days a week, to hear the 106 most serious cases. 56

One of those cases was Brian Pirko's. He sat at a table facing the Allen board and for the first time told the truth. Four of the other six mids in his study group that December night did the same. At the end of his hearing, Pirko—a descendant of three generations of West Pointers—told the board, "Whatever happens, I feel better just knowing that I've come here and cleared my conscience." 57

But the two others in Pirko's group held out. When their cases came up, they claimed they had not been involved. 58

When his turn came, Justin Jones-Lantzy admitted lying to protect his friends, but said he had not cheated. When Duke Ingraham was called, he denied doing anything wrong. 59

On March 31, a line of mids formed outside a first-floor conference room at Bancroft Hall. One by one, they were ushered in and read their fates. "I stood before them," Brian Pirko said. "Allen read the findings: 'You have been separated from the Naval Academy. . . .' I said, 'Aye, aye, sir,' and saluted. About-face and out." 60

Gradually, it emerged that those being expelled were for the most part the hardcore instigators, against whom the evidence was overwhelming, and those who had eventually told the truth. Holes had been blown in the wall of silence, but chunks had held. As Pirko said, "Confession was the strongest piece of evidence against you." In his study group, the five who confessed were out; the two who did not were retained. 61

Justin Jones-Lantzy, to his shock, was expelled. Duke Ingraham was retained. "The ones who kept their mouths shut, who 'played it smart,' are graduating," says one JAG lawyer. "I think this whole class of '94 is shaking their heads. What is the message?" 62

The Allen board recommended twenty-nine expulsions, and punishment, including retaking Double-E and late graduation, for a few dozen more mids. Thirty-five were exonerated. The findings were then sent to Admiral Kelso for review, just at the time when the admiral, tarnished by Tailhook, was negotiating his own early retirement. Kelso, who had steadfastly denied he had been on the hotel floor where the mauling of women occurred, even though more than thirty witnesses placed him there—who, in the view of some, had "lied till he died"—was now judging the integrity of the mids. ("Yeah, some of us found that ironic," said one of the expelled mids.) Kelso kicked back three of the famous first six, who had come forward right away. Secretary Dalton retained two more. The final count: twenty-four midshipmen expelled, sixty-four punished. 63

However, that wasn't quite the end of the story. Back on campus, there were some midshipmen who had not forgotten or forgiven those who had "broken loyalty." 64

"I was really scared for my life for a while," Jones-Lantzy said. He had al-   65
ready been threatened in a local bar by a classmate (in the presence of a JAG
lawyer) with having his legs broken. A few days after the verdicts were announced, he was driving on a highway near Annapolis. "Four football players in
a 4×4 came up behind me. They were moving in on me from the right. They
had their windows down and they were yelling obscenities, trying to run me off
the road. I slammed on the brakes, let them pass, then cut over into the far-right
lane to get away from them." Of the four in the truck, he said, all cheaters, three
had survived and would graduate.

The Allen board was only part of the academy's response. A well-regarded   66
Marine colonel, Michael Hagee, joined the faculty in the newly created post of
ethics officer. "The mission, as I see it," he said, "is to bring focus to character
development." He acknowledged that there had been "too much negative leadership in the past"—too much reliance on harsh methods—and perhaps not a
clear enough understanding among midshipmen that personal integrity tran-
scends all: "There's nothing wrong with classmate loyalty unless it is taken to
an extreme."

Other reforms were promised, including a redesign of the Double-E re-   67
quirement to make it, in the words of the academic dean, "more reasonable."
But the biggest change of all was the assignment of a new superintendent.
Lynch was replaced by Charles Larson, a four-star admiral, commander of the
Navy's Pacific forces, an unquestioned heavyweight whose assignment was de-
signed to trumpet the message of a new era at the Naval Academy.

Next year, that is. On May 25, when the class of '94 graduated, there was the   68
usual happy pomp, but the occasion was laced with a good deal of bitterness.
The mother of one midshipman, who had been cleared after fifteen months of
investigation, said her whole family felt brutalized. "There's no joy for us today,"
she said. "He spent $2,500 on his class ring, and he'll never wear it." □

◢ REREADING FOR UNDERSTANDING

1. Brock notes a distinction between honor violations and conduct violations. What is the difference between behavior covered by the Honor
   Concept and that covered by the Administrative Conduct System? What
   do you think is the rationale for making such a distinction? Do you find it
   a sensible distinction? Explain.

2. Brock cites numerous pressures that contributed to the initial stealing of
   the Double-E exam. What were those pressures?

3. Brock suggests that the Naval Academy administration mishandled the
   initial investigation. How? What were the results of that mishandling?

4. Brock notes that several students refused to be interviewed for his article
   or, in one case, refused to be interviewed unless paid. Why do you think
   he includes this information? What effect does it have on the credibility of

the article? What impression do we get of those students who did not cooperate with the article? of those who did?

5. Brock says that many midshipmen "discover that the Honor Concept can eat them alive" (par. 7). Evaluate the Honor Concept based on the information in Brock's article. If its purpose is to instill integrity and honesty in future leaders, how effective is it? What forces work against it? Would you recommend that the Naval Academy retain its Honor Concept, drop it, or modify it?

6. This article originally appeared in *Esquire*. What would you say is the intention of the article? To what extent is it informative? persuasive? entertaining? Try to draw a rough profile of the intended audience based on specific features of this article.

7. Machiavelli (p. 253) advises that it is acceptable and even necessary to be dishonest with those who are dishonest with you. "If all men were good, this teaching would not be good; but because they are wicked and do not observe faith with you, you also do not have to observe it with them" (par. 3). Is his advice supported by the cheating incident at the Naval Academy and its outcome? What happened to midshipmen like Brian Pirko who told the truth? Would they have been better off to have lied?

◢ RESPONDING

1. One of the midshipmen Brock interviewed indicated that students adhere to the Honor Concept not because of personal integrity but out of fear. How significant a factor is fear in motivating moral behavior? Would more people cheat or be dishonest in other ways if they did not fear the consequences of getting caught?

2. Although some of the students involved in the cheating scandal clearly knew that they were studying a stolen exam, others claimed not to have realized that the test was stolen until they opened their examinations in class the next morning. How credible do you find such claims? Given the circumstances as Brock describes them in this article, do you think it's possible that students at least suspected that they may have been cheating?

3. Brian Pirko, one of the students expelled for cheating, states that when he realized he had cheated, "I froze up. I didn't know what to think or do" (par. 17). What would you have done in Pirko's place?

◢ RESPONDING IN WRITING

How do you suppose an incident like the one described in this article would be handled at your school? If you are not familiar with the system for responding to academic dishonesty at your school, do some research to learn about it. How effective has the policy been in preventing and/or punishing cheating? in teaching honesty and encouraging integrity among students? Write a letter to the editor of your college newspaper in which you critique the current honor system.

ABIGAIL WITHERSPOON

The author of this essay makes a living writing students' papers for a fee. In this essay she describes the work she does. Her name, as well as the names of her employers and colleagues, has been changed.

This Pen for Hire
On Grinding Out Papers for College Students

I am an academic call girl. I write college kids' papers for a living. Term papers, books reports, senior theses; take-home exams. My "specialties": art history and sociology, international relations and comparative literature, English, psychology, "communications," Western philosophy (ancient and contemporary), structural anthropology, film history, evolutionary biology, waste management and disposal, media studies, and pre-Confederation Canadian history. I throw around allusions to Caspar Weinberger and Alger Hiss, Sacco and Vanzetti, Haldeman and Ehrlichman, Joel Steinberg and Baby M. The teaching assistants eat it up. I can do simple English or advanced jargon. Like other types of prostitutes, I am, professionally, very accommodating.

I used to tell myself I'd do this work only for a month or two, until I found something else. But the official unemployment rate in this large Canadian city where I live is almost 10 percent, and even if it were easy to find a job, I'm American, and therefore legally prohibited from receiving a paycheck. So each day I walk up the stairs of a rotting old industrial building to an office with a sign on the window: TAILORMADE ESSAYS, WRITING AND RESEARCH. The owner, whom I'll call Matthew, claims that he started the business for ghostwriters, speechwriters, and closet biographers, and only gradually moved into academic work as a sideline. But even Grace, the oldest surviving writer on Tailormade's staff, can't remember anybody ever writing much other than homework for students at one university or another.

This is a good city for Tailormade. Next door is the city's university and its tens of thousands of students, a school that was once somewhat better when not all of its computer-registered classes numbered in the hundreds. Orders come in from Vancouver, Calgary, Winnipeg. There are plenty of essay services in the States, of course; they advertise in campus newspapers and the back pages of music magazines. Some of the big ones have toll-free phone numbers. They're sprinkled all over: California, Florida, New Jersey. But we still get American business too. Orders come in here from Michigan, Vermont, Pennsylvania; from

Illinois, Wisconsin, upstate New York, sometimes California; from Harvard, Cornell, and Brown. They come in from teachers' colleges, from people calling themselves "gifted students" (usually teenagers at boarding schools), and, once in a while, from the snazzy places some of our customers apparently vacation with their divorced dads, like Paris.

Matthew runs the business with his wife, Sylvia. Or maybe she is his ex-wife, nobody's exactly sure. When you call Tailormade—it's now in the phone book—you hear Sylvia say that Tailormade is Canada's foremost essay service; that our very qualified writers handle most academic subjects; and that we are fast, efficient, and completely confidential. Sylvia speaks loudly and slowly and clearly, especially to Asian customers. She is convinced that everyone who phones the office will be Asian, just as she's convinced that all Asians drive white Mercedes or black BMWs with cellular phones in them. From my personal experience, I find the Asian customers at least more likely to have done the assigned reading.

Matthew and Sylvia are oddly complementary. Matthew, gentle and fumbly, calls out mechanically, "Thank you, sir, ma'am, come again" after each departing back slinking down the hall. Sylvia asks the Chinese customers loudly, "SIMPLE ENGLISH?" She tells the uncertain, "Well, don't show up here till you know what you want," and demands of the dissatisfied, "Whaddya mean you didn't like it? You ordered it, din'cha?"

This afternoon, October 10, I'm here to hand in a paper and fight it out with the other writers for more assignments. Some of us are legal, some aren't. Some have mortgages and cars, some don't. All of us are hungry. The office is jammed, since it's almost time for midterms. Tailormade does a brisk business from October to May, except for January. The chairs are full of customers studiously filling out order forms. You can always tell who is a student and who is a writer. The students are dressed elegantly and with precision; the writers wear ripped concert T-shirts or stained denim jackets with white undershirts peeking out. The students wear mousse and hair gel and nail polish and Tony Lama western boots and Tourneau watches and just the right amount of makeup. They smell of Escape, Polo for men, and gum. The writers smell of sweat, house pets, and crushed cigarettes. Four of the other writers are lolling in their chairs and fidgeting; work usually isn't assigned until all the order forms have been filled out, unless somebody requests a topic difficult to fill. Then Matthew will call out like an auctioneer: "Root Causes of the Ukrainian Famine? Second year? Anyone? Grace?" or "J. S. Mill's Brand of Humane Utilitarianism? Third year? Henry, that for you?" as some customer hovers in front of the desk, eyes straight ahead. Someone else in the room might idly remark that he or she took that course back in freshman year and it was a "gut" or a "real bird."

I suspect that each of us in the Tailormade stable of hacks sorts out the customers differently: into liberal-arts students and business students; into those that at least do the reading and those that don't bother; into those that have trouble writing academic English and those that just don't care about school; into those that do their assignments in other subjects and those that farm every last one of them out to us; into the struggling and inept versus the rich, lazy, and stupid. But for Matthew and Sylvia, the clientele are divisible, even before cash versus credit card, or paid-up versus owing, into Asian customers and non-Asian ones. There's been an influx of wealthy immigrants from Hong Kong in recent years, fleeing annexation. Matthew and Sylvia seem to resent their presence and, particularly, their money. Yet they know that it's precisely this pool of customers—who have limited written English language skills but possess education, sophistication, ambition, cash, and parents leaning hard on them for good grades—that keeps the business going.

When I hand in my twelve pages on "The Role of Market Factors in the   8
Development of the Eighteenth-Century Fur Trade," Matthew tells me, "This lady's been patiently waiting without complaining." I must be very late. Turning to the client, he picks up one of my sheets and waves it. "At least it's a nice bib," he points out to her. "Look at that." Although I wasn't provided with any books for this essay, I managed to supply an extensive bibliography. I can't remember what I put on it.

I'm still waiting for an assignment. In fact, all the writers are still waiting. We   9
often wait at the bar around the corner; Tailormade has its own table there, permanently reserved. But we all have to get ourselves to the office eventually to pick up assignments. Grace, the oldest writer and by now, probably, the best, sits sorrowfully by the window, her long gray hair falling into her lap and her head jammed into her turtleneck, on her thin face a look of permanent tragedy. Grace gets up at three in the morning to work; she never forgets a name, a fact, or an assignment; she has a deep, strange love for Japanese history and in ten years here has probably hatched enough pages and research for several doctoral dissertations in that field. Elliott, another writer, reclines near the door, his little dog asleep under his chair. He uses the dog as an icebreaker with the clients, especially young women. He is six and a half feet tall and from somewhere far up in the lunar landscape of northern Ontario. He has a huge head of blond hair down to his eyes and pants as tight as a rock star's. Elliott is the business writer. He specializes in finance, investment, management, and economics. He lives out of a suitcase; he and the little dog, perhaps practicing fiscal restraint, seem to stay with one of a series of girlfriends. When the relationship comes to an end, Elliott and the little dog wind up back in the office, where they sleep in the fax room and Elliott cranks out essays on his laptop. Henry and Russell, two other writers, twist around, changing position, the way travelers do when they're trying to nap on airport lounge chairs. They both look a little like El Greco saints, although perhaps it just seems that way to me because lately I've been doing a lot of art history papers. They both have long skinny legs, long thin white nervous twiddling hands, long thin faces with two weeks' worth of unintentional beard. Henry points out how good Russell looks, and we all agree. Russell is forty. He has a girlfriend half his age who has, he says, provided a spiritual reawakening. Before he met her, Russell drank so much and held it so badly that he had the distinction of being the only staff member to be banned from the bar around the corner for life. Henry, by contrast, looks terrible. He's always sick, emaciated,

coughing, but he invariably manages to meet his deadlines, to make his page quotas, and to show up on time. We used to have another writer on staff, older even than Russell or Grace, who smoked a pipe, nodded a lot, and never said anything. He was a professor who'd been fired from some school, we were never really sure where. Eventually, he went AWOL and started an essay-writing service of his own. He's now Tailormade's main competition. The only other competitors, apparently, worked out of a hot-dog stand parked next to a campus bookstore. Nobody knows whether they're open anymore.

In general, there is a furtiveness about the way we writers talk to one another, the way we socialize. In the office, we're a little like people who know each other from A.A. meetings or rough trade bars encountering each other on a Monday morning at the photocopy machine. It's not because we're competing for work. It's not even because some of us are illegal and everyone else knows it. It is, if anything, collective embarrassment. We know a lot more than Matthew and Sylvia do. They sit dumbly as we bullshit with the clients about their subjects and assignments ("Ah, introductory psychology! The evolution of psychotherapy is a fascinating topic . . . ever read a guy called Russell Jacoby?") in order to impress them and get them to ask for us. This must be the equivalent of the harlots' competitive bordello promenade. But we work for Matthew and Sylvia. They have the sense to pit us against each other, and it works. We can correct their pronunciation of "Goethe" and they don't care. They know it makes no difference. I suspect they have never been farther away than Niagara Falls; neither of them may have even finished high school. It doesn't matter. The laugh's on us, of course: they own the business.

OCTOBER 12, 1994. A tall gangly kid comes in for a twenty-page senior history essay about the ancient local jail. It involves research among primary sources in the provincial archives, and I spend a week there, going page by page through the faded brown script of the warden's prison logbooks of the 1830s. Agitators are being executed for "high treason" or "banished from the realm," which, I assume, means being deported. Once in a while there's a seductive joy to a project. You forget that you've undertaken it for money, that it isn't yours.

Most of the time, though, all I think about is the number of pages done, the number to go. Tailormade charges twenty dollars Canadian a page for first- and second-year course assignments, twenty-two a page for third- and fourth-year assignments, twenty-four for "technical, scientific, and advanced" topics. "Technical, scientific, and advanced" can mean nuclear physics, as it does in September when there is no business. Or it can mean anything Matthew and Sylvia want it to, as it does in March. Most major spring-term essays are due when final exams begin, in April, and so in March kids are practically lined up in the office taking numbers and spilling out into the hall. The writers get half, in cash: ten and eleven bucks a page; twelve for the technical, scientific, and advanced.

There's one other charge: if the client doesn't bring in her or his own books, except in September and January, she or he is "dinged," charged an extra two dollars a page for research. When the writers get an assignment, we ask if there are books. If there are, it saves us time, but we have to lug them home, and often they're the wrong books. If there are no books, we have to go to the libraries and research the paper ourselves. "Client wants twelve pages on clinical social work intervention," Matthew and Sylvia might tell us. "She has a reading list but no books. I think we can ding her." "He wants a book report on something called *Gravity's Rainbow*? Doesn't have the book, though. I'm gonna ding him."

OCTOBER 13. I am assigned a paper on the French philosopher Michel Foucault. The client has been dinged; I have to find some books. Foucault's *Discipline and Punish* and *Madness and Civilization* are hot properties in the public library system. They are not to be found anywhere. Perhaps this is because professors think Foucault is a hot property, too; he's all over everyone's syllabus.   14

I warn the client about this in the office. "If you don't find anything by the guy, call me," he says. He gives me his home phone number. "Only, *please* don't say you're from the essay service. Say you're . . . a classmate of mine." I promise to be discreet. Most of the clients get scared when you call them at home; most never give out their numbers. I don't blame them.   15

It was different, though, when I was a university student in the early 1980s. I wasn't aware of anyone who bought his or her homework anywhere, although it must have happened. It was about that time that Tailormade was putting up signs on the telephone poles outside the university's main classroom buildings. It advertised just outside the huge central library as well as outside the libraries of three or four smaller schools a few minutes' drive away. This burst of entrepreneurial confidence almost led to the service's undoing. In a spectacular cooperative sting operation among the security departments of the various schools, the office was raided. This event has become a sort of fearsome myth at Tailormade, discussed not unlike the way Syrians might occasionally mention the Israeli raid on Entebbe. Matthew and Sylvia were hauled off to court and a dozen or so clients were thrown out of their respective universities. Matthew and Sylvia, however, must have hired the right lawyer: they were allowed to reopen, provided that they stayed away from campuses and that they stamped every page of every essay TAILORMADE ESSAY SERVICE: FOR RESEARCH PURPOSES ONLY. Now the clients take the stamped essays home, retype them, and print them out on high-end laser printers much better than ours. If the client is obnoxious, complains, or is considered a whiner, each typewritten page will be stamped in the middle. If the client is steady and has good credit, each page will be stamped in the margin so that the stamp can be whited out and the pages photocopied.   16

By the time Tailormade reopened, I had moved back to this country after some years at home in the States. I had no money and no prospects of a legal job. I came in, handed Matthew a résumé, spent a couple of weeks on probationary trial, and then began a serious career as a hack. "What are your specialties?" Matthew had asked me. I told him I'd majored in history and political science as an undergraduate. Over time, as my financial situation grew worse, my "specialties" grew to include everything except math, accounting, economics, and the hard sciences. . . .   17

NOVEMBER 8. I will not go into any of the university's libraries. I will not risk running into anyone I know, anyone who might think I'm one of those   18 perpetual graduate students who never finished their dissertations and drift pathetically around university libraries like the undead, frightening the undergraduates. It would be as bad to be thought one of these lifelong grad students as to be suspected of being what I am. So I use the public libraries, usually the one closest to my apartment, on my street corner. It's a community library, with three wonderful librarians, three daily newspapers, and remarkably few books. If I haven't been given the books already, if the client has been dinged and I have to do research on my own, I come here. I have my favorite chair. The librarians assume I am a "mature" and "continuing" community college student, and make kind chitchat with me.

Sometimes, when I can't find any of the sources listed in the library's computer and don't have time to go to a real library, I use books barely appropriate for the essay: books for "young adults," which means twelve-year-olds, or books I have lying around my apartment—like Jane Jacobs's *The Death and Life of Great American Cities,* H. D. F. Kitto's *The Greeks,* Eduardo Galeano's *Open Veins of Latin America,* Roy Medvedev's book on Stalin or T. H. White's on John Kennedy, books by J. K. Galbraith, Lewis Mumford, Christopher Lasch, Erich Fromm. Books somewhere between the classic and the old chestnut; terrific books, yet with no relation to the topic at hand. But they're good for the odd quote and name-drop, and they can pad a bibliography. Sometimes I can't get away with this, though, and then I have no choice but to go back to an actual place of research, like the archives.

The archives are, in fact, a difficult place for me. They are full of oak tables, clicking laptops, whirring microfiche readers, and self-assured middle-aged men working with pretty young women whose hair is pinned up in nineteenth-century styles. Perhaps some of them are lovers, but certainly all of them are graduate students with their profs. I, by contrast, am a virtual student, a simulacrum.

NOVEMBER 16. I have also been pulling at least one or two all-nighters a week for three weeks now. They're very much like the all-nighters I did as an undergraduate. I eat licorice nibs for energy and drink molehill coffee for caffeine. You make molehill coffee by pouring an entire half cup of coffee grounds, the finer the better, in a number 4 paper filter, one filter per cup. At midnight the razzy voice of Tom Waits is temporarily replaced by the BBC news hour. It would be great to be able to speak just like the BBC newscaster, Somebody hyphen-Jones. If I sounded like that I'm sure I would be able to get credit, somehow, for writing about the birth of the Carolingian Renaissance, or the displacement of the samurai in Tokugawa times, or the inadequacies of the Treaty of Versailles.

I know by experience that if I start writing at midnight I can time my output: first page by the BBC's second news summary, second page by the financial news on the half hour, third page finished by the time they read the rugby scores. Except that the first page, the one with the thesis paragraph in it, is the hardest to write, and it clocks in at well over fifteen minutes.

At two-thirty I hit a wall. The molehill coffee still hasn't kicked in yet, or else it did and I didn't notice, and now it's worn off, or else I've just built up a fatal tolerance to the stuff, like a crack addict. I begin to fall asleep in my chair, even with my headphones on. I turn up the music and blast it through the headphones. This works for the time being. I plug along. I can't really remember what I said in my thesis paragraph, but I am not going to worry about it. The client wants fifteen pages, and when I find myself on the fourteenth I'll read the thing over and brace myself, if I have to, for a bow-out. Bow-outs, like legal fine print, allow you to dart gracefully out of the large ambitious thesis statement you've started the essay with: "The topic of bird evolution is an enormous one; I have been able to touch on just one or two interesting controversies within it." "Space does not permit a detailed discussion of all the internal contradictions within Sri Lanka's postcolonial history." And so on. Nine and a half pages down. Five and a half to go. I can still barely remember what I said in my thesis statement. I can barely remember what this paper is *about*. I want to put my head down for a minute on the keyboard, but God only knows what it would end up typing.

NOVEMBER 18. Things are picking up for Christmas vacation; everything, it [24] seems, is due December 5 or December 15. The essay order form asks, "Subject & Level," "Topic," "No. of Pages," "Footnotes," "Bibliography," and then a couple of lines marked "Additional Information," by far the most common of which is "Simple English." As the year rolls on, we hacks will all, out of annoyance, laziness, or just boredom, start unsimplifying this simple English; by April it will approach the mega-watt vocabulary and tortured syntax of the Frankfurt School. But people hand these papers in and don't get caught, people who have difficulty speaking complete sentences in English; perhaps this is because classes and even tutorials are so big they never have to speak. But in December we're all still on pretty good behavior, simple instead of spiteful. I've just handed in an assignment in "Simple English," a paper titled "Mozart's Friendship with Joseph and Johann Michael Haydn and Its Impact on Mozart's Chamber Music." It reads, in part:

> Mozart was undeniably original. He was never derivative. That was part of his genius. So were the Haydn brothers. All of them were totally unique.

The little library on my corner didn't have much on Mozart or the Haydn [25] brothers. As a result, one of the items in my bibliography is a child's book with a cardboard pop-up of a doughy-looking little Mozart, in a funky pigtail and knee breeches, standing proudly beside a harpsichord. . . .

NOVEMBER 23. I am handing in something entitled "Sri Lanka: A Study in [26] Ethnic Division and Caste Co-optation," which Sylvia assigned me, over the phone, a week ago. "The girl says to tell you that *she's* Sri Lankan." Last year I wrote a senior sociology thesis on "The Italian-Canadian Family: Bedrock of Tradition or Agent of Change?" With that one I heard, "The girl says to tell you that *she's* Italian." I wanted to ask Sylvia if the client knew I wasn't, but I was afraid she'd interpret that as meaning I didn't want the work and she'd give it to someone else.

DECEMBER 2. Occasionally there is an assignment the writers fight for. This week   27
somebody—not me—gets to take home *Fanny Hill* and *Lady Chatterley's Lover*,
and get paid for it. I guess some kids really, *really* hate to read.

DECEMBER 5. A bad assignment: unnecessarily obscure, pedantic, pointless. Cer-   28
tain courses seem to consist of teaching kids the use of jargon as though it were
a substitute for writing or thinking well. Often there is an implied pressure to
agree with the assigned book. And many are simply impossible to understand; I
often take home a textbook or a sheaf of photocopies for an assignment and see,
next to a phrase such as "responsible acceptance of the control dimension," long
strings of tiny Chinese characters in ballpoint pen. No wonder the students find
the assignments incomprehensible; they are incomprehensible to me.

DECEMBER 8. I hand in a paper on Machiavelli. "How'd it go?" asked the client, a   29
boy in a leather bomber jacket reading John Grisham. I begin to go on about
how great one of the books was, a revisionist biography called *Machiavelli in
Hell*. I am hoping, with my scholarly enthusiasm, to make the client feel particularly stupid. "It's an amazing book," I tell him. "It makes a case for Machiavelli
actually being kind of a liberal humanist instead of the cynical guy everybody
always thinks he was—amazing." "That's good," the kid says. "I'm glad you're
enjoying yourself on my tab. Did you answer the essay question the way you
were supposed to?" . . .

DECEMBER 27. During Christmas vacation, friends of mine invite me to a party.   30
Some people will be there whom we know from college; they are in the process
of becoming successful, even making it big. It will be important to project confidence, the illusion of fulfilling my abandoned early promise. "What do I say,"
I ask my friends, "when somebody asks me what I do for a living?"
    "Tell them you're a writer."   31
    My friend Lisa sticks by me loyally all evening. When people ask me, "What   32
is it you do?" Lisa answers for me quickly: "She's a writer."
    "Oh, what is it you write?"   33
    "*Essays*," I say, spitefully, drunkenly. Lisa thinks fast.   34
    "Articles," she says. "She writes articles, on Sri Lanka, and Machiavelli, and   35
the English Civil War."
    "Isn't *that* interesting," they say, leaving us for the guacamole.   36

JANUARY 10, 1995. School has been back in session for a week now. The only work   37
that is in are essays from the education students. I hate these assignments. I have
trouble manipulating the self-encapsulated second language in which teaching
students seem compelled to write. But it's after Christmas, and I'm broke.
Education assignments all involve writing up our customers' encounters in
their "practicum." Teaching students work several times a week as assistant
teachers in grade school classrooms; instead of getting paid for this work, they
pay tuition for it. Unfortunately, these expensive practice sessions don't seem to
go well. My first such assignment was to write "reflections" on a "lesson plan"

for a seventh-grade English class. The teaching student had given me some notes, and I had to translate these into the pedagogical jargon used in her textbooks. The idea seems to be that you have to say, as obscurely as possible, what you did with your seventh-grade kids and what you think about what you did:

> Preliminary Lesson Formulations: My objectives were to integrate lesson content with methodology to expand students' receptiveness and responsiveness to the material and to one another by teaching them how to disagree with one another in a constructive way. The class will draw up a T-chart covering "Disagreeing in an Agreeable Way," roughly in the manner of Bennett et al. Check for understanding. When the students discuss this, they are encouraged to listen to one another's language carefully and "correct" it if the wording is unhelpful, negative, or destructive. I shared my objectives with the class by asking them to read a fable and then divide into pairs and decide together what the moral was. Clearly, this is the "Think-Pair-Share" technique, as detailed in Bennett et al. The three strategies in use, then, are: 1) pair and sharing; 2) group discussion of the fable with mind-mapping; 3) group discussion of ways of disagreement. The teacher, modeling, divides the board in two with a line.

"Pair and share" seemed to mean "find a partner." I had no idea what "mind-mapping" or a "T-chart" was supposed to be. And come to think of it, after reading the fable, I had no idea what the moral was.   38

JANUARY 18. Somebody is applying to the graduate program in family therapy at   39
some university somewhere and wants us to write the application. "She's my friend," said the young woman sitting across from Matthew at the desk. "She wants to start her own private practice as a therapist, right? So she can buy a house, right? And if you're a psychiatrist you have to go all the way through med school, right? So she's given me some notes for you about her here—she only needs one credit for her B.A. in psychology, and she volunteered at a shelter one summer. She wants you to tell them all that. Maybe make up some other things."

"See," Matthew tells me after she leaves. "If you ever go to one of those ther-   40
apists, that's something you should think about."

JANUARY 20. When I first started this work, friends of mine would try to comfort   41
me by telling me it would teach me to write better. Actually, academic prostitution, just like any other kind, seems to bring with it diseases, afflictions, vices, and bad habits. There is, for instance, the art of pretending you've read a book you haven't. It's just like every speed-reading course ever offered by the Learning Annex: read the introduction, where the writer outlines what he's going to say, and the conclusion, where he repeats what he's said.

> In his book *The Technological Society,* Jacques Ellul begins by defining the technical simply as the search for efficiency. He claims, however, that technique itself is subdivided into three categories: the social, the organizational, and the economic.

This is all on the book's *first four pages*. Sometimes—often—I find myself   42
eating up as much space as possible. There are several ways to do this. One is to
reproduce lengthy, paragraph-long quotes in full; another is to ramble on about
your own apparently passionate opinion on something. Or you start talking
about the United States and what a handbasket it's going to hell in. This is
equally useful, for different reasons, on either side of the border. You can ask
rhetorical questions to obsessive excess. ("Can Ellul present the technical in
such a reductionist way? Can he really define technique in such a way? And is it
really valid to distinguish between the social and the organizational?" etc.) And
there's always the art of name-dropping as a way to fill pages and convince the
teaching assistant that your client has read *something*, even if it wasn't what was
on the syllabus.

> Certainly, as writers from Eduardo Galeano to Andre Gunder Frank to
> Noam Chomsky to Philip Agee to Allan Frankovich to Ernesto Laclau doc-
> ument, the CIA has long propped up the United Fruit Company.

At least you can make the client feel stupid. It's the third week of January, my
apartment is cold, and I am bitter.

FEBRUARY 8. I'm learning, as the environmentalists tell us, to reuse and recycle.   43
It's easier when I adapt a paper, with minor changes, on the same topic for different classes, or when I use the same paper for the same class again the following year. I've never worried much about a recycled essay being recognized: the
pay for teaching assistants is low enough, and the burnout rate high enough,
that the odds are substantially against the same person reading and grading
papers for the same course two years in a row. Some topics just seem to beg for
recycling: freshmen are forever being asked to mull over the roles of determinism,
hubris, and moral responsibility in the Oedipus cycle; sociology and philosophy
majors, the ethics of abortion. There are essays on shantytowns in developing
countries, export-oriented economies in developing countries, structural adjustment in developing countries, and one only has to make the obvious case
that the three are interrelated to be able to extend the possibilities for parts of
essays in any of those three categories to resurface magically within another.
Other essays can be recycled with just a little tinkering to surmount minor differences in topic or in emphasis: for instance, "Italian Fascists in North
America," to which "The Italian-Canadian Family" lends itself nicely; "Taboo-
Breaking in Racine and Ford," which re-emerges, after minor cosmetic surgery,
as "Master-Slave Relationships in Ford and Racine: What They Tell Us About
Lust, Fate, and Obligation." And so on.

FEBRUARY 15. I'm sitting on the floor with a pile of old magazines, cutting out   44
pictures of Oreo cookies and Wendy's burgers. This is Andy's essay. It's not an
essay, actually, it's a food bingo chart. I have to find a large sheet of cardboard,
divide it into squares, and glue on pictures of what is recognizably food. Andy
is another education student: he wants to teach junior kindergarten, and his
assignment is, apparently, to teach the little tots where food comes from, or

what it is, or that advertising is a vital component of each of the four basic food groups, or something. I come into Tailormade with food bingo under my arm. I've gotten some strange looks on the subway. It nets me twenty-five bucks.

MARCH 7. I was supposed to turn in an essay today, one I don't have. I fell asleep   45
at the keyboard last night and accidentally slept through the whole night, headphones and all.

MARCH 16. There's a regular customer whose course load would be appropriate   46
for the résumé of a U.N. secretary general. She's taking several courses on developing economies, including one referred to by other clients in the same class as "Third World Women." And one on the history of black Americans from Reconstruction to the present. I wrote her a twenty-five-page history of the early years of the civil-rights movement. She was sitting in the office when I handed it in. "Interesting course, isn't it?" she asked. She requested me again. I wrote her a paper on Costa Rica, one on dowry murders in India, one on the black leader W.E.B. Du Bois. "It's a great course, isn't it?" she asked me when she got the paper on dowry murders. "He seems like a fascinating guy," she said the day she collected W.E.B. Du Bois. "Somebody told me he wound up in *Ghana*." Today I take a shortcut across the university campus on my way to the essay service and see her with a group of other students. I make a direct beeline for her and I smile. I watch her blanch, look around, try to decide whether to pretend not to know me, decide that maybe that isn't a good idea. She gives me a stricken look and a big toothy grin. . . .

APRIL 16. Today, working on a paper, I was reminded that there *are* good pro-   47
fessors. They're the ones who either convince the kids the course content is inherently interesting and get them to work hard on the assignments or who figure out ways to make the assignments, at least, creative events to enjoy. But students with shaky language skills falter at surprises, even good ones; lazy students farm the assignments out no matter what they are. Such assignments are oddly comforting for me: I can almost pretend the two of us are talking over the clients' heads. When I'm alone in my room, in front of the computer and between the headphones, it's hard not to want to write something good for myself and maybe even for the imaginary absentee professor or appreciative T.A., something that will last. But when I'm standing in the crowded Tailormade office, next to someone elegant and young and in eight hundred bucks' worth of calfskin leather, someone who not only has never heard of John Stuart Mill and never read Othello but doesn't even know he hasn't, doesn't even mind that he hasn't, and doesn't even care that he hasn't, the urge to make something that will last somehow vanishes.

APRIL 28. The semester is almost at an end. Exams have started; the essays have   48
all been handed in. Elliott and Russell begin their summer jobs as bike couriers. Henry, like me, is illegal; but he confides to me that he's had enough. "You can only do so much of this," he says. I know, I tell him. I know. ☐

◢ REREADING FOR UNDERSTANDING

1. In the opening line, Witherspoon calls herself an "academic call girl," a metaphor she sustains throughout the essay. How apt is this metaphor? What parallels can you see between her work and life and those of a prostitute?

2. The author expresses contempt for her clients throughout the essay. What seems to be the source of this contempt? Do you think it is justified?

3. Witherspoon describes the physical appearance and lives of her coworkers in some detail. Why do you think she does this? What effect does it have on our impression of the business? on our impression of the author?

◢ RESPONDING

1. Witherspoon mentions many of the tricks she uses to write papers with minimal effort. She says, for example, that she adapts content from one paper for another assignment. Have you ever employed any of these strategies yourself when fulfilling writing assignments? Can you think of other shortcut strategies? Would you call these kinds of tricks "cheating"? Why or why not?

2. In elementary school you were probably taught that when you cheat in school, you cheat yourself. Perhaps you were also told that all cheaters are eventually caught. Does your experience validate these claims? Does Witherspoon's essay? Do those who cheat learn less or do less well in school than those who don't? Are cheaters found out most of the time?

3. Have you ever helped someone to cheat? Why did you do it? How did the experience make you feel afterward? Would you do it again?

◢ RESPONDING IN WRITING

Every student has been tempted to cheat or to comply with a cheater. Think of one such incident that was important in shaping your attitude toward cheating, and write an essay describing it. Tell the circumstances surrounding the temptation, how you responded, and the results. Explain the effect of the incident on your willingness or reluctance to cheat again.

CONTROVERSIES

When the Truth Has Consequences: When Should You Keep a Secret?

JOSÉ ZUNIGA

A former Army sergeant, José Zuniga seemed destined for a brilliant military career, but he could not accept the life of secrecy to which such a career would have condemned him. Zuniga, who is gay, left the army and, along with other soldiers like Colonel Margarethe Cammermeyer, publicly challenged the military's ban on homosexuals. Their fight has been somewhat successful. The Department of Defense's "don't ask, don't tell" policy, which went into effect in February 1994, states that "homosexual orientation is not a bar to service entry or continued service. Homosexual conduct, however, is grounds for separation." In other words, although the policy reverses the previous all-out ban on homosexuals in the military and prevents recruiters and investigators from seeking evidence of homosexuality, it nonetheless requires gays and lesbians in uniform to keep much of their lives a secret.

My Life in the Military Closet

L ieut. Gen Glynn C. Mallory, Jr., commander of the Sixth Army and one of the Pentagon's star tacticians during the Persian Gulf war, stood not more than three feet from me addressing a crowd at the noncommissioned officers' club on the Presidio military base of San Francisco. From time to time he paused from his speech to scan the several pale blue index cards onto which my military career had been abbreviated. Unbeknown to him, Mallory had long been my mentor. When I was assigned to the First Cavalry Division at Fort Hood, Tex., Mallory had commanded the nearby rival Second Armored

Division. I had heard and admired his many speeches on the qualities of a good soldier: loyalty, resolve, physical and ethical fitness. Now, on a breezy day in March 1993, Mallory would reward me as an exemplar of just those values.

As I stood at rigid attention, the three-star general eloquently extolled the accomplishments of a 23-year-old Army sergeant.

"You can be justifiably proud of this distinction, and I know you will continue to serve with the same dedication that prompted your selection as the Soldier of the Year," Mallory said, facing the audience. As he pinned a fifth Army Commendation Medal on my freshly pressed uniform, he whispered, "I'm damned proud to serve with you, son."

Barely a week earlier, Mallory sat with me and several colleagues in a conference room watching a CNN report on homosexuals in the military. "Fags," he snorted, did not belong in "this man's Army."

The words rang in my ears as Mallory pinned the award on me. I had kept my mouth shut then, and I did so now; ambition trumped my anger. I continued to smolder, knowing what I alone between us knew: I was one of the "fags" who did not belong

I entered boot camp in September 1989. As I and 20 or so nervous recruits jumped off the bus at the training center in Fort Bliss, Tex., a tyrannical drill sergeant herded us to the quadrangle. We ran to keep up with his angry directions; we flinched as he barked insults and introduced us to "his Army." His vocal cords strained as he assaulted our virility.

"I'm going to make men out of you little faggots," he screamed, ordering us to drop and do more push-ups than seemed physically possible. "You little pansies aren't fit to spit-shine my boots! When I'm done with you mama's boys you'll be real soldiers!"

Although the sergeant intended his message for the group as a whole, his barbs were clearly aimed at one recruit in particular. The unfortunate target of this attack, a farm boy now squirming in formation, wore his naïveté like a neon sign. His innocence became the weakness on which the drill sergeant fed. "Come on, grandma!" the drill sergeant would repeatedly snarl at the recruit, even though the young man would often outperform many of us.

In every formation and at every occasion the recruit was singled out as the weak link due to some undefinable characteristic the drill sergeant directly attributed to homosexuality. Whether the young man was in fact gay I do not know, nor did facts seem to matter. The drill sergeant seized on his plight as an opportunity to build esprit de corps, and the rest of the group dutifully focused our hatred and venom on him. We would bond by purging one of our own.

The strategy achieved the desired effect. Three weeks into basic training the recruit was discharged for "failure to adapt." His dream of one day becoming an Army doctor, a goal he had promised his parents he would accomplish, was dashed because he had been randomly selected to symbolize everything the sergeant sought to extinguish in the rest of us. As for us, we simply redoubled our efforts not to fall behind.

The incident marked my first encounter with an inherent contradiction in   11
military psychology. The Army requires fellow soldiers to form close bonds
founded on caring and concern, yet it forbids them from caring for one another
too much. Thus, slapping each other on the butt with a wet towel is an acceptable gesture only if a "fag" joke follows to defuse it. From buttocks-grabbing to
sexually laden double entendres, the aura of homoeroticism is ever-present. Yet
even as the Army promotes certain of what can only be called gay values, it
teaches its recruits to hate what it is teaching. The message is confusing, to say
the least.

On graduation day we lined up in alphabetical order (a feat we had come   12
to master) behind the ramshackle auditorium that served as the post's movie
house and recreation center. We had learned to rely on one another, to share
close quarters with men we never imagined we would even speak to, to think of
each other as brothers—for in battle, the drill sergeant had reiterated, it was on
our shoulders that responsibility for our buddies' lives would rest. As I walked
across the highly buffed hardwood stage floor and shook the drill sergeant's
hand, I could not help thinking of the lamb whose career we had sacrificed to
learn that lesson. I was well on my way to becoming "all I could be."

I didn't know I was gay when I entered the Army. At the time, I had a girlfriend,   13
whom I met when I was 19. Cheryl was gregarious and social, I was taciturn and
shy; after a few dates we became fast friends. My main interests, however, were
professional, and my aspirations were largely military. Two of my great-grand-
fathers were war heroes, one a Spanish officer under Maximilian (Napoleon's
chosen emperor of Mexico in 1864), and the other a Zapatista in the Mexican
revolution of 1910. My four grandfathers also had served in the Spanish and
Mexican Armies, and my father had been a military officer as well. I knew that
I, too, would become a soldier.

The military life also appealed to an ingrained desire for regimen. Born   14
into a traditional Roman Catholic family, I attended church every Sunday and
during days of holy obligation, and I served as an altar boy whenever one of the
regulars called in sick. I studied the Catholic doctrine in Bible school and eventually attended parochial schools in East Chicago. Yet amid the strictures of
home life I found time for the traditional pursuits of an average American boy:
playing baseball, missing curfew, dating girls.

After boot camp I was assigned to Fort Hood, where I worked first as an   15
ambulance driver, then as editor of the First Cavalry Division newspaper. It was
there that I met Andrea V. She was a top-notch supply technician with a trait
rare among Army supply clerks: an intense desire to help fellow soldiers
through any bind. She was also gay, the first homosexual I had met in the military. Everyone in the company had heard about her lesbianism. Because of her
generosity, we chose to overlook it.

That state of affairs ended, however, with the arrival of a gung-ho staff   16
sergeant. He was a welcome addition to our unit: he brought field experience,

enthusiasm and intelligence. He also brought a voracious sexual appetite and a legacy of sexual-harassment complaints to prove it.

What seemed at first to be a platonic friendship between Andrea and the   17
sergeant soon erupted into one of the most talked-about scandals on the post: she had agreed to have sex with him, it was viciously rumored, in order to prove her femininity. When she refused to continue the sexual relationship, the irate sergeant taunted her for being a lesbian. To safeguard our own reputations, the rest of us joined in, mocking the sergeant's involvement with a known "dyke."

We stood by as the sergeant selectively enforced Army policy to preserve his   18
sense of manhood. Thus it came as no surprise when, three weeks later, Andrea was expelled from the military with "homosexual" stamped on her record. In watching her life fall into havoc, however, I became aware of an inner conflict of my own—a conflict that, given the message of Andrea's discharge, I preferred not to acknowledge.

During my assignment to Fort Hood, I struck a bond with a certain soldier.   19
Ours was the classic military friendship: car-pooling to and from work, sharing a six-pack on a Friday night. Together we helped one another adjust to the rigors of military life. We served together for six months in Texas before deploying with the First Cavalry Division to the Persian Gulf in September 1990.

We worked together, well behind the front lines: I as a military journalist,   20
editing one of three tabloid newspapers published by the Army during the Persian Gulf conflict, he as a radio technician. The climate was inhospitable, and the stress of the situation was tremendous. My friend and I spent most of our time together, and our friendship intensified. We shared our fears, we shared our mail during times when one of us received none, we shared every facet of our lives. He talked about his girlfriend in Texas; I talked about mine.

Cheryl, meanwhile, wrote constantly to boost my spirits and remind me   21
of the happy life that awaited me upon my return to the States. I longed for the security she promised. One night, from a telephone deep in the Saudi desert, I proposed.

With the impending start of the ground war I volunteered for reassignment   22
as a combat medic on the front line; my friend stayed behind. Living conditions on the front were brutal—filthy clothes, cold food, news blackouts and "whore's baths," in which we rinsed ourselves off with frigid water. I craved companionship. Through some feat of technological wizardry, my friend contacted me by radio to share, long-distance, in my misery. I began to feel a closeness to this man that I could never imagine feeling for anyone else, a closeness so seemingly unnatural that it frightened me.

I don't know if my friend ever realized the depth of my affection for him. Back   23
in Texas, I tested him in code, trying discreetly to draw him out, aware all the

while that he could turn me in if I went too far. A native Californian, he confessed to having seen and heard it all, and would casually mention gay friends. Was he trying to tell me something? Yet other times he would adopt a mocking lisp and effeminate body language. Even if he did feel the same as I did, I rationalized, he would never admit it, for fear of reprisal. I never did learn if he was gay; looking back, I am almost certain he was not. A month after my marriage, he was reassigned.

I refused to believe I might really be gay, both because it so clashed with my   24
stereotypes of gay people and, I suppose, because the consequences to what was shaping up as a very promising Army career would have been devastating. Instead I returned to editing the First Cavalry newspaper and immersed myself in work. And I dedicated myself to making my new marriage succeed; I sought refuge in the glossy photo of my wife that sat on my desk. But with the marriage as a cover, I was suddenly free to introspect, and certain doubts quietly gathered force.

One night, obviously depressed, I went out drinking with a good friend, a   25
female officer. Paradoxically, in the Army, drinking with a woman is not considered unusual, since military life effectively reduces everyone, men and women alike, to the same hypertrophied sex. My friend asked me what was wrong. I had heard she was a lesbian and, taking the risk, confided that I thought I might be gay. She insisted that I drive with her that night to a gay bar in Austin.

The bar was loud and crowded; strobe lights flashed as we tossed back   26
drink after drink, not caring that first call was at 5 A.M. for a three-mile run around the post. Standing in a corner of the bar I looked around me at a crowd of patrons, including a few muscular young men in telltale military haircuts, who all dressed like me, talked like me and did not throw themselves at me in the manner of the predators described in my Army buddies' gay jokes.

This enlightening experience came to a crashing halt, though, when some-   27
one came running into the bar, screaming for all the military types to run to the back room. Within seconds several of us were whisked into a liquor stockroom, the slam of a heavy dead bolt and our breathing the only sounds echoing through the room. Probably military police coming to check if any Army queers were here, my lesbian friend intimated. After a few minutes we were let out; the coast was clear.

"There is no safe house in which the C.I.D. [Criminal Investigation   28
Division] or military police can't reach us," she said squarely. They're out there taking down license-plate numbers right now."

In that moment the term "coming out of the closet" became clear in all its   29
literal meaning, and with it came an urge to exit. I drove home, desperate to share my pain with my wife, but I found her sleeping and could not bear to wake her.

Gradually, secretly, I pursued a new set of friends. Finding them posed little   30
problem: once I made one gay friend, I soon met the majority of gays and lesbians at the installation. For homosexuals in the military, such networks are

critical, as they provide mutual support and defense against the various indignities and humiliations of daily life.

One afternoon several of us listened in amazement as a friend, Marc S., [31] described a nightmare interrogation he had recently endured. Two days earlier his lover, a Medical Service Corps officer, had been hauled in for questioning by the C.I.D. In exchange for an honorable discharge, the lover had agreed to provide military authorities with details of his relationship with Marc. Shortly thereafter Marc had been pulled side for questioning and presented with a similar bargain: he, too, could depart with an honorable discharge if he gave the C.I.D. a list of all his gay and lesbian friends.

"This is not a threat," he tearfully recalled the softer of the two agents say- [32] ing after reading Marc his Miranda rights. "But if you don't cooperate we'll have to expand the investigation."

Marc resisted the Army's scare tactics, but already word had spread and [33] made him a pariah among his friends. He had anticipated that reaction from his straight friends, but he didn't realize his gay friends also would run for cover. He became afraid to venture out, knowing he was being watched. He feared for us, urging us not to associate with him and risk our careers. So we, his best friends, stayed away.

Marc's refusal to cooperate only spurred the C.I.D.'s efforts to snare other [34] offenders in its net. His discharge was delayed two months while an extensive investigation was conducted, but in the end Marc, like thousands of homosexuals before him, was discharged and branded with a mark on his papers that will stigmatize him forever. We witnessed from afar the slow death of his career, afraid even to send a note of sympathy.

Six months after my return from the Persian Gulf, Cheryl and I moved from [35] Killeen, Tex., a military town with nothing to offer but pawn shops, liquor stores and strip joints, to San Francisco. Outwardly, our social life in Killeen adhered to the conventions of married coupledom: we attended neighborhood picnics and traveled to nearby Belton Lake for organized marital retreats. Because we lived off-post, few people knew how little time Cheryl and I actually spent together. That changed with my reassignment to the Presidio. The expense of living in San Francisco forced us to move into military housing. As much as the arrangement helped our finances, it increased the tension developing between us.

I was treated well at the Presidio; my combat record as a journalist and the [36] Combat Medical Badge I proudly wore on my uniform set me apart from other soldiers assigned there, many of whom were either first-time recruits or seasoned officers awaiting retirement. As I had in the past, I buried myself in work, convinced that by doing so I could avoid my moral dilemma and carry on with my married life. But the strategy didn't work. I realized, reluctantly, that I could no longer hide from someone I loved as much as I loved Cheryl. One night after dinner I confessed that I thought I might be gay. She responded with a melancholy smile. "I know."

In early 1992 Cheryl and I separated. She returned to Ohio and I again im-   37
mersed myself in work. But I maintained the facade of a happily married
heterosexual: the wedding photo remained on my desk, and I lied about
Cheryl's whereabouts, making excuses when she could not attend social functions. I constructed a life of duplicity to dispel any rumor that might arise.

In the weeks before being named Sixth Army Soldier of the Year, I watched with   38
admiration as Petty Officer Keith Meinhold, Lieut. (j.g.) Tracy Thorne, Col.
Margarethe Cammermeyer and several other brave military men and women
came out and challenged the ban against homosexuals in the military. Though
in some ways my homosexuality was still abstract, my fear of being discovered,
and my shame from that fear, was not. I struggled with the thought of also coming out, but I was painfully aware of the consequences.

Two weeks after the award, I watched a production of David Drake's one-   39
man play, "The Night Larry Kramer Kissed Me," with a group of civilian gay
friends I had met in San Francisco. A monologue in the play presented a portrait of a society in which diversity is a cherished value, and my silence began
to eat at me. In the audience that night was Elizabeth Birch, the head of litigation for Apple Computer and a chairwoman of the National Gay and Lesbian
Task Force board. After the play a mutual friend introduced us. I told her I
thought I might be ready to come out and asked for her help.

After several meetings with the task force, a plan was devised. They would   40
present me as the surprise speaker at an event being organized for the weekend of the Gay and Lesbian March on Washington. My coming out clearly
would be a public relations coup for homosexuals fighting the military prohibitions, but the task force wanted to be sure I was prepared to sacrifice my
career. I assured them that I was. Once we had a plan we quickly realized how
easily it could be foiled. I had already arranged for military leave for that weekend: if anyone in my command caught wind of my impending disclosure, I
could be given a "lawful order" to remain on base, and thereby sequestered from
the press. Fearing that the task-force phone lines might be tapped, my attorney,
James Kennedy, a former Army prosecutor, advised code names; I became
Luke, he became Obi-Wan Kenobi—and General Mallory became Darth Vader.
Our code was successful, as was the public relations assault: the task force
arranged for more than 20 embargoed interviews to take place before my official coming out.

I signed out on leave the morning of April 23 and flew to Washington that   41
afternoon. As I left the plane at Dulles Airport I realized that that would be my
last night as a public servant with a private life; thereafter I would become a public figure famous for my expulsion into the civilian world. I can't remember
much of what happened during my speech, only what seemed like hours of applause, followed by an inner feeling of sheer terror. The next morning I marched
with the veterans' contingent in the 1993 March on Washington. I was now a part
of the gay, lesbian and bisexual military family, fighting for the right to serve

openly and with dignity, joining arms with Meinhold, Thorne, Cammermeyer and the others.

Immediately upon my return to San Francisco I was isolated from my peers and assigned to live in an empty building with a private bathroom and shower; the privacy of the other soldiers with whom I had shared a community shower, it seemed, was now compromised. I was not allowed to return to my job as a journalist, and I was reassigned to answer telephones in a supply stockroom. I was advised to check in twice a day with my unit so that the command could keep a tight rein on my activities. And I was forced to endure an hourlong sermon from a chaplain, once friendly, who now asked me to define morality and compared homosexuality to bestiality and child pornography. I was relieved to learn I would receive an honorable discharge. 42

My trials, however, did not end there. In the days that followed, I was accused of wearing an unauthorized medal during the Washington ceremony (an award that had been posted in my record, although the Army insists the medal had only been recommended and approved) and stripped of my noncommissioned-officer status. But the Army's retaliatory action ultimately backfired; the local press learned of it and elevated me to martyr status. I followed the news in bewilderment, as almost overnight I was transformed into a celebrity activist. Soon I was out on the streets, ready to assume my new role as a symbol and outspoken critic in the fight for gay civil rights. 43

I have since thought a great deal about what homosexuals are fighting for. We have never asked the military to lead the way in social change; we simply ask that the military catch up with modern society. The issue at stake is not whether gay service members exist or even perform well—I think my case, among others, proves that we not only exist but also excel. Rather, the question is whether heterosexual service members can tolerate the presence of their gay colleagues without resorting to violence or falling to pieces. To ban homosexuals from the military out of fear that acknowledging them would damage morale is a disingenuous attempt to blame the messenger for the message. 44

And the truth is that if the ban were lifted today, homosexuals in the military, already conservative by nature, would continue their lives of discretion, pursuing excellence but without fear of investigation and sanctioned hatred. Intolerance will not disappear overnight, and few gay soldiers would be willing to risk the abuse, both overt and subtle, that disclosure would bring. Nevertheless, for the Government to place a stamp of approval on discrimination of any sort is to make a mockery of the very values it asks its citizens to uphold and its military to defend. 45

I am on a national speaking tour now, and while my new role is sometimes thrilling, it has not come without personal cost. Shortly after my announcement, 46

I spoke with my father, who told me that he loved me. Several weeks later I came across an article in a Texas paper where I had worked many years before. The article was a profile of my life, and it said that my father had disowned me. Stunned, I called the editor of the article, my former boss, and asked how the reporter could have stated as fact something that plainly was not true. The editor told me the paper had contacted my father. "He told our reporter that he had no son named José."

Has all this attention been worth losing my career, and more important, my   47
family? I wonder, sometimes. But I remember a story a 72-year-old veteran, a combat medic in the Second World War and later an Army general, told me not long ago. For more than a week in November 1944, he and his platoon had borne the brunt of a German offensive. At last, relief arrived in the form of a company-size unit of infantrymen, but with it came word that his lover, a rifleman in another battalion, had been mortally wounded in a firefight a week earlier.

"You know what allowed me to pick up my weapon and go on?" the veteran   48
asked me. "The realization that the man who wields the hammer is the one who drives the nails. I vowed someday to make a difference in Roy's memory." Now a gay rights activist in Florida, the veteran urged me to continue the battle, not only for future generations of gay, lesbian and bisexual service members but also in the memory of the thousands who sacrificed their lives for what they believed was right and just.

I have strived to fulfill that duty. One night recently, I went to a gay dance   49
club in a town where I was speaking. I needed to forget the loneliness of the road and my disappointment at not seeing more people my age actively fighting for gay rights. At the club I caught sight of two young lovers holding each other in a corner of the dance floor. Their crew cuts gave them away as military. As the night wore on, the two approached me and introduced themselves.

"We're both in basic training here, José," said the 18-year-old with a shy   50
smile. "We saw you on CNN when you came out." His lover added, his eyes shifting from mine to his partner's: "Thanks for doing what you did. It took a lot of guts." As they walked back onto the dance floor to rejoin their friends.

I wondered what would happen to these airmen. What could I do to insure   51
that the opportunity to excel was not stolen from them? When will the day come when qualified and dedicated service members are allowed to serve without having to deny their identity and their love? Soon, my heart told me. But not without a fight. ☐

◢ REREADING FOR UNDERSTANDING

1. Zuniga tells about another recruit who failed to finish boot camp. According to Zuniga, why did this young man fail? Zuniga says this incident revealed to him an "inherent contradiction in military psychology" (par. 11). Explain that contradiction.

2. According to Zuniga, why did it take him a long time to realize and acknowledge that he was gay?

RESPONDING

1. Zuniga's essay does not begin with his entry into the army. Instead he starts by telling about an incident that occurred just a month before his discharge. Why do you think he chose to tell about receiving the Army Commendation Medal first? How effectively does this episode introduce the rest of the essay?

2. Zuniga says he does not expect the military to "lead the way in social change; we simply ask that the military catch up with modern society." Do you agree that the military lags behind the rest of the culture in its attitude toward homosexuality?

3. Adrienne Rich says in "Women and Honor" (p. 264), "Men have been expected to tell the truth about facts, not about feelings. They have not been expected to talk about feelings at all" (par. 5). Discuss this observation as it applies to Zuniga's story. Do you agree that men have traditionally been taught to deny and conceal their feelings? Can you think of other traditionally male institutions like the military that discourage self-knowledge and openness, even as they encourage honor and integrity?

RESPONDING IN WRITING

Do you think the "don't ask, don't tell" policy is a practical first step toward ending discrimination against gays and lesbians or do you think it forces gays and lesbians in the military to lead dishonest lives? Do some research about the policy, examining the arguments for and against it and its effects since 1993. Write an argumentative essay defending the policy as is or explaining why and how it should be changed.

LETTY COTTIN POGREBIN

A founding editor of *Ms.* magazine, Letty Pogrebin has written extensively on family matters and women's concerns. In this essay, which originally appeared in *The New York Times Magazine*, Pogrebin reflects on her discovery of a family secret that led to the writing of her most recent book, *Deborah, Golda and Me*.

To Tell the Truth

When I was a child, I loved my family's secrets. Each of my parents had six siblings, and the tales they told about one another seemed to rescue the whole clan from the curse of the ordinary. It took me years to notice the suffering behind their revelations or to consider why certain facts get transformed into secrets and how they imprint a person's future.

At first, I was simply delighted to know, for instance, that my grandmother 2 had been a runaway bride. Repulsed by the husband her parents had chosen for her in Hungary at the turn of the century, she jumped out of the window of the bridal chamber on her wedding night and ran off with the man who was to become my grandfather. Why classify this marvelous melodrama as a family secret, I wondered, when the image of that sober old couple as inflamed lovers should have been a treasured legacy.

But most secrets arise out of shame, and shame is defined by the values of 3 the era in which an event takes place. In 1899, a woman who fled from an arranged marriage brought disgrace upon her family; Grandma's rebellion was the scandal of every *shtetl* within miles. In America 50 years later, when I could have used a proud model of female passion, my Grandma's story was still being presented as a shame and a secret because that is how she experienced it—and because the story was meant to warn girls of my generation that, regardless of romantic motivation, a woman who breaks the rules pays for it with her reputation.

My mother and aunts doled out the underground family lore sparingly, as 4 if times were hard and they were rationing butter. Secrets were female currency. While men controlled commerce and the history of nations, women used family history as their negotiable instruments. Knowledge is power, but clandestine knowledge is power squared; secrets could be withheld, exchanged and leveraged as tools of intimacy and woman-to-woman advice. Secrets clarified the limits of feminine propriety by defining what can be felt and known —but not revealed.

I took it as a sign of my maturity when—instead of shooing me out of the 5 room or shifting into Yiddish—my mother let me stay and listen. That's how I learned that the aunt and uncle who wore glamorous clothes and won tango contests were actually miserable in their marriage; that another aunt was a card-carrying Communist throughout the McCarthy period; that still another aunt, a childless woman who'd been the subject of collective pity, was actually quite fertile. She used contraception and had once had an abortion but had chosen to call herself barren rather than admit she didn't *want* any children.

At a time when the female paragon was either virginal, domestic or mater- 6 nal, women blamed themselves for falling short of the ideal and kept quiet if they felt "too sexual," or dissatisfied with marriage or motherhood.

Families, on the other hand, typically chose to hide other perceived inade- 7 quacies, like their poverty, unacknowledged adoptions, suicides, alcoholism, mental illness, domestic violence, whatever disturbed the image of homey perfection. Unlike women's privatized cover-ups, family secrets often required group complicity. If you've ever been party to such a collaborative effort, you know there are two kinds of secrets: those you keep from the world and those that are kept from you.

In my family, the biggest secret—the secret that destroyed my belief in 8 truth, reality and all adults—was the one kept from me until I was almost 12. To my horror, in 1951, I inadvertently discovered that my parents had not really been married for 28 years as they claimed; their wedding date had been a flat-out fiction. Both had been previously divorced and had met each other only 14 years before. What's more, the 26-year-old woman I knew as my "big sister" was actually my half sister, my mother's daughter from her first marriage. And somewhere on the planet I had another half-sister, my father's daughter from *his* first marriage, whom he had stopped seeing shortly after I was born. That was when he and my mother decided to reinvent their past: to blot out the divorces that had seemed so shameful and to backdate their wedding to 1923 so that my father could reasonably present himself as the father of my mother's daughter.

There is nothing quite as unsettling as catching your parents in a lie, nothing as disorienting as finding that your family history is an elaborate mythography complete with conspiratorial relatives and a phony 25th anniversary celebration. The discovery of my parents' charade left its mark. I became an inveterate doubter, always peeling the onion trying to get at the truth beneath the "facts." I suppose this decoding instinct has served me well as a writer, but I will never know how much it has damaged my capacity to trust. 9

The most positive thing I can say about my family's secrets is that they set the stage for my later involvement in the women's movement. Feminism's challenge to sexual hypocrisy and sex-role coercion seemed to directly address my experience growing up with a mother, grandmother and aunts who had to cloak themselves in deception before they could face the world. 10

Nowadays, we've upped the ante on secret subjects. To be sure, the wagons of denial are still pulled in close around the incest perpetrator. And despite the gay rights movement, many parents still keep the fact of their lesbian and gay offspring closeted and often relegate people with AIDS to the symbolic family attic. In this era when bisexual bigamists appear on the talk shows, my parents' divorces would not be worthy of a cover-up. Nevertheless, since going public with my secrets in my latest book, I have been the repository of other people's stories—and there is no end to them. 11

Letter writers describe how they found out they were adopted, a parent was a Holocaust survivor, a father hadn't been killed in Korea but was living in a mental institution, a white woman learned her great-grandmother was black. Wherever I speak around the country, an audience member invariably approaches me afterward to share a secret, as did the man who told me that for his 40th birthday his mother confessed the reason why she had always been so cold and undemonstrative to him. She'd been afraid to express affection because *her* father had been sexually abusive to her and she thought such behavior might be hereditary. 12

By now, I wouldn't be surprised if every one of us is either keeping a secret or has had one kept from us. Paradoxically, what we most have in common may be the stuff we hide from each other. And confronting our secrets may be less important than understanding the shame that feeds them and how our reactions to them shape the rest of our lives. ☐ 13

◢ REREADING FOR UNDERSTANDING

1. Pogrebin says (par. 4) that in her family, "secrets were female currency." What does this metaphor suggest about the value of secrets? What does it suggest about the power of women within the family?

2. According to Pogrebin, there are two kinds of secrets. What are they?

3. In what way did Pogrebin's experience with secrets in her family prepare her to take part in the women's movement as an adult?

◢ RESPONDING

1. The family secrets that Pogrebin discovered in her family—her parents' divorces, her aunt's decision not to have children—are not the kinds of facts that most of us would hide today. Does that mean that we are more open than Pogrebin's parents' generation or simply that we are ashamed of or embarrassed by different things? What kinds of facts are kept secret today?

2. In "To Do the Right Thing" (p. 256), Harriet Goldhor Lerner observes that keeping secrets takes considerable time and energy and commits the secret-holder to further duplicity. She says, "When we must 'watch ourselves,' even when we do so automatically and seemingly effortlessly, the process dissipates our energy and erodes our integrity." How does Pogrebin's article illustrate Lerner's claim? Can you think of secrets that you have kept—or that have been kept from you—that required considerable effort and layers of dishonesty?

3. Pogrebin's essay seems to suggest that family secrets are ultimately destructive to the family as a whole and to individual members. Are there ever times when keeping secrets is necessary? Should small children be told that their parents are having marital difficulties, for example? Should an elderly grandparent be told that a grandson or granddaughter is gay? Should someone be told they have a terminal illness? Should a suicide be hushed up as a death by natural causes? What information, if any, should be kept secret from other family members? What information, if any, should be kept within the family?

◢ RESPONDING IN WRITING

1. Every family or close group tells stories about itself, such as the one about Pogrebin's grandparents' elopement. And, as this narrative suggests, as we grow older, we gain new insight into those family stories, sometimes coming to understand them in very different ways than we did when we were young. Try to think of such a story that is told in your own family or in a group you know well. When did you first hear the story? What did it mean to you then? How has your understanding or interpretation of that story changed? Why has it changed?

2. Pogrebin says that the discovery of her parents' prior marriages shattered her faith in adults and had a lasting impact on her ability to trust others. Write about a time when you discovered a secret. What was the information you learned and how? Why had the information been kept from you? How did the discovery affect you?

SHIRLEE TAYLOR HAIZLIP

Passing, the practice of concealing certain parts of one's identity in order to fit in or avoid persecution, is a seldom discussed but not uncommon fact of human existence. As Shirlee Taylor Haizlip notes in this essay, many blacks have passed for whites throughout American history, leaving behind family and friends and creating entirely new identities for themselves in order to enjoy the freedom and opportunity denied them as blacks. Haizlip's interest in passing began with her search for her mother's brothers and sisters, all of whom had literally disappeared into white society some time earlier.

Passing

In 1916, when Margaret Morris was a little girl living in Washington, D.C., she lost her family and they lost her. First her mother died at the age of forty-one. Then her father, uncles, aunts, sister, brothers, cousins, and even grandmother vanished. This family cleaving left in its turbulent wake a frightened four-year-old who would become my mother.

She was raised by some distant cousins on her mother's side. And although she married into a vibrant, large, welcoming family, she grieved for the people she had known so briefly. Some of that sorrow she passed on to me. She also passed on all the questions that those who are abandoned or adopted have: Why me? What did I do? Wasn't I good, beautiful, sweet, or smart enough?

And so when I was twelve, I told my mother that someday I would find her family. I was determined that through me she would find out why they had left and what sorts of lives they had led. Through me she would finally embrace her only sister. I believed I could give her that most special gift—the gift of family. The mission became a fifteen-year quest, a successful journey through time, across continents, and over the gulf we know as race, for it was race that had precipitated my mother's abandonment. Her vanished family had left her and deliberately set out to try their luck living as white people in a white world.

I began with the knowledge that my mother came from a background that included Irish, Italian, Native American, and African strains. But there were virtually no traces of color or physical traits that have traditionally been thought of as Negroid. All of her family looked like white people. They had fair skin, straight hair in shades ranging from blond to red, and eyes also of every imaginable hue. Her own mother's eyes were said to have been gray.

What I subsequently learned was that her ancestors included English aristocrats, Scottish poets, and Virginia gentry. It had always been a certainty that my father's genetic lines included African and Native American roots, but I learned that he too, like most black Americans, included the descendants of white European immigrants in his family tree. The family that I knew had dramatically enlarged, and it began to look like much of America. In the end I reconciled the two sides of my mother's family, bringing them together across the deep, wide canyon we call race in America. In the end family transcended race.

There was another result. In January of 1994 Simon & Schuster published   6
my book *The Sweeter the Juice* (whose title comes from the old African-
American saying "The blacker the berry, the sweeter the juice"). It chronicled
my search for my mother's family and documented the life and times of six generations of my father's family.

Once the book was out, letters began to arrive in a stream that grew to a   7
torrent. By now I have received thousands, and they have revealed to me in the
most intimate and moving way the extent to which our family's experience is
shared. "'Gram, we got this kinky hair from someplace,'" one letter began. "My
wife remembers her cousin making that remark to the cousin's grandmother
many years ago. At this point we still don't know where or, more properly, who
that someplace was, but reading *The Sweeter the Juice* has aroused my interest
in finding out. . . . We hope that you will accept us as a couple more of your
cousins. . . ."

The anthropologist Ashley Montagu was long an advocate of abolishing race as   8
a concept. He never used the term except in quotation marks. Last year Dr.
Luigi Cavalli-Sforza, a geneticist at Stanford University, confirmed that DNA is
a potpourri of genes deriving from myriad ethnic sources. And Jonathan
Beckwith, a microbiologist at Harvard Medical School, argues that scientists
cannot measure genetic differences between the races.

Yet "race," that socially constructed entity, was the reason for the breach in   9
my mother's family. Although the two sisters had the same parents and skin
color, one lived all her life as a black woman, and the other lived hers as a white
woman, keeping her black heritage a secret from her white husband, their only
child, and their grandchildren. The sister was not alone in the choices she made.
My mother's other siblings and the rest of her family had also abandoned their
race. They acted on the complexly simple infinitive "to be," and in fact they "became," they "were," and their descendants still "are" . . . "white."

Some would say these relatives have "one drop" of black blood, so they are   10
in fact black. But except in Louisiana all of the "one drop" racial laws have been
rescinded since 1986. So if you look white, marry white, live in a white community, attend a white church and a white school, join white associations, have
white-looking children and grandchildren, you are "white," as defined by the
majority in this country.

Hundreds of thousands of blacks passed for white, starting in the days of   11
slavery and continuing into the present. Because of the secret nature of the
transaction, no records were kept of the exact numbers who created new places
for themselves in American society. Population experts tell us that large numbers of black people are "missing." I doubt they were abducted by aliens.

According to Carla K. Bradshaw, a clinical psychologist and professor at the   12
University of Washington, "Passing is the word used to describe an attempt to
achieve acceptability by claiming membership in some desired group while
denying other racial elements in oneself thought to be undesirable. The concept
of passing uses the imagery of camouflage, of concealing true identity or group

membership and gaining false access. Concealment of 'true' identity is considered synonymous with compromised integrity and impostorship.... If an ideal world existed free from the psychology of dominance, where racial differences carried no stigma and racial purity was irrelevant, the concept of passing would have no meaning. In fact, passing of any kind loses meaning in the context of true egalitarianism."

In his history of the subject, *Mixed Blood*, Paul Spickard finds that passing   13
has been going on in this country since the first contact between Africans and Europeans. He describes two distinct forms: discontinuous and continuous passing. Discontinuous passing is defined as being "white" only part of the time—on the job, for instance, at cultural or entertainment events, or in segregated facilities, such as schools, shops, and transportation. Continuous passing, as happened in my mother's family, means a complete break with the African-American community. Such racial alchemy doesn't happen without great emotional and psychological cost. Cutting oneself off from one's culture, one's family, and one's community is tantamount to shutting oneself into a racial closet whose door is never securely locked.

This is not a subject that has received much attention in popular literature,   14
perhaps because it is simply too unsettling. We saw it treated on the Broadway stage in *Show Boat*, whose most riveting character is Julie, the beautiful light-skinned mulatto singer married to a white man. Her racial "secret" is exposed, causing her to lose her marriage, her job, and ultimately her more privileged way of life. A few films, including *Pinky, Imitation of Life*, and, more recently, *Shadows*, deal with "white" heroines whose dark genetic pasts return to haunt and undo their lives. Of course millions of light skinned blacks never have chosen to pass. And some have become national figures, such as the New York City congressman Adam Clayton Powell, Jr., and the civil rights leader Walter White. For millions of others, however, passing has been a way to cope with the poisonous legacy of slavery.

Some geneticists claim that as many as 80 percent of black Americans have   15
white bloodlines and that a surprising 95 percent of white Americans have some black ancestry. These statistics are based not on guesswork but on the direct clinical examination of nucleotides and microsatellites, genetic components common to all human blood. Dr. Luigi Cavalli-Sforza tells us in *The History and Geography of Human Genes*, the first genetic atlas of the world, just published by Princeton University Press, that all ethnic groups hold an array of overlapping sets and subsets of mixed gene pools. He notes that modern Europeans (the ancestors of America's immigrants) have long been a mixed population whose genetic ancestry is 65 percent Asian and 35 percent African. There never has been any such thing as a "Caucasoid" gene. Nor is there such a creature as a "pure" white or black American. During recent hearings of the Senate Committee on Government Affairs on the Human Genome Diversity Project, Dr. Cavelli-Sforza and Dr. Mary-Claire King, a geneticist at the University of California at Berkeley, discussed the implications of their work. They called

racism "an ancient scourge of humanity" and expressed the hope that further extensive study of world populations would help "undercut conventional notions of race and underscore the common bonds between all humans."

Just from looking at archival records of my family, I know that every census has measured race differently. In different periods the same people in my family were listed as mulatto, black, or white. The designation could depend on the eye of the beholder or the neighborhood where they lived. In the meantime, their neighbors, their coworkers, and their communities at large saw them as either black or white, depending on who decided what. (Currently, a multiracial activist group is lobbying Congress to add a "mixed race" category for all those who do not wish to chose one side or the other of their gene pools.)   16

Because of the newness and yet somehow remembered, dreamed, imagined, or experienced familiarity of this story, *The Sweeter the Juice* has captured the interest of white and blacks all over the country. Thus the flood of letters and phone calls. Many of the callers begin their conversations with the phrase "I'm white, I think." And with the letters come copies of old photographs, census documents, family trees, family secrets, and family confessions.   17

"I could have written your story," many black people say. And I know that to be true, for what happened in my family happened in most black families. A woman who reported she was "in [my] mother's generation" wrote: "Your family memoirs brought to the surface long-buried memories of incidents in my life as a Negro who could have chosen to 'go over.' I recall seeing, only once, an uncle who went over; I also recall racial jokes and slurs made in my presence by ones who thought I was white. . . . One of the largest department stores in Pittsburgh hired me as the first black saleslady, unaware that a black lady had been working in its jewelry department for years."   18

From the hills of Appalachia came a three-page letter with a bibliography and seven pages of genealogical charts. It began: "Allow me to say on the first line of this letter that I am a seventy-eight-year-old white woman who has lived in Kentucky all my life. . . . I noted that your name was Haizlip and at some time your people had lived in North Carolina. As the enclosed chart shows, my husband's grandmother was born a Haizlip and married a Morris from North Carolina. . . . I was completely fascinated with your book and read it from 'kiver to kiver' in two days."   19

Culver City is a part of Los Angeles where movie studios continue to crank out their versions of the American dream. From there a woman wrote: "I feel that I am probably somehow distantly related to you. Three of my four grandparents were of Irish ancestry. My mother's grandparents were from County Tipperary, as was your great grandmother. . . . My mother says the name Morris was derived from 'Moorish,' which would suggest racial intermixture even before arrival in the New World. . . . I would be very proud to have African blood in my lineage, and after reading your book, I now know that I probably do, since part of my family, at least, has lived in this country since colonial days."   20

An eighty-nine-year-old woman in Lorain, Ohio, began her lengthy letter by saying: "My grandmother looked like any ol' white woman. If she was or not, I have no way of knowing, but she had brown children and some light, straight-haired ones. In my own gang three of my brothers in the West passed   21 for something other than black Americans. They married Mormon, at least two Mexicans, and they raised their umpteen children not black, but a few became curious about four years ago and started prying. We have met four of them, and they were as 'happy as kings.' The one nephew is a bigwig in the Navy as a white." She signed it "your 'Ohio Cousin.'"

I was a keynote speaker at the banquet my thirty-fifth reunion class held at   22
Wellesley College last June. Before the dinner I chatted with my classmates and their spouses, children, and guests. A dark-haired, blue-eyed woman who had retained her college prettiness came up to me, giggling like a freshman. "You'll never guess what my husband just asked me!" She laughed. "He wanted to know if you were Jewish. Boy, is he going to be embarrassed when he hears your talk."

During my book tour across the country, hundreds of people volunteered   23
stories about gaps in their identity. In Seattle an ostensibly white broadcaster in his sixties told me on the air that except for the color of his grandfather's skin, he had always thought his grandfather had what he described as "Negroid features." When he added that his grandfather's first name was Washington, I said, "I hate to tell you this, but I never knew any white family that named its children Washington. That was always a popular name with black people." Startled, my interviewer said he was going to check the census information on his grandfather in the next few weeks.

At a book signing in a Southern California shopping mall, an older woman   24
with dark red hair and amber eyes bought the book, asked me to autograph it, and then said, "I understand this story, because it happened in my family. But it stopped with my father." I was curious about this gene stoppage and intrigued by this woman's unconscious denial of her heritage. "You see," she continued, "I was raised white, but when I went to Texas for Founders' Day in my hometown, I saw a picture of my great-grandmother for the first time. There was no doubt about it: She was colored. There was no way she could even pass for Indian. I was told she died after giving birth to my grandfather. Later my father was born, and nothing was ever said about his heritage. So everything stopped with him."

There are infinite ways of dealing with denial. Some are not subtle. In   25
Boston I knew there was no balm I could offer the black man with freckles, green eyes, and blondish brown hair—the tightly coiled hair some call "rhiney." Clutching my book to the middle of his chest as if protecting an ancient wound that would not heal, he told me that he remembers as an eight-year-old holding his mother's hand while walking through St. Louis on a summer afternoon. An apparently white man came strolling toward them, and as the three drew close enough to see one another's faces, the boy's mother began to tremble violently. At that moment the man bolted and ran across the street. He sprinted around the corner and out of sight. At this point in his story, the book holder took a deep breath, clearly close to tears. "My mother, who was also light-skinned, had turned red and was crying silently as she looked at the corner where the man had just vanished. 'That was my brother,' she said. 'He's passing, and I haven't seen him in twenty-two years.' That was their last encounter. I

never saw him again. But I will never, ever forget the deep pain and the tears on my mother's face."

Chicago welcomed me during 1994's coldest weather. Only a little less frigid   26
was the greeting from the media aide assigned to me during my visit, who met me at the airport. This young woman quickly informed me that she had graduated from Princeton and that her father and grandfather also had graduated from Princeton. I thought surely that she would add that her great-grandfather had founded Princeton, but she didn't. On my second day, however, her personal freeze began to thaw. She said excitedly that she had begun reading my book and had just discovered that she was probably related to me. "How's that?" I asked. "Well, I see that you are related to Martha Washington, and so am I, so I guess that makes us distant cousins." She continued, "When I told my father about it last night, he was excited until I got to the part about your being black." Then he said, 'Maybe this explains that lost branch Aunt Suzie hasn't been able to find.'"

The themes of these tales create a story quilt of repeated patterns. And between   27
the patches, strong connecting seams began to emerge. From a city slowly recovering from racial paroxysms, a Los Angeles resident wrote: "Our families are so similar. Like yours, we are racially mixed, predominantly European (Irish) and African. And we too had many members who passed for white. . . . To have America confront the fact of black genes in the white population, as you have done, is also therapeutic. Why should a person, on learning he has black ancestry, feel distressed about it? And why should the person in question face betrayal from associates who learn of his black heritage? Thank you for your contribution to racial healing."

A black Detroit woman suggested she felt ethnically liberated: "It validated   28
my right to wonder and even to discuss my multi-ethnicities. Like you, I am proud to be a black American, but why should that mean I have to deny what is not black? Most black Americans descend from at least one white relative, yet many blacks are offended when one discusses anything but one's blackness. You have announced, 'It's OK.'"

Obsession is often the word used to describe the American fascination with   29
race. Just as I wondered all my life about white people I thought might be related to me, so too did this black woman: "Growing up in central Virginia, I often wondered which of the white people I knew as neighbors were related to my black family."

And a black woman from Maryland wrote to me about the time she first   30
learned about passing. "I must have been about ten years old when one day our doorbell rang and my mother told me to answer it. Standing there was a tall, pale man with gray eyes and thin blond hair. He asked for my mother. 'Mama, mama, there's a white man at the door looking for you.' My mother went into the door and then led the man into the parlor. She called me in. 'This is my

brother and your uncle Ted,' she said. After the visitor had left, she told me that her brother was living as a white man in another place and could come to see us only every once in a while. I don't remember ever seeing my uncle again."

Frequently citing the phenomenon of "passing for Gentile," Jews have re- 31 sponded to *The Sweeter the Juice* in similar ways. My mother accompanied me to a signing at a bookstore in an Orange County mall. Sitting on the floor was a cherubic, curly-haired young woman who immediately brought to mind romantic images of a European Gypsy. When she spied my mother approaching behind me, she jumped to her feet, grabbed my mother's hand, and began sobbing. My mother, who wears her emotions just under her skin, also began to cry. Seeing this stranger and my mother hold hands and silently weep, I, too, began to cry. There we were, a mother, a daughter, and a woman unknown to either of us, wailing as if we were professional mourners at an Irish funeral. Finally the young woman cleared her last sob and poured out her story.

She had grown up a member of the only Jewish family in her small town in 32 Orange County. Pained by the prejudice she experienced as a child, she decided never again to reveal her Jewish heritage. She would become a Gentile. She straightened her hair, bobbed her nose, changed her name, and left both Orange County and her Jewishness behind. But, she told my mother, the break did her more harm than good. She recanted her choice and returned to the bosom of her family and her religion. She could not "pass" any longer. Touched by the sorrow that passing had brought to my mother's life and to her own, she had come to the mall to tell her so, face-to-face. She cried, she said, for the pain they both knew.

From Dallas, Texas, came a haunting letter to which I keep returning: "I was 33 particularly interested in your book because of my own life. I grew up in New York. My maiden name was Myersen. [The name is changed here for privacy.] When you grow up in New York and your name is Myersen, you are asked several times a month if you are Jewish. It was seldom an ugly question. It was just informational. The answer to this question was 'Oh, no. It is an old Danish name. Jews spell it "O-N." We are Danish.' In 1983 my mother told me that she discovered a letter indicating my father's family was Jewish (Danish Jews). I have been dealing with the amputation of my heritage and recovery of my heritage since 1983. I will become a Jew in a formal ceremony quite soon."

A Harvard Ph.D. living in Cambridge, Massachusetts, wrote, "Your book 34 raised such basic issues about identity. . . . After we move from our own personality and reality that we take from our genetic makeup, our family, our marriage, work, et cetera and move into the community to which we think we belong, how much is intrinsic, and how much is imposed from the external world? It is hard for me to rely on genetic contributions from my ancestors as supporting my identity, perhaps because I can trace my background back only two generations on one level and almost six thousand years on another. Because

Jews were expelled from so many countries and continents in their history yet lived all over the world and intermarried with every population, physical appearance is meaningless to identity. One has only to go to Israel to see this. . . . We all are linked through history and common belief. Should that not be the linkage between all of us, regardless of our skin color?"

In the Point Loma section of San Diego there is a vast bookstore that has   35 been converted from one of the city's vintage theaters. Bordered in triple rows of Caribbean-colored neon light bars, the curving Art Deco marquee bore my name as the guest author. In this arresting setting an equally arresting, elegant pale woman with large gray eyes and a croquignole wave pressed her business card into my hand. On one side the print read, "Ethnic hair specialist." On the other, a quickly scribbled note: "I will call you to tell you my story." And call she did, the next day. As an adopted child she had always wondered about her ethnicity because she did not feel she was either black or white. Just this year, she said, she managed to have her adoption records unsealed and saw for the first time a picture of her long-dead mother: a teenage Jewish girl who had conceived an out-of-wedlock child by a young black man. The girl's family prevailed on her to give the child up for adoption. In the file was a letter from the mother saying that she wanted to reclaim her baby. She never did, seemingly because of the daunting adoption process at that time. She later died in an mental institution. Speaking in a near whisper, the daughter ended the conversation, "You don't know what it meant to me as a grown woman to see my mother's face, to touch her handwriting, to learn that she really did want me, and to know about my mother." I knew.

Back in Los Angeles, I had an urgent telephone message that a young woman   36 had to speak with me immediately. When I returned the call, the woman told me that she had not known she was black until she was twelve years old. Her hair was blonde, her eyes green, and her skin fair. All her family had passed for white in San Diego. And that's what she had assumed she was until the day she found an old family scrapbook with some yellowed photographs of people who were clearly brown. She asked her parents about them. Her mother refused to discuss the photographs or anything related to them; her father admitted they were relatives but said he had left "that life" behind.

At seventeen this girl went East to meet some of her dark relatives, and   37 upon returning to the West Coast, she decided, she said, "to embrace her blackness." She was the only member of her family to do so, although the rest of her siblings had been informed of their heritage. Now the director of a large and flourishing human-service facility in Watts, the expansive African-American neighborhood in Los Angeles, she stays in touch with her family but lives across the color line.

How would the book be received in the heart of Dixie? I wondered a little ner-   38 vously while being driven to a radio interview on the far outskirts of Atlanta.

The small-scale station occupied the second floor of a two-story boxlike building. My interviewer, a heavyset, jovial middle-aged man in a short-sleeved shirt, eyed me with a curiosity that matched my own. Yes, I thought, he does fit my image of a good ol' boy. Now what?

I sensed it was important to establish common ground quickly. I told my radio host that I had just visited another beautiful Southern area, Hertford, North Carolina, in the eastern end of the state where my father was born. "By jiminy," he drawled, "I don't believe it! That's where I'm from. Isn't it truly God's country! Now don't tell too many people about it, because we want to keep it small and secret. By jiminy! I knew I was going to like you." His interview was straightforward, with no blind curves or cul-de-sacs. When it was over, I asked him how he thought white Southerners would respond to my story. "Well, Shirlee," he said, "we've all known this for years. Some of the ol'-timers may not like to see it in print, but what the heck, it's all part of that devilish thing we call history." 39

Early one Saturday morning the graceful Southern voice of an elderly man told me [he] was sorry to interrupt my weekend privacy but he had just finished my book and could not wait until Monday to talk with me. He had called directory assistance for my telephone number. 40

Since regional accents often disguise race, I couldn't tell whether he was black or white. He wanted to know more about the Halyburton side of my family, which he had researched and said he was related to, thus making him distantly related to me. I was pleased to be able to supply him with facts about two Halyburton generations of which he had no knowledge, dating back to the late 1600s in Scotland. After we had talked a bit, he told me how close he felt to various aspects of the book, because, like my father, he was a Baptist preacher. 41

I asked him what he called himself. 42

"My family is mixed like yours, and I think of myself as a mulatto. I know I had two black aunts, but somehow we got whiter." 43

"What does your community call you?" I queried. 44

"Oh, white, of course." 45

"And your congregation?" 46

"My congregation is white." 47

The minister told me that he lived in a small town in the Blue Ridge Mountain area of North Carolina and that he was going to preach about my book on Sunday. I would like to have been in that audience. 48

It comforts me to think there is a sea change in America. It is surely a new day when white Americans are willing to look at their roots and find that some of them are possibly colored. Perhaps some of us are beginning to do what one anthropologist suggested would be the first step in eliminating racism: separating our need to belong from the dangerous temptation to hate others. 49

I doubt whether these letters would have been written even five years ago. I doubt if strangers would have been calling and talking softly about these most private aspects of their lives. It has buoyed me that all the response so far has 50 been positive, open, and curious. And perhaps the ultimate reconciliation came in a letter from a white woman in a small town in Illinois. She wrote of the man I had discovered to be one of the progenitors of my family, a white Virginia judge who sired and raised my great-grandfather, Edward Everett Morris, a mulatto slave. "One of your ancestors, James Dandridge Halyburton, is my husband's great-great-grandfather. Should you care to correspond with us, we would be delighted. I truly enjoyed your book and am glad that I have found another part of the family."

Recently, Pat Shipman, a paleoanthropologist and the author of several   51 books on evolutionary biology, wrote: "We all agree that we will face the truth together. . . . We have only one joint fate, and we must create it together." At the confidences shared and the secrets disclosed I am not surprised. In America I believe there is now a profound need, a deep preternatural yearning to connect—to feel related, to be part of that special group we call family. ☐

◢ REREADING FOR UNDERSTANDING

1. Haizlip says it is impossible to know how many blacks passed into white society. Why?

2. What is the difference between continuous and discontinuous passing? Why do you think Haizlip's relatives chose continuous passing?

3. Haizlip offers a number of observations that seem contrary to our assumed notions of race. She reports, for example, that some geneticists believe as many as 95 percent of white Americans have some black ancestry. Reread Haizlip's essay, making note of her contradictions to commonly held beliefs about race.

◢ RESPONDING

1. Haizlip's essay calls into question the very concept of race as a distinguishing characteristic among human beings. How would you define "race"? Is it as arbitrary a distinction as Haizlip claims? Do you think it would be beneficial to abolish the concept of race? Would it be detrimental in any way?

2. The response that Haizlip received to her book suggests that passing is a widespread practice. Does this surprise you? Have you heard similar stories within your own family or community?

3. Although Haizlip focuses on the practice of blacks passing for white, there are many circumstances in which people, for one reason or another, conceal part of their identity or pretend to be something that they are not. In "My Life in the Military Closet," for example, José Zuniga describes his struggle to conceal the fact that he was gay from most of his army colleagues. Think of other conditions in which passing occurs. What kind of fear/temptation leads someone to try to pass? Can you think of times in your own life when you have attempted to pass for something you were not?

◢ RESPONDING IN WRITING

We have all experienced, to greater or lesser degrees, the discomfort of being different from the group, and from time to time we have all tried to pretend that we were different in order to fit in. Write about a time when you could have or did pass as something or someone else in order to be accepted. What part of your identity did you conceal? Why? What was the result? Did you gain acceptance or avoid ridicule? Did you ever reveal the truth to that group? As you look back on the experience, how do you think it shaped your sense of identity?

JUDITH ORTIZ COFER

Judith Ortiz Cofer was born in Puerto Rico and grew up in Paterson, New Jersey. A poet and essayist as well as a fiction writer, Cofer says she learned the power of the imagination from her mother and grandmother. For them, she says, "Storytelling played a purpose. When my *abuela* sat us down to tell a story, we learned something from it, even though we always laughed. That was her way of teaching. So early on, I instinctively knew storytelling was a form of empowerment, that the women in my family were passing on power from one generation to another through fables and stories." As you read this selection from *The Latin Deli*, think about how storytelling in its various forms serves as a source of power.

By Love Betrayed

As a little girl I imagined my father was a genie that came out of a magic bottle at night. It was a green bottle of cologne that he splashed on his face before leaving the house. I thought it was the strong smell that made my mother cry.

I loved him more than anyone. He was beautiful to me with his dark, shiny black hair combed back like one of the handsome men on the *telenovelas* my mother watched while she waited for him to come home at night. I was allowed to stay up for the early one: *Traicionado por el amor:* By Love Betrayed.

My *papi* had a mustache like a thin brush that tickled me when he kissed me. If they had not been shouting at each other, he would sometimes come into my room and say good-night before he left for his job at the nightclub. Then his perfume would get on my blanket and I would hold it to my face until I fell asleep. I dreamed of him and me walking on a beach. I had never been to the ocean, but he told me stories about growing up in a house on the beach in Puerto Rico. It had been blown away by a hurricane.

When my mother got angry at my father, she made me think of a hurricane. Blowing him away from us with her screams and her tears. Once, she scratched his cheek. He covered it with her makeup before he left for work.

Another time I heard a sound like a slap, but I did not know who hit whom, because my mother always cried, and he always left.

Sometimes I would hear her saying the rosary aloud, the dozens of Hail Marys and Our Fathers was a song that would put me to sleep better than any lullaby. She had come back to the church after leaving it when she had run away with Papi. My mother said that Tito had taken her away from God but that now she was back to stay. She had the priest come to our apartment and sprinkle it with holy water, which doesn't smell like anything.

My mother made our apartment look like a church too: she put a cross with Christ on it over their bed and mine—Papi liked to say that one day it would fall on their heads and kill them, and my mother would answer, "Well, Tito, I'm ready to go to my Dios any time, are you?" He would just laugh. She hung a picture of the Holy Mother and Baby Jesus on the wall facing my bed, and one of Christ knocking at a door in the hallway. On her dresser she had a painted statue of the Virgin May crushing a black snake. When you saw it on the mirror it looked as if she was a real little person who was about to trip over a snake because she wasn't looking where she was going. I used to play pretend and try to take the snake out. But it was glued on under her little foot. My mother did not like me to play with the saint dolls, though, and I had to sneak into their room when she was busy in the kitchen or watching TV.

My parents argued a lot. Our apartment was small, and I heard them saying the same things over and over in as many different hurting words as was possible. I learned my fighting words in Spanish then: the words to hurt and also the words of the church that my mother taught me so that I would not turn out a sinner like my father.

"Who made you?"

"God made me."

"Why did He make you?"

"To glorify His Name and to obey His commands and those of His Church."

We said this lesson over and over in our catechism class with Sister Teresa who was preparing us for First Communion.

When I got older, I tried to ask my mother questions about my father. Her answers were always the same:

"Where does Papi go at night?"

"To his job."

"But he has a job during the day. He's the super of our building, right?"

"He has two jobs. Finish your cereal. It's getting late for school."

When she made up her mind not to talk about my father, I could not make her say a word. For many years I could not talk to him, since the only time he was at home, in between his jobs, she was also there, watching me. Finally I got my chance to see my papi alone after she started volunteer work at the church several mornings a week when I was in third grade.

One day she had to leave early to help plan a women's religious retreat. She put a bowl of cereal in front of me and told me to walk carefully to school. I was big enough to walk the four blocks alone, especially since there were crossing guards at every corner. I kissed her good-bye and asked for my blessing: "Dios te bendiga, Hija," she said and crossed herself.

"Amén," I said and crossed myself.   20

I ran to the living room window from where I could see her come out on   21
the street and walk toward the church. After she disappeared around the corner, I took the house key and left our apartment to look for my father. I was not sure what I would do when I found him. I felt scared and excited, though, knowing that I was doing something that would make my mother angry if she found out. I knew that Papi would not tell.

It was a big building with long dark hallways that wound around each other   22
for seven floors. I had never been above our third floor. When I reached the fifth floor, I smelled his cologne. I followed it to the door of 5-A. I knew for sure that he was somewhere near because his toolbox was in the corner of the landing. I stood in front of the door with my knees shaking, afraid to knock and afraid to turn back. The building was quiet at that hour. All the children were in school and most people at work. I put my head to the door and listened.

First I heard a woman's voice saying my father's name in a strange way: 23
"Tito, Tito . . ." She said it as if they were playing a game. Then I heard his voice, but I could not understand the words. Then they both laughed. I decided to knock.

The woman who opened the door was wearing a red robe and her hair was   24
a mess. Her lipstick was purple. I remember thinking that she looked like a vampire. I felt like running away, especially since she looked a little wild with her blonde-streaked hair all over her face. She had dark skin and blonde-streaked hair. I remember that.

"What do you want?" she said in an angry voice.   25

"I . . . I'm looking for my father."   26

"Your *father*?" She looked behind her. He had come out of her bedroom. I   27
knew it was her bedroom because her apartment was just like ours, except for the furniture. Her sofa was black, and she had no curtains on her windows. My father was combing his hair with the black comb he always carried in his shirt pocket. He looked really surprised to see me at the door.

"Eva, what are you doing here?" Before I could answer, though, he closed the   28
door behind him—right on the woman's face. I was really nervous. I couldn't tell him what I was doing there because I didn't know myself. He bent down and looked at me. He looked nervous too. I could tell because his left eye twitched when he was upset; I've seen it do that after he and my mother had a fight. "Are you sick, Evita? Why aren't you at school? Where is your mother?" He looked around as if he thought she was behind me somewhere.

"I stayed home, Papi. I had a headache. She's gone to church." He had been   29
squeezing my shoulder with his hand, but he let go of me then. He smiled in a way my mother called his "devil smile." She said that meant he thought he knew it all. That nobody could fool him. He claimed that he always knew when somebody had a secret around the house. And that's how he found the money she had been saving behind her underwear drawer.

"Are you really sick or just taking the day off, *mi amor*?"   30

I just smiled, trying for a "devil smile" myself.   31

"I thought so. Well, maybe I'll do the same. The señora's clogged sink can   32
wait another day. How about a hamburger at the White Castle for lunch?"

"It's only 9:30, Papi. Not time for lunch."   33

"Says who? Today *we* decide everything by ourselves. Deal?" He gave me his   34
hand and I took it. □

◢ REREADING FOR UNDERSTANDING

1. In paragraph 1 and 4, the narrator, Eva, offers a metaphor for each of her
parents. What does she imagine her father to be? her mother? What do
these metaphors suggest about each parent and about her relationship with
them?

2. There are different degrees of deceit in this story, from deliberate lying to
refusing to see or acknowledge the truth. Skim the story, making note of
the ways in which characters practice deception. In each case, what do you
think is the motivation for each deceptive act or statement?

3. When Eva decides to skip school and find her father, she says, "I knew that
Papi would not tell" (par. 21). What makes her so sure that her father will
protect her secret?

◢ RESPONDING

1. In "In What Mode Faith Should Be Kept by Princes" (p. 253), Machiavelli
offers the following advice for dealing with liars: "Because they are wicked
and do not observe faith with you, you also do not have to observe faith
with them." Do you think this line of reasoning explains and/or justifies
Eva's actions? Does she deceive only those who have deceived her? Is she
truthful to those who are honest with her?

2. Consider Judith Ortiz Cofer's observation that storytelling is a means of empowerment. To what extent do Eva, her father, and her mother use stories to
gain power?

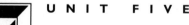

UNIT FIVE

Responsibility

INTRODUCTION

*I*n the last decade, politicians, media pundits, religious leaders, and even ordinary citizens have found much to say about rights and responsibilities. We hear voices urging us to be more responsible, to be more concerned with the needs of others. At every turn, we hear of rights—fathers' rights, gay and lesbian rights, children's rights, animal rights, and even plants' rights. As you read in this unit, you will have the opportunity to listen to and evaluate some of the claims and counterclaims made concerning rights and responsibilities.

The unit on Responsibility opens with A Way In science fiction fantasy by Ursula K. Le Guin. She presents us with life in a utopian city called Omelas. The social world of Omelas appears, on the surface, to be a paradise on earth. Everyone is free to pursue whatever personal whims or desires he or she might have. The story asks us to consider the costs involved when each individual considers only his/her desires without a sense of responsibility toward others. Thus the theme of this unit is set forth: What is the relationship between an individual's right to self-fulfillment as opposed to an individual's responsibility toward helping others live a fulfilled and productive life?

The Contexts essays offer different definitions of what this balance between rights and responsibility should be, from conservative writer Ayn Rand, who claims that one's only responsibility is to oneself, to environmentalist Aldo Leopold, who believes that we are responsible not just to our immediate families or communities, but to all living things with whom we share the earth, as well as to those who will inherit the planet from us.

The Controversies section looks at specific situations in which we are forced to weigh our own rights and desires against the rights and needs of others. A first group of essays asks, "What Is My Responsibility in an Intimate Relationship?" These essays allow us to see different perspectives on rights and responsibilities in intimate male-female relationships. The second group of essays asks, "What Are My Responsibilities Within the Family?" From the perspectives of parents' responsibility toward children, children's responsibility toward parents, and the larger society's responsibility toward children, each of these essays analyzes how much and what kind of responsibility we owe to others in our family. The final group of essays raises the question, "What Are

My Responsibilities to the Environment?" At what point does my right to water my lawn or swim in my pool or even flush my toilet infringe upon the rights of those who also depend upon the same water supply? Does my right to earn a living, to have children, or to produce and consume the goods I desire outweigh my responsibility to conserve the limited resources that sustain others and that future generations will need?

This never ending tug-of-war between rights and responsibilities is one with which you are no doubt well acquainted. Even if you have not already considered the particular problems set forth in these essays, you have certainly faced similar conflicts. Considering the questions raised in this unit will not give you a magic formula for achieving a balance between rights and responsibilities, but perhaps it will give you a useful context for weighing choices you inevitably will face.

A W A Y I N

URSULA K. LE GUIN

Ursula K. Le Guin was born in 1929. Since the 1960s Le Guin has published twenty novels, a half-dozen children's stories, and scores of poems and essays. She says of her own writing that it ranges from "fantasy" to "realist." Critics have noted her fantasy worlds are frequently used as a means to explore social and cultural issues in our "real" world. Our selection is exactly that sort of work. In the fantasy land of Omelas individual happiness seems to be the only concern of the entire community. One member of Omelas suffers terribly, but none in the community are willing to sacrifice their own happiness for that one in need. Omelas gives us "a way in" to the entire issue of rights and responsibilities. How far may we pursue our rights, and when must our individual rights give way in order for us to act responsibly toward another?

The Ones Who Walk Away from Omelas

With a clamor of bells that set the swallows soaring, the Festival of Summer came to the city Omelas, bright-towered by the sea. The rigging of the boats in harbor sparkled with flags. In the streets between houses with red roofs and painted walls, between old moss-grown gardens and under avenues of trees, past great parks and public buildings, processions moved. Some were decorous: old people in long stiff robes of mauve and gray, grave master workmen, quiet, merry women carrying their babies and chatting as they walked. In other streets the music beat faster, a shimmering of gong and tambourine, and the people went dancing, the procession was a dance. Children dodged in and out, their high calls rising like the swallows' crossing flights over the music and the singing. All the processions wound towards the north side of the city, where on the great water-meadow called the Green Fields boys and girls, naked in the bright air, with mudstained feet and ankles and long, lithe arms, exercised their restive horses before the race. The horses wore no gear at all but a halter without bit. Their manes were braided with streamers of silver, gold, and green. They flared their nostrils and pranced and boasted to one another; they were vastly excited, the horse being the only animal who has adopted our ceremonies as his own. Far off to the north and west the mountains stood up half encircling Omelas on her bay. The air of morning was so clear that the snow still crowning the Eighteen Peaks burned with white-gold fire across the miles of sunlit air, under the dark blue of the sky. There was just enough wind to make the banners that marked the racecourse snap and flutter now and then. In the silence of the broad green meadows one could hear the music winding through the city streets, farther and nearer and ever approaching, a cheerful faint sweetness of the air that from time to time trembled and gathered together and broke out into the great joyous clanging of the bells.

Joyous! How is one to tell about joy? How describe the citizens of Omelas?   2

They were not simple folk, you see, though they were happy. But we do not   3
say the words of cheer much any more. All smiles have become archaic. Given a description such as this one tends to make certain assumptions. Given a description such as this one tends to look next for the King, mounted on a splendid stallion and surrounded by his noble knights, or perhaps in a golden litter borne by great-muscled slaves. But there was no king. They did not use swords, or keep slaves. They were not barbarians. I do not know the rules and laws of their society, but I suspect that they were singularly few. As they did without monarchy and slavery, so they also got on without the stock exchange, the advertisement, the secret police, and the bomb. Yet I repeat that these were not simple folk, not dulcet shepherds, noble savages, bland utopians. They were not less complex than us. The trouble is that we have a bad habit, encouraged by pedants and sophisticates, of considering happiness as something rather stupid. Only pain is intellectual, only evil interesting. This is the treason of the artist: a refusal to admit the banality of evil and the terrible boredom of pain. If you can't lick 'em, join 'em. If it hurts, repeat it. But to praise despair is to condemn delight, to embrace violence is to lose hold of everything else. We have almost lost hold, we can no longer describe a happy man, nor make any celebration of joy. How can I tell you about the people of Omelas? They were not naïve and happy children—though their children were, in fact, happy. They were mature, intelligent, passionate adults whose lives were not wretched. O miracle! but I wish I could describe it better. I wish I could convince you. Omelas sounds in my words like a city in a fairy tale, long ago and far away, once upon a time. Perhaps it would be best if you imagined it as your own fancy bids, assuming it will rise to the occasion, for certainly I cannot suit you all. For instance, how about technology? I think that there would be no cars or helicopters in and above the streets; this follows from the fact that the people of Omelas are happy people. Happiness is based on a just discrimination of what is necessary, what is neither necessary nor destructive, and what is destructive. In the middle category, however—that of the unnecessary but undestructive, that of comfort,

luxury, exuberance, etc.—they could perfectly well have central heating, subway trains, washing machines, and all kinds of marvelous devices not yet invented here, floating light-sources, fuelless power, a cure for the common cold. Or they could have none of that: it doesn't matter. As you like it. I incline to think that people from towns up and down the coast have been coming in to Omelas during the last days before the Festival on very fast little trains and double-decked trams, and that the train station of Omelas is actually the handsomest building in town, though plainer than the magnificent Farmers' Market. But even granted trains, I fear that Omelas so far strikes some of you as goody-goody. Smiles, bells, parades, horses, bleh. If so, please add an orgy. If an orgy would help, don't hesitate. Let us not, however, have temples from which issue beautiful nude priests and priestesses already half in ecstasy and ready to copulate with any man or woman, lover or stranger, who desires union with the deep godhead of the blood, although that was my first idea. But really it would be better not to have any temples in Omelas—at least, not manned temples. Religion yes, clergy no. Surely the beautiful nudes can just wander about, offering themselves like divine soufflés to the hunger of the needy and the rapture of the flesh. Let them join the processions. Let tambourines be struck above the copulations, and the glory of desire be proclaimed upon the gongs, and (a not unimportant point) let the offspring of these delightful rituals be beloved and looked after by all. One thing I know there is none of in Omelas is guilt. But what else should there be? I thought that first there were no drugs, but that is puritanical. For those who like it, the faint insistent sweetness of *drooz* may perfume the ways of the city, *drooz* which first brings a great lightness and brilliance to the mind and limbs, and then after some hours a dreamy languor, and wonderful visions at last of the very arcana and inmost secrets of the Universe, as well as exciting the pleasure of sex beyond all belief; and it is not habit-forming. For more modest tastes I think there ought to be beer. What else, what else belongs in the joyous city? The sense of victory, surely, the celebration of courage. But as we did without clergy, let us do without soldiers. The joy built upon successful slaughter is not the right kind of joy; it will not do; it is fearful and it is trivial. A boundless and generous contentment, a magnanimous triumph felt not against some outer enemy but in communion with the finest and fairest in the souls of all men everywhere and the splendor of the world's summer: this is what swells the hearts of the people of Omelas, and the victory they celebrate is that of life. I really don't think many of them need to take *drooz*.

Most of the processions have reached the Green Fields by now. A marvelous   4
smell of cooking goes forth from the red and blue tents of the provisioners. The faces of small children are amiably sticky; in the benign grey beard of a man a couple of crumbs of rich pastry are entangled. The youths and girls have mounted their horses and are beginning to group around the starting line of the course. An old woman, small, fat, and laughing, is passing out flowers from a basket, and tall young men wear her flowers in their shining hair. A child of nine or ten sits at the edge of the crowd, alone, playing on a wooden flute. People pause to listen, and they smile, but they do not speak to him, for he

never ceases playing and never sees them, his dark eyes wholly rapt in the sweet, thin magic of the tune.

He finishes, and slowly lowers his hands holding the wooden flute.   5

As if that little private silence were the signal, all at once a trumpet sounds   6
from the pavilion near the starting line: imperious, melancholy, piercing. The horses rear on their slender legs, and some of them neigh in answer. Sober-faced, the young riders stroke the horses' necks and soothe them, whispering, "Quiet, quiet, there my beauty, my hope. . . ." They begin to form in rank along the starting line. The crowds along the racecourse are like a field of grass and flowers in the wind. The Festival of Summer has begun.

Do you believe? Do you accept the festival, the city, the joy? No? Then let   7
me describe one more thing.

In a basement under one of the beautiful public buildings of Omelas, or   8
perhaps in the cellar of one of its spacious private homes, there is a room. It has one locked door, and no window. A little light seeps in dustily between cracks in the boards, secondhand from a cobwebbed window somewhere across the cellar. In one corner of the little room a couple of mops, with stiff, clotted, foul-smelling heads, stand near a rusty bucket. The floor is dirt, a lit-tle damp to the touch, as cellar dirt usually is. The room is about three paces long and two wide: a mere broom closet or disused tool room. In the room a child is sitting. It could be a boy or a girl. It looks about six, but actually is nearly ten. It is feeble-minded. Perhaps it was born defective, or perhaps it has become imbecile through fear, malnutrition, and neglect. It picks its nose and occasionally fumbles vaguely with its toes or genitals, as it sits hunched in the corner farthest from the bucket and the two mops. It is afraid of the mops. It finds them horrible. It shuts its eyes, but it knows the mops are still standing there; and the door is locked; and nobody will come. The door is always locked; and nobody ever comes, except that sometimes—the child has no understanding of time or interval—sometimes the door rattles terribly and opens, and a person, or several people, are there. One of them may come in and kick the child to make it stand up. The others never come close, but peer in at it with frightened, disgusted eyes. The food bowl and the water jug are hastily filled, the door is locked, the eyes disappear. The people at the door never say anything, but the child, who has not always lived in the tool room, and can remember sunlight and its mother's voice, sometimes speaks. "I will be good," it says. "Please let me out, I will be good!" They never answer. The child used to scream for help at night, and cry a good deal, but now it only makes a kind of whining, "eh-haa, eh-haa," and it speaks less and less often. It is so thin there are no calves to its legs; its belly protrudes; it lives on a half-bowl of corn meal and grease a day. It is naked. Its buttocks and thighs are a mass of festered sores, as it sits in its own excrement continually.

They all know it is there, all the people of Omelas. Some of them have   9
come to see it, others are content merely to know it is there. They all know that it has to be there. Some of them understand why, and some do not, but they all understand that their happiness, the beauty of their city, the tenderness of their friendships, the health of their children, the wisdom of their scholars, the

skill of their makers, even the abundance of their harvest and the kindly weathers of their skies, depend wholly on this child's abominable misery.

This is usually explained to children when they are between eight and twelve, whenever they seem capable of understanding; and most of those who come to see the child are young people, though often enough an adult comes, or comes back, to see the child. No matter how well the matter has been explained to them, these young spectators are always shocked and sickened at the sight. They feel disgust, which they had thought themselves superior to. They feel anger, outrage, impotence, despite all the explanations. They would like to do something for the child. But there is nothing they can do. If the child were brought up into the sunlight out of that vile place, if it were cleaned and fed and comforted, that would be a good thing, indeed; but if it were done, in that day and hour all the prosperity and beauty and delight of Omelas would wither and be destroyed. Those are the terms. To exchange all the goodness and grace of every life in Omelas for that single, small improvement: to throw away the happiness of thousands for the chance of the happiness of one: that would be to let guilt within the walls indeed.

The terms are strict and absolute; there may not even be a kind word spoken to the child.

Often the young people go home in tears, or in a tearless rage, when they have seen the child and faced this terrible paradox. The may brood over it for weeks or years. But as time goes on they begin to realize that even if the child could be released, it would not get much good of its freedom: a little vague pleasure of warmth and food, no doubt, but little more. It is too degraded and imbecile to know any real joy. It has been afraid too long ever to be free of fear. Its habits are too uncouth for it to respond to humane treatment. Indeed, after so long it would probably be wretched without walls about it to protect it, and darkness for its eyes, and its own excrement to sit in. Their tears at the bitter injustice dry when they begin to perceive the terrible justice of reality, and to accept it. Yet it is their tears and anger, the trying of their generosity and the acceptance of their helplessness, which are perhaps the true sources of the splendor of their lives. Theirs is no vapid, irresponsible happiness. They know that they, like the child, are not free. They know compassion. It is the existence of the child, and their knowledge of its existence, that makes possible the nobility of their architecture, the poignancy of their music, the profundity of their science. It is because of the child that they are so gentle with children. They know that if the wretched one were not there snivelling in the dark, the other one, the flute-player, could make no joyful music as the young riders line up in their beauty for the race in the sunlight of the first morning of summer.

Now do you believe in them? Are they not more credible? But there is one more thing to tell, and this is quite incredible.

At times one of the adolescent girls or boys who go to see the child does not go home to weep or rage, does not, in fact, go home at all. Sometimes also a man or woman much older falls silent for a day or two, and then leaves home. These people go out into the street, and walk down the street alone. They keep walking, and walk straight out of the city of Omelas, through the beautiful gates. They keep walking across the farmlands of Omelas. Each one goes alone, youth or girl, man or woman. Night falls; the traveler must pass down village streets, between the houses with yellow-lit windows, and on out into the darkness of the fields. Each alone, they go west or north, towards the mountains. They go on. They leave Omelas, they walk ahead into the darkness, and they do not come back. The place they go towards is a place even less imaginable to most of us than the city of happiness. I cannot describe it at all. It is possible that it does not exist. But they seem to know where they are going, the ones who walk away from Omelas. □

◢ REREADING FOR UNDERSTANDING

1. At one point the narrator comments, "We have almost lost hold, we can no longer describe a happy man" (par. 3). Who are the "we" to whom the narrator refers?

2. Also in paragraph 3, the narrator suggests that "only pain is intellectual, only evil interesting. This is the treason of the artist: a refusal to admit the banality of evil and the terrible boredom of pain." What ironic commentary is the narrator directing against the people of Omelas in this passage? (Reread the whole piece with that question in mind before you answer.)

3. What is the narrator's attitude toward the people of Omelas and their values? How can you tell?

4. Why does the "child" have to be in the small room for the "happy" world of Omelas to exist?

◢ RESPONDING

1. Clearly Omelas is intended to be an allegory for our own culture. In what ways is the relationship between individual suffering and collective happiness portrayed in the story evident in the lives we lead? Try to think of specific comforts or luxuries you enjoy. From where and whom do they come? Does anyone suffer in order for you to enjoy those pleasures?

2. Why do a few individuals who see the child decide to leave Omelas?

3. Where do those who "walk away from Omelas" go?

◢ RESPONDING IN WRITING

Create a sequel to Omelas. Decide whether or not to rescue the child. Develop scenes and dialogue that will help a reader understand who should be responsible for the child (or why no one need feel responsible). Try to show why people leave Omelas and what they create wherever they go. If a fictional writing seems too complex, write an essay that explains what kinds of responsibility are absent from Omelas and what positive or negative effects result from the way the citizens of Omelas interact.

ALDO LEOPOLD

Aldo Leopold (1886–1948) is regarded by many as one of the founding fathers of the modern environmental movement. One of the first graduates of Yale's Forestry School, Leopold worked for the U.S. Forestry Services, finally becoming a professor of wildlife management at the University of Wisconsin in 1933. Leopold's ideas of a land ethic were compiled in a book he called *Sand County Almanac,* based on records of the biotic community in and around his small Wisconsin farm. Published after his death in 1948, *Sand County Almanac* presented a radical thesis for the time, that land use should be based on environmental rather than economic principles. His sense of humankind's responsibility for the land is captured in this straightforward observation: "A thing is right when it tends to preserve the integrity, stability, and beauty of the biotic community. It is wrong when it tends otherwise."

The Land Ethic

When god-like Odysseus returned from the wars in Troy, he hanged all on one rope a dozen slave-girls of his household whom he suspected of misbehavior during his absence.

This hanging involved no question of propriety. The girls were property. The disposal of property was then, as now, a matter of expediency, not of right and wrong.

Concepts of right and wrong were not lacking from Odysseus' Greece: witness the fidelity of his wife through the long years before at last his black-prowed galleys clove the wine-dark seas for home. The ethical structure of that day covered wives, but had not yet been extended to human chattels. During the three thousand years which have since elapsed, ethical criteria have been extended to many fields of conduct, with corresponding shrinkages in those judged by expediency only.

This extension of ethics, so far studied only by philosophers, is actually a process in ecological evolution. Its sequences may be described in ecological as well as in philosophical terms. An ethic, ecologically, is a limitation on freedom of action in the struggle for existence. An ethic, philosophically, is a differentiation of social from anti-social conduct. These are two definitions of one thing. The thing has its origin in the tendency of interdependent individuals or groups to evolve modes of co-operation. The ecologist calls these symbioses. Politics and economics are advanced symbioses in which the original free-for-all competition has been replaced, in part, by co-operative mechanisms with an ethical content.

The complexity of co-operative mechanisms has increased with population density, and with the efficiency of tools. It was simpler, for example, to define the anti-social uses of sticks and stones in the days of the mastodons than of bullets and billboards in the age of motors.

The first ethics dealt with the relation between individuals; the Mosaic Decalogue is an example. Later accretions dealt with the relation between the individual and society. The Golden Rule tries to integrate the individual to society; democracy to integrate social organization to the individual.

There is as yet no ethic dealing with man's relation to land and to the animals and plants which grow upon it. Land, like Odysseus' slave-girls, is still property. The land-relation is still strictly economic, entailing privileges but not obligations.

The extension of ethics to this third element in human environment is, if I read the evidence correctly, an evolutionary possibility and an ecological necessity. It is the third step in a sequence. The first two have already been taken. Individual thinkers since the days of Ezekiel and Isaiah have asserted that the despoliation of land is not only inexpedient but wrong. Society, however, has not yet affirmed their belief. I regard the present conservation movement as the embryo of such an affirmation.

An ethic may be regarded as a mode of guidance for meeting ecological situations so new or intricate, or involving such deferred reactions, that the path of social expediency is not discernible to the average individual. Animal instincts are modes of guidance for the individual in meeting such situations. Ethics are possibly a kind of community instinct in-the-making.

THE COMMUNITY CONCEPT

All ethics so far evolved rest upon a single premise: that the individual is a member of a community of interdependent parts. His instincts prompt him to compete for his place in the community, but his ethics prompt him also to co-operate (perhaps in order that there may be a place to compete for).

The land ethic simply enlarges the boundaries of the community to include soils, waters, plants, and animals, or collectively: the land.

This sounds simple: do we not already sing our love for and obligation to the land of the free and the home of the brave? Yes, but just what and whom do we love? Certainly not the soil, which we are sending helter-skelter down-river. Certainly not the waters, which we assume have no function except to turn turbines, float barges, and carry off sewage. Certainly not the plants, of which we exterminate whole communities without batting an eye. Certainly not the animals, of which we have already extirpated many of the largest and most beautiful species. A land ethic of course cannot prevent the alteration, management, and use of these "resources," but it does affirm their right to continued existence, and, at least in spots, their continued existence in a natural state.

In short, a land ethic changes the role of *Homo sapiens* from conqueror of the land-community to plain member and citizen of it. It implies respect for his fellow-members, and also respect for the community as such.   13

In human history, we have learned (I hope) that the conqueror role is eventually self-defeating. Why? Because it is implicit in such a role that the conqueror knows, *ex cathedra*, just what makes the community clock tick, and just what and who is valuable, and what and who is worthless, in community life. It always turns out that he knows neither, and this is why his conquests eventually defeat themselves.   14

In the biotic community, a parallel situation exists. Abraham knew exactly what the land was for: it was to drip milk and honey into Abraham's mouth. At the present moment, the assurance with which we regard this assumption is inverse to the degree of our education.   15

The ordinary citizen today assumes that science knows what makes the community clock tick; the scientist is equally sure that he does not. He knows that the biotic mechanism is so complex that its workings may never be fully understood.   16

That man is, in fact, only a member of a biotic team is shown by an ecological interpretation of history. Many historical events, hitherto explained solely in terms of human enterprise, were actually biotic interactions between people and land. The characteristics of the land determined the facts quite as potently as the characteristics of the men who lived on it. ▢   17

◪ REREADING FOR UNDERSTANDING

1. Why does Leopold begin his essay on environmental responsibility with an allusion to the return of Odysseus from the Trojan Wars? What point about responsibility in general does Leopold make with the Odysseus story? What particular point from the story can we apply to our responsibility toward the land?

2. Leopold must overcome his readers' potential hostility or indifference to the notion of a "land ethic." What strategies does he employ to engage his readers' interest, to give credibility to his voice? From your perspective, how effective are those strategies?

◪ RESPONDING

1. In the opening paragraphs, Leopold presents the dramatic example of Odysseus hanging his slave-girls for their "misbehavior"—after all, his slaves were

his property to do with as he chose. From that example, Leopold makes the point that what was acceptable, even responsible, behavior at one time becomes unacceptable and irresponsible behavior at another time. Certainly, no one in our society would be hanged for "misbehaving." Our ethical standards have evolved over time: we agree that such behavior would be grossly inappropriate, even inhuman. Can you imagine an evolution of our ethics that might change our definition of property? We own land, trees, water, and we have a "right" (our current ethic) to do what we want with our property. Or do we? Should we push along the evolution of our ethic, our sense of responsibility toward property like land and animals. Or is our current ethic the culmination of the evolutionary process?

2. We want, says Leopold, to compete for a place in the community. We all want to succeed, to be in charge, to move up the ladder. At the same time, we must cooperate within our communities. At work, the desire to rise must be balanced by the need to cooperate with other employees. This same need for balance characterizes other communities like the family, male/female relationships, sports teams, labor unions, political parties, and on and on. How effectively does our culture balance the desires of individuals with the needs of communities? Consider, for instance, the various natural communities of land and animals. How well do we balance our desires within "the biotic community"? Or consider your family as a community. How easy (or necessary) is it to balance your desires with your responsibilities toward your siblings and parents?

AYN RAND

Born Alice Rosenbaum in St. Petersburg, Russia, in 1905, Ayn Rand died in New York in 1982. In between, she led an amazing life. She left Russia after the Bolshevik Revolution, coming to the United States in 1926 with a degree in history and a desire to be a writer, even though she spoke almost no English. A few months after her arrival, she went to Hollywood. On her second day there, filmmaker Cecil B. De Mille gave her work as an extra. Rand later became a successful novelist and screenwriter, with at least three of her novels (We the Living, The Fountainhead, and Atlas Shrugged) selling multimillion editions. At age 52, she launched a new career as a self-appointed spokesperson for capitalism and individual rights. Her basic ideas about individual rights were incorporated in all of her fiction and public lectures. She attacked communism or any collectivist movement. In her fiction, lectures, and other writings, Rand made many enemies among both liberal and conservative intellectuals by asserting that rational self-interest is the only basis for freedom.

Because of her first-hand experiences with Bolshevism, Rand felt strongly that the protection of individual rights was essential for individual liberty. Keep that in mind as you read her piece.

Man's Rights

If one wishes to advocate a free society—that is, capitalism—one must re-   1
alize that its indispensable foundation is the principle of individual rights.
If one wishes to uphold individual rights, one must realize that capitalism
is the only system that can uphold and protect them. And if one wishes to
gauge the relationship of freedom to the goals of today's intellectuals, one may
gauge it by the fact that the concept of individual rights is evaded, distorted,
perverted and seldom discussed, most conspicuously seldom by the so-called
"conservatives."

"Rights" are a moral concept—the concept that provides a logical transi-   2
tion from the principles guiding an individual's actions to the principles guiding his relationship with others—the concept that preserves and protects
individual morality in a social context—the link between the moral code of a
man and the legal code of a society, between ethics and politics. *Individual
rights are the means of subordinating society to moral law.*

Every political system is based on some code of ethics. The dominant   3
ethics of mankind's history were variants of the altruist-collectivist doctrine
which subordinated the individual to some higher authority, either mystical or
social. Consequently, most political systems were variants of the same statist
tyranny, differing only in degree, not in basic principle, limited only by the
accidents of tradition, of chaos, of bloody strife and periodic collapse. Under
all such systems, morality was a code applicable to the individual, but not to
society. Society was placed *outside* the moral law, as its embodiment or source
or exclusive interpreter—and the inculcation of self-sacrificial devotion to social
duty was regarded as the main purpose of ethics in man's earthly existence.

Since there is no such entity as "society," since society is only a number of   4
individual men, this meant, in practice, that the rulers of society were exempt
from moral law; subject only to traditional rituals, they held total power and
exacted blind obedience—on the implicit principle of: "The good is that which
is good for society (or for the tribe, the race, the nation), and the ruler's edicts
are its voice on earth."

This was true of all statist systems, under all variants of the altruist-   5
collectivist ethics, mystical or social. "The Divine Right of Kings" summarizes
the political theory of the first—"*Vox populi, vox dei*" of the second. As witness:
the theocracy of Egypt, with the Pharaoh as an embodied god—the unlimited
majority rule or *democracy* of Athens—the welfare state run by the Emperors
of Rome—the Inquisition of the late Middle Ages—the absolute monarchy of
France—the welfare state of Bismarck's Prussia—the gas chambers of Nazi
Germany—the slaughterhouse of the Soviet Union.

All these political systems were expressions of the altruist-collectivist   6
ethics—and their common characteristic is the fact that society stood above the
moral law, as an omnipotent, sovereign whim worshiper. Thus, politically, all
these systems were variants of an *amoral* society.

The most profoundly revolutionary achievement of the United States of   7
America was *the subordination of society to moral law.*

The principle of man's individual rights represented the extension of   8
morality into the social system—as a limitation on the power of the state, as
man's protection against the brute force of the collective, as the subordination
of *might* to *right*. The United States was the first *moral* society in history.

All previous systems had regarded man as a sacrificial means to the ends of   9
others, and society as an end in itself. The United States regarded man as an end
in himself, and society as a means to the peaceful, orderly, *voluntary* coexistence
of individuals. All previous systems had held that man's life belongs to society,
that society can dispose of him in any way it pleases, and that any freedom he
enjoys is his only by favor, by the *permission* of society, which may be revoked
at any time. The United States held that man's life is his by *right* (which means:
by moral principle and by his nature), that a right is the property of an individual, that society as such has no rights, and that the only moral purpose of a
government is the protection of individual rights.

A "right" is a moral principle defining and sanctioning a man's freedom of   10
action in a social context. There is only *one* fundamental right (all the others are
its consequences or corollaries): a man's right to his own life. Life is a process of
self-sustaining and self-generated action; the right to life means the right to
engage in self-sustaining and self-generated action—which means: the freedom
to take all the actions required by the nature of a rational being for the support,
the furtherance, the fulfillment and the enjoyment of his own life. (Such is the
meaning of the right to life, liberty and the pursuit of happiness.)

The concept of a "right" pertains only to action—specifically, to freedom of   11
action. It means freedom from physical compulsion, coercion or interference by
other men.

Thus, for every individual, a right is the moral sanction of a *positive*—of his   12
freedom to act on his own judgment, for his own goals, by his own *voluntary,
uncoerced* choice. As to his neighbors, his rights impose no obligations on them
except of a *negative* kind: to abstain from violating his rights.

The right to life is the source of all rights—and the right to property is their   13
only implementation. Without property rights, no other rights are possible.
Since man has to sustain his life by his own effort, the man who has no right to
the product of his effort has no means to sustain his life. The man who produces while others dispose of his product, is a slave.

Bear in mind that the right to property is a right to action, like all the   14
others: it is not the right *to an object*, but to the action and the consequences of
producing or earning that object. It is not a guarantee that a man *will* earn any
property, but only a guarantee that he will own it if he earns it. It is the right to
gain, to keep, to use and to dispose of material values.

The concept of individual rights is so new in human history that most   15
men have not grasped it fully to this day. In accordance with the two theories
of ethics, the mystical or the social, some men assert that rights are a gift of
God—others, that rights are a gift of society. But, in fact, the source of rights
is man's nature.

The Declaration of Independence stated that men "are endowed by their   16
Creator with certain unalienable rights." Whether one believes that man is the
product of a Creator or of nature, the issue of man's origin does not alter the

fact that he is an entity of a specific kind—a rational being—that he cannot function successfully under coercion, and that rights are a necessary condition of his particular mode of survival.

"The source of man's rights is not divine law or congressional law, but the 17
law of identity. A is A—and Man is Man. *Rights* are conditions of existence required by man's nature for his proper survival. If man is to live on earth, it is *right* for him to use his mind, it is *right* to act on his own free judgment, it is *right* to work for his values and to keep the product of his work. If life on earth is his purpose, he has a *right* to live as a rational being: nature forbids him the irrational." (*Atlas Shrugged.*)

To violate man's rights means to compel him to act against his own judg- 18
ment, or to expropriate his values. Basically, there is only one way to do it: by the use of physical force. There are two potential violators of man's rights: the criminals and the government. The great achievement of the United States was to draw a distinction between these two—by forbidding to the second the legalized version of the activities of the first.

The Declaration of Independence laid down the principle that "to secure 19
these rights, governments are instituted among men." This provided the only valid justification of a government and defined its only proper purpose: to protect man's rights by protecting him from physical violence.

Thus the government's function was changed from the role of ruler to the 20
role of servant. The government was set to protect man from criminals—and the Constitution was written to protect man from the government. The Bill of Rights was not directed against private citizens, but against the government—as an explicit declaration that individual rights supersede any public or social power.

The result was the pattern of a civilized society which—for the brief span 21
of some hundred and fifty years—America came close to achieving. A civilized society is one in which physical force is banned from human relationships—in which the government, acting as a policeman, may use force *only* in retaliation and *only* against those who initiate its use.

This was the essential meaning and intent of America's political philos- 22
ophy, implicit in the principle of individual rights. But it was not formulated explicitly, nor fully accepted nor consistently practiced.

America's inner contradiction was the altruist-collectivist ethics. Altruism 23
is incompatible with freedom, with capitalism and with individual rights. One cannot combine the pursuit of happiness with the moral status of a sacrificial animal.

It was the concept of individual rights that had given birth to a free society. 24
It was with the destruction of individual rights that the destruction of freedom had to begin.

A collectivist tyranny dare not enslave a country by an outright confisca- 25
tion of its values, material or moral. It has to be done by a process of internal corruption. Just as in the material realm the plundering of a country's wealth is accomplished by inflating the currency—so today one may witness the process of inflation being applied to the realm of rights. The process entails such a growth of newly promulgated "rights" that people do not notice the fact that

the meaning of the concept is being reversed. Just as bad money drives out good money, so these "printing-press rights" negate authentic rights.

Consider the curious fact that never has there been such a proliferation, all 26 over the world, of two contradictory phenomena: of alleged new "rights" and of slave-labor camps.

The "gimmick" was the switch of the concept of rights from the political to 27 the economic realm.

The Democratic Party platform of 1960 summarizes the switch boldly and 28 explicitly. It declares that a Democratic Administration "will reaffirm the economic bill of rights which Franklin Roosevelt wrote into our national conscience sixteen years ago."

Bear clearly in mind the meaning of the concept of *"rights"* when you read 29 the list which that platform offers:

"1. The right to a useful and remunerative job in the industries or shops or farms or mines of the nation.

"2. The right to earn enough to provide adequate food and clothing and recreation.

"3. The right of every farmer to raise and sell his products at a return which will give him and his family a decent living.

"4. The right of every businessman, large and small, to trade in an atmosphere of freedom from unfair competition and domination by monopolies at home and abroad.

"5. The right of every family to a decent home.

"6. The right to adequate medical care and the opportunity to achieve and enjoy good health.

"7. The right to adequate protection from the economic fears of old age, sickness, accidents and unemployment.

"8. The right to a good education."

A single question added to each of the above eight clauses would make the 30 issue clear: *At whose expense?*

Jobs, food, clothing, recreation (!), homes, medical care, education, etc., do 31 not grow in nature. These are man-made values—goods and services produced by men. *Who* is to provide them?

If some men are entitled *by right* to the products of the work of others, it 32 means that those others are deprived of rights and condemned to slave labor.

Any alleged "right" of one man, which necessitates the violation of the 33 rights of another, is not and cannot be a right.

No man can have a right to impose an unchosen obligation, an unrewarded 34 duty or an involuntary servitude on another man. There can be no such thing as *"the right to enslave."*

A right does not include the material implementation of that right by 35 other men; it includes only the freedom to earn that implementation by one's own effort.

Observe, in this context, the intellectual precision of the Founding Fathers: 36 they spoke of the right to *the pursuit* of happiness—*not* of the right to happiness. It means that a man has the right to take the actions he deems necessary to achieve his happiness; it does *not* mean that others must make him happy.

The right to life means that a man has the right to support his life by his 37 own work (on any economic level, as high as his ability will carry him); it does *not* mean that others must provide him with the necessities of life.

The right to property means that a man has the right to take the economic 38 actions necessary to earn property, to use it and to dispose of it; it does *not* mean that others must provide him with property.

The right of free speech means that a man has the right to express his ideas 39 without danger of suppression, interference or punitive action by the government. It does *not* mean that others must provide him with a lecture hall, a radio station or a printing press through which to express his ideas.

Any undertaking that involves more than one man, requires the *voluntary* 40 consent of every participant. Every one of them has the *right* to make his own decision, but none has the right to force his decision on the others.

There is no such thing as "a right to a job"—there is only the right of free 41 trade, that is: a man's right to take a job if another man chooses to hire him. There is no "right to a home," only the right of free trade: the right to build a home or to buy it. There are no "rights to a 'fair' wage or a 'fair' price" if no one chooses to pay it, to hire a man or to buy his product. There are no "rights of consumers" to milk, shoes, movies or champagne if no producers choose to manufacture such items (there is only the right to manufacture them oneself). There are no "rights" of special groups, there are no "rights of farmers, of workers, of businessmen, of employees, of employers, of the old, of the young, of the unborn." There are only *the Rights of Man*—rights possessed by every individual man and by *all* men as individuals.

Property rights and the right of free trade are man's only "economic rights" 42 (they are, in fact, *political* rights)—and there can be no such thing as "an *economic* bill of rights." But observe that the advocates of the latter have all but destroyed the former.

Remember that rights are moral principles which define and protect a 43 man's freedom of action, but impose no obligations on other men. Private citizens are not a threat to one another's rights or freedom. A private citizen who resorts to physical force and violates the rights of others is a criminal—and men have legal protection against him.

Criminals are a small minority in any age or country. And the harm they 44 have done to mankind is infinitesimal when compared to the horrors—the bloodshed, the wars, the persecutions, the confiscations, the famines, the enslavements, the wholesale destructions—perpetrated by mankind's governments. Potentially, a government is the most dangerous threat to man's rights: it holds a legal monopoly on the use of physical force against legally disarmed victims. When unlimited and unrestricted by individual rights, a government is men's deadliest enemy. It is not as protection against *private* actions, but against governmental actions that the Bill of Rights was written.

Now observe the process by which that protection is being destroyed.   45

The process consists of ascribing to private citizens the specific violations   46
constitutionally forbidden to the government (which private citizens have no
power to commit) and thus freeing the government from all restrictions. The
switch is becoming progressively more obvious in the field of free speech. For
years, the collectivists have been propagating the notion that a private individual's refusal to finance an opponent is a violation of the opponent's right of free
speech and an act of "censorship."

It is "censorship," they claim, if a newspaper refuses to employ or publish   47
writers whose ideas are diametrically opposed to its policy.

It is "censorship," they claim, if businessmen refuse to advertise in a maga-   48
zine that denounces, insults and smears them.

It is "censorship," they claim, if a TV sponsor objects to some outrage per-   49
petrated on a program he is financing—such as the incident of Alger Hiss being
invited to denounce former Vice-President Nixon.

And then there is Newton N. Minow who declares: "There is censorship by   50
ratings, by advertisers, by networks, by affiliates which reject programming
offered to their areas." It is the same Mr. Minow who threatens to revoke the
license of any station that does not comply with his views on programming—
and who claims that *that* is not censorship.

Consider the implications of such a trend.   51

"Censorship" is a term pertaining only to governmental action. No private   52
action is censorship. No private individual or agency can silence a man or sup-
press a publication; only the government can do so. The freedom of speech of
private individuals includes the right not to agree, not to listen and not to
finance one's own antagonists.

But according to such doctrines as the "economic bill of rights," an indi-   53
vidual has no right to dispose of his own material means by the guidance of his
own convictions—and must hand over his money indiscriminately to any
speakers or propagandists, who have a "right" to his property.

This means that the ability to provide the material tools for the expression   54
of ideas deprives a man of the right to hold any ideas. It means that a publisher
has to publish books he considers worthless, false or evil—that a TV sponsor
has to finance commentators who choose to affront his convictions—that the
owner of a newspaper must turn his editorial pages over to any young hooligan
who clamors for the enslavement of the press. It means that one group of men
acquires the "right" to unlimited license—while another group is reduced to
helpless irresponsibility.

But since it is obviously impossible to provide every claimant with a job, a   55
microphone or a newspaper column, *who* will determine the "distribution" of
"economic rights" and select the recipients, when the owners' right to choose
has been abolished? Well, Mr. Minow has indicated *that* quite clearly.

And if you make the mistake of thinking that this applies only to big prop-   56
erty owners, you had better realize that the theory of "economic rights" includes
the "right" of every would-be playwright, every beatnik poet, every noise-
composer and every nonobjective artist (who have political pull) to the financial

support you did not give them when you did not attend their shows. What else is the meaning of the project to spend your tax money on subsidized art?

And while people are clamoring about "economic rights," the concept of 57 political rights is vanishing. It is forgotten that the right of free speech means the freedom to advocate one's views and to bear the possible consequences, including disagreement with others, opposition, unpopularity and lack of support. The political function of "the right of free speech" is to protect dissenters and unpopular minorities from forcible suppression—*not* to guarantee them the support, advantages and rewards of a popularity they have not gained.

The Bill of Rights reads: "Congress shall make no law . . . abridging the free- 58 dom of speech, or of the press . . ." It does not demand that private citizens provide a microphone for the man who advocates their destruction, or a passkey for the burglar who seeks to rob them, or a knife for the murderer who wants to cut their throats.

Such is the state of one of today's most crucial issues: *political* rights versus 59 "*economic* rights." It's either-or. One destroys the other. But there are, in fact, no "economic rights," no "collective rights," no "public-interest rights." The term "individual rights" is a redundancy: there is no other kind of rights and no one else to possess them.

Those who advocate *laissez-faire* capitalism are the only advocates of man's 60 rights. ☐

◢ REREADING FOR UNDERSTANDING

1. What does Rand mean when she says (par. 15) rights are not a gift of God nor of society but instead that rights come from "man's nature"? The explanation lies in paragraphs 30–40 and is key to understanding Rand's perspective on "rights."

2. Why does Rand attack the eight "economic" rights listed in the 1960 Democratic Party platform? How is her attack related to what she calls "altruistic-collectivist" ideas?

3. Explain what Rand means by "political rights" versus "economic rights." Why is the difference significant? Do you agree with her distinction? If not, how would you categorize rights?

◢ RESPONDING

1. Many students might believe that they have a right to a college education. Would Rand call this a political right, or would she view such a notion as false, as one of those "economic rights" that she insists do not exist? As you consider this question, you may wish to read Jonathan Kozol's essay in Unit Three; Kozol argues that everyone *is* entitled to an equal education, that a public school in the Bronx should have the same facilities and curriculum as the private academy Exeter. Speculate on Rand's reaction to such an idea.

2. Do you agree with Rand that collective altruism "is incompatible with freedom, with capitalism and with individual rights" (par. 23)? Consider a government program like Social Security, for example, which mandates that all workers contribute part of their wages toward sustaining the elderly. Does such a program threaten our freedom? Is it compatible or incompatible with our vision of ourselves as a democracy? Can you think of other examples of collective altruism?

MARIAN WRIGHT EDELMAN

Marian Wright Edelman (1939–   ) is an African-American lawyer (Yale, 1963) who has spent much of her career working for the betterment of the poor—children, in particular. Since founding the Children's Defense Fund in 1968, Edelman has worked continuously in and out of Washington to help poor children move out of poverty and into the mainstream of economic and social life. In the latter half of the 1990s, Edelman's sense of social responsibility harkens back to the late sixties and early seventies. As you read through this essay, reflect on your own sense of responsibility toward others in your community.

If the Child Is Safe

A Struggle for America's Conscience and Future

If the child is safe everyone is safe.
—G. CAMPBELL MORGAN,
"THE CHILDREN'S PLAYGROUND IN THE CITY OF GOD,"
THE WESTMINSTER PULPIT (CIRCA 1908)

There is no finer investment for any country than putting milk into babies.
—WINSTON CHURCHILL

The most important work to help our children is done quietly—in our homes and neighborhoods, our parishes and community organizations. No government can love a child and no policy can substitute for a family's care, but clearly families can be helped or hurt in their irreplaceable roles. Government can either support or undermine families as they cope with the moral, social, and economic stresses of caring for children.

There has been an unfortunate, unnecessary, and unreal polarization in discussions of how best to help families. Some emphasize the primary role of moral values and personal responsibility, the sacrifices to be made and the personal behaviors to be avoided, but often ignore or de-emphasize the broader forces which hurt families, e.g., the impact of economics, discrimination, and anti-family policies. Others emphasize the social and economic forces that undermine families and the responsibility of government to meet human needs, but they often neglect the importance of basic values and personal responsibility.

The undeniable fact is that our children's future is shaped both by the values of their parents and the policies of our nation.

—PUTTING CHILDREN AND FAMILIES FIRST:
A CHALLENGE FOR OUR CHURCH, NATION, AND WORLD,
NATIONAL CONFERENCE OF CATHOLIC BISHOPS
PASTORAL LETTER, NOVEMBER 1991

The 1990s' struggle is for America's conscience and future—a future that is being determined right now in the bodies and minds and spirits of *every* American child—white, African American, Latino, Asian American, Native American, rich, middle class, and poor. Many of the battles for this future will not be as dramatic as Gettysburg or Vietnam or Desert Storm, but they will shape our place in the twenty-first century no less.

Ironically, as Communism is collapsing all around the world, the American Dream is collapsing all around America for millions of children, youths, and families in all racial and income groups. American is pitted against American as economic uncertainty and downturn increase our fears, our business failures, our poverty rates, our racial divisions, and the dangers of political demagoguery.

Family and community values and supports are disintegrating among all races and income groups, reflecting the spiritual as well as economic poverty of our nation. All our children are growing up today in an ethically polluted nation where instant sex without responsibility, instant gratification without effort, instant solutions without sacrifice, getting rather than giving, and hoarding rather than sharing are the too-frequent signals of our mass media, business, and political life.

All our children are threatened by pesticides and toxic wastes and chemicals polluting the air, water, and earth. No parent can shut out completely the pollution of our airwaves and popular culture, which glorify excessive violence, profligate consumption, easy sex and greed, and depict deadly alcohol and tobacco products as fun, glamorous, and macho.

All our children are affected by the absence of enough heroines and heroes in public and daily life, as the standard for success for too many Americans has become personal greed rather than common good, and as it has become enough to just get by rather than do one's best.

All our children are affected by escalating violence fueled by unbridled trafficking in guns and in the drugs that are pervasive in suburb, rural area, and inner city alike.

Young families of all races, on whom we count to raise healthy children for America's future, are in extraordinary trouble. They have suffered since the early 1970s a frightening cycle of plummeting earnings, a near doubling of birth rates among unmarried women, increasing numbers of single-parent families, falling income—the median income of young families with children fell by 26 percent between 1973 and 1989—and skyrocketing poverty rates.

Forty percent of all children in families with a household head under thirty are poor. While many middle-class youths and young families see the future as a choice between a house and a child, many undereducated, jobless, poor youths and young adults trapped in inner-city war zones see the future as a choice between prison or death at the hands of gangs and drug dealers.

More and more Americans feel their children are being left behind. But poor children suffer most, and their numbers are growing—841,000 in 1990 alone. They are the small, faceless victims who have no one to speak and fight for them. We were mesmerized by the 1987 death of Lisa Steinberg, a child whose adoption was never completed or abuse detected by our overburdened, inadequate child welfare system. We cheered when Jessica McClure was rescued from an open well shaft in the yard of an unregulated family day care center run by a relative, a danger she should not have come close to in the first place. But when eight-month-old Shamal Jackson died in New York City from low birthweight, poor nutrition, and viral infection—from poverty and homelessness—we didn't hear much about him. During his short life, he slept in shelters with strangers, in hospitals, in welfare hotels, in the welfare office, and in the subways he and his mother rode late at night when there was no place else to go. In the richest nation on earth, he never slept in an apartment or house. Nor have we heard about two-pound "Jason" fighting for his life at Children's Hospital in Washington, D.C., or about thousands of other babies in similar neonatal intensive care wards all over America. At birth—three months before he was due—Jason weighed just over one pound. He lives because tubes connect his lungs and every available vein to the many machines that are needed to feed him and keep him warm and enable him to take his next breath. He has a heart problem and has already suffered seizures because of damage to his nervous system caused by bleeding into his head—damage that, if he lives, will probably be permanent.

What exactly led to Jason's premature birth will never be known. We do know, however, that unless a mother receives early and ongoing prenatal care, conditions that lead to prematurity cannot be detected or treated. A third of our mothers do not receive the care they need because our health care system, unlike that of every other major industrialized nation, does not provide universal basic coverage for mothers and children.

Remember these children behind the statistics. All over America, they are the small human tragedies who will determine the quality and safety and economic security of America's future as much as your and my children will. The decision you and I and our leaders must make is whether we are going to invest in every American child or continue to produce thousands of school dropouts, teen parents, welfare recipients, criminals—many of whom are alienated from a society that turns a deaf ear to the basic human needs and longings of every child.

If recent trends continue, by the end of the century poverty will overtake one in every four children, and the share of children living with single parents will also rise. One in every five births and more than one in three black births in the year 2000 will be to a mother who did not receive cost-effective early prenatal care. One of every five twenty-year-old women will be a mother, and more than four out of five of those young mothers will not be married. And the social security system that all of us count on to support us in our old age will depend on the contributions of fewer children—children we are failing today.

If we do not act immediately to protect America's children and change the   12
misguided national choices that leave too many of them unhealthy, unhoused, ill-fed, and undereducated, during the next four years

1,080,000	American babies will be born at low birthweight, multiplying their risk of death or disability,
43,619	babies will die before their first birthday,
4,400,000	babies will be born to unmarried women,
2,000,000	babies will be born to teen mothers,
15,856	children 19 or younger will die by firearms,
2,784	children younger than 5 will die by homicide,
9,208	children 19 or younger will commit suicide,
1,620,000	young people ages 16 to 24 will fail to complete high school,
3,780,000	young people will finish high school but not enroll in college,
599,076	children younger than 18 will be arrested for alcohol-related offenses, 359,600 for drug offenses, and 338,292 for violent crimes,
7,911,532	public school students will be suspended, and
3,600,000	infants will be born into poverty.

It is a spiritually impoverished nation that permits infants and children to be the poorest Americans. Over 13 million children in our rich land go without the basic amenities of life—more than the total population of Illinois, Pennsylvania, or Florida. If every citizen in the state of Florida became poor, the president would declare a national disaster. Yet he and Congress have yet to recognize child and family poverty and financial insecurity as the national disaster it is and to attack it with a fraction of the zeal and shared commitment we now apply to digging out after a devastating hurricane or earthquake or fire. We moved more than 1.7 million elderly persons out of poverty in the three years following the 1972 revisions to the Social Security Act that indexed senior citizens' benefits to inflation. Surely we can provide families with children equitable treatment.

It is a morally lost nation that is unable and unwilling to disarm our chil-   13
dren and those who kill our children in their school buses, strollers, yards, and schools, in movie theaters, and in McDonald's. Death stalks America's playgrounds and streets without a declaration of war—or even a sustained declaration of concern by our president, Congress, governors, state and local elected officials, and citizens.

Every day, 135,000 children bring a gun to school. In 1987, 415,000 violent   14
crimes occurred in and around schools. Some inner-city children are exposed to violence so routinely that they exhibit post-traumatic stress symptoms similar to those that plague many Vietnam combat veterans. Still, our country is

unwilling to take semiautomatic machine guns out of the hands of its citizens. Where are the moral guerrillas and protesters crying out that life at home is as precious as life abroad? Isn't it time for a critical mass of Americans to join our law enforcement agencies and force our political leaders to halt the proliferation of guns? Every day twenty-three teens and young adults are killed by firearms in America.

In response to a distant tyrant, we sent hundreds of thousands of American mothers and fathers, sons and daughters, husbands and wives, sisters and brothers to the Persian Gulf. According to Secretary of State James Baker, the Gulf War was fought to protect our "life style" and standard of living and the rights of the Kuwaiti people. No deficit or recession was allowed to stand in the way. How, then, can we reconcile our failure to engage equally the enemies of poverty and violence and family disintegration within our own nation? When are we going to mobilize and send troops to fight for the "life style" of the 100,000 American children who are homeless each night, to fight for the standard of living of thousands of young families whose earning capacity is eroding and who are struggling to buy homes, pay off college loans, and find and afford child care? Where are the leaders coming to the rescue of millions of poor working- and middle-class families fighting to hold together their fragile households on declining wages and jobs? Why are they not acting to help the one in six families with children headed by a working single mother—29 percent of whom are poor? Isn't it time to tell our leaders to bail out our young families with the same zeal as they bailed out failed thrift and banking institutions to the tune of an estimated $115 billion by 1992?

What do we *really* value as Americans when the president's 1992 budget proposed only $100 million to increase Head Start for *one year* and no addition for child care for working families, but $500 million *each day* for Desert Storm, $90 million *each day* to bail out profligate savings and loan institutions, and hundreds of millions more to give capital gains tax breaks to the rich? Between 1979 and 1989, the average income (adjusted for inflation) of the bottom fifth of families dropped by 6 percent while that of the top fifth surged upward by 17 percent. The poorest fifth of American families with children lost 21 percent of their income.

Why were we able to put hundreds of thousands of troops and support personnel in Saudi Arabia within a few months to fight Saddam Hussein when we are unable to mobilize hundreds of teachers or doctors and nurses and social workers for desperately underserved inner cities and rural areas to fight the tyranny of poverty and ignorance and child neglect and abuse?

Isn't it time for the president and Congress and all of us to redefine our national security and invest as much time and leadership and energy to solving our problems at home as we do to our problems abroad?

It is an ethically confused nation that has allowed truth-telling and moral example to become devalued commodities. Too many of us hold to the philosophy that "government is not the solution to our problems, government is the problem." If government is seen as an illegitimate enterprise, if the public purposes of one's job are not considered a high calling, and if government has no purpose other than its own destruction, the restraints against unethical behavior in both the public and private sectors quickly erode. As a result, for every Michael Deaver and for every Elliot Abrams, from the public sector, there is an Ivan Boesky or a Reverend Jim Bakker in the private sector. If the only principle our society adheres to is economist Adam Smith's "Invisible Hand," it leaves little or no room for the human hand, or the hand of God, whom the prophet Micah said enjoined us "to be fair and just and merciful." There is a hollowness at the core of a society if its members share no common purpose, no mutual goals, no joint vision—nothing to believe in except self-aggrandizement.

Isn't it time for us to hold our political leaders to their professed beliefs and   20
promises about getting children ready for school and providing them health care and education?

It is a dangerously short-sighted nation that fantasizes absolute self-sufficiency   21
as the only correct way of life. Throughout our history, we have given government help to our people and then have forgotten that fact when it came time to celebrate our people's achievements. Two hundred years ago, Congress granted federal lands to the states to help maintain public schools. In 1862, President Lincoln signed the Morrill Land-Grant Act, granting land for colleges. The first food voucher and energy assistance programs came, not during the New Deal or the War on Poverty, but at the end of the Civil War, when Congress and President Lincoln created the Freedman's Bureau. Federal help for vaccinations, vocational education, and maternal health began, not with Kennedy, Johnson, and Carter, but under Madison, Wilson, and Harding, respectively.

Our parents, grandparents, and great-grandparents benefited from this   22
government help just as we all do today. Only the most blind of economists could doubt that American prosperity, like Japan's, is built on the synergistic relations between government and private initiative. But it is some of the most blind economists, political scientists, and "moral philosophers" who have the ear of many of our leaders or are themselves political leaders. Too many of them suffer from the peculiarly American amnesia or hypocrisy that wants us to think that poor and middle-class families must fend entirely for themselves; that makes us forget how government helps us all, regardless of class; and that makes us believe that the government is simply wasting its billions supporting a wholly dependent, self-perpetuating class of poor people, while doing nothing but taxing the rest of us.

Chrysler and Lee Iacocca didn't do it alone. Defense contractors don't do   23
it alone. Welfare queens can't hold a candle to corporate kings in raiding the public purse. Most wealthy and middle-class families don't do it alone. Yet some begrudge the same security for low- and moderate-income families with children who must grow up healthy, educated, and productive to support our aging population.

The president and Congress and public must take the time and have the   24
courage to make specific choices and not wield an indiscriminate budget ax or hide behind uniform but unjust freezes of current inequalities. They must also take time to distinguish between programs that work (like immunization, preventive health care, and Head Start) and programs that don't (like the B2 stealth bomber). They must apply the same standards of accountability for programs

benefiting the rich and poor and middle class alike. They must hold the Pentagon to the same standards of efficiency as social programs. And isn't it time for the president and Congress to invest more in preventing rather than trying to mop up problems after the fact? Isn't it time to reassess national investment priorities in light of changing national and world needs? Does it make sense for our federal government to spend each hour this fiscal year $33.7 million on national defense, $23.6 million on the national debt, $8.7 million on the savings and loan bailout, $2.9 million on education, and $1.8 million on children's health?

Making hard choices and investing in our own people may help restore the   25
confidence of citizens in government. The overarching task of leadership today in every segment of American society is to give our youths, and all Americans, a sense that we can be engaged in enterprises that lend meaning to life, that we can regain control over our families and our national destiny, and that we can make a positive difference individually and collectively in building a decent, safe nation and world.

America cannot afford to waste resources by failing to prevent and curb the   26
national human deficit, which cripples our children's welfare today and costs billions in later remedial and custodial dollars. Every dollar we invest in preventive health care for mothers and children saves more than $3 later. Every dollar put into quality preschool education like Head Start saves $4.75 later. It costs more than twice as much to place a child in foster care as to provide family preservation services. The question is not whether we can afford to invest in every child; it is whether we can afford not to. At a time when future demographic trends guarantee a shortage of young adults who will be workers, soldiers, leaders, and parents, America cannot afford to waste a single child. With unprecedented economic competition from abroad and changing patterns of production at home that demand higher basic educational skills, America cannot wait another minute to do whatever is needed to ensure that today's and tomorrow's workers are well prepared rather than useless and alienated— whatever their color.

We cannot go back and change the last decade's birth rates. But we can pre-   27
vent and reduce the damages to our children and families and ensure every child a healthy start, a head start, and a fair start right now. In the waning years of the twentieth century, doing what is right for children and doing what is necessary to save our national economic skin have converged.

When the new century dawns with new global economic and military   28
challenges, America will be ready to compete economically and lead morally only if we

1. stop cheating and neglecting our children for selfish, short-sighted, personal, and political gain;

2. stop clinging to our racial past and recognize that America's ideals, future, and fate are as inextricably intertwined with the fate of its poor and non-white children as with its privileged and white ones;

3. love our children more than we fear each other and our perceived or real external enemies;

4. acquire the discipline to invest preventively and systematically in all of our children *now* in order to reap a better trained work force and more stable future *tomorrow;*

5. curb the desires of the overprivileged so that the survival needs of the less privileged may be met, and spend less on weapons of death and more on lifelines of constructive development for our citizens;

6. set clear, national, state, city, community, and personal goals for child survival and development, and invest whatever leadership, commitment, time, money, and sustained effort are needed to achieve them;

7. struggle to begin to live our lives in less selfish and more purposeful ways, redefining success by national and individual character and service rather than by national consumption and the superficial barriers of race and class.

The mounting crisis of children and families is a rebuke to everything   29
America professes to be. While the cost of repairing our crumbling national foundation will be expensive in more ways than one, the cost of not repairing it, or of patching cosmetically, may be fatal.

The place to begin is with ourselves. Care. As you read about or meet some   30
of the children and families in this country who need your help, put yourself in their places as fellow Americans. Imagine you or your spouse being pregnant, and not being able to get enough to eat or see a doctor or know that you have a hospital for delivery. Imagine your child hungry or injured, and you cannot pay for food or find health care. Imagine losing your job and having no income, having your unemployment compensation run out, not being able to pay your note or rent, having no place to sleep with your children, having nothing. Imagine having to stand in a soup line at a church or Salvation Army station after you've worked all your life, or having to sleep in a shelter with strangers and get up and out early each morning, find some place to go with your children, and not know if you can sleep there again that night. If you take the time to imagine this, perhaps you can also take the time to do for them what you would want a fellow citizen to do for you. Volunteer in a homeless shelter or soup kitchen or an afterschool tutoring or mentoring program. Vote. Help to organize your community to speak out for the children who need you. Visit a hospital neonatal intensive care nursery or AIDS and boarder baby ward and spend time rocking and caring for an individual child. Adopt as a penpal a lonely child who never gets a letter from anyone. Give a youth a summer job. Teach your child tolerance and empathy by your example.

Essential individual service and private charity are not substitutes for pub-   31
lic justice, or enough alone to right what's wrong in America. Collective mobilization and political action are also necessary to move our nation forward in the quest for fairness and opportunity for every American.

So pledge to take responsibility not only for your child but for all children   32
or at least for one child who may not be your own. Finally, as you read the prayer below by Ina J. Hughs, include with every "we pray" the promise "I take responsibility for":

We pray for children
  who sneak popsicles before supper,
  who erase holes in math workbooks,
  who can never find their shoes.
And we pray for those
  who stare at photographers from behind barbed wire,
  who can't bound down the street in a new pair of sneakers,
  who never "counted potatoes,"
  who are born in places we wouldn't be caught dead,
  who never go to the circus,
  who live in an X-rated world.
We pray for children
  who bring us sticky kisses and fistfuls of dandelions,
  who hug us in a hurry and forget their lunch money.
And we pray for those
  who never get dessert,
  who have no safe blanket to drag behind them,
  who watch their parents watch them die,
  who can't find any bread to steal,
  who don't have any rooms to clean up,
  whose pictures aren't on anybody's dresser,
  whose monsters are real.
We pray for children
  who spend all their allowance before Tuesday,
  who throw tantrums in the grocery store and pick at their food,
  who like ghost stories,
  who shove dirty clothes under the bed, and never rinse out the tub,
  who get visits from the tooth fairy,
  who don't like to be kissed in front of the carpool,
  who squirm in church or temple and scream in the phone,
  whose tears we sometimes laugh at and whose smiles can make us cry.
And we pray for those
  whose nightmares come in the daytime,
  who will eat anything,
  who have never seen a dentist,
  who aren't spoiled by anybody,
  who go to bed hungry and cry themselves to sleep,
  who live and move, but have no being.
We pray for children who want to be carried
  and for those who must,
  for those we never give up on and for those
  who don't get a second chance.
For those we smother . . . and those who will grab
  the hand of anybody kind enough to offer it.

Please offer your hands to them so that no child is left behind because we did
not act. □

◢ REREADING FOR UNDERSTANDING

1. What is the nature of current social and cultural threats to the well-being of our nation's children according to Edelman? According to Edelman, who is responsible or should be responsible for meeting those threats?

2. Edelman goes to some length to dispute the current notion that until recently, Americans were completely self-sufficient. What evidence does she offer that our government has always played a role in helping individual citizens create successful lives?

3. Edelman is a liberal thinker writing in a time of conservative reaction to past liberal social policies. In order to engage a potentially hostile audience, Edelman seeks to evoke pity and compassion in her audience. Find passages in which you recognize this rhetorical strategy. How effective are these emotional appeals? How well does Edelman balance her emotional appeal with logical arguments and hard evidence like facts and figures?

◢ RESPONDING

1. What is the significance of the title "If the Child Is Safe"? How does the title relate to Edelman's sense of responsibility?

2. At your library, find out what has happened to social welfare programs aimed at children since Edelman wrote her article in 1990. You might also wish to consult the 1995 Carnegie Commission report on the preadolescent youth of America (ages 10–13). Does your research indicate that we, as a society, have acted more or less responsibly toward children since the appearance of Edelman's report?

◢ RESPONDING IN WRITING

Ayn Rand and Marian Wright Edelman seem to have opposing views on the degree of responsibility the community should assume for the well-being of its individual members. In a short essay discuss the relative merits of Rand's and Edelman's ideas. Focus on determining what the likely effects would be if Rand's or Edelman's vision of responsibility were actually realized. Which society would you choose to live in, grow old in, or rear children in? Address your essay to your class, and help them to understand your response to the ideas and implications in these two Context essays.

CONTROVERSIES

What Is My Responsibility in an Intimate Relationship?

ANDREW MARVELL

Andrew Marvell (1621–1678) is considered a metaphysical poet, for his poems are concerned with tensions between such forces as body and soul, self and others, and transience and permanence As you read "To His Coy Mistress," think about the various tensions it presents.

To His Coy Mistress

Had we but world enough, and time,
This coyness, lady, were no crime.
We would sit down, and think which way
To walk, and pass our long love's day.
Thou by the Indian Ganges' side   5
Should'st rubies find: I by the tide
Of Humber would complain. I would
Love you ten years before the Flood,
And you should, if you please, refuse
Till the conversion of the Jews;   10
My vegetable love should grow
Vaster [than] empires and more slow;
An hundred years should go to praise
Thine eyes, and on thy forehead gaze;
Two hundred to adore each breast,   15
But thirty thousand to the rest;
An age at least to every part,
And the last age should show your heart.
For, lady, you deserve this state,

Nor would I love at lower rate.   20
    But at my back I alwaies hear
Time's wingèd chariot hurrying near;
And yonder all before us lye
Desarts of vast Eternity.
Thy beauty shall no more be found,   25
Nor, in thy marble vault, shall sound
My ecchoing song; then, worms shall try
That long preserv'd virginity;
And your quaint honour turn to dust,
And into ashes all my lust: 30
The grave's a fine and private place,
But none, I think, do there embrace.
    Now therefore, while the youthful hew
Sits on thy skin like morning dew,
And while thy willing soul transpires   35
At every pore with instant fires,
Now let us sport us while we may,
And now, like am'rous birds of prey,
Rather at once our time devour,
Than languish in his slow-chapt pow'r.   40
Let us roll all our strength, and all
Our sweetness up into one ball;
And tear our pleasures with rough strife,
Thorough the iron gates of life;
Thus, though we cannot make our sun   45
Stand still, yet we will make him run.

◢ REREADING FOR UNDERSTANDING

1. The poem opens at the point of a dramatic moment between the speaker and his mistress. What is that dramatic moment?

2. What is the focus of each of the three stanzas? What is the interrelationship between and among the stanzas? How are the stanzas like parts of an argument?

3. Which of the speaker's arguments are most effective? least effective? Why?

◢ RESPONDING

1. What is the speaker's attitude toward the woman in the poem? Is his attitude responsible or irresponsible?

2. The central theme in Marvell's poem is *carpe diem,* or "seize the day." He is saying that life is short, so we should consume what pleasures are available while they are available. Is that a reasonable, responsible approach to intimate relationships?

RESPONDING IN WRITING

1. Write a response to the speaker in Marvell's poem in which you persuade him of his irresponsibility—or commend his responsibility—in his relationship with his "mistress."

2. Write a response from the mistress's perspective. Imagine what she would say back to the speaker, and fully explain "your" feelings as you answer your suitor's plea.

WENDELL BERRY

Wendell Berry (1934–) is frequently compared to Henry David Thoreau because of his fierce allegiance to and respect for the natural world and his criticism of our urban, technological, consumer-driven lives. He urges us to contrast the frenetic pace of modern life to the slower pace of traditional, agrarian community. Besides writing about nature and our place in nature, Berry is also a poet, novelist, and essayist, as well as an English professor. He farms 125 acres in Kentucky without modern machinery. Like Thoreau, Berry pursues independence and individualism. In this excerpt from his book, *Sex, Economy, Freedom, and Community*, Berry challenges the reader to consider what is for most of us a radical perspective on the origins of the troubles that plague our intimate personal and sexual relationships. He argues that responsible behavior in love and intimate relations must be a function of community-created values which in turn mold individual behavior and values.

Sex, Economy, Freedom, and Community

> *"It all turns on affection now," said Margaret.*
> *"Affection. Don't you see?"*
> —E. M. FORSTER, *HOWARDS END*

The sexual harassment phase of the Clarence Thomas hearing was handled by the news media as if it were anomalous and surprising. In fact, it was only an unusually spectacular revelation of the destructiveness of a process that has been well established and well respected for at least two hundred years—the process, that is, of community disintegration. This process has been well established and well respected for so long, of course, because it has been immensely profitable to those in a position to profit. The surprise and dismay occasioned by the Thomas hearing were not caused by the gossip involved (for that, the media had prepared us very well) but by the inescapable message that this process of disintegration, so little acknowledged by politicians and commentators, can be severely and perhaps illimitably destructive.

In the government-sponsored quarrel between Clarence Thomas and Anita Hill, public life collided with private life in a way that could not have been resolved and that could only have been damaging. The event was depressing and fearful both because of its violations of due process and justice and because it was an attempt to deal publicly with a problem for which there is no public solution. It embroiled the United States Senate in the impossible task of adjudicating alleged offenses that had occurred in private, of which there were no witnesses and no evidence. If the hearing was a "lynching," as Clarence Thomas said it was, that was because it dealt a public punishment to an unconvicted and unindicted victim. But it was a peculiar lynching, all the same, for it dealt the punishment equally to the accuser. It was not a hearing, much less a trial; it was a story-telling contest that was not winnable by either participant.

Its only result was damage to all participants and to the nation. Public life obviously cannot be conducted in that way, and neither can private life. It was a public procedure that degenerated into a private quarrel. It was a private quarrel that became a public catastrophe.

Sexual harassment, like most sexual conduct, is extremely dangerous as a public issue. A public issue, properly speaking, can only be an issue about which the public can confidently know. Because most sexual conduct is private, occurring only between two people, there are typically no witnesses. Apart from the possibility of a confession, the public can know about it only as a probably unjudgeable contest of stories. (In those rare instances when a sexual offense occurs before reliable witnesses, then, of course, it is a legitimate public issue.)

Does this mean that sexual conduct is *only* private in its interest and meaning? It certainly does not. For if there is no satisfactory way to deal publicly with sexual issues, there is also no satisfactory way to deal with them in mere privacy. To make sense of sexual issues or of sex itself, a third term, a third entity, has to intervene between public and private. For sex is not and cannot be any individual's "own business," nor is it merely the private concern of any couple. Sex, like any other necessary, precious, and volatile power that is commonly held, is everybody's business. A way must be found to entitle everybody's legitimate interest in it without either violating its essential privacy or allowing its unrestrained energies to reduce necessary public procedures to the level of a private quarrel. For sexual problems and potentialities that have a more-than-private interest, what is needed are common or shared forms and solutions that are not, in the usual sense, public.

The indispensable form that can intervene between public and private interests is that of community. The concerns of public and private, republic and citizen, necessary as they are, are not adequate for the shaping of human life. Community alone, as principle and as fact, can raise the standards of local health (ecological, economic, social, and spiritual) without which the other two interests will destroy one another.

By community, I mean the commonwealth and common interests, commonly understood, of people living together in a place and wishing to continue to do so. To put it another way, community is a locally understood interdependence of local people, local culture, local economy, and local nature. (Community, of course, is an idea that can extend itself beyond the local, but it only does so metaphorically. The idea of a national or global community is meaningless apart from the realization of local communities.) Lacking the interest of or in such a community, private life becomes merely a sort of reserve in which individuals defend their "right" to act as they please and attempt to limit or destroy the "rights" of others to act as they please.

A community identifies itself by an understood mutuality of interests. But   8
it lives and acts by the common virtues of trust, goodwill, forbearance, self-restraint, compassion, and forgiveness. If it hopes to continue long as a community, it will wish to—and will have to—encourage respect for all its members, human and natural. It will encourage respect for all stations and occupations. Such a community has the power—not invariably but as a rule—to enforce decency without litigation. It has the power, that is, to influence behavior. And it exercises this power not by coercion or violence but by teaching the young and by preserving stories and songs that tell (among other things) what works and what does not work in a given place.

Such a community is (among other things) a set of arrangements between   9
men and women. These arrangements include marriage, family structure, divisions of work and authority, and responsibility for the instruction of children and young people. These arrangements exist, in part, to reduce the volatility and the danger of sex—to preserve its energy, its beauty, and its pleasure; to preserve and clarify its power to join not just husband and wife to one another but parents to children, families to the community, the community to nature; to ensure, so far as possible, that the inheritors of sexuality, as they come of age, will be worthy of it.

But the life of a community is more vulnerable than public life. A community cannot be made or preserved apart from the loyalty and affection of its   10
members and the respect and goodwill of the people outside it. And for a long time, these conditions have not been met. As the technological, economic, and political means of exploitation have expanded, communities have been more and more victimized by opportunists outside themselves. And as the salesmen, saleswomen, advertisers, and propagandists of the industrial economy have become more ubiquitous and more adept at seduction, communities have lost the loyalty and affection of their members. The community, wherever you look, is being destroyed by the desires and ambitions of both private and public life, which for want of the intervention of community interests are also destroying one another. Community life is by definition a life of cooperation and responsibility. Private life and public life, without the disciplines of community interest, necessarily gravitate toward competition and exploitation. As private life casts off all community restraints in the interest of economic exploitation or ambition or self-realization or whatever, the communal supports of public life also and by the same stroke are undercut, and public life becomes simply the arena of unrestrained private ambition and greed.

As our communities have disintegrated from external predation and internal disaffection, we have changed from a society whose ideal of justice was trust   11 and fairness among people who knew each other into a society whose ideal of justice is public litigation, breeding distrust even among people who know each other.

Once it has shrugged off the interests and claims of the community, the public language of sexuality comes directly under the influence of private lust, ambition, and greed and becomes inadequate to deal with the real issues and problems of sexuality. The public dialogue degenerates into a stupefying and useless contest between so-called liberation and so-called morality. The real issue and problems, as they are experienced and suffered in people's lives, cannot be talked about. The public language can deal, however awkwardly and perhaps uselessly, with pornography, sexual hygiene, contraception, sexual harassment, rape, and so on. But it cannot talk about respect, responsibility, sexual discipline, fidelity, or the practice of love. "Sexual education," carried on in this public language, is and can only be a dispirited description of the working of a sort of anatomical machinery—and this is a sexuality that is neither erotic nor social nor sacramental but rather a cold-blooded, abstract procedure that is finally not even imaginable. 12

The conventional public opposition of "liberal" and "conservative" is, here as elsewhere, perfectly useless. The "conservatives" promote the family as a sort of public icon, but they will not promote the economic integrity of the household or the community, which are the mainstays of family life. Under the sponsorship of "conservative" presidencies, the economy of the modern household, which once required the father to work away from home—a development that was bad enough—now requires the mother to work away from home, as well. And this development has the wholehearted endorsement of "liberals," who see the mother thus forced to spend her days away from her home and children as "liberated"—though nobody has yet seen the fathers thus forced away as "liberated." Some feminists are thus in the curious position of opposing the mistreatment of women and yet advocating their participation in an economy in which everything is mistreated. 13

The "conservatives" more or less attack homosexuality, abortion, and pornography, and the "liberals" more or less defend them. Neither party will oppose sexual promiscuity. The "liberals" will not oppose promiscuity because they do not wish to appear intolerant of "individual liberty." The "conservatives" will not oppose promiscuity because sexual discipline would reduce the profits of corporations, which in their advertisements and entertainments encourage sexual self-indulgence as a way of selling merchandise. 14

The public discussion of sexual issues has thus degenerated into a poor attempt to equivocate between private lusts and public emergencies. Nowhere in public life (that is, in the public life that counts: the discussions of political and corporate leaders) is there an attempt to respond to community needs in the language of community interest. 15

And although we seem more and more inclined to look on education, even as it teaches less and is more overcome by violence, as the solution to all our problems (thus delaying the solution for a generation), there is really not much use in looking to education for the help we need. For education has become 16 increasingly useless as it has become increasingly public. Real education is determined by community needs, not by public tests. Nor is community interest or community need going to receive much help from television and the other public media. Television is the greatest disrespecter and exploiter of sexuality that the world has ever seen; even if the network executives decide to promote "safe sex" and the use of condoms, they will not cease to pimp for the exceedingly profitable "sexual revolution." It is, in fact, the nature of the electronic media to blur and finally destroy all distinctions between public and community. Television has greatly accelerated the process, begun long ago, by which many communities have been atomized and congealed into one public. Nor is government a likely source of help. As political leaders have squirmed free of the claims and responsibilities of community life, public life has become their private preserve. The public political voice has become increasingly the voice of a conscious and self-serving duplicity: it is now, for instance, merely typical that a political leader can speak of "the preciousness of all life" while armed for the annihilation of all life. And the right of privacy, without the intervening claims and responsibilities of community life, has moved from the individual to the government and assumed the name of "official secrecy." Whose liberation is that?

In fact, there is no one to speak for the community interest except those people who wish to adhere to community principles. The community, in other words, must speak in its own interest. It must learn to defend itself. And in its self-defense, it may use the many powerful arguments provided for it by the failures of the private and public aims that have so nearly destroyed it. [17]

The defenders of community should point out, for example, that for the joining of men and women there need to be many forms that only a community can provide. If you destroy the ideal of the "gentle man" and remove from men all expectations of courtesy and consideration toward women and children, you have prepared the way for an epidemic of rape and abuse. If you depreciate the sanctity and solemnity of marriage, not just as a bond between two people but as a bond between those two people and their forebears, their children, and their neighbors, then you have prepared the way for an epidemic of divorce, child neglect, community ruin, and loneliness. If you destroy the economies of household and community, then you destroy the bonds of mutual usefulness and practical dependence without which the other bonds will not hold. . . . [18]

We thus can see that there are two kinds of human economy. There is the kind of economy that exists to protect the "right" of profit, as does our present public economy; this sort of economy will inevitably gravitate toward protection of the "rights" of those who profit most. Our present public economy is really a political system that safeguards the private exploitation of the public wealth and health. The other kind of economy exists for the protection of gifts, beginning with the "giving in marriage," and this is the economy of community, which now has been nearly destroyed by the public economy. [19]

There are two kinds of sexuality that correspond to the two kinds of economy. The sexuality of community life, whatever its inevitable vagaries, is centered on marriage, which joins two living souls as closely as, in this world, they can be [20] joined. This joining of two who know, love, and trust one another brings them in the same breath into the freedom of sexual consent and into the fullest earthly realization of the image of God. From their joining, other living souls come into being, and with them great responsibilities that are unending, fearful, and joyful. The marriage of two lovers joins them to one another, to forebears, to descendants, to the community, to Heaven and earth. It is the fundamental connection without which nothing holds, and trust is its necessity.

Our present sexual conduct, on the other hand, having "liberated" itself   21 from the several trusts of community life, is public, like our present economy. It has forsaken trust, for it rests on the easy giving and breaking of promises. And having forsaken trust, it has predictably become political. In private life, as in public, we are attempting to correct bad character and low motives by law and by litigation. "Losing kindness," as Lao-tzu said, "they turn to justness." The superstition of the anger of our current sexual politics, as of other kinds of anger, is that somewhere along the trajectory of any quarrel a tribunal will be reached that will hear all complaints and find for the plaintiff; the verdict will be that the defendant is entirely wrong, the plaintiff entirely right and entirely righteous. This, of course, is not going to happen. And because such "justice" cannot happen, litigation only prolongs itself. The difficulty is that marriage, family life, friendship, neighborhood, and other personal connections do not depend exclusively or even primarily on justice—though, of course, they all must try for it. They depend also on trust, patience, respect, mutual help, forgiveness—in other words, the *practice* of love, as opposed to the mere *feeling* of love.

As soon as the parties to a marriage or a friendship begin to require strict   22 justice of each other, then that marriage or friendship begins to be destroyed, for there is no way to adjudicate the competing claims of a personal quarrel. And so these relationships do not dissolve into litigation, really; they dissolve into a feud, an endless exchange of accusations and retributions. If the two parties have not the grace to forgive the inevitable offenses of close connection, the next best thing is separation and silence. But why should separation have come to be the virtually conventional outcome of close relationships in our society? The proper question, perhaps, is not why we have so much divorce, but why we are so unforgiving. The answer, perhaps, is that, though we still recognize the feeling of love, we have forgotten how to practice love when we don't feel it.

Because of our determination to separate sex from the practice of love in   23 marriage and in family and community life, our public sexual morality is confused, sentimental, bitter, complexly destructive, and hypocritical. It begins with the idea of "sexual liberation": whatever people desire is "natural" and all right, men and women are not different but merely equal, and all desires are equal. If a man wants to sit down while a pregnant woman is standing or walk through a heavy door and let it slam in a woman's face, that is all right. Divorce on an epidemic scale is all right; child abandonment by one parent or another is all right; it is regrettable but still pretty much all right if a divorced parent neglects or refuses to pay child support; promiscuity is all right; adultery is all right. Promiscuity among teenagers is pretty much all right, for "that's the way it is"; abortion as birth control is all right; the prostitution of sex in advertise-ments and public entertainment is all right. But then, far down this road of freedom, we decide that a few lines ought to be drawn. Child molestation, we wish to say, is not all right, nor is sexual violence, nor is sexual harassment, nor is pregnancy among unmarried teenagers. We are also against venereal diseases, the diseases of promiscuity, though we tend to think that they are the govern-ment's responsibility, not ours.

In this cult of liberated sexuality, "free" of courtesy, ceremony, responsibil-ity, and restraint, dependent on litigation and expert advice, there is much that is human, sad to say, but there is no sense or sanity. Trying to draw the line where we are trying to draw it, between carelessness and brutality, is like insist-ing that falling is flying—until you hit the ground—and then trying to outlaw hitting the ground. The pretentious, fantastical, and solemn idiocy of the pub-lic sexual code could not be better exemplified than by the now-ubiquitous phrase "sexual partner," which denies all that is implied by the names of "hus-band" or "wife" or even "lover." It denies anyone's responsibility for the conse-quences of sex. With one's "sexual partner," it is now understood, one must practice "safe sex"—that is, one must protect oneself, not one's partner or the children that may come of the "partnership."   24

But the worst hypocrisy of all is the failure of the sexual libertarians to come to the defense of sexually liberated politicians. The public applies strenu-ously to public officials a sexual morality that it no longer applies to anyone pri-vately and that it does not apply to other liberated public figures, such as movie stars, artists, athletes, and business tycoons. The prurient squeamishness with which the public and the public media poke into the lives of politicians is surely not an expectable result of liberation. But this paradox is not the only one. According to its claims, sexual liberation ought logically to have brought in a time of "naturalness," ease, and candor between men and women. It has, on the contrary, filled the country with sexual self-consciousness, uncertainty, and fear. Women, though they may dress as if the sexual millennium had arrived, hurry along our city streets and public corridors with their eyes averted, like hunted animals. "Eye contact," once the very signature of our humanity, has become a danger. The meeting ground between men and women, which ought to be safeguarded by trust, has become a place of suspicion, competition, and violence. One no longer goes there asking how instinct may be ramified in affection and loyalty; now one asks how instinct may be indulged with the least risk to personal safety.   25

Seeking to "free" sexual love from its old communal restraints, we have "freed" it also from its meaning, its responsibility, and its exaltation. And we have made it more dangerous. "Sexual liberation" is as much a fraud and as great a failure as the "peaceful atom." We are now living in a sexual atmosphere so polluted and embittered that women must look on virtually any man as a potential assailant, and a man must look on virtually any woman as a potential accuser. The idea that this situation can be corrected by the courts and the police only compounds the disorder and the danger. And in the midst of this acid rainfall of predation and recrimination, we presume to teach our young   26 people that sex can be made "safe"—by the use, inevitably, of purchased drugs and devices. What a lie! Sex was never safe, and it is less safe now than it has ever been.

What we are actually teaching the young is an illusion of thoughtless free- 27 dom and purchasable safety, which encourages them to tamper prematurely, disrespectfully, and dangerously with a great power. Just as the public economy encourages people to spend money and waste the world, so the public sexual code encourages people to be spendthrifts and squanderers of sex. The basis of true community and household economy, on the other hand, is thrift. The basis of community sexuality is respect for everything that is involved—and respect, here as everywhere, implies discipline. By their common principles of extravagance and undisciplined freedom, our public economy and our public sexuality are exploiting and spending moral capital built up by centuries of community life—exactly as industrial agriculture has been exploiting and spending the natural capital built up over thousands of years in the soil.

In sex, as in other things, we have liberated fantasy but killed imagination, 28 and so have sealed ourselves in selfishness and loneliness. Fantasy is of the solitary self, and it cannot lead us away from ourselves. It is by imagination that we cross over the differences between ourselves and other beings and thus learn compassion, forbearance, mercy, forgiveness, sympathy, and love—the virtues without which neither we nor the world can live.

Starting with economic brutality, we have arrived at sexual brutality. Those 29 who affirm the one and deplore the other will have to explain how we might logically have arrived anywhere else. Sexual lovemaking between humans is not and cannot be the thoughtless, instinctual coupling of animals; it is not "recreation"; it is not "safe." It is the strongest prompting and the greatest joy that young people are likely to experience. Because it is so powerful, it is risky, not just because of the famous dangers of venereal disease and "unwanted pregnancy" but also because it involves and requires a giving away of the self that if not honored and reciprocated, inevitably reduces dignity and self-respect. The invitation to give oneself away is not, except for the extremely ignorant or the extremely foolish, an easy one to accept.

Perhaps the current revulsion against sexual harassment may be the begin- 30 ning of a renewal of sexual responsibility and self-respect. It must, at any rate, be the beginning of a repudiation of the idea that sex among us is merely natural. If men and women are merely animals, it is hard to see how sexual harassment could have become an issue, for such harassment is no more than the instinctive procedure of male animals, who openly harass females, usually by unabashed physical display and contact; it is their way of asking who is and who is not in estrus. Women would not think such behavior offensive if we had not, for thousands of years, understood ourselves as specifically human beings— creatures who, if in some ways animal-like, are in other ways God-like. In asking men to feel shame and to restrain themselves—which one would not ask of an animal—women are implicitly asking to be treated as human beings in that full sense, as living souls made in the image of God. But any humans who wish to be treated and to treat others according to that definition must understand that this is not a kindness that can be conferred by a public economy or by a public government or by a public people. It can only be conferred on its members by a community. ☐

◢ REREADING FOR UNDERSTANDING

1. Explain Berry's concept of community. What is the source of its authority? What are its responsibilities? How does Berry's definition of community match the reality of your home community? your college community?

2. What causes are at work, according to Berry, to undermine community in contemporary America? Do you agree? Can you recognize any of these causes at work in your home community? in your college community?

3. Assume you are discussing Berry's essay with a peer who has not read it. Describe the interrelationship between sexual behavior, values, and a viable community. Be prepared to explain what forces Berry believes are destroying the community's ability to teach the young how to balance individual sexual desires with community norms.

4. What does Berry mean when he observes that "marriage, family life, neighborhood" do not depend on "justice"? On what *do* they depend, as Berry sees it? Do you agree?

◢ RESPONDING

1. Berry observes that marriage, family life, and friendship do not depend on "justice—though, of course, they must all strive for it. They [marriage, etc.] depend also on trust, patience, respect, mutual help, forgiveness—in other words, the *practice* of love as opposed to the mere *feeling* of love" (par. 21). Examine the distinction Berry makes between "the practice of love and the feeling of love." Can you find an example from your own experience, observation, or popular culture to illustrate the difference?

2. Briefly list what Berry argues are essential values and behaviors in sexual relationships, marriage, friendships, and in neighborhoods. If you have read Ellen Willis's argument (page 418), compare Berry's ideas to Willis's argument that community standards impose unacceptable restriction on intimate relationships and create "inequality" between men and women. Which way of understanding relationships seems more desirable, more responsible—Berry's or Willis's?

3. In the final paragraph of his essay, Berry observes that "if men and women are merely animals, it is hard to see how sexual harassment could have become an issue. . . ." Reflect on this. What simple insight, with significant implications for our sense of responsibility in sexual relationships, does Berry articulate?

TIMBERLINE

When You're Ready to Fall

▲ REREADING FOR UNDERSTANDING

1. What story is being told in the still-frame shots that compose this Timberline advertisement? Is there a hero? more than one?

2. Who is the target audience? (Consider: age, gender, education level, socioeconomic characteristics, and so on.) How do the text and graphics appeal to the target audience?

▲ RESPONDING

1. Of the two "characteristics" in the advertisement, which one is more aggressive? How does that aggressive image enhance the ad's emotional appeal for the intended audience? How effective is that emotional appeal? Why?

2. What is the purpose of the eagle's image in the Timberline ad? How does it reinforce the intended message?

3. What does this ad imply about responsibility in an intimate relationship?

4. Do you think the image of relationships presented in this ad reflects the general attitude of our culture as a whole? Should our culture accept the values—the sense of responsibility—implied in this ad? Why or why not?

CAMILLE PAGLIA

Camille Paglia (1947–   ) is a college professor and a literary, artistic, and social critic of a rather controversial and provocative style. Part of her controversial character comes from her perspectives on human sexuality, especially male sexuality. Paglia suggests sexuality is a primitive urge, often associated with creative energy in art and literature. This sexual energy, she claims, may lead to perverse or aggressive sexual behavior among men. Paglia sees such "natural" perversity as desirable because of the intense, often creative, energy that sexuality releases. She acknowledges, however, that sexual energy can also lead to criminal, often brutal, behavior of men toward women. Paglia condemns forceful rape but feels that women should assume more responsibility for sexual encounters, taking into account the aggressive character of the male animal. These views, not surprisingly, have angered many feminists. Paglia remains, so far, indifferent to their criticism. Her attitude is captured in the introduction to *Sex, Art, and American Culture*, from which a chapter is presented below. Paglia remarks that "sexuality [is] at odds with current feminism, whose public proponents are in a reactionary phase of hysterical moralism and prudery. . . . We need a new kind of feminism, one that stresses personal responsibility and is open to art and sex in all their dark, unconsoling mysteries."

Rape and Modern Sex War

Rape is an outrage that cannot be tolerated in civilized society. Yet feminism, which has waged a crusade for rape to be taken more seriously, has put young women in danger by hiding the truth about sex from them.

In dramatizing the pervasiveness of rape, feminists have told young women that before they have sex with a man, they must give consent as explicit as a legal contract's. In this way, young women have been convinced that they have been the victims of rape. On elite campuses in the Northeast and on the West Coast, they have held consciousness-raising sessions, petitioned administrations, demanded inquests. At Brown University, outraged, panicky "victims" have scrawled the names of alleged attackers on the walls of women's rest rooms. What marital rape was to the Seventies, "date rape" is to the Nineties.

The incidence and seriousness of rape do not require this kind of exaggeration. Real acquaintance rape is nothing new. It has been a horrible problem for women for all of recorded history. Once fathers and brothers protected women from rape. Once the penalty for rape was death. I come from a fierce Italian tradition where, not so long ago in the motherland, a rapist would end up knifed, castrated, and hung out to dry.

But the old clans and small rural communities have broken down. In our cities, on our campuses far from home, young women are vulnerable and defenseless. Feminism has not prepared them for this. Feminism keeps saying the sexes are the same. It keeps telling women they can do anything, go anywhere, say anything, wear anything. No, they can't. Women will always be in sexual danger.

One of my male students recently slept overnight with a friend in a passageway of the Great Pyramid in Egypt. He described the moon and sand, the ancient silence and eerie echoes. I will never experience that. I am a woman. I am not stupid enough to believe I could ever be safe there. There is a world of solitary adventure I will never have. Women have always known these somber truths. But feminism, with its pie-in-the-sky fantasies about the perfect world, keeps young women from seeing life as it is.

We must remedy social injustice whenever we can. But there are some things we cannot change. There are sexual differences that are based in biology. Academic feminism is lost in a fog of social constructionism. It believes we are totally the product of our environment. This idea was invented by Rousseau. He was wrong. Emboldened by dumb French language theory, academic feminists repeat the same hollow slogans over and over to each other. Their view of sex is naïve and prudish. Leaving sex to the feminists is like letting your dog vacation at the taxidermist's.

The sexes are at war. Men must struggle for identity against the overwhelming power of their mothers. Women have menstruation to tell them they are women. Men must do or risk something to be men. Men become masculine only when other men say they are. Having sex with a woman is one way a boy becomes a man. 7

College men are at their hormonal peak. They have just left their mothers and are questing for their male identity. In groups, they are dangerous. A woman going to a fraternity party is walking into Testosterone Flats, full of prickly cacti and blazing guns. If she goes, she should be armed with resolute alertness. She should arrive with girlfriends and leave with them. A girl who lets herself get dead drunk at a fraternity party is a fool. A girl who goes upstairs alone with a brother at a fraternity party is an idiot. Feminists call this "blaming the victim." I call it common sense. 8

For a decade, feminists have drilled their disciples to say, "Rape is a crime of violence but not of sex." This sugar-coated Shirley Temple nonsense has exposed young women to disaster. Misled by feminism, they do not expect rape from the nice boys from good homes who sit next to them in class. 9

Aggression and eroticism are deeply intertwined. Hunt, pursuit, and capture are biologically programmed into male sexuality. Generation after generation, men must be educated, refined, and ethically persuaded away from their tendency toward anarchy and brutishness. Society is not the enemy, as feminism ignorantly claims. Society is woman's protection against rape. Feminism, with its solemn Carry Nation repressiveness, does not see what is for men the eroticism or fun element in rape, especially the wild, infectious delirium of gang rape. Women who do not understand rape cannot defend themselves against it. 10

The date-rape controversy shows feminism hitting the wall of its own broken promises. The women of my Sixties generation were the first respectable girls in history to swear like sailors, get drunk, stay out all night—in short, to act like men. We sought total sexual freedom and equality. But as time passed, we woke up to cold reality. The old double standard protected women. When anything goes, it's women who lose. 11

Today's young women don't know what they want. They see that feminism has not brought sexual happiness. The theatrics of public rage over date rape are their way of restoring the old sexual rules that were shattered by my generation. Because nothing about the sexes has really changed. The comic film *Where the Boys Are* (1960), the ultimate expression of Fifties man-chasing, still speaks directly to our time. It shows smart, lively women skillfully anticipating and fending off the dozens of strategies with which horny men try to get them into bed. The agonizing date-rape subplot and climax are brilliantly done. The victim, Yvette Mimieux, makes mistake after mistake, obvious to the other girls. She allows herself to be lured away from her girlfriends and into isolation with boys whose character and intentions she misreads. *Where the Boys Are* tells the truth. It shows courtship as a dangerous game in which the signals are not verbal but subliminal. 12

Neither militant feminism, which is obsessed with politically correct language, nor academic feminism, which believes that knowledge and experience 13 are "constituted by" language, can understand preverbal or nonverbal communication. Feminism, focusing on sexual politics, cannot see that sex exists in and through the body. Sexual desire and arousal cannot be fully translated into verbal terms. This is why men and women misunderstand each other.

Trying to remake the future, feminism cut itself off from sexual history. It   14
discarded and suppressed the sexual myths of literature, art, and religion. Those myths show us the turbulence, the mysteries and passions of sex. In mythology we see men's sexual anxiety, their fear of woman's dominance. Much sexual violence is rooted in men's sense of psychological weakness toward women. It takes many men to deal with one woman. Woman's voracity is a persistent motif. Clara Bow, it was rumored, took on the USC football team on weekends. Marilyn Monroe, singing "Diamonds Are a Girl's Best Friend," rules a conga line of men in tuxes. Half-clad Cher, in the video for "If I Could Turn Back Time," deranges a battleship of screaming sailors and straddles a pink-lit cannon. Feminism, coveting social power, is blind to woman's cosmic sexual power.

To understand rape, you must study the past. There never was and never   15
will be sexual harmony. Every woman must take personal responsibility for her sexuality, which is nature's red flame. She must be prudent and cautious about where she goes and with whom. When she makes a mistake, she must accept the consequences and, through self-criticism, resolve never to make that mistake again. Running to Mommy and Daddy on the campus grievance committee is unworthy of strong women. Posting lists of guilty men in the toilet is cowardly, infantile stuff.

The Italian philosophy of life espouses high-energy confrontation. A male   16
student makes a vulgar remark about your breasts? Don't slink off to whimper and simper with the campus shrinking violets. Deal with it. On the spot. Say, "Shut up, you jerk! And crawl back to the barnyard where you belong!" In general, women who project this take-charge attitude toward life get harassed less often. I see too many dopey, immature, self-pitying women walking around like melting sticks of butter. It's the Yvette Mimieux syndrome: make me happy. And listen to me weep when I'm not.

The date-rape debate is already smothering in propaganda churned out by   17
the expensive Northeastern colleges and universities, with their overconcentration of boring, uptight academic feminists and spoiled, affluent students. Beware of the deep manipulativeness of rich students who were neglected by their parents. They love to turn the campus into hysterical psychodramas of sexual transgression, followed by assertions of parental authority and concern. And don't look for sexual enlightenment from academe, which spews out mountains of books but never looks at life directly.

As a fan of football and rock music, I see in the simple, swaggering mas-   18
culinity of the jock and in the noisy posturing of the heavy-metal guitarist certain fundamental, unchanging truths about sex. Masculinity is aggressive, unstable, combustible. It is also the most creative cultural force in history. Women must reorient themselves toward the elemental powers of sex, which can strengthen or destroy.

The only solution to date rape is female self-awareness and self-control. A   19
woman's number one line of defense is herself. When a real rape occurs, she

should report it to the police. Complaining to college committees because the courts "take too long" is ridiculous. College administrations are not a branch of the judiciary. They are not equipped or trained for legal inquiry. Colleges must alert incoming students to the problems and dangers of adulthood. Then colleges must stand back and get out of the sex game. ☐

◢ REREADING FOR UNDERSTANDING

1. Paglia argues that mainstream feminism is naive in its approach to sexuality between men and women. With what particular criticisms does Paglia attack feminists' response to the "date rape crisis" in the first eleven paragraphs of this peace?

2. Look carefully at Paglia's style of writing in a number of paragraphs (choose a sequence of four to five paragraphs). Pay particular attention to length of sentences and word choice. How do those elements affect the audience's response to Paglia as a writer?

◢ RESPONDING

1. Paglia makes a distinction between "real rape"—what one might call criminal rape—and "situational rape," in which a woman has placed herself voluntarily, at least to some extent, in a potentially sexually charged environment. How accurate is Paglia's distinction? how persuasive?

2. Paglia comments (par. 5) that a male student of hers slept in a darkened passageway of the Great Pyramid in Egypt for the sheer thrill of the experience. She goes on to say that such adventures are beyond most women's experience because women alone are always at risk, and always have been. She concludes that feminism keeps young women from seeing life as it is. Apparently Paglia believes life for woman will always be unequal because men will always pose a potential threat to their safety. Is feminism naive to argue that women can have real freedom to experience life as men do? Is Paglia correct in her observation? Why or why not?

HELEN CORDES

Helen Cordes was born in 1954 and received her undergraduate degree in 1983. A free-lance writer since 1982, she has published numerous articles in various national magazines that focus on gender and social issues. She is currently a contributing editor for *Utne* magazine, a liberal, public interest publication. Her article here is a spirited reply to Paglia's perspective on the nature of responsibility in intimate relationships.

Winking at Abusive Sexual Behavior Isn't the Answer

I thought the old "blue balls"" defense—you remember, that's the one where backseat Romeos claimed they couldn't halt their sexual advances because their aching gonads imperiously demanded relief—went out with air raid shelters and doo wop. But now there are those like Camille Paglia who are bringing back blue balls with a vengeance. According to Paglia and her cohorts, men really *can't* control their urges. Rape for men is just doin' what comes naturally. And gals, don't bother fighting it—just get used to it again.

It's not surprising that these anti-feminist screeds seem irresistible to America's magazine editors (mostly male? just a wild guess), but it is ironic. In the past few years, men have become increasingly petulant about "male-bashing," complaining that feminists have accused them—particularly the white and privileged among them—of being responsible for all the world's major woes, including rampant violence against women. Even politically correct guys protest that extremist feminist statements like "all men will rape if they can" just go too far. "Look," they respond indignantly, "I don't rape, no one I know rapes or beats his wife—why do you women keep saying men are such animals? How do you think that makes us feel?" Then along comes Paglia with the same message—that men rape whenever they can—and, curiously enough, many men give her a rousing cheer.

Both extremist views—the contention that men have insistent urges and some feminists' belief that all men rape—are dangerous. Men are right to be outraged at stereotypes about their gender. But they're wrong to accept Paglia's forgiving view of their "biological programming." Lots of men might like to believe that "masculinity is aggressive, unstable, combustible" because that line is a great excuse for self-indulgent behavior. But can most men seriously agree with statements such as "Generation after generation, men must be educated, refined, and ethically persuaded away from their tendency toward anarchy and brutishness"? Do all real men dream of the "fun element in rape, especially the wild, infectious delirium of gang rape"? Do normal men really get off on hurting women? Is this the "truth about sex" we need to tell our sons and daughters?

The truth about sex—and the "sex wars" between men and women—is at once more complicated and more ordinary than that. Sure, I'll buy Paglia's line that men are sexually violent toward women because they fear being dominated by women. I fear (as women have always feared) being dominated by men. So if a man is patronizing me, can I shoot him? ("He led me on, officer. What else could a red-blooded woman do?") And yes, seeking sex *is* usually motivated in part by pure sexual desire, but both men and women also use sex to substitute for other inadequacies in their lives. Honest women are quick to confide that they use sex to shore up their egos or as a bargaining chip for attention and affection. And truly honest men will tell you the same thing.

The reason for the sex wars—for women feeling that men are sex-obsessed predators who will rape at will, and for men feeling that women are distrustful, uptight, and too quick to cry rape—is that too little has changed. Too many men perpetuate the adolescent blue balls theory—and why should they give it up? Pretending that it's uncontrollable sexual urges that make them aggressively demand sex gives men control, power, and a feeling that they are entitled to sexual favors. And who wants to give that up? In the face of abusive behavior from certain men, many women are giving up all too readily, returning to their mothers' attitude that men are after only one thing. And although it's not fair, it's also not surprising that women occasionally act badly to well-meaning men who are genuinely trying to overcome the conditioning that pushed them to be sexually aggressive.

Both sides are retreating into bitterness and antagonism, when in truth the 6
long view reveals real hope for the future. Look at how much closer we've gotten to egalitarianism and harmony between the sexes in the past 25 years. As working women become the norm, men are no longer expected to be wage slaves. Women's experiences of and complaints about abusive behavior have been heard, and institutions have responded—women who have been raped, sexually harassed, and battered can now get help in every region of the country.

Progress like this is what makes it especially annoying and depressing to 7
see Paglia's views gaining legitimacy. Her awestruck view of male sexuality, and her inane suggestion that women view it as a blind force of nature instead of morally accountable behavior, are ludicrous throwbacks to the blue balls days.

Women *should* let men know when their behavior is offensive. But individ- 8
ual complaints are toothless without societal and institutional awareness, dialogue, and censure. The feminist movement that Paglia and others vilify has brought about these critical societal attitudes and structures. For just one example, look to the way rape victims are now treated by the police. When rape victims go to the police they can now hope to be met with respect, thanks to feminist efforts to sensitize officers, many of whom didn't take the crime seriously before.

I agree with Paglia that women would do well to avoid drunken frat parties 9
and solo campouts. But her prescription for "prudent" and "cautious" behavior won't save them from sexual violence. Women are raped and harassed everywhere and anytime—often in situations that are not remotely "dangerous" or "provocative." Instead of cloistering women and allowing men free rein, why don't women and men talk and work together for change, so that they can find ways to be peaceably intimate again? ☐

◢ REREADING FOR UNDERSTANDING

1. What are the main complaints Cordes voices against Paglia's view of male sexuality?

2. According to Cordes, what is the responsibility of a man in a sexual relationship? What is the source of that responsibility?

RESPONDING

1. Cordes suggests that men's sexual behavior is best controlled when "societal and institutional awareness, dialogue, and censure" are factors (par. 8). Paglia suggests that institutional elements (like campus date-rape crisis committees) interfere with individual liberty and freedom. What is the best source of values to define responsibility within intimate or family relationships— the community's or an individual's or some combination of both? Why?

2. If you have time, reread Rand (p. 375) and Berry (p. 395). Both offer multiple perspectives on the values that ought to define and regulate individual behavior. Rand's general argument is captured in her observation (par. 32) that "no man can have a right to impose an unchosen obligation, an unrewarded duty or an involuntary servitude on another man." Berry's ideas focus on the ways in which individual behavior in intimate relationships should be influenced, if not controlled, by community values. Apply Rand's and Berry's perspectives to Responding question 1 above.

3. Cordes takes issue with Paglia's assertion that men's sexual behavior is beyond their control. Why? Whose understanding of sexuality do you think is more accurate, Cordes's or Paglia's?

JULES FEIFFER

Rejection Is Abuse

◢ RESPONDING

1. Who do you think is the intended audience for this cartoon?

2. What contemporary attitude does this cartoon lampoon? How would a feminist like Paglia or Cordes respond—with laughter or irritation? Why?

3. What kinds of responsibility are implied for whom in this cartoon?

CONTROVERSIES

Responsibility

What Are My Responsibilities Within My Family?

RUTH ANSAH AYISI

Ruth Ansah Ayisi is a free-lance journalist currently living in Mozambique, Africa. Her article provides an African cultural perspective on the issue of intergenerational responsibility. She describes how changing cultural and economic conditions in her native culture are redefining responsibility among family members, especially children's responsibility toward their parents. As you read Ayisi's article, consider the role the elderly have traditionally played in our own society. Is that role changing? If so, how? Consider, too, the place of parents and grandparents in your own family and community.

Family Values

In a desperate attempt to save an elderly patient from dying, the doctor tried to trace a family member of the sick man. To the doctor's relief, he managed to track down a son who was working nearby. The doctor explained that his patient needed a blood transfusion and financial assistance. But the son's response came as a shock. "Who is my father? He never cared for me and Mama. I don't know him. Let him die."

Most Ghanaians would be outraged by the son's response, just as they are generally horrified that in Europe, many elderly people are institutionalized rather than taken care of by a relative, however distant. Traditionally in Ghana, as in most African countries, the old are regarded as senior family members who impart wisdom and should at least be held in respect and cared for.

In West African languages, expressions for the elderly mean things like, "he or she who knows," or "he or she who has vision." The Akan of Ghana have a proverb which says: "When children learn to wash their hands, they may eat with the elders."

But the sick man was a Ghanaian and so is his son, and these days although such a case is rare, it is becoming less so. "Twenty years ago, the general view would be that you must look after your father because he fathered you, irrespective," said Nana Apt, a 49-year-old sociologist at the University of Ghana, Legon, and president of the African Gerontological Society. "Now it is the modern economics. The salaries people are getting do not keep them going, neither themselves nor their immediate family, so that now it becomes easier for children to say, 'Look, I can't' because they themselves cannot even cope."

Ghana, like other African countries, has been swallowing the bitter pill of a structural adjustment program sponsored by the World Bank and International Monetary Fund. Nine years after President Jerry Rawlings' government initiated the program, Ghana can boast of having the highest growth rate in black Africa, but prices have soared and the cedi, the national currency, has been drastically devalued. The cash economy gives little room for generosity among the extended family.

While tax exemptions are available for children's education, they are not allowed for supporting the elderly. Moreover, most pension schemes are aimed at those who have worked in the formal sector, which is only a small proportion of the elderly.

Besides financial problems, traditional values are being eroded and the cultural gap between the old and young is widening. Educational opportunities have also split families, which had a history of living together in the countryside in a large family home. Young people have flocked to the towns or emigrated overseas. Research has shown that rural youth are twice as likely to live with their grandparents as urban youth. And fewer young married couples these days are willing to live in the same house as their parents.

The cash economy also puts pressure on young people to earn money fast. Today, everything is money. Young people these days tend to feel less obliged, for example, to look after an elderly aunt or uncle.

Therefore, a particularly vulnerable group are elderly women who have living children, like a pair of unidentical twins, Akwele and Akuokor Dokwi. They live by themselves in a tumbledown shack on the outskirts of the capital, Accra. The shack is bare inside except for a few tins that are used as plates and cups, and some scrawny chickens kept in a coop. The sisters depend on the charity of the church and people in community. "We don't even have enough money to buy food," says Akuokor.

The twins came from a farming family in the Upper West region. They are unable to read or write and worked on a farm until they moved to Accra. "Our mother said our father was too old, so she married another man," said Akuokor, angry tears pouring down her wrinkled cheeks. She brought out a ragged handkerchief and sobbed some more.

A few minutes later, Akuokor reveled in the opportunity to continue chatting. Her days are spent simply. "When I get up the morning, I sweep the house, clean the coop and everything. I want everything to be clean. But because of my legs, I can't go far away. I just stay in the house."

Akwele looks frail, but she too seemed overwhelmed with excitement that they had visitors who were prepared to hear their stories. "We had wanted to go to school, but our father said we must work in the fields," said Akwele.   12

"A teacher even came to our house to try to take us to school." Akwele had two children, both of whom died at a young age. Akuokor never married, but looked after her father until he died.   13

Yet Akwele and Akuokor are luckier than others in that they benefit from Help Age, a non-governmental organization set up three years ago. Help Age fitted a new piece of iron sheeting for a roof so the twins no longer get drenched when it rains. They also have visits and receive some food.   14

The problems that the elderly face are varied, and sometimes even when they have a relative looking after them, they can still be in need, said Veronica Ayisi, one of the volunteers of Help Age.   15

Ayisi regularly visits Emmanuel Anum Tetteh, an elderly man who lives with his brother and niece. His leg had been grotesquely swollen from foot to thigh for two years, but the niece had not taken him to the hospital. Indications are that Tetteh is suffering from an advanced form of elephantiasis.   16

"The niece does not have enough money," said Ayisi. "She has no permanent job. She has children and she has to look after her father, too. There is not enough money to feed them and take him to the hospital."   17

The even more pitiful cases, however, are those begging in the bustling streets of Accra. "God bless you," they say, when coins are thrown at them by a driver stuck in a traffic jam.   18

"You never saw this 10 years ago in Accra," said Dr. Apt.   19

Other African countries, such as those with wars like Mozambique, Somalia, and Sudan, or those with a high number of AIDS cases among the young population, have an even more critical problem of caring for the elderly.   20

In Mozambique, for example, over a decade of war between the government and the Renamo rebels has ripped apart families. Thousands of elderly while away their time in refugee camps in neighboring countries, others in government-controlled accommodation centers or alone in their villages without the comfort of family or enough food to eat.   21

Chilente Simango is a typical tragedy. Silver-haired Chilente appeared to be waiting to die. The worst drought in living memory this year in Mozambique had meant that he had not eaten for two weeks. His interest in life had been sapped out of his body. A grandfather of seven, Simango now lives without any family member in an accommodation center in Chibabava, the heart of the central province of Sofala. "The war has separated me from my family," said Simango. "I don't know where any of them are or who is alive or dead. The rebels did not take me because I'm too old."   22

In Mozambique's cities, prices are so high that even a middle-income wage earner cannot make ends meet. Mozambique is by some estimates one of the poorest countries in the world, with over 70 percent of its 15.7 million people living in absolute poverty. Like Ghana, a structural adjustment program has   23 also meant more goods in the shops, but attached are prices that only the rich can think about.

It is a common sight to see elderly women and men roaming around the cities in rags begging outside banks or in the markets. Some employ children to beg for them. 24

Throughout Africa, it is only gradually being acknowledged that it is not only the West that is failing their elderly population. 25

And the real crisis facing the elderly in Africa has not yet emerged. Ghana, like other African countries, still has a relatively small elderly population because life expectancies are so low, averaging around 49 years. But as medical care is improving, people are beginning to live longer. For example, in 1960 the proportion of people over 60 years of age was 4.2 percent, but by 2025 the proportion should rise to 6.4 percent. Females consistently outnumber men among the elderly. 26

But the solution in Africa is not so easy. Poverty, war, and the breakdown of norms are bewildering for Africa's elderly. They took it for granted that their old age would not be their responsibility but their children's. "During our childhood in Ghana, we stayed in a family house, so we helped the aged," said Ayisi. "We used to do everything for them." 27

Help Age, now in its third year in Ghana, has begun to play a limited but important role, and is aiming to expand its activities. 28

But obviously, Help Age cannot solve the problem alone. The real solution is for governments and the people to change their attitudes, says Dr. Apt. This includes the old and young, men and women. 29

"In Ghana, those who retire from formal employment are talking about their retirement children. And it is really silly because they are dependent and then there will be dependents of the dependents." 30

Studies carried out by Apt show that most young people would like to look after elderly family members, but find that there are serious financial constraints. 31

The ideal situation would be for there to be some assistance for people to continue to care for their elderly family members, said Apt. "People feel guilty that they are not able to look after their elderly." 32

But few people live in an ideal situation. 33

"People in countries like ours, and I always address this to young people, need to begin to look straight into the eye of aging in the sense of planning," said Apt, "because life has changed, and there is no point in saying I am going to have 10 children and they are going to look after me. Most likely, the children will migrate and go elsewhere." □ 34

◢ **REREADING FOR UNDERSTANDING**

I. What causes does Aysisi cite as the forces behind the changing sense of responsibility among some African children toward their parents and other older adult relatives?

2. What traditional family structure and living patterns in Ghanaian society helped to foster a sense of intergenerational responsibility? How essential are those same values to sustaining a sense of responsibility among children toward the elderly in our society?

◢ RESPONDING

1. In paragraph 27, Ayisi notes that the older generation in Ghana "took it for granted that their old age would not be their responsibility but their children's." Jane English, in her essay (p. 424), argues that "filial obligations of grown children are a result of friendship rather than owed for services rendered." Both of these perspectives on children's obligation to their parents are common in our culture. Discuss which one is likely to produce more responsible relationships.

2. In Ghanaian culture, "impart[ing] wisdom" (par. 2) from one generation to the next contributed to the younger generation's sense of responsibility toward the older generation. Is respect for their wisdom a reason to care for older parents and relatives in our culture? Should it be? Should it be a significant one?

ELLEN WILLIS

Ellen Willis (1941–   ) is a journalist, editor, and writer whose work has appeared in magazines such as *The New Yorker, Ms., Rolling Stone,* and the *Village Voice.* In this 1994 article, Willis examines the limitations imposed on women by traditional family responsibilities.

Why I'm Not "Pro-Family"

I n 1992, "family values" bombed in Houston. Right-wingers at the Republican convention, sneering at career women and single mothers, turned voters off. Now the Democrats are in power—yet ironically, the family issue has reemerged, more strongly than ever. Last year, New York's influential Democratic senator, Daniel Patrick Moynihan, suggested that in relaxing the stigma against unmarried childbearing, we had laid the groundwork for the burgeoning crime rate. Then *The Atlantic* published a cover story provocatively titled: "Dan Quayle Was Right." Its author, social historian Barbara Dafoe Whitehead, invoked recent research to argue that high rates of divorce and single parenthood hurt children and underlie "many of our most vexing social problems."

The article hit a nerve. It provoked an outpouring of mail, was condensed for *Reader's Digest* and won an award from the National Women's Political Caucus. Commentators both conservative and liberal praised it in newspapers across the country. Together, Moynihan's and Whitehead's salvos launched a national obsession with "the decline of the family." President Clinton joined the bandwagon: "For 30 years," he declared in his State of the Union message, "family life in America has been breaking down."

The new advocates of the family seem more sympathetic to women than their right-wing precursors. They know women are in the workforce to stay; they are careful to talk about the time pressures faced by "parents"—not "mothers"—with jobs, and they put an unaccustomed emphasis on men's family obligations, such as contributing their fair share of child support. Some advocate liberal reforms ranging from antipoverty programs to federally funded child care to abortion rights, arguing that such measures are pro-family because they help existing families. (A recent Planned Parenthood fundraising letter proclaims, "Pro-choice is pro-family.")

I'm all for reforms that make it easier to give children the care they need, and I'm certainly in favor of men's equal participation in childrearing. My quarrel is with the underlying terms of the discussion, especially the assumption that anyone who cares about children must be "pro-family." I grew up in the fifties, in a family with two committed parents—the kind of home the pro-familists idealize. I had security; I had love. Yet like many of my peers, especially women, I saw conventional family life as far from ideal and had no desire to replicate it. It wasn't only that I didn't want to be a housewife like my mother; I felt that family life promoted self-abnegation and social conformity while stifling eroticism and spontaneity. I thought the nuclear family structure was isolating, and that within it, combining childrearing with other work would be exhausting, even if both parents shared the load—impressions I can now confirm from experience.

To me the alternative that made the most sense was not single parenthood—we needed *more* parents, not fewer, to share the daily responsibilities of childrearing and homemaking. In the seventies, a number of people I knew were bringing up children in communal households, and I imagined someday doing the same. But by the time my companion and I had a child ten years ago, those experiments and the counterculture that supported them were long gone.

From my perspective, the new champions of the family are much like the old. They never consider whether the current instability of families might signal that an age-old institution is failing to meet modern needs and ought to be reexamined. The idea that there could be other possible structures for domestic life and childrearing has been excluded from the conversation—so much so that cranks like me who persist in broaching the subject are used to getting the sort of tactful and embarrassed reaction accorded, say, people who claim to have been kidnapped by aliens. And the assumption that marriage is the self-evident solution to single parents' problems leads to impatience and hostility toward anyone who can't or won't get with the nuclear-family program.

Consider the hottest topic on the pro-family agenda: the prevalence of unwed motherhood in poor black communities. For Moynihan and other welfare reformers, the central cause of inner-city poverty and crime is not urban economic collapse, unemployment or racism, but fatherless households. Which means the solution is to bring back the stigma of "illegitimacy" and restrict or eliminate welfare for single mothers. Clinton has proposed requiring welfare recipients to leave the rolls after two years and look for work, with temporary government jobs as a backup (where permanent jobs are supposed to come from, in an economy where massive layoffs and corporate shrinkage are the order of the day, is not explained).

As the reformers profess their concern for poor children (while proposing   8
to make them even poorer), the work ethic (as jobs for the unskilled get ever scarcer) and the overburdened taxpayer, it's easy to miss their underlying message—that women have gotten out of hand. They may pay lip service to the idea that men too should be held responsible for the babies they father. But in practice there is no way to force poor, unemployed men to support their children or to stigmatize men as well as women for having babies out of wedlock. This is, after all, still a culture that regards pregnancy as the woman's problem and childrearing as the woman's job. And so, predictably, women are the chief targets of the reformers' punitive policies and rhetoric. It's women who will lose benefits; women who stand accused of deliberately having babies as a meal ticket; women who are (as usual) charged with the social failures of their sons. Given the paucity of decently paying jobs available to poor women or the men they're likely to be involved with, demanding that they not have children unless they have jobs or husbands to support them is tantamount to demanding that they not have children at all. (Note the logic: Motherhood is honorable work if supported by a man but parasitic self-indulgence if supported by the public.) Put that demand together with laws restricting abortion for poor women and teenagers, and the clear suggestion is that they shouldn't have sex either.

While this brand of misogyny is specifically aimed at poor black women, it   9
would be a mistake to think the rest of us are off the hook. For one thing (as Whitehead and other pro-familists are quick to remind us), it's all too easy in this age of high divorce and unemployment rates for a woman who imagined herself securely middle-class to unexpectedly become an impoverished single mother. Anyway, there is a thin line between fear and loathing of welfare mothers and moral distaste for unmarried mothers per se. Secretary of Health and Human Services Donna Shalala, a feminist and one of the more liberal members of the Clinton cabinet, has said, "I don't like to put this in moral terms, but I do believe that having children out of wedlock is just wrong." The language the welfare reformers use—the vocabulary of *stigma* and *illegitimacy*—unnervingly recalls the repressive moral climate of my own teenage years.

I can't listen to harangues about illegitimacy without getting posttraumatic   10
flashbacks. Let's be clear about what the old stigma meant: a vicious double standard of sexual morality for men and women; the hobbling of female sexuality with shame, guilt and inhibition; panic over dislodged diaphragms and late periods; couples trapped into marriages one or both never wanted; pregnant girls barred from school and hidden in homes for unwed mothers; enormous pressure on women to get married early and not be too picky about it.

Is it silly to worry that in the post–*Roe v. Wade*, post-Pill nineties some version of fifties morality could reassert itself? I don't think so. Activists with a   11
moral cause can be very persuasive. Who would have imagined a few years ago that there would be a public debate about restricting cigarettes as an addictive

drug? Abortion may still be legal, but its opponents have done a good job of bringing back its stigma (ironically, this is one reason a lot of pregnant teenagers decide to give birth).

Many pro-familists, above all those who call themselves communitarians, are openly nostalgic for a sterner moral order. They argue that we have become a society too focused on rights instead of duties, on personal freedom and happiness instead of sacrifice for the common good. If the welfare reformers appeal to people's self-righteousness, the communitarians tap an equally potent emotion—guilt. In our concern for our own fulfillment, they argue, we are doing irreparable harm to our children. 12

Whitehead's *Atlantic* article cites psychologist Judith Wallerstein and other researchers to support her contention that while adults have benefited from the freedom to divorce and procreate outside marriage, children have suffered. Children in single-parent families, Whitehead warns, are not only at great risk of being poor but are more likely to have emotional and behavioral problems, drop out of school, abuse drugs. She calls on Americans to recognize that our experiment with greater freedom has failed and to "act to overcome the legacy of family disruption." 13

I don't doubt that the fragility of today's family life is hard on kids. It doesn't take a social scientist to figure out that a lone parent is more vulnerable than two to a host of pressures, or that children whose familial world has just collapsed need support that their parents, depleted by the struggle to get their own lives in order, may not be able to give. But Whitehead's response, and that of communitarians generally, amounts to lecturing parents to pull up their socks, stop being selfish, and do their duty. This moralistic approach does not further a discussion of what to do when adults' need for satisfying relationships conflicts with children's need for stability. It merely stops the conversation. 14

Women, of course, are particularly susceptible to guilt mongering: If children are being neglected, if marriages are failing, whose fault can it be but ours? And come on now, who is that "parent" whose career is really interfering with family life? (Hint: It's the one who gets paid less.) While the children Judith Wallerstein interviewed were clearly miserable about their parents' breakups, she made it equally clear that the parents weren't self-indulgent monsters, only people who could no longer stand the emotional deadness of their lives. Are we prepared to say that it's too bad, but their lives simply don't matter? 15

This is the message I get from David Blankenhorn, coeditor of a pro-family anthology and newsletter, who exhorts us to "analyze the family *primarily* through the eyes of children" (my emphasis). I think this idea is profoundly wrongheaded. Certainly we need to take children seriously, which means empathizing with their relatively powerless perspective and never unthinkingly shifting our burdens to their weaker backs. On the other hand, children are more narcissistic than most adults ever dream of being—if my daughter had her way, I'd never leave the house. They too have to learn that other people's needs and feelings must be taken into account. 16

Besides, children are the next generation's adults. There's something tragic about the idea that parents should sacrifice their own happiness for the sake of children who will grow up to sacrifice in turn (in my generation, that prospect 17 inspired pop lyrics like, "Hope I die before I get old"). Instead of preaching sacrifice, we should be asking what it is about our social structure that puts adults and children at such terrible odds, and how we might change this. Faced with a shortage of food, would we decide parents have to starve so their kids can eat—or try to figure out how to increase food production?

Intelligent social policy on family issues has to start with a deeper under- 18 standing of why marriage and the two-parent family are in trouble: not because people are more selfish than they used to be but because of basic—and basically desirable—changes in our culture. For most of history, marriage has not been primarily a moral or an emotional commitment but an economic and social contract. Men supported women and children and had unquestioned authority as head of the household. Women took care of home, children, and men's personal and sexual needs. Now that undemocratic contract, on which an entire social order rested, is all but dead. Jobs and government benefits, along with liberalized sexual mores, allow women and their children to survive (if often meagerly) outside marriage; as a result, women expect more of marriage and are less willing to put up with unsatisfying or unequal relationships. For men, on the other hand, traditional incentives to marry and stay married have eroded.

What's left when the old contract is gone is the desire for love, sexual pas- 19 sion, intimate companionship. But those desires are notoriously inadequate as a basis for domestic stability. Human emotions are unpredictable. People change. And in the absence of the social compulsion exerted by that contract, moral platitudes about sacrifice count for little. Nor is it possible to bring back the compulsion without restoring inequality as well. Restrict divorce? Men who want out will still abandon their families as they did in the past; it's women with young children and less earning power who are likely to be trapped. Punish single parenthood? Women will bear the brunt.

The dogmatic insistence that only the two-parent family can properly pro- 20 vide for children is a self-fulfilling prophecy. As even some pro-familists recognize, the larger society must begin to play an active part in meeting the economic and social needs the family once fulfilled. This means, first of all, making a collective commitment to the adequate support of every child. Beyond that, it means opening our minds to the possibility of new forms of community, in which children have close ties with a *number* of adults and therefore a stable home base that does not totally depend either on one vulnerable parent or on one couple's emotional and sexual bond.

Of course, no social structure can guarantee permanence: In earlier eras, 21 families were regularly broken up by death, war and abandonment. Yet a group that forms for the specific purpose of cooperative child-rearing might actually inspire more long-term loyalty than marriage, which is supposed to provide emotional and sexual fulfillment but often does not. The practical support and help parents would gain from such an arrangement—together with the greater freedom to pursue their own personal lives—would be a strong incentive for staying in it, and the inevitable conflicts and incompatibilities among the group members would be easier to tolerate than the intense deprivation of an unhappy marriage.

It's time, in other words, to think about what has so long been unthinkable,   22
to replace reflexive dismissiveness with questions. What, for instance, can we
learn from the kibbutz—how might some of its principles be adapted to Americans' very different circumstances? What worked and didn't work about the
communal experiments of the sixties and seventies? What about more recent
projects, like groups of old people moving in together to avoid going to nursing
homes? Or the "co-housing" movement of people who are buying land in the
suburbs or city apartment buildings and dividing the space between private
dwellings and communal facilities such as dining rooms and child-care centers?

I'm not suggesting that there's anything like an immediate practical solu-   23
tion to our present family crisis. What we can do, though, is stop insisting on
false solutions that scapegoat women and oversimplify the issues. Perhaps then
a real discussion—worthy of Americans' inventiveness and enduring attraction
to frontiers—will have a chance to begin. □

◢ REREADING FOR UNDERSTANDING

1. Willis argues that "the larger society must begin to play an active part in
   meeting the economic and social needs the family once fulfilled" (par. 20).
   Why does Willis believe this is necessary?

2. Willis points out what she believes to be absurd logic in assigning responsibility for children to unwed mothers (par. 8): "Note the logic: Motherhood is honorable work if supported by a man but parasitic self-indulgence
   if supported by the public." Is that logic indeed "flawed"? Why or why not?

3. In Willis's view, from what perspective should family members' happiness
   be viewed? Does she believe happiness is a greater or lesser goal for parents
   than being responsible to other family members?

4. Willis's article first appeared in *Glamour,* a magazine whose readers are pri-
   marily young middle-class women. It is possible that some segments of
   Glamour's audience would not jump to agree with Willis's ideas. How does
   Willis create a voice to engage skeptical readers?

◢ RESPONDING

1. What qualities of life are lost, according to Willis, as a result of family responsibilities involved in parenting? Are those lost qualities essential to an
   individual's self-fulfillment? Explain.

2. Willis comments, in paragraph 4, "I felt that family life promoted self-abnegation and social conformity while stifling eroticism and spontaneity."
   By contrast, Berry argues in his essay (p. 395) that "seeking to 'free' sexual
   love from its old communal restraints, we have 'freed' it also from its
   meaning, its responsibility, and its exaltation" (par. 26). The disagreement

exemplified in these excerpts is striking. Look for supporting ideas behind these quotations in these writers' articles. Do the ideas of Berry or Willis seem more likely to produce both fulfilled and responsible individuals within family or intimate relationships? Why do you think so?

◢ RESPONDING IN WRITING

What are the virtues of Willis's proposed "communal parenting" as a means to fulfill both family responsibilities and personal desires? How well would such a model work among the adults and children you know? Would greater responsibility toward children result in a shared parenting community? Would "communal parenting" give children what they need most? Write a letter to Willis in which you explain why you believe her ideas would or would not be effective in creating more responsible parenting.

JANE ENGLISH

Jane English (1947–1978) was a philosophy professor whose main philosophical interest was applied ethics. In this essay, English attempts to define the source of responsibility in relationships, particularly in family and friendships.

What Do Grown Children Owe Their Parents?

What do grown children owe their parents? I will contend that the answer is "nothing." Although I agree that there are many things that children *ought* to do for their parents, I will argue that it is inappropriate and misleading to describe them as things "owed." I will maintain that parents' voluntary sacrifices, rather than creating "debts" to be "repaid," tend to create love or "friendship." The duties of grown children are those of friends and result from love between them and their parents, rather than being things owed in repayment for the parents' earlier sacrifices. Thus, I will oppose those philosophers who use the word "owe" whenever a duty or obligation exists. Although the "debt" metaphor is appropriate in some moral circumstances, my argument is that a love relationship is not such a case.

Misunderstandings about the proper relationship between parents and their grown children have resulted from reliance on the "owing" terminology. For instance, we hear parents complain, "You owe it to us to write home (keep up your piano playing, not adopt a hippie lifestyle), because of all we sacrificed for you (paying for piano lessons, sending you to college)." The child is sometimes even heard to reply, "I didn't ask to be born (to be given piano lessons, to be sent to college)." This inappropriate idiom of ordinary language tends to obscure, or even to undermine, the love that is the correct ground of filial obligation.

I. FAVORS CREATE DEBTS

There are some cases, other than literal debts, in which talk of "owing," though metaphorical, is apt. New to the neighborhood, Max barely knows his neighbor, Nina, but he asks her if she will take in his mail while he is gone for a month's vacation. She agrees. If, subsequently, Nina asks Max to do the same for her, it seems that Max has a moral obligation to agree (greater than the one he would have had if Nina had not done the same for him), unless for some reason it would be a burden far out of proportion to the one Nina bore for him. I will call this a *favor*: when A, at B's request, bears some burden for B, then B incurs an obligation to reciprocate. Here the metaphor of Max's "owing" Nina is appropriate. It is not literally a debt, of course, nor can Nina pass this IOU on to heirs, demand payment in the form of Max's taking out her garbage, or sue Max. Nonetheless, since Max ought to perform one act of similar nature and amount of sacrifice in return, the term is suggestive. Once he reciprocates, the debt is "discharged"—that is, their obligations revert to the condition they were in before Max's initial request.

Contrast a situation in which Max simply goes on vacation and, to his surprise, finds upon his return that his neighbor has mowed his grass twice weekly in his absence. This is a voluntary sacrifice rather than a favor, and Max has no duty to reciprocate. It would be nice for him to volunteer to do so, but this would be supererogatory on his part. Rather than a favor, Nina's action is a friendly gesture. As a result, she might expect Max to chat over the back fence, help her catch her straying dog, or something similar—she might expect the development of a friendship. But Max would be chatting (or whatever) out of friendship, rather than in repayment for mown grass. If he did not return her gesture, she might feel rebuffed or miffed, but not unjustly treated or indignant, since Max has not failed to perform a duty. Talk of "owing" would be out of place in this case.

It is sometimes difficult to distinguish between favors and non-favors, because friends tend to do favors for each other, and those who exchange favors tend to become friends. But one test is to ask how Max is motivated. Is it "to be nice to Nina" or "because she did *x* for me"? Favors are frequently performed by total strangers without any friendship developing. Nevertheless, a temporary obligation is created, even if the chance for repayment never arises. For instance, suppose that Oscar and Matilda, total strangers, are waiting in a long checkout line at the supermarket. Oscar, having forgotten the oregano, asks Matilda to watch his for a second. She does. If Matilda now asks Oscar to return the favor while she picks up some tomato sauce, he is obliged to agree. Even if she had not watched his cart, it would be inconsiderate of him to refuse, claiming he was too busy reading the magazines. He may have a duty to help others, but he would not "owe" it to her. But if she has done the same for him, he incurs an additional obligation to help, and talk of "owing" is apt. It suggests an agreement to perform equal, reciprocal, canceling sacrifices.

2. THE DUTIES OF FRIENDSHIP

The terms "owe" and "repay" are helpful in the case of favors, because the sameness of the amount of sacrifice on the two sides is important; the monetary metaphor suggests equal quantities of sacrifice. But friendship ought to be characterized by *mutuality* rather than reciprocity: friends offer what they can give and accept what they need, without regard for the total amounts of benefits exchanged. And friends are motivated by love rather than by the prospect of repayment. Hence, talk of "owing" is singularly out of place in friendship.   6

For example, suppose Alfred takes Beatrice out for an expensive dinner and a movie. Beatrice incurs no obligation to "repay" him with a goodnight kiss or a return engagement. If Alfred complains that she "owes" him something, he is operating under the assumption that she should repay a favor, but on the contrary his was a generous gesture done in the hopes of developing a friendship. We hope that he would not want her repayment in the form of sex or attention if this was done to discharge a debt rather than from friendship. Since, if Alfred is prone to reasoning in this way, Beatrice may well decline the invitation or request to pay for her own dinner, his attitude of expecting a "return" on his "investment" could hinder the development of a friendship. Beatrice should return the gesture only if she is motivated by friendship.   7

Another common misuse of the "owing" idiom occurs when the Smiths have dined at the Joneses' four times, but the Joneses at the Smiths' only once. People often say, "We owe them three dinners." This line of thinking may be appropriate between business acquaintances, but not between friends. After all, the Joneses invited the Smiths not in order to feed them or to be fed in turn, but because of the friendly contact presumably enjoyed by all on such occasions. If the Smiths do not feel friendship toward the Joneses, they can decline future invitations and not invite the Joneses; they owe them nothing. Of course, between friends of equal resources and needs, roughly equal sacrifices (though not necessarily roughly equal dinners) will typically occur. If the sacrifices are highly out of proportion to the resources, the relationship is closer to servility than to friendship.*   8

Another difference between favors and friendship is that after a friendship ends, the duties of friendship end. The party that has sacrificed less owes the other nothing. For instance, suppose Elmer donated a pint of blood that his wife Doris needed during an operation. Years after their divorce, Elmer is in an accident and needs one pint of blood. His new wife, Cora, is also of the same blood type. It seems that Doris not only does not "owe" Elmer blood, but that she should actually refrain from coming forward if Cora has volunteered to   9

---

*Cf. Thomas E. Hill, Jr., "Servility and Self-Respect," *Monist* 57 (1973). Thus, during childhood, most of the sacrifices will come from the parents, since they have most of the resources and the child has most of the needs. When children are grown, the situation is usually reversed.

donate. To insist on donating not only interferes with the newlyweds' friendship, but it belittles Doris and Elmer's former relationship by suggesting that Elmer gave blood in hopes of favors returned instead of simply out of love for Doris. It is one of the heart-rending features of divorce that it attends to quantity in a relationship previously characterized by mutuality. If Cora could not donate, Doris's obligation is the same as that for any former spouse in need of blood; it is not increased by the fact that Elmer similarly aided her. It *is* affected by the degree to which they are still friends, which in turn may (or may not) have been influenced by Elmer's donation.

In short, unlike the debts created by favors, the duties of friendship do not   10
require equal quantities of sacrifice. Performing equal sacrifices does not cancel the duties of friendship, as it does the debts of favors. Unrequested sacrifices do not themselves create debts, but friends have duties regardless of whether they requested or initiated the friendship. Those who perform favors may be motivated by mutual gain, whereas friends should be motivated by affection. These characteristics of the friendship relation are distorted by talk of "owing."

3. PARENTS AND CHILDREN

The relationship between children and their parents should be one of friend-   11
ship characterized by mutuality rather than one of reciprocal favors. The quantity of parental sacrifice is not relevant in determining what duties the grown child has. The medical assistance grown children ought to offer their ill mothers in old age depends upon the mothers' need, not upon whether they endured a difficult pregnancy, for example. Nor do one's duties to one's parents cease once an equal quantity of sacrifice has been performed, as the phrase "discharging a debt" may lead us to think.

· Rather, what children ought to do for their parents (and parents for chil-   12
dren) depends upon (1) their respective needs, abilities, and resources and (2) the extent to which there is an ongoing friendship between them. Thus, regardless of the quantity of childhood sacrifices, an able, wealthy child has an obligation to help his needy parents more than does a needy child. To illustrate, suppose sisters Cecile and Dana are equally loved by their parents, even though Cecile was an easy child to care for, seldom ill, while Dana was often sick and caused some trouble as a juvenile delinquent. As adults, Dana is a struggling artist living far away, while Cecile is a wealthy lawyer living nearby. When the parents need visits and financial aid, Cecile has an obligation to bear a higher proportion of these burdens than her sister. This results from her abilities, rather than from the quantities of sacrifice made by the parents earlier.

Sacrifices have an important causal role in creating an ongoing friendship,   13
which may lead us to assume incorrectly that it is the sacrifices that are the source of the obligation. That the source is the friendship instead can be seen by examining cases in which the sacrifices occurred but the friendship, for some reason, did not develop or persist. For example, if a woman gives up her newborn child for adoption, and if no feelings of love ever develop on either side, it seems that the grown child does not have an obligation to "repay" her for her

sacrifices in pregnancy. For that matter, if the adopted child has an unimpaired love relationship with the adoptive parents, he or she has the same obligations to help them as a natural child would have.

The filial obligations of grown children are a result of friendship, rather than owed for services rendered. Suppose that Vance married Lola despite his parents' strong wish that he marry within their religion, and that as a result, the parents refuse to speak to him again. As the years pass, the parents are unaware of Vance's problems, his accomplishments, the birth of his children. The love that once existed between them, let us suppose, has been completely destroyed by this event and thirty years of desuetude. At this point, it seems, Vance is under no obligation to pay his parents' medical bills in their old age, beyond his general duty to help those in need. An additional, filial obligation would only arise from whatever love he may still feel for them. It would be irrelevant for his parents to argue, "But look how much we sacrificed for you when you were young," for that sacrifice was not a favor but occurred as part of a friendship which existed at that time but is now, we have supposed, defunct. A more appropriate message would be, "We still love you, and we would like to renew our friendship." 14

I hope this helps to set the question of what children ought to do for their parents in a new light. The parental argument, "You ought to do x because we did y for you," should be replaced by, "We love you and you will be happier if you do x," or "We believe you love us, and anyone who loved us would do x." If the parents' sacrifice had been a favor, the child's reply, "I never asked you to do y for me," would have been relevant; to the revised parental remarks, this reply is clearly irrelevant. The child can either do x or dispute one of the parents' claims: by showing that a love relationship does not exist, or that love for someone does not motivate doing x, or that he or she will not be happier doing x. 15

Seen in this light, parental requests for children to write home, visit, and offer them a reasonable amount of emotional and financial support in life's crises are well founded, so long as a friendship still exists. Love for others does call for caring about and caring for them. Some other parental requests, such as for more sweeping changes in the child's lifestyle or life goals, can be seen to be insupportable, once we shift the justification from debts owed to love. The terminology of favors suggests the reasoning, "Since we paid for your college education, you owe it to us to make a career of engineering, rather than becoming a rock musician." This tends to alienate affection even further, since the tuition payments are depicted as investments for a return rather than done from love, as though the child's life goals could be "bought." Basing the argument on love leads to different reasoning patterns. The suppressed premise, "If A loves B, then A follows B's wishes as to A's lifelong career" is simply false. Love does not even dictate that the child adopt the parents' values as to the desirability of alternative life goals. So the parents' strongest available argument here is, "We love you, we are deeply concerned about your happiness, and in the long run you will be happier as an engineer." This makes it clear that an empirical claim is really the subject of the debate. 16

The function of these examples is to draw out our considered judgments as to the proper relation between parents and their grown children, and to show 17 how poorly they fit the model of favors. What is relevant is the ongoing friendship that exists between parents and children. Although that relationship developed partly as a result of parental sacrifices for the child, the duties that grown children have to their parents result from the friendship rather than from the sacrifices. The idiom of owing favors to one's parents can actually be destructive if it undermines the role of mutuality and leads us to think in terms of quantitative reciprocal favors. □

◢ REREADING FOR UNDERSTANDING

1. What, from English's perspective, is the difference between a "debt" and a "free gesture"? How does that difference relate to her overall argument defining responsibility among family members?

2. Why does English regard the concept of "debt" or "owing" as inappropriate for friendships? Why does responsibility end when a friendship ends?

3. According to English, what factors determine the kind of behavior children should adopt toward older parents who have a financial or emotional need?

◢ RESPONDING

1. Do you agree with English's distinctions among "debt," "favors," and "owing"? If those distinctions were followed by you or your friends, would the quality of relationships, your sense of responsibility, improve or decline? In other words, can you apply English's ideas to relationships outside the family? If the answer is yes, would the effects be positive? Explain.

2. Do you believe that adults who are no longer "friends" with their parents are obligated to help their parents if a dire emotional or financial need arises?

◢ RESPONDING IN WRITING

Choose a relationship in your life that you would like to change in some significant way. For example, you might wish your parents would grant you more responsibility for your own decisions. You might wish a friendship would develop into a romance, or a romance cool into a friendship. Write a letter to the other person(s) in the relationship explaining how you would like the relationship to change and why. Tell what steps you are willing to take and what you expect, or hope for, from him or her.

CONTROVERSIES

What Are My Responsibilities Toward the Environment?

ALAN DURNING

Alan Durning writes extensively on environmental issues. A full-time re-searcher for an environmental think tank called the Worldwatch Institute, Durning helped craft the Institute's 1990 report entitled *The State of the World*. In an excerpt from that report, Durning presents ideas and argu-ments showing how the amazing spread and growth of industrial capitalism is altering the behavior and values of cultures around the world. Durning at-tempts to demonstrate that our pursuit of happiness through a materialis-tic, consumer culture leads to irresponsible behavior on a worldwide scale. As you read his essay, consider how accurately he portrays the consumer culture as you personally experience it. Do you agree that consumerism creates environmental problems? Or is Durning wrong to suggest material-istic consumerism is a kind of global irresponsibility?

Asking How Much Is Enough

Early in the age of affluence that followed World War II, an American re-tailing analyst named Victor Lebow proclaimed, "Our enormously pro-ductive economy . . . demands that we make consumption our way of life, that we convert the buying and use of goods into rituals, that we seek our spiritual satisfaction, our ego satisfaction, in consumption. . . . We need things consumed, burned up, worn out, replaced, and discarded at an ever increasing rate." Americans have responded to Mr. Lebow's call, and much of the world has followed.

Consumption has become a central pillar of life in industrial lands, and is even embedded in social values. Opinion surveys in the world's two largest economies—Japan and the United States—show consumerist definitions of success becoming ever more prevalent. In Taiwan, a billboard demands "Why Aren't You a Millionaire Yet?" The Japanese speak of the "new three sacred treasures": color television, air conditioning, and the automobile.

The affluent life-style born in the United States is emulated by those who 3 can afford it around the world. And many can: the average person today is four-and-a-half times richer than were his or her great-grandparents at the turn of the century. Needless to say, that new global wealth is not evenly spread among the earth's people. One billion live in unprecedented luxury; 1 billion live in destitution. Even American children have more pocket money—$230 a year— than the half-billion poorest people alive.

Overconsumption by the world's fortunate is an environmental problem 4 unmatched in severity by anything but perhaps population growth. Their surging exploitation of resources threatens to exhaust or unalterably disfigure forests, soils, water, air, and climate. Ironically, high consumption may be a mixed blessing in human terms too. The time-honored values of integrity of character, good work, friendship, family, and community have often been sacrificed in the rush to riches. Thus, many in the industrial lands have a sense that their world of plenty is somehow hollow—that, hoodwinked by a consumerist culture, they have been fruitlessly attempting to satisfy what are essentially social, psychological, and spiritual needs with material things.

Of course, the opposite of overconsumption—poverty—is no solution to 5 either environmental or human problems. It is infinitely worse for people and bad for the natural world too. Dispossessed peasants slash and burn their way into the rain forests of Latin America, and hungry nomads turn their herds out onto fragile African rangeland, reducing it to desert. If environmental destruction results when people have either too little or too much, we are left to wonder how much is enough. What level of consumption can the earth support? When does having more cease to add appreciably to human satisfaction?

Answering these questions definitively is impossible, but for each of us in 6 the world's consuming class, asking is essential nonetheless. Unless we see that more is not always better, our efforts to forestall ecological decline will be overwhelmed by our appetites.

THE CONSUMING SOCIETY

Skyrocketing consumption is the hallmark of our era. The headlong advance of 7 technology, rising earnings, and consequently cheaper material goods have lifted overall consumption to levels never dreamed of a century ago. The trend is visible in statistics for almost any per capita indicator. Worldwide, since mid-century the intake of copper, energy, meat, steel, and wood has approximately doubled; car ownership and cement consumption have quadrupled; plastic use has quintupled; aluminum consumption has grown sevenfold; and air travel has multiplied 32 times.

Moneyed regions account for the largest waves of consumption since 1950. 8 In the United States, the world's premier consuming society, on average people today own twice as many cars, drive two-and-a-half times as far, use 21 times as much plastic, and travel 25 times as far by air as did their parents in 1950. Air conditioning spread from 15 percent of households in 1960 to 64 percent in 1987, and color televisions from 1 to 93 percent. Microwave ovens and video cassette recorders found their way into almost two thirds of American homes during the eighties alone.

That decade was a period of marked extravagance in the United States; not since the roaring twenties had conspicuous consumption been so lauded. Between 1978 and 1987, sales of Jaguar automobiles increased eightfold, and the average age of first-time fur coat buyers fell from 50 to 26. The select club of American millionaires more than doubled its membership from 600,000 to 1.5 million over the decade, while the number of American billionaires reached 58 by 1990.   9

Japan and Western Europe have displayed parallel trends. Per person, the Japanese of today consume more than four times as much aluminum, almost five times as much energy, and 25 times as much steel as people in Japan did in 1950. They also own four times as many cars and eat nearly twice as much meat. In 1972, 1 million Japanese traveled abroad; in 1990, the number was expected to top 10 million. As in the United States, the eighties were a particularly consumerist decade in Japan, with sales of BMW automobiles rising tenfold over the decade. Ironically, in 1990 a *reja bumu* (leisure boom) combined with concern for nature to create two new status symbols: four-wheel drive Range Rovers from England and cabins made of imported American logs.   10

Still, Japan has come to the high consumption ethos hesitantly. Many older Japanese still hold to their time-honored belief in frugality. Yorimoto Katsumi of Waseda University in Tokyo writes, "Members of the older generation . . . are careful to save every scrap of paper and bit of string for future use." A recent wave of stratospheric spending—cups of coffee that cost $350 and mink coats for dogs—has created a crisis of values in the society. Says one student, "Japanese people are materialistically well-off, but not inside. . . . We never have time to find ourselves, or what we should seek in life."   11

Like the Japanese, West Europeans' consumption levels are only one notch below Americans'. Taken together, France, West Germany, and the United Kingdom almost doubled their per capita use of steel, more than doubled their intake of cement and aluminum, and tripled their paper consumption since mid-century. Just in the first half of the eighties, per capita consumption of frozen prepared meals—with their excessive packaging—rose more than 30 percent in every West European country except Finland; in Switzerland, the jump was 180 percent. As trade barriers come down in the move toward a single European market by 1992, prices will likely fall and product promotion grow more aggressive, boosting consumption higher. . . .   12

Long before all the world's people could achieve the American dream, however, the planet would be laid waste. The world's 1 billion meat eaters, car drivers, and throwaway consumers are responsible for the lion's share of the damage humans have caused to common global resources. For one thing, supporting the life-style of the affluent requires resources from far away. A Dutch person's consumption of food, wood, natural fibers, and other products of the   13 soil involves exploitation of five times as much land outside the country as in-side—much of it in the Third World. Industrial nations account for close to two-thirds of global use of steel, more than two-thirds of aluminum, copper, lead, nickel, tin, and zinc, and three fourths of energy.

Those in the wealthiest fifth of humanity have built more than 99 percent 14
of the world's nuclear warheads. Their appetite for wood is a driving force be-hind destruction of the tropical rain forests, and the resulting extinction of countless species. Over the past century, their economies have pumped out two thirds of the greenhouse gases that threaten the earth's climate, and each year their energy use releases perhaps three fourths of the sulfur and nitrogen oxides that cause acid rain. Their industries generate most of the world's hazardous chemical wastes, and their air conditioners, aerosol sprays, and fac-tories release almost 90 percent of the chlorofluorocarbons that destroy the earth's protective ozone layer. Clearly, even 1 billion profligate consumers is too much for the earth.

Beyond the environmental costs of acquisitiveness, some perplexing find- 15
ings of social scientists throw doubt on the wisdom of high consumption as a personal and national goal: rich societies have had little success in turning con-sumption into fulfillment. Regular surveys by the National Opinion Research Center of the University of Chicago reveal, for example, that no more Americans report they are "very happy" now than in 1957. The share has fluctuated around one-third since then, despite a doubling of personal consumption expenditures per capita. Whatever Americans are buying, it does not seem to be enough.

Likewise, a landmark study in 1974 revealed that Nigerians, Filipinos, 16
Panamanians, Yugoslavians, Japanese, Israelis, and West Germans all ranked themselves near the middle of a happiness scale. Confounding any attempt to correlate affluence and happiness, poor Cubans and rich Americans were both found to be considerably happier than the norm, and citizens of India and the Dominican Republic, less so. As Oxford psychologist Michael Argyle writes, "there is very little difference in the levels of reported happiness found in rich and very poor countries."

Measured in constant dollars, the world's people have consumed as many 17
goods and services since 1950 as all previous generations put together. As noted [earlier], since 1940 Americans alone have used up as large a share of the earth's mineral resources as did everyone before them combined. If the effectiveness of that consumption in providing personal fulfillment is questionable, perhaps environmental concerns can help us redefine our goals.

IN SEARCH OF SUFFICIENCY

In simplified terms, an economy's total burden on the ecological systems that 18
undergird it is a function of three factors: the size of the population, average consumption, and the broad set of technologies—everything from mundane clotheslines to the most sophisticated satellite communications systems—the economy uses to provide goods and services.

Changing agricultural patterns, transportation systems, urban design, en-   19
ergy use, and the like could radically reduce the total environmental damage
caused by the consuming societies, while allowing those at the bottom of the
economic ladder to rise without producing such egregious effects. Japan, for example, uses a third as much energy as the Soviet Union to produce a dollar's
worth of goods and services, and Norwegians use half as much paper and cardboard apiece as their neighbors in Sweden, though they are equals in literacy
and richer in monetary terms.

Eventually, though, technological change will need its complement in the   20
reduction of material wants. José Goldemberg of the University of São Paolo
and an international team of researchers conducted a careful study of the
potential to cut fossil fuel consumption through greater efficiency and use of
renewable energy. The entire world population, Goldemberg concludes, could
live with the quality of energy services now enjoyed by West Europeans—things
like modest but comfortable homes, refrigeration for food, and ready access to
public transit, augmented by limited auto use.

The study's implicit conclusion, however, is that the entire world decidedly   21
could *not* live in the style of Americans, with their larger homes, more numerous electrical gadgets, and auto-centered transportation systems. Technological
change and the political forces that must drive it hold extraordinary potential,
but are ultimately limited by the compulsion to consume. If money saved
through frugal use of materials and energy is simply spent buying private jets
for weekend excursions to Antarctica, what hope is there for the biosphere? In
the end, the ability of the earth to support billions of human beings depends on
whether we continue to equate consumption with fulfillment.

Some guidance on what the earth can sustain emerges from an examina-   22
tion of current consumption patterns around the world. For three of the most
ecologically important types of consumption—transportation, diet, and use of
raw materials—the world's people are distributed unevenly over a vast range.
Those at the bottom clearly fall below the "too little" line, while those at the top,
in what could be called the cars-meat-and-disposables class, clearly consume
too much.

About 1 billion people do most of their traveling, aside from the occa-   23
sional donkey or bus ride, on foot, many of them never going more than 100
kilometers from their birthplaces. Unable to get to jobs easily, attend school, or
bring their complaints before government offices, they are severely hindered
by the lack of transportation options.

The massive middle class of the world, numbering some 3 billion, travels by   24
bus and bicycle. Kilometer for kilometer, bikes are cheaper than any other vehicles, costing less than $100 new in most of the Third World and requiring no
fuel. The world's automobile class is relatively small: only 8 percent of humans,
about 400 million people, own cars. Their vehicles are directly responsible for an
estimated 13 percent of carbon dioxide emissions from fossil fuels worldwide,
along with air pollution, acid rain, and a quarter-million traffic fatalities a year.

Car owners bear indirect responsibility for the far-reaching impacts of their   25
chosen vehicle. The automobile makes itself indispensable: cities sprawl, public
transit atrophies, shopping centers multiply, workplaces scatter. As suburbs

spread, families start to need a car for each driver. One-fifth of American house-holds own three or more vehicles, more than half own at least two, and 65 per-cent of new American houses are built with two-car garages. Today, working Americans spend nine hours a week behind the wheel. To make these homes-away-from-home more comfortable, 90 percent of new cars have air-condition-ing, doubling their contribution to climate change and adding emissions of ozone-depleting chlorofluorocarbons.

Around the world, the great marketing achievement of the auto industry   26
has been to turn its machines into cultural icons. As French philosopher Roland Barthes writes, "cars today are almost the exact equivalent of the great Gothic cathedrals . . . the supreme creation of an era, conceived with passion by un-known artists, and consumed in image if not in usage by a whole population which appropriates them as . . . purely magical object[s]." . . .

THE CULTIVATION OF NEEDS

"The avarice of mankind is insatiable," wrote Aristotle 23 centuries ago,   27
describing the way that as each of our desires is satisfied a new one seems to appear in its place. That observation, on which all of economic theory is based, provides the most obvious answer to the question of why people never seem satisfied with what they have. If our wants are insatiable, there is simply no such thing as enough.

Much confirms this view of human nature. The Roman philosopher   28
Lucretius wrote a century before Christ: "We have lost our taste for acorns. So [too] we have abandoned those couches littered with herbage and heaped with leaves. So the wearing of wild beasts' skins has gone out of fashion. . . . Skins yes-terday, purple and gold today—such are the baubles that embitter human life with resentment." Nearly 2,000 years later, Russian novelist Leo Tolstoy echoed Lucretius: "Seek among men, from beggar to millionaire, one who is contented with his lot, and you will not find one such in a thousand. . . . Today we must buy an overcoat and galoshes, tomorrow, a watch and a chain; the next day we must install ourselves in an apartment with a sofa and a bronze lamp; then we must have carpets and velvet gowns; then a house, horses and carriages, paint-ings and decorations."

What distinguishes modern consuming habits from those of interest to   29
Lucretius and Tolstoy, some would say, is simply that we are much richer than our ancestors, and consequently have more ruinous effects on nature. There is no doubt a great deal of truth in that view, but there is also reason to believe that certain forces in the modern world encourage people to act on their con-sumptive desires as rarely before. Five distinctly modern factors seem to play a role in cultivating particularly voracious appetites: the influence of social pres-sures in mass societies, advertising, the shopping culture, various government policies, and the expansion of the mass market into the traditional realm of household and local self-reliance.

In the anonymous mass societies of advanced industrial nations, daily   30
interactions with the economy lack the face-to face character that prevails in surviving local communities. Traditional virtues such as integrity, honesty, and

skill are too hard to measure to serve as yardsticks of social worth. By default, they are gradually supplanted by a simple, single indicator—money. As one Wall Street Banker put it bluntly to the *New York Times*, "Net worth equals self-worth." Under this definition, consumption becomes a treadmill, with everyone judging their status by who is ahead and who is behind.

Psychological data from several nations confirm that the satisfaction de-   31
rived from money does not come from simply having it. It comes from having more of it than others do, and from having more this year than last. Thus, the bulk of survey data reveals that the upper classes in any society are more satisfied with their lives than the lower classes are, but they are no more satisfied than the upper classes of much poorer countries—nor than the upper classes were in the less-affluent past.

More striking, perhaps, most psychological data show that the main deter-   32
minants of happiness in life are not related to consumption at all: prominent among them are satisfaction with family life, especially marriage, followed by satisfaction with work, leisure, and friendships. Indeed, in a comprehensive inquiry into the relationship between affluence and satisfaction, social commentator Jonathan Freedman notes, "Above the poverty level, the relationship between income and happiness is remarkably small."

Yet when alternative measures of success are not available, the deep human   33
need to be valued and respected by others is acted out through consumption. Buying things becomes both a proof of self-esteem ("I'm worth it," chants one advertising slogan) and a means to social acceptance—as token of what turn-of-the-century economist Thorstein Veblen termed "pecuniary decency."

Beyond social pressures, the affluent live completely enveloped in the pro-   34
consumption advertising messages. The sales pitch is everywhere. One analyst estimates that the typical American is exposed to 50–100 advertisements each morning before nine o'clock. Along with their weekly 22-hour diet of television, American teenagers are typically exposed to 3–4 hours of TV advertisements a week, adding up to at least 100,000 ads between birth and high school graduation.

Marketers have found ever more ways to push their products. Advertise-   35
ments are broadcast by over 10,000 television and radio stations in the United States, towed behind airplanes, plastered on billboards and in sports stadiums, bounced around the planet from satellites. They are posted on chair-lift poles on ski slopes, and played through closed circuit televisions at bus stops, in subway stations, and on wall-sized video screens at shopping malls.

Ads are piped into classrooms and doctors' offices, woven into the plots of   36
feature films, placed on board games, mounted in bathroom stalls, and played back between rings on public phones in the Kansas City airport. Even the food supply may soon go mass media: the Viskase company of Chicago now offers to print edible ad slogans on hot dogs, and Eggverts International is using a similar technique to advertise on thousands of eggs in Israel.

Advertising has been one of the fastest growing industries during the past   37
half-century. In the United States, ad expenditures rose from $198 per capita in 1950 to $498 in 1989. Total global advertising expenditures, meanwhile, rose from an estimated $39 billion in 1950 to $237 billion in 1988, growing far

faster than economic output. Over the same period, per person advertising expenditures grew from \$15 to \$46. In developing countries, the increases have been astonishing. Advertising billings in India jumped fivefold in the eighties, and South Korea's advertising industry has recently grown 35–40 percent annually.

The proliferation of shopping centers has, in a roundabout way, also promoted the compulsion to consume. Mall design itself encourages acquisitive impulses, many critics believe. But perhaps more important, suburban malls and commercial strips suck commerce away from downtown and neighborhood merchants. Shopping by public transit or on foot becomes difficult, auto traffic increases, and sprawl accelerates. In the end, public places such as town squares and city streets are robbed of their vitality, leaving people fewer attractive places to go besides the malls that set the whole shopping process in motion. Perhaps by default, malls have even become popular spots to exercise. Avia, a leading sports footwear manufacturer, introduced a shoe designed for the rigors of mall walking.

Particularly in the United States, shopping seems to have become a primary cultural activity. Americans spend 6 hours a week doing various types of shopping, and they go to shopping centers on average once a week—more often than they go to church or synagogue. Some 93 percent of American teenage girls surveyed in 1987 deemed shopping their favorite pastime. The 32,563 shopping centers in the country surpassed high schools in number in 1987. Just from 1986 to 1989, total retail space in these centers grew by 65 million square meters, or 20 percent. Shopping centers now garner 55 percent of retail sales in the United States, compared with 16 percent in France and 4 percent in Spain.

Shopping centers are sprouting across the landscape in many industrial lands. Spain's 90-odd centers are expected to triple in number by 1992. Britain's bevy of one-stop superstores doubled to about 500 during the eighties. Italy, despite a strong tradition of community merchants, has recently relaxed controls on mall development, leading to predictions that its shopping centers will multiply from 35 to 100 in five years. . . .

A CULTURE OF PERMANENCE

When Moses came down from Mount Sinai he could count the rules of ethical behavior on the fingers of his two hands. In the complex global economy of the late twentieth century, in which the simple act of turning on an air conditioner sends greenhouse gases up into the atmosphere, the rules for ecologically sustainable living run into the hundreds. The basic value of a sustainable society, though, the ecological equivalent of the Golden Rule, is simple: each generation should meet its needs without jeopardizing the prospects of future generations to meet their own needs. What is lacking is the thorough practical knowledge— at each level of society—of what living by that principle means.

Ethics, after all, exist only in practice, in the fine grain of everyday decisions. As Aristotle argued, "In ethics, the decision lies with perception." When most people see a large automobile and think first of the air pollution it causes, rather than the social status it conveys, environmental ethics will have arrived.

In a fragile biosphere, the ultimate fate of humanity may depend on whether we can cultivate deeper sources of fulfillment, founded on a widespread ethic of limiting consumption and finding non-material enrichment. An ethic becomes widespread enough to restrain antisocial behavior effectively, moreover, only when it is encoded in culture, in society's collective memory, experience, and wisdom.

For individuals, the decision to live a life of sufficiency—to find their own   43
answer to the question "How much is enough?"—is to begin a highly personal process. The goal is to put consumption in its proper place among the many sources of personal fulfillment, and to find ways of living within the means of the earth. One great inspiration in this quest is the body of human wisdom passed down over the ages.

Materialism was denounced by all the sages, from Buddha to Muhammad.   44
[See Table 1.] "These religious founders," observed historian Arnold Toynbee, "disagreed with each other in the pictures of what is the nature of the universe, the nature of the spiritual life, the nature of ultimate reality. But they all agreed in their ethical precepts. . . . They all said with one voice that if we made material wealth our paramount aim, this would lead to disaster." The Christian Bible echoes most of human wisdom when it asks "What shall it profit a man if he shall gain the whole world and lose his own soul?" □

Table 1.	Teachings of World Religions and Major Cultures on Consumption
Religion or Culture	**Teaching and Source**
American Indian	"Miserable as we seem in thy eyes, we consider ourselves . . . much happier than thou, in this that we are very content with the little that we have." (Micmac chief)
Buddhist	"Whoever in this world overcomes his selfish cravings, his sorrows fall away from him, like drops of water from a lotus flower." (*Dhammapada*, 336)
Christian	It is "easier for a camel to go through the eye of a needle than for a rich man to enter into the kingdom of God." (Matt. 19:23-24)
Confucian	"Excess and deficiency are equally at fault." (Confucius, XI.15)
Ancient Greek	"Nothing in Excess." (Inscribed at Oracle of Delphi)
Hindu	"That person who lives completely free from desires, without longing . . . attains peace." (*Bhagavad-Gita*, II.71)
Islamic	"Poverty is my pride." (Muhammad)
Jewish	"Give me neither poverty nor riches." (*Proverbs* 30:8)
Taoist	"He who knows he has enough is rich." (*Tao Te Ching*)

SOURCES: Compiled by Worldwatch Institute.

◢ REREADING FOR UNDERSTANDING

1. Durning's article illustrates the magnitude of growth in consumerism across the globe and the environmental consequences of that growth. He implies that consumerism is driven in part by two forces. What are they? Do either of those causes surprise you?

2. Durning quotes Roland Barthes' observation that "cars today are almost the exact equivalent of the great Gothic cathedrals . . . the supreme creation of an era, conceived with passion by unknown artists, and consumed in image if not in usage by a whole population which appropriates them as . . . purely magical object[s]" (par. 26). What point about Americans' relationship does this comparison make? How accurate is this analysis from your personal experience?

◢ RESPONDING

1. In the opening paragraph, Durning quotes Victor Lebow. Reread Lebow's quotation. What insights does it reveal about the "hidden" causes for our cultural definition of happiness and the good life?

2. Between now and your next class meeting, attempt to keep an accurate record of your consumer transactions. Make note not only of consumer purchases, but also how you use automobiles, electricity, hot showers, toilet facilities, and any other activity that consumes natural resources. At your next class, break into small groups. Discuss whether you are more or less inclined to accept Durning's argument in light of what your consumption log reveals.

3. Durning's report itemizes various rates of consumption as of 1989. As a research project, find current data on a few items like per capita waste generated, fossil fuel consumed, or areas of interest to you. What do you discover? Does your research indicate that we are becoming more or less responsible as a consumer culture?

◢ RESPONDING IN WRITING

Think of ways you could reduce your individual consumption, such as forgoing fast food served in disposable, environmentally polluting containers (or some other environmentally threatening behavior cited by Durning that caught your interest). Write an essay addressed to students at your college explaining your decision to be more environmentally thrifty and encouraging them to do the same. Or choose one of the examples of consumption Durning criticizes and write an essay in defense of that practice. Give reasons to show why this particular type and scope of consumption are justified.

BETSY CARPENTER

Betsy Carpenter is a staff writer for *U.S. News & World Report.* In this 1994 article she points to a simple but profound problem: more people inevitably cause more pollution. Carpenter's observation that growing numbers of people have a dramatic impact on the environment seems obvious, yet it is an observation many ignore, perhaps because it calls into question what most would consider to be a fundamental right—the right to have children. As you read, consider what responsibility, if any, individuals and society have to control population growth.

More People, More Pollution

Overpopulation typically brings to mind images of starving children in impoverished Third World countries, smoldering rainforests, crowded slums and barren, eroded hillsides.

It all seems a long way from affluent, industrialized America. Yet even close to home, a mounting environmental bill is coming due that is a direct consequence of population growth. Consider Presly Creek, a small Virginia inlet off the Chesapeake Bay. At first glance, it looks pristine. But, in fact, it is buckling under the strain of the 15 million people (up from 8 million in 1950) who now live in the 64,000-square-mile Chesapeake Bay watershed: Polluted runoff from roads, lawns and farms has turned the water a murky green and decimated underwater sea-grass meadows. The oyster reefs are gone, as are the sturgeon, American wigeon and redhead ducks. Even the creek's curves have been resculpted as silt from plowed fields and construction sites has filled in its coves.

As the population has swelled in the past few decades, places like Presly Creek have become commonplace. While not stinking, burning or dead, they have been irrevocably degraded, and human numbers are largely to blame. "One person's impact isn't a very big deal, but multiply it by 15 million and it adds up," says Michael Hirschfield of the Chesapeake Bay Foundation in Annapolis, Md. New technology has blunted some of the impact of people on the environment. But experts contend that human ingenuity may only have postponed the day of reckoning. As the longstanding efforts to revive the bay suggest, technology is better at cleaning up industrial messes than at solving the intractable problems caused by millions of people going about their everyday activities.

THE ENEMY IS US

Many Americans still hold big industry responsible for the nation's environmental woes. Increasingly, however, people are the source of problems such as air and water pollution and the decline of many species of plants and animals. The Chesapeake watershed stretches from Cooperstown, N.Y., to southern Virginia and includes Richmond, Va., Washington and Baltimore. Much of what enters the rivers, creeks and streams lacing these lands ends up in the bay: outfall of sewage treatment plants, toxic runoff from city streets, waste oil dumped down storm sewers and car exhaust washed out of the sky by rain showers.

As the population of the watershed has grown, so has the environmental impact of each of those additional people. People today drive more, use more energy and take up more land than ever before. Total emissions of nitrogen-oxide gases from vehicles have almost doubled from 1 to almost 2 pounds per person per week between 1952 and 1986. The pollutant is produced by cars and power plants and is implicated in many of the bay's problems. Watershed inhabitants use four times as much land to build homes as they did 40 years ago.

HOE AND AX

Although human impact on the bay has accelerated sharply in recent decades, it began centuries ago during an earlier population boom, says Stephen Potter of the Smithsonian Institution. The first European colonists arrived at Jamestown, Va., in 1607, but for a century they left little imprint on the land. Most clung to the shoreline in small outposts, attacking the wilderness behind them with ax- and hoe-based agriculture that was borrowed from the Indians and minimized soil erosion.

But the arrival of thousands more European settlers—coupled with the rise of slavery and the introduction of the plow—changed everything. Soil erosion became a widespread problem. By the early 1800s, many smaller ports were so clogged with silt that they had to be abandoned. Sediment not only reshapes coastlines, it also clouds the water and smothers fish spawning grounds. And while farmers were changing the coastline, fishermen devastated certain fish and oyster populations. Studies of fish bones and shells found in colonial garbage dumps reveal that by the mid-1700s, watermen had so depleted inshore oyster bars that they had to pluck oysters from the bay's deeper channels with long-handled tongs. By the mid-1800s, fishermen had exhausted sheepshead and drum in certain parts of the bay.

But the environmental consequences of this first population surge pale beside the impacts of the recent explosion. For Robert Costanza, director of the Maryland International Institute for Ecological Economics at the University of Maryland in Solomons, the bay's fundamental problem is best summarized by a simple comparison: Today, for every cubic mile of water in this rich estuary, there are 800,000 people living in the watershed; the Baltic Sea, by contrast, has 16,000 persons per cubic mile of water and the Mediterranean Sea just 350.

The Chesapeake has been brought to its knees by two pollutants in particular, nitrogen and phosphorus, which are released nearly every time people turn around. Besides auto exhaust and power-plant emissions, the sources of nitrogen include animal manure and chemical fertilizer runoff from fields and lawns and prodigious quantities of sewage. Some 2 million watershed residents use septic tanks, which discharge nitrogen into ground water. Conventional sewage treatment plants spew a nitrogen-rich outfall into rivers and produce huge quantities of nitrogen- and phosphorus-laden sludge; the sludge is often spread onto fields as fertilizer, which washes into rivers and streams.

Nitrogen and phosphorus trigger a far-reaching biological chain reaction   10
in the bay, fueling the explosive growth of tiny plankton that, along with sediment flowing from fields and construction sites, choke off sunlight to other
plants, notably aquatic sea grasses. The acreage of sea-grass beds has plunged,
prompting in turn a sharp decline in the diversity of bay waterfowl, according
to Tom Horton and William M. Eichbaum, authors of *Turning the Tide: Saving
the Chesapeake Bay*. Populations of 17 of 20 varieties of duck have dropped in
recent decades; redhead ducks and American wigeon have almost vanished. The
overall waterfowl population has dropped by only 10 to 20 percent, however:
Canada and snow geese have adapted to the sea-grass declines by feeding in
grain fields and now account for 65 percent of total waterfowl, up from 20 percent in the 1950s.

The ecological reverberations of man-made nutrients extend to the bay's   11
deepest channels. When the plankton die, they drop to the bottom and decom-
pose in a process that consumes oxygen, exacerbating a natural oxygen shortage in parts of the bay. Now, in the summer months, large stretches of the
estuary do not have enough oxygen to support aquatic life.

Population pressure also has spurred land development in the watershed   12
that has hampered the bay's natural ability to rebound from environmental
blows. Undeveloped lands buffer human impacts in a number of ways. Forests
act like sponges, moderating water flow and cushioning the impact of floods
and droughts. Wetlands purify water by trapping sediment and filtering out nutrients. But undeveloped land is disappearing: Keeping pace with population
trends, in Maryland the amount of developed land jumped by 38 percent between 1973 and 1990.

The plundering of the bay's oyster beds also has shut down a natural water   13
purification system. To feed, oysters, clams and other bivalves filter water
through their gills, removing plankton and sediment from as many as 50 gallons
of water a day. Scientists estimate that in early colonial times there were so many
oysters in the estuary that the mollusks could filter a volume of water equal to
the entire bay in a matter of days. But overharvesting has slashed the oyster population to about 1 percent of its original total. Oyster harvests are down to 2
million pounds annually from a high of 118 million pounds in the 1880s. Today,
it takes the bay's oysters a year or more to filter a bay's worth of water.

RULES AND TECHNOLOGY HELP

Despite the clear link between a burgeoning population and environmental   14
degradation, more people do not automatically bring more pollution. In the
past few decades, government regulations and pollution-cutting technologies
have helped keep the bay alive. By the late 1980s, for instance, Maryland,
Virginia, Pennsylvania and D.C. banned the use of phosphate laundry deter-
gents, which helped cut phosphorus discharges from sewage treatment plants
by 30 to 50 percent.

Progress has been hindered, however, by the fact that many new rules are   15
either voluntary or poorly enforced. During the 1970s, the bay states enacted

laws to control sediment runoff from construction sites with measures ranging from settling ponds to barriers of straw bales and cloth. But a 1990 survey of sites found that only one fourth had adequate erosion controls.

Technology has also mitigated population's impact, though as George   16
Moffett argues in his recently published *Critical Masses: The Global Population Challenge*, growth ultimately swamps the benefits of technology. Pollution-control devices have made cars dramatically cleaner, for example, but those gains have been overwhelmed by the increase in the number of miles driven.

As the world gains another 5 billion people, preventing Presly Creek and   17
thousands of places like it from degrading further will require a change in consumption patterns, argues Allen Hammond of the World Resources Institute. Americans, he says, need to build a more sustainable society—developing land more carefully, farming more wisely and restructuring industry to be more efficient. Some maintain that Americans are not prepared for such a fundamental shift, but Hammond is more optimistic: "Attitudes can change quickly. Look how fast the Berlin Wall came down." ☐

◢ REREADING FOR UNDERSTANDING

1. What is the relationship between population growth and industrial technology as a cure for environmental problems, according to Carpenter's article?

2. How does population growth itself become a significant factor in widespread environmental degradation?

◢ RESPONDING

1. Can you find ways in which population growth in your own neighborhood has affected the local environment? Begin by considering the very existence of your neighborhood. What natural habitats did it replace? What do you imagine was its impact on various nonhuman populations? Also consider the activities households in your neighborhood now engage in. What impact do such activities have on the local environment?

2. One solution to population growth might be to examine our "right" to have children. Do we have such a right? Where does it come from? What past cultural traditions or beliefs give us our sense of our "right" to have children? Are those traditions and beliefs still valid? You may also wish to consider the definition of rights and responsibilities offered by Ayn Rand (p. 375) and Marian Wright Edelman (p. 383). Would either of these authors agree that having children was a right to which everyone is entitled? Why or why not?

3. If you have read Virginia Postrel's article (p. 444), compare Carpenter's style (voice, pronoun usage, word choice, sentence type and variety) with

Postrel's. How are their writing styles suited to their different purposes (Carpenter's article is a news magazine article whereas Postrel's piece is a persuasive speech)?

 RESPONDING IN WRITING

Beginning in 1995, Congress has moved to repeal existing environmental regulations and to alter the role of the Environmental Protection Agency. What effect will recent deregulation and repeal of environmental laws have on the population/pollution equation? In order to answer the question, research a particular piece of environmental legislation, such as the Clean Water Act, and find out what changes have been made in its restrictions or in the ability of the Environmental Protection Agency to enforce its provisions. After you have completed your research, write to your senator or representative, expressing your views on the issue of environmental protection through legislation.

VIRGINIA I. POSTREL

Virginia I. Postrel is the editor of *Reason* magazine, a social and political commentary publication. Besides editing *Reason*, she writes editorial and commentary pieces for newspapers like the *Washington Post* and the *Los Angeles Times*. Postrel has also worked as a reporter for *Inc.* magazine and for the *Wall Street Journal*. This essay is the text of a speech Postrel delivered to the City Club of Cleveland in 1990. Although the speech was not written as an answer to Alan Durning's essay, many of the ideas it offers directly address and refute Durning's arguments. As you read Postrel's critique of environmentalists' arguments, consider how fairly and fully she has considered those arguments, and how reasonable her criticism is.

The Environmental Movement
A Skeptical View

On Earth Day, Henry Allen of The *Washington Post* published a pointed and amusing article. In it, he suggested that we've created a new image of Mother Nature:

"A sort of combination of Joan Crawford in *Mildred Pierce* and Mrs. Portnoy in *Portnoy's Complaint*, a disappointed, long-suffering martyr who makes us wish, at least for her sake, that we'd never been born."

"She weeps. She threatens. She nags. . . ."

She's a kvetch who makes us feel guilty for eating Big Macs, dumping paint thinner down the cellar sink, driving to work instead of riding the bus, and riding the bus instead of riding a bicycle. Then she makes us feel even guiltier for not feeling guilty enough.

Go ahead, use that deodorant, don't even think about me, God knows I'll be gone soon enough, I won't be here to see you get skin cancer when the ozone hole lets in the ultraviolet rays . . ."

I think all of us can see that Allen is on to something. There's a lot of truth in his picture of the new Mother Nature.

The question is, Where did this New Mother Nature come from? And how does this picture of nature affect—even warp—the way we deal with environmental issues?

Americans have historically been a can-do people, proud of our Yankee ingenuity. We believed in solving problems. Based on our history, you'd expect to see us tackling environmental problems the way John Todd took on sewage sludge.

Todd is an environmental biologist who became concerned about the toxic sludge that comes out of sewage plants. Based on his biological research, he realized that the sludge could be cleaned up by mixing it with certain microbes. The microbes would metabolize it and produce clean water. Todd now has a pilot plant in Providence, Rhode Island, and he estimates that such a system could handle all of that city's sludge with 120 acres of reaction tanks—a modest number.

Now, if you're like me, you think this is great. Here is a bona fide environmental problem. An ingenious man with an environmental conscience has come along, put his ingenuity and training to work, and *solved the problem.* But rather than applauding Todd's solution, many of his friends in the environmental movement have stopped speaking to him. "By discovering a solution to a man-made offense," writes Gregg Easterbrook in *The New Republic,* "he takes away an argument against growth."

Todd's practical environmentalism has run up against what I refer to as "green" ideology. This ideology is distinct from the common desire for a cleaner world—that's why it can lead people to condemn solutions like Todd's. It is also different from the traditional doctrines of either the left or the right: It combines elements from each with a value system of its own.

This green ideology underlies many of the environmentalist critiques and policy recommendations that we see today. Now, I'm not suggesting that environmentalists are engaged in some sort of grand conspiracy or are governed by some lockstep system of thought. What I *am* suggesting is that if you want to understand a political movement, it's a good idea to read its theorists and find out who its intellectual heroes are.

Green ideology is not mysterious. Anybody can go to the library and read the books that define it.

Green ideology is not some fringe theory cooked up in California. Like many important ideas in American history, it is largely imported from Britain and Germany. It is, increasingly, one of the most powerful forces in our culture. We may even adopt parts of it without realizing their origins. To be informed citizens, we ought to know something about it.

First of all, a caveat. Ideologies are messy. They tend to associate disparate ideas in unexpected ways. What's more, people who share the same general ideological viewpoint rarely agree on everything. No two conservatives or liberals or libertarians or even Marxists believe exactly the same thing. And political movements are almost always riven by internal conflict (you should read some of the things the abolitionists said about each other).

The environmental movement is no different. Purist greens who distrust political compromise berate Washington-based groups that lobby for legislation. The Green-Greens, who aren't leftist, attack the Red-Greens, who are. Grassroots activists criticize the "Gang of 10," the large, well-funded environmental groups.

And perhaps the biggest *philosophical* split is between "deep ecology" and other forms of environmentalism. Deep ecologists advocate a mystical view of the natural world as an end in itself, not made for human beings. They criticize traditional conservationism, as well as leftist "social ecology," for emphasizing the environment's value to people.

Most environmental activists—the rank and file—combine some of each outlook to create a personal viewpoint. They can do this because, deep down, the greens aren't as divided as they sometimes like to think.

Every ideology has a primary value or set of values at its core—liberty, equality, order, virtue, salvation. For greens, the core value is stasis, "sustainability" as they put it. The ideal is of an earth that doesn't change, that shows little or no effects of human activity. Greens take as their model of the ideal society the notion of an ecosystem that has reached an unchanging climax stage. "Limits to growth" is as much a description of how things *should* be as it is of how they *are*.

That is why there is no room in the green world for John Todd and his sewage-cleaning microbes. Todd hasn't sought to stop growth. He has found a way to live with it.

The static view has two effects on the general environmental movement: First, it leads environmentalists to advocate policies that will make growth hard on people, as a way of discouraging further development. Cutting off new supplies of water, outlawing new technologies, and banning new construction to increase the cost of housing are common policies. And, second, the static view leads environmentalists to misunderstand how real environmental problems can be solved.

Consider how we regulate air pollution. Since the 1977 Clean Air Act, Americans have spent some $3.5 billion on reducing air pollution—with very little to show for it. Current policy dictates *specific technologies*—for example, smokestack scrubbers for coal-burning power plants. The plants can't just use cleaner coal. And cars have to have catalytic converters. If someone comes up with a cheaper or more efficient way to get the same result, the government says, Sorry. We've picked our one true technology. You can't sell yours.

Now, for decades economists have suggested that we take a different approach to regulating pollution. Set an overall allowable level, they say, then let companies decide how to achieve it. Let them buy and sell permits that regulate the amount of pollution they can emit: If you wanted to build a new plant, you'd have to buy some permits from somebody else who was closing their plant or reducing their pollution. The economy could grow without increasing the total amount of pollution. Companies would have to pay a price for the pollution they put out. And plant managers would have an economic incentive to adopt—or even develop from scratch—pollution-saving technologies.

Most environmentalists, however, hate, loath, and despise this whole idea. 20 They call it a "license to pollute." Emissions trading treats pollution as a cost, a side effect to be controlled, rather than an outright evil, a sin. It allows growth. And it lets individual choice, not politics, determine exactly which technologies will be adopted to control pollution. It takes a *dynamic* view, rather than a static one. Over time, it assumes, people will come up with better and better ways to deal with pollution. And, it assumes, we ought to *encourage* these innovations.

People rarely adopt a new technology because it makes life worse. But 21 nowadays we tend to pay more attention to the dangers or pollution from new technologies. We take the old technologies' disadvantages for granted. So, for example, we forget that the automobile actually made city life cleaner.

By creating a market for petroleum-derived gasoline, the car also encour- 22 aged the production of heating oil and natural gas—much cleaner fuels than the coal people used to use to heat homes and businesses. And, thanks to the automobile, cities no longer have to dispose of tons of horse manure every day.

Extrapolating from his own time, a British writer in 1885 described the 23 future of London:

> "It is a vast stagnant swamp, which no man dare enter, since death would be his inevitable fate. There exhales from this oozy mass so fatal a vapour that no animal can endure it. The black water bears a greenish-brown scum, which forever bubbles up from the putrid mud of the bottom."

Clearly, modern environmentalists have no monopoly on dire predictions 24 of disaster. From this particular fate we were saved by the automobile.

A dynamic view sees the pluses of change as well as the minuses. And it ap- 25 preciates how new, unforeseen technologies or social changes can allay current problems.

By contrast, the environmental movement has been built on crisis. Around 26 the turn of the century, Americans were terrified of the growing lumber short-age. A 1908 New York *Times* headline read: "Hickory Disappearing, Supply of Wood Nears End—Much Wasted and There's No Substitute." Actually, as prices rose, the railroads—the major consumers of wood—did find substitutes. And more-efficient ways of using wood.

Meanwhile, however, Gifford Pinchot used the specter of a "timber short- 27 age" to get the U.S. Forest Service started. There was, of course, no such short-age, unless you take the static view. And a growing number of both economists and environmental activists now see Pinchot's legacy of central planning and federally managed forest lands as an economic and environmental disaster.

Contrary to the doomsayers, both past and present, people have a knack for 28 innovating their way out of "crises"—if they have both the permission and the incentive to do so. So we find that people developed petroleum as whale oil became scarce, that farmers turn to drip irrigation as water prices rise, and that drivers bought fuel-efficient cars when gas prices went up.

To a large degree, however, green ideology is not about facts. It is about *values*, and the environmental movement is about enforcing those values through political action. Green politics, write British greens Jonathon Porritt and David Winner, "demands a wholly new ethic in which violent, plundering humankind abandons its destructive ways, recognizes its dependence on Planet Earth and starts living on a more equal footing with the rest of nature. The danger lies not only in the odd maverick polluting factory, industry, or technology, but in the fundamental nature of our economic systems. It is industrialism itself—a 'super-ideology' embraced by socialist countries as well as by the capitalist West—which threatens us."

If we look around, we can see the effort to remake "violent, plundering humankind" in a number of current initiatives. Take recycling. On one level, it seems like common sense. Why waste resources? That's certainly true with aluminum, which takes huge amounts of electricity to make in the first place and very little energy to recycle. But then there's glass. Both making glass in the first place and melting it down for recycling take about the same amount of energy. The only other thing new glass takes is sand—and we have plenty of that. Unless you're worried about an imminent sand crisis, there's little reason to recycle glass. It doesn't even take up much room in landfills.

But, of course, glass—like other forms of packaging—is convenient. Getting people to recycle it is a way of reminding them of the evils of materialism and the folly of convenience. As Jeremy Rifkin's little booklet *The Greenhouse Crisis: 101 Ways to Save the Earth* advises shoppers: "Remember, if it's disposable and convenient, it probably contributes to the greenhouse effect." On a scientific level, this is ridiculous. But as a value statement it conveys a great deal. Convenient, disposable products are the creations of an affluent, innovative, industrial society that responds to consumer demands. In a static, green world, we would forego incandescent lighting for fluorescent bulbs and clothes dryers for clothes lines. We would give up out-of-season fruits and vegetables, disposable diapers (of course), free-flowing shower heads, and other self-indulgent pleasures.

If green ideology is guilt transformed into politics, we might wonder why people adopt it. Partly, I think, green ideology appeals to many people's sense of frustration with modern life. Technology is too complicated, work too demanding, communication too instantaneous, information too abundant, the pace of life too fast. Stasis looks attractive, not only for nature but also for human beings.

E.F. Schumacher put it this way in *Small Is Beautiful*, a central work of green theory. "The pressure and strain of living," he wrote, "is very much less in, say, Burma, than it is in the United States, in spite of the fact that the amount of labour-saving machinery used in the former country is only a minute fraction of the amount used in the latter."

Jeremy Rifkin describes the green coalition as "time rebels," who "argue that the pace of production and consumption should not exceed nature's ability to recycle wastes and renew basic resources. They argue that the tempo of social and economic life should be compatible with nature's time frame." Rifkin, therefore, can't stand computers. They go too fast.

To slow economy and society to the approved *adagio*, the greens have some   35
fairly straightforward prescriptions: Restrict trade to the local area. Eliminate markets where possible. End specialization. Anchor individuals in their "bio-regions," local areas defined by their environmental characteristics. Shrink the population. Make life simple again, small, self-contained.

It is a vision that can be made remarkably appealing, for it plays on our   36
desire for self-sufficiency, our longing for community, and our nostalgia for the agrarian past. We will go back to the land, back to the rhythms of seedtime and harvest, back to making our own clothes, our own furniture, our own tools. Back to barnraisings and quilting bees. Back to a life we can understand without a string of Ph.D.s.

"In living in the world by his own will and skill, the stupidest peasant or   37
tribesman is more competent than the most intelligent workers or technicians or intellectuals in a society of specialists," writes Wendell Berry, an agrarian admired by both greens and cultural conservatives. Berry is a fine writer; he chooses words carefully; he means what he says. We will go back to being peasants.

These are, of course, harsh words. And we aren't likely to wake up as subsis-   38
tence farmers tomorrow. But an economy, like an ecology, is made up of intri-cate connections. Constantly tinkering with it—cutting off this new technology here, banning that product there—will have unintended consequences. And sometimes, one suspects, the consequences aren't all that unintended.

Take electricity. Environmentalists, of course, rule out nuclear power,   39
regardless of the evidence of its safety. But then they say coal-powered plants can cause acid rain and pollution, so they're out, too. Oil-fired plants release greenhouse gases (and cost a bundle, too). Hydroelectric plants are no good because they disrupt the flow of rivers.

Solar photovoltaic cells have always been the great hope of the future. But   40
making them requires lots of nasty chemicals, so we can expect solar cells to be banned around the time they become profitable. Pretty soon, you've eliminated every conceivable source of electricity. Then your only option is to dismantle your industry and live with less: the environmentalist warning of impending shortages becomes a self-fulfilling prophecy.

And, make no mistake about it, many environmentalists have a truly radi-   41
cal agenda. "It is a spiritual act to try to shut down DuPont," says Randall Hayes, director of the Rainforest Action Network. From the appealing ads his group runs to solicit donations to save the rainforests, you'd never guess he had that goal in mind.

And consider the remarkably frank book, *Whatever Happened to Ecology?*,   42
by longtime environmental activist Stephanie Mills, recently published by Sierra Club Books. Mills garnered national attention in 1969, when she delivered a col-lege commencement address entitled "The Future Is a Cruel Hoax" and declared she'd never have children. The book traces the evolution of the environmental movement and of her ideas since then. Today, she and her husband live on a farm in northern Michigan, where they pursue their bioregionalist ideal of

"reinhabiting" the land by restoring some of its wildness and blocking future development. A journalist, not a theorist, Mills speaks not only for herself but for the intellectual movement of which she is a part. Her words are chilling:

> "We young moderns resort to elaborate means of getting physical experience. Yogic practice, fanatical running, bicycling, competitive sports, bodybuilding. All of these recreations are voluntary and may not cultivate the endurance necessary for the kind of labor required to dismantle industrial society and restore the Earth's productivity."

Are voluntary . . . the endurance necessary . . . the labor required . . . dismantle industrial society. The prose is pleasant, the notions it contains disturbing. She continues: 43

> "One summer afternoon a few days after a freak windstorm, I made a foray out to buy some toilet paper (Every time I have to replenish the supply of this presumed necessity, I wonder what we're going to substitute for it when the trucks stop running.)"

When the trucks stop running. There is a history of the future buried in those words, fodder for several science-fiction novels—but no explanation of when and why the trucks will stop. Or who will stop them.   44

People don't want to be peasants: The cities of the Third World teem with the evidence. And certainly, the typical subscriber to the *Utne Reader* (a sort of green *Reader's Digest* with a circulation of 200,000 after only six years of publication) doesn't envision a future of subsistence farming—much less the hunter-gatherer existence preferred by deep ecologists. More to the reader's taste is, no doubt, the cheery vision offered by Executive Editor Jay Walljasper.   45

> It's 2009. Nuclear weapons have been dismantled. Green publications have huge circulations. Minneapolis has 11 newspapers and its own currency ("redeemable in trout, walleye, or wild rice"). Sidewalk cafés sell croissants and yogurt. A local ordinance decrees a 24-hour workweek. Cars are nearly nonexistent (a delegation from the "People's Independent Republic of Estonia" is in town to help design better ski trails for commuters). Citizens vote electronically. The shopping mall has become a nature preserve.

Walljasper is clearly having fun—after all, he puts Aretha Franklin's face on the $10 bill—and he doesn't consider any of the tough questions. Like how all those magazines and newspapers exist without printing plants or paper mills. How the Estonians got to town without airplanes or the fuel to run them (Jeremy Rifkin specifically names the Boeing 747 as the kind of product that can't be produced in the small-is-beautiful factories of the coming "entropic age.") How the chips to run the electronic voting got etched without chemicals. Where the chips were made. How a 24-hour workweek produced the sustained concentration needed to write software or the level of affluence that allows for restaurant croissants.   46

And, above all, Walljasper doesn't explain why after millenia of behaving otherwise, humans simply gave up wanting *stuff.* If the Walljasper of 2009 still overloads on reading material, why should we assume that people whose fancy   47 runs toward fast food and polyester (or fast cars and silk) would be struck with a sudden attack of bioregionally approved tastes? How *exactly* did that shopping mall disappear?

"The root of the solution has to be so radical that it can scarcely be spoken of," says movie director and British green John Boorman. "We all have to be prepared to change the way we live and function and relate to the planet. In short, we need a transformation of the human spirit. If the human heart can be changed, then everything can be changed." 48

We have heard this somewhere before—in, for example, the promise of a "New Soviet Man." People are forever seeking to change the human heart, often with tragic results. 49

The greens want people to give up the idea that life can be better. They say "better" need not refer to material abundance, that we should just be content with less. Stasis, they say, can satisfy our "vital needs." They may indeed convince some people to pursue a life of voluntary simplicity, and that is fine and good and just the thing a free society ought to allow. Stephanie Mills is welcome to her organic farm. 50

But most of us do not want to give up 747s, or cars, or eyeglasses, or private washing machines, or tailored clothing, or even disposable diapers. The "debased human protoplasm" that Stephanie Mills holds in contempt for their delight in "clothes, food, sporting goods, electronics, building supplies, pets, baked goods, deli food, toys, tools, hardware, geegaws, jim-jams, and knick-knacks" will not happily relinquish the benefits of modern civilization. Many ordinary human beings would like a cleaner world. They are prepared to make sacrifices—*tradeoffs* is a better word—to get one. But ordinary human beings will not adopt the Buddha's life without desire, much as E.F. Schumacher might have ordained it. 51

At its extreme, green ideology expresses itself in utter contempt for humanity. Reviewing Bill McKibben's *The End of Nature* in the *Los Angeles Times*, National Park Service research biologist David M. Graber concluded with this stunning passage: 52

> "Human happiness, and certainly human fecundity, are not as important as a wild and healthy planet. I know social scientists who remind me that people are part of nature, but it isn't true. Somewhere along the line—at about a billion years ago, maybe half that—we quit the contract and became a cancer. We have become a plague upon ourselves and upon the Earth. It is cosmically unlikely that the developed world will choose to end its orgy of fossil-energy consumption, and the Third World its suicidal consumption of landscape. Until such time as Homo sapiens should decide to rejoin nature, some of us can only hope for the right virus to come along."

It is hard to take such notions seriously without sounding like a bit of a kook yourself. But there they are—calmly expressed in the pages of a major, mainstream, Establishment newspaper by an employee of the federal government. When it is acceptable to say such things in polite intellectual company, when feel-good environmentalists tolerate the totalitarians in their midst, when sophisticates greet the likes of Graber with indulgent nods and smiles rather 53 than arguments and outrage, we are one step farther down another bloody road to someone's imagined Eden.

Thank you. □

◢ REREADING FOR UNDERSTANDING

1. What does Postrel mean by the "green ideology"?

2. According to Postrel, what are the main threats that "green ideology" poses to American life as we know it?

3. How reasonable are Postrel's attacks on "green ideology"? Look at her analysis of the electric utility industry, for instance. Is her analysis responsible?

◢ RESPONDING

1. Both Postrel and Durning (p. 430) use facts and figures to lend support to their analysis of environmental issues. Are both equally "responsible" in fairly representing the data they use? For instance, Postrel claims that the Clean Air Act has cost $3.5 billion since 1970 (to 1990) "with very little to show for it" (par. 18). Durning cites various data to argue that air pollution continues to increase because the proliferation of cars far outweighs the positive effects of mandatory, factory-installed clean air devices. Which proponent is using research data more responsibly? Do some research of your own to find out.

2. Postrel observes that many green environmentalists believe that technology is only bad and deny that technology has had any positive effects on human life and the environment. She says in paragraph 21, for instance, "we forget that the automobile actually made city life cleaner." Does this example effectively support Postrel's argument? In what ways has technology actually helped the environment? Can you identify any past or current technological improvements whose benefits justify the negative impact of that technology on the environment?

◢ RESPONDING IN WRITING

Write a script for a speech you would give to a public meeting in your own community (college or home). Help the members of that community understand what balance we should seek among individual rights, responsibility, and the environment. If you focus on one or two issues (such as transportation, recycling, air or water quality, or population growth) and then trace out the consequences of one policy or another, your script will be more focused and easier to prepare.

The Pursuit of Happiness

What Is the Good Life?

INTRODUCTION

*T*his final unit of *Making Choices* contains, in many ways, all the thematic components of the preceding units. Education, work, truth and lying, responsibility—each of us weaves all these threads together into a fabric distinctly ours, hoping the finished product will resemble the good life.

In pursuit of the good life, we pursue pleasure and avoid pain—and call that happiness. Or we embrace struggle, deny ourselves luxuries to pursue some ideal, some social good—and call that happiness. We reject or embrace the material world, we consume objects and experiences as if there were no tomorrow, or we conserve resources and attempt to preserve the natural world—and call that the good life. However we formulate our pursuit, however consciously and deliberately we plan, or however mindlessly we are driven by the culture that shapes us—all of us want a good life and happiness.

As in all of the preceding units, these readings will not provide a final or best answer to the question of what makes a life good or happy. We offer a few perspectives only. We begin with A Way In piece by Voltaire entitled "Story of a Good Brahmin." The tale captures two different approaches people seem to take as we pursue the good life. One is a lifelong attempt to understand what makes life good; the other is a mindless approach to life captured in the cliché "Ignorance is bliss." In one way or another all the writers in this unit argue for some balance between those extremes. The question is, How much knowledge, and what sort, will cause life to be good, will cause one to find "true" happiness?

Each piece argues for a different balance of rational thinking, spiritual experience, or pragmatic materialism as the source of the good life. As you read through the Contexts essays, be aware of the different emphasis and balance all these writers place on one aspect or another of the good life. Consider how you might apply their perspective to any of the Controversies pieces or to reflections on your own life.

The Controversies section of this unit is divided into three subsections: (1) What Is the American Dream? (2) How Is Happiness Discovered? and (3) Does the Good Life Require a Spiritual Dimension? The first section allows you to look at different facets of the American Dream from materialism to social idealism. The second questions whether happiness is found in solitude or community. And the final section presents the role spiritual experiences might play as we attempt to shape a life worth living.

As you read from the group of writers collected in this unit, you will encounter old and new perspectives that seek to persuade readers to choose one road to the good life over another. Listen, absorb, and critique the various perspectives on what constitutes a good life. You may end up with a slightly altered definition yourself. Or you may find and pursue a slightly different path to a good life than the one you now follow.

A W A Y I N

*T*his A Way In piece presents a basic issue common to the selections in this unit: How much understanding of oneself and of life is needed to bring happiness and a sense of having lived well? Voltaire's "Story of a Good Brahmin" allows us to see that question played out. As you read the brief story, reflect on whose approach to life you prefer—the "old automaton's" or the "Good Brahmin's."

VOLTAIRE

François-Marie de Arouet (1694–1778) is known by the familiar pen name of Voltaire. Voltaire read and wrote extensively in politics, philosophy, history, science, drama, and poetry throughout his adult life. By 1760, he was acclaimed throughout Europe as one of the most brilliant, satirical minds of his age. He fought against the barbaric cruelties of the Roman Catholic church, and against the injustice and arbitrary power of government. He also championed the development of empirical science.

Story of a Good Brahmin

On my travels I met an old Brahmin, a very wise man, of marked intellect and great learning. Furthermore, he was rich and, consequently, all the wiser, because, lacking nothing, he needed to deceive nobody. His household was very well managed by three handsome women who set themselves out to please him. When he was not amusing himself with his women, he passed the time in philosophizing. Near his house, which was beautifully decorated and had charming gardens attached, there lived a narrow-minded old Indian woman: she was a simpleton, and rather poor.

Said the Brahmin to me one day: "I wish I had never been born!" On my asking why, he answered: "I have been studying forty years, and that is forty years wasted. I teach others and myself am ignorant of everything. Such a state of affairs fills my soul with so much humiliation and disgust that my life is intolerable. I was born in Time, I live in Time, and yet I do not know what Time is. I am at a point between two eternities, as our wise men say, and I have no conception of eternity. I am composed of matter: I think, but I have never been able to learn what produces my thought. I do not know whether or no my understanding is a simple faculty inside me, such as those of walking and digesting, and whether or no I think with my head as I grip with my hands. Not only is the cause of my thought unknown to me; the cause of my actions is equally a mystery. I do not know why I exist, and yet every day people ask me questions on all these points. I have to reply, and as I have nothing really worth saying I talk a great deal, and am ashamed of myself afterward for having talked.

"It is worse still when I am asked if Brahma was born of Vishnu or if they 3 are both eternal. God is my witness that I have not the remotest idea, and my ignorance shows itself in my replies. 'Ah, Holy One,' people say to me, 'tell us why evil pervades the earth.' I am in as great a difficulty as those who ask me this question. Sometimes I tell them that everything is as well as can be, but those who have been ruined and broken in the wars do not believe a word of it—and no more do I. I retire to my home stricken at my own curiosity and ignorance. I read our ancient books, and they double my darkness. I talk to my companions: some answer me that we must enjoy life and make game of mankind; others think they know a lot and lose themselves in a maze of wild ideas. Everything increases my anguish. I am ready sometimes to despair when I think that after all my seeking I do not know whence I came, whither I go, what I am nor what I shall become."

The good man's condition really worried me. Nobody was more rational or 4 more sincere than he. I perceived that his unhappiness increased in proportion as his understanding developed and his insight grew.

The same day I saw the old woman who lived near him. I asked her if she 5 had ever been troubled by the thought that she was ignorant of the nature of her soul. She did not even understand my question. Never in all her life had she reflected for one single moment on one single point of all those which tormented the Brahmin. She believed with all her heart in the metamorphoses of Vishnu and, provided she could obtain a little Ganges water wherewith to wash herself, thought herself the happiest of women.

Struck with this mean creature's happiness, I returned to my wretched 6 philosopher. "Are you not ashamed," said I, "to be unhappy when at your very door there lives an old automaton who thinks about nothing, and yet lives contentedly?"

"You are right," he replied. "I have told myself a hundred times that I 7 should be happy if I were as brainless as my neighbor, and yet I do not desire such happiness."

My Brahmin's answer impressed me more than all the rest. I set to examin- 8 ing myself, and I saw that in truth I would not care to be happy at the price of being a simpleton.

I put the matter before some philosophers, and they were of my opinion. 9 "Nevertheless," said I, "there is a tremendous contradiction in this mode of thought, for, after all, the problem is—how to be happy. What does it matter whether one has brains or not? Further, those who are contented with their lot are certain of their contentment, whereas those who reason are not certain that they reason correctly. It is quite clear, therefore," I continued, "that we must choose not to have common sense, however little common sense may contribute to our discomfort." Everyone agreed with me, but I found nobody, notwithstanding, who was willing to accept the bargain of becoming a simpleton in order to become contented. From which I conclude that if we consider the question of happiness we must consider still more the question of reason.

But on reflection it seems that to prefer reason to felicity is to be very sense-   10
less. How can this contradiction be explained? Like all the other contradictions. It is matter for much talk. □

◢ REREADING FOR UNDERSTANDING

1. Why is the Brahmin not happy? Be certain you can illustrate your answer with several of the Brahmin's "complaints."

2. Why does the narrator conclude (par. 9) that "if we consider the question of happiness we must consider still more the question of reason"?

◢ RESPONDING

1. In paragraph 4, Voltaire's narrator remarks: "I perceived that his [Brahmin's] unhappiness increased in proportion as his understanding and insight grew." Does that ring true with your own experience?

2. The Good Brahmin and the "old automaton" represent extreme approaches to pursuing the good life. Which "extreme" would you consider more promising? Why?

3. Do you think your college education will cause you to be more like the Good Brahmin or the "old automaton"?

◢ RESPONDING IN WRITING

The narrator in this piece observes that "to prefer reason to felicity [happiness] is to be senseless" (par. 10). Write a brief essay in which you attempt to define and demonstrate an important (perhaps universal) type of happiness that a person might obtain without any rational understanding of its causes. Or, write an essay in which you illustrate an important aspect of happiness or the good life that is impossible to obtain without some understanding of oneself or of life. Address your essay to the Good Brahmin or to the "old automaton," as seems appropriate.

The Pursuit of Happiness

ARISTOTLE

Aristotle was a Greek philosopher born in 384 B.C. He became a pupil of Plato's (another Greek philosopher) and later a member of Plato's Academy in Athens. Aristotle left Athens to become a tutor to the young Alexander the Great and eventually returned to Athens to found his own school, the Lyceum. Late in his life, Aristotle had to flee Athens because of the changing political situation. He died in exile in 321 B.C. During his life, Aristotle wrote widely in philosophy and science. This selection is an excerpt from his philosophical work on ethics called the *Nicomachean Ethics*. In the *Ethics* Aristotle discusses human nature, politics, and what one must understand about human nature in order to live a happy and good life. He focuses particularly on how reason, our rational capacity, should help us to recognize and pursue what will lead to happiness and the good life.

When Aristotle refers to the soul, understand that he considers the soul to be a part of the body. Aristotle believed that the soul dies with the body; it is not a spiritual force living on after the body dies. For Aristotle, the soul has three parts or qualities: rational, appetitive, and vegetative. The rational aspect of the soul is its highest or best quality, giving us the power to reason; the appetitive part of the soul controls our desires and emotions; the vegetative part directs the physical growth of our bodies. As you read, look for Aristotle's careful explanation of the interrelationship between our rational nature and happiness.

Happiness Is the Greatest Good

Every art and every inquiry, and likewise every activity, seems to aim at some good. This is why the good is defined as that at which everything aims. 1

But sometimes the end at which we are aiming is the activity itself while other times the end is something else that we are trying to achieve by means of 2 that activity. When we are aiming at some end to which the activity is a means, the end is clearly a higher good than the activity. . . .

Now if in all our activities there is some end which we seek for its own sake, and if everything else is a means to this same end, it obviously will be our highest and best end. Clearly there must be some such end since everything cannot be a means to something else since then there would be nothing for which we ultimately do anything and everything would be pointless. Surely from a practical point of view it is important for us to know what this ultimate end is so that, like archers shooting at a definite mark, we will be more likely to attain what we are seeking [in all our actions]. . . . 3

Some people think our highest end is something material and obvious, like pleasure or money or fame. One thinks it is this, and another thinks it is that. Often the same person changes his mind: When he is sick, it is health; when he is poor, it is wealth. And realizing they are really ignorant, such men express great admiration for anyone who says deep-sounding things that are beyond their comprehension. . . . 4

Most people think the highest end is pleasure and so they seek nothing higher than a life of pleasure. . . . They reveal their utter slavishness in this for they prefer [as their highest end] a life that is attainable by any animal. . . . Capable and practical men think the highest end is fame, which is the goal of a public life. But this is too superficial to be the good we are seeking since fame depends on those who give it. . . . Moreover, men who pursue fame do so in order to be assured of their own value. . . . Finally, some men devote their lives to making money in a way that is quite unnatural. But wealth clearly is not the good we are seeking since it is merely useful as a means to something else. . . . What, then, is our highest end? 5

As we have seen, there are many ends. But some of them are chosen only as a means to other things, for example, wealth, musical instruments, and tools [are ends we choose only because they are means to other things]. So it is clear that not all ends are ultimate ends. But our highest and best end would have to be something ultimate. . . . 6

Notice that an end that we desire for itself is more ultimate than something we want only as a means to something else. And an end that is never a means to something else is more ultimate than an end that is sometimes a means. And the most ultimate end would be something that we always choose for itself and never as a means to something else. 7

Now happiness seems more than anything else to answer to this description. For happiness is something we always choose for its own sake and never as a means to something else. But fame, pleasure, . . . and so on, are chosen partly for themselves but partly also as a means to happiness, since we believe that they will bring us happiness. Only happiness, then, is never chosen for the sake of these things or as a means to any other thing. 8

We will be led to the same conclusion if we start from the fact that our   9
ultimate end would have to be completely sufficient by itself. . . . By this I
mean that by itself it must make life worth living and lacking in nothing. But
happiness by itself answers this description. It is what we most desire even
apart from all other things. . . .

So, it appears that happiness is the ultimate end and completely sufficient   10
by itself. It is the end we seek in all that we do. . . .

The reader may think that in saying that happiness is our ultimate end we are   11
merely stating a platitude. So we must be more precise about what happiness
involves.

Perhaps the best approach is to ask what the specific purpose or function   12
of man is. For the good and the excellence of all beings that have a purpose—
such as musicians, sculptors, or craftsmen—depend on their purpose. So if
man has a purpose, his good will be related to this purpose. And how could
man not have a natural purpose when even cobblers and carpenters have a purpose? Surely, just as each part of man—the eye, the hand, the foot—has a
purpose, so also man as a whole must have a purpose. What is this purpose?

Our biological activities we share in common even with plants. So these   13
cannot be the purpose or function of man since we are looking for something
specific to man. The activities of our senses we also plainly share with other
things: horses, cattle, and other animals. So there remain only the activities that
belong to the rational part of man. . . . So the specific purpose or function of
man involves the activities of that part of his soul that belongs to reason, or that
at least is obedient to reason. . . .

Now the function of a thing is basic, and its good is something added to   14
this function. For example, the function of a musician is to play music, and the
good musician is one who also plays music but who in addition does it well. So,
the good for man would have to be something added to his function of carrying on the activities of reason; it would be carrying on the activities of reason
but doing so well or with excellence. But a thing carries out its proper functions
well when it has the proper virtues. So the good for man is carrying out those
activities of his soul [which belong to reason] and doing so with the proper
virtue or excellence. . . .

Since our happiness, then, is to be found in carrying out the activities of the soul   15
[that belong to reason], and doing so with virtue or excellence, we will now have
to inquire into virtue, for this will help us in our inquiry into happiness. . . .

To have virtue or excellence, a thing (1) must be good and (2) must be able   16
to carry out its function well. For example, if the eye has virtue, then it must be
a good eye and must be able to see well. Similarly, if a horse has its virtue, then
it must be all that it should be and must be good at running, carrying a rider,
and charging. Consequently, the proper virtue or excellence of man will consist

of those habits or acquired abilities that (1) make him a good man and (2) enable him to carry out his activities well. . . .

Now the expert in any field is the one who avoids what is excessive as well   17
as what is deficient. Instead he seeks to hit the mean and chooses it. . . . Acting well in every field is achieved by looking to the mean and bringing one's actions into line with this standard of moderation. For example, people say of a good work of art that nothing could be taken from it or added to it, implying that excellence is destroyed through excess or deficiency but achieved by observing the mean. The good artist, in fact, keeps his eyes fixed on the mean in everything he does. . . .

Virtue, therefore, must also aim at the mean. For human virtue deals with   18
our feelings and actions, and in these we can go to excess or we fall short or we can hit the mean. For example, it is possible to feel fear, confidence, desire, anger, pity, pleasure, . . . and so on, either too much or too little—both of which extremes are bad. But to feel these at the right times, and on the right occasions, and towards the right persons, and with the right object, and in the right fashion, is the mean between the extremes and is the best state, and is the mark of virtue. In the same way, our actions can also be excessive or can fall short or can hit the mean.

Virtue, then, deals with those feelings and actions in which it is wrong to   19
go too far and wrong to fall short but in which hitting the mean is praiseworthy and good. . . . It is a habit or acquired ability to choose . . . what is moderate or what hits the mean as determined by reason. . . .

But it is not enough to speak in generalities. We must apply this to particular   20
virtues and vices. Consider, then, the following examples.

Take the feelings of fear and confidence. To be able to hit the mean [by hav-   21
ing just enough fear and just enough confidence] is to have the virtue of courage. . . . But he who exceeds in confidence has the vice of rashness, while he who has too much fear and not enough confidence has the vice of cowardliness.

The mean where pleasure . . . is concerned is achieved by the virtue of tem-   22
perance. But to go to excess is to have the vice of profligacy, while to fall short is to have the vice of insensitivity. . . .

Or take the action of giving or receiving money. Here the mean is the virtue   23
of generosity. . . . But the man who gives to excess and is deficient in receiving has the vice of prodigality, while the man who is deficient in giving and excessive in taking has the vice of stinginess. . . .

Or take one's feelings about the opinion of others. Here the mean is the   24
virtue of proper self-respect, while the excess is the vice of vanity, and the deficiency is the vice of small-mindedness. . . .

The feeling of anger can also be excessive, deficient, or moderate. The man   25
who occupies the middle state is said to have the virtue of gentleness, while the one who exceeds in anger has the vice of irascibility, while the one who is deficient in anger has the vice of apathy. ☐

◢ REREADING FOR UNDERSTANDING

1. Aristotle begins by discussing a basic concept: everything we do is either a "means" or an "end." Explain the difference between the two. Perhaps you could begin with Aristotle's example of archery. What is the ultimate end or goal of an archer? What are the means to that end? Why are the means less important than the end? Develop another example from your own experience: first, define the goal (the end), and then trace the means by which that goal is accomplished.

2. According to Aristotle, what quality of our soul must be developed and nurtured in order for us to pursue the ultimate end of happiness? Why is this quality so necessary?

3. What does "virtue" mean for Aristotle? How does Aristotle's concept of virtue help us pursue "the mean"? How does pursuing the mean lead us to happiness—or the good life—according to Aristotle?

◢ RESPONDING

1. Do you agree with Aristotle that happiness is humankind's ultimate goal, a common "end" shared by us all? Can you isolate another, different, commonly pursued ultimate end? Defend your suggestion.

2. Aristotle says (par. 14) that happiness is the "carrying out those activities of [the] soul [which belong to reason] and doing so with the proper virtue or excellence." In what ways would Aristotle's approach to the good life be similar to or different from the approach presented in the Sermon on the Mount (p. 464)? Read what Christ "blesses" as good in the Sermon on the Mount as a possible way to focus your response.

LUKE 6:17–38

The selection from Luke's Gospel comes from the New International Version of the Bible. Although no authorial name is attached to the original text, circumstantial evidence is used to ascribe the Gospel to Luke. Scholars suggest Luke was not Jewish, but he was well educated in Greek culture and a physician by profession. This Gospel, originally in Greek, was probably composed in Rome c. A.D. 60. Luke's Gospel in general emphasizes what values and behaviors are necessary for a Christian to obtain "salvation." Obviously, then, Luke's Gospel is one argument for both happiness and the good life. In this excerpt from Chapter 6, Luke reports the Sermon on the Mount preached by Jesus to a crowd of his followers in Galilee.

The Sermon on the Mount

BLESSINGS AND WOES

[17]He went down with them and stood on a level place. A large crowd of his disciples was there and a great number of people from all over Judea, from Jerusalem, and from the seacoast of Tyre and Sidon, [18]who had come to hear him and to be healed of their diseases. Those troubled by evil spirits were cured, [19]and the people all tried to touch him, because power was coming from him and healing them all.

[20]Looking at his disciples, he said:

> "Blessed are you who are poor,
>   for yours is the kingdom of God.
> [21]Blessed are you who hunger now,
>   for you will be satisfied.
> Blessed are you who weep now,
>   for you will laugh.
> [22]Blessed are you when men hate you,
>   when they exclude you and insult you
>   and reject your name as evil,
>   because of the Son of Man.

[23]"Rejoice in that day and leap for joy, because great is your reward in heaven. For that is how their fathers treated the prophets.

> [24]"But woe to you who are rich,
>   for you have already received your comfort.
> [25]Woe to you who are well fed now,
>   for you will go hungry.
> Woe to you who laugh now,
>   for you will mourn and weep.
> [26]Woe to you when all men speak well of you,
>   for that is how their fathers treated the false prophets.

LOVE FOR ENEMIES

[27]"But I tell you who hear me: Love your enemies, do good to those who hate you, [28]bless those who curse you, pray for those who mistreat you. [29]If someone strikes you on one cheek, turn to him the other also. If someone takes your cloak, do not stop him from taking your tunic. [30]Give to everyone who asks you, and if anyone takes what belongs to you, do not demand it back. [31]Do to others as you would have them do to you.

[32]"If you love those who love you, what credit is that to you? Even 'sinners' love those who love them. [33]And if you do good to those who are good to you, what credit is that to you? Even 'sinners' do that. [34]And if you lend to those from

whom you expect repayment, what credit is that to you? Even 'sinners' lend to 'sinners,' expecting to be repaid in full. [35]But love your enemies, do good to them, and lend to them without expecting to get anything back. Then your reward will be great, and you will be sons of the Most High, because he is kind to the ungrateful and wicked. [36]Be merciful, just as your Father is merciful.

JUDGING OTHERS

[37]"Do not judge, and you will not be judged. Do not condemn, and you will not be condemned. Forgive, and you will be forgiven. [38]Give, and it will be given to you. A good measure, pressed down, shaken together and running over, will be poured into your lap. For with the measure you use, it will be measured to you." □

◢ REREADING FOR UNDERSTANDING

1. What is the central definition of happiness in the Sermon on the Mount?

2. What brings a person happiness, according to this passage? Is the cause singular or multiple?

◢ RESPONDING

1. How does Jesus regard life—as a means or an end?

2. What is the good or happiness to be pursued in life, according to this sermon? Focus on the concept or word "pursued."

3. This passage occurs in our excerpt from the Buddha (p. 479): "There is no fire like passion; there is no evil like hatred; there is no pain like this bodily existence; there is no happiness higher than peace." How are these ideas compatible or incompatible with the message of the Sermon on the Mount?

◢ RESPONDING IN WRITING

Choose one of the passages in the Sermon on the Mount that you are least familiar with or that you find most engaging. How would the ideas lead—or not lead—to a good life for you or your peers? Write a brief essay for your peers, not to convert them to a religious belief, but to show them how the passage may develop or inhibit values and behavior that might produce the "good life."

REM B. EDWARDS

Rem B. Edwards is a professor of philosophy. This selection is an excerpt from a book he devoted to investigating the development of a philosophy called hedonism during the fifth and fourth centuries B.C. You will read detailed definitions of hedonism that should help you to understand the formal elements of a perspective on life that must be universally common—the human animal enjoys pleasure and avoids pain. Hedonism has at least one significant similarity to Aristotle's thoughts on the good life in that it is an attempt to define what is "intrinsically" good. Once that intrinsic good is discovered, then a clear path for the good life will be revealed.

What Is Hedonism?

What in life is really worth living for? This question has intrigued philosophers and nonphilosophers alike from time immemorial. It is one thing to know how to make a living, and another thing altogether to know what makes life worth living. The latter question is not of purely "academic" interest, for how a person answers it can make all the difference in the way he orders his life and activities in the "real world" both inside and outside the confines of academia. In fact, it may be the single most important question that a human being can ever ask or try to answer.

In philosophy, the popular question of what makes life worth living is subjected to analysis, clarification, and refinement; and it comes out as the question of what things are intrinsically good. An intrinsic good, by definition, is something worth having, achieving, choosing, desiring, experiencing, bringing into existence, or sustaining in existence, for its own sake. It is an end in itself and not to be desired or chosen simply as a means to some goal which lies beyond it. An intrinsic bad or evil is something worth avoiding for its own sake. Good things chosen merely as means are extrinsic goods, but intrinsic goods are chosen because of their own inherent or self-contained worth. Some things may be both intrinsically and extrinsically good at the same time. If love, knowledge, and pleasure are intrinsically good, they may also be extrinsically good; for there is a sense in which love may lead to more love, knowledge to more knowledge, and pleasure to more pleasure. But if they are intrinsic goods, none of them can be *merely* a means to an end.

What makes life worth living? This seems to mean: "What is there in life that is worth having, experiencing, choosing, desiring for its own sake?" The question is of almost universal human interest. It is not easily answered and the responses proposed are invariably highly controversial. Hedonism is one such controversial answer. The term is derived from the Greek word *hēdonē*, meaning "pleasure," and hedonism is basically the theory that pleasure is the only intrinsic good. It has been such a fundamental and tenaciously long-lived theory that all the alternatives to it may with some justice be grouped together under the one label of *nonhedonistic* theories. Let us examine more closely what is involved in hedonistic and nonhedonistic views of what is intrinsically good.

THE DEFINITION OF HEDONISM

Although there are psychological versions of hedonism which maintain that the   4
pursuit of pleasure alone or the avoidance of pain alone are the sole activities of which we human beings are capable, our attention in this book will be confined to normative hedonism, which presents the pursuit of pleasure or happiness and the avoidance of pain or unhappiness as *ideals* of action to which there are viable alternatives, rather than as necessities of human nature. Normative hedonism is the theory that:

1. Pleasure, or happiness defined in terms of pleasure, is the *only* thing which is intrinsically good; and pain, or unhappiness defined in terms of pain, is the *only* thing which is intrinsically evil.

2. *Happiness*, hedonistically defined, consists of a positive surplus of pleasure over pain through an extended period of time; *unhappiness*, hedonistically defined, consists of a surplus of pain over pleasure through an extended period of time.

3. I *ought to act* to maximize pleasure or happiness and to minimize pain or unhappiness.

Each of these points needs some explaining.

(1) We are not hedonists merely because we are interested in the pursuit of   5
happiness, or because we regard pleasure or happiness as an intrinsically good thing. To qualify as hedonists, we must be *exclusively* interested in the pursuit of happiness, and must regard pleasure or happiness as the sole intrinsic good. Unless we can accept this stronger claim, we are not hedonists; and if we provide a constructive alternative answer to the question of what is intrinsically good, we are nonhedonists. Nonhedonistic theories may be divided into *antihedonistic* theories and *pluralistic* theories.

Antihedonistic theories assert that pleasure or happiness, hedonistically   6
conceived, are not intrinsically good at all, and that pleasure or happiness should not be pursued. The Greek Cynics and Early Stoics seem to have been antihedonists, though their antihedonism may have rested upon a confusion about the meaning of the word "pleasure" which only qualitative hedonism can clarify, that is, a confusion of "lower" with "higher" qualities of pleasure. The Stoics seemed to want to throw out the latter with the former because the same word "pleasure" covered both. Antisthenes the Cynic is supposed to have said that he would rather go mad than experience the first drop of pleasure. Cleanthes, one of the Early Stoics, taught that all pleasure was contrary to nature, including the pleasures of moral virtue. He suggested that to experience pleasure was the worst thing that could happen to a man. For both the Cynics and the Early Stoics, the good life for man consisted in the development

and exercise of virtue and reason, and all enjoyment, insofar as this involved agreeable feeling, was to be avoided altogether. Even virtue and reason were ideally to be exercised without enjoyment. . . .

(2) Hedonistically conceived, "happiness" consists in a positive surplus of   7
pleasure over pain (ideally no pain at all) over an extended period of time. Particular pleasures are the ingredients of happiness; take them away and there is no happiness at all. It would be awkward to say, "I was happy for five seconds," and less awkward to say "I experienced pleasure for five seconds." The difference between happiness and pleasure is the element of time—five seconds is just not long enough for happiness, though a day, week, month, or season might be. Where between five seconds and a day is the line to be drawn? There is no exact answer to the question of "how long" pleasures must prevail if we are to speak of happiness rather than pleasure, just as there is no exact answer in terms of minutes or even years to the question as to when the Middle Ages began and ended, but vague concepts are often just what we need.

There is no exact answer to the question of how intense or prolonged plea-   8
sures must be in order to compose a positive surplus of pleasure over pain. And the same sort of indefiniteness about duration and intensity is involved in the hedonistic concept of unhappiness, which consists of a surplus of pain or disagreeable feeling over pleasure, at worst no pleasure at all, over an extended period of time. It is appropriate to call ourselves happy in the hedonistic sense if our agreeable feeling ranges anywhere from a minimal positive balance of contentment with our lot to unspeakable ecstasy. When the balance is tipped in favor of disagreeable feeling, unhappiness is the appropriate word for our state of mind. But the point at which the balance is tipped is exceedingly variable from person to person and from time to time for any given person. . . .

(3) . . . Every hedonist advocates the active pursuit of happiness and the   9
avoidance of unhappiness. But hedonism as such is neutral on the questions of for whom this happiness should be achieved and when it should be enjoyed. I should act to maximize happiness and minimize unhappiness, but for whom? To get an answer to this question, hedonism must be combined with other theories of action that try to answer questions of value distribution, such as egoism, universalism, racism, or nationalism. All such theories may be viewed profitably as attempts to answer the question of how we should act to distribute intrinsic value. Egoism says act to distribute it only to oneself. Universalism says act to distribute it to everyone, or, as John Stuart Mill put it, to "the whole sentient creation." Racism says to distribute it only to members of a favored race, nationalism only to members of a favored nation, and so on. But there may be hedonistic and nonhedonistic forms of egoism, universalism, racism, and nationalism, depending on how the question of what things are intrinsically good is answered.

Special care should be taken to distinguish hedonism from egoism. The   10
two are popularly confused; "hedonist" and "egoist" are often treated as synonyms in everyday moralizing. Yet, hedonism and egoism are answers to two entirely different questions: What things are intrinsically good? and How

should I act to distribute intrinsic goods? The egoist holds that he should act to distribute the good things of life, whatever they are, only to himself; but he may give a pluralistic or a hedonistic answer to the question of what they are. The hedonist holds that only pleasure or happiness is intrinsically good, but he may give either an egoistic or a nonegoistic answer to the question of how it should be distributed. In the arena of distribution, the happiness or welfare of me alone lies at one extreme, and the greatest happiness or welfare of the greatest possible number of persons or sentient beings lies at the other. In between lies the happiness or welfare of the members of a race or nation or the like. Jeremy Bentham seems to have been an egoist, but there are moral or universalistic as well as egoistic forms of hedonism, and other nineteenth-century utilitarians including John Stuart Mill and Henry Sidgwick were universalistic hedonists. The realm of the moral is understood by universalistic utilitarians as pertaining to the advantage or welfare of everyone alike or the greatest possible number of persons or sentient beings. If we decide to be hedonists, we do not thereby decide to be (or not to be) egoists, and the reverse is equally true. The two positions are clearly separate and distinct.

Hedonism as such is thus neutral on the question of "for whom" happiness should be sought, egoistic hedonists giving one reply, universalistic hedonists another, and racistic and nationalistic hedonists still others. Many answers are also possible to the question of *when* this maximum of pleasure is to be pursued and experienced, the basic division here being between the hedonists of the present moment, such as the Greek philosopher Aristippus, who say: "Act to maximize pleasure *now* and don't worry about the future," and the hedonists of the long run, such as Epicurus, who say: "Act to maximize pleasure over the entire span of your life." The latter is a reflective and calculating form of hedonism, and the former is neither. To succeed as a long-run hedonist, it is necessary to know a great deal about what causes what in the world and in the realm of human experience. Some pleasures lead to a predominance of pain over pleasure in the long run, and they are to be avoided; other pleasures lead to future enjoyments of like kind and should be cultivated. To identify the acceptable and unacceptable pleasures, we must know a great deal about what causes people in general to enjoy themselves and to suffer. We also need to know what causes us as individuals to enjoy ourselves and to suffer. The successful hedonist of the long run must have a deep knowledge of the general psychology of human nature, and he must also know himself, since it is often the case that one man's pleasure is another man's poison, or to speak more precisely, that what is a source of pleasure for one man is a source of pain for another.

Most philosophical hedonists have been long-range hedonists, and we shall be interested primarily in long-range hedonism in this book. But a couple of remarks need to be made about short-range hedonism. In the first place, we do learn after a while that the future does not just go away simply because we choose to ignore it. "Eat, drink, and be merry, for tomorrow we die," and "Have a blast while you last" may be acceptable philosophies for those who are reasonably certain that they are not going to last very long, that tomorrow they are going to die. But in the absence of such assurance, most of us would be well advised to order our lives and activities in ways that will probably succeed in maximizing pleasure and minimizing pain over the long haul. In the second place, there is an interesting ambiguity in the notion of "the present moment." How long is it? If "the present moment" is very strictly construed to include only the thin knife-edge of the instant at hand, then hedonism of the present moment cannot be a theory of action at all. It cannot say "Act to maximize pleasure in the *present* moment," for all action aims at *future* results, even if these results lie only a few seconds away. "The present moment" usually means "the next few hours." Don't worry about the chances of hangover or pregnancy; just live it up tonight—that is, during the next few hours, if the night is still young. But if the night is still young, then most of it still lies in the future; and the real difference between "present-moment" and "long-run" hedonism lies in the question of *how much* of the future to consider rather than whether to consider the future at all. Long-run hedonism does not say that we should act to maximize merely *future* pleasures, but pleasures over the whole span of life, which includes the present and immediate future as well as the distant future. In a sense, the future never comes; and any philosophy that advocates the actualization of merely distant future pleasures requires a continual postponement of enjoyment for the sake of that future which never comes. Long-run hedonism includes, rather than excludes, present and immediately future enjoyment, however, since its ideal is that of happiness over the *entire* span of life.

THE MEANING OF "PLEASURE" AND "PAIN"

How are pleasure and pain to be identified, as the hedonist understands them? 13 When we are dealing with words like "pleasure" and "pain," it appears that certain normally applicable techniques of definition cannot be used. Pleasures and pains are not sense-objects in the "external" world, and the meaning of "pleasure" and "pain" cannot be communicated ostensively. We cannot hold up or point directly to instances of pleasure and pain and say "Here is one six inches long," "Here is one that weighs eight ounces," or "Here is one that is bright red, or dark blue." Nor can pleasure and pain, as the hedonist understands them, be defined in purely behaviorist terms, though many influential attempts to do this have been made in recent years. "Pain behavior" and "pleasure behavior" may be criteria for the correct or incorrect applications of judgment about pain and pleasure to other minds; but the hedonist is *not* maintaining that overt, publicly observable, behavioristically testable manifestations of pain and pleasure are intrinsically bad or good. In saying that the pain of a toothache is undesirable in and of itself, the hedonist is not taking the position that such pain behavior as holding my jaw, drying, wincing, or pill-swallowing is bad intrinsically. In saying that the enjoyment of nature is intrinsically good, the hedonist is not asserting that merely standing on the seashore with one's eyes open in the direction of a glorious sunset with no feeling at all is intrinsically good. The pleasure and pain in which the hedonist is interested are inner qualities of feeling, and some small introspective ability is required in order to focus attention upon pleasures and pains in the relevant sense. If introspective psychology is thrown out completely, then hedonism in its classical sense is thrown out with it. Pleasure and pain, as intrinsically desirable or undesirable, have been thought of as inner qualities of feeling or awareness, private feelings which we would naturally like to perpetuate or avoid. Pain is not "pain behavior"; it is the quality of inner feeling that prompts us to behave that way, and the same may be said of pleasure. If all sentient beings are eliminated from our solar system, as we may have the power to do with our chemical, biological, or atomic weaponry, the solar system that remains will have no intrinsic value in it. If the thought is any consolation, it will have no intrinsic disvalue in it either. Its value will be entirely neutral without the presence of sentient beings capable of some measure of awareness of those agreeable feelings we call pleasures and those disagreeable feelings we call pains. The actualization of intrinsic goods and ills as the hedonist identifies them is thus parasitic for its mode of existence upon the presence of sentience or awareness in the world. To put it another way, to the hedonist, no "material object" in the popular sense of external object of sense experience is intrinsically good, though such objects may be extrinsically good as sources of agreeable feeling. Thus the hedonist does and must reject three theses of Watsonian metaphysical behaviorism. He cannot accept the claims: (1) that inner awareness or consciousness does not exist, for pleasure and pain as he understands them are qualities of inner awareness and not publicly observable sense-objects or patterns of behavior; (2) that introspection is a totally unreliable and unacceptable source of knowledge, for he must rely upon his own abilities to focus his attention upon his own feelings to tell whether he is experiencing pleasure or pain; and (3) that the words "pleasure" and "pain" can be redefined without loss of sense to be *identical* in meaning with such publicly observable patterns of "pain behavior" as crying, frowning, grimacing, and holding one's side, or such patterns of "pleasure behavior" as smiling and laughing, for it is the inner feelings that may accompany and usually cause such behavior which interest him and which he regards as intrinsically bad or good.

If pleasure and pain cannot be defined ostensively or behavioristically, and if this is true also of all synonyms and roughly equivalent phrases, then how can the meaning of "pleasure" and "pain" as the hedonist understands them be communicated to someone who at least professes to be left in the dark when the hedonist uses the terms? We could not directly point to examples of such entities, as we might if we were teaching the meaning of "yellow" and "green." But we might be able to use an indirect way of combined pointing and speaking. Assuming a kind of common "human nature," we would suggest that our subject try to remember circumstances in which people typically experience pleasure or pain, and that he try to focus his attention on his own remembered feelings in such circumstances. Those feelings that he liked and wanted to sustain, cultivate, repeat would be pleasures; and those feelings that he disliked and wanted to terminate and avoid would be pains. We might approach the problem more directly and try to generate present circumstances that typically cause pleasure or pain, then ask him to focus on any feelings he might wish to sustain or be rid of. A jab with a pin, or a pinch, or a bee sting will typically generate pain. A back rub or sexual stimulation will typically generate pleasure. In such circumstances, if attention is focused on feelings to be eliminated and avoided, or feelings to be sustained and cultivated, then examples of pains and pleasures have been located experientially, and the denotative meaning of these terms has been experientially learned. The assumption of a common human nature that such techniques of communication require is not as doubtful as it appears to be on the surface. Certainly there are many individual and cultural variations in our sources of enjoyment and frustration, but it is also true that a few sources of the same are almost universally human. After all, the person who designs a torture chamber or a weapon of war usually does not have to consider cultural and personal idiosyncrasies to achieve remarkably efficient instruments of suffering and death. . . . □

◢ REREADING FOR UNDERSTANDING

1. Edwards provides an explicit definition of an "intrinsic good" in paragraph 2. Reread that definition slowly, perhaps two or three times. Now, could you explain to a friend what makes something "intrinsically good"? What does it mean to do something for its own sake? For instance, could penmanship be an intrinsic good, or jogging, tennis, reading, planting a garden? Can you suggest three "intrinsic goods" of your own?

2. How do "egotistic" and "universalist" hedonism differ? Distinguish Aristippus' and Epicurus' views of pleasure (par. 11).

3. In the final several paragraphs, Edwards goes to some length to explain that hedonism implies the active psychological capacity to evaluate sensory experience. What point is he trying to make about hedonism? Work in small groups to answer this question. Compare your group's response to others in the class.

◢ RESPONDING

1. Epicurus, as presented by Edwards, warns that some pleasures, if pursued too long or too actively, could eventually lead to pain. Is that true? Can you give examples? Do people change their behavior or values if they recognize the possibility (or likelihood) of pain tomorrow as a consequence of pleasure today? Why or why not?

2. Do you believe Americans in general have more hedonistic values and behaviors than spiritual values and behaviors? Which set of values and behaviors will more likely lead to a "good life"?

ERICH FROMM

Erich Fromm has been described as "at once a sociologist, anthropologist, psychologist—and one is tempted to add, lover of human life, poet and prophet." Obviously he had many interests, yet much of Fromm's professional career was spent in the field of psychoanalysis as a professor in Germany, Mexico, and the United States. He published numerous books and articles during his life (1900–1980). The excerpt included here is from a chapter in his book *To Have or to Be* (1976). In much of his writing, Fromm focuses on the problem of finding meaning or purpose in life. Fromm uses his training and work experience in psychology and psychoanalysis as a basis for calling into question the individualistic and materialistic views of cultures that prevail in America and elsewhere in the world. In this selection, Fromm proposes a method of living that he believes may produce a happier life.

A First Glance

THE IMPORTANCE OF THE DIFFERENCE BETWEEN HAVING AND BEING

The alternative of *having* versus *being* does not appeal to common sense. *To have,* so it would seem, is a normal function of our life: in order to live we must have things. Moreover, we must have things in order to enjoy them. In a culture in which the supreme goal is to have—and to have more and more—and in which one can speak of someone as "being worth a million dollars," how can there be an alternative between having and being? On the contrary, it would seem that the very essence of being is having; that if one *has* nothing, one *is* nothing.

Yet the great Masters of Living have made the alternative between having and being a central issue of their respective systems. The Buddha teaches that in order to arrive at the highest stage of human development, we must not crave possessions. Jesus teaches: "For whosoever will save his life shall lose it; but whosoever will lose his life for my sake, the same shall save it. For what is a man advantaged, if he gain the whole world, and lose himself, or be cast away?" (Luke 9:24–25). Master Eckhart taught that to have nothing and make oneself open and "empty," not to let one's ego stand in one's way, is the condition for achieving spiritual wealth and strength. Marx taught that luxury is as much a vice as poverty and that our goal should be to *be* much, not to *have* much. (I refer here to the real marx, the radical humanist, not to the vulgar forgery presented by Soviet communism.)

For many years I had been deeply impressed by this distinction and was seeking its empirical basis in the concrete study of individuals and groups by the psychoanalytic method. What I saw has led me to conclude that this distinction, together with that between love of life and love of the dead, represents the most crucial problem of existence; that empirical anthropological and psychoanalytic data tend to demonstrate that *having and being are two fundamental modes of experience, the respective strengths of which determine the differences between the characters of individuals and various types of social character.*

EXAMPLES IN VARIOUS POETIC EXPRESSIONS

As an introduction to understanding the difference between the having and   4
being modes of existence, let me use as an illustration two poems of similar
content that the late D. T. Suzuki referred to in "Lectures on Zen Buddhism."
One is a haiku by a Japanese poet, Basho, 1644–1694; the other poem is by a
nineteenth-century English poet, Tennyson. Each poet describes a similar experience: his reaction to a flower he sees while taking a walk. Tennyson's verse is:

> Flower in a crannied wall,
> I pluck you out of the crannies,
> I hold you here, root and all, in my hand,
> Little flower—but *if* I could understand
> What you are, root and all, and all in all,
> I should know what God and man is.

Translated into English, Basho's haiku runs something like this:

> When I look carefully
> I see the *nazuna* blooming
> By the hedge!

The difference is striking. Tennyson reacts to the flower by wanting to *have*   5
it. He "plucks" it "root and all." And while he ends with an intellectual speculation about the flower's possible function for his attaining insight into the
nature of God and man, the flower itself is killed as a result of his interest in it.
Tennyson, as we see him in his poem, may be compared to the Western scientist who seeks the truth by means of dismembering life.

Basho's reaction to the flower is entirely different. He does not want to   6
pluck it; he does not even touch it. All he does is "look carefully" to "see" it.
Here is Suzuki's description:

> It is likely that Basho was walking along a country road when he noticed
> something rather neglected by the hedge. He then approached closer, took
> a good look at it, and found it was no less than a wild plant, rather in-
> significant and generally unnoticed by passersby. This is a plain fact de-
> scribed in the poem with no specifically poetic feeling expressed anywhere
> except perhaps in the last two syllables, which read in Japanese *kana*. This
> particle, frequently attached to a noun or an adjective or an adverb, signi-
> fies a certain feeling of admiration or praise or sorrow or joy, and can
> sometimes quite appropriately be rendered into English by an exclamation
> mark. In the present *haiku* the whole verse ends with this mark.

Tennyson, it appears, needs to possess the flower in order to understand   7
people and nature, and by his *having* it, the flower is destroyed. What Basho
wants is to *see*, and not only to look at the flower, but to be at one, to "one"

himself with it—and to let it live. The difference between Tennyson and Basho is fully explained in this poem by Goethe:

FOUND

I walked in the woods
All by myself,
To seek nothing,
That was on my mind.

I saw in the shade
A little flower stand,
Bright like the stars
Like beautiful eyes.

I wanted to pluck it,
But it said sweetly:
Is it to wilt
That I must be broken?

I took it out
With all its roots,
Carried it to the garden
At the pretty house.

And planted it again
In a quiet place;
Now it ever spreads
And blossoms forth.

Goethe, walking with no purpose in mind, is attracted by the brilliant little flower. He reports having the same impulse as Tennyson: to pluck it. But unlike Tennyson, Goethe is aware that this means killing the flower. For Goethe the flower is so much alive that it speaks and warns him; and he solves the problem differently from either Tennyson or Basho. He takes the flower "with all its roots" and plants it again so that its life is not destroyed. Goethe stands, as it were, between Tennyson and Basho: for him, at the crucial moment, the force of life is stronger than the force of mere intellectual curiosity. Needless to say that in this beautiful poem Goethe expresses the core of his concept of investigating nature.

Tennyson's relationship to the flower is in the mode of having, or posses- [8] sion—not material possession but the possession of knowledge. Basho's and Goethe's relationship to the flower each sees is in the mode of being. By being I refer to the mode of existence in which one neither *has* anything nor *craves to have* something, but is joyous, employs one's faculties productively, is *oned* to the world.

Goethe, the great lover of life, one of the outstanding fighters against hu- [9] man dismemberment and mechanization, has given expression to being as against having in many poems. His Faust is a dramatic description of the conflict between being and having (the latter represented by Mephistopheles), while in the following short poem he expresses the quality of being with the utmost simplicity:

PROPERTY

I know that nothing belongs to me
But the thought which unimpeded
From my soul will flow.
And every favorable moment
Which loving Fate
From the depth lets me enjoy.

The difference between being and having is not essentially that between   10
East and West. The difference is rather between a society centered around persons and one centered around things. The having orientation is characteristic
of Western industrial society, in which greed for money, fame, and power has
become the dominant theme of life. Less alienated societies—such as medieval
society, the Zuni Indians, the African tribal societies that were not affected by
the ideas of modern "progress"—have their own Bashos. Perhaps after a few
more generations of industrialization, the Japanese will have their Tennysons. It
is not that Western Man cannot fully understand Eastern systems, such as Zen
Buddhism (as Jung thought), but that modern Man cannot understand the
spirit of a society that is not centered in property and greed. Indeed, the writings of Master Eckhart (as difficult to understand as Basho or Zen) and the
Buddha's writings are only two dialects of the same language.

IDIOMATIC CHANGES

A certain change in the emphasis on having and being is apparent in the grow-   11
ing use of nouns and the decreasing use of verbs in Western languages in the
past few centuries.

A noun is the proper denotation for a thing. I can say that I *have* things: for   12
instance that I have a table, a house, a book, a car. The proper denotation for an
activity, a process, is a verb: for instance I am, I love, I desire, I hate, etc. Yet ever
more frequently an *activity* is expressed in terms of *having*; that is, a noun is
used instead of a verb. But to express an activity by *to have* in connection with
a noun is an erroneous use of language, because processes and activities cannot
be possessed; they can only be experienced.

HAVING AND CONSUMING

Before discussing some simple illustrations of the having and being modes of   13
existence, another manifestation of having must be mentioned, that of *incorporating*. Incorporating a thing, for instance by eating or drinking, is an archaic
form of possessing it. At a certain point in its development an infant tends to
take things it wants into its mouth. This is the infant's form of taking possession, when its bodily development does not yet enable it to have other forms of
controlling its possession. We find the same connection between incorporation
and possession in many forms of cannibalism. For example: by eating another
human being, I acquire that person's powers (thus cannibalism can be the

magic equivalent of acquiring slaves); by eating the heart of a brave man, I acquire his courage; by eating a totem animal, I acquire the divine substance the totem animal symbolizes.

Of course, most objects cannot be incorporated physically (and inasmuch as they could, they would be lost again in the process of elimination). But there is also *symbolic* and *magic* incorporation. If I believe I have incorporated a god's, a father's, or an animal's image, it can neither be taken away nor eliminated. I swallow the object symbolically and believe in its symbolic presence within myself. This is, for instance, how Freud explained the superego: the introjected sum total of the father's prohibitions and commands. An authority, an institution, an idea, an image can be introjected in the same way: I *have* them, eternally protected in my bowels, as it were. ("Introjection" and "identification" are often used synonymously, but it is difficult to decide whether they are really the same process. At any rate, "identification" should not be used loosely, when one should better talk of imitation or subordination.)   14

There are many other forms of incorporation that are not connected with physiological needs and, hence, are not limited. The attitude inherent in consumerism is that of swallowing the whole world. The consumer is the eternal suckling crying for the bottle. This is obvious in pathological phenomena, such as alcoholism and drug addiction. We apparently single out both these addictions because their effects interfere with the addicted person's social obligations. Compulsive smoking is not thus censured because, while not less of an addiction, it does not interfere with the smokers' social functions, but possibly "only" with their life spans.   15

Further attention is given to the many forms of everyday consumerism later on in this volume. I might only remark here that as far as leisure time is concerned, automobiles, television, travel, and sex are the main objects of present-day consumerism, and while we speak of them as leisure-time activities, we would do better to call them leisure-time *passivities.*   16

To sum up, to consume is one form of having, and perhaps the most important one for today's affluent industrial societies. Consuming has ambiguous qualities: It relieves anxiety, because what one has cannot be taken away; but it also requires one to consume ever more, because previous consumption soon loses its satisfactory character. Modern consumers may identify themselves by the formula: *I am = what I have and what I consume.* □   17

◢ REREADING FOR UNDERSTANDING

1. Explain, in your own words, Fromm's distinction between "having" and "being." Use elements from the poems Fromm cites to support your explanation.

2. How does our living in a consumer culture affect our ability to "be," to create a real self?

3. According to Fromm, what cycle arises from consumerism? Is that cycle positive or negative in its effects?

4. What does Fromm mean by this observation (par. 15): "The attitude inherent in consumerism is that of swallowing the whole world. The consumer is the eternal suckling . . . "?

◢ RESPONDING

1. Fromm points out that "incorporating" is a primitive means of having. According to some ancient beliefs of cannibalism, a warrior can incorporate the bravery of another warrior by eating his heart. Can you identify ways in which our culture encourages us to "incorporate" desirable traits or values into our "identity" through consumerism? Is Fromm correct to suggest that advertising, TV programming, and movies are roughly equivalent modern means of "incorporating" traits and values?

2. Do you believe our American culture is defined by Fromm's concluding equation: "I am = what I have and what I consume"? If so, does that concern you? Explain the nature of your concerns. If not, explain what nonconsumer "being" more accurately characterizes American culture.

3. Do you agree or disagree with Fromm's assertion, "The attitude inherent in consumerism is that of swallowing the whole world. The consumer is the eternal suckling crying for the bottle" (par. 15)? As you consider this question, you may want to read Stringer's essay (p. 481). He presents his own vivid story of one who had bought, then rejected, the consumer definition of the good life. Only after he becomes a street person in New York City does he find a quality of life that "did wonders for, yes, my self-esteem."

◢ RESPONDING IN WRITING

At one point (par. 17), Fromm observes that consuming has ambiguous qualities: It relieves anxiety, because what one has cannot be taken away; but it also requires one to consume ever more, because previous consumption soon loses its satisfactory character." Is Fromm's observation accurate, perhaps insightful? Write a response with your peers as an audience. In several paragraphs, critique Fromm's wisdom or misjudgment about our consumer culture and its promised good life.

BUDDHA

Several different Buddha and Buddhist traditions originated in India, Nepal, and Tibet. The word "Buddha" is not, in our sense, a name like George or Phyllis. Rather it implies "The Enlightened One." When Western Europeans refer to Buddha, we generally refer to Siddartha Gautama of the Sakya tribe of Eastern India. Many suggest this Buddha lived c. 560–480 B.C. Buddha's basic philosophy was called the "Middle Way." The Middle Way attempts to overcome suffering in daily life by breaking out of the cycle of birth, death, and rebirth through a state of "nirvana." Nirvana is a mental state in which one's sense of being is unaffected by change in the external world; it is a transcendental state of oneness with all beings and the universe. While working toward a state of nirvana, Buddha urged his followers to base their daily life on the spirit of good will and love among humanity. By doing so, he taught, they could find contentment and happiness. As you read the excerpts below, consider what specific values and behaviors the Buddha offers as a means to happiness and the good life.

Happiness

We live happily indeed, not hating those who hate us! among men who hate us we dwell free from hatred! We live happily indeed, free from ailments among the ailing! among men who are ailing we dwell free from ailments!   1

We live happily indeed, free from greed among the greedy! among men who are greedy let us dwell free from greed!   2

We live happily indeed, though we call nothing our own! We shall be like the bright gods, feeding on happiness!   3

Victory breeds hatred, for the conquered is unhappy. He who has given up both victory and defeat, he is contented and happy.   4

There is no fire like passion; there is no evil like hatred; there is no pain like this bodily existence; there is no happiness higher than peace.   5

Hunger is the worst of diseases, bodily demands the greatest evil; if one knows this truly, that is Nirvana, the highest happiness.   6

Health is the greatest of gifts, contentedness the best riches; trust is the best of relationships, Nirvana the highest happiness.   7

He who has tasted the sweetness of solitude and tranquility becomes free from fear and free from sin, while he tastes the sweetness of drinking in the law.   8

The sight of the elect is good, to live with them is always happiness; if a man does not see fools, he will be truly happy.   9

He who walks in the company of fools suffers a long way; company with fools, as with an enemy, is always painful; company with the wise is happiness, like meeting with kinsfolk.   10

Therefore, one ought to follow the wise, the intelligent, the learned, the much-enduring, the dutiful, the elect; one ought to follow such a good and wise man, as the moon follows the path of the stars. ☐   11

◢ REREADING FOR UNDERSTANDING

According to this passage, what main human values and activities will lead to happiness and the good life?

◢ RESPONDING

1. Which of an average American college student's values and behaviors would be most in conflict with Buddha's precepts? Why? Which values and behaviors are most compatible? Why?

2. How are Buddha's values similar to those of Christ as represented by Luke (p. 464)? How are they different?

3. Take two or three of the Buddha's precepts that seem particularly puzzling or simply untrue, at least on a quick reading. Analyze them so that you could discuss their weaknesses with someone who thought them clear and true, at least on a first reading.

◢ RESPONDING IN WRITING

Attempt to imitate to some degree both the form and content of the teaching of Buddha or of Jesus Christ. That is, create a series of brief, succinct, and memorable observations on what causes happiness or what will lead to the good life. Organize your "sayings" so that the whole piece is coherent, has a sense of focus, a sense of beginning, middle, and end. Obviously you write from modern experience, reflecting modern values and definitions of the good life. Nevertheless, use ideas from the Buddha, the Bible, Fromm, or Aristotle as they seem relevant, but use them for your purposes in your own language.

CONTROVERSIES

What Is the American Dream?

CAVERLY STRINGER

Caverly Stringer is a free-lance writer, working on a book entitled *Vagrants in Paradise*. He is also co-editor of *Street News*. Before his latest career, he was co-owner of a small business in New York City, a business that seemed to be going well, and seemed to put Stringer on the road to the classic American Dream of hard work leading to success. Suddenly, things began to fall apart. Stringer dropped out; he literally lived on the streets of New York City. This essay is a glimpse of what that life was like as well as a critique of the dream he had been pursuing.

Confessions of an Urban Outlaw

I am at the scene of the purge: 42nd Street between Eighth and Ninth. A tax-paying, law-abiding shopkeeper, ever vigilant to keep this street the show-place of quality-of-life control, takes a broomhandle to a panhandler loitering in front of his triple-X peep palace. "Take a walk, scumbag!" growls the smutmeister. At his flank, in a red jumpsuit emblazoned with the insignia of the modern-day legion of decency, "Times Square Business Improvement District," stands a hulking West Indian street sweeper. He is eager to demonstrate—even at wages that keep him below the poverty line for forty hours' toil—his dedication to the cause by rousting a "no-account" bum. "Get a job!" he exclaims.

Watching this, I happen to look up and my eye catches the marquee of a long-dark second-run movie house down the block. It has been closed down, so we have been promised, to make way for a mighty office tower, which, after three years, has yet to materialize. In the void between the ambitions of commerce and the realities of the marketplace the marquee has become an easel for the practitioners of quote art. It reads:

Many men can bear adversity
But few men can stand contempt

The beggar does not go quietly. First there is his outrage (imagine that!) to   3
vent. But from down the block approaches, with hastening step, a beat cop.
Swiftly calculating the odds against him, the sparechanger gives in with a sagging sigh and trudges westward in search of a more hospitable place.

I had been en route to committing my own quality-of-life offense—armed   4
with a bagful of *Street News* to peddle on the subway (an arrestable offense
these days)—when I had paused to witness the scene. Now, the trio turns its
sour gaze on me. And there it is again (imagine!)—outrage. "Go ahead," I
silently challenge. "Start on me next! Say one fucking word!"

There is an impasse for a few seconds during which a midday muffhound   5
sidles up unnoticed. Sizing up the four of us crowding the doorway, he settles
on me as the one blocking his way into the porn house. He moves as if to walk
through me. There's a little dance as we both move right, then left, then right in
synchronous "you first" gestures.

Again, an assist from New York's Finest.   6

"You were just leaving, weren't you?" the officer says to me. With an exag-   7
gerated bow to the porn patron, I say, "Excuuuuse me, sir! By all means do step
right in, sir. I'm sorry, did you want to go into one of those little rooms back
there and JERK OFF?" I give those last two words all I've got. Passers-by rub-
berneck from as far away as across the street.

I guess they got the antisocial part right regarding guys like me and New   8
York's quality of life. At least in this case, I certainly wasn't promoting the "civil
society" to which the Q-of-L pushers like Mayor Giuliani are so fond of referring. I suppose you can label me incorrigible as well. Not only am I without re-
morse for the nuisance I made of myself to that 42nd Street enterprise but I
regret not having heaved my canvas bag of papers right through its plate-glass
window. Instead, I continue eastward. Glancing back, I glimpse the words on
the other side of the marquee:

Paradise for an environment.
Hell for a society.

I am not altogether devoid of manners, however. Allow me to introduce myself.   9
I am the obscene coda to your Kodak-colored sing-along. The verse that does
not rhyme. I am the spoiler in a last-ditch embrace of the mighty myth. The
nagging sight before your sighs. I am a vagrant in paradise.

I have fallen (nay, leapt) from the Ferris wheel of fortune. Neither con-   10
sumer nor commodity any longer, I confound the game. Of what to do with me
there are many plans and theories, but no real clue. I have power—enough to
affect public policy—yet remain powerless to inform its course. As an outsider,
policy is beyond my benefit; likewise am I beyond policy. For I am an outlaw.

My crime is having lived, for the better part of the past five years, on the   11
streets of this city. For most people this seems a pity, a waste and a cause for despair. But if you ask me . . .

My former employer did just that.   12

"Doesn't your mind stagnate?" he wanted to know, having encountered me   13
humping an industrial-size bag of redeemable cans to the store. *Strange you
should ask,* I thought at the time. *I seem to recall that on the job any proposal I
put forward that remotely resembled a bright idea got drowned in your nitpicking.
And I too was complicit, allowing the salve of a paycheck to temper the ardor with
which I'd fight for my ideas.*

Off the street, I was working sixty hours a week to keep a $984-a-month   14
studio apartment in a five-story walk-up, one scant block south of the projects.
On the street, I lived in the biggest mansion in New York City, right in the hub
of Manhattan: Grand Central Terminal. Off the street, I was spinning in circles,
chasing ambitions so vague and secondhand I couldn't define them if my life
depended on it. On the street, I enjoy a life that is, for once, refreshingly clear
of clutter. Hunger requires action less abstract than reaching for my wallet. In
pursuit of shelter, there is no landlord intervening. Action and consequences
are more purely linked on the street.

Like most people, I used to cringe at the sight of a man lying prone and   15
ragged on the sidewalk, and think, *There but for the grace of God . . .* Secretly,
though, it's often a more selfish matter with all of us—closer to *Thank God that
isn't me.* Off the street, I had this fear in the pit of my stomach that, caught in
the same situation, I would be unable to bear it. It wasn't the adversity of
wretchedness I found so dreadful; it was the prospect of becoming the subject
of people's contempt. For at the time I sought, without discrimination, the
approval of all.

Once on the street, however, I found no great hardship. Nor did I find—ex-   16
cept in the more benign form of pity—much contempt. The street turned out to
be, in fact, just the thing I needed. In the same manner that a person goes on a
fast to purify his system, I needed to purge my psyche of the deceptive markers
by which I had been sighting my way to a false sense of fulfillment. There was
the photograph of the Porsche I had pinned to my office wall. With such "car-
rots" I thought I could entice myself toward "success." The fact that I had never
bothered to learn to drive did not, in my abstruse striving, make any difference.

What I needed was to make friends with myself in the raw. That was five   17
years ago; back then it was possible to find the oblivion within which this could
be done. On the street then you could fend for yourself, keep your own coun-
sel and, if you wanted, be left alone. If things got to where you couldn't cope,
there were emergency shelters, soup kitchens and free clothing outlets to tide
you over. Today, however, facilitation of such an existence has been deemed a
worthless enterprise by society. The operative idea is that vagrants must be
rushed off the streets and injected back into the "mainstream." We are "the
homeless," and implicit in the name is a presumption that salvation for the dis-
franchised is as simple a matter as putting roofs over our heads.

What seems to elude advocates and antagonists alike is the possibility that   18
in the "mainstream" one can get caught up in a cycle with as much potential for
debilitation as all the drugs, alcohol and danger of disease commonly associated
with street life.

Poverty, mental illness, catastrophe, emotional crisis, violence at home, drug and alcohol addiction, are all circumstances that can lead to homelessness. In these cases it is understood that, more than "three hots and a cot," it takes meaningful employment, counseling, medical and rehabilitative treatment and other services to return people to *viable* "mainstream" life. But in my case, and I suspect I am not alone, it was living in the "mainstream" itself that ceased to be viable. So simply being cast back into life's old trappings was not a solution. 19

Before he walked out the door one morning and never came back, my friend and business partner, Barry Foster, was fond of pointing out that if you put a rat at one end of a maze and a piece of cheese at the other, the rat will eventually find its way to the prize by process of elimination. At each dead end it will turn and try a different path. "But man!" Barry would scorn. "Among all the animals, only humans will keep trying the same path expecting that, this time, they will find the cheese." 20

I had been chasing down dead-end alleys myself. And the notion that ever-increasing status, higher pay and more possessions were things of value was perpetually mocked by my misery. I persisted in longing for these things, not knowing what my true longings were. Had I not been jolted out of such passivity, discovering (by losing it) something I did value, I might still be spinning my wheels today. 21

The bad news came in threes. 22

One moment I had a business partner too narrow of vision to endure, a father too easy to despise for a lifetime of neglect, and a brother—much too lacking in guile for this city—to fret over. The next moment they were gone. In the short space of ninety days they had fallen like dominoes. Heart failure. Cancer. Vasculitis. Dead. 23

At the time I was putting in sixty-hour weeks trying to ensconce myself as a big shot in a small corporation. There was, I thought, no time for anything as worthless as grief. When, finally, I cried—for my brother mostly—I couldn't stop. At the end of it I was empty. I couldn't even go through the motions. I didn't go to work, didn't answer the phone and ignored the doorbell. People rang, buzzed. They only wanted to help. I just wanted to be left alone for a while. 24

On the street, I developed genuine confidence. Shorn of the trappings by which people commonly gauge a person's worthiness, I found I could nonetheless capture, inform, inspire and enlighten with nothing to recommend me but the quality of my thought. It did wonders for, yes, my self-esteem—something most people assume is inconsistent with being one of the great unwashed, as if self-esteem can be found in a bar of soap. 25

In the whirlwind of daily events we confront a swirl of human issues. Especially in New York. The temptation to simplify, to throw up our hands and settle for pat solutions, wrestles with our notions of social responsibility. Phrases like *low self-esteem, antisocial behavior, incorrigible homeless,* resonate with that part of us that favors our own interest. In a complex, densely populated, 26 heterogeneous metropolis like this, we try to find sense in common denominators. By doing so, we open the door to a politics of opportunism.

Rather than inspire us to heed our better natures, newly "populist" politicians trawl in the swamp of our anger, frustration and intolerance. In the name of civil decency, quality of life and tough love, we vagrants—in that we so publicly admit we are lost—are worthy of contempt.   27

The fact is, people everywhere seek a purge, a cleansing, an uncluttered perspective. The problem is that loud voices have persuaded us to cease pondering human complexities and, for the sake of smooth commerce, to follow more confined and predictable pursuits. Commodities, competitiveness—by such things does conventional wisdom measure the quality of life. On the streets, where everything is primal and personal, I have learned that wisdom is rarely conventional and that there is no answer of value that does not spawn at least another question. If modern mainstream life is to be nothing more than commerce, then count me out. I'd rather remain an outlaw. As an outlaw you have to think critically, to reject every principle and law that lacks moral authority and, if you wish to survive, to defer to the better part of your nature. Not the worst of codes in these, the "best of times." ☐   28

◢ REREADING FOR UNDERSTANDING

1.   What is the irony in the first paragraph? What is exposed by that irony?

2.   How does the first movie marquis quotation (par. 2) apply to the entire article? How is the second quotation (par. 8) a comment on the scene in front of the porn store?

3.   Why did Stringer leave his job, apartment, and security?

◢ RESPONDING

1.   What insights has Stringer gained about happiness and the good life from his five years on the streets of New York?

2.   Is Stringer's philosophy of the good life similar to that expressed by any of the Contexts authors? Which one (or more) would say to Stringer, "You have found the good life"? Why? Which author(s) would probably tell Stringer that he is a fool? Why?

3.   Stringer rejects modern definitions of happiness and the good life because the good in life is only measured by "commodities and competitiveness." Stringer argues that rejecting those values and living on the street causes him to "think critically, to reject every principle and law that lacks moral authority, and . . . to defer to the better part of your nature." Using ideas and illustrations from his essay and Sidel's essay (p. 490), construct a case for or against "dropping out" of the American Dream race.

MARTIN LUTHER KING, JR.

Many agree that Dr. Martin Luther King, Jr. (1929–1968) was one of the most significant social and political leaders of this century. An ordained minister who became active in nonviolent, civil rights protest movements that sprang up throughout the American South during the 1950s and early 1960s, he soon emerged as the most articulate and charismatic leader of that movement, organizing nonviolent protests that culminated in the massive civil rights protest march on Washington, D.C., in 1963. He delivered this speech from the steps of the Lincoln Memorial as the culminating moment of that march. In 1964, King became the youngest-ever recipient of the Nobel Peace Prize. He was killed by an assassin in Memphis, Tennessee, in 1968.

King's American Dream is not based on vengeance or hatred. Rather, it is based on hope, love, and a sense of shared humanity.

I Have a Dream

Five score years ago, a great American, in whose symbolic shadow we stand, signed the Emancipation Proclamation. This momentous decree came as a great beacon light of hope to millions of Negro slaves who had been seared in the flames of withering injustice. It came as a joyous daybreak to end the long night of captivity.

But one hundred years later, we must face the tragic fact that the Negro is still not free. One hundred years later, the life of the Negro is still sadly crippled by the manacles of segregation and the chains of discrimination. One hundred years later, the Negro lives on a lonely island of poverty in the midst of a vast ocean of material prosperity. One hundred years later, the Negro is still languishing in the corners of American society and finds himself an exile in his own land. So we have come here today to dramatize an appalling condition.

In a sense we have come to our nation's Capitol to cash a check. When the architects of our republic wrote the magnificent words of the Constitution and the Declaration of Independence, they were signing a promissory note to which every American was to fall heir. This note was a promise that all men would be guaranteed the unalienable rights of life, liberty, and the pursuit of happiness.

It is obvious today that America has defaulted on this promissory note insofar as her citizens of color are concerned. Instead of honoring this sacred obligation, America has given the Negro people a bad check; a check which has come back marked "insufficient funds." But we refuse to believe that the bank of justice is bankrupt. We refuse to believe that there are insufficient funds in the great vaults of opportunity of this nation. So we have come to cash this check—a check that will give us upon demand the riches of freedom and the security of justice. We have also come to this hallowed spot to remind America of the fierce urgency of *now*. This is no time to engage in the luxury of cooling off or to take the tranquilizing drug of gradualism. *Now* is the time to make real the promises of Democracy. *Now* is the time to rise from the dark and desolate valley of segregation to the sunlit path of racial justice. *Now* is the time to open the doors of opportunity to all of God's children. *Now* is the time to lift our na-tion from the quicksands of racial injustice to the solid rock of brotherhood.

It would be fatal for the nation to overlook the urgency of the moment and   5
to underestimate the determination of the Negro. This sweltering summer of
the Negro's legitimate discontent will not pass until there is an invigorating
autumn of freedom and equality. 1963 is not an end, but a beginning. Those
who hope that the Negro needed to blow off steam and will now be content will
have a rude awakening if the nation returns to business as usual. There will be
neither rest nor tranquility in America until the Negro is granted his citizenship
rights. The whirlwinds of revolt will continue to shake the foundations of our
nation until the bright day of justice emerges.

But there is something I must say to my people who stand on the warm   6
threshold which leads into the palace of justice. In the process of gaining our
rightful place we must not be guilty of wrongful deeds. Let us not seek to sat-isfy our thirst for freedom by drinking from the cup of bitterness and hatred.
We must forever conduct our struggle on the high plane of dignity and disci-pline. We must not allow our creative protest to degenerate into physical vio-lence. Again and again we must rise to the majestic heights of meeting physical
force with soul force. The marvelous new militancy which has engulfed the
Negro community must not lead us to a distrust of all white people, for many
of our white brothers, as evidenced by their presence here today, have come to
realize that their destiny is tied up with our destiny and their freedom is inex-tricably bound to our freedom. We cannot walk alone.

And as we walk, we must make the pledge that we shall march ahead. We   7
cannot turn back. There are those who are asking the devotees of civil rights,
"When will you be satisfied?" We can never be satisfied as long as the Negro is
the victim of the unspeakable horrors of police brutality. We can never be sat-isfied as long as our bodies, heavy with the fatigue of travel, cannot gain lodg-ing in the motels of the highways and the hotels of the cities. We cannot be
satisfied as long as the Negro's basic mobility is from a smaller ghetto to a larger
one. We can never be satisfied as long as a Negro in Mississippi cannot vote and
a Negro in New York believes he has nothing for which to vote. No, no, we are
not satisfied, and we will not be satisfied until justice rolls down like waters and
righteousness like a mighty stream.

I am not unmindful that some of you have come here out of great trials and   8
tribulations. Some of you have come fresh from narrow jail cells. Some of you
have come from areas where your quest for freedom left you battered by the
storms of persecution and staggered by the winds of police brutality. You have
been the veterans of creative suffering. Continue to work with the faith that un-earned suffering is redemptive.

Go back to Mississippi, go back to Alabama, go back to South Carolina, go   9
back to Georgia, go back to Louisiana, go back to the slums and ghettoes of our
northern cities, knowing that somehow this situation can and will be changed.
Let us not wallow in the valley of despair.

I say to you today, my friends, that in spite of the difficulties and frustra-   10
tions of the moment I still have a dream. It is a dream deeply rooted in the
American dream.

I have a dream that one day this nation will rise up and live out the true   11
meaning of its creed: "We hold these truths to be self-evident; that all men are
created equal."

I have a dream that one day on the red hills of Georgia the sons of former   12
slaves and the sons of former slaveowners will be able to sit down together at
the table of brotherhood.

I have a dream that the state of Mississippi, a desert state sweltering with   13
the heat of injustice and oppression, will be transformed into an oasis of freedom and justice.

I have a dream that my four little children will one day live in a nation   14
where they will not be judged by the color of their skin but by the content of
their character.

I have a dream today.   15

I have a dream that the state of Alabama, whose governor's lips are pres-   16
ently dripping with the words of interposition and nullification, will be transformed into a situation where little black boys and black girls will be able to join
hands with little white boys and white girls and walk together as sisters and
brothers.

I have a dream today.   17

I have a dream that one day every valley shall be exalted, every hill and   18
mountain shall be made low, the rough places will be made plain, and the
crooked places will be made straight, and the glory of the Lord shall be revealed,
and all flesh shall see it together.

This is our hope. This is the faith with which I return to the South. With   19
this faith we will be able to hew out of the mountain of despair a stone of hope.
With this faith we will be able to transform the jangling discords of our nation
into a beautiful symphony of brotherhood. With this faith we will be able to
work together, to pray together, to struggle together, to go to jail together, to
stand up for freedom together, knowing that we will be free one day.

This will be the day when all of God's children will be able to sing with new   20
meaning.

> My country, tis of thee
> Sweet land of liberty,
>   Of thee I sing:
> Land where my fathers died,
> Land of the pilgrims' pride,
> From every mountainside
>   Let freedom ring.

And if America is to be a great nation this must become true. So let free-   21
dom ring from the prodigious hilltops of New Hampshire. Let freedom ring
from the mighty mountains of New York. Let freedom ring from the heighten-
ing Alleghenies of Pennsylvania!

Let freedom ring from the snowcapped Rockies of Colorado!   22
Let freedom ring from the curvaceous peaks of California!   23
But not only that; let freedom ring from Stone Mountain of Georgia!   24

Let freedom ring from Lookout Mountain of Tennessee!　25

Let freedom ring from every hill and molehill of Mississippi. From every　26
mountainside, let freedom ring.

When we let freedom ring, when we let it ring from every village and every　27
hamlet, from every state and every city, we will be able to speed up that day when
all of God's children, black men and white men, Jews and Gentiles, Protestants
and Catholics, will be able to join hands and sing in the words of the old Negro
spiritual, "Free at last! free at last! thank God almighty, we are free at last!" □

◢ REREADING FOR UNDERSTANDING

1. What does King believe is the central cause of the plight of the American
   Negro?

2. What action does King ask of those who gathered to hear his speech?

3. Characterize the "dream" King shares in paragraphs 10–18.

◢ RESPONDING

1. What ideas and passages do you find most moving? Why?

2. Do many of the injustices African-Americans suffered in 1963 still continue today? Has the dream of freedom been achieved?

3. Which author in the Contexts section would be in greatest agreement with
   King's views on the "good life"? Why?

◢ RESPONDING IN WRITING

In a brief essay to your parents' generation, explain to them what might occur
if our society does not incorporate the social and political values King outlines
in his speech. What hope exists for the good life, not just for African-Americans
but for all of us, if the dream expressed here does not come true?

RUTH SIDEL

Ruth Sidel (1933–　　) is a sociologist, a college professor, and a keen
observer of current social issues and trends about which she has written in
numerous books and articles. In one of her books, *On Her Own: Growing Up
in the Shadow of the American Dream*, she interviews 150 young women
aged twelve to twenty-five. Sidel uses the interviews to discover what type
of American Dream these women are pursuing. In the selection below, the

opening chapter from that book, Sidel reveals how young women combine the work ethic with trendy materialism. Sidel suggests women can now pursue more personal and individualistic versions of the American Dream than may have been available to them formerly. As you read Sidel's essay and listen to the interviewees voice their "new" American Dream, compare their dreams to yours. See if you are pleased, puzzled, or depressed by what you read.

The New American Dreamers

It's your life. You have to live it yourself.
. . . If you work hard enough, you will get
there. You must be in control of your life,
and then somehow it will all work out.
—ANGELA DAWSON
HIGH-SCHOOL JUNIOR,
SOUTHERN CALIFORNIA

She is the prototype of today's woman—confident, outgoing, knowledge- 1 able, involved. She is active in her school, church, or community. She may have a wide circle of friends or simply a few close ones, but she is committed to them and to their friendship. She is sophisticated about the central issues facing young people today—planning for the future, intimacy, sex, drugs, and alcohol—and discusses them seriously, thoughtfully, and forthrightly. She wants to take control of her life and is trying to figure out how to get from where she is to where she wants to go. Above all, she is convinced that if she plans carefully, works hard, and makes the right decisions, she will be a success in her chosen field; have the material goods she desires; in time, marry if she wishes; and, in all probability, have children. She plans, as the expression goes, to "have it all."

She lives in and around the major cities of the United States, in the towns 2 of New England, in the smaller cities of the South and Midwest, and along the West Coast. She comes from an upper-middle-class family, from the middle class, from the working class, and even sometimes from the poor. What is clear is that she has heard the message that women today should be the heroines of their own lives. She looks toward the future, seeing herself as the central character, planning her career, her apartment, her own success story. These young women do not see themselves as playing supporting roles in someone else's life script; it is their own journeys they are planning. They see their lives in terms of *their* aspirations, *their* hopes, *their* dreams.

Beth Conant is a sixteen-year-old high-school junior who lives with her 3 mother and stepfather in an affluent New England college town. She has five brothers, four older and one several years younger. Her mother is a librarian, and her stepfather is a stockbroker. A junior at a top-notch public high school, she hopes to study drama in college, possibly at Yale, "like Meryl Streep." She would like to live and act in England for a time, possibly doing Shakespeare. She hopes to be living in New York by the age of twenty-five, in her own apartment or condo, starting on her acting career while working at another job by which she supports herself. She wants to have "a great life," be "really independent," and have "everything that's mine—crazy furniture, everything my own style."

By the time she's thirty ("that's so boring"), she feels, she will need to be sensible, because soon she will be "tied down." She hopes that by then her career will be "starting to go forth" and that she will be getting good roles. By thirty-five she'll have a child ("probably be married beforehand"), be working in New York and have a house in the country. How will she manage all this? Her husband will share responsibilities. She's not going to be a "supermom." They'll both do child care. He won't do it as a favor; it will be their joint responsibility. Moreover, if she doesn't have the time to give to a child, she won't have one. If necessary, she'll work for a while, then have children, and after that "make one movie a year."   4

Amy Morrison is a petite, black, fifteen-year-old high school sophomore who lives in Ohio. Her mother works part-time, and her father works for a local art museum. She plans to go to medical school and hopes to become a surgeon. She doesn't want to marry until she has a good, secure job but indicates that she might be living with someone. She's not sure about having children but says emphatically that she wants to be successful, to make money, to have cars. In fact, originally she wanted to become a doctor "primarily for the money," but now she claims other factors are drawing her to medicine.   5

Jacqueline Gonzalez is a quiet, self-possessed, nineteen-year-old Mexican-American woman who is a sophomore at a community college in southern California. She describes her father as a "self-employed contractor" and her mother as a "housewife." Jacqueline, the second-youngest of six children, is the first in her family to go to college. Among her four brothers and one sister, only her sister has finished high school. Jacqueline's goal is to go to law school and then to go into private practice. While she sees herself as eventually married with "one or two children," work, professional achievement, and an upper-middle-class life-style are central to her plans for her future.   6

If in the past, and to a considerable extent still today, women have hoped to find their identity through marriage, have sought to find "validation of . . . [their] uniqueness and importance by being singled out among all other women by a man," the New American Dreamers are setting out on a very different quest for self-realization. They are, in their plans for the future, separating identity from intimacy, saying that they must first figure out who they are and that then and only then will they form a partnership with a man. Among the young women I interviewed, the New American Dreamers stand apart in their intention to make their own way in the world and determine their own destiny prior to forming a significant and lasting intimate relationship.   7

Young women today do not need to come from upper-middle-class homes such as Beth's or middle-class homes such as Amy's or working-class homes such as Jacqueline's to dream of "the good life." Even young women with several strikes against them see material success as a key prize at the end of   8 the rainbow. Some seem to feel that success is out there for the taking. Generally, the most prestigious, best-paying careers are mentioned; few women of any class mention traditional women's professions such as teaching or nursing. A sixteen-year-old unmarried Arizona mother of a four-and-a-half-month-old baby looks forward to a "professional career either in a bank or with a computer company," a "house that belongs to me," a "nice car," and the ability to buy her son "good clothes." She sees herself in the future as dating but not married. "There is not so much stress on marriage these days," she says.

Yet another young woman, a seventeen-year-old black unmarried mother   9
of an infant, hopes to be a "professional model," have "lots of cash," be "rich," maybe have another child. When asked if a man will be part of the picture, she responds, "I don't know."

An eighteen-year-old Hispanic unmarried mother hopes to "be my own   10
boss" in a large company, have a "beautiful home," send her daughter to "the best schools." She wants, in her words, to "do it, make it, have money."

These young women are bright, thoughtful, personable. And they are quin-   11
tessentially American: they believe that with enough hard work they will "make it" in American society. No matter what class they come from, their fantasies are of upward mobility, a comfortable life filled with personal choice and material possessions. The upper-middle-class women fantasize a life even more upper-middle-class; middle-class and working-class women look toward a life of high status in which they have virtually everything they want; and some young women who come from families with significant financial deprivation and numerous other problems dream of a life straight out of "Dallas," "Dynasty," or "L.A. Law." According to one young woman, some of her friends are so determined to be successful that they are "fearful that there will be a nuclear war and that they will die before they have a chance to live their lives. If there is a nuclear war," she explained, "they won't live long enough to be successful."

Young women are our latest true believers. They have bought into the   12
image of a bright future. Many of them see themselves as professional women, dressed in handsome clothes, carrying a briefcase to work, and coming home to a comfortable house or condo, possibly to a loving, caring husband and a couple of well-behaved children. How widespread is the dream? How realistic is it? What is the function of this latest American dream? What about those young women who cling to a more traditional dream? What about those who feel their dreams must be deferred? What about those with no dream at all? And what about those who "share the fantasy," as the Chanel No. 5 perfume advertisement used to say, but have little or no chance of achieving it?

Perhaps the most poignant example of the impossible dream is Simone   13
Baker, a dynamic, bright, eighteen-year-old black woman from Louisiana. Simone's mother is a seamstress who has been off and on welfare over the years, and her father is a drug addict. Simone herself has been addicted to drugs of one kind or another since she was five. She has been in and out of drug-abuse facilities, and although she attended school for many years and was passed from grade to grade, she can barely read and write. When I met her in a drug rehabilitation center, she was struggling to become drug free so that she

could join the Job Corps, finish high school, and obtain some vocational training. Her dream of the future is so extraordinary, given her background, that she seems to epitomize the Horatio Alger myth of another era. When asked what she would like her life to be like in the future, Simone replies instantly, her eyes shining: "I want to be a model. I want to have a Jacuzzi. I want to have a *big*, BIG house and a BIG family—three girls and two boys."

"And what about the man?" I ask her.   14

"He'll be a lawyer. He'll be responsible, hardworking, and sensitive to my   15
feelings. Everything will be fifty-fifty. And he'll take the little boys out to play football and I'll have the girls inside cooking. That would be a dream come true!"

Simone's dream is an incredible mixture of the old and the new—a Dick-   16
and-Jane reader updated. And she's even mouthing the supreme hope of so many women in this age of the therapeutic solution to personal problems— that she'll find a man who is "sensitive" to her "feelings." She has lived a life far from the traditional middle class and yet has the quintessential image of the good life as it has been formulated in the last quarter of the twentieth century. But for Simone, it is virtually an impossible dream. One wishes that that were not so; listening to her, watching her excitement and hope at the mere thought of such a life, one gets caught up and wants desperately for it all to happen. The image is clear: the white house in the suburbs with the brass knocker on the front door, the leaves on the lawn in the fall, the boys playing football with this incredibly wonderful husband/father, and Simone sometimes the successful model, other times at home, cooking with her daughters. But we know how very unlikely it is that this particular dream will come true. And yet, maybe . . .

How have young women come to take on the American Dream as their   17
own? That this is a relatively new dream for women is clear. Until recent years women, for the most part, did not perceive themselves as separate, independent entities with their own needs and agendas. Women fit themselves into other people's lives, molded their needs to fit the needs of others. For the full-time homemaker the day began early enough to enable husband and children to get to work and school on time. Chores had to be done between breakfast and lunch or between lunch and the end of school. Dinnertime was when the man of the house returned from work. When a woman worked outside of the home, her work hours were often those that fit into the schedules of other family members. Her needs were determined by the needs of others, as often her identity rested on her affiliation with them.

What some women seem to be saying now is that they will form their own   18
identities, develop their own styles, and meet their own needs. They will be the central characters in their stories. They will work at jobs men work at, earn the money men earn; but many of them also plan at the same time to play all the roles women have traditionally played.

What has become clear in talking with young women throughout the   19
country is that many of them are planning for their future in terms of their "public" roles as well as their "domestic" roles, that they are "laying claim to significant and satisfying work . . . as a normal part of their lives and laying

claim also to the authority, prestige, power, and salary that . . . [that] work commands." Historically, women have been confined primarily to the "domestic" sphere of life, particularly to child rearing and homemaking, and men, for the most part, have participated in the "public" sphere—that is, in social, economic, and political institutions and forms of association in the broader social structure. This dichotomy between "public" and "domestic" has led to "an asymmetry in the cultural evaluation of male and female that appears to be universal." Margaret Mead noted this asymmetry when she observed that "whatever the arrangements in regard to descent or ownership of property, and even if these formal outward arrangements are reflected in the temperamental relations between the sexes, the prestige values always attach to the activities of men."

In New Guinea, women grow sweet potatoes and men grow yams; yams are   20
the prestige food. In societies where women grow rice, the staple food, and men hunt for meat, meat is the most valued food. Traditionally, the more exclusively male the activity, the more cultural value is attached to it. Because male activities have been valued over female activities and women have become "absorbed primarily in domestic activities because of their role as mothers," women's work of caring has traditionally been devalued. However, as political scientist Joan Tronto has pointed out, it is not simply the dichotomy between the public and the private that results in the devaluation of the female but the immense difference in power between the two spheres. So long as men have a monopoly on the public sphere and it in turn wields great power within society, women, identified with the private sphere, which is seen as relatively powerless, will be devalued.

Since the emergence of the women's movement in the 1960s, women in the   21
U.S. as well as in many other parts of the world have been questioning the traditional asymmetry between men and women, seeking to understand its roots, its causes, and its consequences, and attempting to modify the male monopoly of power. Many strategies have developed toward this end: laws have been passed in an attempt to eliminate discrimination; groups have formed to elect more women to positions of power; those already in power have been urged to appoint more women to administrative roles; dominant, high-status, high-income professions have been pressured to admit more women to their hallowed ranks; and strategies to bring greater equity to male and female salaries have been developed.

Great stress has been placed on raising the consciousness of both women   22
and men concerning this imbalance of power, but particular attention has been devoted to raising the consciousness of women. Discussion about the relative powerlessness of the non-wage-earning "housewife" has been widespread. Books and articles about the impoverishment of the divorced woman, the problems of the displaced homemaker, and the often desperate plight of the single, female head of household have been directed at women. During the 1970s and 1980s, the message suddenly became clear to many women: perhaps they are entitled to play roles formerly reserved for men; perhaps they would enjoy these challenges; perhaps they have something special to offer and can make a difference in the practice of medicine or law or in running the country. Moreover, it became clear that if women want power, prestige, and paychecks

similar to those men receive, if they want to lessen the asymmetry between male and female, then perhaps they must enter those spheres traditionally reserved for men. If men grow yams, must women grow yams? If men hunt and women gather, must women purchase a bow and arrow? If men are in the public sphere while women are at home caring for children and doing the laundry, the consensus seems to say that women must enter the public sphere. If men are doctors and lawyers and earn great rewards while women are nurses and teachers and earn meager rewards, then women see what they obviously must do. If men have focused on doing while women have focused on caring, then clearly women must become doers.

It is not sufficient, however, to become a doer in a traditionally female   23
occupation, for, as we know, these occupations are notoriously underpaid and underesteemed. Women must become *real* doers in the arena that counts: they must learn to play hardball, or, as Mary Lou Retton says in her breakfast-cereal advertisements, "eat what the big boys eat." For real power, status, money, and "success," it's law, medicine, and finance—also, possibly, acting, modeling, or working in the media, if one is very lucky.

An illustration of the current emphasis on male-dominated careers as the   24
road to success for young women are the career goals of *Glamour* magazine's "Top Ten College Women '88." One woman hopes to become an astronaut; a second plans to work in the area of public policy, another to be a biologist, another to obtain a degree in business administration, yet another to obtain a degree in acting; and one young woman is currently working in journalism. One college senior is undecided between journalism and law, and the last three are planning to go to law school. These young women, according to *Glamour*, "possess the talents and ambition necessary to shape tomorrow's society." It is noteworthy that none of the women *Glamour* chose to honor are entering any traditionally female occupation or any "helping" profession—not even medicine. Don't nurses, teachers, and social workers "possess the talents and ambition necessary to shape tomorrow's society"? The word has gone out and continues to go out that the way to "make it" in American society and the way to "shape tomorrow's society" is the traditional male route.

Once singled out, these young women play their part in spreading the   25
ideology of the American Dream. Three of the ten honorees appeared on NBC's "Today" show. When asked about the significance of their being chosen, one woman replied without hesitation that if you work hard, you can do whatever you want to do. This statement was greeted by smiles and nods; she had clearly given the right message.

In addition to wanting to break out of the mold of a secondary worker re-   26
ceiving inferior wages and benefits and having little authority or opportunity for advancement, women have been motivated to make real money and to acquire valued skills and some semblance of security because of their relatively recent realization that women, even women with children, may well be forced to care for themselves or, at the very least, to participate in providing for the family unit. Women have come to realize that whether because of divorce (which leaves women on the average 73 percent poorer and men on the average 42 percent richer), childbearing outside of marriage, the inability of many men

to earn an adequate "family wage," or their remaining single—either through design or through circumstance—they must be prepared to support themselves and anyone else for whom they feel responsible.

But what of all that caring women used to do—for children, for elderly par-   27 ents, for sick family members, for the home? What about Sunday dinner, baking chocolate-chip cookies with the kids eating up half the batter, serving Kool-Aid in the backyard on a hot summer day? What about sitting with a child with a painful ear infection until the antibiotic takes effect, going with a four-year-old to nursery school the first week until the child feels comfortable letting you leave, being available when there's an accident at school and your second grader must be rushed to the emergency room? Who's going to do the caring? Who is going to do the caring in a society in which few institutions have been developed to take up the slack, a society in which men have been far more reluctant to become carers than women have been to become doers. Members of the subordinate group may gain significantly in status, in self-image, and in material rewards when they take on the activities and characteristics of the dominant group, but there is little incentive for members of the dominant group to do the reverse.

Above all, how do young women today deal with these questions? How do   28 they feel about doing and caring, about power, prestige, and parenting? What messages is society giving them about the roles they should play, and how are they sorting out these messages?

A key message the New American Dreamers are both receiving and send-   29 ing is one of optimism—the sense that they can do whatever they want with their lives. Many Americans, of course—not just young people or young women—have a fundamentally optimistic attitude toward the future. Historically, Americans have believed that progress is likely, even inevitable, and that they have the ability to control their own destinies. A poll taken early in 1988 indicates that while the American public was concerned about the nation's future and indeed more pessimistic about "the way things [were] going in the United States" than they had been at any other time since the Carter presidency in the late 1970s, they nonetheless believed that they could "plan and regulate their own lives, even while the national economy and popular culture appear[ed] to be spinning out of control." As one would expect, those with higher incomes and more education are more optimistic than those with less; Republicans are more optimistic than Democrats or Independents; and, significantly, men are more hopeful than women. In looking toward the future, young men clearly dream of "the good life," of upward mobility and their share of material possessions. While young women historically have had far less control over their lives than men, for the past twenty-five years they have been urged to take greater control, both in the workplace and in their private lives, and they have clearly taken the message very much to heart.

Angela Dawson, a sixteen-year-old high-school junior from southern   30 California, sums up the views of the New American Dreamers: "It's your life. You have to live it yourself. You must decide what you want in high school, plan your college education, and from there you can basically get what you want. If you work hard enough, you will get there. You must be in control of your life, and then somehow it will all work out."

Angela is clearly reflecting widespread changes in young women's expecta-   31
tions. Recent studies indicate that over the past quarter-century there has been significant change in women's educational and career expectations. From 1960 to 1980, for example, the proportion of young women in their senior year of high school who expected to go on to college and complete a degree and the proportion who expected to follow "high level" professional careers increased significantly. Interestingly, the expectation for higher education and careers requiring an undergraduate degree rose more between 1960 and 1972, while the expectation of a professional career requiring a graduate degree rose most steeply between 1972 and 1980. Furthermore, some research indicates that by 1980 the notion of high achievement had become so widespread that even young women with lower academic achievement or without plans for going on to college expected to be able to enter a "high level" profession. One sociologist interprets these data as a fundamental shift in values among young women:

> This suggests less a form of rational calculation than an ideological surge to aim for the top of the career hierarchy, whatever one's chances. It seems that "career feminism"—achieving equality in the labor force for women— had made a major impact on young women by 1980. Instead of responding to a "pull" factor—increased opportunities drawing young women into institutions of higher education—the expectations of women for the highest level careers seem themselves to have represented a "push" factor. Propelled by the pressure to get out of the female job ghetto, by widespread media coverage of women entering male-dominated careers, by the discussion of new strategies and pressures (networking, mentoring) to break down sex segregation in careers, young women's plans to enter high level professions seem more an expression of the new *values* [italics in original] of achieving job equality for women than of recognizing opportunities for such careers.

Other studies also indicate continuing and increasing "profeminist" views   32
among women and men in the late 1970s and early-to-mid-1980s. Despite considerable media discussion of a backlash against feminism, General Social Survey data from the National Opinion Research Center indicate that between 1977 and 1985 an increased percentage of women and men supported women working and felt that "a working mother can establish just as warm and secure a relationship with her children as a mother who does not work." On this latter issue and on a question about working women and the well-being of preschool children ("A preschool child is likely to suffer if his or her mother works"), the percentage of men taking the "profeminist" view increased; nevertheless, men were considerably more traditional in their views than were women.

Thus, support for women entering the labor force, including women with   33
children, has continued to grow. The idea of mothers working has gained such widespread acceptance that poor mothers who do *not* work, particularly those receiving Aid to Families with Dependent Children, are currently seen as deviant.

Under so-called welfare reform legislation passed by the U.S. Congress during the fall of 1988, many of these mothers will be required to go out to work or at least to enter training programs and then to look for work. This action has been rationalized by the statement "It is now the norm for women to work. Why should poor women be any different?"

This increased commitment on the part of women to enter the "public"   34
sphere and, in many cases, to aim for the most prestigious jobs, to reach for the top, to "go for it," is reflected in other aspects of their lives. One of these is young women's increased participation in athletic activities. A recent survey indicates that among a random sample of girls aged seven to eighteen, 82 percent said that they currently participate in sports. Eighty-seven percent of the parents polled believe that sports are as important for girls as for boys.

Young women clearly have a great deal to gain from intense athletic in-   35
volvement: the confidence that comes with the development of skills, an understanding of the importance of teamwork, improved body image, and, of course, the friendships that can develop from continuous commitment to and participation in activities one cares about deeply. But perhaps the most important benefit was spelled out by the mother of a teenage female athlete: The "message of sports," she writes, is to "be aggressive . . . Go for the ball. Be intense." It must be noted that in this case it was the athlete's father who continuously counseled her to really "go for it," not to be content to "sit on the bench." The writer notes how girls have been trained for generations to "Be quiet, Be good, Be still . . . not to get dirty" and that being intense is "neither quiet nor good. And it's definitely not pretty." What participation in athletics can teach a young woman, and what she must learn if she is really to be a force in this society, is to not be "afraid to do her best." This is part of what Angela and some of the other young women seem to be saying—they are going to go out there and not be afraid to do their best.

These women have a commitment to career, to material well-being, to suc-   36
cess, and to independence. To many of them, an affluent life-style is central to their dreams; they often describe their goals in terms of cars, homes, travel to Europe. In short, they want their piece of the American Dream. Many of them plan eventually to weave marriage and children into the superstructure; some of them are not so sure. But for now their priorities are to figure out who they are, get on with their education, and become successful in their chosen field.

What is new about the dreams of many young women today is not only   37
that they are the central characters in their plans for the future but that they believe they must prepare themselves to go it alone. Young women of all classes talk about the need to be independent. Some quote their mothers and other female relatives who are urging them to organize their lives so that they can take care of themselves. A seventeen-year-old midwestern daughter of divorced parents reports, "My mom tells me I have to be self-secure. I don't want to have to depend on anyone." Another says, "My mother wants me to be happy and she wants me to be able to take care of myself." Yet another: "My grandmother says 'Have your own nest egg.'" Several young women in the Southwest agree. A seventeen-year-old whose parents are divorced: "I want to be independent—

financially and emotionally. I want to be stable and independent. I do not want to rely on anyone else," she says emphatically. A twelve-year-old agrees and says her friends talk about the need for women to be able to support themselves and their families. She was five months old when her parents divorced and freely admits she still wishes they would get back together. A sixteen-year-old whose mother is a "housewife" and whose father does "sales-type jobs" but is currently unemployed isn't sure what she wants to do but knows she wants a "decent job" and doesn't want "to end up dependent."

This perception on the part of young women that success is there for the taking, that affluence is a necessary ingredient in any life plan, and that they need to be able to stand on their own can be seen as a coming together of several strands of American thought: the American Dream promises upward mobility to those who plan and work sufficiently hard; the women's movement has taught at least two generations of women that they are entitled to play virtually any roles in society that they are capable of and that they are entitled to reap the appropriate rewards; and the ideology of the Reagan years has both stressed individualism and undermined Americans' belief in the necessity of creating a more humane and equitable environment in which all people can thrive. During the 1980s we have witnessed, I believe, the merging of these three lines of thought against a backdrop of ever-increasing disparities in wealth and well-being between rich and poor, black and white, and ever-increasing emphasis on materialism, often at any cost—what one social critic has called the "empty ostentation and narcissistic culture of the 1980s." Is it any wonder that young women feel they are on their own? The message that they must go it alone is being given to many Americans: the homeless; the hungry; the elderly nursing-home residents; the children who are essentially lost in the foster-care system; the millions who are uninsured for health care and those who do not have access to care because of inadequate or nonexistent services; the numbers of young people receiving inferior education that cannot possibly prepare them for living and working in the next century. Moreover, young women see on a personal level that individuals must be able to care for themselves. They see their divorced parents floundering; they hear the cautionary tales about relying too much on men; they are all too aware of the status and respect given in American society to those who embody the traditional male characteristics of autonomy and power, and know that to protect themselves they must have no less. 38

The feminist movement did not, of course, set out to bolster and extend to yet another group the ideology of individualism and the American Dream. With its appeal to "sisterhood" and its use of consciousness-raising groups, it set out, rather, on a far more collective course, encouraging women to see themselves not simply as individuals but as part of a long, international struggle for equality. But movements do not exist in a vacuum. The women's movement originated within a class system that drew largely middle- and upper-middle-class adherents and then was in part shaped by their concerns and their needs. It exists today within an individualistic, hierarchical system committed for the most part to private enterprise and profit making. Once it became clear that the 39 movement was not going to disappear, elements of that structure began admitting "the best and the brightest" to their hallowed halls. Leaders of the movement might call for widely available day care, paid parental leave, larger welfare grants, and more money for prenatal care, but what was picked up by the media were the upper-middle-class women in the courtrooms, the board rooms, and the emergency rooms, often putting off marriage and children in order to go for the brass ring of success.

This ideology of independence and individualism can be seen to some degree in all three groups, but it is far more prevalent among the New American Dreamers, and adds significantly to the pressure these young women already feel. They feel pressure to succeed not only for the status and material rewards success bestows but because they recognize the likelihood that they may be the sole support of themselves and their children.   40

This sense of responsibility, of aloneness, brings a new intensity to the need to be "successful." Many young women see the choices as "making it" or "not making it," being "independent" versus being "dependent." Understood in those terms, the pressure is to work out a way for oneself to live the good life.   41

Nancy Delmonico exemplifies the young woman under pressure to achieve because she realizes she may well be out there on her own. She is a thoughtful, articulate, seventeen-year-old high-school senior who lives in Arizona. Nancy's parents are divorced; her father was raised on a farm and now has his own business, and her mother is an administrator of a community agency. Nancy feels considerable anxiety over both her choice of college and her choice of career. She is currently undecided between acting and criminal law. She says with obvious anxiety that she finds the decision "overwhelming."   42

Nancy expects to have an established career by the time she is in her mid-twenties, probably in law or in politics, and at some point to marry and have "a kid or two." She hopes eventually to be a "judge or a Supreme Court justice, travel a lot, see the world, and experience a lot of things." She sums up by saying, "Today you've got to be able to take care of yourself."   43

Some young women have an almost magical attitude about success—somehow they'll get there. Others have a clear picture of what they need to do to get where they want to go. These young women, with their dreams for achievement and success, recognize that they are under significant pressure to achieve. Not only must they get good grades and be accepted into a good college, but most of them anticipate graduate school as well.   44

"What is the key issue facing young women today?" I ask four high-school students as we sit around a table in the beautifully proportioned library on the third floor of an Episcopal church in the Midwest. The young women—a sophomore, two juniors, and a senior—reflect a minute; then the senior, a thoughtful, quiet, composed, articulate young black woman, responds: "College. That's what I'm worrying about. Everyone is worried about where they'll go, where they'll get the money." A fifteen-year-old junior chimes in, saying she is "hyper" about grades. She wants to get into a "good college"—she "wouldn't mind MIT." The fifteen year old sophomore, who hopes to go to medical school, worries about grades, too. She recognizes that it is going to take her a long time   45 to pay for medical school and thinks she'll eventually specialize in some kind of surgery, an area of medicine known for its high income.

These young women are well aware that if they are going to be successful and independent, they need to start putting it together right now. One young woman from a New England college town states that the young people in her high school are *very* competitive about getting into college. She feels her school is not developing individuals but, rather, producing "Ivy League machines."

Billy Dreskin, a young rabbi who works with high-school students in a small community in Westchester County, outside New York City, comments on the pressures young people face today: "Their lives are consumed with doing well in school. They think they'll die if they don't make a good living, and school is their ticket to success. The pressures here are not so much economic as academic," he continues. "[There's] pressure to take AP [advanced placement] courses. They convey a certain status, and kids are taking them who shouldn't be. The kids can't do any of the things they want to do without money, and in order to earn the money, they need to succeed academically."

Several young women from Arizona describe some of the pressures they feel. Nancy Delmonico says, "Grades are a big pressure. I feel the pressure from teachers and from my parents. They are concerned about our being successful—about what we'll be doing with the rest of our lives." She states, moreover, that this enormous amount of pressure on young people is a key factor in adolescent alcohol and drug abuse. As a young woman who has attended both public and private schools, she feels that there is a much greater problem with drugs and alcohol among private-school kids, partly because they have the money to pay for the substances and partly because they are under such great pressure.

A high-school junior interjects, "I pressure myself! I get down on myself. I see a C as an F. And I feel I'm not worrying about college enough!" A twelve-year-old seventh grader says, "My mom and dad pressure me about grades. My sister is a gymnast—that's what she's good at, so lousy grades don't matter. I'm not good at anything special, so school has to be my thing." Another twelve-year-old says her greatest concern is choosing which of two high schools to attend. Her mother wants her to go to the more academically prestigious school. She's more concerned with where her friends are going. And she also worries about grades. Her father is a doctor, and her mother is a lawyer; she feels she must get good grades for them.

Stacy Steinberg, a soft-spoken yet articulate seventeen-year-old high-school junior, whose mother is a school nurse and whose father is an auditor, analyzes the pressures young women feel: "It's so hard to be an adolescent today, and it's only going to get harder. Kids today have to worry about liquor, drugs, sex, *and* their academic work. And your parents want you to do better than they did, but it's harder to do better today than when they were growing up."

She goes on: "Guys have different pressures; they're more into sexual experiences. But it's harder to be a girl. You see models in ads and say, 'I don't look like that; how can I fit into that?' Parents say, 'When you lose a few more pounds, you can get a new outfit.' And the pressure about grades—the girls who cry if they don't do perfectly on a quiz!

"You want to be feminine but independent. What's an independent woman? 52
Someone who if left on her own could fend for herself.

"The world is changing and it's hard to figure out where you belong. I have 53
an anorexic friend; she just wants control over her life. What with competition,
SATs, parents pressuring kids, and divorce, kids need their parents more than
ever but they just can't communicate with them."

While the emphasis among the New American Dreamers is on doing, on ca- 54
reer, on material rewards, these young women almost always include commitment to family as one of their central concerns. Although they have taken on the
goals of high achievement, success, and independence, they have for the most
part kept the values of caring for others. They now see a dual responsibility, at
work and at home, both public and private. The New American Dreamers may
at this time in their lives place their career goals first, but as they look ahead it
becomes clear that many fully expect to care for family and children as well.

Alexandra Morgan, a black seventeen-year-old from the Midwest, whose 55
mother is a high-school teacher and whose father is a chemist, hopes to be an
oceanographer. She plans to "settle down" after she completes a B.S. and an
M.S. in science and oceanography, but only when she finds the right person,
one with whom she wants to "share the future." He must be "what I want in a
guy"; what is important is "how he carries himself and if he knows what he
wants out of life." She plans to have "no more than two children" and worries
about "juggling work and coming home to the children—they need to know
they are loved." She recalls that her mother always worked but was always there.
But her mother had a work life based on the school calendar—Christmas and
spring vacations, summers off. How will Alexandra manage to do both? In her
plans for the future the doing is clear and concrete; the caring is hazier, harder
to imagine.

Wendy Jackson has the dream, too. A twenty-year-old junior from one of 56
the campuses of the University of North Carolina, Wendy is the youngest of
three children and comes from a working-class family. Her father, now retired,
was a supervisor in a local textile plant, and her mother still works as a winder
in another textile plant. Wendy's dream seems in many ways to be at odds with
the life she is leading. An undergraduate major in social work, she plans to work
with handicapped people, probably as a school social worker. She is also engaged; her fiancé is studying, in her words, "ag ed"—agricultural education—
and they plan to live in Raleigh. But Wendy does not see herself marrying until
she is at least twenty-six. "The most important thing is independence," she says.
"You have to be secure within yourself before making a connection with someone else. If something ever happens, you must be able to stand alone.

"I want to expand, to see things and meet people. I don't want to stay in one 57
place. I don't want to hold back. I want to be released into a new world. I know
social work might put me back because of the money; it might not allow me to
do the things I want to do. I plan to go on and get an MSW so that I can make
more money."

Wendy isn't sure whether she wants children. She does know that she wants 58
to travel and that she wants a different kind of marriage than her mother had.

"My father came home and lay on the couch." What kind of relationship does she want? "I'm selfish—call me greedy. I'm not going to come home and wash his clothes. I'd rather not get married than be someone's maid!"

Wendy is on course for a very different life than the one she says she wants. 59 She's studying for a bachelor's degree in social work; as she comments, she is likely to be paid a meager salary and have few opportunities for promotion. Her professional options will improve somewhat with an MSW, but will these opportunities get her where she wants to go? She's engaged at the age of twenty and yet has an image of independence and adventure that seems at odds with the life of a married social worker living in a small city in North Carolina. Wendy's relatively unconventional ideas and dreams seem directly in conflict with her far more conventional life choices. It is almost as though Wendy's hopes for the future were taken from *Ms.* magazine while her real options were rooted in *Good Housekeeping.*

Other young women have this inner drive, this vision of what they want to 60 become that impels them onward when others from similar backgrounds might choose more modest goals. Sandra Curran grew up in New York City, the youngest of four children. Her parents came to this country from Trinidad when Sandra was ten; they have both worked in a hospital for many years—her father as a security guard, her mother as a unit secretary. From the time she was a junior in college, Sandra has had a vision of her future life: she planned to get her master's degree in social work, work a couple of years, and then go on to law school. And she has done exactly that. Along the way she married a young man who is working in computers and also getting his master's degree; she is currently holding down a full-time, extremely demanding job in foster care while attending law school at night. Why is she doing all this? Where does the drive, the impetus come from? Sandra tries to explain:

"I have a picture of a certain life-style that I want. By the time I'm forty I 61 want to be able to enjoy my family, live in the suburbs. I want to work by choice rather than out of necessity.

"Law will enable me to speak out—to advocate for individuals and families. 62 I plan to practice either family or criminal law, and with my MSW and my law degree I can deal with counseling, advocating, and legal issues in a holistic way.

"I just have an image of how I see myself in the future, how I will be com- 63 fortable emotionally. I have always had high expectations."

Like many other New American Dreamers, Sandra is clear about how to de- 64 velop her career but far less clear about how she will manage family and career. As with so many women who are firmly set on their quest, she sees what she must do to get where she wants to be professionally, but while she is also committed to children, to family, and to caring, that aspect of life is less mapped out, more sketchily drawn. One of the characteristics of the New American Dreamers is their focus on what they need to accomplish *before* they become emotionally involved. Their focus is on their professional lives, on doing; caring is part of the picture but less clearly visualized. Nonetheless it is always there, in the background, for though young women understand that they must be active participants in society, they also understand that new arrangements have yet to be worked out to provide the caring that women once provided. The New American Dreamers know that they want to be prepared to take on new roles and responsibilities even as they suspect they will still be expected to perform the old ones as well. The Neotraditionalists know the demands of the domestic role all too well. □

◢ REREADING FOR UNDERSTANDING

1. What, according to Sidel, are the distinguishing characteristics of young women today as they define their American Dream?

2. How has the American Dream changed for contemporary young women?

3. Sidel describes what she calls the "impossible dream" of some young American women. Why does Sidel consider those dreams impossible? Is she right?

◢ RESPONDING

1. Would young men pursuing their American Dream have different goals and means for attaining them than the young women interviewed by Sidel?

2. If, as Sidel seems to imply, more and more young women are following young men by pursuing individual happiness through material success, what may happen to nonmaterial, caring values like concern for community, the environment, law and order, welfare of our elderly and very young?

3. Sidel quotes one young woman who fears nuclear war because she and her friends will not "live long enough to be successful." A generally shared perspective among the New American Dreamers is that money and possessions are significant, if not the main, causes of success, and (presumably) happiness and the good life. Contrast that view with Stringer's (p. 481) perspective on success. Which perspective do you believe is likely to produce more individual happiness? Why?

4. How do you respond to the New American Dream of these young women? Is their dream your dream, whether or not you are female? What elements are most appealing? least appealing? Why?

TONI CADE BAMBARA

Toni Cade Bambara (1939–95) was a writer and filmaker. Her work includes a 1986 documentary about the police bombing of the radical group MOVE; a novel, *The Salt Eaters,* which won the National Book Award, and a collection of short stories, *Gorilla My Love,* from which this story is taken. Critics have noted her brilliant narrative style that captures the rhythm and life of "street language" of the inner city. "The Lesson" gives us a fine sample of her literary gifts and her sense of how one generation can help another understand what qualities are essential to the "good life."

The Lesson

Back in the days when everyone was old and stupid or young and foolish and me and Sugar were the only ones just right, this lady moved on our block with nappy hair and proper speech and no makeup. And quite naturally we laughed at her, laughed the way we did at the junk man who went about his business like he was some big-time president and his sorry-ass horse his secretary. And we kinda hated her too, hated the way we did the winos who cluttered up our parks and pissed on our handball walls and stank up our hallways and stairs so you couldn't halfway play hide-and-seek without a goddamn gas mask. Miss Moore was her name. The only woman on the block with no first name. And she was black as hell, cept for her feet, which were fish-white and spooky. And she was always planning these boring-ass things for us to do, us being my cousin, mostly, who lived on the block cause we all moved North the same time and to the same apartment then spread out gradual to breathe. And our parents would yank our heads into some kinda shape and crisp up our clothes so we'd be presentable for travel with Miss Moore, who always looked like she was going to church, though she never did. Which is just one of things the grown-ups talked about when they talked behind her back like a dog. But when she came calling with some sachet she'd sewed up or some gingerbread she'd made or some book, why then they'd all be too embarrassed to turn her down and we'd get handed over all spruced up. She'd been to college and said it was only right that she should take responsibility for the young ones' education, and she not even related by marriage or blood. So they'd go for it. Specially Aunt Gretchen. She was the main gofer in the family. You got some old dumb shit foolishness you want somebody to go for, you send for Aunt Gretchen. She been screwed into the go-along for so long, it's a blood-deep natural thing with her. Which is how she got saddled with me and Sugar and Junior in the first place while our mothers were in a la-de-da apartment up the block having a good ole time.

So this one day Miss Moore rounds us all up at the mailbox and it's puredee hot and she's knockin herself out about arithmetic. And school suppose to let up in summer I heard, but she don't never let up. And the starch in my pinafore scratching the shit outta me and I'm really hating this nappy-head bitch and her goddamn college degree. I'd much rather go to the pool or to the show where it's cool. So me and Sugar leaning on the mailbox being surly, which is a Miss Moore word. And Flyboy checking out what everybody brought for lunch. And Fat Butt already wasting his peanut-butter-and-jelly sandwich like the pig he is. And Junebug punchin on Q.T.'s arm for potato chips. And Rosie Giraffe shifting from one hip to the other waiting for somebody to step on her foot or ask her if she from Georgia so she can kick ass, preferably Mercedes'. And Miss Moore asking us do we know what money is, like we a bunch of retards. I mean real money, she say, like it's only poker chips or monopoly papers we lay on the grocer. So right away I'm tired of this and say so. And would much rather snatch Sugar and go to the Sunset and terrorize the West Indian kids and take their hair ribbons and their money too. And Miss Moore files that remark away for next week's lesson on brotherhood, I can tell. And finally I saw we oughta get to the subway cause it's cooler and besides we might meet some cute boys. Sugar done swiped her mama's lipstick, so we ready.

So we heading down the street and she's boring us silly about what things   3
cost and what our parents make and how much goes for rent and how money ain't divided up right in this country. And then she gets to the part about we all poor and live in the slums, which I don't feature. And I'm ready to speak on that, but she steps out in the street and hails two cabs just like that. Then she hustles half the crew in with her and hands me a five-dollar bill and tells me to calculate 10 percent tip for the driver. And we're off. Me and Sugar and Junebug and Flyboy hangin out the window and hollering to everybody, putting lipstick on each other cause Flyboy a faggot anyway, and making farts with our sweaty armpits. But I'm mostly trying to figure how to spend this money. But they all fascinated with the meter ticking and Junebug starts laying bets as to how much it'll read when Flyboy can't hold his breath no more. Then Sugar lays bets as to how much it'll be when we get there. So I'm stuck. Don't nobody want to go for my plan, which is to jump out at the next light and run off to the first bar-b-que we can find. Then the driver tells us to get the hell out cause we there already. And the meter reads eighty-five cents. And I'm stalling to figure out the tip and Sugar say give him a dime. And I decide he don't need it bad as I do, so later for him. But then he tries to take off with Junebug foot still in the door so we talk about his mama something ferocious. Then we check out that we on Fifth Avenue and everybody dressed up in stockings. One lady in a fur coat, hot as it is. White folks crazy.

"This is the place," Miss Moore say, presenting it to us in the voice she uses   4
at the museum. "Let's look in the windows before we go in."

"Can we steal?" Sugar asks very serious like she's getting the ground rules   5
squared away before she plays. "I beg your pardon," say Miss Moore, and we fall out. So she leads us around the windows of the toy store and me and Sugar screamin, "This is mine, that's mine, I gotta have that, that was made for me, I was born for that," till Big Butt drowns us out.

"Hey, I'm goin to buy that there."   6

"That there? You don't even know what it is, stupid."   7

"I do so," he say punchin on Rosie Giraffe. "It's a microscope."   8

"Watcha gonna do with a microscope, fool?"   9

"Look at things."   10

"Like what, Ronald?" ask Miss Moore. And Big Butt ain't got the first   11
notion. So here go Miss Moore gabbing about the thousands of bacteria in a drop of water and the somethinorother in a speck of blood and the million and one living things in the air around us is invisible to the naked eye. And what she

say that for? Junebug go to town on that "naked" and we rolling. Then Miss Moore ask what it cost. So we all jam into the window smudgin it up and the price tag say $300. So then she ask how long'd take for Big Butt and Junebug to save up their allowances. "Too long," I say. "Yeh," adds Sugar, "outgrown it by that time." And Miss Moore say no, you never outgrow learning instruments. "Why, even medical students and interns and," blah, blah, blah, And we ready to choke Big Butt for bringing it up in the first damn place.

"This here costs four hundred eighty dollars," say Rosie Giraffe. So we pile 12 up all over her to see what she pointin out. My eyes tell me it's a chunk of glass cracked with something heavy, and different-color inks dripped into the splits, then the whole thing put into a oven or something. But for $480 it don't make sense.

"That's a paperweight made of semi-precious stones fused together under 13 tremendous pressure," she explains slowly, with her hands doing the mining and all the factory work.

"So what's a paperweight?" asks Rosie Giraffe. 14

"To weigh paper with, dumbbell," say Flyboy, the wise man from the East. 15

"Not exactly," say Miss Moore, which is what she say when you warm or 16 way off too. "It's to weigh paper down so it won't scatter and make your desk untidy." So right away me and Sugar curtsy to each other and then to Mercedes who is more the tidy type.

"We don't keep paper on top of the desk in my class," say Junebug, figuring 17 Miss Moore crazy or lyin one.

"At home, then," she say. "Don't you have a calendar and a pencil case and 18 a blotter and a letter-opener on your desk at home where you do your home-work?" And she know damn well what our homes look like cause she nosys around in them every chance she gets.

"I don't even have a desk," say Junebug. "Do we?" 19

"No. And I don't get no homework neither," say Big Butt. 20

"And I don't even have a home," say Flyboy like he do at school to keep the 21 white folks off his back and sorry for him. Send this poor kid to camp posters, is his specialty.

"I do," says Mercedes. "I have a box of stationery on my desk and a picture 22 of my cat. My godmother bought the stationery and the desk. There's a big rose on each sheet and the envelopes smell like roses."

"Who wants to know about your smelly-ass stationery," say Rosie Giraffe 23 fore I can get my two cents in.

"It's important to have a work area all your own so that . . ." 24

"Will you look at this sailboat, please," say Flyboy, cuttin her off and pointin 25 to the thing like it was his. So once again we tumble all over each other to gaze at this magnificent thing in the toy store which is just big enough to maybe sail two kittens across the pond if you strap them to the posts tight. We all start reciting the price tag like we in assembly. "Handcrafted sailboat of fiberglass at one thousand one hundred ninety-five dollars."

"Unbelievable," I hear myself say and am really stunned. I read it again for 26 myself just in case the group recitation put me in a trance. Same thing. For some reason this pisses me off. We look at Miss Moore and she looking at us, waiting for I dunno what.

"Who'd pay all that when you can buy a sailboat set for a quarter at Pop's,   27
a tube of glue for a dime, and a ball of string for eight cents? "It must have a motor and a whole lot else besides," I say. "My sailboat cost me about fifty cents."

"But will it take water?" say Mercedes with her smart ass.   28

"Took mine to Alley Pond Park once," say Flyboy. "String broke, Lost it.   29
Pity."

"Sailed mine in Central Park and it keeled over and sank. Had to ask my   30
father for another dollar."

"And you got the strap," laugh Big Butt. "The jerk didn't even have a string   31
on it. My old man wailed on his behind."

Little Q.T. was staring hard at the sailboat and you could see he wanted it   32
bad. But he too little and somebody'd just take it from him. So what the hell. "This boat for kids, Miss Moore?"

"Parents silly to buy something like that just to get all broke up," say Rosie   33
Giraffe.

"That much money it should last forever," I figure.   34

"My father'd buy it for me if I wanted it."   35

"Your father, my ass," say Rosie Giraffe getting a chance to finally push   36
Mercedes.

"Must be rich people shop here," say Q.T.   37

"You are a very bright boy," say Flyboy. "What was your first clue?" And he   38
rap him on the head with the back of his knuckles, since Q.T. the only one he could get away with. Though Q.T. liable to come up behind you years later and get his licks in when you half expect it.

"What I want to know is," I say to Miss Moore though I never talk to her. I   39
wouldn't give the bitch that satisfaction, "is how much a real boat costs? I figure a thousand'd get you a yacht any day."

"Why don't you check that out," she says, "and report back to the group?"   40
Which really pains my ass. If you gonna mess up a perfectly good swim day least you could do is have some answers. "Let's go in," she say like she got something up her sleeve. Only she don't lead the way. So me and Sugar turn the corner to where the entrance is, but when we get there I kinda hang back. Not that I'm scared, what's there to be afraid of, just a toy store. But I feel funny, shame. But what I got to be shamed about? Got as much right to go in as anybody. But somehow I can't seem to get hold of the door, so I step away for Sugar to lead. But she hangs back too. And I look at her and she looks at me and this is ridiculous. I mean, damn, I have never ever been shy about doing nothing or going nowhere. But then Mercedes steps up and then Rosie Giraffe and Big Butt crowd in behind and shove, and next thing we all stuffed into the doorway with only Mercedes squeezing past us, smoothing out her jumper and walking right down the aisle. Then the rest of us tumble in like a glued-together jigsaw done all wrong. And people looking at us. And it's like the time me and Sugar crashed into the Catholic church on a dare. But once we got in there and everything so

hushed and holy and the candles and the bowin and the handkerchiefs on all the drooping heads, I just couldn't go through with the plan. Which was for me to run up to the altar and do a tap dance while Sugar played the nose flute and messed around in the holy water. And Sugar kept givin me the elbow. Then later teased me so bad I tied her up in the shower and turned it on and locked her in. And she'd be there till this day if Aunt Gretchen hadn't finally figured I was lyin about the boarder takin a shower.

Same thing in the store. We all walkin on tiptoe and hardly touchin the   41
games and puzzles and things. And I watched Miss Moore who is steady watchin us like she waitin for a sign. Like Mama Drewery watches the sky and sniffs the air and takes note of just how much slant is in the bird formation. Then me and Sugar bump smack into each other, so busy gazing at the toys, 'specially the sailboat. But we don't laugh and go into our fat-lady bump-stomach routine. We just stare at that price tag. Then Sugar run a finger over the whole boat. And I'm jealous and want to hit her. Maybe not her, but I sure want to punch somebody in the mouth.

"Watcha bring us here for, Miss Moore?"   42

"You sound angry, Sylvia. Are you mad about something?" Givin me one of   43
them grins like she tellin a grown-up joke that never turns out to be funny. And she's lookin very closely at me like maybe she plannin to do my portrait from memory. I'm mad, but I won't give her that satisfaction. So I slouch around the store being very bored and say, "Let's go."

Me and Sugar at the back of the train watchin the tracks whizzin by large   44
then small then gettin gobbled up in the dark. I'm thinkin about this tricky toy I saw in the store. A clown that somersaults on a bar then does chin-ups just cause you yank lightly at his leg. Cost $35. I could see me askin my mother for a $35 birthday clown. "You wanna who that costs what?" she'd say, cocking her head to the side to get a better view of the hole in my head. Thirty-five dollars could buy new bunk beds for Junior and Gretchen's boy. Thirty-five dollars and the whole household could go visit Granddaddy Nelson in the country. Thirty-five dollars would pay for the rent and the piano bill too. Who are these people that spend that much for performing clowns and $1,000 for toy sailboats? What kinda work they do and how they live and how come we ain't in on it? Where we are is who we are, Miss Moore always pointin out. But it don't necessarily have to be that way, she always adds then waits for somebody to say that poor people have to wake up and demand their share of the pie and don't none of us know what kind of pie she talkin about in the first damn place. But she ain't so smart cause I still got her four dollars from the taxi and she sure ain't gettin it. Messin up my day with this shit. Sugar nudges me in my pocket and winks.

Miss Moore lines us up in front of the mailbox where we started from, seem   45
like years ago, and I got a headache for thinkin so hard. And we lean all over each other so we can hold up under the draggy-ass lecture she always finishes us off with at the end before we thank her for borin us to tears. But she just looks at us like she readin tea leaves. Finally she say, "Well, what did you think of F.A.O. Schwarz?"

Rosie Giraffe mumbles, "White folks crazy."   46

"I'd like to go there again when I get my birthday money," says Mercedes, 47
and we shove her out the pack so she has to lean on the mailbox by herself.

"I'd like a shower. Tiring day," say Flyboy. 48

Then Sugar surprises me by sayin, "You know, Miss Moore, I don't think all 49
of us here put together eat in a year what that sailboat costs." And Miss Moore
lights up like somebody goosed her. "And?" she say, urging Sugar on. Only I'm
standin on her foot so she don't continue.

"Imagine for a minute what kind of society it is in which some people can 50
spend on a toy what it would cost to feed a family of six or seven. What do you
think?"

"I think," say Sugar pushing me off her feet like she never done before, 51
cause I whip her ass in a minute, "that this is not much of a democracy if you
ask me. Equal chance to pursue happiness means an equal crack at the dough,
don't it?" Miss Moore is besides herself and I am disgusted with Sugar's treach-
ery. So I stand on her foot one more time to see if she'll shove me. She shuts up,
and Miss Moore looks at me, sorrowfully I'm thinkin. And somethin weird is
goin on, I can feel it in my chest.

"Anybody else learn anything today?" lookin dead at me. I walk away and 52
Sugar has to run to catch up and don't even seem to notice when I shrug her
arm off my shoulder.

"Well, we got four dollars, anyway," she says. 53

"Uh hunh." 54

"We could go to Hascombs and get half a chocolate layer and then go to the 55
Sunset and still have plenty more for potato chips and ice-cream sodas."

"Uh hunh." 56

"Race you to Hascombs," she say. 57

We start down the block and she gets ahead which is O.K. by me cause I'm 58
goin to the West End and then over to the Drive to think this day through. She
can run if she want to and even run faster. But ain't nobody gonna beat me at
nuthin. □

◢ REREADING FOR UNDERSTANDING

1. What is Sylvia's attitude toward Miss Moore early in the story?

2. What attitude toward family do Sylvia and her friends seem to have before
   they go to the store? What is their sense of the good life?

3. Why does Sylvia end the story with this thought: "But ain't nobody gonna
   beat me at nuthin"?

◢ RESPONDING

1. How did the use of elements from black English affect your initial response
   to the story? Did your response to the characters and overall story change
   as you read further? If so, how do you account for the change?

2. Why did Miss Moore take the children to the upscale toy store? Is the title a clue?

3. What does Miss Moore mean by "Where we are is who we are" (par. 44)?

4. What is Miss Moore's lesson for the children? Is it a lesson only for poor black children?

CONTROVERSIES

How Is Happiness Discovered?

DAVID E. SHI

David Shi (1951–   ) has been a college history professor for almost twenty years and is now academic dean at Furman University in South Carolina. He has written widely on how individuals and groups within American culture have developed particular philosophies of living. In this essay, Shi explores the "simple life" as a recurring theme in American history. This theme may be a useful perspective for discovering and pursuing happiness.

The Simple Life

Simplicity has been one of this nation's scarcest yet most renewable moral resources. From the colonial period to the present, Americans as diverse as Thomas Jefferson, Henry David Thoreau, Scott and Helen Nearing, and Wendell Berry have rejected the sumptuous life in favor of some version of simplicity. Now, amid acute concerns about the environment and an epidemic of stress-related disorders, many Americans are embracing "simpler" ways of living. In doing so they are sustaining an elevated vision of the good life that has demonstrated perennial appeal and provoked continual confusion.

The simple life is almost as difficult to define as it is to practice, for it is not so much a single idea as it is an omnibus label encompassing an array of ideals and activities. These include a concern for family nurture and community cohesion; a hostility toward luxury and a suspicion of riches; a belief that the primary reward of work should be well-being rather than money; a desire for maximum personal self-reliance and creative leisure; a nostalgia for the supposed simplicities of the past and an anxiety about the technological and bureaucratic complexities of the present and future; a taste for the plain and functional, especially in the home; a reverence for nature and a preference for country living; and a sense of both religious and ecological responsibility for the proper use of the world's resources.

Over the years individuals and groups have varied greatly in the empha-   3
sis placed on these values and practices. As a result, there have been, and still are, many *forms* of simple living representing a wide spectrum of motives and methods. Their common denominator is the core assumption that the making of money and the accumulation of things should not compromise the purity of the soul, the life of the mind, the cohesion of the family, or the good of the commonweal. As Thoreau once advised, "Simplify your life. Do not devote your life to nonessentials or the acquisition of unnecessary possessions. Avoid clutter."

Of course, such a philosophy of living is by no means unique to American   4
culture. Simplicity is an ancient and universal ideal, perhaps primordially old. Most of the world's great religions and philosophies have advocated some form of simple living that elevates activities of the mind and spirit over material desires and activities. The great spiritual teachers of Asia—Zarathustra, Buddha, Lao-Tse, and Confucius—all stressed that material self-control was essential to the good life. . . .

In the American experience this ethic of plain living and high thinking has   5
also encompassed a wide spectrum of motives and behavior, a spectrum bounded on one end by religious asceticism and on the other by refined gentility. Some proponents of simplicity have been quite conservative in appealing to traditional religious values and or classical notions of republican virtue; others have been liberal or radical in their assault on corporate capitalism and its ethos of compulsive consumerism. In addition, class biases, individual personality traits, and historical circumstances have also combined to produce many differing versions of simple living in the American experience.

The history of simplicity has been a festival of irony, for the ideal of en-   6
lightened restraint has always been linked in an awkward embrace with the nation's phenomenal abundance and relentless work ethic. Since the colonial era, advocates of simple living have been professing a way of life at odds with an American environment full of bountiful resources, entrepreneurial opportunities, and increasingly powerful institutions that combine to exalt the glories of self-indulgence and war against contentment.

Puritan and Quaker settlers who arrived in America during the seventeenth   7
and eighteenth centuries brought with them a delicately balanced social ethic stressing hard work, self-control, plain living, civic virtue, and spiritual devotion. Their goal was to create model societies in which simplicity of worship, dress, manners, and speech would be practiced and enforced. Yet in both Puritan Massachusetts and Quaker Pennsylvania, the champions of collective simplicity soon found themselves waging a losing battle against the corrupting influence of rapid population growth, religious pluralism, and secular materialism.

The lesson in both Massachusetts and Pennsylvania seemed to be that   8
pious simplicity as a *societal* ethic was impossible to sustain in the midst of such a fluid and dynamic American environment blessed with so many opportunities for economic gain and social display. Certainly that was the assumption

of the many pietistic sects that settled in America in the eighteenth century and after. The so-called "plain people"—Mennonites, Amish, Dunkers, Brethren in Christ, Moravians, Shakers, and others—shared a strong commitment to communal simplicity and a strict non-conformity to the ways of the larger world.

In the New World these various religious groups set themselves apart   9
from mainstream society by establishing small, isolated, homogeneous, and self-sustaining rural communities. Through mutual aid, intensive agriculture, thrift, and diligence, their settlements prospered. Some verged on asceticism, practicing celibacy and renunciation of sensual and material pleasures; others allowed cohabitation and a comfortable sufficiency. All of them, however, insisted upon the priorities of faith and family and community. In other words, these religious non-conformists required social conformity.

American history is strewn with dozens of communal efforts at simple liv-   10
ing, ranging from the Transcendentalist utopias at Fruitlands and Brook Farm in the 1840s to the hippie communes of the 1960s and 1970s. Few of them, however, lasted more than a few months. Many of the participants in such alternative communities were naive about the hardships involved and lacked experience in the basic skills necessary for self-reliant living.

Yet the history of the simple life in the United States includes victories as   11
well as defeats. That many of the "plain people" have managed to retain much of their initial ethic testifies to their spiritual strength and social discipline. There have also been many successful and inspiring individual practitioners of simple living. As a guide for personal living and as a myth of national purpose, simplicity has thus displayed remarkable resiliency, showing that it can be a living creed. Aspiring, despairing, yet persistently striving to elevate the nation's priorities, diverse exemplars of simple living such as the Quaker saint John Woolman, the Transcendentalist philosopher Henry Thoreau, the feisty naturalist John Muir, and the Catholic activist Dorothy Day have dignified the ideal and invested it with relevance. In the process they have displayed an enlivening sense of wonder and an ennobling sense of purpose. As Emerson wrote of the Transcendentalists—they served as "collectors of the heavenly spark, with power to convey the electricity to others." During periods of war, depression, or social crisis, statesmen, ministers, and reformers have invoked the merits of simplicity to help revitalize public virtue, self-restraint, and mutual aid. In this way simplicity continues to exert a powerful influence on the nation's conscience.

The ideal of simplicity, however ambiguous, however fitfully realized, sur-   12
vives largely because its attempt to elevate aspirations beyond the material and the mundane is ennobling. Who has not yearned for simplicity, for a reduction of the complexities and encumbrances of life? In the American experience the simple life remains particularly enticing because it reminds us of what so many of our founding mothers and fathers hoped America would become—a nation of practical dreamers devoted to spiritual, and civic purposes, a "city upon a hill," a beacon to the rest of the world.

Today, simplicity remains what it has always been: an animating vision of   13
moral purpose that seizes and nourishes ethically sensitive imaginations. It offers people a way to recover personal autonomy and transcendent purpose by stripping away faulty desires and extraneous activities and possessions.

For simplicity to experience continued vitality, its advocates must learn 14
from the mistakes of the past. Proponents of simplicity have often been naively
sentimental about the quality of life in olden times, narrowly anti-urban in
outlook, and disdainful of the liberating and enlightening effects of prosperity
and technology. After all, most of the "high thinking" of this century has been
facilitated by prosperity. The expansion of universities and libraries, the demo-
cratization of the fine arts, and the ever-widening impact of philanthropic
organizations—all of these developments have been supported by the rising
pool of national wealth. This is no mean achievement. "A creative economy,"
Emerson once wrote, can be "the fuel of magnificence."

And, any virtue pressed too far can become counterproductive: some sim- 15
plifiers, for example, have reverted to a fanatical survivalism in order to live out
their version of the good life; others have displayed a self-righteous, prickly
individualism that has alienated potential supporters and impeded attempts
at collective social or political action. Still others have adopted an affluent rus-
ticity that seems more style than substance. Showy plainness is the red spider in
the rose of simple living.

Americans have repeatedly espoused the merits of simple living, only to be- 16
come enmeshed in its opposite. People have found it devilishly hard to limit
their desires to their needs so as to devote most of their attention to "higher"
activities. This should not surprise us. Socrates pointed out centuries ago that
"many people will not be satisfied with the simpler way of life. They will be for
adding sofas, and tables, and other furniture; also dainties, and perfumes, and
incense, and courtesans and cakes." He knew that all notions of moral excellence and spiritual commitment are by their very nature the province of a
minority, since few can live up to their dictates for long. Thoreau likewise noted
that simplicity was for the few rather than for the many. He recognized at the
beginning of *Walden* that the simple life he described would have little appeal
to "those who find their encouragement and inspiration in precisely the present
condition of things, and cherish it with the fondness and enthusiasm of lovers."
Many Americans have not wanted to lead simple lives, and not wanting is the
best reason for not doing so. "Simplicity," observed the Quaker reformer
Richard Gregg, "seems to be a foible of saints and occasional geniuses, but not
something for the rest of us."

Happily, modern simplicity demands neither an end to national economic 17
growth nor a vow of personal poverty. If the decision to lead a simple life is fundamentally a personal matter, then so, too, is the nature and degree of simplifi-
cation. There is no cosmic guidebook or universal formula to follow. Although
some prominent enthusiasts have verged on rigid self-denial, they have been the
exception rather than the rule. Simplicity in its essence demands neither a vow
of poverty nor a life of rural homesteading. Money or possessions or activities
in themselves do not corrupt simplicity, but the love of money, the craving of
possessions, the lure of conformity, and the prison of activities do.

As an ethic of self-conscious material moderation rather than radical re- 18
nunciation, simplicity can be practiced in cities and suburbs, townhouses and
condominiums. It requires neither a log cabin nor a hairshirt but a deliberate ordering of priorities so as to distinguish between the necessary and superfluous,

the useful and wasteful, the beautiful and vulgar. Wisdom, the philosopher William James once remarked, is knowing what to overlook. Indeed, the key to mastering the fine art of simple living is discovering the difference between personal trappings and personal traps. In this sense, simplicity is ultimately a state of mind, a well-ordered inner harmony among the material, sensual, and ideal, rather than a particular standard of living.

For those living in a press of anxieties, straining desperately, often miserably after more money, more things, and more status, only to wonder in troubled moments how to get off such a treadmill, the rich tradition of simplicity in the American experience still offers an enticing path to a better life. Those hesitant to change the trajectory of their runaway lifestyles might want to ask with the poet Adrienne Rich, "With whom do you believe your lot is cast? From where does your strength come?" 19

Those who voluntarily choose an outwardly more simple and inwardly more fulfilling style of living discover that pressures are reduced, the frenetic pace of life is slowed, and daily epiphanies are better appreciated. Simpler living also benefits us all by reducing demands on our increasingly fragile and besieged environment. In addition, winnowing one's money-making and money-spending activities can provide more opportunities for activities of intrinsic worth—family, faith, civic and social service, aesthetic creativity, and self-culture. The saintly naturalist John Burroughs acknowledged this fact in 1911 when the superintendent of the New York City schools asked him to share with the students the secret of his good life. "With me," he remarked, "the secret of my youth [at age seventy-four] is the simple life—simple food, sound sleep, the open air, daily work, kind thoughts, love of nature, and joy and contentment in the world in which I live. . . . I have had a happy life. . . . May you all do the same." □ 20

◢ REREADING FOR UNDERSTANDING

1. What point is Shi making (par. 6) when he observes that, throughout America's history, "the ideal of enlightened restraint has always been linked in an awkward embrace with the nation's phenomenal abundance and relentless work ethic"?

2. According to this essay, has the ideal of the "simple life" survived in our culture?

3. What does Shi cite as the main weaknesses of living the "simple life"? the main strengths?

◢ RESPONDING

1. In paragraph 16, Shi quotes Quaker reformer Richard Gregg: "Simplicity seems to be a foible of saints and occasional geniuses, but not something

for the rest of us." Is Gregg correct in his observation of human nature? Why or why not?

2. If Shi were to visit your class, what two or three of his ideas, values, or perspectives on life would you challenge or question? Why? By contrast, which of Shi's ideas do you applaud? Why?

3. Have you, or has anyone you know, ever attempted to simplify life in order to be happy, to lead a better life? What did you "simplify"? Did it work? Why or why not?

◢ RESPONDING IN WRITING

Socrates, Christ, and Thoreau are a few notable individuals who argued that the simpler life is, the better. Consider your own daily life. If it were less complicated, would you be happier? Would your life be "better"? Write your response to this question as a diary entry. Deliberately observe your life—your activities—for a week, and record what you observe. Then, in a brief essay, write out how your life would or would not improve if some aspects of your routine were simplified. Assume your essay will be published in a college literary magazine devoted to nonfiction commentaries on life.

MAY SARTON

May Sarton was born in Belgium in 1912. Her parents brought her to America in 1916. From the late forties to her death in 1996, she had a widely recognized career as a poet, novelist, and teacher of creative writing, publishing hundreds of poems and over twenty novels. Our piece is an excerpt from her prose piece entitled *Journal of a Solitude*, published in 1973. Listen to Sarton's description of the happiness to be found in life alone.

The Rewards of Living a Solitary Life

The other day an acquaintance of mine, a gregarious and charming man, told me he had found himself unexpectedly alone in New York for an hour or two between appointments. He went to the Whitney and spent the "empty" time looking at things in solitary bliss. For him it proved to be a shock nearly as great as falling in love to discover that he could enjoy himself so much alone.

What had he been afraid of, I asked myself? That, suddenly alone, he would discover that he bored himself, or that there was, quite simply, no self there to meet? But having taken the plunge, he is now on the brink of adventure; he is about to be launched into his own inner space, space as immense, unexplored and sometimes frightening as outer space to the astronaut. His every perception will come to him with a new freshness and, for a time, seem startlingly original. For anyone who can see things for himself with a naked eye becomes, for a moment or two, something of a genius. With another human being present vision becomes double vision, inevitably. We are busy wondering, what does my companion see or think of this, and what do I think of it? The original impact gets lost, or diffused.

"Music I heard with you was more than music." Exactly. And therefore music *itself* can only be heard alone. Solitude is the salt of personhood. It brings out the authentic flavor of every experience.   3

"Alone one is never lonely: the spirit adventures, walking/In a quiet garden, in a cool house, abiding single there."   4

Loneliness is most acutely felt with other people, for with others, even with a lover sometimes, we suffer from our differences of taste, temperament, mood. Human intercourse often demands that we soften the edge of perception, or withdraw at the very instant of personal truth for fear of hurting, or of being inappropriately present, which is to say naked, in a social situation. Alone we can afford to be wholly whatever we are, and to feel whatever we feel absolutely. That is a great luxury!   5

For me the most interesting thing about a solitary life, and mine has been that for the last twenty years, is that it becomes increasingly rewarding. When I can wake up and watch the sun rise over the ocean, as I do most days, and know that I have an entire day ahead, uninterrupted, in which to write a few pages, take a walk with my dog, lie down in the afternoon for a long think (why does one think better in a horizontal position?), read and listen to music, I am flooded with happiness.   6

I am lonely only when I am overtired, when I have worked too long without a break, when for the time being I feel empty and need filling up. And I am lonely sometimes when I come back home after a lecture trip, when I have seen a lot of people and talked a lot, and am full to the brim with experience that needs to be sorted out.   7

Then for a little while the house feels huge and empty, and I wonder where my self is hiding. It has to be recaptured slowly by watering the plants, perhaps, and looking again at each one as though it were a person, by feeding the two cats, by cooking a meal.   8

It takes a while, as I watch the surf blowing up in fountains at the end of the field, but the moment comes when the world falls away, and the self emerges again from the deep unconscious, bringing back all I have recently experienced to be explored and slowly understood, when I can converse again with my hidden powers, and so grow, and so be renewed, till death do us part. □   9

◢ REREADING FOR UNDERSTANDING

1. Can you explain what Sarton means when she observes (par. 2) that having experiences with another person causes one's vision to be "double"? She implies that "double vision" is negative. Why?

◪ **RESPONDING**

1. Examine your current daily schedule for the amount of time, if any, you spend in absolute solitude. Look back over the last four years or so of your life. Make a list of memories of being solitary. What did you do? How did you react to your solitude emotionally?

2. What differences exist between Sarton's pursuit of happiness (how she defines happiness and how she pursues it) and the pursuit of happiness presented by the young women Sidel interviewed in "The New American Dreamers" (p. 489)? After examining the differences, which pursuit do you prefer? Why?

3. Sarton declares that solitude yields happiness. If this is true, why don't more people live solitary lives? (Stringer's essay [p. 481] may offer useful perspectives to help you respond to this question.)

◪ **RESPONDING IN WRITING**

Consider this observation by May Sarton (par. 3): "Solitude is the salt of personhood." Write an essay in which you discuss the obstacles by which our contemporary, mass-media culture prevents our enjoying solitude and thus the good life. Your peers are your audience.

Or, write a response to Sarton in which you point out the flaws in her belief that solitude is the essence of the good life.

DYMPNA UGWU-OJU

Dympna Ugwu-Oju came to the United States because of war in her native Nigeria. After completing her Ph.D. in English in this country, she returned to Nigeria and her Ibo tribe. There she recognized that her culture placed little value on her education or on her as a single woman. While in Nigeria, she accepted an arranged marriage because, as she said, love is "synonymous with duty" in Ibo culture. She has since returned to the United States where she is a college English professor in California. Her essay provides a different cultural perspective on the source of happiness. Ugwu-Oju neatly compares her own conformity to the Ibo way with the experience of another Ibo woman who chooses the "American way" to happiness.

Pursuit of Happiness

My best friend called me late on Saturday night to tell me she was leaving her husband. It was completely unexpected, but yes, she was definitely leaving him. Her mind was made up—16 long years of marriage, 4 children—and she was leaving.

"Why? What happened?" I asked on reflex. Something must have hap- 2
pened; why else would she be so resolute. It had to be something devastating.

"Nothing really," she answered, "nothing I can put my finger on." 3

"Is he having an affair? Is he involved with someone else?" He didn't strike 4
me as the cheating type, but why else would she be leaving?

"No, nothing like that." I was amazed at how calm she sounded. 5

"Did he beat you up?" I was not prepared yet to accept her dismissive atti- 6
tude. Women don't end marriages for nothing. She just wasn't leveling.

"It's nothing in particular." She spoke haltingly, weighing every word. "All I 7
know is that I've been very unhappy lately."

"Uhm, I'm listening," I nudged her, waiting for the litanies of abuse, of 8
deprivation. But she said no more. "I just thought you should hear it from me,"
she added as we said our goodbyes.

I waited two days and called her back. I knew I had to tread very lightly. 9
"Just tell me one thing and I'll leave you alone: Are *you* having an affair?" That
wasn't the question I wanted to ask, but it popped out.

"No! Are you crazy? How can you even ask me that?" She laughed out loud. 10
Then sensing my need to come to terms with her news, she said she'd call back
after her husband was asleep.

As I waited, I pondered the inquisition our friends would put me through. 11
My friend and I and both our husbands, like a majority of our friends, are
Nigerians. While we've lived in the United States for most of our adulthood and
for all intents and purposes live like Americans, we identify closely with our traditional Ibo culture. An Ibo woman is born (educated if she is lucky), marries,
procreates (a definite must, male children preferably) and dies when her time
comes, God rest her soul. Women of our generation, educated and all, are expected to live through our husbands and children as our mothers and grand-
mothers did before us.

An Ibo woman has very little personal identity, even if she lives in the 12
United States and has success in her career. Our culture takes very little pride in
a woman's accomplishment. At an Ibo gathering a woman is more likely to be
asked whose wife or mother she is before she is asked her name or what she
does for a living. If the woman is accomplished but unmarried, people will say,
"But where is she going with all that success?" Ibos cling to the adage that a
woman is worth nothing unless she's married and has children.

I am as guilty as any other Ibo woman living in the United States in per- 13
petuating this. Professionally, I am more successful than the majority of Ibo
men I've met in this country, yet when we gather for a party, usually to celebrate
a marriage or birth, I join the women in the kitchen to prepare food and serve
the men. I remember to curtsy just so before the older men, looking away to
avoid meeting their eyes. I glow with pride when other men tease my husband
about his "good wife." I often lead the women in the Ibo wedding song: "It is as
it should be; give her the keys to her kitchen." At birth ceremonies, I start the
chant: "Without a child, what would a woman be?" It is a song my mother sang
and one which every Ibo woman knows like her own name.

I know the rules and the consequences of breaking them. Our culture is unforgiving of a stubborn woman. She always gets the maximum punishment—ostracism. "She thinks she's smart; let's see if she can marry herself" is how mistreatment of a noncompliant woman is justified.

To the surprise of my American friends, I've never had difficulty separating my Ibo self from my professional and everyday American life. At work, I'm as assertive as any American-born female. I raise my voice as loud as necessary to be heard in meetings. At conferences where I present papers on "Women From the Third World," I make serious arguments about the need for international intervention in countries where women are deprived of all rights, where women are subjected to clitorectomies, where baby girls are killed to make room for boys. Yet as easily as I switch from speaking English to Ibo, I am content to slide into the role of the submissive and obedient wife. I never confuse my two selves.

Hundreds of thousands of women from the third world and other traditional societies share my experience. We straddle two cultures, cultures that are often in opposition. Mainstream America, the culture we embrace in our professional lives, dictates that we be assertive and independent—like men. Our traditional culture, dictated by religion and years of socialization, demands that we be docile and content in our roles as mothers and wives—careers or not.

But suddenly, my best friend, steeped in the Ibo culture as much as I am, tells me she's leaving her husband—not for any offenses he's committed but because she is unhappy. I think of the question my mother and her mother would ask: "What on earth does she want?" She has everything any woman (Ibo woman, that is) would want: a professional husband (from a good family back home) with a good income, who allows her to pursue her own career; not one, not two, but *three* sons and a daughter; a huge house in the suburbs. And she tells me she's unhappy.

"Whoever told her a woman needs to be happy?" her mother would ask. Everyone knows that the happy part of a marriage is brief. After her first child, she is well on her way to fulfillment. This may sour a little if her first and second babies are girls. Her husband will drop subtle hints that he'll marry someone who can produce a son. But a good Ibo woman devises ways to hold his interest until she produces a son. My friend has three sons, and she's not happy?

"What about the children?" I heard her muffled sobs and sensed her struggle to regain composure. "They'll stay with their father," she said. She has no right to the children. That is the Ibo tradition, American laws or not. A woman departs from her husband's home as she came into it—empty-handed. She must refund the bride price her husband paid—plus interest—and may even have to refund the cost of the master's degree she obtained during their marriage.

My friend knows all that. And now she was going to leave without the children she had lived for, her guarantee of protection in her marriage. She had been lucky birthing three sons in a row, delighting her husband, winning praise in our community. Had she not consoled me when my first child was born female? "Don't worry, the next one will be a boy; you'll see." And when my

14

15

16

17

18

19

20

second child was born male, had my friend not screamed louder than I with joy? Why would she now walk away from the secure future she had earned?

"How can you do this to yourself?" I lost all control. "Have you gone mad?"   21

"I need to try to find happiness. I really thought that you, of all people,   22 would understand," she said coldly, hanging up before I could reply.

Later, I realized what was going on with my friend. She thinks herself   23 American. She has bought into America's concept of womanhood—personal satisfaction, no matter the cost. She wants to be happy. I wonder if she knows what she's getting into. □

◢ REREADING FOR UNDERSTANDING

1. Ugwu-Oju provides a narrative summary of the role Ibo women are expected to play in Ibo society. Describe some central aspects of that role. Compare it to the "proper" role of a traditional, middle-class American woman.

2. What, as reported by Ugwu-Oju, causes an Ibo woman with traditional Ibo values to be happy?

◢ RESPONDING

1. Assuming that Ugwu-Oju's friend's domestic situation is reported accurately, is her friend justified to "try to find happiness" (par. 22) by giving up her traditional Ibo role of loyal wife and responsible mother?

2. In what ways does the role women are expected to play in Ibo culture define happiness for them? Do you think it's possible to derive happiness from a role you are more or less *required* to play? Consider some role you live out before you respond to this question. Focus on roles you adopt to make others or yourself happy.

◢ RESPONDING IN WRITING

1. "She [Ugwu-Oju's friend] has bought into America's concept of womanhood—personal satisfaction, no matter the cost" (par. 23). Perhaps many Americans, both male and female, feel that "personal satisfaction" is a good life to be purchased "no matter the cost." Write an essay that might appear as a guest feature in a popular news magazine like *Time* or *Newsweek*. Critique or support the idea that personal satisfaction ought (ought not) to be sought "no matter the cost." (You may argue a middle ground, of course.)

EDWARD SOREL

Dereliction of Duty

EDWARD SOREL

WHEN I WAS YOUNG I'D WALK THE CITY STREETS FOR HOURS DREAMING ABOUT WHAT I WOULD DO WITH MY LIFE...

... I LIKED TO IMAGINE MYSELF AS THE REALIST PAINTER WHO RESCUED AMERICA FROM ABSTRACT EXPRESSIONISM...

...OR THE UNION ORGANIZER WHO FINALLY BROUGHT SAFE CONDITIONS TO THE WEST VIRGINIA COAL MINES.

BUT SOMETIMES AFTER SEEING A DOUBLE FEATURE ON 42ND STREET, I'D WONDER IF I COULD BE A SCREENWRITER – IF *I* COULD BE THE ONE TO RETURN AMERICAN MOVIES TO THEIR FORMER GLORY.

OTHER TIMES I'D IMAGINE MYSELF AS A MERCHANT SEAMAN WHO SECRETLY WRITES POETRY – POEMS THAT DEFINE THE AMERICAN EXPERIENCE

I'D EVEN SEE MYSELF AS A CHARISMATIC POLITICAL LEADER – A SPOKESMAN FOR THE AMERICAN UNDERCLASS.

WHAT I ACTUALLY DID WAS GET MARRIED, HAVE CHILDREN, AND MAKE MONEY ANY WAY I COULD. I DON'T HAVE MANY REGRETS...

...BUT SOMETIMES I FEEL I'VE LET MY COUNTRY DOWN.

◢ RESPONDING

1. Look again at the title Sorel gave his cartoon. What duty is avoided? Is that duty recognized and accepted by the audience for this cartoon—individuals like yourself? Why or why not?

2. The cartoon suggests that the main character has missed the good life. What is the implied good life?

3. The second to the last frame of the cartoon is a brief summary of the "standard" American Dream. What would your parents say if they saw this cartoon? Would they or you argue for that standard? Would they or you argue that a life of public service is a better "good life"? Why or why not?

4. In "Pursuit of Happiness" (p. 519), Ugwu-Oju suggests that her friend left her husband to pursue her American Dream despite her Ibo tribal heritage and its definition of the good life. What do you think Sorel's response would be to the friend's move? What is your response?

5. Create a cartoon story board like Sorel's. Here are two possible titles: "My American Dream" or "The American Dream that Became a Nightmare." Be sure your story has a beginning, a middle, and an end. Keep the text brief but packed with as much content as possible.

CONTROVERSIES

Does the Good Life Require a Spiritual Dimension?

LEO TOLSTOY

Count Leo Tolstoy (1828–1910) was a Russian novelist, playwright, and philosopher. Born into a landed, aristocratic family, he went to university but did not graduate. While in the Russian army (1851–1855), he began writing and his work met with immediate acclaim. Later he traveled in Europe, meeting princes, writers, and intellectuals. Around 1861, he returned to his estate, Yasnaya Polyana. Tolstoy continued to write, and he also worked to develop his large land holdings. But by 1879, the man who had written *War and Peace* and *Anna Karenina*, who had a family, wealth, and international recognition, was in a state of despair. He felt all he had done, and the day-to-day life he lead, were meaningless. The work you are about to read is Tolstoy's story of the journey from success to despair to a new sense of meaning through his discovery of faith as a basis for a good life.

As you read, you may be somewhat confused by Tolstoy's description and discussion of "his peasants." Hundreds of peasants lived and worked on Tolstoy's estate. The peasants had been serfs (like slaves) until 1861 when they were freed in Russia. Even after 1861, however, peasants continued to work very hard just to live a subsistence life. Yet Tolstoy found in the lives of these peasants a spirituality that became a model for creating meaning and achieving happiness in this own life. Pay close attention to Tolstoy's discussion of the peasant's life late in this essay. It will help you to grasp how Tolstoy saw religion as a means to happiness and the good life.

My Confession

Although I regarded authorship as a waste of time, I continued to write during those fifteen years. I had tasted of the seduction of authorship, of the seduction of enormous monetary remunerations and applauses for my insignificant labour, and so I submitted to it, as being a means for improving my material condition and for stifling in my soul all questions about the meaning of my life and life in general.

In my writings I advocated, what to me was the only truth, that it was necessary to live in such a way as to derive the greatest comfort for oneself and one's family.

Thus I proceeded to live, but five years ago something very strange began to happen with me: I was overcome by minutes at first of perplexity and then of an arrest of life, as though I did not know how to live or what to do, and I lost myself and was dejected. But that passed, and I continued to live as before. Then those minutes of perplexity were repeated oftener and oftener, and always in one and the same form. These arrests of life found their expression in over the same questions: "Why? Well, and then?"

At first I thought that those were simply aimless, inappropriate questions. It seemed to me that that was all well known and that if I ever wanted to busy myself with their solution, it would not cost me much labour,—that now I had no time to attend to them, but that if I wanted to I should find the proper answers. But the questions began to repeat themselves oftener and oftener, answers were demanded more and more persistently, and, like dots that fall on the same spot, these questions, without any answers, thickened into one black blotch.

There happened what happens with any person who falls ill with a mortal internal disease. At first there appear insignificant symptoms of indisposition, to which the patient pays no attention; then these symptoms are repeated more and more frequently and blend into one temporally indivisible suffering. The suffering keeps growing, and before the patient has had time to look around, he becomes conscious that what he took for an indisposition is the most significant thing in the world to him,—is death.

The same happened with me. I understood that it was not a passing indisposition, but something very important, and that, if the questions were going to repeat themselves, it would be necessary to find an answer for them. And I tried to answer them. The questions seemed to be so foolish, simple, and childish. But the moment I touched them and tried to solve them, I became convinced, in the first place, that they were not childish and foolish, but very important and profound questions in life, and, in the second, that, no matter how much I might try, I should not be able to answer them. Before attending to my Samára estate, to my son's education, or to the writing of a book, I ought to know why I should do that. So long as I did not know why, I could not do anything. I could not live. Amidst my thoughts of farming, which interested me very much during that time, there would suddenly pass through my head a question like this: "All right, you are going to have six thousand desyatínas of land in the Government of

Samára, and three hundred horses,—and then?" And I completely lost my senses and did not know what to think farther. Or, when I thought of the education of my children, I said to myself: "Why?" Or, reflecting on the manner in which the masses might obtain their welfare, I suddenly said to myself: "What is that to me?" Or, thinking of the fame which my works would get me, I said to myself: "All right, you will be more famous than Gógol, Púshkin, Shakespeare, Molière, and all the writers in the world,—what of it?" And I was absolutely unable to make any reply. The questions were not waiting, and I had to answer them at once; if I did not answer them, I could not live.

I felt that what I was standing on had given way, that I had no foundation   7
to stand on, that that which I lived by no longer existed, and that I had nothing
to live by. . . .

All that happened with me when I was on every side surrounded by what is   8
considered to be complete happiness. I had a good, loving, and beloved wife, good children, and a large estate, which grew and increased without any labour on my part. I was respected by my neighbours and friends, more than ever before, was praised by strangers, and, without any self-deception, could consider my name famous. With all that, I was not deranged or mentally unsound,—on the contrary, I was in full command of my mental and physical powers, such as I had rarely met with in people of my age: physically I could work in a field, mowing, without falling behind a peasant; mentally I could work from eight to ten hours in succession, without experiencing any consequences from the strain. And while in such condition I arrived at the conclusion that I could not live, and, fearing death, I had to use cunning against myself, in order that I might not take my life.

This mental condition expressed itself to me in this form: my life is a stu-   9
pid, mean trick played on me by somebody. Although I did not recognize that "somebody" as having created me, the form of the conception that some one had played a mean, stupid trick on me by bringing me into the world was the most natural one that presented itself to me.

Involuntarily I imagined that there, somewhere, there was somebody who   10
was now having fun as he looked down upon me and saw me, who had lived for thirty or forty years, learning, developing, growing in body and mind, now that I had become strengthened in mind and had reached that summit of life from which it lay all before me, standing as a complete fool on that summit and seeing clearly that there was nothing in life and never would be. And that was fun to him—

But whether there was or was not that somebody who made fun of me, did   11
not make it easier for me. I could not ascribe any sensible meaning to a single act, or to my whole life. I was only surprised that I had not understood that from the start. All that had long ago been known to everybody. Sooner or later there would come diseases and death (they had come already) to my dear ones and to me, and there would be nothing left but stench and worms. All my affairs, no matter what they might be, would sooner or later be forgotten, and I myself

should not exist. So why should I worry about all these things? How could a man fail to see that and live,—that was surprising! A person could live only so long as he was drunk; but the moment he sobered up, he could not help seeing that all that was only a deception, and a stupid deception at that! Really, there was nothing funny and ingenious about it, but only something cruel and stupid.

Long ago has been told the Eastern story about the traveller who in the steppe is overtaken by an infuriated beast. Trying to save himself from the animal, the traveller jumps into a waterless well, but at its bottom he sees a dragon who open his jaws in order to swallow him. And the unfortunate man does not dare climb out, lest he perish from the infuriated beast, and does not dare jump down to the bottom of the well, lest he be devoured by the dragon, and so clutches the twig of a wild bush growing in a cleft of the well and holds on to it. His hands grow weak and he feels that soon he shall have to surrender to the peril which awaits him at either side; but he still holds on and sees two mice, one white, the other black, in even measure making a circle around the main trunk of the bush to which he is clinging, and nibbling at it on all sides. Now, at any moment, the bush will break and tear off, and he will fall into the dragon's jaws. The traveller sees that and knows that he will inevitably perish; but while he is still clinging, he sees some drops of honey hanging on the leaves of the bush, and so reaches out for them with his tongue and licks the leaves. Just so I hold on to the branch of life, knowing that the dragon of death is waiting inevitably for me, ready to tear me to pieces, and I cannot understand why I have fallen on such suffering. And I try to lick that honey which used to give me pleasure; but now it no longer gives me joy, and the white and the black mouse day and night nibble at the branch to which I am holding on. I clearly see the dragon, and the honey is no longer sweet to me. I see only the inevitable dragon and the mice, and am unable to turn my glance away from them. That is not a fable, but a veritable, indisputable, comprehensible truth. 12

The former deception of the pleasures of life, which stifled the terror of the dragon, no longer deceives me. No matter how much one should say to me, "You cannot understand the meaning of life, do not think, live!" I am unable to do so, because I have been doing it too long before. Now I cannot help seeing day and night, which run and lead me up to death. I see that alone, because that alone is the truth. Everything else is a lie. 13

The two drops of honey that have longest turned my eyes away from the cruel truth, the love of family and of authorship, which I have called an art, are no longer sweet to me. 14

"My family—" I said to myself, "but my family, my wife and children, they are also human beings. They are in precisely the same condition that I am in: they must either live in the lie or see the terrible truth. Why should they live? Why should I love them, why guard, raise, and watch them? Is it for the same despair which is in me, or for dulness of perception? Since I love them, I cannot conceal the truth from them,—every step in cognition leads them up to this truth. And the truth is death." 15

"Art, poetry?" For a long time, under the influence of the success of human praise, I tried to persuade myself that that was a thing which could be 16 done, even though death should come and destroy everything, my deeds, as well as my memory of them; but soon I came to see that that, too, was a deception. It was clear to me that art was an adornment of life, a decoy of life. But life lost all its attractiveness for me. How, then, could I entrap others? So long as I did not live my own life, and a strange life bore me on its waves; so long as I believed that life had some sense, although I was not able to express it,—the reflections of life of every description in poetry and in the arts afforded me pleasure, and I was delighted to look at life through this little mirror of art; but when I began to look for the meaning of life, when I experienced the necessity of living myself, that little mirror became either useless, superfluous, and ridiculous, or painful to me. I could no longer console myself with what I saw in the mirror, namely, that my situation was stupid and desperate. It was all right for me to rejoice so long as I believed in the depth of my soul that life had some sense. At that time the play of lights—of the comical, the tragical, the touching, the beautiful, the terrible in life—afforded me amusement. But when I knew that life was meaningless and terrible, the play in the little mirror could no longer amuse me. No sweetness of honey could be sweet to me, when I saw the dragon and the mice that were nibbling down my support. . . .

In my search after the question of life I experienced the same feeling which a man who has lost his way in the forest may experience.   17

He comes to a clearing, climbs a tree, and clearly sees an unlimited space before him; at the same time he sees that there are no houses there, and that there can be none; he goes back to the forest, into the darkness, and he sees darkness, and again there are no houses.   18

Thus I blundered in this forest of human knowledge, between the clearings of the mathematical and experimental sciences, which disclosed to me clear horizons, but such in the direction of which there could be no house, and between the darkness of the speculative sciences, where I sunk into a deeper darkness, the farther I proceeded, and I convinced myself at last that there was no way out and could not be.   19

By abandoning myself to the bright side of knowledge I saw that I only turned my eyes away from the question. No matter how enticing and clear the horizons were that were disclosed to me, no matter how enticing it was to bury myself in the infinitude of this knowledge, I comprehended that these sciences were the more clear, the less I needed them, the less they answered my question.   20

"Well, I know," I said to myself, "all which science wants so persistently to know, but there is no answer to the question about the meaning of my life." But in the speculative sphere I saw that, in spite of that fact that the aim of the knowledge was directed straight to the answer of my question, or because of that fact, there could be no other answer than what I was giving to myself: "What is the meaning of my life?"—"None." Or, "What will come of my life?"—"Nothing." Or, "Why does everything which exists exist, and why do I exist?"—"Because it exists."   21

Putting the question to the one side of human knowledge, I received an   22
endless quantity of exact answers about what I did not ask: about the chemical
composition of the stars, about the movement of the sun toward the constella-
tion of Hercules, about the origin of species and of man, about the forms of infinitely small, imponderable particles of ether; but the answer in this sphere of
knowledge to my question what the meaning of my life was, was always: "You
are what you call your life; you are a temporal, accidental conglomeration of
particles. The interrelation, the change of these particles, produces in you that
which you call life. This congeries will last for some time; then the interaction
of these particles will cease, and that which you call life and all your questions
will come to an end. You are an accidentally cohering globule of something. The
globule is fermenting. This fermentation the globule calls its life. The globule
falls to pieces, and all fermentation and all questions will come to an end." Thus
the clear side of knowledge answers, and it cannot say anything else, if only it
strictly follows its principles.

With such an answer it appears that the answer is not a reply to the question.   23
I want to know the meaning of my life, but the fact that it is a particle of the infinite not only gives it no meaning, but even destroys every possible meaning.

Those obscure transactions, which this side of the experimental, exact sci-   24
ence has with speculation, when it says that the meaning of life consists in evolution and the cooperation with this evolution, because of their obscurity and
inexactness cannot be regarded as answers.

The other side of knowledge, the speculative, so long as it sticks strictly to   25
its fundamental principles in giving a direct answer to the question, everywhere
and at all times has answered one and the same: "The world is something infinite and incomprehensible. Human life is an incomprehensible part of this incomprehensible *all....*"

I lived for a long time in this madness, which, not in words, but in deeds, is par-   26
ticularly characteristic of us, the most liberal and learned of men. But, thanks
either to my strange, physical love for the real working class, which made me
understand it and see that it is not so stupid as we suppose, or to the sincerity
of my conviction, which was that I could know nothing and that the best that I
could do was to hang myself,—I felt that if I wanted to live and understand the
meaning of life, I ought naturally to look for it, not among those who had lost
the meaning of life and wanted to kill themselves, but among those billions departed and living men who had been carrying their own lives and ours upon
their shoulders. And I looked around at the enormous masses of deceased and
living men,—not learned and wealthy, but simple men,—and I saw something
quite different. I saw that all these billions of men that lived or had lived, all,
with rare exceptions, did not fit into my subdivisions,* and that I could not

---

* In a passage omitted here, Tolstoy characterized four attitudes that people have towards life: living
in ignorance of the problem of the meaning of life; ignoring it and trying to attain as much pleasure
as possible; admitting that life is meaningless and committing suicide; admitting that life is meaningless but continuing to live aimlessly. (Ed.)

recognize them as not understanding the question, because they themselves put it and answered it with surprising clearness. Nor could I recognize them as Epicureans, because their lives were composed rather of privations and suffering than of enjoyment. Still less could I recognize them as senselessly living out their meaningless lives, because every act of theirs and death itself was explained by them. They regarded it as the greatest evil to kill themselves. It appeared, then, that all humanity was in possession of a knowledge of the meaning of life, which I did not recognize and which I contemned. It turned out that rational knowledge did not give any meaning to life, excluded life, while the meaning which by billions of people, by all humanity, was ascribed to life was based on some despised, false knowledge.

The rational knowledge in the person of the learned and the wise denied   27
the meaning of life, but the enormous masses of men, all humanity, recognized this meaning in an irrational knowledge. This irrational knowledge was faith, the same that I could not help but reject. That was God as one and three, the creation in six days, devils and angels, and all that which I could not accept so long as I had not lost my senses.

My situation was a terrible one. I knew that I should not find anything on   28
the path of rational knowledge but the negation of life, and there, in faith, nothing but the negation of reason, which was still more impossible than the negation of life. From the rational knowledge it followed that life was an evil and men knew it,—it depended on men whether they should cease living, and yet they lived and continued to live, and I myself lived, though I had known long ago that life was meaningless and an evil. From faith it followed that, in order to understand life, I must renounce reason, for which alone a meaning was needed.

There resulted a contradiction, from which there were two ways out: either   29
what I called rational was not so rational as I had thought; or that which to me appeared irrational was not so irrational as I had thought. And I began to verify the train of thoughts of my rational knowledge.

In verifying the train of thoughts of my rational knowledge, I found that it   30
was quite correct. The deduction that life was nothing was inevitable; but I saw a mistake. The mistake was that I had not reasoned in conformity with the question put by me. The question was, "Why should I live?" that is, "What real, indestructible essence will come from my phantasmal, destructible life? What meaning has my finite existence in this infinite world?" And in order to answer this question, I studied life.

The solutions of all possible questions of life apparently could not satisfy me,   31
because my question, no matter how simple it appeared in the beginning, included the necessity of explaining the finite through the infinite, and vice versa.

I asked, "What is the extra-temporal, extra-causal, extra-spatial meaning of   32
life?" But I gave an answer to the question, "What is the temporal, causal, spatial meaning of my life?" The result was that after a long labour of mind I answered, "None."

In my reflections I constantly equated, nor could I do otherwise, the finite   33
with the finite, the infinite with the infinite, and so from that resulted precisely

what had to result: force was force, matter was matter, will was will, infinity was infinity, nothing was nothing,—and nothing else could come from it.

There happened something like what at times takes place in mathematics: 34 you think you are solving an equation, when you have only an identity. The reasoning is correct, but you receive as a result the answer: $a = a$, or $x = x$, or $o = o$. The same happened with my reflection in respect to the question about the meaning of my life. The answers given by all science to that question are only identities.

Indeed, the strictly scientific knowledge, that knowledge which, as Descartes 35 did, begins with a full doubt in everything, rejects all knowledge which has been taken on trust, and builds everything anew on the laws of reason and experience, cannot give any other answer to the question of life than what I received,—an indefinite answer. It only seemed to me at first that science gave me a positive answer,—Schopenhauer's answer: "Life has no meaning, it is an evil." But when I analyzed the matter, I saw that the answer was not a positive one, but that it was only my feeling which expressed it as such. The answer, strictly expressed, as it is expressed by the Brahmins, by Solomon, and by Schopenhauer, is only an indefinite answer, or an identity, $o = o$, life is nothing. Thus the philosophical knowledge does not negate anything, but only answers that the question cannot be solved by it, that for philosophy the solution remains insoluble.

When I saw that, I understood that it was not right for me to look for an 36 answer to my question in rational knowledge, and that the answer given by rational knowledge was only an indication that the answer might be got if the question were differently put, but only when into the discussion of the question should be introduced the question of the relation of the finite to the infinite. I also understood that, no matter how irrational and monstrous the answers might be that faith gave, they had this advantage that they introduced into each answer the relation of the finite to the infinite, without which there could be no answer.

No matter how I may put the question, "How must I live?" the answer is, 37 "According to God's law." "What real result will there be from my life?"— "Eternal torment or eternal bliss." "What is the meaning which is not destroyed by death?"—"The union with infinite God, paradise."

Thus, outside the rational knowledge, which had to me appeared as the 38 only one, I was inevitably led to recognize that all living humanity had a certain other irrational knowledge, faith, which made it possible to live.

All the irrationality of faith remained the same for me, but I could not help 39 recognizing that it alone gave to humanity answers to the questions of life, and, in consequence of them, the possibility of living.

The rational knowledge brought me to the recognition that life was mean- 40 ingless,—my life stopped, and I wanted to destroy myself. When I looked around at people, at all humanity, I saw that people lived and asserted that they knew the meaning of life. As to other people, so even to me, did faith give the meaning of life and the possibility of living.

Looking again at the people of other countries, contemporaries of mine 41 and those passed away, I saw again the same. Where life had been, there faith, ever since humanity had existed, had given the possibility of living, and the chief features of faith were everywhere one and the same.

No matter what answers faith may give, its every answer gives to the finite existence of man the sense of the infinite,—a sense which is not destroyed by suffering, privation, and death. Consequently in faith alone could we find the meaning and possibility of life. What, then, was faith? I understood that faith was not merely an evidence of things not seen, and so forth, not revelation (that is only the description of one of the symptoms of faith), not the relation of man to man (faith has to be defined, and then God, and not first God, and faith through him), not merely an agreement with what a man was told, as faith was generally understood,—that faith was the knowledge of the meaning of human life, in consequence of which man did not destroy himself, but lived. Faith is the power of life. If a man lives he believes in something. If he did not believe that he ought to live for some purpose, he would not live. If he does not see and understand the phantasm of the finite, he believes in that infinite; if he understands the phantasm of the finite, he must believe in the infinite. Without faith one cannot live. . . . 42

In order that all humanity may be able to live, in order that they may continue living, giving a meaning to life, they, those billions, must have another, a real knowledge of faith, for not the fact that I, with Solomon and Schopenhauer, did not kill myself convinced me of the existence of faith, but that these billions had lived and had borne us, me and Solomon, on the waves of life. 43

Then I began to cultivate the acquaintance of the believers from among the poor, the simple and unlettered folk, of pilgrims, monks, dissenters, peasants. The doctrine of these people from among the masses was also the Christian doctrine that the quasi-believers of our circle professed. With the Christian truths were also mixed in very many superstitions, but there was this difference: the superstitions of our circle were quite unnecessary to them, had no connection with their lives, were only a kind of an Epicurean amusement, while the superstitions of the believers from among the labouring classes were to such an extent blended with their life that it would have been impossible to imagine it without these superstitions,—it was a necessary condition of that life. I began to examine closely the lives and beliefs of these people, and the more I examined them, the more did I become convinced that they had the real faith, that their faith was necessary for them, and that it alone gave them a meaning and possibility of life. In contradistinction to what I saw in our circle, where life without faith was possible, and where hardly one in a thousand professed to be a believer, among them there was hardly one in a thousand who was not a believer. In contradistinction to what I saw in our circle, where all life passed in idleness, amusements, and tedium of life, I saw that the whole life of these people was passed in hard work, and that they were satisfied with life. In contradistinction to the people of our circle, who struggled and murmured against fate because of their privations and their suffering, these people accepted diseases and sorrows without any perplexity or opposition, but with the calm and 44 firm conviction that it was all for good. In contradistinction to the fact that the more intelligent we are, the less do we understand the meaning of life and the more do we see a kind of a bad joke in our suffering and death, these people live, suffer, and approach death, and suffer in peace and more often in joy. In contradistinction to the fact that a calm death, a death without terror or despair, is the greatest exception in our circle, a restless, insubmissive, joyless death is one of the greatest exceptions among the masses. And of such people, who are deprived of everything which for Solomon and for me constitutes the only good of life, and who withal experience the greatest happiness, there is an enormous number. I cast a broader glance about me. I examined the life of past and present vast masses of men, and I saw people who in like manner had understood the meaning of life, who had known how to live and die, not two, not three, not ten, but hundreds, thousands, millions. All of them, infinitely diversified as to habits, intellect, culture, situation, all equally and quite contrary to my ignorance knew the meaning of life and of death, worked calmly, bore privations and suffering, lived and died, seeing in that not vanity, but good.

I began to love those people. The more I penetrated into their life, the life   45
of the men now living, and the life of men departed, of whom I had read and heard, the more did I love them, and the easier it became for me to live. Thus I lived for about two years, and within me took place a transformation, which had long been working within me, and the germ of which had always been in me. What happened with me was that the life of our circle,—of the rich and the learned,—not only disgusted me, but even lost all its meaning. All our acts, reflections, sciences, arts,—all that appeared to me in a new light. I saw that all that was mere pampering of the appetites, and that no meaning could be found in it; but the life of all the working masses, of all humanity, which created life, presented itself to me in its real significance. I saw that that was life itself and that the meaning given to this life was truth, and I accepted it. □

◤ REREADING FOR UNDERSTANDING

1. Tolstoy begins by revealing a somber realization about life, and he provides the tale of the "traveler" (par. 12) to illustrate this revelation. Summarize what Tolstoy thinks about life and what causes him to think that way. Use the material from the opening of this "confession" up to and including the fable.

2. What one inescapable truth does Tolstoy discover that causes him to search for something new to live by?

3. Why does Tolstoy reject family, art, and science as sources for happiness?

4. Tolstoy says that the "masses" of humankind have found a basis for being happy. Explain what that basis is.

5. Explain what Tolstoy means by "faith." How is his concept of faith similar to or different from yours or your peers?

 **RESPONDING**

1. Is Tolstoy convincing when he argues that faith provides "extra-rational" reasons for living and therefore a basis for meaning and happiness in this life? How useful is his analysis as a way of finding happiness in life? Do many individuals whom you know find happiness this way, regardless of whether they have ever read Tolstoy?

2. Is Tolstoy's philosophy similar to the old woman's in Voltaire's "Story of a Good Brahmin" (p. 456)? Don't answer too quickly: this is a difficult question—more so than first glance would suggest. How does a yes or no answer reflect on your response to Tolstoy's ideas?

 **RESPONDING IN WRITING**

Tolstoy was driven by the question, "Why should I live?" This can be either a potentially foolish or a very profound inquiry. Construct a tentative answer to Tolstoy's question in a few paragraphs. Then choose one writer in Unit Six you disagree with and one you find intriguing. Use their ideas to revise your first response to Tolstoy. Draft your revised response to a close friend, teacher, or parent. Help your audience understand what you think the good life might be and how it ought to be lived.

 WALT WHITMAN

Walt Whitman (1819–1892) was born in Long Island, New York. Despite his six years of grammar school education, he spent most of his professional life working as a writer. His poetry was considered radical by many of his contemporaries, but now his poetry speaks to us with familiarity and energy. The excerpt below is from "Song of Myself." Look for ways in which the narrator presents us with the relative worth of the natural world and the spiritual life as possible guides to happiness.

From "Song of Myself"

I think I could turn and live with animals, they are so placid and self-contain'd,
I stand and look at them long and long.

They do not sweat and whine about their condition,
They do not lie awake in the dark and weep for their sins,
They do not make me sick discussing their duty to God,

5

Not one is dissatisfied, not one is demented with the mania of owning things,
Not one kneels to another, nor to his kind that lived thousands of years ago,
Not one is respectable or unhappy over the whole earth.

 REREADING FOR UNDERSTANDING

1. The narrator has a strong presence in this piece. How does Whitman create a narrator whom many readers might find admirable?

2. If you do not find the narrator admirable, explain what you object to.

3. We infer from this excerpt from "Song of Myself" that the narrator would find happiness "living with" animals. What reasons are given? Do these reasons define what happiness ought to be? Do you agree? Would many of your peers agree? Why or why not?

BERTRAND RUSSELL

Lord Bertrand Russell (1872–1970) was a significant mathematician, philosopher, writer, social, and political activist throughout most of his long life. His collected writings run to twenty-eight volumes. He received the Nobel Prize for literature in 1950. He taught at several American universities including Harvard, University of Chicago, and University of California at Los Angeles. He was to teach at City College of New York but his appointment was withdrawn because of his controversial views on "free love" among other things. Russell was also a life-long pacifist. He was jailed at the age of eighty-nine for organizing a demonstration in support of world disarmament. His philosophy of the good life is summed up in his own words, "The good life is inspired by love and guided by knowledge."

The essay included here is based on a speech he later adapted as the first chapter of his book by the same name. In it, Russell takes up traditional arguments for the existence of God and then demonstrates their error in the light of knowledge. He places his hope for his and humankind's happiness in our intelligence, and our capacity for kindness, compassion, and love.

Why I Am Not a Christian

As your Chairman has told you, the subject about which I am going to speak to you tonight is "Why I Am Not a Christian." Perhaps it would be as well, first of all, to try to make out what one means by the word *Christian*. It is used these days in a very loose sense by a great many people. Some people mean no more by it than a person who attempts to live a good life.

In that sense I suppose there would be Christians in all sects and creeds; but I do not think that that is the proper sense of the word, if only because it would imply that all the people who are not Christians—all the Buddhists, Confucians, Mohammedans, and so on—are not trying to live a good life. I do not mean by a Christian any person who tries to live decently according to his lights. I think that you must have a certain amount of definite belief before you have a right to call yourself a Christian. The word does not have quite such a full-blooded meaning now as it had in the times of St. Augustine and St. Thomas Aquinas. In those days, if a man said that he was a Christian it was known what he meant. You accepted a whole collection of creeds which were set out with great precision, and every single syllable of those creeds you believed with the whole strength of your convictions.

WHAT IS A CHRISTIAN?

Nowadays it is not quite that. We have to be a little more vague in our meaning of Christianity. I think, however, that there are two different items which are quite essential to anybody calling himself a Christian. The first is one of a dogmatic nature—namely, that you must believe in God and immortality. If you do not believe in those two things, I do not think that you can properly call yourself a Christian. Then, further than that, as the name implies, you must have some kind of belief about Christ. The Mohammedans, for instance, also believe in God and in immortality, and yet they would not call themselves Christians. I think you must have at the very lowest the belief that Christ was, if not divine, at least the best and wisest of men. If you are not going to believe that much about Christ, I do not think you have any right to call yourself a Christian. Of course, there is another sense, which you find in *Whitaker's Almanack* and in geography books, where the population of the world is said to be divided into Christians, Mohammedans, Buddhists, fetish worshipers, and so on; and in that sense we are all Christians. The geography books count us all in, but that is a purely geographical sense, which I suppose we can ignore. Therefore I take it that when I tell you why I am not a Christian I have to tell you two different things: first, why I do not believe in God and in immortality; and, secondly, why I do not think that Christ was the best and wisest of men, although I grant him a very high degree of moral goodness.

But for the successful efforts of unbelievers in the past, I could not take so elastic a definition of Christianity as that. As I said before, in olden days it had a much more full-blooded sense. For instance, it included the belief in hell. Belief in eternal hell-fire was an essential item of Christian belief until pretty recent times. In this country, as you know, it ceased to be an essential item because of a decision of the Privy Council, and from that decision the Archbishop of Canterbury and the Archbishop of York dissented; but in this country our religion is settled by Act of Parliament, and therefore the Privy Council was able to override their Graces and hell was no longer necessary to a Christian. Consequently I shall not insist that a Christian must believe in hell.

THE EXISTENCE OF GOD

To come to this question of the existence of God: it is a large and serious ques-   4
tion, and if I were to attempt to deal with it in any adequate manner I should
have to keep you here until Kingdom Come, so that you will have to excuse me
if I deal with it in a somewhat summary fashion. You know, of course, that the
Catholic Church has laid it down as a dogma that the existence of God can be
proved by the unaided reason. That is a somewhat curious dogma, but it is one
of their dogmas. They had to introduce it because at one time the freethinkers
adopted the habit of saying that there were such and such arguments which
mere reason might urge against the existence of God, but of course they knew
as a matter of faith that God did exist. The arguments and the reasons were set
out at great length, and the Catholic Church felt that they must stop it. Therefore they laid it down that the existence of God can be proved by the unaided
reason and they had to set up what they considered were arguments to prove it.
There are, of course, a number of them, but I shall take only a few.

THE FIRST-CAUSE ARGUMENT

Perhaps the simplest and easiest to understand is the argument of the First   5
Cause. (It is maintained that everything we see in this world has a cause, and as
you go back in the chain of causes further and further you must come to a First
Cause, and to that First Cause you give the name of God.) That argument, I
suppose, does not carry very much weight nowadays, because, in the first place,
cause is not quite what it used to be. The philosophers and the men of science
have got going on cause, and it has not anything like the vitality it used to have;
but, apart from that, you can see that the argument that there must be a First
Cause is one that cannot have any validity. I may say that when I was a young
man and was debating these questions very seriously in my mind, I for a long
time accepted the argument of the First Cause, until one day, at the age of eighteen, I read John Stuart Mill's Autobiography, and I there found this sentence:
"My father taught me that the question 'Who made me?' cannot be answered,
since it immediately suggests the further question 'Who made God?'" That very
simple sentence showed me, as I still think, the fallacy in the argument of the
First Cause. If everything must have a cause, then God must have a cause. If
there can be anything without a cause, it may just as well be the world as God,
so that there cannot be any validity in that argument. It is exactly of the same
nature as the Hindu's view, that the world rested upon an elephant and the elephant rested upon a tortoise; and when they said, "How about the tortoise?" the
Indian said, "Suppose we change the subject." The argument is really no better
than that. There is no reason why the world could not have come into being
without a cause; nor, on the other hand, is there any reason why it should not
have always existed. There is no reason to suppose that the world had a beginning at all. The idea that things must have a beginning is really due to the
poverty of our imagination. Therefore, perhaps, I need not waste any more time
upon the argument about the First Cause.

THE NATURAL-LAW ARGUMENT

Then there is a very common argument from natural law. That was a favorite   6
argument all through the eighteenth century, especially under the influence of
Sir Isaac Newton and his cosmogony. People observed the planets going around
the sun according to the law of gravitation, and they thought that God had
given a behest to these planets to move in that particular fashion, and that was
why they did so. That was, of course, a convenient and simple explanation that
saved them the trouble of looking any further for explanations of the law of
gravitation. Nowadays we explain the law of gravitation in a somewhat complicated fashion that Einstein has introduced. I do not propose to give you a lecture on the law of gravitation, as interpreted by Einstein, because that again
would take some time; at any rate, you no longer have the sort of natural law
that you had in the Newtonian system, where, for some reason that nobody
could understand, nature behaved in a uniform fashion. We now find that a
great many things we thought were natural laws are really human conventions.
You know that even in the remotest depths of stellar space there are still three
feet to a yard. That is, no doubt, a very remarkable fact, but you would hardly
call it a law of nature. And a great many things that have been regarded as laws
of nature are of that kind. On the other hand, where you can get down to any
knowledge of what atoms actually do, you will find they are much less subject
to law than people thought, and that the laws at which you arrive are statistical
averages of just the sort that would emerge from chance. There is, as we all
know, a law that if you throw dice you will get double sixes only about once in
thirty-six times, and we do not regard that as evidence that the fall of the dice
is regulated by design; on the contrary, if the double sixes came every time we
should think that there was design. The laws of nature are of that sort as regards
a great many of them. They are statistical averages such as would emerge from
the laws of chance; and that makes this whole business of natural law much less
impressive than it formerly was. Quite apart from that, which represents the
momentary state of science that may change tomorrow, the whole idea that natural laws imply a lawgiver is due to a confusion between natural and human
laws. Human laws are behests commanding you to behave a certain way, in
which way you may choose to behave, or you may choose not to behave; but
natural laws are a description of how things do in fact behave, and being a mere
description of what they in fact do, you cannot argue that there must be somebody who told them to do that, because even supposing that there were, you are
then faced with the question "Why did God issue just those natural laws and no
others?" If you say that he did it simply from his own good pleasure, and without any reason, you then find that there is something which is not subject to
law, and so your train of natural law is interrupted. If you say, as more ortho-
dox theologians do, that in all the laws which God issues he had a reason for
giving those laws rather than others—the reason, of course, being to create the
best universe, although you would never think it to look at it—if there were a
reason for the laws which God gave, then God himself was subject to law, and
therefore you do not get any advantage by introducing God as an intermediary.
You have really a law outside and anterior to the divine edicts, and God does not

serve your purpose, because he is not the ultimate lawgiver. In short, this whole argument about natural law no longer has anything like the strength that it used to have. I am traveling on in time in my review of the arguments. The arguments that are used for the existence of God change their character as time goes on. They were at first hard intellectual arguments embodying certain quite definite fallacies. As we come to modern times they become less respectable intellectually and more and more affected by a kind of moralizing vagueness.

THE ARGUMENT FROM DESIGN

The next step in this process brings us to the argument from design. You all   7
know the argument from design: everything in the world is made just so that we can manage to live in the world, and if the world was ever so little different, we could not manage to live in it. That is the argument from design. It sometimes takes a rather curious form; for instance, it is argued that rabbits have white tails in order to be easy to shoot. I do not know how rabbits would view that application. It is an easy argument to parody. You all know Voltaire's remark, that obviously the nose was designed to be such as to fit spectacles. That sort of parody has turned out to be not nearly so wide of the mark as it might have seemed in the eighteenth century, because since the time of Darwin we understand much better why living creatures are adapted to their environment. It is not that their environment was made to be suitable to them but that they grew to be suitable to it, and that is the basis of adaptation. There is no evidence of design about it.

When you come to look into this argument from design, it is a most as-   8
tonishing thing that people can believe that this world, with all the things that are in it, with all its defects, should be the best that omnipotence and omniscience have been able to produce in millions of years. I really cannot believe it. Do you think that, if you were granted omnipotence and omniscience and millions of years in which to perfect your world, you could produce nothing better than the Ku Klux Klan or the Fascists? Moreover, if you accept the ordinary laws of science, you have to suppose that human life and life in general on this planet will die out in due course: it is a stage in the decay of the solar system; at a certain stage of decay you get the sort of conditions of temperature and so forth which are suitable to protoplasm, and there is life for a short time in the life of the whole solar system. You see in the moon the sort of thing to which the earth is tending—something dead, cold, and lifeless.

I am told that that sort of view is depressing, and people will sometimes tell   9
you that if they believed that, they would not be able to go on living. Do not believe it; it is all nonsense. Nobody really worries much about what is going to happen millions of years hence. Even if they think they are worrying much about that, they are really deceiving themselves. They are worried about something much more mundane, or it may merely be a bad digestion; but nobody is really seriously rendered unhappy by the thought of something that is going to happen to this world millions and millions of years hence. Therefore, although it is of course a gloomy view to suppose that life will die out—at least I suppose

we may say so, although sometimes when I contemplate the things that people do with their lives I think it is almost a consolation—it is not such as to render life miserable. It merely makes you turn your attention to other things.

THE MORAL ARGUMENTS FOR DEITY

Now we reach one stage further in what I shall call the intellectual descent that   10 the Theists have made in their argumentations, and we come to what are called the moral arguments for the existence of God. You all know, of course, that there used to be in the old days three intellectual arguments for the existence of God, all of which were disposed of by Immanuel Kant in the *Critique of Pure Reason*; but no sooner had he disposed of those arguments than he invented a new one, a moral argument, and that quite convinced him. He was like many people: in intellectual matters he was skeptical, but in moral matters he believed implicitly in the maxims that he had imbibed at his mother's knee. That illustrates what the psychoanalysts so much emphasize—the immensely stronger hold upon us that our very early associations have than those of later times.

Kant, as I say, invented a new moral argument for the existence of God, and   11 that in varying forms was extremely popular during the nineteenth century. It has all sorts of forms. One form is to say that there would be no right or wrong unless God existed. I am not for the moment concerned with whether there is a difference between right and wrong, or whether there is not: that is another question. The point I am concerned with is that, if you are quite sure there is a difference between right and wrong, you are then in this situation: Is that difference due to God's fiat or is it not? If it is due to God's fiat, then for God himself there is no difference between right and wrong, and it is no longer a significant statement to say that God is good. If you are going to say, as theologians do, that God is good, you must then say that right and wrong have some meaning which is independent of God's fiat, because God's fiats are good and not bad independently of the mere fact that [He] made them. If you are going t o say that, you will then have to say that it is not only through God that right and wrong came into being, but that they are in their essence logically anterior to God. You could, of course, if you liked, say that there was a superior deity who gave orders to the God who made this world, or could take up the line that some of the gnostics took up—a line which I often thought was a very plausible one—that as a matter of fact this world that we know was made by the devil at a moment when God was not looking. There is a good deal to be said for that, and I am not concerned to refute it.

THE ARGUMENT FOR THE REMEDYING OF INJUSTICE

Then there is another very curious form of moral argument, which is this: they   12 say that the existence of God is required in order to bring justice into the world. In the part of this universe that we know there is great injustice, and often the good suffer, and often the wicked prosper, and one hardly knows which of those is the more annoying; but if you are going to have justice in the universe as a whole you have to suppose a future life to redress the balance of life here on earth. So they say that there must be a God, and there must be heaven and hell in order that in the long run there may be justice. That is a very curious argument. If you looked at the matter from a scientific point of view, you would say, "After all, I know only this world. I do not know about the rest of the universe, but so far as one can argue at all on probabilities one would say that probably this world is a fair sample, and if there is injustice here the odds are that there is injustice elsewhere also." Supposing you got a crate of oranges that you opened, and you found all the top layer of oranges bad, you would not argue, "The underneath ones must be good, so as to redress the balance." You would say, "Probably the whole lot is a bad consignment"; and that is really what a scientific person would argue about the universe. He would say, "Here we find in this world a great deal of injustice, and so far as that goes that is a reason for supposing that justice does not rule in the world; and therefore so far as it goes it affords a moral argument against deity and not in favor of one." Of course I know that the sort of intellectual arguments that I have been talking to you about are not what really moves people. What really moves people to believe in God is not any intellectual argument at all. Most people believe in God because they have been taught from early infancy to do it, and that is the main reason.

Then I think that the next most powerful reason is the wish for safety, a sort   13
of feeling that there is a big brother who will look after you. That plays a very
profound part in influencing people's desire for a belief in God.

THE CHARACTER OF CHRIST

I now want to say a few words upon a topic which I often think is not quite suf-   14
ficiently dealt with by Rationalists, and that is the question whether Christ was the best and the wisest of men. It is generally taken for granted that we should all agree that that was so. I do not myself. I think that there are a good many points upon which I agree with Christ a great deal more than the professing Christians do. I do not know that I could go with Him all the way, but I could go with Him much further than most professing Christians can. You will remember that He said, "Resist not evil: but whosoever shall smite thee on thy right cheek, turn to him the other also." That is not a new precept or a new principle. It was used by Lao-tse and Buddha some 500 or 600 years before Christ, but it is not a principle which as a matter of fact Christians accept. I have no doubt that the present Prime Minister [Stanley Baldwin], for instance, is a most sincere Christian, but I should not advise any of you to go and smite him on one cheek. I think you might find that he thought this text was intended in a figurative sense.

Then there is another point which I consider excellent. You will remember   15
that Christ said, "Judge not lest ye be judged." That principle I do not think you would find was popular in the law courts of Christian countries. I have known in my time quite a number of judges who were very earnest Christians, and none of them felt that they were acting contrary to Christian principles in what

they did. Then Christ says, "Give to him that asketh of thee, and from him that would borrow of thee turn not thou away." That is a very good principle. Your Chairman has reminded you that we are not here to talk politics, but I cannot help observing that the last general election was fought on the question of how desirable it was to turn away from him that would borrow of thee, so that one must assume that the Liberals and Conservatives of this country are composed of people who do not agree with the teaching of Christ, because they certainly did very emphatically turn away on that occasion.

Then there is one other maxim of Christ which I think has a great deal in it, but I do not find that it is very popular among some of our Christian friends. He says, "If thou wilt be perfect, go and sell that which thou hast, and give to the poor." That is a very excellent maxim, but, as I say, it is not much practiced. All these, I think, are good maxims, although they are a little difficult to live up to. I do not profess to live up to them myself; but then, after all, it is not quite the same thing as for a Christian.   16

DEFECTS IN CHRIST'S TEACHING

Having granted the excellence of these maxims, I come to certain points in which I do not believe that one can grant either the superlative wisdom or the superlative goodness of Christ as depicted in the Gospels; and here I may say that one is not concerned with the historical question. Historically it is quite doubtful whether Christ ever existed at all, and if He did we do not know anything about Him, so that I am not concerned with the historical question, which is a very difficult one. I am concerned with Christ as He appears in the Gospels, taking the Gospel narrative as it stands, and there one does find some things that do not seem to be very wise. For one thing, He certainly thought that His second coming would occur in clouds of glory before the death of all the people who were living at that time. There are a great many texts that prove that. He says, for instance, "Ye shall not have gone over the cities of Israel till the Son of Man be come." Then He says, "There are some standing here which shall not taste death till the Son of Man comes into His kingdom"; and there are a lot of places where it is quite clear that He believed that His second coming would happen during the lifetime of many then living. That was the belief of His earlier followers, and it was the basis of a good deal of His moral teaching. When He said, "Take no thought for the morrow," and things of that sort, it was very largely because He thought that the second coming was going to be very soon, and that all ordinary mundane affairs did not count. I have, as a matter of fact, known some Christians who did believe that the second coming was imminent. I knew a parson who frightened his congregation terribly by telling them that the second coming was very imminent indeed, but they were much consoled when they found that he was planting trees in his garden. The early Christians did really believe it, and they did abstain from such things as plating trees in their gardens, because they did accept from Christ the belief that the second coming was imminent. In that respect, clearly He was not so wise as some other people have been, and he was certainly not superlatively wise.   17

THE MORAL PROBLEM

Then you come to moral questions. There is one very serious defect to my mind   18
in Christ's moral character, and that is that He believed in hell. I do not myself
feel that any person who is really profoundly humane can believe in everlasting
punishment. Christ certainly as depicted in the Gospels did believe in everlasting punishment, and one does find repeatedly a vindictive fury against those
people who would not listen to His preaching—an attitude which is not uncommon with preachers, but which does somewhat detract from superlative
excellence. You do not, for instance find that attitude in Socrates. You find him
quite bland and urbane toward the people who would not listen to him; and it
is, to my mind, far more worthy of a sage to take that line than to take the line
of indignation. You probably all remember the sort of things that Socrates was
saying when he was dying, and the sort of things that he generally did say to
people who did not agree with him.

You will find that in the Gospels Christ said, "Ye serpents, ye generation of   19
vipers, how can ye escape the damnation of hell." That was said to people who
did not like His preaching. It is not really to my mind quite the best tone, and
there are a great many of these things about hell. There is, of course, the familiar text about the sin against the Holy Ghost: "Whosoever speaketh against the
Holy Ghost it shall not be forgiven him neither in this World nor in the world
to come." That text has caused an unspeakable amount of misery in the world,
for all sorts of people have imagined that they have committed the sin against
the Holy Ghost, and thought that it would not be forgiven them either in this
world or in the world to come. I really do not think that a person with a proper
degree of kindliness in his nature would have put fears and terrors of that sort
into the world.

Then Christ says, "The Son of Man shall send forth His angels, and they   20
shall gather out of His kingdom all things that offend, and them which do iniq-
uity, and shall cast them into a furnace of fire; there shall be wailing and gnashing of teeth"; and He goes on about the wailing and gnashing of teeth. It comes
in one verse after another, and it is quite manifest to the reader that there is a
certain pleasure in contemplating wailing and gnashing of teeth, or else it would
not occur so often. Then you all, of course, remember about the sheep and the
goats; how at the second coming He is going to divide the sheep from the goats,
and He is going to say to the goats, "Depart from me, ye cursed, into everlasting
fire." He continues, "And these shall go away into everlasting fire." Then He says
again, "If thy hand offend thee, cut it off; it is better for thee to enter into life
maimed, than having two hands to go into hell, into the fire that never shall be
quenched; where the worm dieth not and the fire is not quenched." He repeats
that again and again also. I must say that I think all this doctrine, that hell-fire
is a punishment for sin, is a doctrine of cruelty. It is a doctrine that put cruelty
into the world and gave the world generations of cruel torture; and the Christ of
the Gospels, if you could take Him as His chroniclers represent Him, would certainly have to be considered partly responsible for that.

There are other things of less importance. There is the instance of the   21
Gadarene swine, where it certainly was not very kind to the pigs to put the

devils into them and make them rush down the hill to the sea. You must re-member that He was omnipotent, and He could have made the devils simply go away; but He chose to send them into the pigs. Then there is the curious story of the fig tree, which always rather puzzled me. You remember what happened about the fig tree. "He was hungry; and seeing a fig tree afar off having leaves, He came if haply He might find anything thereon; and when He came to it He found nothing but leaves, for the time of figs was not yet. And Jesus answered and said unto it: 'No man eat fruit of thee hereafter for ever' . . . and Peter . . . saith unto Him: 'Master, behold the fig tree which thou cursedst is withered away.'" This is a very curious story, because it was not the right time of year for figs, and you really could not blame the tree. I cannot myself feel that either in the matter of wisdom or in the matter of virtue Christ stands quite as high as some other people known to history. I think I should put Buddha and Socrates above Him in those respects.

THE EMOTIONAL FACTOR

As I said before, I do not think that the real reason why people accept religion   22
has anything to do with argumentation. They accept religion on emotional grounds. One is often told that it is a very wrong thing to attack religion, be-cause religion makes men virtuous. So I am told; I have not noticed it. You know, of course, the parody of that argument in Samuel Butler's book, *Erewhon Revisited*. You will remember that in *Erewhon* there is a certain Higgs who ar-rives in a remote country, and after spending some time there he escapes from that country in a balloon. Twenty years later he comes back to that country and finds a new religion in which he is worshiped under the name of the "Sun Child," and it is said that he ascended into heaven. He finds that the Feast of the Ascension is about to be celebrated, and he hears Professors Hanky and Panky say to each other that they never set eyes on the man Higgs, and they hope they never will; but they are the high priests of the religion of the Sun Child. He is very indignant, and he comes up to them, and he says, "I am going to expose all this humbug and tell the people of Erewhon that it was only I, the man Higgs, and I went up in a balloon." He was told, "You must not do that, because all the morals of this country are bound round this myth, and if they once know that you did not ascend into heaven they will all become wicked"; and so he is per-suaded of that and he goes quietly away.

    That is the idea—that we should all be wicked if we did not hold to the   23
Christian religion. It seems to me that the people who have held to it have been for the most part extremely wicked. You find this curious fact, that the more intense has been the religion of any period and the more profound has been the dogmatic belief, the greater has been the cruelty and the worse has been the state of affairs. In the so-called ages of faith, when men really did be-lieve the Christian religion in all its completeness, there was the Inquisition, with its tortures; there were millions of unfortunate women burned as witches; and there was every kind of cruelty practiced upon all sorts of people in the name of religion.

You find as you look around the world that every single bit of progress in   24
humane feeling, every improvement in the criminal law, every step toward the
diminution of war, every step toward better treatment of the colored races, or
every mitigation of slavery, every moral progress that there has been in the
world, has been consistently opposed by the organized churches of the world. I
say quite deliberately that the Christian religion, as organized in its churches,
has been and still is the principal enemy of moral progress in the world.

HOW THE CHURCHES HAVE RETARDED PROGRESS

You may think that I am going too far when I say that that is still so. I do not   25
think that I am. Take one fact. You will bear with me if I mention it. It is not a
pleasant fact, but the churches compel one to mention facts that are not pleasant. Supposing that in this world that we live in today an inexperienced girl is
married to a syphilitic man; in that case the Catholic Church says, "This is an
indissoluble sacrament. You must endure celibacy or stay together. And if you
stay together, you must not use birth control to prevent the birth of syphilitic
children." Nobody whose natural sympathies have not been warped by dogma,
or whose moral nature was not absolutely dead to all sense of suffering, could
maintain that it is right and proper that that state of things should continue.

That is only an example. There are a great many ways in which, at the pre-   26
sent moment, the church, by its insistence upon what it chooses to call morality, inflicts upon all sorts of people undeserved and unnecessary suffering. And
of course, as we know, it is in its major part an opponent still of progress and
of improvement in all the ways that diminish suffering in the world, because it
has chosen to label as morality a certain narrow set of rules of conduct which
have nothing to do with human happiness; and when you say that this or that
ought to be done because it would make for human happiness, they think that
has nothing to do with the matter at all. "What has human happiness to do with
morals? The object of morals is not to make people happy."

FEAR, THE FOUNDATION OF RELIGION

Religion is based, I think, primarily and mainly upon fear. It is partly the terror   27
of the unknown and partly, as I have said, the wish to feel that you have a kind
of elder brother who will stand by you in all your troubles and disputes. Fear is
the basis of the whole thing—fear of the mysterious, fear of defeat, fear of
death. Fear is the parent of cruelty, and therefore it is no wonder if cruelty and
religion have gone hand in hand. It is because fear is at the basis of those two
things. In this world we can now begin a little to understand things, and a little
to master them by help of science, which has forced its way step by step against
the Christian religion, against the churches, and against the opposition of all
the old precepts. Science can help us to get over this craven fear in which
mankind has lived for so many generations. Science can teach us, and I think
our own hearts can teach us, no longer to look around for imaginary supports,

no longer to invent allies in the sky, but rather to look to our own efforts here below to make this world a fit place to live in, instead of the sort of place that the churches in all these centuries have made it.

WHAT WE MUST DO

We want to stand upon our own feet and look fair and square at the world— 28
its good facts, its bad facts, its beauties, and its ugliness; see the world as it is and be not afraid of it. Conquer the world by intelligence and not merely by being slavishly subdued by the terror that comes from it. The whole conception of God is a conception derived from the ancient Oriental despotisms. It is a conception quite unworthy of free men. When you hear people in church debasing themselves and saying that they are miserable sinners, and all the rest of it, it seems contemptible and not worthy of self-respecting human beings. We ought to stand up and look the world frankly in the face. We ought to make the best we can of the world, and if it is not so good as we wish, after all it will still be better than what these others have made of it in all these ages. A good world needs knowledge, kindliness, and courage; it does not need a regretful hankering after the past or a fettering of the free intelligence by the words uttered long ago by ignorant men. It needs a fearless outlook and a free intelligence. It needs hope for the future, not looking back all the time toward a past that is dead, which we trust will be far surpassed by the future that our intelligence can create. □

◢ REREADING FOR UNDERSTANDING

1. After defining what he thinks being a Christian means, Russell tells why he does not accept the existence of God. He presents four traditional arguments for the existence of God and goes on to analyze these arguments for weaknesses. Summarize each argument, both the points for and against as Russell presents them.

2. Toward the end of the paragraph on "The First-Cause Argument," Russell points to a serious flaw. What is the flaw? How persuasive is Russell's rebuttal?

3. Explain how "chance" is a counterargument against "The Natural-law Argument" for God's existence.

4. How does Russell attack the argument that natural law (order and purpose within the universe) is an explanation for God's existence? Many theorists argue that we can infer God's existence by the "design" of the universe. How does Russell undermine that argument?

5. Russell's refutation of "The Moral Arguments for Deity" is, perhaps, the most difficult to understand. In his response, look for definitions of what causes right or wrong. Then look for an analysis of the "sequence of causes"

argument. If you find those, you may be able to comprehend Russell's meaning. "The Argument for the Remedying of Injustice" spurs Russell to suggest two counterarguments. What are they?

6. According to Russell, why does Christ's teaching about hell cause Christ to lose a degree of moral authority?

◢ RESPONDING

1. In "The Character of Christ" (par. 14), Russell admits to agreeing with certain precepts of Christ. However, he charges that most Christians aren't Christians because they do not follow those precepts. Is Russell correct? Must all of Christ's teaching be followed to be a Christian, or may an individual choose which principles to follow or ignore? What beliefs do you think are indispensable to Christianity?

2. Russell contends in paragraph 21 that most people "accept religion on emotional grounds." He cites fear as the principle emotion. How accurate is this observation?

3. Russell concludes by telling us "What We Must Do": rely on basic human qualities like intelligence, kindness, and courage—not religious dogma—to improve the well being of humankind. He argues, for example, that religious dogma has caused women to be burned to death as witches, allied with the devil. Does religious dogma still cause suffering? Is Russell too optimistic about humanity's ability to do without religious teachings? (Answer this question again after reading Moore's essay, "Care of the Soul," p. 549.)

◢ RESPONDING IN WRITING

Imagine you could write a letter to Lord Russell. What questions about his thinking would you want to ask—how he found happiness, what he thought life's purpose to be, whatever other question you may have. Write your essay-letter so that your imaginary audience can understand your questions, confusions, or interest in Lord Russell's ideas and point of view. Have one of your peers assume the role of Lord Russell. He or she should attempt to answer your questions based on Russell's essay.

THOMAS MOORE

Thomas Moore (1940–   ) was a college professor of psychology and religion before going into private practice as a psychotherapist. He has written numerous articles on religion and psychology, especially Jungian and archetypal psychology. He now writes in a more popular vein about the interactions and conflicts between psychology and religion. In this excerpt from his book *Care of the Soul,* you will see these concerns. Moore calls for a return to a division between the mind and the soul. The soul, he believes, has particular needs that, if satisfied, will help one's psychological well-being. Clearly Moore's view of the soul is "new age" and traditional at the same time. Equally clearly, Moore suggests we shouldn't expect to be deeply happy if we choose to ignore the soul.

Care of the Soul

The Benefits—and Costs—of a More Spiritual Life

In the modern world we tend to separate psychology from religion. We like to think that emotional problems have to do with the family, childhood, and trauma—with personal life but not with spirituality. We don't diagnose an emotional seizure as "loss of religious sensibility" or "lack of spiritual awareness." Yet the soul—the seat of our deepest emotions—can benefit greatly from the gifts of a vivid spiritual life, and can suffer when it is deprived of them.

The soul, for example, needs an articulated world-view, a carefully worked-out scheme of values and a sense of relatedness to the whole. It needs a myth of immortality and an attitude toward death. It also thrives on spirituality that is not so transcendent—such as the spirit of family, arising from traditions and values that have been part of the family for generations.

Spirituality doesn't arrive fully formed without effort. Religions around the world demonstrate that spiritual life requires constant attention and a subtle, often beautiful technology by which spiritual principles and understandings are kept alive. For good reason we go to church, temple, or mosque regularly and at appointed times: it's easy for consciousness to become lodged in the material world and to forget the spiritual.

Just as the mind digests ideas and produces intelligence, the soul feeds on life and digests it, creating wisdom and character out of experience. Renaissance Neoplatonists said that the outer world serves as a means of deep spirituality and that the transformation of ordinary experience into the stuff of soul is all-important. If the link between life experience and deep imagination is inadequate, then we are left with a division between life and soul, and such a division will always manifest itself in symptoms.

"PSYCHOLOGICAL MODERNISM"

Professional psychology has created a catalog of disorders, known as the Diagnostic and Statistical Manual, or DSM, which is used by doctors and insurance companies to help diagnose and standardize problems of emotional life and behavior with precision. For example, in the current edition, there is a category called "adjustment disorders." The problem is that adjusting to life, while perhaps sane to all outward appearances, may sometimes be detrimental to the soul.

One day I would like to make up my own DSM, in which I would include   6
the diagnosis "psychological modernism," an uncritical acceptance of the values of the modern world. It includes blind faith in technology, inordinate attachment to material gadgets and conveniences, uncritical acceptance of the march of scientific progress, devotion to the electronic media, and a lifestyle dictated by advertising. This orientation toward life also tends toward a mechanistic and rationalistic understanding of matters of the heart.

In this modernist syndrome, technology becomes the root metaphor for   7
dealing with psychological problems. A modern person comes into therapy and says, "Look, I don't want any long-term analysis. If something is broken, let's fix it. Tell me what I have to do and I'll do it." Such a person is rejecting out of hand the possibility that the source of a problem in a relationship, for example, may be a weak sense of values or failure to come to grips with mortality.

There is no model for this kind of thinking in modern life, where almost   8
no time is given to reflection and where the assumption is that the psyche has spare parts, an owner's manual, and well-trained mechanics called therapists. Philosophy lies at the base of every life problem, but it takes soul to reflect on one's own life with genuine philosophical seriousness.

The modernist syndrome urges people to buy the latest electronic gear and   9
to be plugged in to news, entertainment, and up-to-the-minute weather reports. It's vitally important not to miss out on anything.

Yet there seems to be an inverse relationship between information and wis-   10
dom. We are showered with information about living healthily, but we have largely lost our sense of the body's wisdom. We can tune in to news reports and know what is happening in every corner of the world, but we don't seem to have much wisdom in dealing with these world problems. We have many demanding academic programs in professional psychology, yet there is a severe dearth of wisdom about the mysteries of the soul.

The modernist syndrome also tends to literalize everything it touches. For   11
example, ancient philosophers and theologians taught that the world is a cosmic animal, a unified organism with its own living body and soul. Today we literalize that philosophy in the idea of the global village. The world soul today is created not by a dem-iurge or semi-divine creator as in ancient times, but by fiber optics. In the rural area where I live there are huge television reception dishes in the backyards of small homes, keeping villagers and country folk tuned into every entertainment and sports event on Earth.

We have a spiritual longing for community and relatedness and for a cos-   12
mic vision, but we go after them with literal hardware instead of with sensitivity of the heart. We want to know all about people from far away places, but we don't want to feel emotionally connected to them.

Therefore, our many studies of world cultures are soulless, replacing the   13
common bonding of humanity and its shared wisdom with bytes of information that have no way of getting into us deeply, of nourishing and transforming our sense of ourselves. Soul has been extracted from the beginning, because we

conceive education to be about skills and information, not about depth of feeling and imagination.

EVERYDAY SACREDNESS

Another aspect of modern life is a loss of formal religious practice in many people's lives, which is not only a threat to spirituality as such, but also deprives the soul of valuable symbolic and reflective experience. Care of the soul might include a recovery of formal religion in a way that is both intellectually and emotionally satisfying. One obvious source of spiritual renewal is the religious tradition in which we were brought up.   14

Some people are fortunate in that their childhood tradition is still relevant and lively to them, but others feel detached from their religion because it was a painful experience for them, or because it seems just too naive and simple-minded. Yet the fundamental insights of every tradition are ever subjected to fresh imagination in a series of reformations, and what might otherwise be a dead tradition becomes the base of a continually renewing spiritual sensibility.   15

There are two ways of thinking about church and religion. One is that we go to church in order to be in the presence of the holy, to learn and to have our lives influenced by that presence. The other is that church teaches us directly and symbolically to see the sacred dimension of everyday life. In this latter sense, religion is an "art of memory," a way of sustaining mindfulness about the religion that is inherent in everything we do. For some, religion is a Sunday affair, and they risk dividing life into the holy Sabbath and the secular week. For others, religion is a weeklong observance that is inspired and sustained on the Sabbath. For them, it is not insignificant that in our language each day of the week is dedicated to a god or goddess, from Saturn's Saturday to Thursday's Thor to Monday's Moon.   16

Yet how can we catch the appearance of the sacred in the most ordinary objects and circumstances? For one thing, we can all create sacred books and boxes —a volume of dreams, a heartfelt diary, a notebook of thoughts—and thus in a small but significant way can make the everyday sacred. This kind of spirituality, so ordinary and close to home, is especially nourishing to the soul. Without this lowly incorporation of the sacred into life, religion can become so far removed from the human situation as to be irrelevant. People can be extremely religious in a formal way and yet profess values in everyday life that are thoroughly secular.   17

An appreciation for vernacular spirituality is important because, without it, our idealization of the holy—making it precious and too removed from life—can actually obstruct a genuine sensitivity to what is sacred. Church-going can become a mere aesthetic experience or, psychologically, even a defense against the power of the holy. Formal religion, so powerful and influential in the establishment of values and principles, always lies on a cusp between the divine and the demonic. Religion is never neutral. It justifies and inflames the emotions of a holy war, and it fosters profound guilt about love and sex. The   18

Latin word *sacer*, the root of sacred, means both "holy" and "taboo," so close is the relationship between the holy and the forbidden.

Spirituality is seeded, germinates, sprouts, and blossoms in the mundane. [19] It is to be found and nurtured in the smallest of daily activities. The spirituality that feeds the soul and ultimately heals our psychological wounds may be found in those sacred objects that dress themselves in the accoutrements of the ordinary.

MAINTENANCE OF THE HOLY

While mythology is a way of telling stories about felt experience that are not [20] literal, ritual is an action that speaks to the mind and heart but doesn't necessarily make sense in a literal context. In church, people do not eat bread in order to feed their bodies but to nourish their souls.

If we could grasp this simple idea, that some actions may not have an effect [21] on actual life but speak instead to the soul, and if we could let go of the dominant role of function in so many things we do, then we might give more to the soul every day. A piece of clothing may be useful, but it may also have special meaning in relation to a theme of the soul. It is worth going to a little trouble to make a dinner a ritual by attending to the symbolic suggestiveness of the food and the way it is presented and eaten. Without this added dimension, which requires some thought, it may seem that life goes on smoothly. But slowly the soul is weakened and can make its presence known only in symptoms.

It's worth noting that neurosis, and certainly psychosis, often takes the [22] form of compulsive ritual. Yet when we can't stop ourselves from eating certain foods or pull ourselves away from the television set, isn't this also a compulsive ritual? Could it be that these neurotic rituals appear when imagination has been lost and the soul is no longer cared for? In other words, neurotic rituals could signify a loss of ritual in daily life that, if present, would keep the soul in imagination and away from literalism.

Neurosis could be defined, then, as a loss of imagination. We say we "act [23] out," meaning that what should be kept in the realm of image is lived out in life as if it were not poetry. The cure, in fact, for neurotic ritualism could be the cultivation of a more genuine sense of ritual in our daily life.

Ritual maintains the world's holiness. Knowing that everything we do, no [24] matter how simple, has a halo of imagination around it and can serve the soul enriches life and makes the things around us more precious, more worthy of our protection and care. As in a dream, a small object may assume significant meaning, so in a life that is animated with ritual there are no insignificant things.

When traditional cultures carve elaborate faces and bodies on their chairs [25] and tools, they are acknowledging the soul in ordinary things, as well as the fact that simple work is also ritual. When we stamp out our mass-made products with functionality blazoned on them but no sign of imagination, however, we are denying ritual a role in ordinary affairs. We are chasing away the soul that could animate our lives.

We go to church or temple in order to participate in that strong traditional ritual, but also to learn how to *do* rituals. Tradition is an important part of ritual because the soul is so much greater in scope than an individual's consciousness. Rituals that are "made up" are not always just right, or, like our own interpretations of our dreams, they may support our pet theories but not the eternal truths. If we are going to give ritual a more important place in life, it is helpful to be guided by formal religion and tradition. 26

How interesting it would be if we could turn to priests, ministers, and rabbis in order to get help in finding our own ritual materials. These spiritual professionals might be better schooled in ritual rather than in sociology, business, and psychology, which seem to be the modern preferences. The soul might be cared for better through our developing a deep life of ritual rather than through many years of counseling for personal behavior and relationships. We might even have a better time of it in such soul matters as love and emotion if we had more ritual in our lives and less psychological adjustment. We confuse purely temporal, personal, and immediate issues with deeper and enduring concerns of the soul. 27

The soul needs an intense, full-bodied spiritual life as much as and in the same way that the body needs food. That is the teaching and imagery of spiritual masters over centuries. But these same masters demonstrate that the spiritual life requires careful attention, because it can be dangerous. It's easy to go crazy in the life of the spirit, warring against those who disagree, proselytizing for our own personal attachments rather than expressing our own soulfulness, or taking narcissistic satisfactions in our beliefs rather than finding meaning and pleasure in spirituality that is available to everyone. 28

The history of our century has shown the proclivity of neurotic spirituality toward psychosis and violence. Spirituality is powerful, and thus has the potential for evil as well as for good. The soul needs spirit, but our spirituality also needs soul—intelligence, a sensitivity to the symbolic and metaphoric life, community, and attachment to the world. 29

We have no idea yet of the positive contribution that could be made to us individually and socially by a more soulful religion and theology. Our culture in is need of theological reflection that does not advocate a particular tradition, but tends the soul's need for spiritual direction. In order to accomplish this goal, we must gradually bring soul back to religion. □ 30

◢ REREADING FOR UNDERSTANDING

1. What does Moore want the reader to understand by his term "psychological modernism" (par. 5)?

2. What insight into modern life is captured by Moore when he observes that, today, a person in therapy demands "If something is broken, let's fix it." What troubles Moore about this attitude?

3. What does Moore imply by the word "soul"? Is his meaning of "soul" similar to or different from what the "average" person means by the word "soul"? In what specific ways?

◢ RESPONDING

1. Moore argues that ritual can sustain the soul and our imagination; that is, a symbolic act, repeated again and again in a similar form, can cause those who participate to feel some ideas or values with particular intensity. If you or your family eat dinner or breakfast with the TV on, try mealtime without the TV accompaniment; the resulting empty silence will no doubt change the mood. Does that exercise help you appreciate Moore's notion that the soul needs ritual in order to thrive? If our soul thrives only on technological rituals in the modern world, as Moore argues, can we still have a soul?

2. Moore defines and describes spiritual life and religious experience. Compare his ideas to Christ's "Sermon on the Mount" (p. 463) and Buddha's in "Happiness" (p. 478). What similarities or differences do you find?

3. Explain what kind of happiness Moore suggests will result if the soul is nurtured. Do you find that appealing? Would acting on his ideas add to or detract from the happiness in your life? Explain.

TEXT CREDITS

ARISTOTLE: "Nicomachean Ethics," translated by Manuel Velasquez, *Philosophy: A Text with Readings*, pp. 123–125. Copyright © 1994. Reprinted by permission of the author.

AYISI, RUTH ANSAH: "Family Values," by Ruth Ansah Ayisi, *African Report*, Vol. 38, Issue 1, January 1993, pp. 64–66. Reprinted by permission of the African-American Institute.

BAMBARA, TONI CADE: From *Gorilla, My Love* by Toni Cade Bambara. Copyright © 1972 by Toni Cade Bambara. Reprinted by permission of Random House, Inc.

BERRY, WENDELL: "Looking Ahead" from *The Gift of the Good Land: Further Essays Cultural and Political* by Wendell Berry. Copyright © 1981 by Wendell Berry. Reprinted by permission of North Point Press, a division of Farrar, Straus & Giroux, Inc.

BERRY, WENDELL: From *Sex, Economy, Freedom & Community* by Wendell Berry. Copyright © 1993 by Wendell Berry. Reprinted by permission of Pantheon Books, a division of Random House, Inc.

BIRKERTS, SVEN: "Perseus Unbound" from *The Gutenberg Elegies: The Fate of Reading in an Electronic Age*. Copyright © 1994 by Sven Birkerts. Published by Faber & Faber Inc.

BOK, SISSELA: From *Lying: Moral Choice in Public and Private Life* by Sissela Bok. Copyright © 1978 by Sissela Bok. Reprinted by permission of Pantheon Books, a division of Random House, Inc.

BOOTH, WAYNE: Wayne Booth, *The Vocation of a Teacher*. Reprinted by permission of The University of Chicago Press.

BRANDT, BARBARA: "Less Is More," by Barbara Brandt, *Between Worlds: A Reader, Rhetoric and Handbook*, edited by Susan Bachman and Melinda Barth. Copyright © 1995. Reprinted by permission of Barbara Brandt.

BROCK, POPE: "The Extremes of Honor," by Pope Brock, *Esquire*, Vol. 122, Issue 4, October 1994, pp. 114–120. Reprinted by permission of the Ellen Levine Literary Agency.

BURTLESS, GARY: "It's Better than Watching Oprah," by Gary Burtless. Reprinted with permission of The Wall Street Journal © 1990 Dow Jones & Company, Inc. All rights reserved.

BURTT, E. A.: From E. A. Burtt, *The Teachings of the Compassionate Budda*. Copyright © 1955. Reprinted by permission.

CARPENTER, BETSY: Copyright, Sept. 12, 1994, *U. S. News & World Report*.

CHAVEZ, LINDA: "The Real Aim of Cultural Diversity," by Linda Chavez, *The Chronicle of Higher Education*, July 18, 1990, pp. B1–B2. Reprinted by permission of the author.

CHUBB, JOHN E. AND MOE, TERRY M.: "Choice Is a Panacea" by John E. Chubb and Terry M. Moe, *The Brookings Review*, Vol. 8, Summer, 1990, pp. 4–12. Copyright © 1990. Reprinted by permission.

MACHIAVELLI, NICCOLO: Niccoló Machiavelli, *The Prince,* translated by Harvey C. Mansfield, Jr.. Reprinted by permission of The University of Chicago Press.

MARVELL, ANDREW: From *The Complete Works of Andrew Marvell,* edited by John Hopper. Copyright © 1966. Reprinted courtesy of AMS Press, Inc.

MOHR, NICHOLASA: "The English Lesson" by Nicholasa Mohr is reprinted with permission from the publisher of *In Nueva York* (Houston: Arte Público Press–University of Houston, 1988).

MOORE, THOMAS: Excerpt (as it appeared in *Psychology Today*) from *Care of the Soul* by Thomas Moore. Copyright © 1992 by Thomas Moore. Reprinted by permission of HarperCollins Publishers, Inc.

MORGAN, ELIZABETH SEYDEL: "Economics," by Elizabeth Seydel Morgan, *The Virginia Quarterly.* Copyright © 1991. Used by permission.

MORGENTHAU, HANS J.: Reprinted by permission of *The New Republic.* © 1994, The New Republic, Inc.

NEGROPONTE, NICHOLAS: From *Being Digital* by Nicholas Negroponte. Copyright © 1995 by Nicholas Negroponte. Reprinted by permission of Alfred A. Knopf Inc.

NYE, NAOMI SHIHAB: "The Use of Fiction" by Naomi Shihab Nye, from *The Morrow Anthology of Younger American Poets,* edited by Dave Smith and David Bottoms, published in 1985 by Quill Publishing. Copyright © Naomi Shihab Nye.

PAGLIA, CAMILLE: From *Sex, Art and American Culture* by Camille Paglia. Copyright © 1992 by Camille Paglia. Reprinted by permission of Vintage Books, a Division of Random House, Inc.

PASCARELLA, PERRY: Reprinted with the permission of The Free Press, a division of Simon & Schuster from *The New Achievers: Creating a Modern Work Ethic* by Perry Pascarella. Copyright © 1984 by Perry Pascarella.

POGREBIN, LETTY COTTIN: Copyright © 1992 by The New York Times Co. Reprinted by permission.

POSTMAN, NEIL: Reprinted with permission from *Technos: Quarterly for Education & Technology,* Vol. 2, No. 4; Agency for Institutional Technology.

POSTMAN, NEIL AND STEVE POWERS: "Reenactments and . . . Still News," pp.87–95, from *How to Watch TV News* by Neil Postman and Steve Powers. Copyright © 1992 by Neil Postman and Steve Powers. Used by permission of Viking Penguin, a division of Penguin Books USA Inc.

POSTREL, VIRGINIA I.: "The Environmental Movement: A Skeptical View" by Virginia I. Postrel, *Vital Speeches of the Day,* September 15, 1990, pp. 729–732. Reprinted by permission.

RAND, AYN: "Man's Rights,"pp. 108–17, from *The Virtue of Selfishness* by Ayn Rand. Copyright © 1961, 1964 by Ayn Rand. Used by permission of Dutton Signet, a division of Penguin Books USA, Inc.

REICH, ROBERT: "Jobs: Skills Before Credentials," by Robert B. Reich, *The Wall Street Journal,* February 2, 1994. Reprinted with permission of the Wall Street Journal © 1994 Dow Jones & Company, Inc. All rights reserved.

RICH, ADRIENNE: "Women and Honor: Some Notes on Lying" from *On Lies, Secrets, and Silence: Selected Prose 1966–78* by Adrienne Rich. Copyright © 1979 by W. W. Norton & Company, Inc. Reprinted by permission of the author and W. W. Norton & Company, Inc.

ROSE, MIKE: Reprinted with the permission of The Free Press, a division of Simon & Schuster, from *Lives on the Boundary: The Struggles and Achievements of America's Underprepared* by Mike Rose. Copyright © 1989 by Mike Rose.

INDEX

559